OAK RIDGES

MORAINE

OAK RIDGES
MORAINE

COMPILED BY THE STORM COALITION

The BOSTON
MILLS PRESS

Canadian Cataloguing in Publication Data

Oak Ridges Moraine

ISBN 1-55046-191-5

1. Oak Ridges Moraine (Ont.). 2. Natural History - Ontario
- Oak Ridges Moraine. I. STORM Coalition.

FC3095.0196024 1997   917.13'5   C97-930519-5
F1059.024024 1997

Copyright STORM Coalition, 1997

Published by
THE BOSTON MILLS PRESS
132 Main Street
Erin, Ontario, Canada
N0B 1T0
Tel 519-833-2407
Fax 519-833-2195
www.boston-mills.on.ca

An affiliate of
Stoddart Publishing Company Ltd.
34 Lesmill Road
North York, Ontario, Canada
M3B 2T6

Design by Taylor Design Group
Copyediting by James Bosma
Pencil sketches by Paul Harpley
Ink sketches by Gordon Berry
Major maps by Mason Kirkpatrick
Photo editing by Ian Deslauriers
General editing by Gordon Berry, Margaret Cranmer-Byng, Fred Helleiner and David McQueen

The publisher gratefully acknowledges the support of Consumers Gas, the Durham chapter of the Canada Trust Friends of the
Environment Foundation, DuPont Canada, and Paul Harpley.

BOSTON MILLS PRESS books are available for bulk purchase for sales promotions, premiums, fundraising, and seminars.
For details contact:

SPECIAL SALES DEPARTMENT, Stoddart Publishing Company Ltd., 34 Lesmill Road, North York, Ontario, Canada, M3B 2T6
Tel. 416-445-3333 Fax 416-445-5967

Printed in Hong Kong

Opposite: A carpet of trilliums in a maple forest. Photo by D. McQueen

CONTENTS

Acknowledgments. 9

Introduction: Welcome to the Moraine, *Hon. David Crombie*. 11

1. A Legacy of Ice, Water and Wind, *Frederick Johnson* 15

2. Changing Landscapes, *John R. Fisher and Donald H.M. Alexander*. 19

3. Caledon Heritage, *Heather Broadbent* 23

4. Water beneath Our Feet, *Debbe Crandall* 25

5. Secret Trail on the Moraine, *Ian Deslauriers* 29

6. Birds of the Oak Ridges Moraine, *Brian Henshaw*. 33

7. Purple Woods Conservation Area, *Christopher L. Conti* 37

8. A Hike through Mary Lake Monastery, *Fiona Cowles* 41

9. Zephyr Tract—York Regional Forest, *Paul Harpley*. 43

10. The Ridges at Long Sault, *Dale Hoy* 47

11. The Rice Lake Plains, *James Kamstra* 51

12. Where the Moraine Meets the Escarpment, *Susan Powell*. 55

13. Sand and Gravel, *Margaret Cranmer-Byng* 59

14. Pangman Springs Conservation Area, *Dan Zilstra* 61

15. The Ganaraska Story, *Susan Erskine Elgear* 65

16. The Ganaraska Forest, *Jim Tedford and Niva Rowan* 67

17. The Wildlife Habitat Trail, *Gordon Berry* 71

18. Singers and Sun Lovers: Amphibians and Reptiles, *James Kamstra* 73

19. Palgrave Forest and Wildlife Area, *Bill Kilburn* 79

20. Thornton Bales King Conservation Area, *Peter Seibert*. 83

21. The York Regional Forest, *Kevin R. Reese* 85

22. Hiking the Oak Ridges Trail in Uxbridge, *Anne Shier* 89

23. Oak Ridges Trail — Seneca College Section, *Jack Seigel* 93

24. A Vision of Trails, *David McQueen* 97

25. Albion Hills Conservation Area, *Brad Cundiff* 99

26. The Durham Demonstration Forest, *David McQueen* 103

27. Ski the Moraine, *Peter Attfield* 107

28. Fish of the Oak Ridges Moraine, *Mike Stoneman* 111

Conclusion: The Future of the Moraine, *David McQueen*. 115

Organizations 119

Index 120

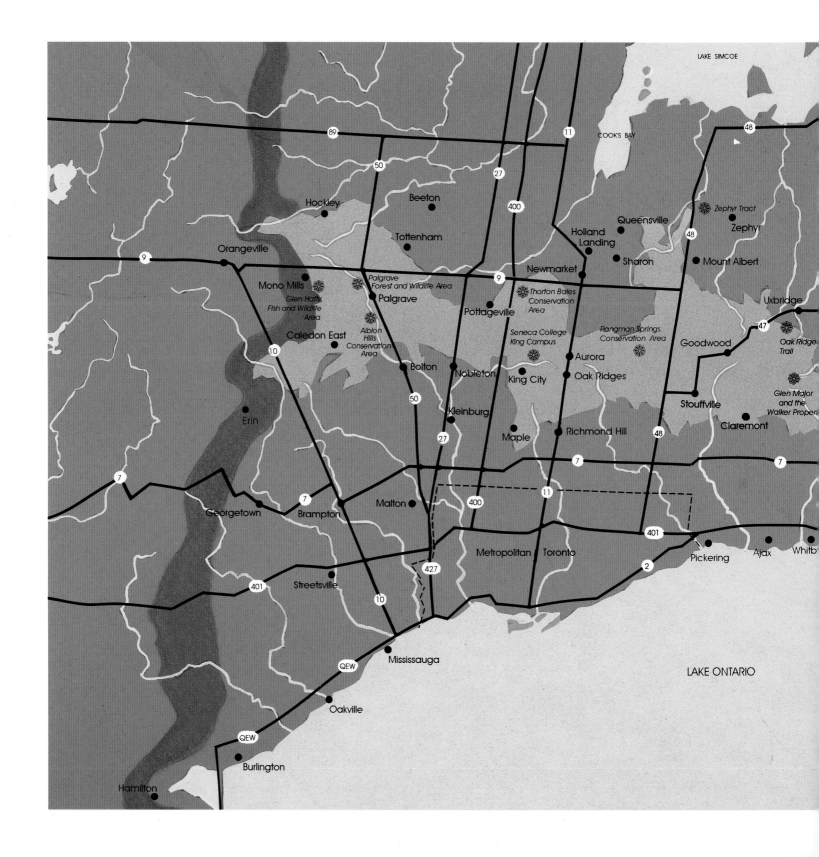

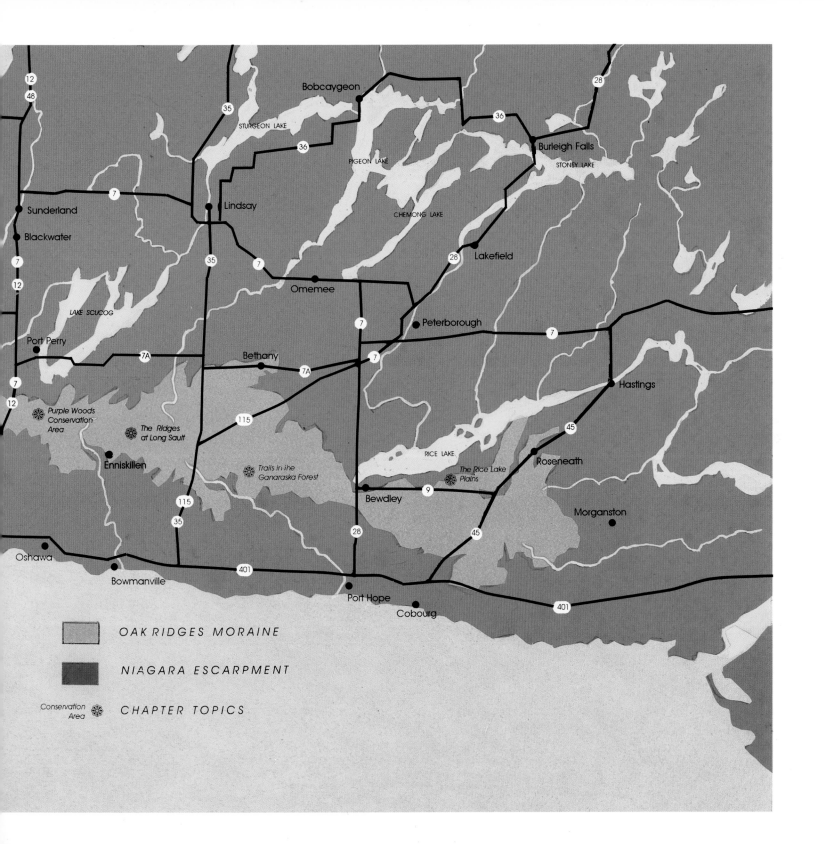

Bobcaygeon

STURGEON LAKE

35

36

PIGEON LAKE

28

Burleigh Falls

STONEY LAKE

12

48

CHEMONG LAKE

7

Sunderland

Lindsay

Blackwater

7

28

Lakefield

12

7

Omemee

LAKE SCUCOG

7

Peterborough

7

Port Perry

7A

Bethany

7A

7

7

12

115

Hastings

Purple Woods
Conservation
Area

The Ridges
at Long Sault

45

RICE LAKE

Roseneath

Enniskillen

Trails in the
Ganaraska Forest

The Rice Lake
Plains

115

9

Bewdley

Morganston

35

28

45

Oshawa

401

Bowmanville

Port Hope

Cobourg

401

OAK RIDGES MORAINE

NIAGARA ESCARPMENT

Conservation
Area

CHAPTER TOPICS

ACKNOWLEDGMENTS

Right up to the point of delivering a complete manuscript to the Boston Mills Press, this book has been a totally volunteer effort. Authors, photographers, artists and designers — including many freelancers who normally do this kind of thing for pay — have freely donated their services.

That is eloquent testimony to the breadth of informed support that exists for the Oak Ridges Moraine. It also merits, on behalf of the book committee, a profound thank you to all of our many contributors.

Special thanks are due to John Fisher, who originally conceived the idea of the book and saw the project through its early stages. We would also like to thank the officers and members of the STORM (Save the Oak Ridges Moraine) Coalition, the Federation of Ontario Naturalists, and the Metropolitan Toronto and Region Conservation Authority for much encouragement and assistance.

I would like to personally thank my fellow members of the book committee — Gordon Berry, Margaret Cranmer-Byng, Ian Deslauriers, Paul Harpley, Fred Helleiner and Mason Kirkpatrick — for the very long hours they put in to elicit and edit text and otherwise pull the project together. Special mention should be made of the sheer energy, backed by years of authorship and editorial experience, that Gordon Berry brought to our group, and of his travelling many uncompensated kilometres between Peterborough and Toronto. Special also was Paul Harpley's interruption of a busy spare-time career as a wildlife artist to help us both with artwork and fund raising.

Finally, we wish to sincerely thank the team assembled by Boston Mills, who worked so cheerfully and competently with us: James Bosma, Gillian Stead, Walter Pick and Adele Taylor-Pick.

David McQueen
Chair, book committee
STORM Coalition

Opposite: Fall colours at the Glen Haffy Lookout.
Photo courtesy of MTRCA

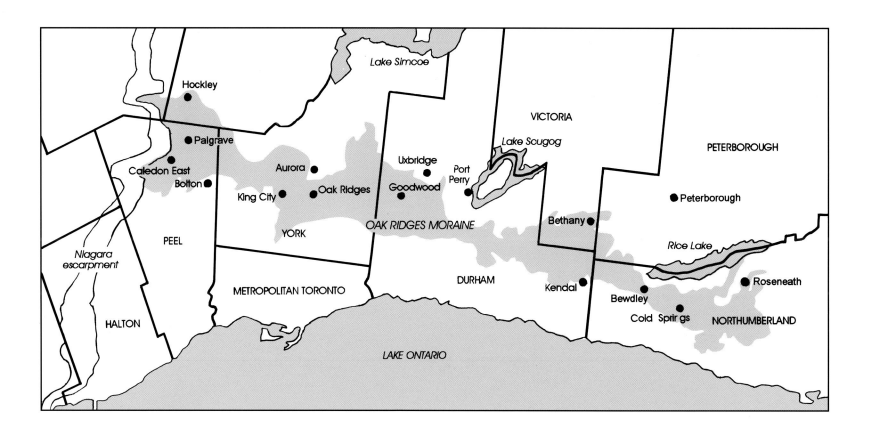

The Moraine varies in width, from 4 kilometres (near Bewdley, south of Rice Lake) to 24 kilometres (near Ballantrae). In Richmond Hill, where the Moraine fills a pre-glacial valley, it is more than 240 metres thick.

INTRODUCTION:
WELCOME TO THE MORAINE

Hon. David Crombie

rive north from Lake Ontario, almost anywhere along its length, and the pattern is the same: a fringe of urban life near the lake that gradually gives way to suburbs, and a flat, square grid of roads and farms laid out with careful precision. But a little farther north yet, the land begins to rise in an irregular ridge of sandy hills. Woodlands crowd farm fields, and the roads dip and weave through hummocky terrain. You have reached the Oak Ridges Moraine.

Continue north and the Moraine is quickly passed, for it is but a narrow band in most places. But travel west to east, along its length, and you get quite a different picture of this fascinating piece of Southern Ontario landscape. At its westerly end, the Moraine spills, in the confused jumble of Caledon hill country, over the buried limestone edge of the Niagara Escarpment. Follow the ridge eastward and it

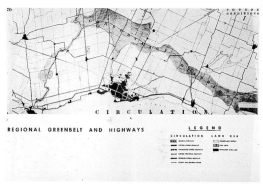

This historic highway planning map (1943) shows the Oak Ridges Moraine greenbelt. Waterfront Regeneration Trust (Ontario Archives)

Former mayor of Toronto and federal cabinet minister Hon. David Crombie is today chair of the Waterfront Regeneration Trust. As chair of the Royal Commission on the Future of the Toronto Waterfront, Mr. Crombie recognized, and emphasized in the Commission's reports, the ecological importance of the Oak Ridges Moraine. He also played a leading role in founding the Oak Ridges Trail Association.

Agriculture remains a dominant activity on the Moraine. Photo by S. Russell

Hackett Lake … a typical kettle lake. Photo by L. Wise

The Oak Ridges Moraine takes its name from the many fine oaks that once grew along the ridge. These oaks were harvested and sent to Britain to build the wooden ships of the British navy. Not only were the trunks valued for their strength and size, but bent and crooked limbs were prized for the curved rib and prow parts that could be cut from them. Large, straight pines were needed for the masts of naval ships, and many of these great timbers were cut along the Moraine and hauled by wagon to Port Hope for shipment to England.

leads you, past Aurora and Uxbridge, to the southern edges of Lake Scugog and Rice Lake. Finally, near Trenton, over 200 kilometres from Caledon, the gravel hills become less distinct and the Moraine reaches its end.

The Moraine is not just an attractive place to visit or to live. In fact, it is an environmental treasure — part of the Greater Toronto bioregion — the value of which ought not be underestimated. Let me explain why.

The Moraine acts as a giant rain barrel for the bioregion. Its porous sands and gravels soak up water from rain and melting snow, which percolates into underground reservoirs known as aquifers. At least ten communities, and hundreds of farms and rural residences, draw upon these aquifers as a source of drinking water. Along the flanks of the Moraine, this cool, clean water bubbles out in springs that are the source of over thirty rivers and streams. This steady supply of ground water, which comprises over a third of the flow of the Humber, Don, Rouge and Ganaraska Rivers, is vital to the ecological health of these waterways. It is also vital to their future.

In their lower reaches, many of these streams suffer greatly from the intrusion of silt, fertilizer and other pollutants that wash off streets and farmland or are discharged through urban storm sewers. The destruction of trees and wetlands has allowed water to rush downstream, eroding streambanks and further altering natural rhythms. Ultimately, the near-shore areas of Lake Ontario have been affected, as many of the pollutants present there arrive through these tributaries.

An enormous amount of effort and money has been invested to correct conditions downstream. Yet without stabilizing the influence of the Moraine on these watersheds (i.e. the ability of these gravel hills to contribute a strong base of clean water) these restoration activities will be in vain.

The rivers of the Moraine have long been used for transportation and industry. Native peoples took advantage of their steady flow, using them as travel corridors, especially the Humber, as a link to the Holland River and Lake Simcoe, and the Ganaraska, as a shortcut to Rice Lake and the Trent system. European settlers used river mouths as harbours, and soon built mills along almost every stream for water power. Ironically, the clearing of trees from Moraine watersheds resulted in the silting of harbours and mill ponds, which caused such destructive flooding that much of this early industry was short-lived. In many parts of the Moraine, however, the steep slopes and poor soils discouraged land clearing.

In the headwaters of the Ganaraska River, and several other areas that had previously been cleared, blowing sands prompted extensive reforestation. As a result, the Oak Ridges Moraine now has many of the largest remaining blocks of natural habitat within the bioregion. These blocks provide critical habitat for species including the scarlet tanager and the rose-breasted grosbeak, as well as many species of thrush and wood warbler. The Moraine is also rich in other specialized habitats, such as the kettle-bog wetlands scattered across its length, and the remnants of the prairie communities south of Rice Lake.

The woodlands of the Moraine are an important reservoir of wildlife and vegetation that could potentially be used to repopulate depleted habitats to the south. Habitat connections to allow the movement of species are vital to this process. The Moraine may be able to provide these connections at a regional scale.

With sound management, the Moraine will provide even better wildlife habitats in the future. Conifer plantations could be gradually converted to native forests, and some of the areas that are now open fields could be regenerated into a wide variety of habitats. As urban growth continues on the Lake Ontario plains south of the Moraine, the ecological value of this corridor of green will become ever greater.

Chalk Lake. Photo by D. McQueen

The Oak Ridges Moraine will become increasingly important for people as well. This quiet oasis of green, offering opportunities for healthful recreation close to the city, will be an essential counterpoint to the urban landscape. Already the Moraine is known as a place for walking, skiing, mountain biking and horseback riding. As more trails are developed, linking together the public lands on the Moraine, it will surely become even more popular for recreation.

As you page through this book, you will learn that the Oak Ridges Moraine is more than just an assortment of interesting and attractive places; it is also an essential part of a broad bioregion, the protection of which is key to the regeneration of the bioregion as a whole.

The rolling hills of Caledon. Photo by D. McQueen

1. A LEGACY OF ICE, WATER AND WIND

Frederick Johnson

The Oak Ridges Moraine is an immense ridge of land that runs east to west through the Southern Ontario landscape, north of and parallel to Lake Ontario. It stretches over 200 kilometres, from the Niagara Escarpment in the west to almost the Trent River in the east. It is a rolling landscape, amply supplied with forests, fields, wetlands and lakes. In marked contrast, lands to the north and south are gently rolling to flat plains that have been almost entirely converted to agricultural or urban land use.

The Moraine is a testament to the forces of nature. It was created less than fifteen thousand years ago, during the last great ice age, and is probably the thickest and most extensive deposit of glacially derived material anywhere in Ontario. In some places it is over 300 metres in elevation and over 200 metres thick.

Despite its impressive dimensions, the majority of the Oak Ridges Moraine was formed within only a few thousand years. The Niagara Escarpment, by contrast, has taken hundreds of millions of years to reach its present form. Most of the Moraine is the result of the direct deposition of material by glacial ice or of sediments carried by meltwater from the terminus of the ice sheets.

At least four times in the last million years, massive sheets of glacial ice over 1.5 kilometres thick advanced over the northern half of North America and subsequently melted back. The landscape of Southern Ontario, including the Oak Ridges Moraine, is a product of these continual advances and "retreats".

In some places, the ice would scrape and excavate the landscape. The Great Lakes, Lake Simcoe and the Kawartha Lakes are examples of large basins, now water-filled, that were gouged out of the bedrock through glacial action. In other areas, where the glacial ice had become supersaturated with eroded materials, the ice would release this material or would indirectly deposit it from water that flowed off the edge of the glacial ice. The Oak Ridges Moraine acted as a huge dumping ground for glacial debris scraped up from other parts of the countryside.

The Oak Ridges Moraine is referred to as an interlobate moraine, because it was formed between two lobes of receding ice. As the glaciers

The retreating glaciers deposited silt, sand, gravel and rock all along the Moraine. Photo by P. Harpley

More than 15,000 years ago, Southern Ontario was locked beneath a massive sheet of glacial ice similar to those that exist today in Greenland and Antarctica.

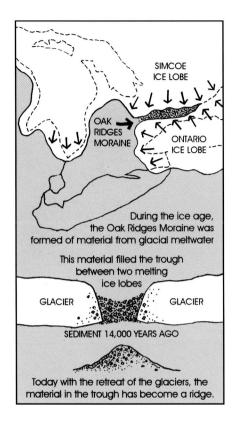

SIMCOE ICE LOBE

OAK RIDGES MORAINE

ONTARIO ICE LOBE

During the ice age, the Oak Ridges Moraine was formed of material from glacial meltwater

This material filled the trough between two melting ice lobes

GLACIER   GLACIER

SEDIMENT 14,000 YEARS AGO

Today with the retreat of the glaciers, the material in the trough has become a ridge.

began to melt (approximately fifteen thousand years ago), a crevasse or split in the ice was created in the area of the Moraine. Two distinct lobes of ice emerged, the Simcoe ice lobe to the north and the Ontario ice lobe to the south.

Eventually, the crevasse widened to create a large trough. This trough received water and associated sands, silts and gravels previously locked in the glacial ice. Over hundreds or even thousands of years, huge blankets of stratified sands, gravel and silt filled the trough. Minor readvances of the ice lobes into the trough caused the interlayering of these layers with non-sorted till material. When the ice melted from the area, a large ridge of glacial debris remained to form the core of the Moraine.

Although the Oak Ridges can be generally defined as a ridge formed by an interlobate Moraine, a great deal of variation exists in the form and character of the landscape within the Moraine, reflecting localized differences in the geologic process.

About two-thirds of the Oak Ridges Moraine consists of sandy plains. These are areas where the core material of the Moraine occurs at the surface. Recent work conducted by the Ontario Geological Survey suggests that much of the stratified sands may have been delivered from the north by large rivers beneath the glacial ice. This material would have been initially laid down as broad, flat deposits such as those found in the vicinity of Ballantrae and Goodwood. In many other areas, especially along the northern slopes of

the Moraine, subsequent water and wind erosion has created an irregular rolling landscape. The internal structure of the deposits is typified by even-layered deposits of sand and silt, which indicates that they were formed as deltas or lake sediments in shallow-water settings. Sometimes, contorted or irregular layers are encountered, indicating collapse within the deposit caused by the melting of pieces of ice trapped within or underneath the sediment. Such material is collectively referred to as ice-contact stratified drift.

After the development of the initial Oak Ridges Moraine core, there were several minor readvances of the ice lobes from the north and south. In some areas, along the north and south slope, the ice deposited a thin veneer of non-sorted till material to form relatively flat till deposits. These deposits represent some of the better-quality farmland within the Moraine.

Along the south slope of the Moraine, a later readvance of the Lake Ontario ice lobe created a

Till plains at the base of the Oak Ridges Moraine, near Pangman Springs. Photo by E. Gillan

The rolling hills of the Moraine, looking south toward Lake Ontario. Photo by J. Kamstra

The Moraine has more than two dozen kettle lakes, most of them in the western half.

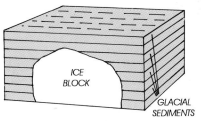

KETTLE LAKE FORMATION

ICE BLOCK

GLACIAL SEDIMENTS

KETTLE SHAPE FORMS AFTER ICE BLOCK MELTS

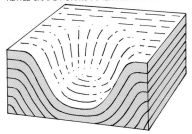

secondary "end," or terminal moraine, just to the south of the crest of the Moraine. This secondary deposit is marked by a distinctive hummocky terrain with scattered conical hills known as kames and depressional areas, known as kettles. This terrain is well defined and can be traced from the Caledon area across to the southeastern portion of Uxbridge Township. The soil here is dominated by till, with localized pockets of sand and gravel. The poor surface drainage and irregular topography render this area generally unsuitable for large-scale mechanized farming. Much of the irregularity in the surface was caused by the entrapment and subsequent melting out of stagnant glacial ice. This hummocky terrain area is also typified by the presence of numerous kettle lakes and wetlands. These depressed areas were formed by the melting out of large entrapped blocks of glacial ice. Musselman Lake, Lake Wilcox and Bond Lake are among the kettle lakes found in the Moraine.

The ice lobes that were instrumental in forming the Oak Ridges Moraine melted away from this part of Ontario about twelve thousand years ago. However, this did not mark the end to the constant shaping and reshaping of the Moraine surface. Even

Bond Lake in Richmond Hill, is next to Yonge Street and is the deepest kettle lake on the Moraine at 30 metres.
Photo by L. Wise

today, the actions of wind, water, plants, animals and people are changing the face of the Moraine.

Streams continue to cut valleys into the north and south slopes of the Moraine and rework glacial material into stream-bed (alluvial) sediments.

Kettle lakes are slowly being converted into wetlands through natural successional processes and will eventually become dry land. This process usually takes place over thousands of years, but, with the influence of people, it may occur more quickly.

Wind continues to re-sort and shift the sands and silts of the Moraine and in some places forms large tracts of sand dunes. This process

was accelerated in the 1920s and 1930s, after much of the protective tree cover of the Moraine was removed for farming.

People are perhaps the greatest modifiers of the Moraine as they excavate, grade and recontour the land surface to meet their own particular needs.

The Oak Ridges Moraine is the product of a large, complex and still poorly understood geological past. In spite of the fact that over four million people live on or near this amazing geological legacy, it is still wrapped in mystery and still has much to teach us about our rich and varied natural heritage.

Reforestation of farm fields during the 1940s saved thousands of acres from continued erosion.
Photo courtesy of Ganaraska Region Conservation Authority

2. CHANGING LANDSCAPES

John R. Fisher and Donald H.M. Alexander

Adapted and abridged from "The Symbolic Landscape of the Oak Ridges Moraine: Its Influence on Conservation in Ontario, Canada," Environments: A Journal of Interdisciplinary Studies, *University of Waterloo, vol. 22, no. 1, 1993.*

The landscape history of the Oak Ridges Moraine speaks of a resilient and dynamic place. Both natural processes and people have played a role in it. The Moraine's story is constantly evolving and challenges even the most idle observer into active participation; it is impossible to know and understand the Oak Ridges Moraine fully and not become a participant in its saga.

The next time you find yourself on the Moraine, bend a knee and thrust your hand into the sandy soil. Raise your hand high above your head and extend your fingers so as to expose the fine grains to the wind or rain. Watch carefully as the powder-like particles of sand pass into the air and disappear. This is the story of erosion.

Walk into the forest and ask yourself why it is that here, under the canopy, springs bubble to the surface. Walk into the valleys, dip your cup into the babbling brooks, and taste the cold, clean water where once there was none. If you listen carefully, you will hear the life returning to this healing landscape in every bird call, every splash of spawning trout, every crash of fleeing deer. This is the living story of the Oak Ridges Moraine. But there have also been invasion, exploitation, and destruction.

The famous regional planner, Benton MacKaye, speculated in 1928 that the landscapes of northeastern North America have been shaped by three major invasions. In the context of the Oak Ridges Moraine, the first invasion comprised the advance and final disappearance of the Wisconsin glacier about twelve thousand years ago, which ultimately produced the Moraine's physical structure.

After the glaciers, the first humans to arrive on the Moraine were the Native peoples. But so light and nature-respecting was their touch that MacKaye did not classify them as "invaders."

Much more perturbing, however, was the second invasion, which involved the advance of European settlers and ideologies, first along the north shore of Lake Ontario, then up the south slope of the Moraine itself.

Now, in the twentieth century, a third invasion has carved into the landscape, as bulldozers push nature back to make room for metropolitan sprawl.

canopy: the topmost layer of leaves, branches and twigs of the forest trees.

Urban sprawl near the Oak Ridges Moraine. Photo by L. Wise

The community of Oak Ridges, part of the Town of Richmond Hill since 1971, has grown from a few hundred people at the turn of the century to its current population of 6,500. Over the next ten to fifteen years, planned development could increase that population to as many as 23,500.

INDIAN ARTIFACTS OF THE MORAINE

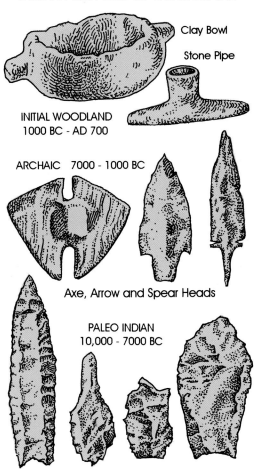

Clay Bowl

Stone Pipe

INITIAL WOODLAND
1000 BC - AD 700

ARCHAIC 7000 - 1000 BC

Axe, Arrow and Spear Heads

PALEO INDIAN
10,000 - 7000 BC

Stone Scrapers and Projectile points

Perhaps there will be a fourth invasion, that will involve the restoration of natural areas and the development of low-impact recreational corridors, so that a growing population may better appreciate the ecological value of these incredible places. But this remains to be seen.

The general nature of the first, glacial, invasion of the Moraine has been described in the preceding chapter. It is important to note that early advances of the Wisconsin ice sheet created a significant moraine. There followed, however, a period of melting, and then a renewed advance of the ice sheet. This final assault, though relatively short-lived by geological standards, was sufficiently thick to override the earlier moraine, destroying many of its previously dramatic features and leaving a new cap of till deposits.

The characteristic vegetation that grew up in the aftermath of all this formed the basis for the hunting, gathering, and horticultural activities of the Native populations who came to occupy the Great Lakes lowlands.

One of our best sources of information about their way of life comes from an archeological dig on the southern shore of Rice Lake. The dig indicated that the Moraine uplands were primarily used as a hunting and gathering ground by the several Native cultures that made use of the site between 170 b.c. and a.d. 1690. Major sources of food included deer and fish, and there was also some reliance on locally available plant foods. Charcoal analysis indicates that many hardwood tree species, such as white and red oak, ash, maple,

elm, hickory and beech, grew on the Moraine and were used as firewood.

In the early 1600s, Europeans introduced the fur trade. This greatly intensified intertribal warfare between the Hurons and the Iroquois, which, in turn, restricted settlement on and around the Moraine. Already, in his journal of 1615, Samuel de Champlain noted the depopulation of the Trent valley, and by 1650 this entire area had been abandoned as a result of periodic Iroquois incursions. The Hurons of the district migrated to join their fellows living near Georgian Bay; but there, too, the Hurons were destined to be routed by the Iroquois.

Meanwhile, near the eastern reaches of the Moraine, the Cayuga Nation of the Iroquois established the village of Ganaraska, in 1666, at the mouth of the Ganaraska River in what is today Port Hope. They were displaced with the southward push of the Mississaugas in about 1700.

During this period of intertribal tensions and warfare, the Oak Ridges Moraine proper was devoid of permanent settlement, and was mainly perceived as a hunting and gathering area. Researchers estimate that the Moraine was crisscrossed by at least five major trail systems, and reference is also made to a trail along the crest of the Moraine near Uxbridge. There may well be places where the hikers on the modern Oak Ridges Trail are treading in the very footsteps of Native hunters and warriors of long ago!

The second invasion of the Moraine was cultural, as European settlers, together with their techniques, their technologies and their ideologies, moved into what was then the pristine environment of Upper Canada. In the beginning, these settlers sought to subdue the land in order to reap the harvests of an agricultural economy. They believed that heavy forest cover indicated fertile land beneath. But this was not necessarily true, for the Moraine.

Pressure for deforestation and land settlement was especially intense in the early 1800s. Between 1830 and 1833 the population of Ontario increased by fifty percent. So great was the pressure for land that a new settlement policy was adopted against the advice of the colonial office. Settlers were enabled to put down a ten-percent deposit on land and pay off the balance in instalments. Many settlers, lacking capital, bought the land, and then, rather than suffer forfeiture, either sold it to land speculators or stripped it of its timber and abandoned it. One way or another, much forest was recklessly stripped from the Oak Ridges Moraine.

Effectively, this led to the creation of deserts, as the removal of forest cover, in conjunction with poor agricultural practices, resulted in the formation of blowsand and shifting dunes. As early as the 1870s, foresters were calling for extensive replanting of such areas. Eventually, priority tracts were acquired and planted as county agreement forests in the 1920s.

The next major move towards recovery came with the Guelph Conference of 1941, convened largely through the efforts of the Federation of Ontario Naturalists and the Ontario Conservation and Reforestation Association. There it was decided to initiate a demonstration survey that could serve as a special example of conservation research and rehabilitation. In 1941, the Ganaraska Watershed, which has its headwaters in the Oak Ridges Moraine, was selected for the survey.

The result of the survey was a landmark study by A.H. Richardson, published in 1944, and leading to a massive reforestation project that began two years later. But, as intended, the Richardson study had influence well beyond the Ganaraska. It became the model upon which conservation surveys for other areas in the province would be based, with the report from each survey becoming a working plan for conservation efforts in the future. With the Ganaraska survey, conservation began to move from a focus on a single resource (water) towards integrated resource management.

Thus the slow desiccation of the Oak Ridges Moraine, with the resulting alternation of flooding and drought, was a big factor affecting conservation policy in Southern Ontario. So too, in 1954, was Hurricane Hazel, which struck with particular force in the populated and heavily deforested Humber and Etobicoke watersheds. The damage, and the loss of human lives, added an enormous impetus to conservation efforts.

The third invasion of the Moraine was technological in origin, spawned by the invention of the automobile. A quotation from J. Coleman in the Toronto Star Weekly (May 2, 1924) illustrates this well: "Motoring north from Toronto one soon comes to hills, the tumbled oak ridges... where the

A First Nation dugout canoe was found by divers in Bond Lake. It is displayed at the Marine Museum in Toronto.

The Carrying Place Trail was an ancient trading route linking the aboriginal people of the Lake Ontario region with other Native groups living near Lake Huron, Georgian Bay and Lake Superior. From the seventeenth century onward, the trail was also used by European explorers, fur traders and early settlers. In the south, the trail passed through the Humber River valley, with portions of Weston and Islington Roads following the original route.

The gravel of the Moraine is mined extensively for use in roads and buildings in the Greater Toronto Area. Photo by L. Wise

Forest Regeneration. Photo by I. Deslauriers

Many of the agreement forests on the Moraine are open to the public, notably in York and Durham Regions. A major part of the Durham Demonstration Forest lies just south of Uxbridge and offers interpretive information as well as pleasant woodland walks.

wooded knobs and kettle-shaped basins make a fine contrast with the flat or gently rolling surface to the south."

The reforestation of the Moraine and the abandonment of farms occurred at a time when people, in a reaction against the constraints of urban life, were beginning to seek the peace and quiet of the countryside. Initially, this involved the acquisition of farms, the occupation of existing farmhouses, and the building of some new dwellings. By and large, the countryside was left unharmed. Indeed, the new residents often contributed to reforestation efforts.

Today, however, the trickle of immigration onto the Moraine is fast becoming a flood. Whole new subdivisions, along with malls and industrial parks, are springing up, threatening not only the scenic beauty of the area, but also the quality and quantity of both surface and ground water.

Woodlots, which once sheltered wildlife and recharged streams, have fallen to the chain saw, and the permeable surfaces through which rainwater and snowmelt once passed and were cleaned and cooled are being covered in concrete.

A secondary impact of the automobile has been a quantum leap in the extraction of aggregates — sand and gravel — on the Moraine, with much of it going into the construction of superhighways and other roads.

All of this has provoked a response, not only from those who moved to the Moraine to seek peace and quiet, but from conservationists who fear that the irreplaceable natural heritage of the Moraine will be lost forever. Organizations such as the STORM Coalition have sprung up, and public pressure has forced a variety of government commissions and study groups to address the issues.

3. CALEDON HERITAGE

Heather Broadbent

The Town of Caledon is a rural municipality at the west end of the Oak Ridges Moraine, where the Moraine runs up and over the lower slopes of the Niagara Escarpment. It is a sought-after residential, educational and recreational area for migrants from the city, day visitors and vacationers. There are also several thousand acres of publicly held lands that provide numerous recreational opportunities. In addition, there is a fascinating diversity of early structures, built of materials drawn from both the Moraine and the Escarpment.

On this part of the Moraine, the original landscape has been entirely taken over by the cultural (human-created) landscape. Many areas have been reforested, both through natural regeneration and by mid-twentieth-century plantations. Also, as the century has progressed and we have learned the importance of environmental protection, valleys, streams and small rivers have been allowed to take on a less regimented appearance. Wildflowers are even returning.

With a little imagination, and a certain persistence in exploring concessions and sideroads, the visitor to Caledon can gain some keen insights into what life was like for the original European settlers on the Moraine.

Whether on a hobby or a full-time commercial basis, much of the land is still farmed, with considerable areas devoted to dairy, beef and horses. It is partly for this reason that so many heritage buildings and artifacts of the original settlers abound.

Though surveying and settlement began rather later in Caledon than in areas to the east, they gathered momentum in the 1820s, as people were attracted by the thick old-growth forests and the Humber River. Because of the forest cover, the Humber was then a bigger stream than it is today, and provided water power for numerous grist mills and sawmills.

As elsewhere on the Moraine, tree clearing and unwise agriculture led to blowing sand and siltation of the Humber. But soils were better in some parts of Caledon, notably in the northeast, and it is in those parts that you will still see one-, one-and-a-half- and two-storey buildings with large squared logs and medium gable roofs. Some of these buildings are nearly 175 years old. In many cases, two hand-spreads do not suffice to span

Squared-timber log cabins can still be found on the Moraine.
Photo by D. McQueen

No Native groups inhabit Caledon today, but, as late as the 1870s, one family still wintered on Mount Wolfe, a sacred, ancestral place believed to have been frequented by Natives for thousands of years.

Common historic construction techniques used along the Oak Ridges Moraine:

Round logs and round notches, usually unchinked. Used in barns and out buildings.

Squared logs, dove-tailed, chinked with white plaster. Used in houses.

Clapboard homes with casements.

Stone buildings of limestone, sandstone, and occasionally granite rocks brought down and left by the glaciers. Sometimes the stone was dressed, but more commonly it was only partially or roughly shaped.

Common fence construction techniques used along the Oak Ridges Moraine:

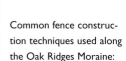

Stump fences, mostly of pine roots.

Straight split-rail cedar fences, erected without nails

Split-rail snake fences.

their squared pine logs; eighteen square inches is quite common, and twenty-four is not unusual.

The first farm buildings (some still in use) were of squared- or whole-log framing. Sometimes these buildings had foundations and cellars built of water-worn river stones and glacial boulders.

As sawmilling became more efficient and large barns became necessary, enough big trees remained to provide the enormous planks — (some 24 inches wide or more) — still visible on many Caledon farm buildings. Other locally available construction materials, from the Escarpment as well as the Moraine, included limestone and sandstone, and clay suitable for bricks.

As the forest receded and buildings became more exposed to wind and sun, people began to pay closer attention to the orientation of structures. In the later 1800s, the rears of buildings were built toward the prevailing wind. Elegant porches and wide eaves also appeared, which helped to stop the summer sun from beating on walls and windows, but still let in the lower winter sun. How ironic that when the energy crunch of the 1970s and 1980s struck we had to relearn many of the things our predecessors already knew!

One of few remaining mill-pond dams on the Oak Ridges Moraine.
Photo by D. McQueen

4. WATER BENEATH OUR FEET

Debbe Crandall

When I was a child, nothing was quite so wonderful as skipping from stone to stone in a creek bed in my own backyard. After school I'd dump the books, grab a snack, and run past the barn to the Stone Bridge. The creek flowed past cedar and hemlock, under the Stone Bridge and through a culvert. To the left, the creek was wide and meandering and then narrowed to a canyon. For a child, the canyon walls — at least a hundred feet high — were almost unscalable, with crisscrossing dead and leaning trees. The water was cold and clear, and the little pools that formed behind rocks were perfect to drink from. The source of the water was a wondrous little pool of water that had frogs and algae, and birds flitting after bugs. What a magical place for a child whose after-school life was with the fairies that surely lived there!

Even when there has been no rain for days, the rivers of the Moraine are always flowing. Where does all the water come from? It was years later that the magic of this little creek was explained to me in the context of the physiography of the Oak Ridges Moraine and that I began to understand its significance more fully.

The Oak Ridges Moraine is a long ridge of small hills called kames. This ridge forms the headwaters for twenty-two watersheds, which include the Credit, Humber, Don, Rouge, Ganaraska, Black, Holland and Nottawasaga Rivers (to name the biggest). While its most noticeable features are the many rivers and streams that flow north and south from these slopes, and the large stands of maple, white pine and oak that are scattered along its length, the most significant feature of the Moraine lies hidden below the ground surface.

The Moraine plays a major role in the water cycle of south-central Ontario. It forms a watershed divide, so that streams and rivers flow from the hills of the Moraine toward Lake Simcoe, Lake Ontario and Georgian Bay. If you could slice open the Moraine from end to end, you would see three main sand-and-gravel layers separated by clays and tills — something like a triple-decker sandwich — situated at different depths below the ground surface. Of these three, the middle layer, referred to as the Oak Ridges Moraine aquifer complex, is the largest and most extensive.

The movement of precipitation and meltwater

Ground water seeps out at the base of a hill. Such discharge often results in ponds and wetlands. Photo by I. Deslauriers

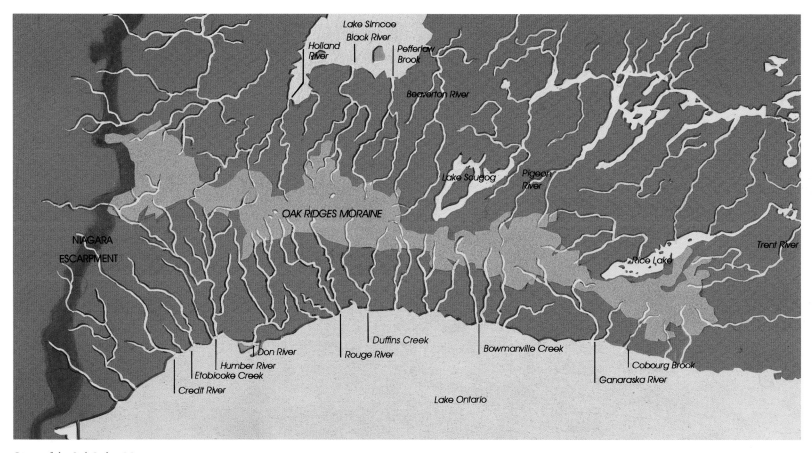

Rivers of the Oak Ridges Moraine.

below the surface of the ground is highly complex, and difficult to map. Whether this water flows along shallow paths to bubble to the surface in springs or small streams, or seeps down into aquifers hundreds of metres below the ground, is largely determined by the porosity of the underground soil layers. The Moraine is composed primarily of sands and gravels, which are much more porous than silts or clays. Because of this, up to eighty percent of surface water on the Moraine sinks down through these sands and gravels to the aquifers below.

The aquifer complex is a system of natural reservoirs that receives and stores infiltrating water, which is filtered and cleansed on its downward path. The water is slowly released from the sands and gravels at various depths, moving down from the high ridge of land toward the lower slopes, where it is discharged. Water discharges from the ground all along the Moraine, seeping into marshy wetlands, springs and intermittent streams that start off as thin ribbons of water and end up as full-blown rivers.

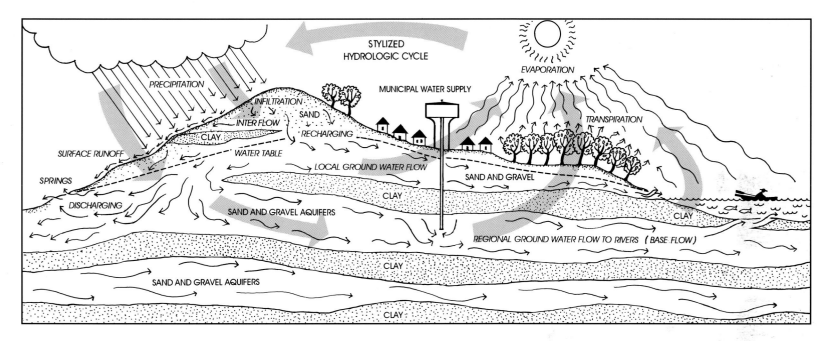

Stylized Hydrologic Cycle showing precipitation, infiltration, interflow, surface runoff, springs, discharging, recharging, evaporation, transpiration, water table, municipal water supply, local ground water flow, regional ground water flow to rivers (base flow), and sand and gravel aquifers separated by clay layers.

The Oak Ridges Moraine, with its combination of hill-and-valley topography and flatter upland and lowland areas, contributes to both local and regional ground-water flow. Local ground-water systems tend to occur where the topography forms rolling hills and valleys, with the result that water discharges from the ground a relatively short distance from where it entered. Because of the short, steep slopes of the Moraine (an average 130-metre vertical drop over 8 kilometres), these headwater areas have a relatively rapid rate of recharge.

At a regional scale, the Oak Ridges Moraine aquifer complex discharges ground water well to the north and south of the Moraine. Ground water may travel for longer distances, discharging many kilometres from the recharge areas. This action provides water to headwater streams on

and off the Moraine, and to the rivers to the north and south. In times of drought, all of the stream-flow is provided by this ground-water supply.

Over ten communities along the Moraine derive their supplies of municipal drinking water from deep wells, and most of the rural population has private wells sunk into Moraine aquifers. In fact, the classic model of the water cycle ought to be updated to include water taking as an important outflow of water from the watershed.

The combination of recharge and discharge maintains the Moraine as a natural, working ecosystem. The Moraine supplies cold, clear and clean water to rivers and streams all year, providing viable fish habitats. Where urban development has not intruded, healthy rivers and attendant valley systems provide linked corridors for wildlife migration, resulting in healthy biodiversity. Trees lining

In the Greater Toronto Area (GTA), approximately 431,000 people rely on ground water, from both private and municipal wells, to supply their water needs.

The Water Cycle

The water cycle is the constant circulation of water through the biosphere. From lakes, rivers and oceans, water evaporates into the atmosphere. It is then returned to the earth through condensation.

While the run-off from rain and snow finds its way into streams and rivers, and, finally, into the oceans, other water is stored in swamps and lowlands, huge, sponge-like layers of porous sand and gravel beneath the surface of the ground. This underground water eventually finds its way to the surface through springs and wells, or is used by plants.

Development disturbs the natural flow of groundwater on the Moraine.
Photo by L. Wise

Ground water seeps out from the lower slopes of the Moraine to steadily feed the headwaters of more than fifteen major watersheds.

hydrogeology: the science of sub-surface waters and their movement underground.

hydrology: the study of inland water, both liquid and frozen, above and below the ground.

aquifer: water deposits held below the ground in sand or gravel beds, or trapped in porous bedrock.

watershed: the land drained by a stream or river system.

recharge: water that passes downward or laterally through the soil. Recharge supplies water to aquifers.

discharge: water that seeps or bubbles from the ground. Discharge is supplied by aquifers.

water table: the upper level of ground water held in aquifers.

streams and river valleys shade the water, keeping it cool, reducing evaporation, and releasing water back to the atmosphere through transpiration. Their roots stabilize the riverbanks and help to check flowing water. The wetlands, ponds and springs act as natural flood and erosion controls to catch and store excess water. They also filter and clean surface water before it is released into the watershed basin. Kettle lakes, although not always directly connected to the underlying aquifers, have peripheral wetlands from which streams also originate.

Human impact has resulted in changes to the earth's surface that are now disrupting the water cycle of the Moraine, and this balanced, working ecosystem is beginning to fail. The construction of roads and parking lots, as well as residential, commercial and industrial developments, has disturbed and compacted the soil, preventing water from sinking into the ground. Surface water is forced to flow laterally, channeled via curbs, culverts and pipes, to the nearest flowing-water system. Along the way, it becomes contaminated with road salts, fertilizers, pesticides, herbicides, human effluent and silt. This water, reduced to waste, flows directly into streams and rivers and finally into Lake Ontario, by-passing the natural filtering process that the Moraine would otherwise provide.

But urban sprawl is not the only factor that compromises the efficiency of the water cycle. Rural communities are frequently serviced by septic systems, and improper placement, construction,

design and use allow contaminated water to enter ground-water systems. The extraction of sand and gravel also reduces and impairs the filtering ability of the Moraine. Deforestation of the steep slopes of the Moraine has resulted in soil erosion and an increased rate of run-off. Even more devastating has been the removal of the forest floor and grass cover, which is the first step in the recharge process. Excessive use of fertilizers and pesticides, by farmers, home owners and golf-course operators, is another constant assault on the system. As the population grows, water is used faster than it can be replenished.

The significant role of the Moraine in the local and regional water cycle is under extreme pressure. The health of this entire ecosystem will depend on our future use of this land. In light of our own dependence on the fresh water the Moraine provides, we must do what we can to restore and preserve this watershed.

The kettle lakes of Bond (foreground), Wilcox (middle) and St. George (background) form the headwaters of the eastern branch of the Humber River. Photo by L. Wise

5. SECRET TRAIL ON THE MORAINE

Ian Deslauriers

It's one of life's great mysteries how Glen Major has remained so green, secluded and peaceful so close to Toronto. It is just thirty minutes northeast of the city limits. Take Highway 401 to Pickering and turn north on Brock Road (Durham Road #1). Travel north to Claremont and turn right onto Regional Road 5. At Balsam, make a left turn and head north on what begins as Pickering Sideroad 4. Across a set of tracks and over the crest of a hill you will find Glen Major.

Some homes, a church and a private lodge still remain in this former hamlet, but the real treasure of this community is beyond the road, in the forest. As you pass through Glen Major, you will see a mix of pine, maple and oak forest. The trees on the left, behind the few house lots, are all on public land. The Metropolitan Toronto and Region Conservation Authority (MTRCA) owns thousands of hectares, acquired back in the late 1950s and early 1960s through the efforts of the late Charles Sauriol, one of Canada's leading conservationists. Duffins Creek has its headwaters there, and there are so many trails that you can easily get lost if you're not careful.

Once you pass through the hamlet of Glen Major, the road winds up and around some more hills. You will see a telecommunications tower on a hill on your right. Just before you reach the entrance road to the tower, you will see a gravel road on your left. Here you will find the beginning of the trail.

The old Methodist church at Glen Major. Photo by D. McQueen

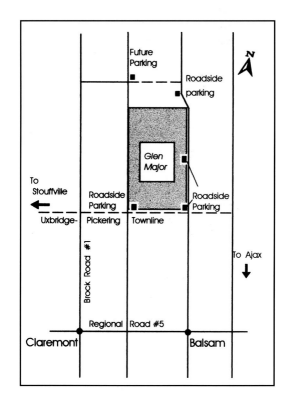

How to get there:
Take Brock Road to Claremont. Turn east on Regional Road 5. Turn north at Balsam and park on the west side of the road.

The original Walker farm with his "crops" of larch, white pine, spruce and red pine. Photo by L. Wise

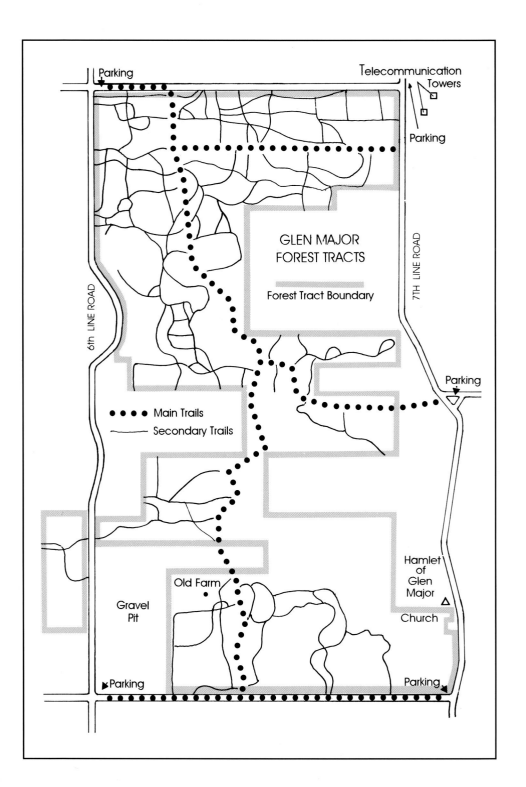

GLEN MAJOR
FOREST TRACTS

Forest Tract Boundary

Telecommunication
Towers

Parking

Parking

Parking

●●●● Main Trails

—— Secondary Trails

6th LINE ROAD

7TH LINE ROAD

Hamlet
of
Glen
Major

Church

Old Farm

Gravel
Pit

Parking

Parking

The forest here is a mix of natural woodlots and reforestation. The reforestation was carried out largely by one man: James Walker. As a young lawyer, in the 1930s, Walker visited this area. He witnessed its barren farm fields and blowing sands—the result of decades of poor farming practices combined with light sandy soils and a number of years of drought.

James Walker bought his first farm and started to plant some trees. He did some reading and soon believed he could make trees work for him and the landscape. Walker foresaw a continuous and sustainable harvest of wood fibre from a forest that would restore the landscape, bring back the wildlife, and hold more water in the ground to feed the springs that supplied Duffins Creek. Today, the Walker property provides all of those things, and one thing more: trails.

Walker eventually sold this land — about 450 hectares — to the MTRCA, bringing its total land holdings in the area to almost 1,200 hectares. Add another 200 hectares of York Region forest to that and you can see why this is one of the largest public forest land holdings in the Greater Toronto Area.

There are two ways that you can access these trails. One is to follow the road allowance directly west once you have entered the orange gate. This white-blazed section of the main Oak Ridges trail is easy to follow. For an even more scenic route with some fine vistas, walk south beyond the orange gate for a little over 200 metres until

Hikers can enjoy scenic vistas at the southern end of Glen Major.
Photo by I. Deslauriers

Trail User's Code:

- Hike only along marked routes.
- Respect the privacy of people living along the trail.
- Do not climb fences. Use stiles provided.
- Walk around the edge of fields. Do not cross them.
- Control your dog on a leash, and carry a small plastic bag for droppings.
- Do not disturb wildlife.
- Leave flowers and plants for others to enjoy.
- Carry out all garbage. Bring a plastic bag and pick up stray litter left by others.
- Light no fires.
- Carry a compass. (It is surprisingly hard to find North on a grey day.)
- Dress in clothing appropriate for the season.
- Take nothing but photographs, and leave only your thanks.

you come to a broad east–west trail. Follow this trail west.

The thin lines on the map represent cleared firebreak roads. Walking through the forest, you will see interesting combinations of larch, red pine, oak, white pine and spruce — all planted by Mr. Walker and his staff. Work your way along one of these trails in a westerly direction for just over a kilometre until you reach a major north–south trail.

If you have a few extra hours, follow the north–south trail farther south. It will take you through rolling hills and eventually lead you to an open meadow. This was once a farm field, and you can still find the foundation of the barn if you turn west at the base of the hill. The view is impressive; you can just imagine the farmer struggling to get a crop in and then watching it wash away with every driving rain on those sandy hills. Now the tall grass and wildflowers await the slow succession of ash, pine and maple trees.

On your way back, turn east at the main trail and follow it to the 7th Line. From there, walk north along the road to your car. If you choose to stay on the north–south route, pick a different trail to the east. You can't get too badly lost as long as you keep heading east until you hit the road.

So why has Glen Major remained such a big secret? For one thing, there is no natural body of water to attract swimmers and picnickers. Another reason is the slow growth of the forest. Once just a series of young pine plantations spread amongst a few remnant hardwood forests,

The haunting remains of a struggling farm in the Glen Major Forest. Photo by I. Deslauriers

this area is now covered in mature forest, with a few wild meadows hidden in the rolling hills. Finally, there has been little promotion of the area by the Conservation Authority. It was only recently that the map of firebreaks was completed as part of an inventory of the property. But with over sixty percent of Ontarians walking for fitness and fun, the next several years should see a marked change in the profile and use of Glen Major.

6. BIRDS OF THE OAK RIDGES MORAINE

Brian Henshaw

Each spring, the excited exclamations of bird-watchers ring out from Lake Erie and Lake Ontario shoreline woodlots as countless millions of returning migrant birds pour into the vast hinterland of Canada. Many of these colourful travellers are bound for the higher latitudes of the great boreal forests; however, the majority of species flooding in from their winter stays in warmer climes will stay in Southern Ontario. Many have wintered in the southern United States, but others have travelled from as far afield as Argentina, Costa Rica and the Caribbean.

The Oak Ridges Moraine is home to a surprising variety of birdlife. In this part of the province, the undulating upland forests, old fields and isolated wetlands of the Moraine represent a significant island of green amidst a sea of developed lands. The ecosystems here provide a refuge not only for the smallest of warblers and flycatchers, but also for the large and powerful birds of prey, such as hawks, and for woodpeckers, thrushes, sparrows and finches. The Moraine ecosystems do not end at arbitrarily defined boundaries. This area provides nourishing streamside habitats and wetlands. The relative

ecosystem: the community of living organisms in a certain area and its interaction with the physical environment.

BIRDS COMMONLY ENCOUNTERED IN FOUR MORAINE HABITATS:

MORAINE FOREST

red-shouldered hawk
ruffed grouse
pileated woodpecker
eastern wood pewee
least flycatcher
veery
wood thrush
red-eyed vireo
black-and-white warbler
American redstart
ovenbird
scarlet tanager
purple finch

Red-shouldered hawk.
Photo by J. Seigel

33

KETTLE PONDS

green-backed heron
wood duck
mallard
blue-winged teal
sora
willow flycatcher
yellow warbler
common yellowthroat

OPEN FIELDS

black-billed cuckoo
eastern kingbird
eastern bluebird
brown thrasher
mourning warbler
indigo bunting
rufous-sided towhee
field sparrow
vesper sparrow

Ovenbirds. Photo by J. Richards

accessibility of the Moraine's natural areas provides an excellent opportunity for people to experience some of the incredible diversity of birdlife that, at least for part of the year, calls the Oak Ridges Moraine home.

The birds that breed on the Moraine are more difficult to find during early summer, when they disperse to seek out suitable nesting territories. Naturalists are often dissuaded by a powerful combination of mosquitoes, black-flies and dense foliage. For those willing to brave these conditions, many spectacular birds can be found getting about the business of procreation. In any given year, approximately 130 species of birds breed on the Moraine, and at least another sixty pass through, as visitors. Within the GTA there are many species that breed almost exclusively on the Moraine.

There are several major habitat types on the Moraine, and each is characterized by a particular group of birds that is adapted to it. The mixed deciduous/coniferous forests are an important component of the Moraine. These forests, including the

Long Sault Conservation Area, in Durham Region, offer some of the largest remaining blocks of this habitat type in the GTA.

Perhaps the most significant aspect of these woodlands is size. Large blocks of forest reduce competition between those species of birds and animals that feed and breed at the edge of a forest and those birds that nest well inside it. American crows, brown-headed cowbirds, raccoons, eastern chipmunks, grey squirrels and other wildlife are often more numerous in areas of fragmented forest. The presence of any of these species can decrease the breeding success of birds that require deep forest sites for breeding. In addition, there are some

Pileated woodpecker. Photo by J. Richards

34

species that require large areas of suitable habitat within which to place their nesting territories.

In larger forests, we find many of our scarcer birds of prey: sharp-shinned hawk, Cooper's hawk, northern goshawk, red-shouldered hawk and broad-winged hawk. The presence of so many predatory hawks on the Moraine attests to the high productivity of this ecosystem.

The red-shouldered hawk, often seen soaring over our larger forests in mid-April, nests in large-crowned deciduous trees. Such trees can be scarce in areas that are selectively cut.

Barred owls breed in several locations on the Moraine. Another vocal nocturnal summer resident is the whippoorwill. But perhaps the most noticeable of small birds in these forests are the ever-present ovenbird, with its loud "tee-cher tee-cher tee-cher," and the vocal wood thrush, with its beautiful song that rings out from the forest floor. Other species include the dazzling warblers of the understorey, including the black-throated blue warbler and the canopy-feeding blackburnian warbler. Occasionally, species more typical of forests farther north can be found, such as the magnolia warbler and the purple finch.

Among important Moraine habitats are the many small kettle ponds and other isolated wetlands that dot the landscape. These are home to the wood duck and the mallard, while surrounding shrubs harbour the brightly coloured yellow warbler. Larger ponds and wetlands provide refuge for several scarcer species, which are often shy and difficult to see, such as the pied-billed grebe and the

least bittern. More visible might be the graceful black tern, a species that has declined markedly.

Even more species can be found in areas of transition from one habitat to another, known as ecotones. Between open wetlands and swampy forests are found the northern waterthrush, the Canada warbler and the white-throated sparrow.

Open areas of early succession, young plantations, clearcuts and old meadows are also important elements of the landscape. During an early morning walk in these habitats, one is sure to be greeted by the "drink-your-tea-ee" song of the rufous-sided towhee, the mellow, doubled-up song of the brown thrasher, the "chuwy-chuwy-chuwy" of a mourning warbler, or the emphatic "quick-quick, fire-fire, water-water!" of the dapper indigo bunting.

Recent reforestation efforts, coupled with natural regeneration, have placed additional stresses on several of the species adapted to this habitat, especially the various sparrows. These open areas should be viewed as ecosystems in their own right, and not as waste spaces to be developed or even reforested.

Eastern bluebird. Photo by J. Richards

Scarlet tanager. Photo by J. Richards

PLANTATION FORESTS

red-breasted nuthatch
hermit thrush
solitary vireo
yellow-rumped warbler
black-throated green warbler
pine warbler
chipping sparrow

Red-eyed vireo. Photo by J. Richards

Great blue heron. Photo by J. Richards

Let us hope that the eastern bluebird, with its flashing colours, will never be allowed to go the way of the endangered loggerhead shrike and Henslow's sparrow.

A relatively recent addition to the changing landscape of the Moraine are the large areas of commercially planted timber and abandoned pine plantations. These forests have introduced a group of birds that are more typically found on the Canadian Shield. The haunting flute-like song of the hermit thrush, recently well established as a Moraine-breeding bird, is surely one of the most beautiful songs in the bird world. To hear it, one must wait until dusk on a calm summer's evening. Several other species have readily adapted to this new niche. The most common are the brown creeper, the golden-crowned kinglet, the solitary vireo and the black-throated green warbler.

Some birds use the Moraine for very specific purposes. Several species, including the great blue heron, feed in small Moraine wetlands, but may nest several miles away in their heronries. Belted kingfishers dart along streams and rivers that are fed by Moraine discharge and surface creeks.

The Moraine is also important to a wide variety of birds in search of food and shelter while on their long migrations every spring and fall. Some species even find food and shelter on the Moraine throughout the winter months. When northern food crops fail, birds that would otherwise stay in the north often arrive in huge numbers looking for alternative sources of food.

The birdlife of the Oak Ridges Moraine is vibrant and varied. It is my hope that we can share this sanctuary with them for generations to come.

Evening grosbeak. Photo by J. Richards

7. PURPLE WOODS CONSERVATION AREA

Christopher L. Conti

A modest 17 hectares, Purple Woods is nevertheless considered one of the most interesting and significant conservation areas along the Oak Ridges Moraine. It is located on the crest of the Moraine, and marks the watershed divide between the headwaters that drain north to the massive wetland that feeds into Lake Scugog, and the streams that flow south toward Lake Ontario via Oshawa Creek.

Just south of the parking lot, the wooden viewing platform, which stands 320 metres above sea level, affords one of the most extensive views of Lake Ontario anywhere in the GTA, with visibility of more than 20 kilometres. The incredibly varied topography of the Moraine can be seen from this vantage point — hills, valleys, lakes, rivers and forest. Try to time your visit for a clear, sunny day.

Located at the headwaters of Oshawa Creek, Purple Woods is a combination of forests, meadows and rolling hills. The Central Lake Ontario Conservation Authority (CLOCA) established the conservation area through property purchases in the mid-to-late 1970s. Its long-term goal is to purchase another 9 hectares of land when funds are available.

In purchasing the area, the Conservation Authority recognized the need to protect forested portions of the Moraine. Since the Moraine is the headwaters area for the major streams within the CLOCA watershed, protection of the existing forest and regeneration of natural areas help to ensure the future integrity of ground and surface waters in the watershed. The forest captures a share of the rain that falls on it. This promotes infiltration by helping to prevent the rain from running quickly into streams and rivers, where the flow would be quickly discharged downstream and eventually into Lake Ontario.

Purple Woods contains a variety of forest and meadow habitats, a small picnic area, and a maple syrup operation. Roughly half the area is hardwood forest and the other half is meadow. With its mix of forest and field, the area is an excellent place to see a variety of wildlife. Even the uncommon black-throated blue warbler has been reported to breed in the area.

Eastward from the viewing platform, the Sugarbush Nature Trail provides a short interpretive hike through the forest. The species composition

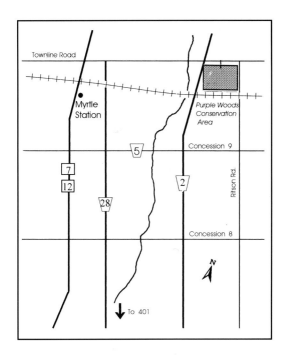

How to get there:
Turn north onto Simcoe Street from either the 401 or Highway 2 and head north to just within Oshawa city limits. After passing under the CPR bridge, you are getting close. Ample signage will direct you to the conservation area.

Old-style sugar-bush demonstration.
Photo courtesy of Central Lake Ontario Conservation Authority

of maple, beech and ash, with some mature specimens of black cherry, red oak and other hardwoods, provides one of the few examples of this type of mature woodlot in this section of the Moraine.

Just past Post 5 on the trail, a few steps south along Ritson Road, you will see a mature beech and a mature maple growing up against each other. Both these species do well in the deep-shaded understorey of mature forest, and this accounts for their increasing dominance over the red oak, which needs more light.

In autumn, the beeches produce large quantities of edible nuts, a favourite food of chipmunks and squirrels. Another interesting characteristic of this tree is that it can produce new shoots from its own roots and from old stumps. This allows the tree to regenerate without depending solely on its seeds.

The Nature Trail branches out to the southeast, leading to the Sugar Shack. Every year, in March and April, the Conservation Authority

Sugar maple

Beech

To tell sugar maples from other maples, look for opposite branching of the twigs, and vertical strips of bark that curl at the edges on mature trees.

Opposite: Maple and Beech trees fused together.
Photo by D. McQueen

A carpet of trilliums in a maple forest. Photo by D. McQueen

Spring beauty, a pretty spring perennial, grows from an underground tuber rather like a small potato. This tuber has a sweet, chestnut-like flavour, and Native people and early settlers used it for food.

Chipmunk

Squirrel corn

More information can be obtained from the Central Lake Ontario Conservation Authority (CLOCA), 100 Whiting Avenue, Oshawa, Ontario L1H 3T3.

Spring beauty. Photo by G. Berry

operates a maple syrup demonstration that attracts thousands of people. The trees are tapped through a series of plastic lines, and also with individual buckets. There is an annual pancake breakfast during maple syrup season, and maple products are available for purchase in the area.

A little later in the spring, the forest floor erupts with red and white trilliums and other woodland spring flowers. Among the plants in this area are the less common spring beauty and squirrel corn.

Purple Woods Conservation Area provides us an opportunity to learn the importance of the Moraine, to understand our connection to its watersheds, and to enjoy and appreciate its beauty. Areas like this are critical not only to the protection of the natural systems of the Moraine and the watershed, but also to our continued interaction with nature.

8. A HIKE THROUGH MARY LAKE MONASTERY

Fiona Cowles

A new trail across the Oak Ridges Moraine was a visionary idea fostered by a group of volunteers who saw its potential for both recreation and education. From this beginning the Oak Ridges Trail Association (ORTA) was formed. This hike, through Mary Lake Monastery, in King Township, is part of the trail developed by ORTA.

This walk is at its best in the spring, when the new leaves are bursting, and in the fall, when the array of colours in the mixed deciduous woodland is a delight. Good footwear is essential because of occasional wet spots.

The access point for this section of the trail is at the intersection of Jane Street and the 16th Sideroad (about 4 kilometres north of the King Sideroad). You can either park on the shoulder or in the churchyard on the southeast corner. This is the centre of a small hamlet known as Sacred Heart, which began as a colony established during the Depression by the Catholic Church. The Church provided thirty-five needy Toronto families with ten acres each, a small house, chickens and seed for planting. The colony became self-supporting

and operated a number of co-operative ventures.

From the intersection, walk east for about 500 metres along the 16th Sideroad, known as "Green Lane" because the trees extend an arch of foliage over the dirt road. Look for a tree on your right with white blazes indicating a right turn. Just beyond, deep in the bush, a stile over a fence will lead you to the beginning of the trail. A little farther, you will see a sign that lists some rules of the trail — very important, since you will be walking over private property. You are asked to stay on the blazed trail and to control your dog on a leash at all times.

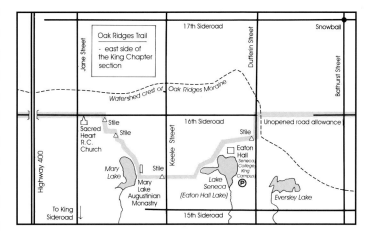

The Oak Ridges Trail Association (ORTA) was formed in October 1991 with the long-term goal of developing a trail, section by section, along the full length of the Moraine, from the Niagara Escarpment in the west, to Northumberland forest in the east. When complete, this trail will link the Bruce Trail, the Ganaraska Trail and adjacent valley trails such as the Humber and the Rouge. ORTA welcomes everyone interested in helping with this project.

For the address of ORTA and other organizations relating to the Oak Ridges Moraine, please consult the list at the back of this book.

Mary Lake is a kettle lake that drains into the east branch of the Humber River. Photo by L. Wise

Pileated woodpecker

Follow the white blazes down the wide grassy path, through tall spruce and birch, until you reach an open field and the remnants of an apple orchard. Arrow signs along the western and southern edges of the field lead to a stile over a tall fence.

This is the entrance to the Mary Lake Monastery, the property of the Augustinian Fathers since 1935, formerly owned by Sir Henry Pellatt of Casa Loma fame. The high fencing in the corner of this 1,000-acre farm was originally erected to enclose a herd of elk and deer that was kept for hunting. The concrete fence posts have survived remarkably intact since the early 1920s. The Augustinians have kindly allowed the trail to pass through their institutional lands, and care should be taken to respect the privacy of the monks by staying on the marked trail.

After hopping the stile, take a left turn along a woodland path. The trail here is rough and steep in places, and winds through cedar, hickory and birch woodland, up hill and down dale, until you get a glimpse of a large expanse of water through the trees.

Mary Lake (or Lake Marie, as it was known for many years) is a kettle lake. It was formed by a block of ice that was buried in the glacial deposits of the Oak Ridges Moraine at the end of the last ice age. The trail, wet in places, especially during the spring runoff, follows the lakeside until it comes quite close to the Mary Lake shrine, a striking church with a tower reminiscent of some old Scottish churches. The monastery buildings, which house about thirty monks, are nestled beside the church, and overlook the lake. As you walk through the woodlands and marshy area at the head of the lake, you may be lucky enough to see a great blue heron swooping over the water. You may also hear the distinctive call of the pileated woodpecker from a perch high on a hollow tree.

On reaching the lakeside pump house, take a sharp left turn and head up the slope towards an enormous brick barn. This impressive structure was built by Pellatt and is still used by the Augustinians, housing their dairy herd of brown, soft-eyed Jersey cows and black-and-white Holsteins. Follow the white blazes across the farmyard area and watch for the electric fence, or hop over the stile at the side of the trail. This will lead you to a raised lane that used to be the spur of an old rail line to the Pellatt estate. As there are cattle and pigs in this area, dogs must be leashed.

There are marshy areas on either side of the raised pathway, and the weeds grow high through the summer, so wear long sleeves and pants to keep the mosquitoes at bay. The lane leads toward Keele Street, through more fields and woodlands, to another stile. Directly opposite the stile, the trail continues into Seneca College's King Campus.

9. ZEPHYR TRACT—
YORK REGIONAL FOREST

Paul Harpley

The Zephyr Tract of the York Regional Forest system is an 85-hectare tract located on the northern extremity of the Oak Ridges Moraine. There is a gravel lot on the north side of Holborn Road, where visitors can park. Leading from the north end of this lot, the trail follows an abandoned rail line. The rail ties and track have been removed, so walking is easy. Where the rail line swings to the north, enter the path into the thick cedar forest and ascend the sloping trail to the west. In a few minutes, the main north–south walking trail will appear near the top of a ridge in a thick jack pine reforestation area. After a ten-minute walk to the north, you will be sufficiently deep in the forest that the sandy trail and the smell of pine needles will tempt you to forget the daily concerns of life, and you will be free to experience the beauty and serenity of nature.

Many side trails branch off through a variety of forest habitats, from pine reforestation, through open forest meadow, to mature maple/beech glades. On warm June days, the sun filters through the trees, casting elaborate shadows on the forest floor. Small bluffs are exposed along the trail at what seem like regular intervals. These bluffs, beneath a thick, acidic pine-needle duff, are composed of the light brown sandy soil so characteristic of parts of the Oak Ridges Moraine, with not a pebble to be found anywhere. The soil is dry here, and the sand quickly absorbs any rainwater, which filters down into deep aquifers within this natural ridge of glacial till.

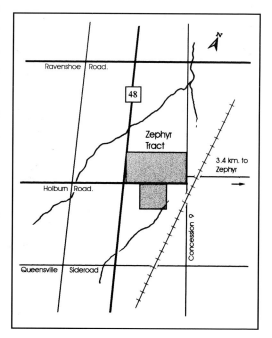

How to get there:
From the south, take Highway 404 to Newmarket and turn right onto Davis Drive. After a ten-minute drive, turn left onto Highway 48. About twenty minutes later you will reach Holborn Road. Turn right. The Zephyr Tract is located on either side of Holborn Road, just west of Concession 9, East Gwillimbury.

43

Red-shouldered hawk

The jack pines were planted over fifty years ago to settle the sand that had blown out of control following the original clearing of this land just before the turn of the twentieth century. The pine trees grow in regular lines, as they were planted, and the distinct lack of bird songs is a reminder that nature does not always appreciate our efforts. Even here, where nature has long since reclaimed the land, the effects of human influence on the landscape can be seen: evidence of past wildfires, old tree stumps from logging, and split-rail fences of farm fields returned to forest.

In the spring and summer, hikers can hear the

Opposite: Surrounded by forest, these cedar rails are evidence of long-abandoned farm pasture. Photo by S. Russell

Red pine are common in plantations. Photo by G. Berry

calls and songs of many bird species, both in the open forest meadows and in the green, breezy maple/beech forest. Black-capped chickadees, common flickers, American robins and ovenbirds make their presence known through melodious songs and flitting movements among the trees and on the forest floor.

The Zephyr Tract is at the very end of a long, sinuous geomorphic feature that snakes its way across the landscape in the northern GTA. The high, sandy slopes, many of them now wooded, stand in stark contrast to the wide lowland Lake Simcoe plain that stretches to the north, with its wide, meandering rivers and sensitive wetlands. Many small trout streams originate here from woodland springs at the base of the Moraine slopes, and flow down to the Black River and Pefferlaw Brook, eventually arriving at the shining waters of Lake Simcoe.

Environmental awareness of the north slope of the Moraine is relatively poor. These areas provide habitat for mammals that are rarely seen near the large urban centres to the south. River otters and porcupines are routinely encountered here, and bobcats can be heard yowling in the night. In the Lake Simcoe wetlands and wildlands, just off the Moraine, moose and black bear are occasionally seen. They come into the area from time to time from the near north of Muskoka and the Kawarthas.

You might be lucky enough to catch a glimpse of a red-shouldered hawk, a provincially significant breeding bird in the area. In past years, several nests have been found here in the mature forest. This iso-

Bobcat

lated locale, with clean, flowing rivers, is an ideal habitat.

About an hour in, the trail becomes overgrown. You descend into the low cedar scrub and wetlands at the base of the Moraine slope. Here the trail meets numerous informal paths, many of which exhibit extreme erosion damage. These are evidence of one of the most devastating of human activities on the Moraine: dirt biking. This scourge of natural areas threatens wildlife and seriously degrades the land base.

In late summer, among the cedars and around the lowland springs and wet places, are shy displays of delicate orchids. Helleborine, an introduced orchid, has spread widely and is now a common plant. It stands about 25 centimetres high, with greenish flowers, and is now often found growing with native woodland species.

The Zephyr Tract offers a rich opportunity to escape the pace and noise of the city — a chance to refresh the spirit and establish perspective in our harried lives. To those who had the foresight to establish the many parks and conservation areas along the Moraine, we owe a debt of gratitude. The efforts of these early conservation pioneers produced a magnificent legacy, but a legacy that is under siege from reduced funding and the constant threat of pollution and urban development. We all have an urgent duty to see that this inheritance is not lost through indifference or neglect.

10. THE RIDGES AT LONG SAULT

Dale Hoy

From Durham Road 20, just east of Grasshopper Park Road, turn north on Woodley Road, which winds up a hill through old farm fields to the Long Sault parking lot. A short walk to the west takes you up to a knoll from which you can gaze south over the Bowmanville Creek watershed clear on down to Lake Ontario. Behind the trees, to the west, lies an active quarry. To the north is one of the best examples of today's typical Moraine forest.

After the glaciers disappeared from these hills about ten thousand years ago, white and black spruce and tamarack covered the gravelly soils. As the climate warmed, the water drained away from the porous soils, and the spruces made way for the mixed deciduous/coniferous forests of American

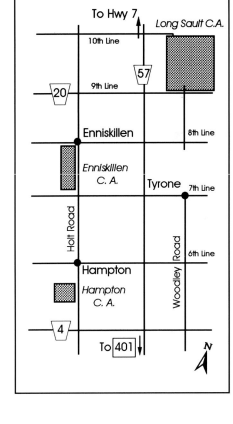

The naked limbs of deciduous trees dominate the forests of Long Sault. Photo by L. Wise

47

How to get there:

The main entrance and parking are off Sideroad 20, northeast of Enniskillen. There is also a northwest entrance to the property at Concession 10 and Avery Road; this provides ample parking and immediate access to the trails.

Facilities:

Interpretive trails
Toilets
Parking available
Cross-country skiing

The fall colours of a young maple forest. Photo by G. Berry

beech, sugar maple, ironwood, red oak, yellow birch, white pine and hemlock. The white pines were huge, the kind that take four men with arms outstretched to surround.

During the logging heyday, the great white pines were taken from the Moraine ridges for use as planking and masts on nineteenth-century sailing ships. Lumber was shipped along a route from Manvers Township to Port Darlington. The old road suffered periodic flooding and thus became known as *Sault* (French for "rapids").

Today, the Conservation Area at Long Sault is a remnant of the great forests that once covered the Moraine. Fragments of this forest still persist, at Happy Valley, Glenville Hills, Jefferson, York Region, Glen Major and Ganaraska, and form the headwaters of the Humber River. Long Sault is nestled between Glen Major and Ganaraska and boasts well-marked and easily accessible walking and skiing trails of varying lengths.

The logging and farming history of the area is evident in the variety of plant communities that exist. Old fields have filled with shrubs and pioneering trees, and pine plantations now occupy areas once cleared for farming. The original settlers did not realize that the occurrence of pine on these ridges was indicative of poor agricultural soils. In many places, clearing of the forest resulted in exposed sand, which the wind massaged into restless dunes. Plantations of red, Scots, white and jack pines were used to calm and anchor the shifting sands, but this limited variety of tree species also limited wildlife habitat. In the south, eastern

white cedar thickets and a small pond mark two, small spring-fed wetlands. In the north lies the largest forested area on Central Lake Ontario Conservation Authority land.

Entering the deciduous forest from the north entrance is like entering a cathedral. The canopy, comprised of sugar maple, American beech and red oak, soars high above the sparse ground cover. Some of the white birch and aspen that originally colonized the cut-over forest and sheltered the seedlings of the maples and beeches that followed, still remain. Much of the low cover is sugar maple, persisting as small shrubs unable to grow taller in the deep shade of the canopy. When one of the elder maples succumbs to wind or disease, the gap in the canopy will admit shafts of light, triggering a life-and-death race among the shrubby maples on the forest floor. Of the dozens that compete for space, only one or two will live to fill the gap.

Occasional dark copses of eastern hemlock cling to the cooler, north-facing slopes of the forest. The elegant branches droop daintily, shading out almost all the ground cover beneath. Under the deciduous trees, a great array of wildflowers thrives. Trilliums, bloodroot, hepatica, Canada mayflower, shinleaf, pipsissewa, Solomon's seal and sarsaparilla brightly clothe the spring forest floor. These flower buds are set in the previous fall, enabling them to thrust up as the snow melts with spring's warm rays of sun. Later in the season, they are followed by wild columbine, white baneberry, woodland asters and zigzag goldenrod. Framing it all are the ferns — lady, bracken, spinulose wood and

Red maple

Red oak

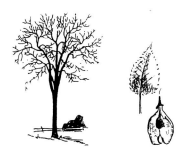

White elm

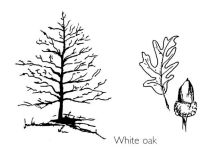

White oak

Hepatica

Solomon's seal

White baneberry

Bracken fern

Rattlesnake fern. Photo by J. Seigel

rattlesnake — which silently produce and disperse millions of spores during the course of the summer.

Walking the north trail at evening, you will hear the birds begin to sing again after an afternoon respite. Ovenbirds are all around. Red-eyed vireos sing monotonously, and black-capped chickadees and ovenbirds are never far away.

An array of warblers flits through the trees, and a flash of scarlet and black indicates the presence of the scarlet tanager. Five species of woodpecker nest here: a tribute to the age of the trees and the size of the forested area. The total number of bird species has never been inventoried, but during spring migration this is among the best of places to see birds, and is a lot less cluttered with birders than the better-known places.

Chipmunks, moles and white-tailed deer are among the mammals here, and there are many species of amphibians and snakes. Watch for

bright orange salamanders among the leaf litter. These salamanders are efts — red-spotted newts in the juvenile stage. After hatching from eggs laid in ponds, they leave for dry land. They roam the forest floor for three to seven years before they return to the pond as adults, and they remain completely aquatic thereafter.

Long Sault, a place of history and great beauty, is unique in Durham Region. The mosaic of fields, plantations and natural forest provides habitat for a rich and varied sampling of plants and animals. Looking into the distance toward Lake Ontario, one can see the relentless approach of housing and industry. When these hills were first farmed and logged, there were still sufficient wildlands surrounding the cleared areas to provide seed sources for renewal. Since those days, we have lost almost all of the forest in Southern Ontario. As a result, the value of the few remaining fragments is now immeasurable, both in aesthetic and biological terms. It is only with our care and protection that Long Sault will remain.

Red-spotted newt. Photo by J. Kamstra

11. THE RICE LAKE PLAINS

James Kamstra

South of Rice Lake, in Northumberland County, lies an area known as the Rice Lake Plains. To the casual back-road explorer, this area may not seem much different from other areas of the Oak Ridges Moraine. It is a pleasant rolling landscape of woodlots, hedgerows, sand hills and old fields. For the botanist, however, this is one of the most intriguing areas of the Moraine.

Catharine Parr Traill (in *The Backwoods of Canada*, 1836) was the first to describe the Rice Lake Plains in writing. On September 1, 1832, near the village of Cold Springs, she wrote, "We now ascend the plains, a fine elevation of land, for many miles scantily clothed with oaks, and here and there bushy pines. A number of exquisite flowers and shrubs adorn these plains which rival any garden in beauty." In her later works, she describes many of the plants she encountered, including lupines, blazing stars, Indian paintbrush and prairie grasses.

The pioneers quickly converted the original grasslands into cropland and pasture. Because there were few trees, the Rice Lake Plains were easier to clear and cultivate than the surrounding

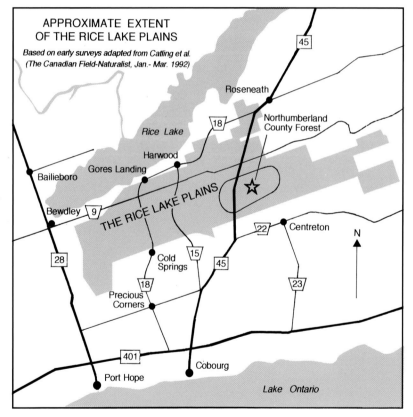

APPROXIMATE EXTENT OF THE RICE LAKE PLAINS

Based on early surveys adapted from Catling et al. (The Canadian Field-Naturalist, Jan.- Mar. 1992)

We do not usually associate prairies with Ontario. However, true grasslands were an original feature of parts of Ontario and covered large portions of the southwestern section of the province. Small pockets of prairie and associated oak savanna vegetation occurred where soil conditions were suitable. Today, remnants exist in several sites, including London, Brantford, Holland Landing and Toronto's High Park.

forest. When looking at today's landscape of farms and woodlots, it is hard to believe that natural prairie and savanna once covered several hundred square kilometres prior to European settlement. How was that possible in the humid climate of

51

Rice Lake, near Harwood. Photo by J. Kamstra

One of the earliest forms of wildlife management was practised by the Mississaugas on the Rice Lake Plains. In *The Backwoods of Canada*, Catharine Parr Traill writes, "These plains were formerly famous hunting grounds of the Indians, who, to prevent the growth of timbers, burned them year after year." In fact, the Mississaugas' original name for Rice Lake was *pem-a-dash-da-dota*, meaning "Lake of the Burning Plains."

Purple lupines. Photo by J. Kamstra

Black oak. Photo by J. Kamstra

Southern Ontario, which was primarily covered with unbroken forest? Two critical factors allowed a flora more typical of Western Canada to thrive here: sand and fire.

The Oak Ridges Moraine is a ridge of sand, gravel and clay. Soils of the Rice Lake Plains have a particularly high sand component. Sand particles are large and do not hold moisture for as long as finer grained soils. In addition, when sand is exposed to sunlight, a hot microclimate results. Consequently, only plants that can tolerate drought and heat will survive there. Prairie plants are superbly adapted to dry conditions and require a lot of sunlight. Although plant succession is much slower on sandy soils than on clay or loam soils, shrubs and trees will eventually establish themselves. Sun-loving plants are then shaded out. Periodic fires, however, burn off the woody plants and recreate a suitable habitat for the sun-loving plants.

The Natives who inhabited this area before the settlers managed their hunting grounds by regularly putting the torch to the dry vegetation, burning off the woody plants and accumulated humus. Prairie herbs and grasses returned, which in turn were favoured by deer.

Wide expanses of rolling grassland, festooned with the purple of lupines and the red of Indian paintbrush, can no longer be found on the Rice Lake Plains, but most of the fifty or so species of prairie and savanna plants can still be found in remnant patches of habitat. Ironically, in the area near Cold Springs, virtually no original habitat remains, for these lands are now intensively cropped. Further east, however, the soil is poorer; this has allowed pockets of the unique flora to persist.

To me, the two species that best characterize the dry habitat of the Rice Lake Plains are black oak and butterfly milkweed. Black oak is the most drought resistant of all of Ontario's oak species. Although common here, the Northumberland black oak population is separated from the nearest known site by about 100 kilometres (to the southwest). At first glance, the black oak appears very similar to the familiar red oak. The leaves of the black oak possess more deeply notched lobes, however, giving the canopy a spiky look. In addition, with its gnarled trunk and low-hanging branches, the black oak has a somewhat ragged character.

Butterfly milkweed is scattered among many of the neglected fields in the eastern portions of the plain. It is most noticeable in mid-July, when the plants are topped with brilliant orange clusters of flowers. Where the milkweed abounds, less conspicuous prairie plants can often be found, including hoary vervain, prairie cinquefoil, bush clover, yellow flax and Bicknell's frostweed. In late summer, the tall prairie grasses show off their

Black oak

Butterfly milkweed. Photo by J. Kamstra

Like the prairie flora of the Rice Lake Plains, butterflies also find dry, open and sunny habitats to their liking. Monarchs, aphrodite fritillaries, painted ladies, common wood nymphs, and skippers of several species can be seen there. The flowers of the butterfly milkweed are a favourite place for butterflies to alight and sip nectar, and New Jersey tea is another excellent nectar source. Other plants are eaten by the butterfly larvae. Black oak, for example, provides food for caterpillars of several species including Edward's hairstreak and Juvenal's duskywing skipper.

Prairie cinquefoil. Photo by J. Kamstra

It is believed that prairie vegetation moved into what is now Ontario from the southwest during a warmer, drier time about 5,000 years ago. As the climate cooled, small patches of prairie vegetation remained only where habitat conditions favoured it. The Natives' use of fire is believed to have been a critical factor in preventing forests from colonizing most of the prairie sites. Probably the best example of prairie/savanna in Ontario today — still burned regularly by the Native population — is on Walpole Island.

flowers. Perhaps best known are the big bluestem, with its turkey-foot top, and the slightly smaller little bluestem. Sky-blue and heath asters, mixed with several species of goldenrod, and Indian grass, with its lustrous golden-brown seed clusters, colour the savanna pockets in early autumn.

The flowering plants seen here in spring are quite different. Appearing in early May, the prairie buttercup, early buttercup, arrow-leaved violet and hairy rock cress are among the earliest flowers on the plain. In early June, the eastern lupine shows its spectacular display in the few areas where it still occurs.

Remnant pockets of prairie flora can be found in other parts of the Oak Ridges Moraine. Dry, sandy soil is a common feature throughout, so it is not surprising that the occasional patches of prairie cinquefoil, hoary vervain and dropseed occur. But the Rice Lake Plains are special because of the unusually high diversity of prairie flora found on them.

While the flora of the Rice Lake Plains makes the area botanically unique, the wildlife is also worth noting. These black-oak savannas are a favourite haunt of the eastern bluebird, the

Early buttercup. Photo by J. Kamstra

Smooth green snake. Photo by J. Kamstra

rufous-sided towhee, the brown thrasher and the field sparrow. Smooth green snakes, although rarely seen, are common in the dry meadows, and the sand-loving eastern hognose snake is known only on this portion of the Moraine.

There are many interesting sites containing prairie flora on the back roads of the Rice Lake Plains. Northumberland County Roads 9, 15, 18 and 22 provide access to this area, which lies roughly between the villages of Gores Landing, Baltimore, Castleton and Roseneath. Most of the lands here are privately owned and are not open to the public. But the Northumberland County Forest, bisected by Highway 45, is public land and contains a maze of sand roads. While most of the forest consists of reforested pine plantations, there are pockets of open habitat here and there, where the prairie flora can be found. A good place to look is anywhere along the hydro-electric transmission line that crosses through the southern part of the forest. Who knows? Maybe you will find a yet-undiscovered patch of lupine or blazing star.

12. WHERE THE MORAINE MEETS THE ESCARPMENT

Susan Powell

In Southern Ontario, two significant bedrock features dominate the landscape: the Niagara Escarpment and the Oak Ridges Moraine. These features are a source of outstanding geological information, great beauty, and a wealth of ecological diversity. They also offer numerous recreational opportunities for the adventurer and inspirational landscapes for the artist.

An ideal place to explore both of these glacial legacies is Glen Haffy Conservation Area (formerly known as Glen Haffy Forest and Wildlife Area) in Caledon. Owned and managed by the Metropolitan Toronto and Region Conservation Authority (MTRCA), this 325-hectare area is located on the eastern edge of the Niagara Escarpment Orangeville-Caledon outlier, and at

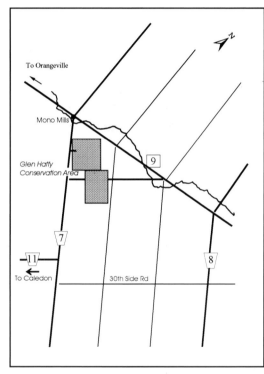

How to get there:	Facilities:
The entrance is on the east side of Airport Road, just south of Highway 9.	Trails
	Toilets
	Well
	Parking
	Fishing (fee)
	Closed in winter

Fall colours at the Glen Haffy lookout.
Photo courtesy of MTRCA

Forest trails are perfect for quiet family walks. Photo courtesy of MTRCA

outlier: an isolated mass of bedrock resting on an older rock

the western end of the Oak Ridges Moraine, between the Humber and Credit River valleys. Glen Haffy C.A. is one of over 105 parks in the continuous Niagara Escarpment Parks and Open Space System.

Glen Haffy C.A. offers several opportunities to learn about geology, ecology and forestry. Note the irregular, rolling landscape opposite the entrance on the east side of Airport Road. This is part of the Singhampton Moraine, formed by the Georgian Bay ice lobe. Upon entering the park, the road slopes down into a depression where a channel was formed by the meltwater of a huge mass of glacial ice. The channel begins south of Glen Haffy, in Sleswick, and ends up near Mono Mills at Highway 9 and Airport Road.

If you drive toward the lookout point, you will cross yet another Moraine, called the

Gibraltar. This moraine was formed when the margin of the glacier stood for a time near the present edge of the Niagara Escarpment. The view from the lookout point is incredible. The scattered boulders, and those used to make up the stone wall, are erratics, differing in composition from the existing bedrock. These rocks, mostly granite, were carried by the glaciers from the Precambrian shield, a distance of at least 100 kilometres. Here you can also see deposits of sand and gravel that the glaciers left behind in the form of small hills or kames, which mantle the face of the Escarpment.

Glen Haffy Conservation Area is one of the most popular areas for trout fishing in Southern Ontario. Two stocked public ponds provide a superb recreational opportunity for the whole family. Glen Haffy is also home to the MTRCA's fish-rearing facility. Thousands of rainbow trout are raised to angling size and used to stock the Glen Haffy ponds (and other MTRCA waters). The ponds at Glen Haffy are spring fed, with cold, clean water from the Escarpment.

A nature trail through the area takes you into a magnificent forest filled with a variety of native tree species. This is home to many migrating and breeding birds, including ovenbirds and wood thrushes, and a variety of wildflowers, including trout lily, jack-in-the-pulpit, red and white trilliums, wild ginger and spring beauty, as well as many fern species.

A section of the Bruce Trail enters the conservation area and joins the Glen Haffy Loop, which offers a circular hiking route. From the open parkland, the trail descends the Escarpment, crosses a small stream, and then enters a mature wood.

Red trillium. Photo by S. Russell

Jack-in-the-pulpit. Photo by J. Seigel

Unmarked paths to the west lead to vantage points from which the rolling countryside can be viewed. The trail then merges with a wider path that leads from the top of the Escarpment down to the group camping area. Camping is permitted in designated areas only. The trail leaves the campsite at the edge of a mixed forest and emerges into open and reforested fields before reaching Highway 9.

Whether you are a hiker, picnicker, birder, fishing enthusiast, photographer, painter or geographer, or just enjoy a walk with your dog, be sure to explore and experience Glen Haffy Conservation Area.

Wild ginger. Photo by J. Seigel

58

13. SAND AND GRAVEL

Margaret Cranmer-Byng

The Oak Ridges Moraine is rich in aggregate resources, which include sand, gravel, crushed rock or stone, or any combination of these. Aggregates are a non-renewable resource, and there are few areas with the same quality or quantity as the Oak Ridges Moraine. They are the basic material for all kinds of construction, including highways and bridges, residential, commercial, and industrial buildings and parking lots, and sewage and storm-water systems.

Sand and gravel extraction has been going on for over a hundred years on the Oak Ridges Moraine. In the early days, pits were small, but as

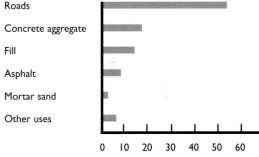

SAND AND GRAVEL USE IN ONTARIO (in percent)

Roads
Concrete aggregate
Fill
Asphalt
Mortar sand
Other uses

0 10 20 30 40 50 60

(From Energy, Mines and Resources Canada)

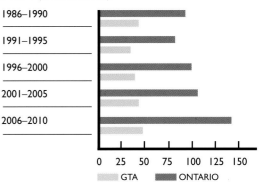

FORECASTED SAND AND GRAVEL DEMAND FOR ONTARIO AND THE GTA AVERAGED FOR THE FIVE-YEAR PERIOD (in million tonnes).

1986–1990
1991–1995
1996–2000
2001–2005
2006–2010

0 25 50 75 100 125 150

GTA   ONTARIO

(From "A State of the Resource" Study. Planning Initiatives Ltd., 1993)

Gravel extraction next to Glen Major forests. Photo by I. Deslauriers

59

A large manmade lake south of Goodwood. Photo by L. Wise

towns and villages grew and as Metropolitan Toronto spread into the countryside, aggregate operations expanded. The Moraine is now a major source of supply — one that is economically attractive, as greater proximity to markets means lower transportation costs and a lower cost for the final product.

The trend towards larger operations continues. Today, many sites cover huge expanses of land, and the work could span decades before the resource is exhausted. The dilemma is that this valuable material is often located beneath woodlands, wetlands, headwater areas and forests. With the extraction of sand and gravel, the unique fil-tering ability of these sections of the Moraine is lost, which adversely affects the water quality of the Moraine. This is a major concern, since, in the rehabilitation of these areas, large amounts of chemical fertilizer are often used.

Rehabilitation is now required by law, which means that the land is to be restored to its former condition, or changed so that it is compatible with adjacent land. Unfortunately, even with human help, the distinctive landform of the Moraine may be impossible to reproduce. The gravel and sand are needed, but so are the Moraine's other natural resources. Hard choices and tough decisions lie ahead.

14. PANGMAN SPRINGS CONSERVATION AREA

Dan Zilstra

Pangman Springs is a remarkably diverse area; with its woods, fields and ponds, it is an oasis of natural beauty. Wide, well-worn paths permit easy access for families and groups. The gently rolling terrain, characteristic of the Moraine, is excellent for gentle hikes in summer, or for cross-country skiing and snowshoeing in winter.

Located on the north face of the Oak Ridges Moraine, the Pangman Springs property is comprised of 98 hectares of forest, meadows, hills, ponds and streams. As the name suggests, you are never far from water. An aquifer under the Moraine is a constant source of waters for both Bogart Creek and the Black River.

From the east entrance, just north of the Porritt Tract of the York Regional Forest, the trail starts off through a typical cedar lowland forest. The cedars are very dense and block out much of the light, making the air quite cool and damp. A

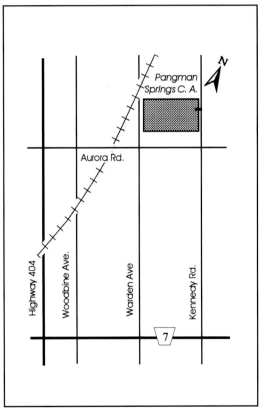

Trout lily. Photo by G. Berry

How to get there:
Travel north on Kennedy Road from Aurora Road. The entrance is about 1 kilometre along on the west side of the road.

Facilities:
Roadside parking only

61

Raccoon — the bandit of the forest. Photo by F. Clauer

The acquisition of this property was made possible by donations from private individuals, from the Nature Conservancy of Canada, and from the Ministry of Natural Resources. Pangman Springs was purchased by the Lake Simcoe Region Conservation Authority in 1986. It is named after a family who donated funds for the land purchase.

Shortly after its purchase, a master plan by the Lake Simcoe Region Conservation Authority (LSRCA) recommended an Outdoor Education Centre for the site. Given the poor economic climate, this could not be achieved until 1996, when a partnership between the (LSRCA) and Trails Youth Initiatives was developed. This partnership will provide much-needed income to ensure that the property is conserved and maintained in public ownership.

Opposite: A lush forest floor in Pangman Springs.
Photo by I. Deslauriers

quiet stillness surrounds you, but if you are fortunate, you may hear the drumming of a ruffed grouse. Grouse are often heard but rarely seen, as the forest is so dense. Black-capped chickadees and winter wrens are abundant among the sheltering cedars.

Next you enter the majestic, mature beech and maple hardwood forest that covers much of the drier uplands of the park. The forest is very different here, with the openness created by the lofty canopy. This patch of forest is typical of what once covered much of Southern Ontario. In late April and early May, before the canopy leafs out, the forest is carpeted with wildflowers. Trillium, spring beauty, jack-in-the-pulpit, trout-lily and Dutchman's-breeches, among others, light up the floor, and the air is perfumed by these spring gems.

On the annual hike of the Richmond Hill Naturalists, the botanists are kept busy identifying flower after flower, while the birders crane their necks to the treetops trying to spot spring warblers as they pass through on their way to northern nesting grounds. Mature forests always contain a large population of dead and dying trees, which attract a variety of woodpeckers. All of the common Southern Ontario woodpeckers can be seen in the park: downy and hairy woodpeckers, yellow-bellied sapsuckers, common flickers, red-headed woodpeckers and pileated woodpeckers.

After you have made your way through the hardwood forest (and caught your breath, since the trail climbs straight up the side of the Moraine), the trail leads to yet another ecosystem. Breaking free of the forest's cool grasp, you enter a dry grassland studded with sumac and Scots pine. The area is very sandy and always seems hot and dry in comparison to the forest. As stark as it appears, this area contains plenty of life. Among the four-footed inhabitants of the park are white-tailed deer, raccoon, red fox, and cotton-tail rabbit. Birds also

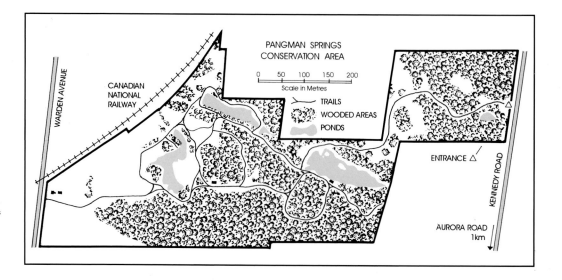

PANGMAN SPRINGS
CONSERVATION AREA

0   50   100   150   200
Scale in Metres

TRAILS
WOODED AREAS
PONDS

WARDEN AVENUE

CANADIAN
NATIONAL
RAILWAY

ENTRANCE △

KENNEDY ROAD

AURORA ROAD
1km

Jack-in-the-pulpit

Hairy woodpecker

Red-headed woodpecker

love it here. At least seven species of sparrow have been spotted: savannah, grasshopper, vesper, chipping, field, white-throated and song. This is also hawk country, and if you are fortunate you might spot a Cooper's hawk, a broad-winged hawk, a kestrel or an osprey.

As the trail continues, the secret of Pangman Springs is revealed. Many years ago, a previous owner dammed several creeks to form three sizable ponds. The backdrop to these ponds is a mixed forest of hardwoods and cedar.

In late spring and early summer, the forest is alive with the calls of thrushes, flycatchers and warblers. Canada geese and great blue herons search the ponds for food, and if you are quiet you may see a beaver swim by.

In June, a diligent search may be rewarded with the discovery of several orchid species, including nodding lady's-tresses, helleborine, showy and yellow lady's-slipper and bog twayblade, as well as at least a dozen species of ferns. By the time you get to this point, it is time to take off your backpack and sit back to enjoy the scenery. On the west side of the first pond is a clearing with an old cottage and several inviting picnic tables. When birding, it is often just as effective to sit back and let the birds come to you, as opposed to hunting them and disturbing them with your approach.

Once rested, you can explore the many trails that lead to and from the cottage. Most of the forest around here is either hardwood (including a large stand of black cherry) or damp woodland of cedar, poplar, birch and maple. Northeast of the

Man-made ponds at Pangman Springs. Photo by I. Deslauriers

cottage, the forest opens up again into abandoned pasture. In the spring and summer, there is the constant calling of bobolinks, eastern meadowlarks and northern orioles. If you visit this area in late summer, you will probably see a botanist or two looking for fringed and closed gentians, as this is virtually the only known location in all of York Region for these unique pale-blue flowers.

15. THE GANARASKA STORY

Susan Erskine Elgear

We put our feet on the backs of shovels and slide down into the earth once again, slipping the seedlings into the slices of space, then bringing the shovels back up out of the ground. Tamp, tamp, tamp — secured.

There is time to pause, to listen to the drumming of the ruffed grouse, to watch the blue jay, to smell, to hear, to witness. Our act of planting trees is no longer urgent. The urgency is passed. Most of the trees have been planted.

In 1944, the Province of Ontario wrote a prescription for conservation. In language that would become the jargon of conservation, "A Report on the Ganaraska Watershed" described the impoverished state of a settled landscape and the means to its resurrection.

The author, A.H. Richardson, dared to suggest that human activity and settlement created this rural barrens, disturbing all other forms of life in the watershed. The Ganaraska could not sustain life in the absence of trees. The same clearing, cutting and farming practices applied in other regions destroyed the watershed, and soil erosion, flooding and silting resulted. The need to understand and to respond was indeed urgent.

The Ganaraska report was a business plan — a strategic plan — "a study in land use with recommendations for the rehabilitation of the area in the postwar period." It was a risk, a gamble, a make-work project. It was full of "herewith's," "therefore's" and "furthermore's." It was an admission of guilt and an offer to amend. It was an alternative. It worked. It taught us to behave.

Richardson's report advocated the stabilization of the watershed to further exploit and extract from it in future. The Ganaraska watershed was to be restored in order that it could be used again. The planned resurrection, however, failed, for the watershed responded with life itself. The watershed is now valuable because it is alive — moving, flowing, ever present, ever changing, life sustaining.

The act of planting trees has not changed, but our reasons for doing so now go beyond resourcism. In the 1990s, we are engaged in the preservation of life in all its forms and processes for its own sake, and ours.

This watershed exists both because of conservation and in spite of it. From land use and resource

management we have come to realize that the meaning of conservation lies within. If you must "settle," then you must also comply with the area in which you live. Give to your place, do not take away. Contribute to life as a member of your watershed.

Manage your own behaviour ... plant trees.

Sugar maple in full fall colour. Photo by F. Clauer

16. THE GANARASKA FOREST

Jim Tedford and Niva Rowan

Mantling the Oak Ridges Moraine in the northeastern corner of the Municipality of Clarington, and spreading eastward into Hope, Manvers, and Cavan Townships, the 4,500-hectare Ganaraska Forest enriches these communities with a diversified historical, cultural and natural heritage that goes back many generations. Its proud history encompasses the genesis of the conservation movement in Ontario, and it is seen today as one of the most successful rehabilitation projects anywhere in the world.

The first Ganaraska Forest was part of a much larger forest stretching from Lake Ontario northward over the Oak Ridges Moraine. These forested hills provided lumber for a burgeoning market

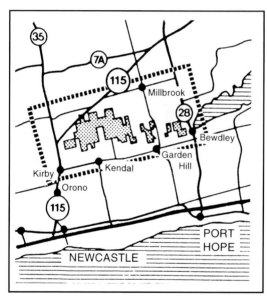

How to get there:

From the west, exit Highway 115 at Kirby and travel east approximately 10 km on Regional Road 9. Turn left (north) at Cold Springs Camp Road and proceed 4 km to the Forest Centre.
From the east, exit Highway 28 onto Regional Road 9. Travel approximately 16 km (2 kilometres west of Elizabethville). Turn right (north) onto Cold Springs Camp Road and proceed 4 km to the Forest Centre.

Facilities:

Ski and hiking trails
Toilets
Forest Centre
Water available
User fees

The Ganaraska Forest — one of the largest forest tracts in Southern Ontario. Photo by L. Wise

Forest Memberships:
General-use or skiing passes are required. Day passes and seasonal and family memberships are available from the Ganaraska Region Conservation Authority, P.O. Box 328, Port Hope, Ontario L1A 3W4, (905) 885-8173.

The memory of A.H. Richardson is preserved at Richardson's Lookout, which offers sweeping views over the Ganaraska valley and Forest. Look for the signs along Durham/Northumberland Road 9, between Elizabethville and Garden Hill.

at home and abroad through the late eighteenth and most of the nineteenth centuries. Once cleared, the area developed into a briefly prosperous but short-lived agricultural community.

By the early 1900s, this rural community on the Moraine north of Port Hope had largely disappeared. In its place were abandoned farms, severely eroded soils, and hundreds of hectares of blowsand dunes. With the loss of forest cover, many tributaries of the Ganaraska River dried up, resulting in increasing annual alternations of water shortage and seasonal and flash flooding at the mouth of the river in the town of Port Hope. The same scene was being enacted all along the Oak Ridges Moraine. The Richardson report of 1944 on the Ganaraska Watershed recommended addressing this serious conservation problem, and the result was the creation of a new Ganaraska Forest.

Today, the Ganaraska Forest stretches from Highway 115/35 eastward to Rice Lake. It is the largest forest on the Moraine. Crucial to its establishment was the creation of a new type of agency in Ontario with the responsibility of undertaking conservation projects at the local level. In 1946, the Ganaraska Region Conservation Authority became one of the first in the province to be established for this purpose.

White-tailed deer (large buck). Photo by F. Clauer

Showy lady-slipper. Photo by S. Russell

Earthstar fungus. Photo by J. Seigel

More than five million trees, mostly red and white pine and some spruce, have been planted over a fifty–year period to stabilize the blowsand and dunes. These plantations, representing almost half of the forest (the rest being subsequent spontaneous growth), are now home to a variety of wildlife, including the rare green trillium, and flocks of wild turkeys. They also provide, through carefully selective cutting, logs for homes, utility poles, and lumber. Today, many of these plantations are gradually returning to what they were originally: a mixed forest of oak, pine, maple, and beech.

Potential flooding in Port Hope has been greatly reduced, and in this and other respects Richardson's vision of the Ganaraska Forest has become a reality. The once-desolate landscape is now home to deer, rabbit, and grouse, as well as flocks of wild turkey. There are hundreds of kilometres of roads and trails for visitors to explore. Activities include hiking, cross-country skiing and horseback riding. Hunting, snowmobiling, dirt biking are also permitted in certain restricted areas, but are carefully monitored to ensure that the health of the forest is maintained.

Children have a unique opportunity to live and learn in the forest, witnessing at first hand through outdoor education programs, the lessons that nature has to offer.

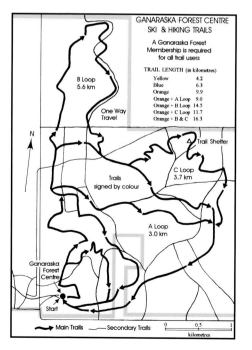

17. THE WILDLIFE HABITAT TRAIL

Gordon Berry

In the Iroquois language, *ganaraske* is believed to mean "at the spawning place," an appropriate description, for each spring, the banks of the Ganaraska River are crowded with hopeful anglers. The waters of this river flow from the Oak Ridges Moraine and drain much of the Ganaraska Forest.

The Ganaraska Forest Centre caters to school, Scout, and other groups by providing classrooms, dormitories and recreational facilities, as well as access to many kilometres of forest roads and trails. The centre provides space for parking and is the easiest access point to many of the trails on the Moraine.

Starting behind the dormitories of the Centre, the Wildlife Habitat Trail offers a relatively short hike, well within the capabilities of most families. It runs through reforested areas that are shady and cool in summer. While serried ranks of pine dominate the landscape, some interesting places along the trail reveal where attempts have been made to speed up the restoration of forest diversity by planting selected species of trees and shrubs that will attract wildlife.

Most animals and birds attempt to find a niche in the environment, where they can live without undue stress and competition from other species. Special adaptations enable certain species to live in specific parts of the forest. For example, some birds live high in the tree canopy and have beaks that are specialized for opening seeds, while others such as ruffed grouse and wild turkeys are adapted to life on the forest floor.

The more diverse the forest, both in species and age of trees, the greater the variety of life it can support. Old or fallen trees are often full of cavities. These provide homes for both birds and small mammals. When a new forest is planted few such home sites are available, and the variety of species that survive there is thus limited.

The trees in the Ganaraska Forest were planted for two reasons: to control the erosion of the exposed sandy soils that had resulted from poor agricultural practices, and to control the flooding of the Ganaraska River at Port Hope. Trees were needed that could adapt to impoverished soils. White pine, Scots pine and spruce were selected, and they have fulfilled their purpose admirably.

Rebuilding a forest takes a very long time. The Ganaraska Forest is in the early stages of a new

Ruffed Grouse. Photo by J. Seigel

Helleborine
Common, not native.
Strongly veined leaves.
Greenish flowers.
Heart-shaped lip. Found in
woods, ravines and thickets.

Crested Clavaria, "Fairy Clubs"
A common saprophytic species found in coniferous forests. Whitish, but colouring may vary. Inedible.

Cortinarius
Many similar species. One of the most common autumn fungi found in coniferous forests. It has a white or slightly purple colouring. Older specimens turn brown. Inedible and smells slightly of acetylene.

Emetic Russula, "the Sickener"
Inedible and extremely acrid in taste. Blood-red or pinkish-red caps grow in acidic soils and are often found in coniferous forests.

Indian Pipe
Wintergreen family. White stem, leaf and flower (black later). Waxy, translucent pipes. Found in shady woods.

chapter in its history. The second stage, in which diversity is established, requires a gradual buildup of decaying vegetation in the soil to provide the humus and nutrients needed by many broad-leafed plants. Along the Wildlife Habitat Trail, this transition is already taking place. Foresters and the Ontario Federation of Anglers and Hunters have worked together to introduce species of plants that animals and birds require both for cover and for food. These plants — honeysuckle, nannyberry, coral berry, autumn olive, serviceberry and grey dogwood — are found in small clearings along the Wildlife Habitat Trail. Highbush cranberry is also evident, established by both natural and organized planting.

As the ground cover develops, there are increasing numbers of ruffed grouse, and in the shrubs, cedar waxwings find shelter. Wild turkeys have been very successfully introduced here, and from the initial twenty to twenty-four birds, the flocks have prospered. Now some are being trapped and transferred to other forests in the Peterborough area. To suddenly come across these large red-necked birds on a trail is startling. Deer winter here in the shelter of the forest and are often spotted by cross-country skiers.

When humans disturb the environment, they often make it possible for species not native to the habitat to establish themselves. As you walk, you may be contributing to this process by dispersing seeds from other areas that are stuck to the soles of your shoes. There are a lot of common plants along the trails — mullein, beebalm, wild rasp-berries, milkweed — but sometimes there are also surprises. While picking some sweet wild raspberries in August, I found two species of orchid in bloom, and several clumps of Indian pipe (a plant that is all white, has no chlorophyll, and gets its nutrients from decaying vegetation in the soil).

The Ganaraska Forest produces a rich variety of fungi. These plants push their way up between the needles that carpet the forest floor, and can be readily seen from the trail, especially in late summer and fall. Painted cups, earthstars, morels, inkcaps, puffballs, and beautiful tufts of small coral-like fungi grow beside the paths.

Near the end of this trail is a brook with crystal-clear water flowing under a small bridge. The cool waters that bubble from the ground only a short distance from the bridge are typical of the fresh-water streams and springs that rise from aquifers deep in the ground all along the Oak Ridges Moraine.

You do not have to know the names of all the rare forest species to enjoy them; nature has a beauty that appeals to the spirit as well as the mind. But consider taking along a bird or plant guide book, or even one just on fungi, because the more you know about nature, the greater your ability to preserve it for future generations to enjoy.

18. SINGERS AND SUN LOVERS: AMPHIBIANS AND REPTILES

James Kamstra

While a variety of reptiles and amphibians lives on the Oak Ridges Moraine, the casual observer may be disappointed at seeing so few, since many species are secretive, well camouflaged or only seasonally detectable. Some frogs call conspicuously during their breeding season, then seem to vanish when they move to their summer range. Salamanders live most of their lives unnoticed in leaf litter or burrowing in the upper soil layer. Even snakes can detect vibrations on the ground and usually move off the trail before we see them.

Wetlands and kettle ponds dot the landscape of the Moraine, creating ideal habitats for frogs. In early spring, wood frogs and spring peepers crawl out of the thawing ground and move en masse to these ancestral breeding sites. During the first warm rains in late March or early April, the annual mating chorus begins. Wood frogs call feverishly for a mere two or three weeks, then lie silent. But peepers will continue to call for up to two months. The higher elevations of the Moraine

Bullfrog. Photo by S. Russell

The following amphibian and reptile species have been found on the Oak Ridges Moraine, although some are known only from sparse records. Only the adult habitat is noted.

Amphibians	Habitat	Status
American toad	field, thicket, forest	common
western chorus frog	field, thicket	uncommon
spring peeper	thicket, forest	common
eastern grey tree frog	thicket, forest	common
wood frog	wet forest	common
northern leopard frog	pond, field	common
pickerel frog	cold streams	rare
green frog	permanent ponds	common
bullfrog	large pond, lake	uncommon
red-spotted newt	pond, field, stream	uncommon
red-back salamander	forest	uncommon
spotted salamander	upland forest	uncommon
blue-spotted salamander	forest	uncommon

Reptiles		
common snapping turtle	ponds	common
Midland painted turtle	ponds, marsh	common
Blanding's turtle	ponds, lakes	rare
eastern garter snake	upland and wetland	common
northern water snake	large pond, lake	rare
eastern hognose snake	upland meadow	rare
northern brown snake	field, forest	rare
northern redbelly snake	field, forest	common
smooth green snake	upland meadow	uncommon
eastern milk snake	field, thicket	uncommon

Eastern grey tree frog. Photo by J. Seigel

create a slightly cooler climate than the Lake Ontario plain to the south; this extends the spring peeper's breeding season here. The Moraine truly is peeper country, for they are far more abundant here than on the fragmented and often urbanized lands to the south.

By late April, leopard frogs and American toads are singing in the ponds. Later, in May, they are joined by grey tree frogs and green frogs. Many frog species move out of the ponds once they have finished breeding. Wood frogs move to moist woodlands, tree frogs into the canopy of trees, leopard frogs into open meadows, and toads towards dry areas. Having upland habitats adjacent to wetlands is critical to the survival of many of these amphibians.

Salamanders are less obvious, since they do not call and they spend most of their time under logs or moss or in the soil. One species, the red-spotted newt, prefers sand-bottomed wetlands.

Consequently many of the Moraine's ponds provide ideal habitat. Newts are unique among our amphibians in that they have a three- instead of two-stage life cycle. The aquatic larva transforms into the landlubber red eft stage for about two years before returning to the water as an adult newt. The redback salamander is also unique, being our only amphibian that does not breed in water. The female guards her small clutch of eggs within the moist seclusion of a rotten log. The larval stage is passed within the egg itself. Redbacks occur in some of the woodlands on the Moraine, although they are not as common as in other parts of the province.

Two other rarely seen species, spotted and blue-spotted salamanders, are known as mole salamanders because they spend most of their lives underground. These salamanders migrate to their favourite breeding ponds as soon as the ice is off, but after mating and egg laying the adults return to their solitary, burrowing lifestyle. You may be fortunate enough to come across such a pond on one of the few nights of the year when the salamanders are engaged in their breeding frenzy. Otherwise, these creatures can occasionally be found in the summer under rotting logs in the forest. While both species certainly occur in the larger forested tracts on the Moraine, it is difficult to determine how common or widespread they are.

The reptiles of the Oak Ridges Moraine are fewer in number and species than amphibians. Both snapping turtles and midland painted turtles occur in nearly all wetlands of any size. Snapping turtles spend most of their time under water and are therefore less frequently observed. In June, however, adult females leave the water and wander overland,

Spring peeper. Photo by S. Russell

often for several kilometres, to find a suitable nesting site. It is at this time of year that turtles of both species are often seen crossing roads. Too many wind up as casualties in the process.

Turtles require dry, open areas of loose sand in which to lay their eggs. Sunshine warms the

Pickerel frog

Northern leopard frog. Photo by S. Russell

ground, incubating the eggs. After two or three months in the ground, the eggs will hatch and the hatchlings must find their way to water. Potential nesting sites are numerous in the sandy soils of the Moraine. No doubt, today's landscape provides more suitable nesting areas than in pre-settlement days, when forest cover was more complete.

Painted turtles are more conspicuous than snappers, since they frequently haul themselves out onto logs to bask in the sun. In early spring and autumn, when water temperatures are low, dozens of turtles can be seen sunning together in one small area of a wetland, while none appear to be basking elsewhere. This is because turtles tend to congregate where the microclimate is warmest. Basking raises the turtle's body temperature, which is critical to the survival of this cold-blooded creature. When the water turns warmer, the turtles will disperse throughout the wetland.

Among the snakes on the Moraine, the eastern garter is best known and most common. It is a versatile species, inhabiting a variety of areas, from woodlands and thickets to wetlands, but open meadows are its favourite haunt. Milk snakes can occasionally be found in old foundations and rock piles, or under boards. The milk snake, boldly patterned with reddish brown blotches set on an overall light grey colour, is secretive and rarely encountered in the open. The smooth green snake, on the other hand, is out by day in dry open meadows, but its uniform green colouration provides excellent camouflage, so it too is rarely

Spotted salamander. Photo by J. Kamstra

seen. The redbelly snake, Canada's smallest species, is widespread in the area. It is chiefly a woodland species, unlike the other snakes, which thrive in sunnier environs. Redbellies are most often encountered in spring or autumn, when they lie on trails or roads to bask in the sun.

As a group, reptiles and amphibians form a significant yet subtle link in the local ecosystem. They create burrows that can later be used by other animals. They also help to control insect and rodent populations. Amphibians, by their sheer numbers and reproductive capabilities, are themselves an important food source for many higher predators. In addition, amphibians are

Opposite: Painted turtle. Photo by S. Russell

Garter snake. Photo by J. Kamstra

excellent indicators of environmental quality, since most require the presence of two adjacent habitats.

As long as the range of wet and dry, and open and forested habitats is maintained, the Oak Ridges Moraine will continue to provide many reptiles and amphibians with an ideal home. If you open your ears to learn the common frog calls and keep a watchful eye for the occasional sun-basking snake or turtle, your hiking experience will certainly be enhanced.

19. PALGRAVE FOREST AND WILDLIFE AREA

Bill Kilburn

There is no better time of year than winter to get a sense of the rolling, rambling nature of the Oak Ridges Moraine, and no better way to experience it than by following the contours of the land on a pair of cross-country skis. The perfect place for such an adventure is Palgrave Forest and Wildlife Area (PFWA).

There are three ski loops at PFWA, comprising 16 kilometres of groomed and track-set ski trails. The loops range in difficulty from beginner to expert. The 3.9-kilometre beginners' loop is generally flat, with a couple of small hills toward the end. It is perfect for a leisurely family outing.

In contrast, the 8.4-kilometre experts' loop includes several challenging hills and is well suited for the experienced skier.

For those who appreciate natural forest beauty, PFWA has much to offer. The jack pine, a dominant tree of our northern forests, lines the forest edge. It has short needles in bundles of two and sharply curved cones that remain attached to the tree for several years. Jack pine, balsam fir (with singular flat needles on smooth twigs), and tamarack (the only naturally occurring tree in eastern Canada that loses its needles every winter) were all planted here. The most conspicuous

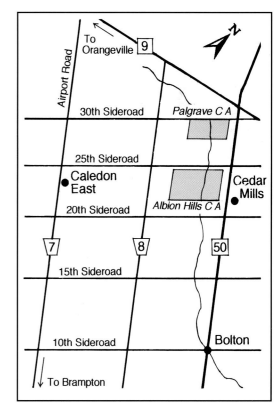

The Palgrave forest is a mix of planted conifer and natural-growth deciduous trees. Photo courtesy of MTRCA

79

How to get there:

Palgrave Forest and Wildlife Area is located on Highway 50, just north of Palgrave, 12 kilometres north of Bolton. As you leave Palgrave heading north, there is a gentle curve in the road as it crosses over the Humber River. The entrance comes up immediately on your left. It is not well marked, so watch carefully.

Facilities:
Trail fees for skiing
Toilets
Picnic sites
Ski trails (16 kilometres)
Open weekends only
Parking lot

Balsam fir

Winter snow on a pine plantation. Photo by I. Deslauriers

planted trees, however, are those that form the dense, orderly stands that dominate PFWA. These stands consist of white spruce (with singular bluish-green needles), eastern white pine (Ontario's official tree, with needles in bundles of five), and red pine (with long needles in bundles of two). The abundance of these trees indicates the extensiveness of reforestation efforts in this area.

In addition to the planted trees, remnants of the original forests that once covered the area still remain. Deciduous trees, including sugar maple, beech, white and yellow birch, basswood and poplar, grow alongside the coniferous eastern hemlock. In the wet, low-lying areas, including the flood plain of the Humber River, are small stands composed entirely of eastern white cedar. This tree is distinguished by small, scale-like leaves arranged on flattened shoots. White cedar is a favourite winter food of white-tailed deer, but deer are by no means the only animal to take advantage of the well-treed Moraine.

Winter provides an excellent opportunity to observe animal tracks and trails. Many of the animals on the Moraine are nocturnal, but the tracks they leave in the snow at night reveal much about their movements and activities.

One of the most distinctive animal trails is that of the red fox. The red fox is a member of the canine family and thus leaves dog-like prints, but there are several differences that will allow you to distinguish the two. First, look at the manner in which the trail has been laid down. If the prints appear sloppy, show signs of foot dragging, and appear to reflect a carefree attitude, they were probably made by a domestic dog. In contrast, the tracks of a fox will appear tidy and careful, the feet being placed rather than dragged. A red fox trail will also appear fairly straight, with a width seldom greater than ten centimetres.

Another sign of a fox trail is scent. The scent of a fox is pungent and skunk-like, although not nearly so strong. It is believed that the scent is left as a means of communicating with other foxes in the area.

The porcupine, while its tracks are rarely seen, also leaves a very distinctive trail. For signs of a porcupine's presence, look up at the trees that line the trails. Some trees will have large patches of bare wood on the trunks or limbs. This is because the porcupine has been sitting up on the limb and scraping off the bark to get at the tasty layer just below. If you look closely at these patches you may be able to see the gnaw marks left by the porcupine's teeth.

The track of a porcupine is laid down in a waddling motion and is characterized by pigeon-toed steps. The oval prints are each approximately eight centimetres long and are often connected by drag marks. The heavily quilled tail also leaves drag marks. In snow more than a few centimetres deep, the short legs of the porcupine cause the belly to drag, creating a trough of 15 centimetres or more in width. The trail often ends at a tree. If this is the case, and there are scattered shoots around the trunk, there is a good chance that you will see the dark shape of a porcupine on a tree limb.

PFWA boasts several other rodents in addition to the porcupine. Red and grey squirrels exhibit

Red pine

White pine

White spruce

Deer

Deer mouse

Dog

Red fox

Cottontail rabbit

Squirrel

Cross-country skiing on firebreak roads at Palgrave Forest.
Photo courtesy of MTRCA

paired tracks. Within a squirrel trail, each set of tracks is made up of two pairs of prints. The front pair is the much larger of the two, having been made by the hind feet, which land ahead of the front feet. Squirrel trails usually lead from tree to tree.

Deer mice and white-footed mice leave a track pattern similar to that of squirrels, although much smaller. As they scurry through the snow, these rodents often leave drag marks between their tracks from their long tails. Mouse trails frequently end at barely perceptible openings in the snow, or sometimes at miniature ice tunnels.

Mice are not alone in burrowing into the snow. Both meadow voles and shrews construct long meandering tunnels just below the surface of the snow. Meadow voles are rodents, whereas shrews, which are slightly smaller, belong to a lesser-known group of mammals that feeds largely on insects. The tunnels of both these creatures become more visible as the snow begins to melt. Sometimes these tunnels break the surface as they are being made, causing them to resemble small troughs. A tunnel that is 4 centimetres wide or more was probably made by a vole; if it is 2.5 centimetres or less, it is probably the work of a shrew.

The eastern cottontail rabbit has tracks similar to those of a rodent. Like the squirrel's, the cottontail's track is made up of two pairs of prints. There is, however, an easy way to tell the tracks of these two animals apart. In a cottontail's tracks, the second pair of prints in each set, made by the front feet, is staggered (i.e. one of the front feet lands on the

ground slightly ahead of the other). In a squirrel's track, the front feet land exactly beside each other.

If you would like to visit PFWA to try to interpret animal tracks, or just to enjoy a pleasurable cross-country ski, it is open on weekends throughout the winter for as long as conditions allow. Skating is not permitted, and dogs are not allowed on the trails during the winter season.

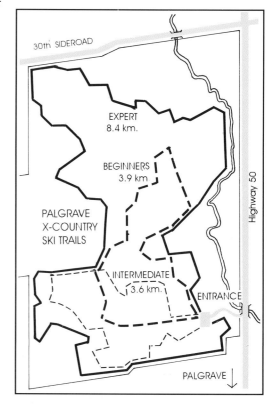

20. THORNTON BALES KING CONSERVATION AREA

Peter Seibert

On maps and in official records it's known as Thornton Bales King Conservation Area, but many people who visit the area call it Ninety-nine Steps. The Conservation Area occupies twenty rugged hectares in the northeastern part of King Township, and is located on the north side of Mulock Drive, 4 kilometres west of Newmarket.

Standing on the ridge of sand and gravel that forms the southern boundary of the conservation area, looking northward, one sees a forest of sugar maple and American beech fanning out toward Lake Simcoe. Vegetation on the forest floor is sparse, as the sun's rays cannot penetrate the dense leaf cover. Shade-loving maple and beech saplings, mixed with a variety of shrubs, are found on the forest floor. Spring also produces a vast array of wildflowers. The display starts in April, with the hepatica pushing up through last year's leaves, closely followed by a variety of native flowers. Red and white trilliums, yellow violets, lilies of the valley, Canada violets, wild ginger and spring beauty grow abundantly on the slopes. In the moist, low-lying areas, mitrewort and foamflower are found.

The show is over by early summer, when the trees fill out with leaves overhead, blocking the sun and causing deep shade.

Most of the site is heavily wooded, with only the occasional small opening. In summer, a variety of ferns grow on the forest floor, including Christmas fern, rattlesnake fern, sensitive fern and marginal fern. In the open areas, wild strawberry, bracken, pussytoes and a variety of grasses are common. Goldenrod, asters and black-eyed Susan occupy the open sites in late summer, but very few wildflowers bloom under the dense forest canopy at this time of the year. The only abundant species

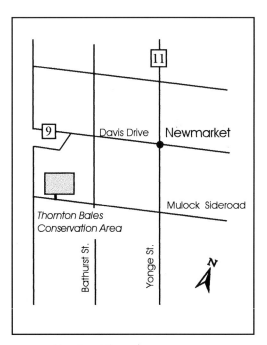

Paths wind through majestic oak, maple and pine at Thornton Bales Conservation Area.
Photo courtesy of Lake Simcoe Region Conservation Authority

How to get there:
Access to the conservation area is off the north side of Mulock Sideroad, 4 kilometres west of Highway 11 (Yonge Street).

Facilities:
Hiking trails
No entrance fee
Parking available

Christmas fern

Enchanter's nightshade

Trout lily

Rugged slopes well forested with mature maple. Photo by D. McQueen

is enchanter's nightshade. With few exceptions, and those primarily found in the open spaces, the wildflowers that grow at Thornton Bales King Conservation Area are native to North America. In much of Southern Ontario where the original forest cover has been removed, the present-day wildflowers are immigrants, brought here from other parts of the world by the European immigrants who settled here.

No doubt, aboriginal people visited this area. History books tell us that Native North Americans and early explorers passed just a few miles to the west of the property on their journeys from Lake Ontario to Lake Simcoe and beyond. The first person known to have held a deed for the property was Rufus Rogers, who made the purchase in 1804. Rogers was the leader of Rogers' Rangers, a military group formed in the American colonies. Rogers' Rangers later joined with the York volunteers to form the Queen's York Rangers, 1st American Regiment. The regiment's

present-day headquarters is in Aurora, just a few kilometres south of this property.

Several owners succeeded Rogers before Thornton J. Bales, a prominent resident of the area, purchased the property in 1911. Mr. Bales's interests in conservation led to his donation of the property to King Township. In 1961, the Township turned the property over to the Lake Simcoe Region Conservation Authority. Originally known as the King Conservation Area, it was renamed in 1970 in honour of Thornton Bales.

Visitors to the Conservation Area have a chance to enjoy the beauty of quiet woodland trails that run through the hardwood forest. But be forewarned: the area is not for the faint of heart. The steep slopes at the southern edge of the property give way to the valley floor 53 metres below. You can visit the area throughout the year and experience the changes that the seasons bring. Explore the property and enjoy the wildlife, and don't forget to count the steps.

21. THE YORK REGIONAL FOREST

Kevin R. Reese

Within the boundaries of York Region lie eighteen tracts of public land known as the York Regional Forest. These tracts comprise over 2,000 hectares, containing both natural and plantation forests, creeks, and forested wetlands. First established in 1924, the forest is owned by the Region of York and has been managed under a long-term agreement by the Ontario Ministry of Natural Resources. Thirteen of these tracts are located on the Oak Ridges Moraine.

To fully appreciate these tracts, it helps to understand the basic principles of forest succession. Forests change over time, both in the patterns of tree species present and in the physical conditions of the environment in which they grow. Each stage of forest succession produces specific levels of light intensity, temperature and even soil chemistry that influence which species will flourish in the next stage of succession.

The ability of a particular tree species to grow in a given amount of available sunlight is known as shade tolerance. Early stages of succession are characterized by pioneer species of shrubs and trees, which are intolerant of shade and grow vigorously in high levels of light. As the forest matures, the forest floor becomes shaded and cool, and only more shade tolerant species can become established.

Over a long period of time a stable pattern of interactive species develops called a climax community. This stage is characterized by shade-tolerant species that regenerate in the canopy gaps caused by the decline or loss of single trees. The species of trees and plants present at this stage will likely remain without change for long periods, unless interrupted by a major disturbance. Wind storms, flooding and forest fires, as well as human activities such as clearing land for agriculture and heavy logging, are all capable of causing drastic change.

York Regional Forest is part of over 110,000 hectares of Agreement Forest in Ontario. Early settlement and economic growth resulted in the clearing of much of the original forest cover. Where the soils were light in texture, they could not support the loss of the forest or sustain agricultural practices. Wind and water erosion resulted in the loss of precious topsoil and, with it, the land's productivity.

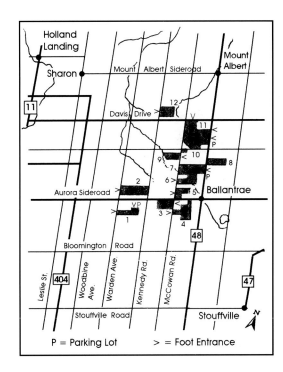

Zephyr Tract, another tract of the York Regional Forest that is also on the Moraine, is not shown on this map. It lies farther north, and is described in Chapter 10.

Tract	Map Location	Area (hectares)	Trails	Parking lot	Toilets	Well
Robinson	1	43	*	*	*	*
Porrit	2	81	*	*	*	*
Dainty	3	41	*			
Clarke	4	63	*			
Patterson	5	48	*			
Hall	6	85	*			
West Main	7	217	*	*	*	*
‡ Hollidge	8	83				
Scout	9	48	*			
Mitchell	10	22				
‡ North	11	333	*	*	*	*
‡ Bendor & Graves	12	81	*			

‡ no snowmobiling

Shade-Intolerant Tree Species:
trembling aspen
balsam poplar
white birch

Mid-tolerant Tree Species:
black cherry
bitternut hickory
red maple
white elm
white ash
red oak
basswood
white pine

Shade-Tolerant Tree Species:
sugar maple
American beech
hemlock

A few years after a red pine plantation was clearcut, this mixture of replanted deciduous and coniferous trees is beginning to take over.
Photo by I. Deslauriers

The land lost its capacity to retain moisture and support plant growth, and these areas became wastelands.

A municipal reforestation committee was formed, and, in cooperation with the provincial government, began to purchase and reforest the lands most in need. In 1924, an agreement under the Forestry Act was signed. The task of reestablishing a new forest had begun. Millions of seedlings were planted, and species were selected according to their ability to survive in the harsh, dry, nutrient-poor conditions. Red and white pine were planted, with some oak and poplar. The pine were found to be most successful, but where red and white pine could not grow, Scots and jack pine were established, and spruce were planted in the lower areas. With some exceptions, most of the deciduous trees planted did not survive; however, pockets of remnant natural forest can be found throughout many of the tracts, and a few decayed stumps still bear witness to the grandeur of the original forest.

Plantation forests have been carefully managed since their establishment. The trees are selectively thinned from time to time to ensure that they remain vigorous and healthy. As the trees

Recreational opportunities change with the seasons. The winter months offer snowshoeing, cross-country skiing and snowmobiling. Spring, summer and fall offer hiking, horseback riding, bird-watching and mountain biking.

The York Regional Forest is there for your enjoyment, but there are some rules. Cutting or removing trees or plants is prohibited, as are fires and overnight camping. No motorized wheeled vehicles are allowed within the forest; however, snowmobiling is allowed in some of the tracts.

Forest trails follow firebreak roads through most Regional Forests. Photo by J. Seigel

Poison ivy grows well in sandy soil. Photo by I. Deslauriers

grow, the crowns develop a solid canopy providing shade for the forest floor. Fallen leaves, needles and branches are deposited and begin to decay, creating a layer of humus. Many small insects, fungi and other organisms assist in the process, and a healthy nutrient cycle begins in the new forest soil.

The combination of shade and soil provides perfect conditions for the natural establishment of many native, shade-tolerant tree species. Seeds are dispersed by wind, birds, and animals. The plantations are actually managed to promote the restoration of these natural ecological processes, as late successional forests cannot be replaced by planting, but must develop slowly over time.

A wide variety of plants and animals now exists in the York Regional Forest. However, the naturally established understoreys will take many more decades of careful management before they can be called mature forests.

A network of access roads and walking trails provides for diverse recreational opportunities in the York Regional Forest. Because of the varied topography of the Moraine, each of the forest tracts has its own character. Trails in some of the tracts are flat or gently rolling, while others offer steeper and more challenging climbs.

The York Regional Forest is a wonderful place to escape to. With every change in season, the forest offers something new. Some of the seasonal changes are obvious, such as the fall colours and the arrival of winter snow. But some are more subtle, such as the appearance of fragile spring wildflowers and the return of migrant birds. The more time you spend in the forests and the more carefully you look, the more you will see and learn.

22. HIKING THE OAK RIDGES TRAIL IN UXBRIDGE

Anne Shier

This hike, covering about 11 kilometres from west to east across Uxbridge Township, offers a small-scale version of most of the typical landscapes of the Moraine. There are cedar swamps and other wetlands, lakes, ponds, rolling meadows, pine plantations and hardwood forests. Almost the only missing element is the oak savanna topography of the Rice Lake plains.

For those who have never hiked this territory before, it might be a good idea to join one of the periodic group hikes that are organized by the Oak Ridges Trail Association (ORTA). This will familiarize you with the various twists and turns of the trail, and with access points on concession roads. You can then come back later and hike segments you particularly liked.

The starting point of the trail lies just south of Highway 47, on Regional Road 30 (which is also the York/Durham Line and Concession 1, Uxbridge). As you drive south on 30, look for an

Several rail lines crisscross the Moraine, including this one, which is still used. Several abandoned rail lines have been converted into first-class hiking and ski trails.
Photo by D. McQueen

Great blue heron

Marsh marigold

Much of the abundant forestation of Uxbridge Township consists of plantation forest. Photo by D. McQueen

unopened road allowance that takes off to the east. You can park your car on the shoulder.

Walking east on the road allowance, you will glimpse a large pond on your right. After crossing the CNR line (along which the York/ Durham Heritage Railway has begun to run excursion trains), you will see the St. Lawrence grain depot on the left, and a field bounded by a three-bar horse fence on the right. The trail is hard to follow at this point, so look carefully for the white blazes. You cannot see the archway through the dense cedar woods until you are right up to it. Eventually you will come to a swamp — always a special place to be. If you are

lucky, you may witness a great blue heron taking off, or a muskrat swimming for cover.

When you reach Concession 2, Uxbridge, turn right and go south for 1.2 kilometres. Then turn left and go east through the Metro Conservation Authority's Goodwood Tract.

On reaching Concession 3, Uxbridge, go north for 1.2 kilometres to the Secord Road, then turn right, following the road. A short distance in, on the right, is the extensive pet cemetery established by veterinarian Dr. Alan Secord in 1949. There are some fairly elaborate and recent monuments, most of which commemorate dogs.

Before the cemetery was established, this site

was occupied by White's sawmill, built around the turn of the nineteenth century. Old maps indicate that, at times during the last half of the 1800s, as many as a dozen sawmills were operating in Uxbridge Township. Some were steam driven, while others utilized locally available water power. The latter, with their dams and water wheels, were observed to have an adverse effect on the salmon population of Lake Ontario, as they blocked some of the more important spawning runs of these fish.

When the big trees were all cut, the sawmills shut down and farmers moved onto the cleared land. They took off perhaps one good crop before discovering the discouraging realities of the sandy Moraine soil. Many people do not realize that the present abundant forestation of much of Uxbridge Township consists largely of plantation forest and natural regeneration.

Near the cemetery, the trail branches left into some dense woodland, where more trail development

The hills of Glen Major, near the Walker property.
Photo by I. Deslauriers

is needed. A lot of work has been carried out on this section already by a group of enthusiastic people from the British Trust for Conservation Volunteers, with the help of some Canadian trail builders.

The trail emerges from the woods into a wheat field. Keep to the edge of the field until you reach the top corner, then turn left on the track and out onto Concession 4. Heading north, you will have to walk about 1 kilometre before turning right, into the Metro Conservation Authority's Clubline Tract. Near the end of this tract, close to Concession 5, there is an interpretive sign about the Durham Forest Demonstration Project. Part of this project is being conducted here.

After crossing Concession 5, walk south along the wide shoulder on the east side until you reach the gate that opens eastward into forest lands owned by Uxbridge Township. Before you pass this, you may wish to cross over to Mason Hogue's Gardens on the west side — well worth a visit.

Continuing eastward through the Uxbridge lands, you come to a high stile over a tall fence. This is a particularly good area for deer, and often there are woodpeckers at work. After climbing the stile, you are on the north part of the Walker property, now owned by the Metropolitan Toronto and Region Conservation Authority. Mr. Walker and his wife started with a small piece of land in 1933, planted thousands of trees of many different species, and maintained and selectively harvested them. The Walkers then continued to assemble land for reforestation, leaving a remarkable area of forest to posterity. There are many trails through these extensive woodlands, one of which has been identified and blazed as the main Oak Ridges Trail.

This hike ends at Concession 6, approximately halfway across the Uxbridge section of the Oak Ridges Trail. Eventually, the Oak Ridges Trail will continue across the rolling hills of the Moraine into Scugog Township and on towards the Ganaraska Forest. ORTA hopes to complete it in the near future with the help of like-minded people who enjoy the outdoors.

23. OAK RIDGES TRAIL— SENECA COLLEGE SECTION

Jack Seigel

The King Campus of Seneca College, just south of the Oak Ridges Moraine crest, is fortunate in occupying more than 300 hectares of scenic rolling land with two kettle lakes. The property, located on the northwest corner of Dufferin Street and the Bloomington Sideroad, is rich in both human and natural history. The physical diversity of fields, forests, lakes and gardens provides exceptional opportunities for courses in outdoor recreation, natural science, and trail and landscape studies. During the winter, Seneca College maintains groomed trails for cross-country skiing. Winter access is via the main gate with the purchase of a trail ticket.

This land was originally acquired by Sir John Eaton, the son of department store founder Timothy Eaton. After years of planning, a large, majestic stone mansion was completed in 1940 on the north shore

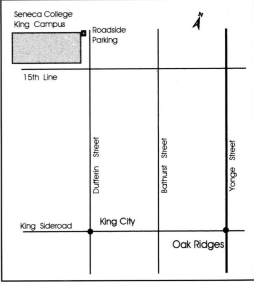

How to get there:
Follow King Sideroad to Dufferin Street. Turn north on Dufferin Street and travel approximately 3 kilometres to the entrance of Seneca College.

Facilities:
Washrooms and vending machines available in the building complex
Fee for parking on campus
Free parking available in the northeast corner of the property along Dufferin Street
Cross-country ski trails

Eaton Hall Lake is a kettle lake on property formerly owned by the Eaton family and now home to Seneca College. Photo by L. Wise

The variegation of trilliums may be caused by chemicals found in the roots of nearby nut-bearing trees. Photo by I. Deslauriers

of the lake, although this was unfortunately preceded by John's untimely death. Lady Flora McCrae Eaton remained on and allowed the mansion to be used as a naval rehabilitation hospital during the war. After its purchase by Seneca College, the house was initially used for offices and classrooms. As the student population grew, Garriock Hall was added south of the lake, in 1978, and Eaton Hall was restored as a management training and conference centre.

The Oak Ridges Trail crosses the northern half of the campus, from Dufferin Street to Keele Street, providing access to four natural zones: the northeast reforested area, the old-growth forest surrounding Eaton Hall, the lake margin and the western fields. The trail thus offers summer hikers and winter skiers many opportunities for wildlife viewing and nature appreciation. As the area is a nature reserve, dogs and bicycles are not permitted on the trail.

Enter the property in the northeast corner via a fence stile. The trail follows the north perimeter along the edge of fields and reforested stands of ash and pine. At the base of a steep hill, the trail crosses the old rail bed of the Schomberg & Aurora Railway (1902–1927). Originally cleared for farming, the hilly terrain and sandy soils of this area soon proved unsuitable for agriculture. Scots pines were planted on the hills, and ash on pockets of better soil. The stands of this reforested area are not managed and many other species have invaded. Poison ivy is common along the section of the trail, and wildflowers, including asters, goldenrod and coneflower, are most evident in late summer and fall.

As the trail turns south and downslope, the plantation gives way to the deep, cool shade of a stand of hemlock, cedar and yellow birch. This microclimate is created by the many cold springs that find their way to the surface, creating the small stream that flows under the footbridge. The moist ground is covered with mosses, liverworts and bulblet ferns, and northern waterthrush have nested in the upturned, moss-draped stumps.

Continue along the gravel road on the right. This was once the main entrance to the mansion. In winter, deer beds can often be seen in the shallow snow under the hemlocks. Small hills of cone scales are common on the forest floor. These are the winter storage middens of red squirrels. In spring, a dense colony of edible ostrich fern lines the route, and clumps of red-flowering raspberry

and red-berried elder reach through the canopy over the trail.

Adjacent to the mansion, rich soils boast a forest of beautiful, mature maples, beeches and red oaks. The larger trees are over 250 years old. Other tree species here include ironwood and black cherry. The college designated these woodlots and the lake as a campus nature reserve.

In the spring, before the tree canopy leafs out to block the sun, the forest floor is a mosaic of colour. Trilliums, bloodroot, blue cohosh, wild ginger and jack-in-the-pulpit are just a few of the many species of wildflowers, and beneath beech trees you can find the fragile, whitish-pink beechdrop, a parasitic wildflower that lives on tree roots. The profusion of flowers is related closely to light. Forest-floor wildflowers finish blooming as the emerging leaves reduce the light to below ten percent.

In addition to maintaining a variety of interesting native plants, Lady Eaton hired a grounds staff to develop gardens and manicured walkways with species from around the world. Some of these gardens are still maintained, with unusual species such as the maidenhair tree or ginkgo (considered a "living fossil"), as well as West Coast Douglas fir and Oregon grape. In other areas, forgotten rhododendrons peek from shrub-lined trails, and periwinkle invades wooded hillsides, competing with native species.

The forest is extensive enough to provide habitat for many interior and forest-edge bird species. The pileated woodpecker and the rare red-shouldered hawk nest on campus, and in the

Spotted salamander

95

Trumpeter swan. Photo by J. Seigel

numerous cavities produced by aging and dead trees, wood ducks may be seen. The forest is vibrant with migrating warblers as they search the tree bark for insects awakened in the warmth of spring sun. Mammals are also common, and both coyotes and foxes den on campus.

Dead trees and fallen branches, rather than being removed for firewood within the reserve area, are allowed to accumulate, providing nutrients for the soil, habitat for fungi, and shelter for wildlife. Cool, moist weather in the spring and fall encourages the fruiting of a great variety of mushrooms. Yellow- and blue-spotted salamanders, spring peepers and grey tree frogs are often seen shortly before hibernation, in the leaf litter of fall.

The trail continues south over steep hills to an extensive lowland adjacent to Little Lake. Mountain maple, dogwood and Canada yew occupy a dense shrub layer, and black ash and tamarack trees can be seen along the lake margin. With spring come wildflowers, including foamflower and goldthread, and

ferns, such as maidenhair, rattlesnake and royal. The large basin known as Seneca Lake is 14 metres deep, with a narrow fringe of aquatic vegetation. Little Lake is less than 2 metres deep; the shoreline is a rich habitat of shrubs and aquatic plants. In spring and fall, migrating ospreys can be seen hovering and diving to catch fish. Shoreline logs provide hunting perches for green-backed herons, and mammals such as mink, muskrat and beaver are common.

Seneca is currently participating in the Ontario Trumpeter Swan Reintroduction Program. A breeding pair can be seen on the pond adjacent to the Veterinary Science building. Two-year-old captive-bred trumpeters have been released on the lake. It is hoped that they will return to breed in years to come.

The southern portion of the property is relatively flat and fertile, and is still farmed today. Many of the original farm buildings are in evidence, and new campus buildings have been added. The trail follows a patchwork of fields and small woodlots linked by shrubby fencerows that provide good "edge" habitat for small mammals and birds. Weasels hunt the fencerows for rodents, and rabbits are pursued by coyotes. Students maintain a trail of bluebird boxes along the route, and, while you may see a bluebird, tree swallows and house wrens are more common.

Seneca is proud of the wild nature it protects on King Campus and is pleased to make this area available to the public by participating in the Oak Ridges Trail.

24. A VISION OF TRAILS

David McQueen

ew people know just how extensive the network of hiking trails in Southern Ontario is. Fewer still realize how much more extensive (and readily accessible) it could become.

When the Oak Ridges Trail is completed, the GTA will be bounded on the north by the Oak Ridges Trail, on the east by the Ganaraska Trail, on the south by the Waterfront Trail, and on the west by the Bruce Trail. These four trails will connect not only with each other, but also with other trails west of the Bruce (see the first map).

The Metropolitan Toronto and Region

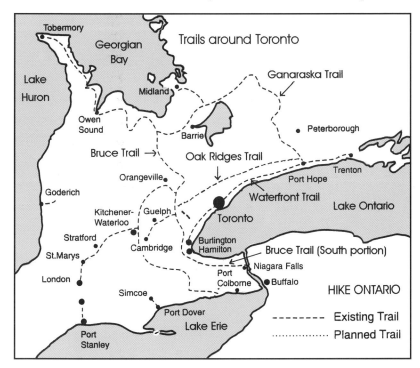

Trails around Toronto

Tobermory
Georgian Bay
Lake Huron
Midland
Owen Sound
Barrie
Bruce Trail →
Oak Ridges Trail
Orangeville
Goderich
Kitchener-Waterloo
Guelph
Toronto
Stratford
St.Marys
Cambridge
Burlington
Hamilton
London
Simcoe
Port Colborne
Port Dover
Lake Erie
Port Stanley

Ganaraska Trail
Peterborough
Trenton
Port Hope
Waterfront Trail
Lake Ontario
Bruce Trail (South portion)
Niagara Falls
Buffalo
HIKE ONTARIO

------- Existing Trail
·········· Planned Trail

The GTA is customarily defined in terms of political boundaries. It comprises the Municipality of Metropolitan Toronto and the Regional Municipalities of Halton, Peel, York and Durham.

The Oak Ridges Moraine lies partly inside and partly outside the GTA. Inside the GTA, it is located in Peel, York and Durham Regions. At its west end, it extends into Simcoe and Dufferin Counties, and, at its east end, into Victoria, Peterborough and Northumberland Counties.

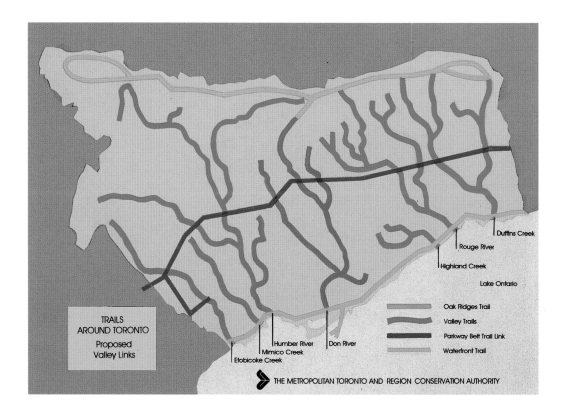

TRAILS AROUND TORONTO
Proposed Valley Links

Duffins Creek
Rouge River
Highland Creek
Lake Ontario

Oak Ridges Trail
Valley Trails
Parkway Belt Trail Link
Waterfront Trail

Humber River
Mimico Creek
Don River
Etobicoke Creek

THE METROPOLITAN TORONTO AND REGION CONSERVATION AUTHORITY

Conservation Authority has envisaged, within the GTA, a further development of valley trails along the Humber, Don and Rouge Rivers, among others (see the second map). Portions of these trails, including the Humber Trail, already exist. These valley greenways would provide additional north–south linkages between the Oak Ridges Trail and the Waterfront Trail.

Combine the two maps, and what an impressive picture emerges! No nature-loving citizen of the GTA would be more than a short transit ride away from this network of trails — the hiker's superhighway. With multiple access points, people from all over the GTA could abandon their built-up urban surroundings for natural green ones every weekend, and hike continuously for just a few kilometres, or all the way to Tobermory, Niagara Falls or Trenton. Such a network, constructed and maintained through volunteer labour, would be an inexpensive yet invaluable public asset.

25. ALBION HILLS CONSERVATION AREA

Brad Cundiff

Anchoring the Moraine's west end is the 516-hectare Albion Hills Conservation Area, a core area of significant habitat on the Humber River system.

It is thanks to the mighty Humber that this conservation area exists. The land was first acquired by the Humber River Conservation Authority in 1955, with the intention of building flood-control works that would prevent a repeat of the disastrous flooding caused by Hurricane Hazel in 1954. The Authority, which later merged with other smaller authorities to form the Metropolitan Toronto and Region Conservation Authority (MTRCA), soon realized, however, that

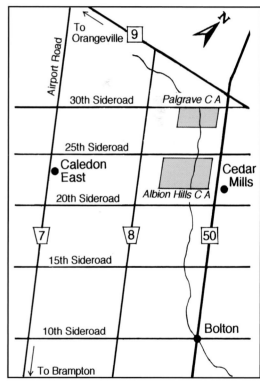

How to get there:
Follow Highway 50 North. The park entrance is on the west side of the highway, just north of the hamlet of Cedar Mills.

Facilities:
Washrooms
Fishing
Nature trails
Refreshments
Camping
Cross-country skiing
Tobogganing
Admission fee

Old farm fields are gradually being converted to forest cover in much of Albion Hills. Photo courtesy of MTRCA

Trail bridge over a well-hidden creek. Photo by D. McQueen

the downstream works at Claireville and elsewhere were sufficient. Albion Hills Conservation Area would instead enjoy a more passive role in flood control, with a stretch of natural habitat that could absorb and slowly release precipitation, and gentle river meanders that could help to hold back the Humber's flow.

Like the Don valley to the east, the Humber River valley is an important corridor linking the Moraine and the Niagara Escarpment to Lake Ontario. Birds use it as a flyway, small mammals as habitat, and larger animals, such as deer, as a movement corridor between larger habitat blocks.

For walkers and skiers, the gently rolling terrain of Albion Hills provides endless variety and breathtaking views. In the past, some parts of the conservation area were heavily planted with rows of pines, while open areas were extensively mowed. In recent years, however, the MTRCA has adopted a more laissez-faire management philosophy. Combined with the enthusiasm of those working to rehabilitate the Humber River valley property, this could mean a brighter and more diverse ecological future for Ontario's first conservation area.

A large field of goldenrod. Photo by I. Deslauriers

101

American toad

Plantain grows at the edge of nearly every path. It is originally from Europe. The Native people called it "white man's foot," because it seemed to spring up magically wherever the Europeans walked.

Two clusters of prehistoric artifacts were unexpectedly discovered at the Albion Hills Conservation Area in 1995, when a new campground access road was in the planning stage. Members of the MTRCA's archeological unit found evidence of campfires and a variety of tools used to process animals for food and clothing. The artifacts are being analyzed at the Royal Ontario Museum.

Albion Hills is at its best in the late summer or fall, when views across the Caledon Hills are at their most colourful. Walkers can enjoy gentle hikes on the area's many trails (which double as ski trails in the winter). The longest combined ski/nature trail is the 6-kilometre Rabbit Trail, which starts from behind the north parking lot and passes through an area of mostly pine plantation. Signs are posted to explain interesting natural features along the way. Near the end, on its way back to the trailhead, the trail cuts through a forest of white ash, black cherry and birch.

If the Rabbit Trail has not satisfied your hiking needs, then park near the ski chalet and pick up the Red Trail, which starts behind the chalet. This 9-kilometre trail heads through a reforested area before eventually crossing Centreville Creek (a tributary of the Humber). The trail then follows the creek past the Albion Hills outdoor education centre, which is set in a lovely meadow that

is at its finest when the asters and goldenrods are in bloom in late summer and in the fall. On quiet days, you might see pheasant or white-tailed deer. Just after the Red Trail meets the Blue Trail, you will reach a spot where the red trail makes a ninety-degree turn. From here, there is a great view of the Caledon Hills stretching out across the Moraine. It is a short stretch from this spot back to the trail's starting point.

It is also possible to connect to the Bruce Trail from the Albion Hills group camping area. The Bruce Trail skirts the western edge of the Conservation Area and continues north to the back end of Palgrave Conservation Area. It then runs on to Glen Haffy Conservation Area as it pushes its way north toward the Bruce Peninsula. On the stretch past Albion Hills, the Bruce Trail follows the Caledon Trailway, a recently developed rail trail with a wide path and gentle grade suitable for hikers, wheelchairs and bicycles.

26. THE DURHAM DEMONSTRATION FOREST

David McQueen

A visit to the Durham Demonstration Forest can be done for pure pleasure. For just this reason, its complex of well-maintained trails and its varieties of terrain and trees have, for many years, attracted hikers, equestrians, mountain bikers, cross-country skiers and school groups. But it is also a giant outdoor laboratory, where visitors can witness numerous ongoing experiments in modern forest management.

The best place to start any exploration of this area is the well-signed third entrance on the east side of Concession 7, Uxbridge, south of Durham Regional Road 21. This leads to the Head of Trails, where you'll find ample parking and two large interpretive plaques with trail maps and other useful information.

As on several other parts of the Moraine, reforestation began here in the 1920s in an effort to stabilize the sandy wasteland that reckless tree cutting and poor agricultural practices had left behind. The effort was successful, with the straight-trunked red pine proving to be the most effective plantation species in dry, sandy conditions. The pines thrived, and with their heightening top canopies and accumulating branch and needle droppings on the ground, created a shaded and enriched forest floor where other tree species would in time find welcome.

Today, with the soil stabilized, forest management has more complex, second-stage objectives. In particular, it aims to create a more diverse forest of deciduous and coniferous trees similar to the natural forest that existed here before European settlement. This is not something that can be done overnight through bureaucratic regulations or massive replanting. Instead, over a much longer

The entrance to Durham Region Demonstration Forest.
Photo by D. McQueen

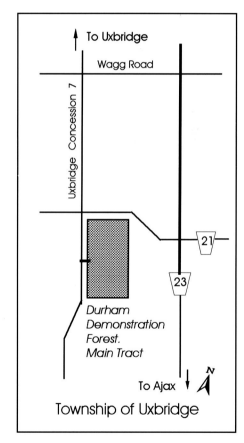

Township of Uxbridge

How to get there:	Facilities:
The entrance is on the east side of Concession 7, south of Uxbridge and Wagg Road.	parking interpretive signage trail maps

Red pine was not commercially valued until the pressure-treating process was developed. Red pine is more susceptible to rot than other types of pine.

See Chapter 21 for more information on shade tolerance and its role in forest succession.

Both the familiar native eastern tamarack and the European larch are members of the larch family, but in North America the European larch is an exotic, imported species. It has found some favour for replanting purposes.

The well-maintained trails of Durham Forest have for many years attracted hikers, equestrians, mountain bikers and cross-country skiers. Photo by I. Deslauriers

Red squirrel. Photo by G. Berry

Forestry Terms
(From the Ministry of
Natural Resources)

Clearcutting: all trees in a
stand are removed. The area
may then be replanted or
left to regenerate naturally.

Selective cutting: individual
trees or groups of mature
and/or unhealthy trees are
removed. With regeneration,
the result can be a more
varied forest, in both the age
and species mix.

Shelterwood cutting: this is
more drastic and large-scale,
involving two or more cuts.
The first cut takes out about
half of the mature trees. The
remaining mature trees
develop larger crowns, providing seeds and shade for
natural regeneration. Finally,
the rest of the mature trees
are cut, giving to the regener-
ative saplings sunlight and
room to grow.

time horizon, and with continuous experimenta-
tion, it relies heavily on the natural processes of
forest succession and natural regeneration. As a
forest floor becomes naturally enriched, more of
the tree and shrub seeds brought in by birds,
mammals and winds will germinate and flourish
there.

If we want a healthy, diversified forest, not
only do red pines and other trees have to be
thinned from time to time, but account must also
be taken of the shade tolerances of different
species. For example, young red oaks do not grow
well in deep shade under the overhead canopy
provided by more mature trees. Where red oaks
are wanted, therefore, holes of appropriate size in
the canopy must be created by removing some of
those mature trees. These cuts effectively mimic
what nature periodically does via disease, wind-
storm and fire.

You can witness the various reforestation techniques by visiting the stations on the loop trails.
At station P3, on the Blue Loop, you will see an
example of clearcutting. A whole stand of diseased
Scots pine was taken out in 1985 and replaced

Original forest

Selective cut

Shelterwood cut

with seedlings of white pine, Norway spruce and European larch.

At station P8, on the Red Loop, a more elaborate experiment is in progress to determine the best way to transform plantations of red pine and other coniferous species into mixed hardwood forest. There are seven tracts, one of which is a control or comparison tract to which nothing is done. On the other six tracts, small selective gaps in the pine canopy have been created, as well as larger shelterwood areas.

In the understorey, the height and variety of trees and shrubs are carefully controlled. This allows researchers to study timing and growth rates, and to determine optimum mixtures of forest.

Modern forestry does not focus exclusively on trees. It takes a broader, holistic approach, looking upon forests as complex ecosystems in which every living organism plays a vital role. In this broader context, the major aim is to establish biodiversity, and to "bank" this against future needs.

For more information about the projects being carried out in the Durham Forest, consult the *Field Guide to the Durham Regional Demonstration Forest*, issued by the Ministry of Natural Resources.

To obtain a copy, contact the Ministry of Natural Resources (416) 314-2000.

27. SKI THE MORAINE

Peter Attfield

The Oak Ridges Moraine often has plenty of good snow for skiing, even when surrounding areas are bare. Its elevation and sheltering woods help to trap and hold the snow, and many of the conservation areas and other public properties along its length provide excellent trails for skiers of all abilities.

ALBION HILLS CONSERVATION AREA
(Town of Caledon, north of Bolton)

- 14 kilometres of track-set trails, with loops of 2, 3, 6 and 9 kilometres, suitable for all levels, plus a skate-skiing loop of 7 kilometres.
- 450 hectares of hardwood forest, conifer plantation and meadows. Trails along Centreville Creek and the Humber River.
- Fee.
- Trail maps provided.
- Chalet open daily, with ski rentals and heated lunchroom; snack bar open weekends.
- Toboggan hills.
- Operated by the Metropolitan Toronto and Region Conservation Authority.
- For trail conditions call (416) 661-6600.
- Access is on the west side of Highway 50, 9 kilometres north of Bolton or 5.5 kilometres south of Highway 9.

DAGMAR RESORT
(Uxbridge Township, south of Town of Uxbridge)

- 14 kilometres of track-set trails, with loops of 1, 2, 3, 4, 5, and 8 kilometres, suitable for all levels.
- 140 hectares of hardwood forest, fields and conifer plantation.
- Trail maps provided, but some trails are not well marked.
- Fee.
- Ski rentals, lunchroom and snack bar open daily. There is also downhill skiing and snowboarding on site.
- For trail conditions call (905) 649-2002.
- Access is on the west side of Lakeridge Road (Durham Regional Road 23), 6 kilometres south of Durham Regional Road 21 or 9 kilometres north of Highway 7.

DURHAM REGIONAL FOREST — MAIN TRACT
(Uxbridge Township, south of Town of Uxbridge)

- 25 of trails suitable for all levels. Some trails suitable for skate skiing. (Trails are also popular in winter with hikers, snowmobilers, equestrians and even mountain bikers, so don't expect good ski tracks.)
- 375 hectares of mostly red- and jack-pine plantation, with hardwood forest and some steep hills in the south end.

Cross-country skiing. Photo courtesy of MTRCA

- Trail map sign and outhouses at parking lot. No markers on trails.

- No fee.

- The forest is owned by the Regional Municipality of Durham, and managed by the Ontario Ministry of Natural Resources.

- Access is on the east side of Concession 7, Uxbridge, 0.7 kilometres south of Durham Regional Road 21 or 7.6 kilometres north of Durham Regional Road 5.

GANARASKA FOREST CENTRE
(Hope Township, northwest of Port Hope)

- 24 kilometres of track-set trails, with loops of 3, 4, 6, 9, 10, 12, 15 and 16 kilometres, suitable for intermediate and advanced skiers.

- 880 hectares of conifer plantation and hardwood forest.

- Trail maps provided.

- Fee.

- Lunchroom open weekends only.

- Operated by the Ganaraska Region Conservation Authority.

- For trail conditions call (905) 797-2721.

- Take Northumberland County Road 9 to the Forest Centre sign at Cold Springs Camp Road (12.2 kilometres east of Highway 35/115 or 14.3 kilometres west of Highway 28), then go 4 kilometres north.

LONG SAULT CONSERVATION AREA
(Town of Clarington, north of Bowmanville)

- 18 kilometres of trails, with loops of 2, 4, 6 and 8 kilometres, suitable for intermediate and advanced skiers. Trails are not groomed or track set, but are marked and usually well skied. (Highlights include a ruined homestead and a scenic climb up the spine of a narrow ridge.)

- 340 hectares of hardwood forest, with some conifer plantation and meadows.

- Trail map sign at parking lot (paper maps are sometimes available there).

- No fee.

- A lunchroom and snack bar may be open some Sundays.

- Operated by the Central Lake Ontario Conservation Authority.

- For trail conditions call (905) 263-2041 or (905) 579-0411.

- Access is on the north side of Durham Regional Road 20, 2.5 kilometres east of Durham Regional Road 57, or 10 kilometres west of Highway 35. A second parking lot 1 kilometre east provides access to 4 kilometres of the trails.

NORTHUMBERLAND COUNTY FOREST
(Haldimand Township, northeast of Cobourg)

- 23 kilometres of trails, with loops of 2, 3, 4, 5, 10 and 15 kilometres, suitable for all levels. Trails are not groomed or track-set, but are well marked.

- 350 hectares of mostly conifer plantation, with some mixed forest.

- Trail maps provided.

- No fee. (Please contribute to the donation box.)

- Forest owned by Northumberland County and managed by Ontario Ministry of Natural Resources, but ski trails are marked and maintained by volunteers.

- For trail conditions call (905) 372-5644 or (905) 372-5831.

- Take Highway 45 for 13.7 kilometres northeast of Highway 401 (or 4.5 kilometres southwest of Northumberland County Road 9), to Beagle Club Road, then go north 0.8 kilometres to parking lot on west side.

PALGRAVE FOREST AND WILDLIFE AREA
(Town of Caledon, north of Palgrave)

- 14 kilometres of track-set trails, with loops of 3, 4 and 8 kilometres, suitable for intermediate and advanced skiers.
- 230 hectares of mostly pine plantation.
- Open weekends only.
- Trail maps provided.
- Fee.
- Outhouses, but no buildings or shelters.
- Operated by the Metropolitan Toronto and Region Conservation Authority.
- For trail conditions call (416) 661-6600.
- Access is on the west side of Highway 50, 1 kilometre north of Palgrave or 2.4 kilometres south of Highway 9.

PLEASURE VALLEY
(Uxbridge Township, north of Claremont)

- 25 kilometres of track-set trails, with loops of 4, 8 and 14 kilometres, suitable for all levels. Fifteen kilometres are wide enough for skate skiing.
- 260 hectares of mostly hardwood forest.
- Fee.
- Ski rentals, lunchroom and snack bar open daily.
- For trail conditions call (905) 649-3334.
- Access is on the east side of Brock Road (Durham Regional Road 1), 5 kilometres north of village of Claremont (Durham Regional Road 5) or 3 kilometres south of Durham Regional Road 21.

SENECA COLLEGE — KING CAMPUS
(King Township, northeast of King City)

- 10 kilometres of track-set trails, with loops of 4, 5 and 6 kilometres, suitable for all levels, plus a skate-skiing loop of 2 kilometres.
- 280 hectares of forest, field and plantation,

and a kettle lake. Trails follow rail bed, and pass stately Eaton Hall.

- Trail maps are provided.
- Fee.
- Ski rentals, lunchroom and snack bar are open weekends only.
- Operated by Seneca College. For trail conditions call (905) 833-3333, extension 5024.
- Access is on the west side of Dufferin Street (York Regional Road 53), 2.5 kilometres north of King Road (York Regional Road 11).

TRILLIUM TRAILS
(North of Oshawa)

- 16 kilometres of track-set trails, with loops of 2, 4, 6, 7 and 13 kilometres, suitable for all levels. (Drive just 1 kilometre north to Purple Woods Conservation Area for great views from a lookout platform on the crest of the Moraine.)
- 55 hectares of conifer plantation, meadows and hardwood forest.
- Fee.
- Ski rentals, lunchroom and snack bar open daily.
- For trail conditions call (905) 655-3754.
- Access is on the west side of Simcoe Street (Durham Regional Road 2), 0.2 kilometres north of Durham Regional Road 5, or 9 kilometres south of Port Perry.

WALKER WOODS
(Uxbridge Township, south of Town of Uxbridge)

- 35 kilometres of skiable forest access roads and firebreaks, but no official trails or signs. (The dense network of trails is bewildering — there are more than 150 intersections and no signs to guide you. Explore cautiously, and bring a compass to help find your way back to the road you parked on. For a map of the vicinity, which includes small-scale maps of all trails in Walker Woods and Durham Forest, contact the Oak Ridges Trail Association.)

- 285 hectares of conifer plantation, hardwood forest, and even a red-oak plantation.

- No facilities, services, or fee.

- Managed by the Metropolitan Toronto and Region Conservation Authority.

- Access is from the east side of Concession 6, Uxbridge, 3.2 kilometres north of the Uxbridge/Pickering Townline or 2.9 kilometres south of Durham Regional Road 21. Another is from the west side of Concession 7, Uxbridge, 5.8 kilometres north of Durham Regional Road 5 or 2.5 kilometres south of Durham Regional Road 21. No parking lots. Park on the shoulder.

YORK REGIONAL FOREST

York Regional Forest tracts are owned by the Regional Municipality of York and managed by the Ontario Ministry of Natural Resources. There are several York Regional Forest tracts on the Moraine. All have trails, but none provide any facilities (trail signs, outhouses or shelters) or services (track-setting or regular trail maintenance). Skiing is most peaceful on the following three tracts, on which snowmobiling is prohibited. Admission is free.

HEADQUARTERS TRACT
(Town of Whitchurch-Stouffville, east of Newmarket)

- 8 kilometres of unmarked flat and rolling trails through 80 hectares of red-pine plantation and hardwood forest. These pretty trails are used mostly by skiers, and often have very good tracks.

- Access is on the east side of Highway 48 opposite Cherry Street, 0.9 kilometres south of Vivian Road (York Regional Road 74) or 3.2

kilometres north of Aurora Road (York Regional Road 15).

NORTH TRACT
(Town of Whitchurch-Stouffville, east of Newmarket)

- 22 kilometres of unmarked flat and rolling trails through 330 hectares of pine plantation and hardwood forest. The area southwest of the parking lot is less heavily logged, and has more hardwood forest.

- Access is on the west side of Highway 48, 0.8 kilometres north of Vivian Road (York Regional Road 74).

PORRITT TRACT
(Town of Whitchurch-Stouffville, east of Aurora)

- 5 kilometres of unmarked rolling trails on 80 hectares of red- and jack-pine plantation and hardwood forest.

- Access is on the west side of Kennedy Road (York Regional Road 3), 0.6 kilometres north of the Aurora Road (York Regional Road 15).

28. FISH OF THE OAK RIDGES MORAINE

Mike Stoneman

Today, walking along the banks of a small headwater stream on the Oak Ridges Moraine on a summer afternoon, a casual observer could be forgiven for thinking that the stream contained no fish. The sparkling waters cascading over rocks and logs, combined with the sun-dappled shadows, make it very difficult to see the many fish hiding in the stream. In fact, in a stream only 2 metres wide, several hundred fish could be living, largely unseen, in every 100-metre section. These fish include trout and salmon ranging from 3-centimetre juveniles less than a year old, to 50-centimetre adults that can weigh 2.5 kilograms! A bewildering variety of minnows, shiners, chub and dace, all members of the minnow family, share space with sculpins, darters, sticklebacks, catfish, and even bass.

In late April or early September there is an even more impressive array of fish. During the spring spawning run, adult rainbow trout up to a metre long and weighing up to 10 kilograms leave Lake Ontario and travel up streams to shallow, gravelly spawning areas. There the fish dig shallow pits, or redds, and bury their fertilized eggs in the

Extensive damming of streams in the late 1800s and 1900s had an adverse effect on the fish population in the rivers and streams of the Moraine. But today, without dams, and forestation and the reintroduction of fish species, population and diversity continue to improve.
Photo by D. McQueen

gravel. Nurtured by the cool water that percolates through the gravel, the eggs hatch to release the next generation of trout. In the fall, the same spectacle is repeated by brown trout, chinook salmon, coho salmon and even Atlantic salmon. Obstructions such as log jams and waterfalls are no barrier to the prodigious jumping ability of these animals. The fish congregate by the hundreds in a pool below the obstruction and take turns attempting to jump the obstacle.

Fish ladders have been constructed on many man-made barriers to allow fish to pass, creating spectacular viewing opportunities for people eager to see these magnificent creatures. Ladders at Port Hope, on the Ganaraska River, and at Bowmanville, on Bowmanville Creek, are particularly popular. Spawning runs of this magnitude also attract huge numbers of anglers from all over Ontario, Quebec and the northern United States. Bowmanville Creek, Wilmot Creek, Shelter Valley Creek and the Ganaraska River rank as some of the best trout- and salmon-fishing destinations in the world.

The streams owe their abundant trout and salmon populations to the unique geology of the Oak Ridges Moraine. Trout and salmon are very temperature sensitive and can survive only in cold streams. Along the Moraine, the streams are fed by the constant flow of cold, clear ground water that seeps out of the gravel deposits. Ground water maintains a constant temperature year-round, buffering the streams against the extremes of summer heat and winter cold. Even on the

hottest days the streams remain relatively cool, rarely exceeding 12 degrees Celsius at their origins. As the water flows downstream it gradually warms up, heated both by the sun's rays and by the inflow of warmer surface runoff. This continuum from very cold conditions at the headwaters to warmer conditions further downstream, allows a spectrum of fish species to occupy the stream, each located at its preferred temperature range. As the stream warms, the trout and salmon give way to suckers, minnows, bass and pike. If the stream heats up too much, however, the fish population will disappear altogether.

The rate at which the stream warms is largely determined by the amount of sunlight that falls on the water's surface and by the ratio of ground water to surface water that flows into the stream. Both of these factors are influenced by the amount of forest cover in the watershed. Trees reduce warm surface runoff by intercepting rainwater and slowing surface flow, which encourages water to soak into the ground and replenish underground aquifers. Trees also shade the stream and the surrounding area, reducing solar heating. The cutting down of forests contributes to stream warming and causes a shift in fish species. Likewise, urbanization harms trout streams by removing shade and preventing rainwater from replenishing the aquifers. Paved surfaces prevent infiltration, directing rainfall directly into streams as warm surface runoff. With a reduction in ground water, trout populations are sure to diminish.

Atlantic salmon. Photo by Gilbert Von Rykersvol

The original species composition of the Oak Ridges Moraine streams consisted of brook trout, which lived their whole life in the stream, and Atlantic salmon, which spent one or two years in the stream and then migrated to Lake Ontario to mature. Salmon were so abundant that early settlers used wagon loads of them to fertilize their fields!

However, human activity has caused a profound change in the fish populations of the Oak Ridges Moraine streams in the late 1800s and early 1900s. Land was cleared along the Moraine for farming and ranching, removing the shading effect of the trees. Stream temperatures began to rise and the trout and salmon had to move farther upstream to remain in cool water. Without the protection of the tree roots, the fine sandy soils of the Moraine were rapidly eroded by wind and rain and washed into the streams. Large amounts of fine sand in the river settled in the gaps in the rocks and gravel, blocking the percolation of water that is so crucial for the incubation of the buried eggs. Along with rising temperatures, this greatly reduced the numbers of fish.

At the same time that land was being cleared for farming, dams were built on the streams.

In the 1890s, Samuel Wilmot, of Newcastle, noticed the falling numbers of Atlantic salmon and started a hatchery program at his home in an attempt to save them. Despite his best efforts, and the production of millions of young salmon, the loss of habitat was too severe, and the Atlantic salmon disappeared from the Lake Ontario basin by the early 1900s.

Some streams had over a dozen dams along their lengths, powering sawmills and grist mills. No thought was given to allowing fish over the dams, so the spawning runs of the Atlantic salmon were completely blocked. With the increased temperatures, the short sections between the lake and the first dam were generally unsuitable for spawning, so the salmon population dwindled rapidly.

By the 1930s, erosion and the generally poor fertility of the Moraine soils rendered farming unprofitable. The reforestation of the Oak Ridges Moraine was undertaken by the provincial government beginning with the founding of the Orono Provincial Forestry Station. Trees raised at Orono were used to replant large areas of the Moraine, gradually returning the forest cover and stabilizing the shifting soils. As the forests were reestablished, the sand input to the streams was reduced, and the ground water input increased, creating ideal conditions for trout and salmon. The widespread availability of electricity meant that most dams were gradually abandoned and removed, and fish ladders were built on the remaining ones. With the habitat gradually improving and access restored, the stage was set for the recovery of the trout and salmon in the Oak Ridges Moraine streams.

But attempts to reestablish Atlantic salmon in Lake Ontario during the 1950s and 1960s met with little success, perhaps because of the limited information available on their requirements. Introductions of other species have been more fruitful. Early introductions of brown trout from Europe and rainbow trout from the west coast of North America were particularly successful, creating self-sustaining naturalized populations in many of the Moraine streams. More recently, chinook and coho salmon have been imported from the west coast, and they have established themselves in many streams as well. The introduction of other species seems to suggest that the conditions are appropriate for trout and salmon, so there is hope that another reintroduction of Atlantic salmon could be successful. However, the presence of these other species means that the Atlantics will have to compete for food and shelter.

In the late 1980s, the Ontario Ministry of Natural Resources began conducting experimental introductions to examine the effects of other species on young Atlantics. Early results appear promising, as the young are able to survive in the presence of competitors and grow from less than 3 centimetres in April to over 15 centimetres by October. If this carries over into adult growth and survival, the streams of the Oak Ridges Moraine may once again contain self-sustaining populations of Atlantic salmon.

CONCLUSION:
THE FUTURE OF THE MORAINE

David McQueen

In this book we have attempted to provide not only a description and history of the Oak Ridges Moraine and its ecology but also information of interest to hikers, naturalists and other outdoor enthusiasts. Our overriding objective has been to better acquaint people — through essays, pictures, maps and diagrams — with the Moraine, but above all, to encourage people to visit and experience it first-hand.

This book may leave you asking certain questions. What now? How well protected is this ecological treasure you have described for us? Will it still be there in the future for us, our children, and our grandchildren? What can I do?

Ironically, one of the Moraine's greatest advantages — its accessibility — may also be its undoing. Much of the Moraine is within an hour's drive of the more thickly populated portions of the GTA.

The Moraine thus affords us a perfectly situated breathing space. More than that, it is a greenbelt that helps greatly to clean and stabilize key rivers, including the Humber, Don, Rouge and Holland. As William Granger, former chair of the

Morning dew on a pussy willow bud. Photo by F. Clauer

core area: area possessing ecological features that provide significant habitat for wildlife

corridor areas: area providing vital connection between core areas for wildlife.

What you can do:
- Plant more trees and shrubs on your land.
- Get involved with trail and environmental groups such as the Oak Ridges Trail Association (ORTA) and the Save the Oak Ridges Moraine Coalition (STORM).
- Ask questions about land development at your local council meetings (all the more important now that more planning responsibility has been shifted to the local level).

Some steps already taken to protect the Oak Ridges Moraine:

Before 1989

Some measures are taken to restore and protect particular parts of the Moraine (i.e. agreement forests and the Ganaraska Forest).

1989

Two graduate students in environmental studies, John Fisher and Don Alexander, propose at a public hearing that the Moraine be addressed as a whole. The STORM Coalition (Save the Oak Ridges Moraine) is formed to do just this, and press for legislated protection for the Moraine.

1990

Hon. Ron Kanter, MPP, in his "Options for a Greater Toronto Area Greenlands Strategy," urges the Ontario government to declare a provincial interest in the Moraine.

The Royal Commission on the Future of the Toronto Waterfront, chaired by Hon. David Crombie, expands its mandate to include the Oak Ridges Moraine. The Ontario government expresses a provincial interest in the Moraine.

The proximity of the Oak Ridges Moraine to the Greater Toronto Area makes further urbanization seem inevitable. Photo by L. Wise

Metropolitan Toronto and Region Conservation Authority, points out, it also cleans the air:

> We are critically dependent on the fresh oxygen and cooler summer air temperatures produced by forested areas north, west and east of Metropolitan Toronto. Trees capture particulate pollutants and carbon dioxide expelled by human activity, and return cool, fresh oxygen to the atmosphere. The forested areas around our cities literally act as our green lungs, and are indispensable.

But the Moraine's proximity to Toronto also powerfully attracts other kinds of land use. By far, the two most detrimental of these are urbanization and aggregate extraction. At first in ribbons and then more generally, urban sprawl extends northward all too easily, often overriding significant natural features

A mat of jewelweed covers surface springs in a sensitive forest wetland. Photo by I. Deslauriers

in the process. As to aggregates, while there are large amounts of them in many Ontario locations, both the quality of Moraine sand and gravel and the relatively low cost of transporting them to major markets in the GTA make them especially attractive to the aggregate mining and trucking industries.

Environmentalists, as well as government ministers, public servants and private citizens, have at various times urged more compact and less costly patterns of urban development. They have also advocated a shift away from our current heavy reliance on automobiles and the aggregate-based roads on which they travel.

But changing how we develop lands and roads

116

The scenic vista from the Uxbridge hills. Photo by I. Deslauriers

will take time. Meanwhile, we find ourselves looking at a situation of strong competition between three future uses of this landform: conservation, urbanization, and aggregate extraction. That is the basic political problem of the Moraine.

Yet, despite the special difficulty of expressing long-run environmental value in dollar terms, natural heritage proponents have succeeded in gaining a certain degree of governmental and general recognition for their point of view. So some progress has been made, but it has not been easy. Unremitting efforts by volunteer groups such as the Save the Oak Ridges Moraine Coalition (STORM) and Save the Ganaraska Again (SAGA) have been necessary to get even this far. Much more remains to be done.

Consider, for example, the outcome of the exercise conducted by the Oak Ridges Moraine Technical Working Committee. The committee marked up some major accomplishments: the geographical boundaries of the GTA portion of the Moraine were established; three inter-connected systems on the Moraine were identified (Natural Heritage, Water Resources, and Landform Conservation); the Natural Heritage System was mapped as a chain of sensitive "core" and "corridor" areas, accounting for twenty-six percent of the total Moraine surface; and some useful commissioned research was completed, though largely on a foundation of already-existing data (more up-to-date information is badly needed, notably with regard to ground water resources).

But on some other key issues the committee failed to reach consensus. One was governance. Three plans, with differing degrees of protective "teeth," were on the table, but none was agreed

1991

The Ontario government establishes Interim Planning Guidelines for the part of the Moraine lying within the GTA. It appoints a multi-stakeholder Technical Working Committee to "develop a long-term strategy for the protection and management of the ecological integrity of the Oak Ridges Moraine." In this context, the earlier expression of a provincial interest and the guidelines are to be regarded as "an interim measure remaining in effect until a long-term strategy for the Oak Ridges Moraine within the GTA is developed."

What later becomes known as the Oak Ridges Trail Association is formed to create a trail along the full 160-kilometre length of the Moraine, and begins to work to put initial trail segments in place.

1992

The Royal Commission on the Future of the Toronto Waterfront, in its final reported, "Regeneration," recommends stronger policies for permanent protection of the Moraine.

Aggregate extraction will continue as long as urban centres continue to grow. Photo by L. Wise

117

1993

The Province appoints a Citizens' Advisory Committee on the Moraine to work in conjunction with the Technical Working Committee.

1994

In April, the Technical Working Committee circulates a draft for public discussion entitled, "The Oak Ridges Moraine Strategy for the Greater Toronto Area." In November, it submitted a revised version of this document to the Minister of Natural Resources, but he did not make it public.

upon. Another issue was whether aggregate extraction should be allowed on the twenty-six percent of the Moraine identified as part of the important Natural Heritage System. Aggregate industry representatives maintained that it should be allowed; others disagreed.

Having received the committee's report, the Ontario government, as of this writing, has taken no specific action regarding it. Meanwhile, however, via Bills 20 and 26, highly significant changes have been made in general provincial legislation and policy affecting planning and the environment. These have major implications for the Moraine.

One such change has been a drastic downsizing of the powers, independence and funding of conservation authorities. More than half of the location-specific chapters of this volume, focusing on areas chosen for their natural interest and attractiveness, deal with lands under the jurisdiction of con-

servation authorities. The future of these authorities now appears directly linked to how much local community support they can command.

Generally, there has been a major devolution of planning responsibilities from conservation and other authorities, and from the provincial government itself, to municipalities.

What is likely to happen to the Oak Ridges Moraine in the next century? At this point, nobody really knows. But public involvement in the Moraine, public opinion based on that involvement, and the force with which that opinion is expressed, will surely be influential in the long run. Our fondest hope is that this book will contribute to a significant improvement in everybody's knowledge and understanding of the Moraine, and to an outcome that our descendants will respect and thank us for.

Large portions of the Oak Ridges Moraine remain quiet, pastoral landscapes. Photo by J. Kamstra

ORGANIZATIONS

The following organizations can provide you with more information about the Oak Ridges Moraine:

Aggregate Producers Association of Ontario
365 Brunel Road, Unit 2
Mississauga, Ontario L4Z 1Z5

Conservation Council of Ontario
489 College Street, Suite 506
Toronto, Ontario M6G 1A5

Federation of Ontario Naturalists
355 Lesmill Road
Don Mills, Ontario M3B 1S4

Ganaraska Region Conservation Authority
Box 328
Port Hope, Ontario L1A 3W4

Lake Simcoe Region Conservation Authority
Box 282
120 Bayview Parkway
Newmarket, Ontario L3Y 4X1

Save the Ganaraska Again (SAGA)
4627 Ganaraska Road
R.R. 1 Newtonville, Ontario L0A 1S0

Metropolitan Toronto and Region Conservation
Authority (MTRCA)
5 Shoreham Drive
Downsview, Ontario M3N 1S4

Ministry of Environment and Energy
135 St. Clair Avenue West, Suite 100
Toronto, Ontario M4V 1P5

Ministry of Municipal Affairs
777 Bay Street, Floor 17
Toronto, Ontario M5G 2E5

Ministry of Natural Resources
99 Wellesley Street West, Whitney Block
Toronto, Ontario M7A 1W3

Oak Ridges Trail Association (ORTA)
Box 28544
Aurora, Ontario L4G 6S6

Save the Oak Ridges Moraine Coalition
(STORM)
Box 2209, Station B
Richmond Hill, Ontario L4E 1A4

Urban Development Institute
2025 Sheppard Avenue East
Willowdale, Ontario M2J 1V6

INDEX

aggregate extraction 28, 59–60, 116, 117

agreement forests 21, 22, 54, 85, 86

amphibians 50, 73–78, 96

animal tracks 81, 82

aquifer 12, 25–28, 43, 61, 72, 112

artifacts 20, 23, 102

birds 33–36, 42, 44, 50, 54, 62, 64, 70–72 88, 90, 92, 95, 96, 100, 102

butterflies 53

Carrying Place Trail 21

Central Lake Ontario Conservation Authority 37, 39, 49

Champlain, Samuel de 20

Crombie, Hon. David 11, 116

deforestation 28, 112, 113

Duffin's Creek 26, 29, 30

Eaton family 93–96

erosion 19, 28, 46, 65, 71, 85, 113, 114

European settlers 20–23, 40, 49, 51, 85, 113

ferns 50, 64, 83, 96, 96

fire 52–54

fish 44, 57, 70, 91, 111–114

flooding 71, 68, 70, 99

forest succession 85, 86, 63, 105

forestry terms 105, 106

forests 21, 24, 29, 30–35, 43–49, 57, 60, 61 64, 65–72, 83, 85–88, 89, 103–105, 116

fungi 70–73, 88, 96

Ganaraska Region Conservation Authority 68, 70

glacier, glacial action 15–17, 24, 47, 56, 57

Granger, William 115, 116

Guelph Conference, 1941 21

International Year of the Child Forest 65

kames 17, 25, 57

kettle lakes 12, 13, 17, 18, 28, 42, 93

Lake Simcoe Region Conservation Authority 62–64, 83–84

mammals 44, 50, 62, 70–72, 81–82, 88, 90, 92, 95–96, 100, 102

Metropolitan Toronto and Region Conservation Authority 29–30, 32, 55, 90, 92, 97, 99–102, 107, 116

mills 12, 23–24, 91, 113

Native peoples 12, 19–21, 23, 40, 52–54, 71, 84, 102

Niagara Escarpment 11, 15, 23–24, 55–58

Oak Ridges Moraine
    characteristics 11–14, 15, 17, 73–74
    history 15–18, 19–22, 51–54, 67–68, 113–114

Oak Ridges Trail 11, 21, 31, 41–42, 89–92, 97, 117

poison ivy 88, 95

prairie plants 51–54

reforestation 21–23, 31, 36, 43, 58, 65–68

reptiles 50, 54, 73–78

Richardson, A.H. 21, 65, 68

rivers 26

    Black 25, 26, 61

    Bogart Creek 61

    Bowmanville Creek 47, 112

    Credit 25, 26, 56

    Don 12, 25, 26, 98, 100, 115

    Duffin's Creek 26, 29, 30

    Ganaraska 12, 20, 21, 25, 65–68, 112

    Holland 12, 25, 26

    Humber 12, 21–23, 26, 42, 49, 56, 81, 98–100, 115

Nottawasaga 25

Pefferlaw Brook 44

Rouge 12, 25, 98, 115

Shelter Valley Creek 112

Trent 12, 15, 26

Wilmot Creek 112

sand and gravel 12, 15–16, 22, 26, 28, 53, 57, 59–60, 83, 116

Sauriol, Charles 29

trail development 92

Trail Users' Code 32

Trail, Catharine Parr 51

urban development 19, 22, 27, 28

Walker, James 29–31, 92

water 12, 21, 25–28, 34, 112
    ground water 12, 22, 27, 28, 37, 60, 112, 114, 117
    water contamination 12, 28
    water cycle 25–27
    water discharge and recharge 26–28
    water table 28
    watershed 28
    watershed divide 37

wetlands 17, 35, 73–75, 77, 89

wildflowers 23, 32, 39–40, 46, 49–50, 51–54, 57, 64, 70, 72, 83, 95, 96, 102

York/Durham Heritage Railway 90

E S S E N T I A L S   O F
Nuclear Medicine
Imaging THIRD EDITION

FRED A. METTLER, Jr., M.D., M.P.H.
Professor of Radiology and Chairman
Department of Radiology
University of New Mexico School of Medicine
Albuquerque, New Mexico

MILTON J. GUIBERTEAU, M.D.
Clinical Associate Professor of Radiology
University of Texas Medical School
Chairman, Department of Radiology
St. Joseph Hospital
Houston, Texas

W. B. SAUNDERS COMPANY
Harcourt Brace Jovanovich, Inc.
Philadelphia • London • Toronto • Montreal • Sydney • Tokyo

W. B. SAUNDERS COMPANY
Harcourt Brace Jovanovich, Inc.

The Curtis Center
Independence Square West
Philadelphia, PA 19106

Library of Congress Cataloging-in-Publication Data

Mettler, Fred A.

Essentials of nuclear medicine imaging/Fred A. Mettler, Jr.,
Milton J. Guiberteau.—3rd ed.

p. cm.

Includes bibliographical references.

Includes index.

ISBN 0–7216–3996–8

1. Radioisotope scanning.   2. Diagnostic imaging.
  3. Nuclear medicine.   I. Guiberteau, Milton J.
  II. Title. [DNLM: 1. Nuclear Medicine.
  2. Radionuclide Imaging.]

RC78.7.R4M47 1991   616.07′57—dc20

DNLM/DLC   90–8873

Editor: W. B. Saunders Staff
Designer: Bill Donnelly
Production Manager: Ken Neimeister
Manuscript Editor: Alison Kelley
Illustration Coordinator: Brett MacNaughton
Indexer: Ella Shapiro

ESSENTIALS OF NUCLEAR MEDICINE IMAGING   ISBN 0–7216–3996–8
Third Edition

Printed in the United States of America.

Last digit is the print number: 9   8   7   6   5   4   3

This book is dedicated to
James H. Christie, M.D., a great
teacher and friend, and to our
parents and families.

PREFACE
TO THE FIRST EDITION

This book is intended to be used as an introductory text and to provide the reader with basic competence in nuclear medicine imaging. Rapid changes in the field have necessitated a departure from the content of other introductory texts, which is reflected by the inclusion in this volume of chapters on quality assurance, computers, and cardiovascular nuclear medicine. We have included only essential concepts and examinations, and even though there are many approaches to the various problems encountered in nuclear medicine, we often have described only a single approach, one that we have found useful and easy to understand. An effort has been made to include information that we hope will be useful to physicians in the course of practice.

For descriptions of rarely performed examinations and older forms of instrumentation, the reader must consult other texts. In these cases appropriate references have been provided. In some instances particular review articles have been specifically mentioned in the text because they are felt to be valuable reading. Additional reading in nuclear medicine physics is essential if the reader is to have a firm scientific basis.

We hope that this volume will provide a firm basis of knowledge in nuclear medicine imaging on which the reader can build using additional readings and experience.

PREFACE
TO THE THIRD EDITION

Four years have elapsed since the second edition of *Essentials of Nuclear Medicine Imaging* was published. During this period a number of techniques and procedures have evolved, whereas others have been less commonly used. The current edition addresses these changes in the clinical practice of nuclear medicine. For example, there has been more emphasis placed on single photon emission computed tomography (SPECT) instrumentation and on new radiopharmaceuticals such as those developed recently for brain imaging. Although we are always tempted to significantly expand each new edition of the text, it remains our firm resolution to keep this book devoted to essential aspects of nuclear medicine imaging.

Fred A. Mettler, Jr., M.D.
Milton J. Guiberteau, M.D.

ACKNOWLEDGMENTS

We are indebted to James H. Christie for guidance and encouragement, as well as to Barry A. Siegel and numerous colleagues, residents, and technologists for their useful suggestions during manuscript preparation.

CONTENTS

CHAPTER 1

Radioactivity and Radionuclides 1

BASIC ISOTOPE NOTATION, 1
NUCLEAR STABILITY AND DECAY, 1
RADIONUCLIDE PRODUCTION, 3
RADIOACTIVE DECAY, 4
RADIONUCLIDE GENERATOR SYSTEMS, 5
RADIONUCLIDES, 5
Technetium 99m, 5
Iodine, 7
Xenon, 8
Gallium, 8
Indium, 9
Thallium, 9
Positron-Emitting Radionuclides, 9
RADIOPHARMACEUTICALS, 9
Adverse Reactions, 10
Investigational Radiopharmaceuticals, 10

CHAPTER 2

Basic Instrumentation 15

ANGER OR GAMMA SCINTILLATION CAMERA, 15
Collimator, 15
Crystal, 17
Photomultiplier Tubes, 19
Pulse Height Analyzer, 19
Console Controls, 20
Resolution, 20
Specialized Gamma Cameras, 24
EMISSION-COMPUTED TOMOGRAPHY, 24
SODIM IODIDE WELL COUNTER, 24
SINGLE PROBE COUNTING SYSTEM, 26
DOSE CALIBRATOR, 26

CHAPTER 3

Basic Quality Control 27

INSTRUMENTATION, 27
Dose Calibrator, 27
Gamma Cameras, 28
RADIOPHARMACY QUALITY CONTROL, 30
Generator and Radionuclide Purity, 31
Radiochemical Tagging, 32
Sterility, 36

CHAPTER 4

Single Photon Emission Computed Tomography 37
PRINCIPLES OF ROTATIONAL SPECT, 37
Instrumentation, 37
Data Acquisition, 38
Tomographic Image Production, 39
Image Filtering, 39
Image Display, 40
SPECT Quality Control, 40
Field Uniformity Assessment and Correction, 41
Center of Rotation Determination and Correction, 42
X and Y Gain (Pixel Size) Calibration, 42
Detector Head Alignment with the Axis of Rotation, 43
Collimator Evaluation, 43
System Performance, 43

CHAPTER 5

Computers 45
HARDWARE, 46
CAMERA-COMPUTER INTERFACE AND TERMINAL, 47
SOFTWARE, 47
IMAGE ACQUISITION: MEMORY AND MATRIX SIZE, 48
IMAGE DISPLAY AND PROCESSING, 49
OPERATOR INTERACTION, 50
BULK INFORMATION STORAGE, 51
PURCHASE CONSIDERATIONS, 51
Software Considerations, 52
Service, 52
Camera-Computer Interface, 52
CPU, 53
Display, 53
Bulk Information Storage, 53

CHAPTER 6

Cerebrovascular System 55
CONVENTIONAL BRAIN IMAGING, 55
Physiology, 55
Radiopharmaceuticals, 55
Technique of Imaging, 57
   Preparation of the Patient, 57
   Radionuclide Angiogram, 57
   Static Images, 57
   Delayed Static Images, 57
CLINICAL APPLICATIONS, 58
The Normal Brain Scan, 58
   Radionuclide Angiogram, 58
   Static Images, 58
The Abnormal Brain Scan, 59
   Neoplasms, 59
   Cerebrovascular Occlusive Disease, 60
   Cerebral Death, 62
   Intracranial Inflammatory Disease, 63
   Trauma, 63

FUNCTIONAL BRAIN IMAGING, 66
Iodinated Radiopharmaceuticals, 66
Technique, 66
Normal Examination, 67
Pathologic States, 67
Positron-Emitting Agents, 67
CEREBROSPINAL FLUID IMAGING, 68
Radiopharmaceuticals, 70
Technique, 70
Normal Examination, 71
Pathologic States, 71

>Communicating Hydrocephalus, 71
>Noncommunicating Hydrocephalus, 73
>CSF Leaks, 73
>Shunt Patency, 74

CHAPTER 7

Thyroid and Parathyroid **75**
RADIOPHARMACEUTICALS, 75
Iodine 131, 75
Iodine 123, 75
Iodine 125, 76
Technetium 99m, 76
DOSIMETRY, 76
IODINE UPTAKE TEST, 77
Principle and Technique, 77
Procedure, 77
Factors Affecting Uptake, 78
Clinical Considerations, 78

>Elevated 131I Uptake, 78
>Reduced 131I Uptake, 79

SPECIAL TESTS OF THYROID FUNCTION, 79
Thyroid Suppression Test, 79
TSH Stimulation Test, 80
Perchlorate Washout Test, 81
CLINICAL APPLICATIONS, 81
Technical Considerations, 81
Normal Thyroid Images, 82
Abnormal Images, 82

>Histologically Normal Ectopic Thyroid Tissue, 82
>Thyroid Nodules, 83
>Multinodular Gland, 84
>Diffuse Toxic Goiter, 85
>Thyroiditis, 87
>Thyroid Carcinoma, 87

131I THERAPY IN THYROID DISEASE, 90
Principle, 90
Hyperthyroidism, 91

>Patient Preparation, 92

131I IN TREATMENT OF THYROID CARCINOMA, 93
Postsurgical Ablation, 93
Functioning Metastases, 93
PARATHYROID IMAGING, 93

CHAPTER 8

Cardiovascular System 95

ANATOMY AND PHYSIOLOGY, 95

MYOCARDIAL INFARCT IMAGING (PYROPHOSPHATE IMAGING), 96

Pathophysiology, 97

Radiopharmaceuticals, 98

Imaging Technique, 98

New Infarct-Avid Radiopharmaceuticals, 99

Scan Interpretation, 99

    Diffuse Uptake, 100
    Focal Uptake, 101
    Persistent Uptake, 102
    Sensitivity and Specificity, 102

Clinical Applications, 102

    Diagnosis of Acute Myocardial Infarction, 102
    Prognosis and Risk Stratification, 103

MYOCARDIAL PERFUSION SCINTIGRAPHY, 103

Physical Characteristics, 103

Biokinetics, 103

THALLIUM EXERCISE IMAGING, 104

Planar Technique, 104

Planar Image Interpretation, 106

The Abnormal Scan, 107

    Reversible Abnormalities, 107
    Nonreversible Abnormalities, 109
    Reverse Redistribution, 110
    Lung Activity, 111
    Right Ventricular Activity, 111

Dipyridamole Thallium Imaging, 111

    Technique, 112
    Dipyridamole Thallium Image Interpretation, 112

Quantitative Analysis of Thallium, 112

Clinical Applications of Thallium Exercise Imaging, 113

    Coronary Artery Disease, 113
    Prognostication and Risk Stratification in Coronary Artery Disease, 116
    Noncoronary Disease States, 116
        Valvular Lesions, 116
        Left Bundle Branch Block, 117
        Idiopathic Hypertrophic Subaortic Stenosis (IHSS), 117
        Cardiomyopathy, 117
        Hypertensive Myocardial Hypertrophy, 117

SPECT Thallium Imaging, 117

    Technique, 118

RESTING THALLIUM SCINTIGRAPHY, 122

New Myocardial Perfusion Agents, 122

TESTS OF CARDIAC FUNCTION, 123

Computer Methods, 123

    Qualitative Data Display, 123
    Functional (Parametric) Images, 124
    Quantitative Data Display, 127

First-Transit Studies, 129

    Principle, 129
    Radiopharmaceutical, 129
    Technique, 130
    Interpretation, 131

Equilibrium or Blood Pool Radionuclide Ventriculography, 131
Principle, 131
Radiopharmaceutical, 131
Technique, 132
Interpretation, 133
Clinical Applications, 135

CHAPTER 9

Respiratory System 141
ANATOMY AND PHYSIOLOGY, 141
RADIOPHARMACEUTICALS, 143
Perfusion Agents, 143
Ventilation Agents, 143
TECHNIQUE, 146
Perfusion Imaging, 146
Ventilation Imaging, 147
NORMAL LUNG SCAN, 148
Perfusion Scan, 148
Ventilation Scan, 151
CLINICAL APPLICATIONS, 151
Pulmonary Embolism, 151
Ventilation-Perfusion (V/Q) Scan Findings, 152
Approaches to Scan Interpretation, 164
Lung Scan Versus Pulmonary Angiography, 166
Follow-up, 167
COPD, 167
Asthma, Bronchiectasis, and Bronchitis, 170
Lung Neoplasms, 173
Inflammatory Disease, 173
Cardiovascular Abnormalities, 175
Deep Venous Imaging and Thrombus Detection, 175

CHAPTER 10

Gastrointestinal Tract 177
LIVER–SPLEEN IMAGING, 177
Radiopharmaceutical, 177
Technique, 177
Single-Photon Emission Computed Tomography (SPECT)
Imaging, 178
CLINICAL APPLICATIONS, 179
Normal Liver Scan, 179
Abnormal Liver Scan, 180
Specific Disease Entities, 183
Alcoholic Liver Disease, 183
Diffuse and Infiltrative Disorders, 183
Metastatic Disease, 187
Primary Liver Neoplasms, 188
Miscellaneous, 188
Normal Spleen Imaging, 190
Abnormal Spleen Imaging, 190
Focal Lesions, 190
Splenomegaly, 192
Trauma, 192
Nonvisualization of the Spleen, 193

GASTROINTESTINAL BLEEDING, 193
Lower Gastrointestinal Hemorrhage, 193
Technique, 194
Interpretation, 195
Meckel's Diverticulum, 195
HEPATOBILIARY IMAGING, 196
Radiopharmaceuticals, 196
Technique, 197
The Normal Scan, 198
Clinical Manifestations, 198
   Acute Cholecystitis, 198
   Chronic Cholecystitis, 200
   Biliary Obstruction, 201
   Post-traumatic and Post-surgical Scans, 201
   Biliary Atresia, 202
   Evaluation of Defects on Sulfur Colloid Scans, 202
GASTROESOPHAGEAL FUNCTION, 202
ESOPHAGEAL TRANSIT, 202
Radiopharmaceuticals, 203
Technique, 203
Normal and Abnormal Esophageal Transit, 204
GASTROESOPHAGEAL REFLUX STUDIES, 204
Radiopharmaceuticals, 204
Technique, 204
Normal and Abnormal Studies, 204
GASTRIC EMPTYING, 205
Radiopharmaceuticals, 205
Technique, 205
Normal and Abnormal Studies, 205
Schilling Test, 206

CHAPTER 11

Skeletal System 209
ANATOMY AND PHYSIOLOGY, 209
RADIOPHARMACEUTICALS, 209
TECHNIQUE, 210
THE NORMAL SCAN, 211
CLINICAL APPLICATIONS, 213
The Abnormal Scan, 213
   Metastatic Disease, 213
   Malignant Bone Tumors, 219
   Benign Osseous Neoplasms, 221
   Soft Tissue Uptake, 221
   Trauma, 224
   Osteomyelitis Versus Cellulitis, 230
   Benign Non-neoplastic Disease, 231
BONE MARROW SCANNING, 231
BONE MINERAL MEASUREMENTS, 231

CHAPTER 12

Genitourinary System 237
PHYSIOLOGY, 237
RADIOPHARMACEUTICALS, 237

RENAL IMAGING TECHNIQUES, 239
IMAGING TECHNIQUES FOR THE URETERS AND BLADDER, 240
CLINICAL APPLICATIONS, 242
Anatomic Variants, 242
Intrarenal Mass Lesions, 242
Vascular Abnormalities, 242
Renovascular Hypertension, 242
Diffuse Renal Disease, 243
Obstructive Uropathy, 243
Evaluation of Renal Transplants, 247
SCROTAL IMAGING, 249
ADRENAL IMAGING, 249

CHAPTER 13

Tumor and Inflammation Imaging 253
GALLIUM, 253
Biologic Behavior, 253
Imaging Technique, 254
CLINICAL APPLICATIONS, 254
Normal Gallium Scan, 254
Neoplasms, 256
Inflammatory Disease, 257
Immunosuppressed Patients, 260
Osteomyelitis, 260
INDIUM 111 LABELED LEUKOCYTES, 260
Labeling and Biologic Behavior, 260
Imaging Technique, 262
Normal Scan, 262
Abnormal Scan, 262
Osteomyelitis, 263
Immunosuppressed Patients, 263
LABELED ANTIBODIES, 266

CHAPTER 14

Legal Requirements and Radiation Safety 269
REGULATORY AGENCIES, 269
RADIATION SAFETY OFFICER, 269
RADIATION SAFETY COMMITTEE, 270
TYPES OF LICENSES, 270
TRAINING, 271
Supervision and Visiting Authorized User, 271
TRANSPORTATION, 272
RECEIPT OF RADIOACTIVE SHIPMENTS, 272
Record Keeping, 273
Instrumentation, 273
PREPARATION OF RADIOPHARMACEUTICALS, 274
MISADMINISTRATION OF RADIOPHARMACEUTICALS, 275
LABORATORY AREAS, 275
SURVEYS, 276
PERSONNEL MONITORING, 276
WASTE DISPOSAL, 277

Appendices

APPENDIX A
Glossary 281

APPENDIX B-1
Characteristics of Radionuclides for
Imaging and Therapy 290

APPENDIX B-2
Radioactivity Conversion Table for International
System (SI) Units (Becquerels to Curies) 292

APPENDIX B-3
Radioactivity Conversion Table for International
System (SI) Units (Curies to Becquerels) 293

APPENDIX C-1
Technetium 99m Decay and
Generation Tables 294

APPENDIX C-2
Iodine 131 Decay Chart 295

APPENDIX D
Injection Techniques and
Pediatric Dosage 296

APPENDIX E
Sample Techniques for Nuclear Imaging 299

APPENDIX F
Radionuclide Imaging During Pregnancy 320

APPENDIX G-1
General Considerations for Patients Receiving
Radionuclide Therapy 322

APPENDIX G-2
Special Considerations and
Requirements for Iodine 131 Therapy 323

APPENDIX H
Emergency Procedures for Radioactive Spills ... 325

Index 327

CHAPTER 1

Radioactivity and Radionuclides

This chapter is intended to provide an introduction to the field of radioactivity and radionuclides.

Basic Isotope Notation

The atom may be thought of as a collection of protons, neutrons, and electrons. The protons and neutrons are found in the nucleus, and there are shells of electrons, which orbit the nucleus with discrete energy levels. The number of neutrons is usually designated by N. The number of protons is represented by Z (also called the atomic number). The atomic mass number or the total number of nuclear particles is represented by A and is simply the sum of N and Z. The symbolism used to designate atoms of a certain element having the chemical symbol X is given by $_Z^A X_N$. For example, the notation $_{53}^{131} I_{78}$ refers to one isotope of iodine. In this instance, 131 refers to the total number of protons and neutrons in the nucleus. By definition, all isotopes of a given element have the same number of protons and differ only in the number of neutrons. For example, all isotopes of iodine have 53 protons.

Nuclear Stability and Decay

There may be many isotopes of a given element, and some of these isotopes have unstable nuclear configurations of protons and neutrons. Such isotopes often seek greater stability by decay or disintegration of the nucleus to a more stable form. Of the known stable nuclides, most have even numbers of neutrons and protons. Nuclides with odd numbers of neutrons and protons are usually unstable. Nuclear instability may result from either neutron or proton excess.

Nuclear decay may involve a simple release of energy from the nucleus or may actually cause a change in the number of protons or neutrons within the nucleus. When decay involves a change in the number of protons, there is a change of element. This is termed a *transmutation*. Isotopes attempting to reach stability by emitting radiation are *radionuclides*.

There are several mechanisms of decay to achieve stability. One of these is *alpha emission*. In this case, an alpha particle (α) consisting of two protons and two neutrons is released from the nucleus, with a resulting decrease in the atomic mass number (A) by 4 and reduction of both Z and N by 2. The mass of the released alpha particles is so great that they travel only a few centimeters in air and are unable to penetrate even thin paper. These properties cause alpha emitters to be essentially useless for imaging purposes.

Beta particle ($\beta-$) emission is another process for achieving stability and is found primarily in nuclides with a neutron excess. In this case, a $\beta-$ particle (electron) is emitted from the nucleus accompanied by an antineutrino, with the result that one of the neutrons may be thought of as being transformed into a proton, which remains in the nucleus. Thus, beta particle emission decreases the number of neutrons (N) by 1 and increases the number of protons (Z) by 1, so that A remains unchanged (Fig. 1–1A). When Z is increased, the arrow in the decay scheme points toward the right, and the downward direction indicates a more stable state. The energy spectrum of beta particle emission ranges from a certain maximum down to zero, with the mean energy of the spectrum being about a third of the maximum. A 2-MeV beta particle has a range of approxi-

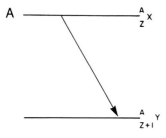

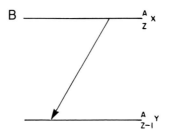

BETA PARTICLE EMISSION
(Z increases by I, N decreases by I)

ELECTRON CAPTURE
(N increases by I, Z decreases by I)

Figure 1–1. Decay schemes of radionuclides from unstable states (top line of each diagram) to more stable states (bottom line).

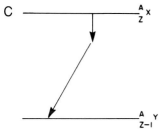

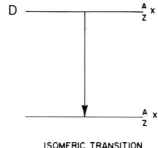

POSITRON EMISSION
(N increases by I, Z decreases by I)

ISOMERIC TRANSITION
(no change in N or Z)

mately 1 cm in soft tissue and is therefore not useful for imaging purposes.

In cases in which there are too many protons in the nucleus (neutron-deficient nuclide), decay may proceed in such a manner that a proton may be thought of as being converted into a neutron. This results in *positron* (β+) emission, which is always accompanied by a neutrino. This obviously increases N by 1 and decreases Z by 1, again leaving A unchanged (Fig. 1–1C). The downgoing arrow in the decay scheme again indicates a more stable state, and the fact that it goes to the left indicates that Z is decreased. Positron emission cannot occur unless at least 1.02 MeV of energy is available to the nucleus. When positron emission occurs, the positron usually only travels a very short distance and combines with an electron in an annihilation reaction. When this happens, two photons of 511 keV are emitted in exactly opposite directions (annihilation radiation). This radiation results from the conversion of the masses of the positron and electron to energy.

Electron capture occurs in a neutron-deficient nuclide when one of the inner orbital electrons is captured by a proton in the nucleus, forming a neutron and a neutrino. This can occur when not enough energy is available for positron emission and is therefore an alternative to positron decay. Since a nuclear proton is essentially changed to a neutron, N increases by 1 and Z decreases by 1, so again A remains unchanged (Fig. 1–1B). Electron capture may be accompanied by gamma emission and is always accompanied by characteristic radiation, either of which may be used in imaging.

If, in any of these attempts at stabilization the nucleus still has excess energy, it may be emitted as nonparticulate radiation, with Z and N remaining the same. Any process in which energy is given off as gamma rays and the numbers of protons and neutrons are not changed is called *isomeric transition* (Fig. 1–1D). An alternative to isomeric transition is *internal conversion.* In internal conversion, the excess energy of the nucleus is transmitted to one of the orbital electrons and the electron may be ejected from the atom, followed by characteristic radiation when the electron is replaced. This process usually competes with gamma ray emission and can only occur if the amount of energy given to the orbital electron exceeds the binding energy of that electron in its orbit.

The ratio of internal conversion electrons to gamma ray emissions for a particular radioisotope is designated by the symbol α. (This should not be confused with the symbol for an alpha particle.) For an isotope such as technetium 99m (^{99m}Tc) α is quite low, indicating that most emissions occur as gamma rays with little internal conversion. A low conversion ratio is preferable for in vivo usage because it implies a greater number of gamma emissions for imaging and a reduced number of conversion electrons which are absorbed by the body, adding to the patient's radiation dose.

In many instances a gamma ray photon is emitted almost instantaneously following particulate decay. However, if there is a measurable delay in the emission of the gamma ray photon and the resulting decay process is an isomeric transition, this intermediate excited state of the isotope is referred to as *metastable*. The most well-known metastable isotope is ^{99m}Tc (the "m" refers to metastable). This isotope decays by isomeric transition to a more stable state, as indicated in Figure 1–2. In the decay scheme, the arrows point straight down, showing that there is no change in Z. It should also be noted that ^{99m}Tc may decay by one of several routes of gamma ray emission.

Radionuclide Production

Most radioactive material that does not occur naturally can be produced by particulate bombardment or fission. Both methods

alter the neutron–proton ratio in the nucleus to produce an unstable isotope. Bombardment essentially consists of the irradiation of the nuclei of selected target elements with neutrons in a nuclear reactor or with charged particles (alpha particles, protons, or deuterons) from a cyclotron. Bombardment reactions may be summarized by equations in which the target element and bombarding particle are listed on the left side of the equations and the product and any accompanying particulate or gamma emissions are indicated on the right. For example:

$$^{A}_{Z}X + n(\text{neutron}) \rightarrow ^{A+1}_{Z}X + \gamma$$
$$\text{or more specifically,}$$
$$^{98}_{42}Mo + n(\text{neutron}) \rightarrow ^{99}_{42}Mo + \gamma$$

Such equations may be further abbreviated using parenthetical notation. The above reaction is thus represented as ^{98}Mo $(n, \gamma)^{99}$Mo. The target and product are noted on each side of the parentheses, which contain the bombarding particle on the left and any subsequent emissions on the right.

Once bombardment is completed, the daughter isotope must be physically separated from any remaining and unchanged target nuclei as well as from any target contaminants. Thus, it is obvious that the completeness of this final separation process as well as the initial elemental purity of the target are vital factors in obtaining a product of high specific activity. Because cyclotron isotope production almost always involves a transmutation (change of Z) from one element to another, this process aids greatly in the separation of the radionuclides producing *carrier-free* isotopes. (A carrier-free isotope is one that has none of the stable element

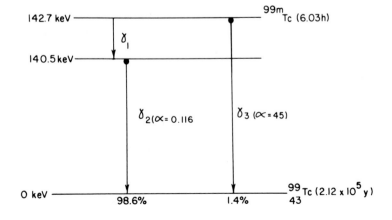

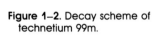

Figure 1–2. Decay scheme of technetium 99m.

accompanying it.) Radionuclides made by neutron bombardment, which does not result in a change of elemental species [e.g., ^{98}Mo (n, γ) ^{99}Mo], are not carrier-free since the chemical properties of the products are identical and thus not as easily separated.

Fission isotopes are simply the daughter products of nuclear fission of uranium 235 or plutonium 239 in a reactor and represent a multitude of radioactive materials, with atomic numbers in the range of roughly half that of uranium 235. These include ^{131}I, ^{133}Xe, ^{90}Sr, ^{99}Mo, and ^{137}Cs, among others. Because many of these isotopes are present together in the fission products, the desired isotope must be carefully isolated to exclude as many contaminants as possible. Although this is sometimes difficult, many carrier-free isotopes are produced in this manner.

Neutron bombardment and nuclear fission almost always produce isotopes with a neutron excess, which decay by β^- emission. It should be evident that some isotopes, such as molybdenum 99, may be produced by either method. Cyclotron-produced isotopes are usually neutron-deficient and decay by electron capture or position emission. Some common examples of cyclotron-produced isotopes include ^{123}I, ^{18}F, ^{67}Ga, ^{111}In, and ^{201}Tl. In general, cyclotron-generated radionuclides are more expensive than those produced by neutron bombardment or fission.

Radioactive Decay

The amount of radioactivity present (the number of disintegrations per second) is referred to as *activity*. In the past, the unit of radioactivity has been the Curie (Ci), which is 3.7×10^{10} disintegrations per second. Since this is somewhat of an inconvenient unit, it is being replaced by an international unit called a Bequerel (Bq), which is 1 disintegration per second. Conversion tables are found in Appendices B-2 and B-3. *Specific activity* refers to the activity per unit mass of material (mCi/gm or Bq/gm). For a carrier-free isotope, the longer the half-life of the isotope the lower the specific activity.

Radionuclides decay in an exponential fashion, and the term *half-life* is often used casually to characterize decay. Half-life usually refers to the *physical half-life,* which is the amount of time necessary for a radionuclide to be reduced to half of its existing activity.

The physical half-life (T_p) is equal to $0.693/\lambda$ where λ is the decay constant. λ and therefore the physical half-life have characteristic values for each radioactive nuclide.

A formula the nuclear medicine physician should be familiar with and be able to use is

$$A = A_0 e^{\frac{-.693}{T_p}(t)}$$

This formula can be utilized to find the activity *(A)* of a particular radioisotope present at a given time *(t)*, given a certain activity *(A_0)* at time 0. For instance, if you had 5 mCi (185 MBq) of ^{99m}Tc at 9:00 A.M. this morning, how much would remain at 9:00 A.M. tomorrow? In this case, T_p of ^{99m}Tc is 6 hours, t is 24 hours and e is a mathematical constant. Thus,

$$A = A_0 e^{\frac{-.693}{T_p}(t)}$$

$$A = A_0 e^{\frac{-.693}{6\ hr}(t)}$$

$$A = 5\ \text{mCi}\ e^{\frac{-.693}{6}(24\ hr)}$$

$$A = 5\ \text{mCi}\ e^{-0.1155(24\ hr)}$$

$$A = 5\ \text{mCi}\ (e^{-2.772})$$

$$A = 5\ \text{mCi}\ e^{\frac{1}{2.772}}$$

$$A = 5\ \text{mCi}\left(\frac{1}{15.99}\right)$$

$$A = 5\ \text{mCi}\ (.0625)$$

$$A = 0.31\ \text{mCi}\ (11\ \text{MBq})$$

Thus, after 24 hours, the amount of ^{99m}Tc remaining is 0.31 mCi (11 MBq).

It should be mentioned that in addition to the physical half-life or physical decay of a radionuclide, two other half-life terms are commonly used. The *biologic half-life* refers to the time it takes an organism to eliminate half of an administered compound or chemical on a strictly biologic basis. Thus, if a stable chemical compound were given to an individual and half of it was eliminated by the body (perhaps in the urine) within 3 hours, the biologic half-life would be 3 hours. The *effective half-life* incorporates both the physical and biologic half-lives. Thus, in speaking of the effective half-life of a particular radiopharmaceutical in humans, one needs to know the physical half-life of the radioisotope used as a tag or label as well as the biologic half-life of the tagged compound. If these are known, the following formula can be used to calculate the effective half-life:

$$T_e = \frac{T_p \times T_b}{T_p + T_b}$$

where:
  T_e = effective half-life
  T_p = physical half-life
  T_b = biologic half-life

If the biologic half-life is 3 hours and the physical half-life is 6 hours, then the effective half-life is 2 hours. Note that the effective half-life is *always shorter* than either the physical or biologic half-life.

Radionuclide Generator Systems

A number of radionuclides of interest in nuclear medicine are short-lived isotopes that emit only gamma rays and decay by isomeric transition. Because it is impractical for an imaging laboratory to be located near a reactor or a cyclotron, generator systems that permit on-site availability of these isotopes have achieved wide use. Some isotopes available from generators include ^{99m}Tc, ^{113m}In, ^{87m}Sr, and ^{68}Ga.

Inside a generator, a radionuclide "parent" with a relatively long half-life is firmly affixed to an ion exchange column. A ^{99}Mo–^{99m}Tc generator consists of an alumina column on which ^{99}Mo is bound. The parent isotope decays to a radioactive daugher (in this case ^{99m}Tc), which is a different element with a shorter half-life. Because the daughter is only loosely bound on the column, it may be removed or "washed off" with an elution liquid such as saline. After the daughter is separated from the column, the "build-up" process is begun again by the residual parent isotope. Uncommonly, some of the parent isotope (^{99}Mo) or alumina will be removed from the column during elution and appear in the eluate containing the daughter isotope. This is termed *breakthrough* and its significance and consequences are addressed in Chapter 3.

In order to make efficient use of a generator, elution times should be spaced appropriately to allow for reaccumulation of the daughter isotope on the column. The short-lived daughter will reach maximum activity at the point when the rate of decay of the daughter equals its rate of production. At this equilibrium point, for instance, the amount of daughter technetium 99m will be slightly less than the activity of the parent molybdenum 99 (Fig. 1–3). When the parent isotope has a half-life slightly greater than that of the daughter, the equilibrium attained is said to be a *transient equilibrium*. This is the case in a ^{99}Mo–^{99m}Tc generator.

The amount of ^{99m}Tc in the generator will reach about half the theoretical maximum in one half-life (6 hours). It will reach about three-fourths of the theoretical maximum in approximately two half-lives, and so on (see Appendix C). This indicates that if one elutes all of the ^{99m}Tc daughter from an ^{99}Mo generator, 24 hours later (four half-lives), the amount of ^{99m}Tc present in the generator will be back to approximately 95 percent of the theoretical maximum.

Radionuclides

In evaluating the choice of a radionuclide to be utilized in the nuclear medicine laboratory, the following characteristics are desirable:

- Minimum of particulate emission
- Primary photon energy between 50 and 500 keV
- Physical half-life greater than the time required to prepare material for injection
- Effective half-life longer than the examination time
- Suitable chemical form and reactivity
- Low toxicity
- Stability or near-stability of the product

TECHNETIUM 99m

Technetium 99m fulfills many of the criteria of an ideal radionuclide and accounts for over 70 percent of nuclear imaging procedures in the United States. It has no particulate emission, a 6-hour half-life, and a predominant (98 percent) 140-keV photon with only a small amount (10 percent) of internal conversion.

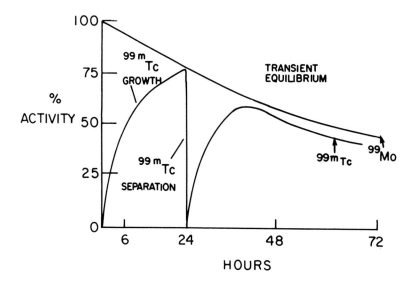

Figure 1–3. Radionuclide buildup and decay in a ^{99}Mo—^{99m}Tc generator, eluted at 0 hours and again at 24 hours.

Technetium 99m is obtained by separating it from the parent molybdenum 99 (67-hour half-life) in a generator system, which may be either an alumina column type or a solvent extraction type. Molybdenum 99 for generators is generally produced by neutron irradiation of ^{98}Mo or by chemical separation of ^{235}U fission products. In the latter case, ^{99}Mo is nearly carrier-free and has a high specific activity.

In the alumina generator system the molybdenum activity is absorbed on an alumina column. By passing physiologic saline over the column, ^{99m}Tc is eluted or washed off the column as *sodium pertechnetate* (Na ^{99m}TcO$_4^-$). This type of generator is commonly used in hospital nuclear medicine departments. In the solvent extraction method, technetium is separated from a solution of aluminum hydroxide containing the equilibrium pair (^{99}Mo–^{99m}Tc). Separation of the two species is possible using methyl ethyl ketone because sodium pertechnetate is highly soluble in the organic solvent. This method produces highly concentrated quantities of ^{99m}Tc and is usually only utilized by commercial radiopharmacies.

Technetium can exist in a variety of valence states, ranging from -1 to $+7$. When eluted from an alumina column generator, ^{99m}Tc is present primarily as heptavalent ($+7$) pertechnetate (TcO$_4^-$). In the preparation of radiopharmaceuticals, ^{99m}Tc pertechnetate can be reduced from $+7$ to a lower valence state, usually $+4$, to permit the labeling of various chelates. This is generally accomplished with stannous (tin) ions.

As pertechnetate, the technetium ion is a singly charged anion and is very similar in size to the iodide ion. Following intravenous injection, ^{99m}Tc pertechnetate is loosely bound to protein and rapidly leaves the plasma compartment. Over half leaves the plasma within several minutes and is distributed in the extracellular fluid. It rapidly concentrates in the salivary glands, choroid plexus, thyroid gland, gastric mucosa, and functioning breast tissue; during pregnancy, it crosses the placenta.

Excretion is by the gastrointestinal and renal routes. Although ^{99m}Tc pertechnetate is excreted by glomerular filtration, it is partially reabsorbed by the renal tubules, with the result that only 30 percent is eliminated in the urine during the first day. The ion is also secreted directly into the colon, with a much smaller amount coming from the small bowel. The colon is the critical organ and receives 1 to 2 rad per 10 mCi (0.02 mGy per MBq) of ^{99m}Tc pertechnetate administered.

The biodistribution of ^{99m}Tc pertechnetate is markedly influenced by pretreatment of patients with potassium perchlorate, sodium perchlorate, or potassium iodide (Figs. 1–4 and 1–5). Since these ions are approximately the same size as pertechnetate, there is direct competition for the binding sites in the choroid plexus, salivary glands, thyroid, and gastric mucosa. Another well-known alteration in the biodistribution of ^{99m}Tc pertech-

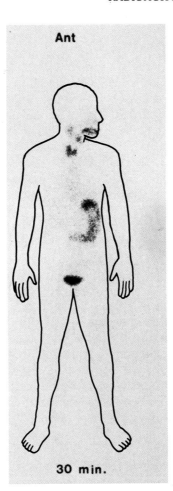
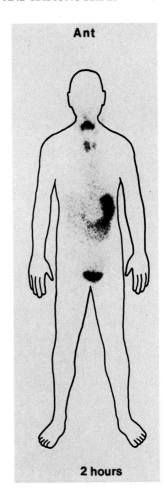

Figure 1–4. Whole-body distribution of ^{99m}Tc sodium pertechnetate without perchlorate blocking. Activity is seen in the thyroid gland, salivary glands, mouth, stomach, and bladder.

netate occurs with pretreatment of patients with stannous chloride causing reduction of the ^{99m}Tc pertechnetate with resultant binding to the red cells. Specific technetium radiopharmaceuticals will be discussed in the chapters on imaging.

IODINE

Two isotopes of iodine (iodine 123 and iodine 131) are clinically useful for imaging and may be administered as iodide. Iodine 123 has a 13.3-hour half-life and decays by electron capture to tellurium 123. The photons emitted are 28-keV (92 percent) and 159-keV (84 percent) gamma rays. Iodine 123 is usually produced in a cyclotron by bombardment of ^{121}Sb, ^{122}Te, or ^{124}Te. Another method is to bombard ^{127}I to produce ^{123}Xe and let this decay to ^{123}I. The cyclotron production and short half-life make ^{123}I expensive and distribution of it on a nationwide basis difficult. Iodine 123 has a whole body dose of 0.04 rad/mCi (0.01 mGy/MBq) and a thyroid dose of 16 rad/mCi (4.3 mGy/MBq). Contamination with ^{124}I may increase the radiation dose; since ^{124}I is long-lived, its proportion in an ^{123}I preparation increases with time.

Iodine 131 is a much less satisfactory isotope from an imaging viewpoint because of the high radiation dose to the thyroid and its relatively high photon energy. However, it is widely available, is relatively inexpensive, and has a relatively long shelf life. Iodine 131 has a half-life of 8.06 days and decays by β^- emission to stable xenon 131. The principal mean beta energy (90 percent) is 192 keV. Several gamma rays are also emitted, with the predominant photon being 364 keV (82 percent abundance). Iodine 131 gives a whole-body dose of 0.5 to 3.5 rad/mCi (0.14 to 0.95 mGy/MBq) and a thyroid dose of 1000 to 2000 rad/mCi (270 to 540 mGy/MBq).

When iodine is orally administered as the iodide ion, it is readily absorbed from the gastrointestinal tract and distributed in the

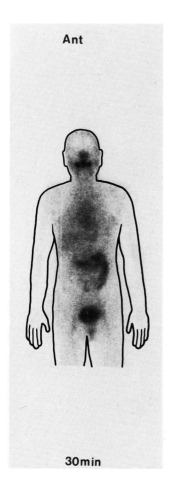

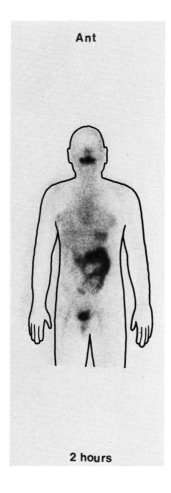

Figure 1–5. Whole-body distribution of ^{99m}Tc sodium pertechnetate with perchlorate blocking. Thyroid activity is no longer seen.

extracellular fluid. It is concentrated in a manner similar to ^{99m}Tc pertechnetate in the salivary glands, thyroid, and gastric mucosa. As with pertechnetate, there is renal filtration with significant tubular reabsorption. Urinary excretion is the predominant route (35 to 75 percent in 24 hours) although there is some fecal excretion as well. Iodide trapped and organified by the normal thyroid has an effective half-life of 7 days. Iodine is an extremely useful radionuclide because it is chemically reactive and is used to produce a variety of radiopharmaceuticals, which will be discussed in later clinical chapters.

XENON

Xenon is a relatively insoluble and inert gas and is most commonly used for pulmonary ventilation studies. Xenon is commercially available in unit-dose vials or in 1-Ci (40-GBq) glass ampules. Xenon is highly soluble in oil and fat, and there is some adsorption of xenon onto plastic syringes.

Xenon 133 has a physical half-life of 5.3 days. The principal gamma photon has an energy of 81 keV. There is also emission of a 374-keV beta particle. With normal pulmonary function, the biologic half-life is approximately 30 seconds. Some disadvantages of xenon 133 include its relatively low photon energy, beta particle emission, and some solubility in both blood and fat.

Xenon 127, which is occasionally used, has the advantages of a higher energy gamma ray (203 keV) and a longer physical half-life (36.4 days).

GALLIUM

Gallium is a metal with only one stable valence state (+3) in aqueous solution. Like iron, gallium binds to the plasma protein transferrin. Two isotopes of gallium have proved useful as imaging agents: gallium 67 and gallium 68. Gallium 67 has a half-life of 78 hours. It can be produced by a variety of reactions in a cyclotron. The principal gamma photons from gallium 67 are: 93 keV (40 percent), 184 keV (24 percent), 296 keV (22 percent), and 388 keV (7 percent). An easy way to remember these energies is to round off the figures (i.e., 90, 190, 290, and 390 keV).

Gallium 68 can be generator-produced in a germanium 68/gallium 68 generator. Gallium 68 has a 68-minute half-life and is a positron emitter. Since the germanium 68 for the gallium 68 generator as well as gallium 67 are cyclotron-produced, isotopes of gallium are relatively expensive.

Gallium is usually administered as a citrate and has a 12-hour half-life in the blood pool, where it is largely bound to plasma proteins, especially transferrin, lactoferrin, and ferritin. It ultimately leaves the blood pool to localize primarily in the liver, spleen, bone marrow, and skeleton. Tumor localization is not well understood, but lysosome binding appears to be involved as well as possible tumor concentration of the previously mentioned gallium protein complexes. The biologic half-life of gallium is approximately 2 to 3 weeks, with approximately 40 percent of the dose excreted in the first five days. Renal excretion (10 to 30 percent) is most common in the first 24 hours. Fecal excretion (about 10 percent) occurs primarily through the bowel wall.

INDIUM

Indium is a metal that can be used as an iron analog; it is quite similar to gallium. Isotopes of interest are indium 111 and indium 113m. Indium 111 has a physical half-life of 67 hours and is cyclotron-produced. The principal photons are 173 keV (89 percent) and 247 keV (94 percent). Indium 113m can be conveniently produced using a ^{113}Sn generator system. It has a physical half-life of 1.7 hours and a photon of approximately 392 keV. Indium 111 can be prepared as a chelate with DTPA. Due to its long half-life, the ^{111}In chelate is used for intracranial cisternography. Indium 111 is also used to label platelets and white cells.

THALLIUM

When a thallium metal target is bombarded with protons in a cyclotron, lead 201 is produced, which can be separated from the thallium target and allowed to decay to thallium 201. Thallium 201 has a physical half-life of 73.1 hours and decays by electron capture to mercury 201. Mercury 201 emits characteristic x-rays from 68 to 80 keV (94.5 percent) and much smaller amounts of gamma rays with higher energies. Since thallium 201 is cyclotron-produced, it is quite expensive. Thallium 201 is normally administered as a chloride and rapidly clears from the blood with a half-life of between 30 seconds and 3 minutes. Because it is roughly a potassium analog, it is rapidly distributed throughout the body, particularly in muscle. Thallium 202 (95 percent photon at 439 keV) contamination should be less than 0.5 percent and if present in greater quantities can significantly degrade images.

POSITRON-EMITTING RADIONUCLIDES

Several radionuclides are used for imaging due to their chemical and positron-emitting properties. Among these are carbon 11 (half-life 20.4 minutes), nitrogen 13 (half-life 10.0 minutes), oxygen 15 (half-life 124 seconds), fluorine 18 (half-life 110 minutes), and bromine 75 (half-life 101 minutes). These are produced using a cyclotron; therefore, they are very expensive, and their use is generally limited to research applications. Several positron emitters can be produced in a generator system, including copper 62, gallium 68, rubidium 82, and iodine 122. All positron-emitting radionuclides are of interest because of their potential use in transaxial tomography.

Radiopharmaceuticals

A radionuclide that has desirable imaging properties can usually be used to make a variety of radiopharmaceuticals. This is done by coupling the radionuclide with various stable compounds that are localized by organs or disease states. Mechanisms of localization for some of these radiopharmaceuticals are listed in Table 1–1. The various radiopharmaceuticals used in imaging procedures are discussed in the appropriate chapters. Although the localizing properties of radiopharmaceuticals are generally sufficient to obtain adequate diagnostic images, the localizing mechanisms may be altered by various conditions in an individual patient, including the administration of other medications. A list of these and their effects on

Table 1–1. MECHANISMS OF LOCALIZATION

- Capillary blockade
  Macroaggregated albumin or microspheres
- Diffusion
  Filtration of DTPA by kidney
  Technetium pertechnetate, DTPA, and gluco-
    heptonate in abnormal brain scans
- Sequestration
  Leukocytes for abscess scanning
  Labeled platelets (damaged endothelium)
  Heat-damaged red cells for splenic scanning
- Phagocytosis
  Colloid scanning for liver and spleen, bone
    marrow, and lymph nodes
- Active transport
  Iodocholesterol in adrenal scanning
  Iodine or pertechnetate (accumulation by cho-
    roid plexus, Meckel's diverticulum, salivary
    gland, stomach, and thyroid)
  Technetium 99m IDA iminodiacetic acid ana-
    logs in liver
  Orthoiodohippurate in renal tubules
  Thallous ions in myocardium
- Compartmental localization
  Labeled red blood cells
- Physicochemical adsorption
  Phosphate bone-scanning agents
- Antibody antigen reactions

the distribution of particular radiopharmaceuticals is given in Table 1–2.

ADVERSE REACTIONS

As drugs, radiopharmaceuticals are extremely safe. Even mild reactions are uncommon and severe reactions are very rare. An *adverse reaction* may be defined as an unanticipated patient response to the nonradioactive component of a radiopharmaceutical. This reaction is not due to the radiation itself. Overdoses of radioactivity represent misadministrations and are not adverse reactions. Misadministrations must be reported to the proper authority. The only adverse effect of a radiopharmaceutical that is required to be reported is that associated with an investigational drug.

The incidence of reactions to radiopharmaceuticals in the United States is probably between 1 and 10 per 100,000 administrations. Most reported adverse reactions are allergic in nature, although some vasovagal reactions have occurred. The clinical manifestations of most reactions are rash, itching, dizziness, nausea, chills, flushing, hives, and vomiting. These reactions may occur within 5 minutes or up to 48 hours post-injection. The late-onset rash or itching has most commonly been reported with technetium 99m bone agents. Severe reactions involving anaphylactic shock or cardiac arrest are reported in less than 3 percent of adverse reactions. In addition to allergic or vasomotor reactions, adverse effects with albumin particulates have been reported due to pulmonary capillary vascular blockage in patients with diminished pulmonary vascular capacity.

Reactions related to pyrogens or additives have become exceedingly rare because of the extensive quality control employed in the manufacture and preparation of radiopharmaceuticals. Pyrogen reactions may be suspected if more than one patient with a dose from a single vial of a radiopharmaceutical has experienced an adverse effect.

INVESTIGATIONAL RADIOPHARMACEUTICALS

Any new radiopharmaceutical must be treated as an investigational new drug (IND) and must go through the process outlined in the *Guidelines for the Clinical Evaluation of Radiopharmaceutical Drugs* of the Food and Drug Administration (FDA). Either manufacturers or health practitioners can file an IND application. Initially, the application must include complete composition of the drug, source, manufacturing data, and preclinical investigations including animal studies.

Clinical investigation occurs in three phases. Phase one is early testing in humans to determine toxicity, pharmacokinetics, and effectiveness. These studies usually involve a small number of persons and are conducted under carefully controlled circumstances. Phase two trials are controlled trials both for effectiveness in treatment of a specific disease and for evaluation of risk. Phase three, clinical investigation, involves extensive clinical trials, provided that information obtained in phases one and two testing demonstrates reasonable assurance of safety and effectiveness. Phase three studies acquire necessary information for complete drug labeling, including the most desirable dose and the drug's safety and effectiveness. It should be noted that most reimbursement organizations and third party payers will not pay for a drug unless it is fully approved by the FDA.

Table 1–2. ABNORMAL RADIOPHARMACEUTICAL DISTRIBUTION DUE TO MEDICATION AND OTHER EXTRINSIC FACTORS

	CAUSE	
FINDING	*Medications*	*Other*
BONE IMAGING—^{99m}Tc DIPHOSPHONATES		
Renal uptake	Amphotericin B	Al^{+++} ions in preparation
	Aluminum antacids	Radiation therapy
	Iron preparations	Radiographic contrast—sodium diatrizoate
	Chemotherapy agents	Alkaline pH
	Vincristine	
	Doxorubicin	
	Cyclophosphamide	
	Gentamicin	
	Dextrose	
Breast uptake	Gynecomastia-producing drugs	
	Digitalis	
	Estrogens	
	Cimetidine	
	Spironolactone	
	Diethylstilbestrol	
Liver uptake	Aluminum antacids	Al^{+++} ions in preparation
	Iron preparations	Excess Sn^{++} ions in preparation
		Radiographic contrast—sodium diatrizoate
		Alkaline pH
Spleen uptake	Aluminum preparations	
Excessive blood pool activity	Aluminum preparations	Too little Sn^{++} ions in preparation
Myocardial activity	Doxorubicin	Recent electrocardioversion
Excessive soft tissue uptake	Iron dextran injections (focal)	
	Iodinated antiseptics	
	Calcium gluconate injections	
	Heparin injections (focal)	
	Meperidine injections (focal)	
Muscle activity	ϵ-aminocaproic acid	
	Intramuscular injections	
Decreased skeletal uptake	Corticosteroids	
	Iron compounds	
	Phospho-Soda	
	Recent cold diphosphonate (hours)	
	Vitamin D$_3$	
Increased calvarial activity ("sickle sign")	Cytotoxic chemotherapy	
Regionally increased skeletal uptake	Regional chemoperfusion	
	Melphalan	
	Actinomycin	
LABELED LEUKOCYTE IMAGING—^{111}In-WBCs		
Reduced or absent abscess uptake (false negative)	Antibiotics	Hyperalimentation
	Lidocaine	
	Procainamide	
	Corticosteroids	
Lung activity		Cell clumping due to excessive agitation
Colon activity	Antibiotic-induced pseudomembranous colitis	
LIVER–SPLEEN IMAGING—^{99m}Tc SULFUR COLLOID		
Increased bone marrow uptake	Nitrosoureas	Colloid size too small
Increased spleen uptake	Nitrosoureas	
	Halothane	
	Methylcellulose	
Decreased spleen uptake	Chemotherapy	Thorium dioxide (Thorotrast)
	Epinephrine	
	Antimalarials	
Lung uptake	Aluminum antacids	Colloid size too large
	Iron preparation	Al^{+++} in preparation
	Virilizing androgens	Particle clumping
	Mg^{++} preparation	

Table continued on following page

Table 1–2. ABNORMAL RADIOPHARMACEUTICAL DISTRIBUTION DUE TO MEDICATION AND OTHER EXTRINSIC FACTORS *Continued*

| | CAUSE | |
FINDING	*Medications*	*Other*
Focal areas of decreased liver activity	Estrogens	
Increased free pertechnetate		Alkaline pH
		Sterilization with iodinated antiseptics
		Incorrect order of mixing
HEPATOBILIARY IMAGING—^{99m}Tc IDA DERIVATIVES		
Delayed biliary to bowel transit	Narcotic analgesics	
	Morphine	
	Demerol	
	Phenobarbital	
Decreased liver uptake and excretion	Chronic high-dose nicotinic acid therapy	
Enhanced hepatobiliary excretion	Phenobarbital	
Nonvisualization of the gallbladder (false positive)	Hepatic artery chemotherapy infusion	
Prolonged gallbladder activity and decreased contractile response to stimulation	Atropine	
^{67}GALLIUM-CITRATE IMAGING		
Excessive bone uptake	Iron preparation	Hemodialysis
	Chemotherapy	
	Methotrexate	
	Cisplatin	
	Vincristine	
	Mechlorethamine	
Excessive liver uptake	Iron dextran	
	Phenobarbital	
Lymph node uptake		Recent lymphangiography
Excessive renal uptake	Doxorubicin	
	Bleomycin	
	Cisplatin	
	Vinblastine	
	Furosemide	
	Phenytoin	
	Allopurinol	
	Cephalosporin	
	Ampicillin	
	Ibuprofen	
	Sulfonamides	
	Methicillin	
	Erythromycin	
	Rifampin	
	Pentamidine	
	Phenylbutazone	
	Phenobarbital	
	Phenazone	
Stomach uptake	Chemotherapy	
	Doxorubicin	
	Bleomycin	
	Cisplatin	
	Vinblastine	
Breast uptake	Estrogens	
	Diethylstilbestrol	
	Oral contraceptives	
	Reserpine	
	Phenothiazines	
	Metoclopramide	

Table continued on opposite page

Table 1–2. ABNORMAL RADIOPHARMACEUTICAL DISTRIBUTION DUE TO MEDICATION AND OTHER EXTRINSIC FACTORS *Continued*

	CAUSE	
FINDING	*Medications*	*Other*
Colon uptake	Antibiotic-induced pseudomembranous colitis, especially Clindamycin Cephalosporins Ampicillin	
Decreased abscess uptake	Prior treatment with iron dextran, deferoxamine	
Prolonged whole body clearance	Vincristine Steroid treatment Mechlorethamine	
Mediastinal and hilar lymph node uptake	Phenytoin (Dilantin)	
Lung uptake	Cyclophosphamide Amiodarone Bleomycin Busulfan BCG	Lymphangiographic contrast
Thymus activity	Chemotherapy Antibiotics	
BLOOD POOL IMAGING—^{99m}Tc-LABELED RBCs		
Reduced RBC labeling efficiency	Heparin Methyldopa Hydralazine Quinidine Digoxin Prazocin Propranolol Doxorubicin	Iodinated contrast media
MYOCARDIAL PERFUSION IMAGING—^{201}THALLIUM CHLORIDE		
Increased myocardial uptake	Dipyridamole Furosemide Isoproterenol Sodium bicarbonate (IV) Dexamethasone	
Decreased myocardial uptake	Propranolol Digitalis Doxorubicin Phenytoin (Dilantin) Lidocaine Minoxidil	
MECKEL'S DIVERTICULUM IMAGING—^{99m}Tc PERTECHNETATE		
Increased gastric mucosa activity	Pentagastrin Cimetidine	
Decreased gastric mucosa activity	Al^{+++} ion (antacids) Perchlorate	
LUNG PERFUSION IMAGING—^{99m}Tc-LABELED MAA		
Focal hot spots or patchy distribution in lungs	Mg^{++} sulfate therapy	Clot formation in syringe, clumping of particles
Increased liver uptake		Particles too small
MYOCARDIAL INFARCTION IMAGING—^{99m}Tc PYROPHOSPHATE		
Similar to diphosphonates		
THYROID UPTAKE AND IMAGING—RADIONUCLIDES (^{131}I, ^{123}I)		
See Chapter 7, Table 7–3.		
GASTRIC EMPTYING STUDIES—ANY RADIOPHARMACEUTICAL		
Delayed gastric emptying	Aluminum hydroxide Propantheline	
Shortened gastric emptying	Metoclopramide	
CEREBRAL CISTERNOGRAPHY—^{111}In DTPA		
Ventricular entry and stasis (false positive study)	Diamox (acetazolamide)	

Suggested Readings

Chandra R: Introductory Physics of Nuclear Medicine (ed 3). Philadelphia, Lea & Febiger, 1987

McAfee JG, Subramanian G: Radioactive agents for im-aging. In: Freeman and Johnson's Clinical Radio-nuclide Imaging (ed 3, Vol. 1). New York, Grune & Stratton, 1984:55–165

Sorenson JA, Phelps ME: Physics in Nuclear Medicine (ed 2). New York, Grune & Stratton, 1987

CHAPTER 2

Basic Instrumentation

Since this book is confined to nuclear medicine imaging, many instruments utilized for research purposes and radiation detection will not be included here. The most widely utilized imaging device at the moment is the Anger or gamma scintillation camera. Several other instruments are utilized in the nuclear medicine laboratory, including the dose calibrator and the well counter. Because these are essential to the daily practice of nuclear medicine they will also be discussed here. Single photon emission tomography is considered in Chapter 4.

Anger or Gamma Scintillation Camera

A gamma camera converts photons emitted by the radionuclide in the patient into a light pulse and subsequently into a voltage signal. This signal is used to form an image of the distribution of the radionuclide. The basic components of a gamma camera system (Fig. 2–1) are the collimator, scintillation crystal, an array of photomultiplier tubes, a pulse height analyzer, a cathode ray tube, and the control console. A computer may also be an integral part of the system. Gamma cameras may be classified as either analog or digital types. An analog signal is used throughout the analog camera; this signal has an infinite range of values and is inherently noisy. A digital signal, on the other hand, only has a discrete number of values. Most of the newer cameras incorporate some digital features. The main advantages of digital cameras are that they are much faster, can interact directly with the computer, and generally require less maintenance. Even the most advanced digital cameras, however, must start with the analog signal in the scintillation crystal and return to an analog signal for cathode ray tube (CRT) display of the image.

COLLIMATOR

The collimator is made of perforated lead and is interposed between the patient and the scintillation crystal. It is designed to reduce scatter and thus allows the gamma camera to localize the radionuclide in the patient. Collimators are able to perform this function by absorbing and stopping most radiation except that arriving almost perpendicular to the detector face: radiation striking the collimator at oblique angles will not be included in the final image. There are two basic types of collimators: *pinhole* and *multihole*.

A *pinhole collimator* operates in a manner very similar to that of a box camera (Fig. 2–2). Radiation must pass through the pinhole aperture in order to be imaged, and the image is always inverted on the scintillation crystal. Since very little of the radiation coming from the object of interest will be allowed to pass through the pinhole over a given time period, the pinhole collimator has very poor sensitivity. Collimator sensitivity refers to the percentage of incident-photons that passes through the collimator. The poor sensitivity of a pinhole collimator makes placement near the organ of interest critical. It is also apparent that bringing the object of interest close to the pinhole will magnify the image. Since magnification is a function of distance, if the object of interest is not relatively flat or thin the image may be distorted. Pinhole collimators are routinely used for very high-resolution images of small organs, such as the thyroid, and certain skeletal regions.

The holes in a *multihole collimator* may be aligned in such a way as to be diverging, parallel, or converging (see Fig. 2–2). The parallel-hole collimator is probably the most widely used in nuclear medicine laboratories. It consists of parallel holes with a long axis perpendicular to the plane of the scintillation crystal. The lead walls between the holes are

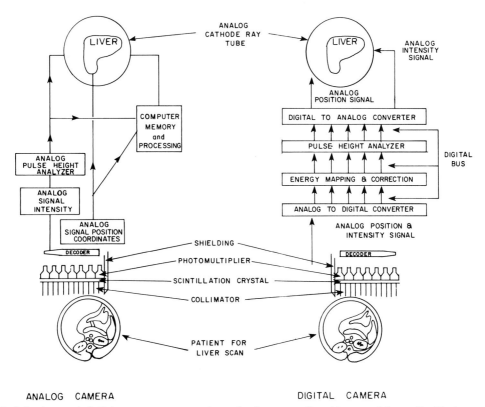

Figure 2–1. Analog and digital gamma camera schematic. A cross-sectional image of the patient is shown at the bottom, with a final image of the liver seen on the cathode ray tube at the top.

referred to as *septa*. The septa absorb gamma rays that do not emanate from the direction of interest; therefore a collimator for use with high-energy gamma rays has much thicker septa than a collimator for low-energy rays. The septa are generally designed so that septal penetration by unwanted gamma rays does not exceed 10 to 25 percent.

A *parallel-hole collimator* should be chosen corresponding to the energy of the isotope being imaged. Low-energy collimators generally refer to a maximum energy of 150 keV, whereas medium-energy collimators have a maximum suggested energy of approximately 400 keV. Collimators are available with different lengths and different widths of septa. In general, the longer the septa, the better the resolution but the lower the count rate (sensitivity) for a given amount of radionuclide. The count rate is inversely proportional to the square of the collimator hole length. If the length of the septa is decreased, the count rate increases and resolution decreases.

The difference between typical low-energy general purpose collimators and low-energy

high-sensitivity collimators is that high-sensitivity collimators may allow about twice as many counts to be imaged, although the spatial resolution is usually degraded about 50 percent. Thus, a high-resolution low-energy collimator has approximately twice the resolving ability of a high-sensitivity low-energy collimator. Most collimators are now designed with hexagonal rather than round holes. Since they have overall thinner septae they have greater sensitivity but more septal penetration than collimators with square or round holes.

With a parallel-hole collimator, neither the size of the image nor the count rate changes significantly with the distance of the object of interest from the collimator. This is due to the fact that as the object is moved small distances away from the crystal, the inverse square law reduces the number of counts. However, this is compensated for by the increased viewing area of the collimator. On the other hand, resolution is best when the object of interest is as close to the collimator face as possible (Fig. 2–3), and scans with multihole collimators are usually obtained

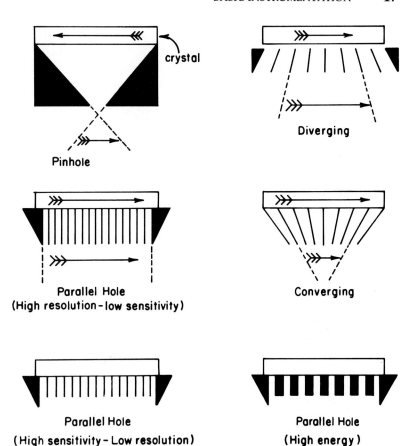

Figure 2-2. Types of gamma camera collimators.

with the collimator in contact with the patient.

A *diverging collimator* is one whose holes and septa begin to diverge away from the crystal face. Generally, use of a diverging collimator increases the imaged area by approximately 30 percent over a parallel-hole collimator. The image itself, however, is slightly minified. With a diverging collimator, both the sensitivity and resolution get worse as one moves away from the collimator. The sensitivity worsens because the area being imaged gets larger, but the object imaged does not get larger and the inverse square law predominates. Diverging collimators are utilized particularly on cameras with small crystal faces, to image large organs, such as the lungs.

A *converging collimator* has holes that converge toward a point (usually 50 cm) in front of the collimator. This convergence results in a magnified image being formed in the crystal. Sensitivity increases as one moves away from the collimator face until one reaches the focal point, beyond which the sensitivity begins to decrease. Resolution, however, decreases with distance. A converging collimator may be used for examination of small areas.

A specialized type of collimator for the Anger scintillation camera is the *seven-pinhole collimator*. Employing a large-field-of-view crystal and multiple pinholes, seven independent projections of an object are obtained. Data are acquired simultaneously from all seven views, and multiple planes are reconstructed using a computer, which then creates a tomographic image of the object. Another type of collimator, known as a *rotating slant hole collimator*, can be used on a standard-field-of-view gamma camera and still provide tomographic images. The planar and depth resolution of both these collimators compare favorably. Both the seven-pinhole and the rotating slant hole collimator are predominantly used for myocardial imaging studies.

CRYSTAL

Radiation emerging from the patient and passing through the collimator may interact

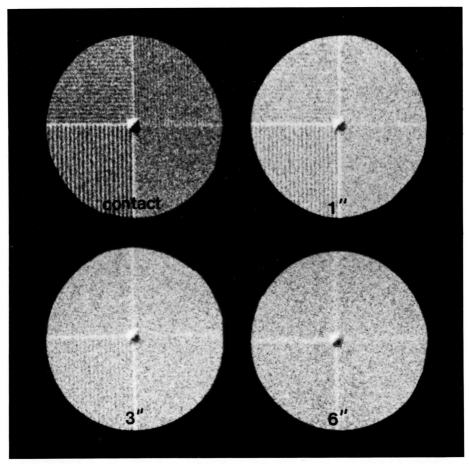

Figure 2–3. Loss of resolution as a function of distance from the collimator. The images are of a bar phantom in contact with and at varying distances from the collimator face. At distances greater than 1 inch, the pattern of the bar phantom essentially disappears.

with a thallium-activated sodium iodide crystal. Interaction of the gamma ray with the crystal may result in ejection of an orbital electron (photoelectric absorption), producing a pulse of fluorescent light (scintillation event) proportional in intensity to the energy of the gamma ray. Photomultiplier tubes (PMTs) along the posterior crystal face detect this light and amplify it. About 30 percent of the light from each event reaches the PMTs. The crystal has an aluminum housing that protects it from moisture, extraneous light, and minor physical damage.

The crystal may be from 10 to 21.5 inches in diameter and from ¼ to ½ inch thick. A larger-diameter crystal has a larger field of view and is more expensive but has the same inherent resolution as a smaller-diameter crystal. The thicker the crystal becomes, the

worse the spatial resolution but the more efficient the detection of gamma rays. In general, with a ½-inch thick crystal, the efficiency for detection of gamma rays from xenon 133 (81 keV) and technetium 99m (140 keV) is almost 100 percent; that is, very few of the photons pass through the crystal without causing a light pulse. As the gamma energy of the isotope is increased, the efficiency of the crystal is markedly reduced. For example, with iodine 131 (364 keV) efficiency is reduced to approximately 20 to 30 percent. Most crystals in new gamma cameras are either ¼ or ⅜ inch thick. With a thinner crystal the overall sensitivity (count rate) decreases by about 10 percent because more photons pass through, but there is approximately a 30 percent increase in spatial resolution, because the PMTs are closer to the event and thus can localize it more accurately and because there is an increase in light collection.

PHOTOMULTIPLIER TUBES

A photomultiplier tube (PMT) converts a light pulse into an electrical signal of measurable magnitude. An array of these tubes is situated behind the sodium iodide crystal and may be placed directly on the crystal, connected to the crystal by light pipes, or optically coupled to the crystal with a silicone-like material. A scintillation event occurring in the crystal is recorded by one or more photomultiplier tubes. Localization of the event in the final image depends on the amount of light sensed by each photomultiplier tube and thus on the pattern of PMT voltage output. The summation signal for each scintillation event is then formed by weighing the output of each tube. This signal has three components: spatial coordinates on X and Y axes as well as a signal (Z) related to intensity. The X and Y coordinates may go directly to instrumentation for display on the cathode ray tube or may be recorded in the computer. The signal intensity is processed by the pulse height analyzer.

The light interaction caused by a gamma ray generally occurs near the collimator face of the crystal. Thus, while a thicker crystal is theoretically more efficient, the PMT is farther away from the scintillation point with a thick crystal and is unable to determine the coordinates as accurately. Therefore, spatial resolution is degraded. The number of PMTs is also very important for the accurate localization of scintillation events and thus for spatial resolution: the greater the number of PMTs the greater will be the resolution. The early gamma cameras used 19 round photomultiplier tubes whereas newer cameras utilize from 37 to 93 hexagonal or round PMTs.

PULSE HEIGHT ANALYZER

The basic principle of the pulse height analyzer (PHA) is to discard signals from background and scattered radiation or radiation from interfering isotopes, so that only photons known to come from the photopeak of the isotope being imaged are recorded. The PHA discriminates between which events occurring in the crystal will either be displayed or stored in the computer and which will be rejected. The PHA is able to make this discrimination because the energy deposited by a scintillation event in the crystal bears a linear relationship to the voltage signal emerging from the photomultiplier tubes.

A typical energy spectrum from a PHA is shown in Figure 2–4. The photopeak is the result of total absorption of the major gamma ray from the radionuclide. If the characteristic K-shell x-ray of iodine (28 keV) escapes from the crystal after the gamma ray has undergone photoelectric absorption, the measured gamma ray energy for technetium 99m would be only 112 keV (140 − 28). This will cause an "iodine escape" peak. A "backscatter" peak may result from primary gamma rays undergoing 180° scatter, then entering the detector and being totally absorbed. This can occur when gamma rays strike material behind the source and scatter back into the detector. It may also occur when gamma rays pass through the crystal without interaction and Compton scatter from the shield or photomultiplier tubes back into the crystal. The "lead x-ray" peak is due to primary gamma rays undergoing photoelectric absorption in the lead of shielding or the collimator with resultant characteristic x-rays (75 to 90 keV) being detected. The effect of Compton scattering in the detector gives a peak from 0 to 50 keV. The sharp edge at 50 keV is called the Compton edge. If the source of radiation is within a patient, Compton scattering occurs within the patient's tissue, and some of these scattered gamma rays travel toward the detector. They will have an energy from 90 to 140 keV. These scattered photons from within the patient cause major imaging difficulties, because the Compton scatter overlaps with the photopeak distribution.

Signal intensity information is matched in the PHA against an appropriate *window*, which is really a voltage discriminator. To allow energy related to the desired isotope photopeak to be recorded, the window has an upper and lower voltage limit that defines the "window width." Thus, a 20 percent symmetric window for 140-keV photopeak means that the electronics will accept 140 ± 14 keV (i.e. 140 keV ± 10 percent) gamma rays. Any signals higher or lower than this, particularly those from scattered radiation, will be rejected. Some cameras have three PHAs, which allow several photopeaks to be utilized at once. This is particularly useful for radionuclides such as gallium 67.

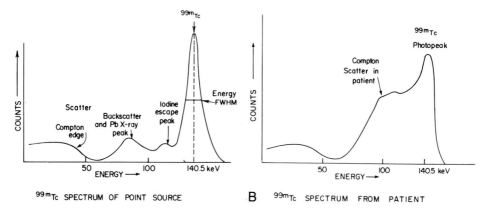

Figure 2–4. Energy spectra for technetium 99m when viewed by the gamma camera as a point source (A) and when viewed in a patient (B). Note the marked amount of Compton scatter near the photopeak that occurs as a result of scatter within the patient.

On newer cameras the signal processing circuitry, such as preamplifiers and pulse height analyzers, is located on the base of each PMT, so that there is little signal distortion between the camera head and the console.

CONSOLE CONTROLS

The position of the PHA window can be visually adjusted using a multichannel analyzer or Z pulse display. The multichannel analyzer display is generally more accurate because it indicates the spectrum of the gamma ray energy and shows both the photopeak and the scatter. For most studies a 20 percent window centered on the photopeak is utilized.

New gamma cameras allow for a fine adjustment known as automatic peaking of the isotope. This essentially divides the photopeak window into halves and calculates the number of counts in each half. If the machine is correctly peaked, each half of the window will have the same number of counts from the upper and lower portions of the photopeak. Occasionally, an asymmetric window is used to improve resolution by eliminating some of the Compton scatter (Fig. 2–5).

Image exposure time is selected by console control and is usually a preset count, a preset time, or preset information density (ID) for the image accumulation. Information density refers to the number of counts per square centimeter of the gamma camera crystal face. The effect of varying information density settings is shown in Figure 2–6. Other console controls are present for orientation and

allow the image to be reversed on the X and Y axes.

In addition, the CRT image may be manipulated by an intensity control, which simply affects the brightness of the image, or by a persistence control, which regulates the length of time the light dots composing the image remain on the screen. Most gamma camera systems have two CRTs—one for operator viewing and another for photographic purposes. The photographic CRT is a nonpersistence type (i.e., the bright spots on the tube display disappear almost immediately).

Hard copy images taken from the photographic CRT may be obtained on Polaroid film or transparent sheet film. Although Polaroid film is exceptionally convenient, it has inferior photographic characteristics and is more expensive than transparency film. In general the Polaroid cameras have three different lenses, each with a different lens aperture, to simultaneously provide images of different intensities. The resulting images are fixed in size and are usually small. Multiformat sheet film recording systems are more versatile, allowing easy variation in the size and number of images displayed.

RESOLUTION

Resolution usually refers to either spatial or energy resolution. *Energy resolution* is the ability to discriminate between light pulses caused by gamma rays of differing energies. *Spatial resolution* refers to the ability to display discrete but contiguous sources of radioactivity. The spatial resolution of various gamma

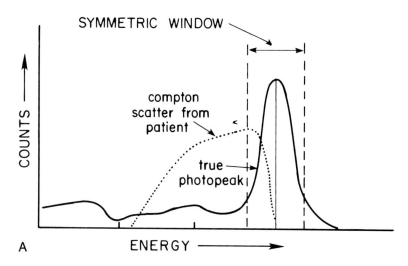

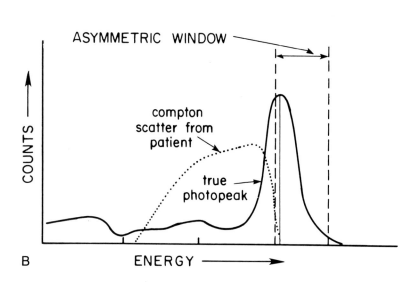

Figure 2–5. Use of a symmetric window (A) allows some of the Compton scatter to be counted and displayed. Theoretically, use of an asymmetric window (B) obviates this problem.

camera systems is usually given in terms of either inherent or overall resolution. Inherent resolution is the ability of the crystal PMT detector and accompanying electronics to record the exact location of the light pulse on the sodium iodide crystal. Marked improvements in gamma cameras have allowed an inherent resolution of about 2 mm.

Statistical variability is particularly important in resolution. An event occurring exactly between two PMTs does not always give the same number of photons to each tube; thus, for any single event the distribution of photons is statistically variable. Statistical variation is relatively greater when fewer light photons are available. In other words, the inherent resolution of a system or its ability to localize an event is directly related to the energy of the isotope being imaged. When radioisotopes with low-energy gamma rays are used the camera has less inherent spatial resolution.

Another factor that affects inherent resolution to a minor extent is Compton scatter. When the gamma ray interacts with the crystal, there is usually photoelectric absorption, which results in a light pulse at the point of interaction. However, with higher-energy gamma rays, the initial event may be a Compton interaction, or scatter (i.e., a collision between a gamma ray and a loosely bound orbital electron). This results in scattered photons with light coming from several points, even though only a single gamma ray interacted with the crystal initially.

Overall spatial resolution is the resolution

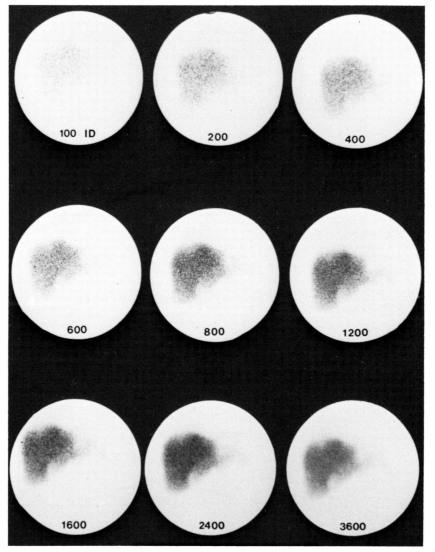

Figure 2–6. Anterior views of the liver obtained with different information density settings. As the information density increases, the defects in the liver are more clearly seen.

capacity of the entire camera system, including such factors as the collimator resolution, septal penetration, and scattered radiation. There are several ways of examining the performance of collimators. The simplest method of examining overall spatial resolution is to determine the full width at half-maximum (FWHM) of the line spread function. This refers to the profile response of the gamma camera to a single point source of radioactivity and reflects the number of counts seen by the crystal at different lateral distances from the source (Fig. 2–7). The source is often placed 10 cm from the crystal for such measurements. The FWHM is ex-

pressed as the width in centimeters at 50 percent of the height of the line spread peak. The narrower the peak, the better the resolution. A typical high-resolution collimator has three times better resolution than a representative high-sensitivity collimator but only allows one-tenth as many counts per minute for a given activity.

Whereas spatial FWHM is useful for comparing collimators, it often does not give other desirable information and does not necessarily relate to the overall clinical performance of the collimator. More difficult but perhaps more encompassing measurements of collimator performance are line-spread and

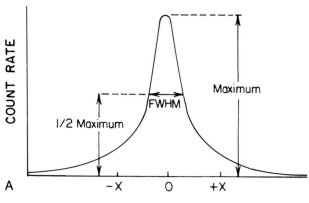

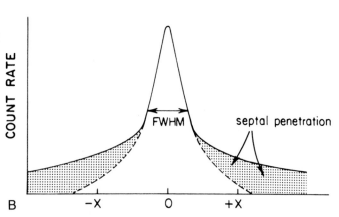

Figure 2–7. (A) The FWHM is the response in count rate to a single point source of radioactivity at different lateral distances from the point source. With septal penetration (B) the image may be significantly degraded even though FWHM is unchanged.

modulation transfer functions. These take into account other factors for optimizing collimator design such as the presence of scattering material and septal penetration. The value of this can be seen in Figure 2–7, which illustrates that the septal penetration occurring in the collimator may be completely undetected by the measurement of FWHM alone.

When the overall spatial resolution of the system with high-energy isotopes is considered, the limiting resolution is that of the collimator. When low-energy isotopes are imaged, the intrinsic resolution becomes more important than the collimator resolution. As the energy of the incident gamma ray decreases, the intrinsic resolution of the crystal decreases markedly, due to the fact that the lower-energy gamma rays provide less light for the PMTs to record; thus, there is more statistical uncertainty regarding the origin of the gamma ray. Although the intrinsic resolution of cameras is often mentioned with great pride by salesmen, the

overall resolution determines the quality of the image, as it is a combination of the resolutions of each of the components in the imaging chain, including the collimator, the inherent resolution, septal penetration, and scatter. The overall system resolution (Rs) is

$$Rs = \sqrt{R_i^2 + R_c^2}$$

where R_i is inherent resolution and R_c is collimator resolution.

Another category of resolution is *energy resolution* or the ability of the imaging system to separate and distinguish between the photopeaks of different radionuclides. If the energy resolution is good the photopeaks will be very tall and narrow; if energy resolution is poor the photopeaks will appear as broad bumps in the energy spectrum. The FWHM concept is also utilized to examine energy resolution and is usually quoted for the relatively high energy (662-keV) photon of cesium 137. With lower-energy photons, the energy resolution is worse.

As with any detection system, it is important not to have scintillation events occurring so fast that the electronic system is unable to count each one of them as a separate event. If two equal light pulses occur too close together in time, the system may perceive this as one event with twice the energy actually present. Such an occurrence would be eliminated by the energy window of the PHA, and none of the information from the two events would be imaged; thus, the sensitivity of the system would be diminished. The time after an event during which the system is unable to respond to another event is referred to as "dead time." Dead time can be important in high-count-rate dynamic studies (in the range of 50,000 counts/sec), particularly with single-crystal cameras. An example is a first-pass cardiac study. Although dead time values of 1 to 2 μsec are reported by some manufacturers, with a 20 percent window and scattering material most cameras have dead times of 5 to 10 μsec with ^{99m}Tc.

SPECIALIZED GAMMA CAMERAS

Whole-body images performed with gamma cameras have become popular, particularly for bone or gallium scanning. Whole-body imaging is accomplished by either placing the patient on a moving table or having the gamma camera detector head move over the patient. The method of movement in either case is usually one to three passes extending from the head to the feet, in both anterior and posterior positions. The number of passes depends upon crystal diameter. The image is generated by keeping the detector output synchronized with the motion of the patient or detector head. This can be done either by moving the film or by moving the display across the face of the CRT in an appropriate fashion.

Portable gamma cameras are now available and are used primarily in cardiac stress laboratories and intensive care units. These cameras require much less space than standard cameras, and most are available with associated computer components. It should be noted that these instruments are designed mainly for use with thallium 201 and technetium 99m and may have limited applicability for general imaging.

Emission-Computed Tomography

The basic principle of emission-computed tomography (ECT) is that the radioactivity being emitted by the patient is measured from many different angles. ECT may be either single photon emission computed tomography (SPECT) using isotopes such as ^{99m}Tc, or positron-emission tomography (PET), in which circuits are used to record high-energy (511-keV) annihilation photons, providing extremely accurate localization. PET generally uses short-lived cyclotron-produced isotopes such as carbon 11, nitrogen 13, oxygen 15, and fluorine 18. PET has therefore been limited to those facilities with rapid access to a cyclotron. Although exciting research studies have been performed concerning cerebral and cardiac metabolism, the ultimate impact of positron-emission tomography remains uncertain. SPECT is more limited than PET, particularly since varying depths of the radiopharmaceutical in the body cause a wide range of tissue attenuation. The advantage of single-photon emission tomography over positron techniques is that the former may be performed using current imaging equipment and can be used with most radiopharmaceuticals. SPECT imaging is covered in detail in Chapter 4.

Sodium Iodide Well Counter

Well counters are very common in nuclear medicine laboratories for performing in vitro studies as well as for quality control and assurance procedures. Many sodium iodide well counters are designed for counting radioactive samples in standard test tubes. Generally there is a solid cylindrical sodium iodide crystal with a cylindrical well cut into the crystal, into which the test tube is placed (Fig. 2–8). A photomultiplier tube is optically coupled to the crystal base. Radiation from the sample interacts with the crystal and is detected by the PMT, which feeds into a scalar. The scalar readout directly reflects the amount of radioactivity in the sample, and is usually recorded in counts for the time period over which the sample is measured.

Reflected light and scattering inside the well surface and the thickness of the crystal limit the energy resolution of the standard

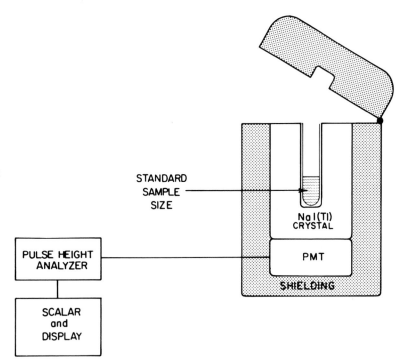

Figure 2–8. Schematic diagram of a standard sodium iodide well counter.

STANDARD SAMPLE SIZE

Na I(TI) CRYSTAL

PMT

SHIELDING

PULSE HEIGHT ANALYZER

SCALAR and DISPLAY

well counter. Since the sample is essentially surrounded by the crystal, the geometrical efficiency for detection of gamma rays is high. Geometrical efficiency is defined as the fraction of emitted radioactivity that is incident upon the detection portion of the counter, in this case, the crystal. Because the crystal is relatively thick, most low-energy photons undergo interaction and very few pass through undetected. Due to these factors, in the energy ranges below 200 keV, the overall crystal detection efficiency is usually better than 95 percent.

Because the top of the well in the crystal is open, it is important to keep the sample volume in the test tube small. If varying sample volumes are placed in the well counter, different amounts of radiation will escape near the top of the crystal, resulting in unequal geometric efficiency. Absorption of gamma rays within the wall of the test tube is a factor when lower-energy sources, such as iodine 125, are counted; therefore, the sample tubes should also be identical.

Because sodium iodide well counters have such a high detection efficiency, there is a

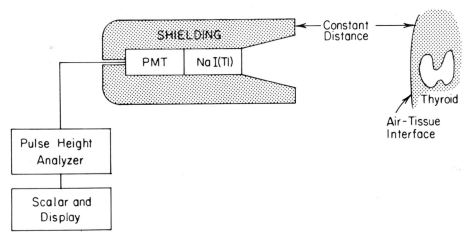

Figure 2–9. Schematic diagram of a single-crystal thyroid probe.

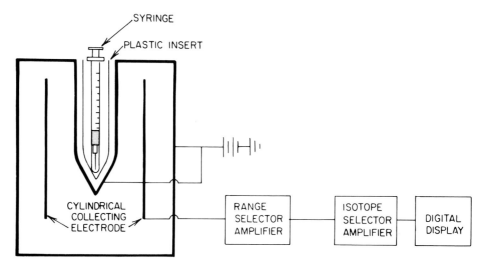

Figure 2–10. Schematic of dose calibrator.

serious problem with electronic dead time. If high levels of activity are employed, much of the radiation is not detected. In general, well counters can typically count only fractions of a microcurie (μCi) or rates of approximately 5000 counts/sec. Attempts to measure amounts of activity greater than this in a well counter can lead to serious errors.

Single Probe Counting System

Single probe counting systems employing only one crystalline detector are quite useful for measuring not only thyroid uptake of radioactive iodine but also cardiac output. The probe used for thyroid counting is actually very similar to the standard well counter in concept (Fig. 2–9), although it does not have the central hole in the sodium iodide crystal. The typical crystal is 5 cm in diameter and 5 cm in thickness, with a cone-shaped (flat field) collimator. As with the well counter, a PMT is at the crystal base. When utilizing such probes for quantitative consistency it is extremely important to maintain a fixed distance from the object being measured to the face of the crystal and to eliminate all extraneous sources of background radiation.

Dose Calibrator

Because it is extremely important to calibrate a dose of isotope prior to injection, the dose calibrator is an essential piece of equipment in any nuclear medicine laboratory. A standard well counter is not useful, since the upper limit of sample activity than can be measured accurately is in the microcurie range. A dose calibrator is essentially a well-type ionization chamber capable of measuring quanitities in the millicurie range. It does not contain a sodium iodide crystal. The chamber is cylindrical and holds a defined volume of inert gas. Within the chamber is a collecting electrode (Fig. 2–10). As radiation emanates from the radiopharmaceutical in the syringe, it enters the chamber and interacts with the gas, causing ionization. An electrical differential applied between the chamber and the collecting electrode causes the ions to be captured and measured.

Most dose calibrators have a digital readout that indicates the amount of activity in microcuries or millicuries once the specific radionuclide being measured has been specified. Since all radionuclides do not generate the same number of photons per radioactive decay, the dose calibrator must be recalibrated for each radionuclide that is to be measured.

The dose calibrator must be linear over the activity range of interest; thus a stable voltage supply is critical. In addition, for patient safety, a dose calibrator must have careful quality control (see Chapter 3).

Suggested Reading

Sorenson JA, Phelps ME: Physics in Nuclear Medicine (ed 2). New York, Grune & Stratton, 1987

CHAPTER 3

Basic Quality Control

A quality control program is especially important in two main areas: instrumentation and radiopharmaceutical preparation. The importance of such a program has been stressed by professional groups, governmental agencies, and hospital accreditation groups.

Instrumentation

Before any equipment is installed, it is important to ensure that there is a suitable environment to house it; otherwise, all attempts at quality control will be fruitless. Most nuclear medicine equipment and computers generate a tremendous amount of heat, and all aspects of ventilation need to be examined. Consoles should never be placed close to a wall. Dust and smoke also cause serious problems, especially for computers. Shutting down newer imaging and computer systems at night prolongs the useful life of many components.

Instrument quality control takes place on several temporal levels. Well counters, dose calibrators, thyroid probes, and gamma cameras should be calibrated upon receipt of a new machine and annually thereafter. For most instruments this can often be done by plotting the energy spectrum of an isotope such as cesium 137. If a narrow window width is used and the number of counts at each 10 keV increment is recorded and plotted, then an energy spectrum is demonstrated. The full-width at half-maximum of the photopeak (see Chapter 2) is then measured and should be less than 10 percent of the peak height. Daily calibration also may be done using a similar source at a specified window and adjusting the voltage so that the maximum count rate is obtained. If this information is recorded daily, subtle changes in the electronics may be identified.

DOSE CALIBRATOR

The dose calibrator is a particularly important instrument for patient protection. It assures the user that the appropriate amount of radiopharmaceutical is about to be administered to the patient. It is the physician's responsibility to determine that the correct dosage is being given to the patient, even if the radiopharmaceutical has been prepared in a central radiopharmacy outside the institution housing the nuclear medicine laboratory. The Nuclear Regulatory Commission requires that all radiopharmaceuticals be assayed for activity prior to administration, and the accuracy must be within 10 percent of the intended dosage.

The dose calibrator should be tested daily. Calibration of the circuits may be done with 100 to 200 μCi (3.7 to 7.4 MBq) of cesium 137 (662 keV) (which is similar in energy to molybdenum 99) and 2 to 5 mCi (74 to 185 MBq) of cobalt 57 (122 keV) (which is similar to technetium 99m). After decay corrections are made the observed activity should agree with the actual calibration source activity by ± 5 percent. Daily background count rates should also be measured and recorded. The dose calibrator must function over a range of 2 μCi (0.07 MBq) to 2 Ci (74 GBq) and must be linear over a wide range of activity. Linearity may be tested by using a high-activity ^{99m}Tc source measured periodically over 24 hours of decay. The dose calibrator readings should closely agree with activity levels calculated from decay tables for ^{99m}Tc. An alternative procedure is to use several lead shields, which attenuate a high-activity ^{99m}Tc source by a known amount. This latter method reduces the time to perform the linearity test from a day to just a few minutes. This will also ensure that the sample size remains the same and that there is no possibility of dilution errors. Such linearity measurements should be made quarterly.

27

The volume of a sample and the type of syringe or vial used can alter the sensitivity of a dose calibrator or scintillation well counter. With low-energy gamma emitters such as thallium 201, xenon 133, and iodine 125, the use of plastic or glass syringes may change readings by as much as 100 percent. When these instruments arrive at the laboratory, measurements are made with the various volumes and syringes used in clinical practice, to derive geometric correction factors. Measurement of the threshold response (lower sensitivity limit) is also important, particularly for molybdenum 99.

GAMMA CAMERAS

Scintillation camera systems are subject to a variety of detector and associated electronic problems that can cause aberrations of the image and that may not be detected by the casual observer. The three parameters usually tested are (1) spatial resolution, or the ability to visualize an alternating, closely spaced pattern of activity; (2) image linearity and distortion, or the ability to reproduce a straight line; and (3) field uniformity, or the ability of the imaging system to produce a uniform image from the entire crystal surface. In general, these determinations can be made with or without the collimator because the collimator is not subject to change.

The sources of activity that are used are either a solid disc (sheet source) with radionuclide dispersed homogeneously throughout, or they are made of Lucite or Plexiglas with a central area filled with radioactive liquid (flood source). The radionuclides used for evaluation of most gamma camera systems are technetium 99m and cobalt 57. ^{99m}Tc has the advantage of being cheap and it tests the electronic circuitry for the photopeak of ^{99m}Tc, which will be used in most of the clinical imaging procedures. Due to its short (6-hour) half-life, ^{99m}Tc has the disadvantage that the flood phantom must be prepared daily. Other disadvantages include nonuniformity if mixing of the ^{99m}Tc liquid is not thorough, and the possibility of contamination if any of the liquid leaks out. Cobalt 57 (122 keV) has a half-life of 270 days and thus does not have to be made daily. It can also be used for sensitivity checks of the instruments. One disadvantage of cobalt 57 is that it is more expensive and does not accurately test the photopeak electronics for ^{99m}Tc. An-

other disadvantage is that the cobalt source initially may have too much activity for electronic handling by the camera system. This may necessitate calibration with the collimator in place to reduce the activity seen by the crystal. Most single-crystal gamma cameras are subject to activity limitations, and a source in excess of 1.2 million counts/min should not be utilized.

To test for spatial resolution, several phantoms have been developed. In general they are either Lucite sheets embedded with lead bars or a sheet of lead with holes in it. The phantom is placed between the camera or collimator face and a radioactive flood or sheet source, and an image is then obtained. Two types of available phantoms (the Hine-Duley and the parallel-line equal-space phantom) have lead bars that extend completely across the detector face. This allows some measurement of detector spatial resolution distortion, uniformity, and linearity. A four-quadrant bar phantom has four sets of bars of different sizes and spacing in each quadrant, which are arranged at 90° angles to each other. Linearity and distortion are difficult to measure with a four-quadrant phantom, and spatial resolution measurements require that the phantom be rotated 90° and reimaged to check all areas of the crystal (Fig. 3–1). All of the above phantoms come in different sizes to best define the resolution capabilities of a particular system.

Field uniformity is generally tested by evaluating the flood-field image. This essentially presents the crystal with a uniform planar source of activity. When obtaining the images for evaluation of uniformity, 1 million counts should be accumulated on a standard-field-of-view camera and 2 million on a large-field-of-view camera. Covering the detector head with a plastic cover is an excellent idea to avoid collimator and crystal contamination if a liquid source is used. A flood-field image may also be obtained by removing the collimator and placing a point source at a sufficient distance (1 to 2 meters) from the detector.

The flood-field image is visually evaluated for uniformity. There is usually an area of increased activity seen around the edge of the image, referred to as *edge-packing*. This artifact results in part from more efficient collection of scintillation events near the edge of the crystal, since there is some reflection from the side of the crystal back toward the

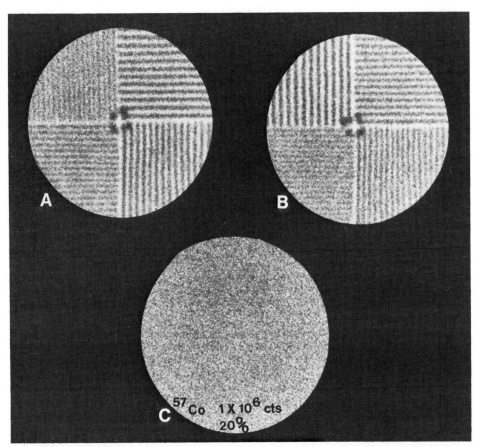

Figure 3–1. Bar phantom and flood-field images. (A, B) Bar phantom with 90° rotation to check all areas of the crystal. (C) Cobalt planar flood source imaged with a 20 percent window.

phototubes. Edge-packing is not normally visible on the cathode ray display. A daily flood image should be placed in a logbook to assess any changes in uniformity and for accreditation inspections. A variety of abnormal images is shown in Figure 3–2.

In an effort to achieve field uniformity, some camera tuning methods involve adjusting the gain of individual photomultiplier tubes or preamplifier circuits. When a particular radionuclide is used to tune a gamma camera, problems such as nonuniformity sometimes arise when imaging is done using other radioisotopes of differing energies.

Most newer cameras have microprocessor and computer circuits to correct for image nonuniformity. An initial flood field image is obtained and stored in the computer memory. Field uniformity is then obtained by adjusting subsequent clinical images based on the initial image in its memory (Fig. 3–3). In general, such correction increases the processing time of data and decreases the maximum usable count rate. A flood field should also be obtained without the use of the computer correction so that the operator can see the status of the detectors themselves and also whether there is degradation over time or need for adjustment. If this is not done, data losses of up to 50 percent may result in prolonged imaging times. Other computer correction systems are available as well.

A number of other steps are required in the daily evaluation of the gamma scintillation camera. These include assurance that the correct energy window for the imaged radionuclide is being selected and that the photopeak is centered symmetrically in the energy window (Fig. 3–4). Centering the energy window too high or too low will result in nonuniform images (Fig. 3–5). Whether the phototubes appear hot or cold when the energy window is off-peak depends upon

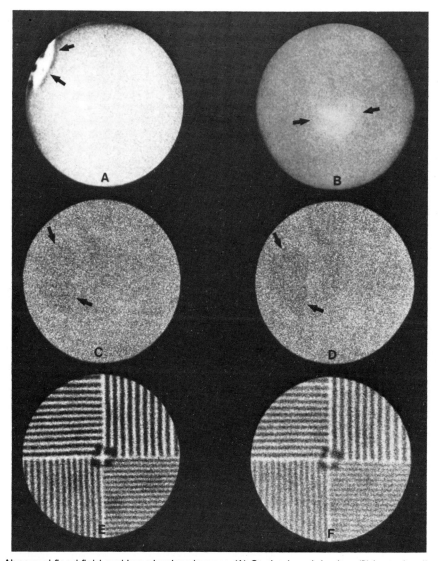

Figure 3–2. Abnormal flood field and bar phantom images. (A) Crushed crystal edge. (B) Loss of optical coupling between crystal and PMTs. (C) Dirt on the cathode ray tube. (D) A 90° electronic orientation change demonstrates that the dirt on the face of the CRT tube does not move. (E) Bar phantom imaged with "hot" photomultiplier tubes are seen better with the collimator in place than with the collimator removed (F). (Images were taken on transparency film.)

the specific manufacturer. Autopeaking should be checked visually on the spectral display. Since scattered radiation may result in improper peaking, peaking should never be done using a patient or a dose syringe in contact with the collimator.

Orientation control, cathode ray tube (CRT) controls, and intensity settings should be kept relatively constant from day to day. If images appear out-of-focus, the CRT should be checked as well as the photographic camera lens. An artifact that doesn't move with electronic orientation changes in the X or Y axis may be dirt or scratches on the CRT face or the camera lens.

A summary of quality control procedures and acceptable parameters is given in Table 3–1.

Radiopharmacy Quality Control

Quality control in radiopharmaceutical preparation is important for patient protection and also so that the radiopharmaceutical

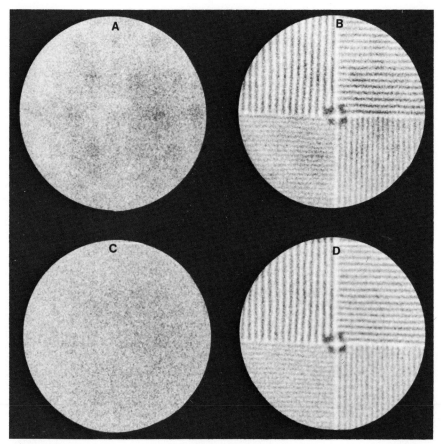

Figure 3–3. Computer correction of flood-field nonuniformity. (A, B) Flood-field and bar-phantom images before computer correction. (C, D) The same images utilizing correction.

will image the intended area. As with any parenteral substance, radiopharmaceuticals must be sterile and free of pyrogens and chemical, radiochemical, or radionuclide impurities.

Regulations and/or recommendations for radiopharmaceutical quality control have been published by at least two groups: the Nuclear Regulatory Commission (NRC) and the United States Pharmacopeia (USP). The USP regulations are important only if a true dedicated pharmacy is being operated, not if a nuclear medicine physician is tagging cold "kits" for injection in the laboratory. The NRC regulations, on the other hand, must be strictly adhered to because they are a provision of licensing.

The quality control of radiopharmaceuticals throughout the preparation process is primarily performed on ^{99m}Tc radiopharmaceuticals. The other radionuclides used are commonly obtained directly from the manufacturer or from a centralized radiopharmacy,

and the only quality control that is usually done in the department is dose calibration and photopeak analysis at the time of imaging.

GENERATOR AND RADIONUCLIDE PURITY

The first step in quality control is to ensure that the radionuclide is pure. This is expressed as the percentage of activity present that is due to the radionuclide of interest. Since ^{99m}Tc normally is obtained by "milking" a molybdenum generator, there must be assurance that only ^{99m}Tc is eluted. Most molybdenum 99–technetium 99m generators are fission-produced, and radionuclide impurities such as molybdenum 99, iodine 131, and ruthenium 103 may be present. The amount of ^{99}Mo contamination or "breakthrough" during elution is normally determined by placing the eluate from the generator in a

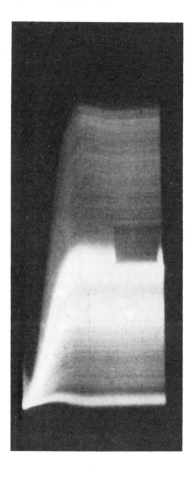 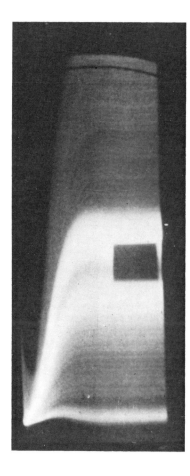

Figure 3–4. Z-mode display of photopeak. The dark square represents the energy window setting. The photopeak is the white band in the middle of the display. The image on the left demonstrates the window centered 50 percent too high, and the image on the right demonstrates the window centered 50 percent too low.

lead shield and measuring the penetration of any ^{99}Mo (740 and 780 keV) photons. The presence of other radionuclides may be determined by multichannel analysis and/or by counting the eluate at different times to allow for decay. This latter method gives an idea of whether the half-life of the contaminant is or is not consistent with that of ^{99}Mo.

The NRC and USP regulations allow no more than 0.15 µCi (0.005 MBq) ^{99}Mo/mCi (37 MBq) ^{99m}Tc at the time of administration. Since ^{99m}Tc decays much faster than ^{99}Mo, the relative amount of any molybdenum contaminant rises with time. Thus, if the ^{99}Mo in an eluent from a generator was barely acceptable at 8:00 A.M., it will likely become unacceptable by later the same day.

The elution column inside the generator is made of alumina (Al$_2$O$_3$). If during elution, sufficient alumina breaks through, the eluate may become cloudy. The presence of aluminum ion (Al^{+3}) should be ascertained at the time of eluting ^{99m}Tc from the generator. Small amounts of aluminum ion may be detected with an indicator paper similar to

the pH paper used in chemistry. If aluminum ion is present, a red color develops. The maximum permissible amount of aluminum ion is 10 µg/ml of ^{99m}Tc eluate with a fission generator. If too much aluminum is present, technetium aluminum particles will be formed which are manifested clinically by hepatic uptake. Excessive aluminum may also cause aggregation of sulfur colloid preparations, resulting in lung uptake. The purpose of ethylenediaminetetra-acetate (EDTA) in sulfur colloid kits is to bind excess Al$^+$ ions and prevent such problems. Agglutination of red blood cells may also occur when inordinate amounts of aluminum ion are contained in ^{99m}Tc pertechnetate solutions.

RADIOCHEMICAL TAGGING

Once radionuclide purity is assured, a prepackaged "kit" containing an unlabeled pharmaceutical may be utilized to produce a radiochemical compound. The biodistribution of that radiochemical in a patient can then easily be visualized with a gamma cam-

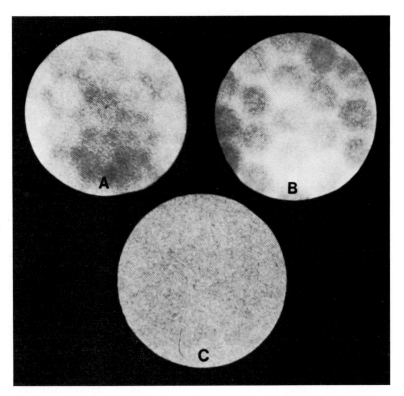

Figure 3–5. Effect of improper setting of the energy window. (A) A flood-field image obtained with the energy window set 50 percent above the photopeak causes the phototubes to appear as cold defects. (B) A flood-field image with the energy window set 50 percent below the photopeak causes the PMTs to appear hot. (C) Image with correct setting. (Images were taken on transparency film.)

era system. Assessment of chemical purity of ^{99m}Tc radiopharmaceuticals is done by determining the degree of successful tagging of the agent contained in the kit and the amount of residual (unbound ^{99m}Tc) in the prepara-

tion. The degree of purity may reflect the proficiency of those who prepare the kits or simply any lot-to-lot or manufacturer-to-manufacturer variability in the kits.

Instant thin-layer chromatography is usu-

Table 3–1. QUALITY CONTROL PARAMETERS

PERFORMANCE PARAMETERS	QUALITY CONTROL PROTOCOL	FREQUENCY
Spatial resolution	Resolution phantom (quadrant bar phantom, rotate 90° between acquisitions)	Weekly
Uniformity	Intrinsic or extrinsic flood evaluated qualitatively	Daily (before first patient)
Linearity	Subjective evaluation from bar phantom resolution test and intrinsic to the uniformity measurement	Weekly
Energy resolution	Full width at half maximum of ^{99m}Tc photopeak expressed as percent	Annually
Count rate response	Twenty percent data loss, resolving time, maximum count rate for 20% window	Annually
Sensitivity	Count rate per microcurie through all collimators with 20% window, calculate absolute sensitivity for available collimators	Annually
Collimator integrity	Ten million count floods through each collimator for evaluation of collimator defects	Annually or when suspicious of damage
Formatter performance	Flood images at all locations and for all image sizes	Annually
Whole-body accessory	Scan bar phantom along diagonal and compare with stationary image, calibrate speed	Annually

ally performed to assess radiochemical purity, using silica gel impregnated in glass fiber sheets or strips. Through the use of various solvents, impurities can be identified by their different migrations in the particular solvent used.

A drop of the radiochemical compound to be analyzed is placed on the strip and the solvent is applied. As the solvent approaches the end of the sheet an assessment is made of the radioactivity present at the point of origin and at the advancing solvent front. Although this may be performed by various scanning methods, the simplest way is to cut the fiber strip into segments and count them individually in a well counter. If this is done, one has to be extremely careful to put only a very small amount of activity at the spot of origin, since well counters are very efficient and it is easy to exceed their count rate capability.

The most common ^{99m}Tc radiopharmaceuticals are prepared by adding ^{99m}Tc freshly eluted from a generator to a "cold" kit as prescribed by the kit manufacturer. The eluate of the generator should be ^{99m}TcO$_4^-$($+7$), i.e., pertechnetate. Since pertechnetate in this valence state is relatively stable, it cannot tag a cold kit preparation and must be reduced to a lower valence state ($+3$, $+4$, $+5$). This is done utilizing a reducing agent such as stannous chloride, which is generally present in the reaction vial.

Most radiochemical impurities obtained in kit preparation are the result of interaction of either oxygen or water with the contents of the kit or vial. If air reaches the vial contents, stannous chloride may be oxidized to stannic chloride even before introduction of ^{99m}Tc into the vial. If this happens, production of reactive technetium is no longer possible and free pertechnetate becomes an impurity. If moisture reaches the vial contents, stannous chloride becomes hydrolyzed, and the formation of stannous hydroxide, a colloid, results.

Reactive reduced technetium may also become hydrolyzed, forming technetium dioxide. This hydrolyzed reduced form of technetium is insoluble and is another impurity that must be tested for. Technetium that has been tagged to a compound can reoxidize and revert back to ^{99m}TcO$_4^-$($+7$).

To minimize oxidation problems, most cold kits are purged with nitrogen, and additional antioxidants such as ascorbic acid may also have been added. It is still extremely important not to inject air into the reaction vial when preparing a radiopharmaceutical. An often overlooked source of problems is the sterile saline used in preparation of the kits. Such saline should be free of preservatives because bacteriostatic agents often interfere with the tagging process.

To check for the presence of free pertechnetate, the radiopharmaceutical is placed on the chromatographic strip and acetone is used as the solvent. Most tagged radiopharmaceuticals remain at the origin while the free pertechnetate advances with the solvent front (Fig. 3–6). To assess the presence of hydrolyzed technetium or technetium dioxide, saline is used as the solvent. In this case technetium dioxide remains at the origin, while those radiopharmaceuticals that are soluble in saline, such as DTPA and ^{99m}TcO$_4^-$($+7$), advance with the solvent front. For some compounds that are insoluble in saline, such as macroaggregated albumin, it is not possible to assess the presence of technetium dioxide using instant thin-layer chromatography.

The USP's lower limit of acceptability for radiochemical purity is 95 percent for pertechnetate, 92 percent for ^{99m}Tc sulfur colloid, and 90 percent for all other ^{99m}Tc radiopharmaceuticals. Once the chromatographic procedures are established, they take very little time to perform and ideally should be done before patient injection.

One reason for performing thin-layer chromatography prior to patient injection is that simple errors can cause the tag to be completely ineffective. For example, in production of sulfur colloid, one kit normally calls first for injection of syringe A and then syringe B into the reaction vial. If these two are reversed, no sulfur colloid is produced and there is a large amount of free ^{99m}Tc pertechnetate. Thus, a liver scan will not be possible with the agent.

The ^{99m}Tc radiopharmaceuticals that are produced with stannous chloride reduction or stannous chelates include MAA, human serum albumin, DTPA, phosphate compounds, and glucoheptonate. The only one in common use produced without reduction or chelation by tin is sulfur colloid. The compounds in which the presence of hydrolyzed technetium (Tc dioxide) may need to be checked are DTPA, phosphate com-

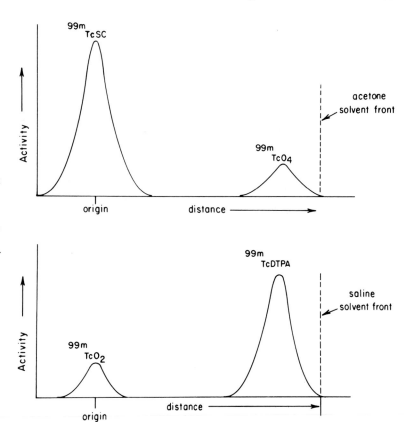

Figure 3–6. (A) Acetone chromatography is used to check for the presence of free pertechnetate, which migrates with the acetone solvent front. (B) To check for technetium dioxide, saline is used and those radiopharmaceuticals that are soluble in saline advance with the solvent.

pounds, glucoheptonate, and IDA derivatives.

Excessive stannous agents can cause quality control problems during radiopharmaceutical preparation that become evident in the actual clinical images. Excess stannous ions (tin) may cause liver uptake on bone scans by formation of a tin colloid (Fig. 3–7). Residual stannous ions in the blood may also cause red cell labeling. Stannous ions may remain

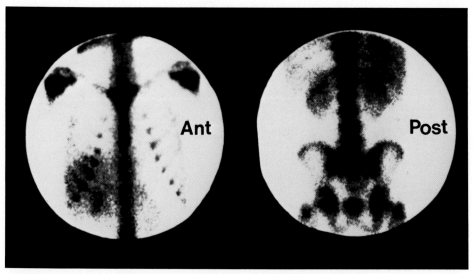

Figure 3–7. Bone scan images demonstrating hepatic activity. In this case, the hepatic activity was probably due to poor quality control and excess tin, causing formation of colloidal-sized particles.

in the blood after a bone scan so that a ^{99m}Tc pertechnetate brain scan attempted within 1 week, may result in red cell labeling.

Particle size of certain compounds may be checked by a hemocytometer as part of the quality control procedure. The USP maximum diameter recommendation for macroaggregated albumin is 150 μ, with 90 percent of particles between 10 μ and 90 μ. Most physicians prefer particles less than 100 μ in size for pulmonary perfusion imaging. Slightly large particle size in preparations of ^{99m}Tc sulfur colloid results in relatively more uptake in the spleen and may give a false impression of hepatocellular dysfunction.

STERILITY

Most compounds provided in kits are sterile and pyrogen-free. USP regulations call for microbiologic testing including growth on a culture media for 14 days. This is clearly a problem for ^{99m}Tc compounds with a 6-hour half-life and is generally not performed. Pyrogen testing as per USP recommendations includes intravenous injection of three rabbits, noting any rise in body temperature over the next 3 hours. This is also clearly impractical for most nuclear medicine laboratories, and thus pyrogen testing is usually limited to the evaluation of gram-negative endotoxins in compounds that are being injected in the central nervous system or cerebral spinal fluid. Gram-negative endotoxins may be conveniently and quickly evaluated by the limulus amebocyte lysate test. This material is derived from the horseshoe crab and in the presence of an extremely small amount of a gram-negative endotoxin, an opaque gel is formed.

Suggested Readings

Murphy PH: Acceptance testing and quality control of gamma cameras, including SPECT. J Nucl Med 28:1221–1227, 1987

Saha GP: Fundamentals of Nuclear Pharmacy (ed 2). New York, Springer-Verlag, 1984

CHAPTER 4

Single Photon Emission Computed Tomography

The successful application of computer algorithms to x-ray imaging in computed tomography (CT) has led to their application to radionuclide techniques and to the advent of single photon emission computed tomography (SPECT). Whereas planar radionuclide organ imaging in multiple views is sufficient for most clinical settings, tomography offers several readily apparent advantages over two-dimensional planar images. The most obvious advantage of tomography is improved image contrast because it focuses on a thin slice of an organ; this minimizes overlaying and underlying activity that may obscure a lesion or area of interest. In addition, SPECT permits absolute three-dimensional localization of radiopharmaceutical distribution with the possibility of quantification and three-dimensional cinematic representation of the organ imaged.

SPECT can be accomplished by either one of two main techniques: (1) transverse or rotational tomography, or (2) longitudinal or limited angle tomography. Although both approaches have been clinically applied with success, only rotational SPECT has enjoyed widespread application.

Principles of Rotational SPECT

INSTRUMENTATION

In its simplest form, rotational SPECT is accomplished by using a conventional Anger (gamma) camera detector head and parallel hole collimator fitted to a rotating gantry such that the detector is capable of orbiting around a stationary patient on a special imaging table with the camera face continually directed toward the patient. The camera head rotates around a central axis called the *axis of rotation* (AOR). The distance of the camera face from this central axis is referred to as the *radius of rotation* (ROR). The orbit is commonly circular with a 360° capacity, although elliptical or body contour motion and arcs of less than 360° may be employed (Fig. 4–1). The detector electronics are coupled with a computer capable of performing acquisition and processing of the image data according to preselected parameters. Unlike x-ray transmission CT, the gamma camera is capable of acquiring data from a large volume of the patient during a single orbit, and multiple slices (sections) are produced from just one data acquisition sequence. More complex systems may employ multiple detectors and more sophisticated computers, but these are not yet in common clinical usage.

As the principal component of the SPECT imaging system, the gamma camera must be state-of-the-art with an intrinsic resolution of at least 3 to 4 mm, an absolute linearity deviation of less than 1 mm, and a basic uniformity deviation of 3 to 5 percent or less across the useful field of view of the detector. A system with excellent energy resolution is needed to permit adequate rejection of scattered radiation, a major degrader of contrast in SPECT images. This is enhanced by an autotune feature, which continually tunes and balances the photomultiplier tubes (PMTs) of the detector during the operation. Whereas count rate capacity of the camera is not critical in SPECT, the system should be able to handle significantly high count rates to avoid any field uniformity distortion because of high count rate effects.

Because the rotation of the detector on the gantry subjects the camera head to thermal, magnetic, and gravitational forces not experienced by planar instruments, the system construction must take these factors into con-

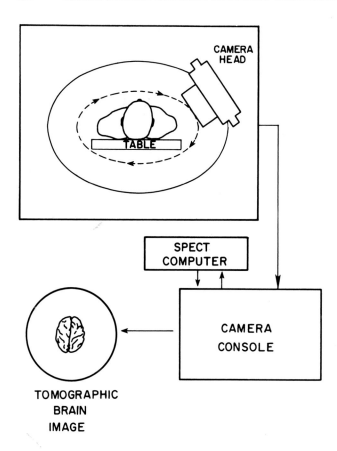

Figure 4–1. Schematic representation of a SPECT system utilizing a single camera head. The camera detector usually rotates about the patient in a noncircular orbit while acquiring data to be fed to the computer. The tomographic computer-reconstructed images are subsequently displayed.

sideration. This includes shielding of the PMTs with a mu metal to protect against changing magnetic fields during rotation.

DATA ACQUISITION

The data required to produce diagnostic SPECT images are usually acquired as a series of multiple planar images collected at discrete angular intervals or in continuous acquisition as the detector head moves around the patient. In the "step and shoot" technique, the camera's orbit is interrupted at regular angular intervals, referred to as azimuth "stops," so that an image may be recorded for a specified period of time at each of the stops. For example, a 360° acquisition orbit using 60 stops yields 60 planar images obtained at 6° intervals. If each image is acquired for 20 seconds then the entire scanning time will require 20 minutes plus the small amount of time needed to move the detector head from each stop to the next. For practical reasons a compromise must be reached regarding the number of stops and the scanning time at each stop needed to produce tomographic images of good statistical quality. These factors are largely dictated by the type of study, amount of radiopharmaceutical employed, patient motion considerations, and specific resolution requirements.

A 360° arc is usually required for most SPECT acquisitions. However, an arc of 180° may be preferred for certain studies such as cardiac perfusion imaging. With any given arc, the more individual projections or views obtained, the better the quality of the reconstructed images. Since the time allotted for obtaining each projection multiplied by the number of projections (usually about 15 to 20 seconds per stop in most studies) essentially determines the length of the study, an increase in the number of projections typically results in a decrease in the time at each stop. However, because each planar view obtained must be statistically significant (sufficient counts per pixel) for adequate reconstructed images, fewer views obtained for more time are generally employed in count-poor studies such as perfusion brain imaging, whereas a greater number of images for less time may be used for count-rich examinations (e.g., sulfur colloid liver scans). In typical clinical applications, approximately 32 stops per 180° rotation (64 stops per 360°) are obtained in order to produce acceptable images.

In general, the smaller the orbital radius of rotation (distance of the camera from the patient or ROR), the greater the potential resolution of the tomographic images. Thus, RORs should be kept as small as feasible. Standard circular orbits are frequently not ideally suited for imaging noncircular body parts such as the chest or abdomen because the camera distance varies significantly according to its orbital position. Furthermore, unless the detector head is very small, imaging body parts such as the head may be compromised by the need for a larger than desired ROR dictated by the shoulders and upper torso. Noncircular orbits and body contour orbits have the potential for solving these problems.

Specific parameters for acquisition of clinical SPECT images will be presented in more detail in chapters concerning specific organ systems and procedures, as well as in Appendix E. However, a few generalizations may prove helpful. Optimally, a clinical imaging department seeks the highest quality images with the best resolution achievable in the shortest time. Practically, the usual trade-offs between resolution and sensitivity must be made, which require the selection of a specific set of acquisition parameters for each study.

Acquisition Time. An acquisition time that allows adequate image statistics is mandatory for the production of diagnostic images. This is in large part determined by count rate, matrix size, and number of projections per orbit. Obviously, the longer the acquisition, the more counts collected and the better the image resolution. However, typical patient tolerances for acquisition times make 30 to 45 minutes a realistic maximum. Thus times per projection (stop) must be predicated on an appraisal of the patient's ability to remain still. Any significant motion of the patient during acquisition may render the results unusable.

Image Matrix Size. Under most circumstances, image resolution is directly proportional to matrix size. The two matrix sizes commonly used in SPECT images are 64 × 64 and 128 × 128. With increased matrix size, however, come the trade-offs of substantial increases in acquisition time, processing time, and contiguous disk storage space. Selection of 128 × 128 matrix over 64 × 64 requires a fourfold increase in most acquisition aspects of the study, including time, which may not be worth the added spatial resolution. Furthermore, the count density in tomographic slices acquired in 128 × 128 is reduced by a factor of 8, which adversely affects perceived image contrast. In most clinical studies the 64 × 64 matrix is the best compromise.

Number of Views. Generally, the more views obtained, the better image resolution possible. However, a compromise with total imaging time must be reached so that commonly 64 views over a 360 degree orbit will produce adequate tomograms.

TOMOGRAPHIC IMAGE PRODUCTION

The data available in the multiple digitized images are combined and manipulated by the computer using mathematical algorithms to reconstruct a three-dimensional image of the organ scanned. The most common method to accomplish this is known as *back projection*, which produces a transaxial view of the organ by applying the technique to the data in each of the planar views acquired.

Unfortunately, simple back projection produces a composite image with significant artifacts (principally the "starburst" artifact) that seriously degrade the quality of the image, rendering it clinically unusable. For this reason, a refined technique called *filtered back projection* was developed. This technique essentially eliminates these artifacts from the reconstructed images by applying a digital filter to the data during the back projection. Depending on the filter selected and if enough projections are obtained, the final images produced will be a close three-dimensional representation of the object scanned. Although other reconstruction techniques exist, the filtered back projection algorithm remains the most commonly used method in commercially available SPECT systems primarily because of its speed and simplicity. Once reconstructed, the tomographic views are still in need of further filtering to produce acceptable images for interpretation.

IMAGE FILTERING

Image filtering of raw data has become a standard nuclear technique for producing processed images that are both visually pleasing and yet preserve the integrity of the acquired data. Essentially, filtering algorithms provided for planar studies such as thallium 201 cardiac perfusion images improve image quality by noise reduction.

Filters are mathematical operations designed to enhance, smooth, or suppress all or part of digital image data, ideally without altering their validity. The concept of applying mathematical filters to digitized nuclear images in order to reduce noise and thus improve image quality has become commonplace in planar procedures. In SPECT, however, image filtering not only enhances the data presentation but is also a basic requirement for the production of the reconstructed sections.

Filters used in SPECT are usually expressed in terms of their effect on spatial frequencies; hence the term *frequency filtering*. All spatial domain images may be broken down and described by the spatial frequencies of their components using Fourier transforms to produce frequency images, which may then be manipulated by frequency filters. Thus, filters can be described by the frequencies that they allow to pass through into the final image. Noise in such images is generally predominant at high spatial frequencies. High-pass filters (passing more relatively high frequencies) generally produce sharper, but noisier images with enhanced edge definition, whereas low-pass filters (passing fewer high frequencies) render smoother, less noisy images with less distinct edges. When applied, filtering may be performed in one, two or three dimensions. Three-dimensional filtering allows filtering between transaxial slices and is commonly applied in SPECT image processing.

In SPECT image production, filtering can be done before, during, or after transaxial reconstruction. To avoid artifacts, accurate back projection reconstruction requires correction of all spatial frequencies through the use of a ramp filter, so named because of its characteristic shape (Fig. 4–2A). As previously stated, this is referred to as *filtered back projection*. This generally produces valid images, which nevertheless may be in need of further improvement of resolution or contrast. For this reason, additional filters are usually employed that allow such manipulations as noise reduction, smoothing, or resolution recovery. These filters may be applied

before filtered back projection is performed, and it is then called *prefiltering* (or preprocessing). In post-processing (or post-filtering), additional filtering is used after filtered back projection. Alternatively, the initial filter may be modified to permit additional filtering during the back projection process.

A number of filters are usually available in the computer tomographic software, and selection depends on a number of factors, including the study being performed, the statistical character of the acquired images, and operator bias. Additional filters commonly used for filtering SPECT images include Butterworth, Parzen, Hamming, and Hann filters (Fig. 4–2B–E).

IMAGE DISPLAY

After being processed, the acquired data may be displayed visually as a three-dimensional representation of the part of the body imaged. This is usually presented cinematically as an image of the body turning continually in space, the so-called "rotating man" image. This view is useful in three-dimensional localization and also in determining whether any significant patient motion occurred during the acquisition. In addition to the transaxial tomographic slices provided, the data can also be easily manipulated to render tomographic sections of the body in standard coronal and sagittal planes as well as in any oblique planes required by the organ being imaged. Oblique reconstructions are frequently used in cardiac perfusion imaging. The final set of images is usually interpreted from both transparency film and computer monitor display; this allows any additional needed image manipulation.

Although current methodology allows the production of high-quality diagnostic images for qualitative interpretation, the inherent problems of photon attenuation with depth and the imperfect attenuation methods currently available render absolute quantitation of radionuclide distribution difficult. Semi-quantitative methods of comparing image data with normal distribution as defined by large series of normal patients has met with some success, as has relative quantitation of activity within the same patient over time, such as is performed in thallium washout determinations.

SPECT QUALITY CONTROL

To ensure high performance standards, routine detector quality control procedures

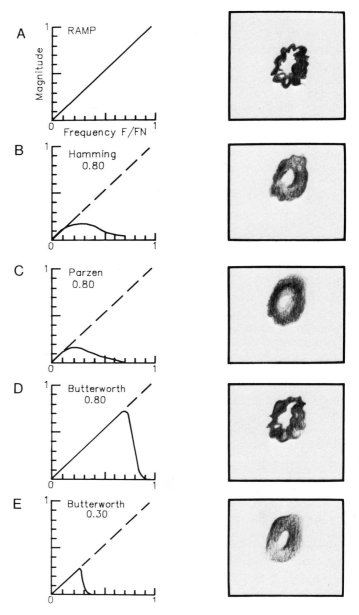

Figure 4–2. (A) A pure ramp filter displayed in frequency space is so called because the value of the filter increases as the spatial frequency increases. The filter is usually applied to the back projection process to attenuate the low frequencies and thus to sharpen edges blurred during the process. (B to E) Additional filters are frequently needed if the images obtained are degraded by the presence of high-frequency noise. In these cases, a window may be applied to the ramp filter, which is set to "cutoff" at a certain frequency (shown here from 0.3 to 0.8). The final reconstruction filters are a product of the ramp filter and the window function. In general, a cutoff value that is too low produces oversmoothed data, which may obscure lesions. A cutoff value that is too high can produce noisy images that have a patchy appearance. The selection of a filter for image processing should consider both the frequency context of the noise in the image as well as the inherent frequency context of the organ being imaged. (Fischer KC: Qualitative SPECT thallium imaging: Technical and clinical applications. In Guiberteau M: Nuclear Cardiovascular Imaging: Current Clinical Practice. New York, Churchill Livingstone, 1990.)

should be performed weekly as with any gamma camera, including tests of intrinsic uniformity, extrinsic uniformity (collimator in place), resolution, and linearity. Regular meticulous quality control of SPECT imaging systems is absolutely essential for the production of clinically useful, artifact-free images. While even significant deviations from optimum performance can be tolerated in routine planar imaging, more minor departures from performance standards in SPECT imaging may produce unacceptable or even misleading images.

FIELD UNIFORMITY ASSESSMENT AND CORRECTION

Because rotational SPECT images are produced from planar views and because that process amplifies any suboptimal characteristics introduced by the instrumentation, quality control of SPECT imaging begins with assurances that the imaging system is operating at the highest intrinsic performance standards. This is especially true of system uniformity, which is governed by multiple factors in the imaging chain: principally detector uniformity of response (intrinsic uniformity), collimator integrity (extrinsic uniformity), and the quality of the analog to digital signal conversion at the camera-computer interface. Significant camera field non-uniformities can result in image artifacts, the most common of which is the *ring artifact.*

In ordinary planar imaging, system uniformity variation of 3 to 5 percent may be acceptable. However, nonuniformities that are not apparent in planar images can give rise to significant errors in the reconstructed tomographic views, which may appear as full or partial ring artifacts. Because the back projection process used in SPECT amplifies nonuniformities inherent in the imaging system, a uniformity deviation in SPECT imaging must be 1 percent or less to produce artifact-free images. Since this is significantly less than that currently achievable because of inherent system inhomogeneity, system nonuniformity must be corrected.

In order to correct system nonuniformity, a superior uniformity correction is needed. This is attained by the weekly acquisition and computer storage of a high-count reference flood-field image performed with the collimator in place to be used for uniformity correction of each planar view acquired before reconstruction. Typically 30,000,000 counts for a 64 × 64 matrix and 120,000,000 counts for a 128 × 128 matrix are required. The flood field must be performed under conditions and acquisition parameters (collimators, matrix size, radioisotope, etc.) specific for the examination to which it will be applied. Thus, separate floods must be acquired for each set of parameters. Cobalt 67 plastic sheet sources with their high intrinsic uniformity and ease of use are best used for this activity. Although high flood-field uniformity correction will rectify inhomogeneity caused by most sources in the imaging chain, it should not be viewed as a substitute for faulty detector electronics or collimators.

CENTER OF ROTATION DETERMINATION AND CORRECTION

The center of rotation (COR) of the imaging system is superficially determined by the mechanical construction of the camera and gantry as well as by the electronics of the system. Thus the apparent center of rotation may be affected either by mechanical aberrations in the detector or gantry alignment,

electronic instabilities in the detector system, or nonlinearities between the camera/computer coupling (ADC). In fact, the apparent COR as perceived by the computer may differ from the actual mechanical COR because of conditions affecting the system electronics. Thus, it is necessary to properly align the electronic center (center of computer matrix) with the mechanical center of rotation (camera COR) in order to prevent COR misalignment artifacts. Any significant misalignment (> 0.5 pixel for a 64 × 64 matrix) results in increasing losses of contrast and resolution in the reconstructed images and often gross image distortion (Fig. 4–3).

Evaluation of the system's COR is a relatively simple procedure typically consisting of imaging a point or line source placed near the center of rotation from several selected angles and then again at the opposing angles (180° apart). Most commercial SPECT systems have software programs capable of calculating the apparent COR and any offset from the computer matrix center and storing it for later COR correction as needed in clinical acquisitions. If a misalignment is found, a correction can be made by the computer software to realign the rotation and matrix centers by shifting the camera's rotational axis to the center of the computer matrix.

COR calibration must be performed for each collimator, zoom factor, and usually matrix size used for clinical imaging. Furthermore, COR calibration factors based on technetium 99m may be valid only for other radionuclides if energy registration circuits have been properly calibrated. With a newly installed camera, COR calibration should probably be performed frequently (perhaps daily) until system stability is established, and then at least weekly. Frequent fluctuations in COR values suggest a problem requiring professional servicing of the instrument.

X AND Y GAIN (PIXEL SIZE) CALIBRATION

The gains in the X and Y directions must be matched so that each pixel has the same size in both dimensions. Dimensional discrepancies may produce inaccurate reconstructions in standard and oblique planes, erroneous attenuation correction, and even shifts in the perceived center of rotation.

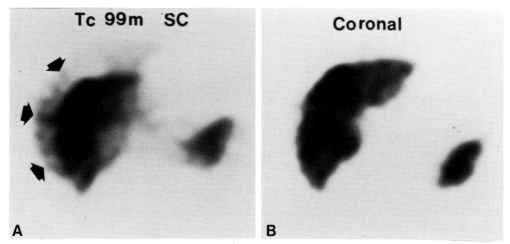

Figure 4–3. (A) Center of rotation artifact demonstrated on a coronal sulfur colloid liver/spleen. An image obtained with a 1 pixel COR misalignment, resulting in blurring and halo artifact. With correction (B), the image is markedly improved.

Usually calibration software is provided by the system vendor. However, X, Y pixel dimensions may be calculated by imaging two-point or line sources separated by a known distance. X and Y gain calibration should be performed monthly.

DETECTOR HEAD ALIGNMENT WITH THE AXIS OF ROTATION

In order to produce accurate back projected images without loss of resolution or contrast, the planar images must be acquired in planes perpendicular to the camera's axis of rotation. This requires the camera face to be level and untilted from the AOR. A 1 percent tilt at a distance of 14 cm will produce a shift of approximately 1 pixel in a 64×64 matrix. Head tilt may be assessed using the camera and computer to collect a set of 36-point source images over 360° and adding together selected frames. If no tilt is present, the images will describe a straight line parallel with the X axis.

Alternatively, a simple check independent of system electronics may be performed by using a carpenter's (bubble) level to evaluate camera face position at the 12 o'clock and 6 o'clock positions on the gantry. The latter test presumes that the crystal face, detector housing, and AOR are all parallel with the earth's surface in the above positions. Camera head tilt should be assessed quarterly with corrections made as necessary.

COLLIMATOR EVALUATION

For optimum image production the collimator should be as close to the manufacturer's specifications as possible and free of obvious defects. Damaged collimator septa may introduce significant field nonuniformity, which can degrade image quality. Various methods have been described to evaluate collimator integrity and may be employed when a serious problem is suspected. Routinely, collimator inspection should be performed through the actual visual examination of the collimator itself and through inspection of high-count extrinsic flood images. Defective collimators should be replaced.

SYSTEM PERFORMANCE

Overall system performance under different acquisition parameters can be assessed by using a variety of commercially available phantoms, including the Jaszczak or Carlson phantoms. These are best employed according to the manufacturer's protocols. Parameters evaluated may include object contrast and image noise, field uniformity, and accuracy of attenuation correction.

Suggested Reading

Freeman LM, Blaufox MD (eds): Single photon emission computed tomography (SPECT). Semin Nucl Med 17(3):183–266, 1987.

CHAPTER 5

COMPUTERS

Within the last several years, computer manipulation of data has led to significant advances in the quantitative analysis of images as well as in providing computer-reconstructed images. It is important for the nuclear medicine practitioner to understand computer terms and basic computer systems, and to be able to define departmental needs. The choice of a system requires careful consideration on the part of the purchaser. Presently, it is extremely difficult to perform state-of-the-art nuclear cardiac imaging and certain other clinical studies without a relatively sophisticated computer system. Additional uses include instrument quality control, image manipulation, and even teaching. The purpose of this section is to provide a basic understanding of minicomputers used in nuclear medicine and to discuss briefly their advantages and limitations.

Most electronic computer systems have circuits that are either on or off, or switching devices that are either open or closed. The arithmetic system used to characterize this circumstance in computers is the *binary system*. This system uses only two symbols, 0 and 1. Conversion from the binary to the decimal system is reasonably simple. As in the decimal system, the digit on the left is of greater magnitude than the digit on the right. In the decimal system, the *base* of the system is 10. In the binary system the base is 2. Thus, for example, the number 123 in the decimal system is:

$$(1 \times 10^2) + (2 \times 10^1) + (3 \times 10^0)$$
$$= 100 + 20 + 3$$
$$= 123$$

The number 10011 in the binary system can be translated into the decimal system as follows:

$$(1 \times 2^4) + (0 \times 2^3) + (0 \times 2^2) + (1 \times 2^1)$$
$$+ (1 \times 2^0)$$
$$= 16 + 0 + 0 + 2 + 1$$
$$= 19$$

Many computers use the *octal system* (base 8) or the *hexadecimal system* (base 16), and the conversion is similar to that already described. For example, the number 11 in the hexadecimal system can be translated as follows into base 10:

$$(1 \times 16^1) + (1 \times 16^0)$$
$$= 16 + 1$$
$$= 17$$

The basic information unit of computers is the *bit* (binary digit) represented either by 0 or 1. A larger unit of information (8 bits) is known as the *byte*. A *word* is a fixed number of bytes (usually 2). Although some small computers (such as personal computers) use 8-bit words, most minicomputers use 32- or 64-bit (2-byte) words.

There are two types of computers, analog and digital. The *analog computer,* which is obsolete, uses continuously varying voltage or current. The *digital computer* allows only for discrete voltage levels, but is much faster than the analog type. Almost all computers used in nuclear medicine are digital computers. The operations are sometimes permanently wired in the machine. Such computers are often referred to as "hard-wired" or "turn-key" systems and are useful only for the particular purpose for which they were designed. They cannot be reprogrammed for other uses. A *general-purpose computer,* on the other hand, has the capability of being easily reprogrammed, which provides great flexibility.

A computer "solves" a problem by referring to a set of instructions in its memory on how to deal with particular information and problems presented. The set of instructions is the *program,* usually provided as a sequence of individual instructions that allow the computer to manipulate information for a desired purpose. The program in a *hard-wired computer* or *microprocessor* is contained in a *read-only-memory* (ROM) so that it cannot be overwritten. General computers have the program stored in a *random-access memory* (RAM), so that the program can be changed as well as read if desired.

Hardware

Hardware refers only to mechanical components and electronic circuits. The basic hardware components of any computer are seen in Figure 5–1. The *central processing unit* (CPU) contains the *supervisor,* which coordinates operations of the computer, interprets the instructions in the program, and directs the rest of the computer to perform these instructions. The CPU also has a main (core) memory, which is divided into *registers* and *buffers.* A register stores information used by the computer. A buffer is a temporary workspace created in the memory to manipulate data. Each division of the memory has an address, which allows the computer to find a particular piece of information. The *main memory,* which utilizes semiconductor chips, is volatile: if the power is suddenly shut off data may be lost unless the system has battery backup power or another safety system.

The *input-output section* consists of hardware that interfaces the CPU with the nuclear gamma camera or other peripheral devices. During acquisition, the program passes data from the camera through the *input section* to the memory. When considering the purchase of a computer system, it is important to find out if the system can acquire or process data from more than one camera simultaneously,

and if so, whether it can be done in a dynamic mode, because some systems are limited in their ability to simultaneously acquire and analyze data.

The *arithmetic and logic unit* (ALU) performs computations and logic operations, functioning like a calculator. An *array processor* is a preprogrammed arithmetic unit usually used for data-filtering routines. The *output section* records the results of the computer manipulation and allows them to be presented to the operator.

In the basic sequence or pattern of an operation, the computer moves instructions from an address in the memory to a CPU register and decodes it. The CPU then carries out the requested operation upon the data. All arithmetic operations and instruction decodings take place in the CPU registers, which are extremely high-speed temporary memories. CPU output is typically placed back in the main memory for future use.

Output devices are generally used for visual display or storage. They include line printers, cathode ray tubes (CRTs), video monitors, disk drives, and magnetic tape drives. For purposes of speed and economy, almost all output display devices at the present time are CRT terminals or video monitors rather than printers. Paper tape readers and card readers find little use in nuclear medicine imaging, because the vast amounts of data involved require rapid acquisition and manipulation as well as efficient storage.

For display, the CPU transfers a matrix of data from main memory to the image or

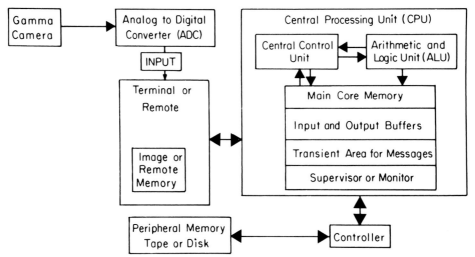

Figure 5–1. Schematic diagram of computer hardware components and information flow.

display memory. This image memory is then scanned 30 times/sec and shown on the display screen. Displays should present image data in at least 256 levels of gray. A color video display allows for color image presentation, whereas CRTs are usually smaller and monochromatic.

Camera-Computer Interface and Terminal

The scintillation pulse seen by the gamma camera is initially a piece of analog information consisting of x and y coordinates and a z-pulse, which is proportional to energy. This information needs to be converted to digital form before being presented to the computer. The gamma camera computer interface has *analog-to-digital converters* (ADCs) to perform this conversion. The interface may also contain several other components, including buffer or image memory, zoom capabilities, and the ability to accept several z-pulses. The buffer or image memory may be used to temporarily store data when the gamma camera sends data faster than it can be stored on disk or put into the main memory. The *zoom capability* allows the image matrix to be inscribed on only a defined portion of the scintillation crystal, which allows for improved spatial resolution. The ability of the interface system to accept several z-pulses allows dual isotope collection and the performance of gated cardiac studies.

The *image memory* is a semiconductor memory, which may be housed in the terminal. This very important piece of temporary storage holds incoming information and allows slow portions of the computer to manipulate the data. A fast portion of the computer might finish its operation on a certain part of the data and then put the data into storage memory while a slow component performs other operations. Important uses of the image memory are (1) to store the scintillation event while the entire image is being accumulated and before the computer begins to perform manipulation on the image, and (2) to store an image recalled from peripheral memory (tape or disk storage).

Points to consider before purchasing interface and computer hardware include the number of terminals supplied and whether the system can support future expansion without a different or larger central processing unit. Since some manufacturers use equipment made by other vendors, it is important to determine who will assume the responsibility for servicing each part of the system.

Software

The most important portion of any gamma camera computer system is the *software*. Programs are referred to as software because they can be changed simply by writing a new program. Software may be divided into three elements: (1) acquisition and analysis (nuclear medicine specific), (2) operating system, and (3) clinical application packages. The hardware supplied by most manufacturers is similar, but the software systems are very different. Some software systems are very restrictive and allow the operator little freedom, while others provide great versatility, and therefore demand more operator input and knowledge. The acquisition and analysis system allows for gated, static, and dynamic acquisition and for analyses such as region of interest, smoothing, etc. Nuclear medicine–specific software is usually developed, supplied, and supported by the nuclear medicine equipment vendor. This is not the case with operating system software. The operating system controls the computer and allows the clinical application package to derive additional information from a completed study. The operating system is usually developed by the basic computer manufacturer, and there is little opportunity to change the system. Clinical application packages are most often developed by the user and deal with a specific program for a specific problem. Most vendors and computer manufacturers are unable to support such limited application programs.

One feature of an operating system that is useful when extensive processing of static images is contemplated is the so-called foreground-background feature. This allows the computer to perform two separate tasks at the same time. One of these tasks (foreground task) is given a higher priority than the other. During periods when the foreground program is idle, the background task is processed. For example, if the foreground task is acquiring a study and there are pauses in the acquisition, the background program may be performing a filtering operation.

Utility programs are provided to allow the operator to perform housekeeping functions. Such functions include copying data from floppy disks to hard disks or magnetic tape; deletion or renaming of files; producing a listing of all the studies or files on a particular portion of the disk or tape, etc.

Once a program is written, it can be loaded into the computer using the binary switches on the front panel of the computer. A short program, permanently stored in the read-only memory of the computer, takes the complicated program from a device such as a storage disk or magnetic tape and places it in the main computer memory for future use. Programs are usually supplied by the manufacturer and either can be a difficult problem, making a system almost unusable, or may make life simple. Optimally, software should provide for patient identification on each data frame and automatically update the patient index each time a new study is performed. Cardiac software packages should include but are not limited to 16 frame-cines, volume curves, emptying and filling rates, filtering, and phase analysis.

Image Acquisition: Memory and Matrix Size

Data may be acquired either by *frame mode* or *list mode*. In the frame mode, incoming data are placed in a spatial matrix in the memory that will be used to generate an image. In the list mode all data are put in the memory as a time sequence list of events. At regular intervals a special code word is inserted into the list. This list is very flexible and can be sorted or divided into images at a later time. The list mode has the disadvantage of a low acquisition rate and a large memory requirement. Frame mode utilizes much less memory than list mode and is more commonly utilized except for gated cardiac studies. All data for images that are collected in the frame mode are acquired in a matrix. The usual image matrix sizes are 64 × 64 and 128 × 128, although 32 × 32 and 256 × 256 are occasionally used. The main disadvantages of frame mode are that the identity of individual events within a time frame is lost and that there is a major dead time loss in transferring frame mode to mass storage.

Matrix size refers to the number of picture

elements along each side of the matrix. These elements may be either "bytes" or "words." In an 8-bit computer, both a "byte" and a "word" are composed of 8 bits. In a 16-bit computer a byte is 8 bits and a "word" is 16 bits. The maximum number of counts that can be represented by an 8-bit picture element (pixel) is 2^8 or 0 through 255 (256 different values). With 16 bits the maximum is 2^{16} or 0 through 65,535 (65,536 different values) per pixel.

The matrix size determines the image resolution. While the matrix size and the number of counts desired have a significant impact on memory required (Table 5–1), the ultimate memory requirements depend upon what the computer system is being used for and how many cameras it is interfaced with simultaneously. The matrix size has nothing to do with the final size of the displayed image. A 32 × 32 matrix has relatively few pixels; therefore the final image will be very coarse. An image obtained in a 256 × 256 acquisition matrix is much more detailed. It should be remembered that "image" resolution of 256 × 256 may refer to either the memory acquisition matrix or the CRT display matrix. Some manufacturers take a 64 × 64 matrix image from the memory and display it on the CRT in a 256 × 256 or 1024 × 1024 matrix, using interpolation methods.

The 32 × 32 matrix will occupy less memory and therefore less disk space. In addition, it can be acquired faster than a finer matrix. Thus, there is a tradeoff between spatial and temporal resolution. In a 32 × 32 matrix, the spatial resolution will be poor, but because it can be acquired rapidly, the temporal resolution will be excellent. For a given computer system, the matrix size desired for acquisition and the read-write speed of the hard disk

Table 5–1. EFFECT OF IMAGE MATRIX SIZE ON MEMORY REQUIRED IN A 16-BIT COMPUTER

MATRIX SIZE	MAXIMUM COUNTS	MEMORY REQUIRED (WORDS)
32 × 32 BYTE	255	0.5 K
32 × 32 WORD	65,535	1 K
64 × 64 BYTE	255	2 K
64 × 64 WORD	65,535	4 K
128 × 128 BYTE	255	8 K
128 × 128 WORD	65,535	16 K
256 × 256 BYTE	255	32 K
256 × 256 WORD	65,535	65 K

dictate the maximum framing rate that is possible.

As mentioned previously, if all 16 bits in a 16-bit computer are utilized, 65,535 (2^{16}) counts per pixel are possible. This allows for statistical identification of small differences in function. If one wishes to increase the matrix size, it is possible to address the memory at the byte level (8 bits per pixel). If this is done, twice as many pixels can be accommodated and the image matrix will be finer, but the number of counts possible in each pixel will be reduced to 255 (2^8).

The amount of memory determines the number of frames that can be collected in the electrocardiographic R-R interval on cardiac studies. For optimum measurement of ejection fraction, at least 25 frames per second are needed. If peak ejection or peak filling rate is to be measured, 50 frames per second are needed. If the main memory is divided into buffers and the size of each buffer is such that each can store one image, the buffer size needed is dependent upon the matrix. In a 32-K (16-K word) system,* if one wishes a 128 × 128 matrix array, the dynamic scanning mode would require at least two 8192-word buffers, leaving no space available in the memory. Thus, only a static image is possible. If the matrix size is reduced to a 64 × 64 byte array, the buffer frame size has to be 2048 words, and thus only 6 frames are possible.

Most nuclear medicine computers have a 16-bit/word memory system containing a total of 128 to 256 K words. Most cardiac studies are performed in acquisition-only mode, with analysis being performed at a later time. A certain portion of the total main memory is used by the operating system and other programs, so that not all the memory is available for image storage.

Image Display and Processing

Image display and processing is necessary in all nuclear medicine computer systems. The computer plays an extremely important role in lesion detectability, and it can perform this function in a number of ways, including reduction of noise, background subtraction,

*In computer terminology, 1 K actually equals 1024 (2^{10}) rather than exactly 1000 and 32 K equals 32,768.

construction of cine loops, and the production of tomographic images. Data are normally collected in 64 × 64 byte images. Although a 32 × 32 byte mode can be used, the decrease in spatial resolution is usually intolerable. Even in 64 × 64 pixel images, there is a noticeable saw-toothed appearance to the image edges. Since the pixel matrix achieved on a display video is 1024 × 1024, the data are usually processed to utilize all the pixels. The simplest method to use is linear interpolation to fill in the extra pixels.

In order to reduce the effects of statistical variation, particularly in low-count images, smoothing of the image can be performed. Smoothing is accomplished through the use of filters. Filters may be either temporal filters or spatial filters. Temporal filters are used for dynamic acquisition, and spatial filters are used on static images. The spatial filters attempt to remove statistical fluctuations of the image by modifying values of data points within various pixels.

The processing performed by spatial filters is done according to the spatial frequencies of the information. It is hoped that by attenuating or augmenting parts of the spatial frequency spectrum, an image is obtained that is easier to interpret or that has more diagnostic value. The simplest smoothing method is 9-point smoothing. This takes 9 pixels of information, and, by taking weighted averages of the 8 pixels on the edge of a central pixel, changes the value of that central pixel. Other kinds of filters that are commonly utilized are low-pass, high-pass, and band-pass filters. A low-pass filter selectively attenuates high frequencies and smooths the image by removing high-frequency noise. An example of this having been applied to data from a SPECT liver scan is shown in Figure 5–2A. Low-pass filtering improves the statistical quality of an image but degrades the sharpness and spatial resolution. High-pass filtering enhances edges to some extent but also augments the noise (Fig. 5–2B). High-pass filtering is important in cardiac nuclear medicine when it is necessary to locate the edge of the ventricle. A band-pass filter is a combination of low- and high-pass filters that effectively suppresses high- and low-frequency signals and only transmits signals that are in a given spatial frequency window.

A simple way of performing low-pass filtering is by addition of dynamic images. It

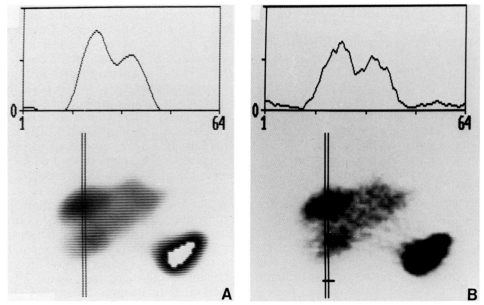

Figure 5–2. Application of spatial filtering to a coronal SPECT image of the liver and spleen. A histogram of the activity defined in a linear region of interest is shown in the upper portion of both A and B. The reconstructed tomographic images are shown in the lower portions (with the liver to the reader's left and the spleen to the reader's right). (A) A low-pass filter removes high frequencies and smooths the image. Rollover artifact is seen as the white area in the central portion of the spleen. (B) A high-pass filter appears more noisy but edges are enhanced. (Case courtesy of Michael Hartshorne, M.D.)

must be remembered that dynamic images have a very low number of counts in each pixel and are therefore usually in the byte mode. Thus, the highest number of counts that can be stored in a pixel is 255. In adding images, it is necessary to change from the byte mode to the word mode so that the maximum number of counts that can be accommodated in each pixel is expanded. If one stays in the byte mode and the number of counts per pixel exceeds 255, the computer will begin counting at zero again for that pixel. This results in a negative defect (rollover artifact) in areas that would normally have a high count rate. An example of this is seen in Figure 5–2A.

Temporal filters are used on dynamic images and involve a weighted averaging technique between each pixel on one image and the same pixel from the frames before and after. Temporal filtering causes a loss of spatial resolution but allows a cine loop to be viewed without flicker. It must be remembered that temporal filtering of dynamic studies does not preclude spatial filtering of the same study, and in fact, the two processes are frequently performed together.

Another common computer image-proc-

essing application is that of frame subtraction. This method may be used for background subtraction and for subtraction of studies performed simultaneously with two different radionuclides. Although less commonly used, additional computer capabilities include frame multiplication and division. Combinations of the maneuvers may be used to produce the so-called functional images obtained from radionuclide ventriculography.

Operator Interaction

The operator interacts with the computer in one of two ways, either by selection from a menu or by using a command structure. The menu system requires sequential choices from a list or menu presented on the video terminal. Although this system is somewhat slower than the command system, it has the advantage that the operator need not be familiar with all of the possible commands. Command structure systems usually have approximately 100 commands that are chosen through use of a two- or three-letter mnemonic. Use of the command system requires

gers; these are essential if cardiac studies are contemplated.

CPU

1. Memory in the CPU should be a minimum of 128 K; for cardiac work, it should be 256 K.
2. Foreground and background regions of the memory are required if simultaneous acquisition and processing is to be done by a single CPU.
3. There are at least three ways to network a computer and several cameras. The least satisfactory way is to have one small CPU networked to different cameras; this requires electronic switching between the cameras. A second method is to have a separate CPU for each camera, which will allow simultaneous acquisition on multiple cameras. The third way is to have a large central CPU with a microprocessor terminal for each camera. The memory in the microprocessor terminal will allow each camera to acquire data independently.

DISPLAY

1. Forward and reverse endless-loop cine display should be provided.

2. The system should be capable of displaying about 20 frames/sec of 128 × 128 image data.
3. It should be capable of displaying 16 images of 64 × 64 simultaneously.
4. The display memory should be 8 bits deep, thus capable of 256 shades of gray or color.

BULK INFORMATION STORAGE

1. The hard disk should be a minimum of 80 megabytes; however, if SPECT studies are contemplated, 1 G byte is desirable.
2. The system should be able to transfer 6.5 × 10^5 bits/sec including disk access time or 20 frames/sec of 64 × 64 byte data.
3. The system should provide for archival storage, either on floppy disk or magnetic tape. One-megabyte floppy disks are most desirable, and if magnetic tape is contemplated, the read-write speed should be 45 inches/sec with a recording density of 600 bits/inch.

Suggested Readings

Gelfand MJ, Thomas SR (eds): Effective Use of Computers in Nuclear Medicine. New York, McGraw-Hill, 1988

Graham MM, Links JM, Lewellen TK, et al: Considerations in the purchase of a nuclear medicine computer system. J Nucl Med 29:717–724, 1988

CHAPTER 6

Cerebrovascular System

Conventional Brain Imaging

Although much of brain scanning has been eclipsed by the widespread availability of computed tomography, there are certain instances in which radionuclide brain imaging provides a different type of information about a suspected cerebral abnormality. Cerebral perfusion and imaging studies may be performed at the bedside or in the nuclear radiology department. For these reasons, an understanding of the techniques and principles involved in radionuclide brain imaging is still important. In addition, newer perfusion agents used in conjunction with SPECT imaging provide an exciting new approach to radionuclide imaging of the brain.

PHYSIOLOGY

In the normal cerebrum, passage of most substances from the cerebral capillaries into the extravascular space is severely restricted, constituting what has been referred to as the "blood–brain barrier." The degree of permeability of this barrier varies with the nature of the material attempting to pass, as well as upon numerous complex carrier mechanisms employed to facilitate or hinder passage through the cell membranes involved. Normally, radiopharmaceuticals commonly used for brain imaging do not traverse the blood–brain barrier. Thus, the radioactivity noted on normal brain images does not lie within the brain itself but rather in the overlying soft tissues and calvarium as well as in the larger blood pool accumulations in the head such as the sagittal and transverse sinuses.

However, in the presence of cerebral pathology such as neoplasm, infarction, or inflammatory processes, sufficient alterations in the blood–brain barrier occur to allow passage of some radioactive tracers into the region of abnormality. This allows for the identification of the lesion on external imaging as a "hot spot"—greater-than-normal activity. Other tracers reflect blood flow with fixation in the tissue. These abnormalities are usually "cold" defects (e.g., stroke and Alzheimer's disease).

RADIOPHARMACEUTICALS

Radiopharmaceutical brain imaging is possible with virtually any radionuclide of sufficient half-life and favorable imaging characteristics that is normally excluded from the brain but which is capable of penetrating a blood–brain barrier altered by underlying pathology. This generally excludes blood pool agents and radiopharmaceuticals largely sequestered by other organ systems. The most commonly employed agents for cerebral imaging are technetium 99m pertechnetate, technetium 99m DTPA, and technetium 99m glucoheptonate (Table 6–1). Technetium 99m pertechnetate probably is the most widely used of these, having the primary advantages of being relatively inexpensive and simple to prepare for use. However, this agent has the notable disadvantage of having slow renal clearance by the body, therefore providing less advantageous target/nontarget ratios at the time of scanning. In addition, pertechnetate is also accumulated by the choroid plexus, making it necessary for a blocking agent to be administered prior to scanning. Though more expensive, technetium 99m DTPA and technetium 99m glucoheptonate are more rapidly excreted by the kidneys, providing higher target/nontarget ratios, a fact that has been used by some investigators to propose earlier imaging with these two agents. Additionally, because these pharmaceuticals are not accumulated in the choroid plexus, the administration of a blocking agent

Table 6–1. RADIOPHARMACEUTICAL AGENTS FOR BRAIN AND CSF IMAGING

RADIOPHARMACEUTICAL	USUAL DOSE	ROUTE OF ADMINISTRATION	PHYSICAL HALF-LIFE	TIME TO IMAGING	ABSORBED DOSE ESTIMATE (RAD/mCi)*			REMARKS
					Whole Body	Gonads	Other	
^{99m}Tc pertechnetate with perchlorate	15–30 mCi (555 MBq–1.1 GBq)	IV	6 hr	1–3 hr	0.01	0.01–0.02	Stomach 0.06 Thyroid 0.01 Colon† 0.13–0.10	Higher with urinary obstruction
^{99m}Tc DTPA	10 mCi (370 MBq)	IV	6 hr	0.5–2.0 hr	0.01–0.02	0.01–0.04	Kidneys† 0.03–0.30 Bladder† 0.07—0.60	
^{99m}Tc glucoheptonate	10 mCi (370 MBq)	IV	6 hr	2–3 hr	0.01	0.004–0.007	Kidneys† 0.15–0.30	
^{99m}Tc DTPA	2 mCi (74 MBq)	Intrathecal	6 hr	0–12 hr				Useful for CSF leak detection
^{111}In DTPA	0.3–1.0 mCi (11–37 MBq)	Intrathecal	67 hr	2–72 hr	0.6		Spinal cord 12.0–20.0	Should have endotoxin testing before injection
^{99m}Tc HMPAO	10–20 mCi (370–740 MBq)	IV	6 hr	0–6 hr	0.013	0.007–0.023		Must be used within 30 min of preparation

*To obtain absorbed doses in mGy/MBq divide values by 3.7.
†Indicates critical organ.

is not required. It must also be mentioned, however, that while technetium 99m DTPA and glucoheptonate require intravenous administration, scanning with pertechnetate may be performed with oral, intramuscular, or intravenous injections, alternatives that may be helpful in uncooperative patients, children, and patients with inaccessible peripheral veins. Furthermore, the slow renal clearance of pertechnetate allows 3- to 4-hour delayed imaging, which may be useful in maximizing the detection of cerebral metastases.

TECHNIQUE OF IMAGING

Radionuclide cerebral imaging generally consists of two phases: (1) a dynamic or angiographic study composed of rapid sequential images of the arrival of the radioactive bolus in the cerebral hemispheres, which essentially constitutes a qualitative measure of perfusion to the brain, and (2) static images obtained approximately 1 hour after the dynamic study, which provide a record of the distribution of the radiopharmaceutical in the cerebral regions, including any abnormal concentrations of the imaging agent. In some instances, delayed static images obtained between 3 and 4 hours after the initial dynamic study better delineate a clinically suspected lesion or an abnormality suggested on the initial static views.

Preparation of the Patient

If any of the above studies are performed using technetium 99m pertechnetate, the choroid plexus must be blocked by the administration of 200 to 500 mg of potassium perchlorate solution, usually administered orally 30 minutes to 1 hour before the administration of the pertechnetate. Perchlorate administration is not necessary when employing technetium DTPA or glucoheptonate.

Radionuclide Angiogram

This study is routinely performed in the anterior position or occasionally by placing a suspected abnormality as close as possible to the collimator. Following a rapid bolus IV injection of 15 to 20 mCi (555 to 740 MBq) of a technetium 99m imaging agent, sequential 2- to 3-second images are obtained for 30 to 60 seconds. Imaging is usually begun when the isotope first appears in the proximal carotid arteries. Using the posterior position for the detection of a suspected abnormality in the posterior fossa is usually unsuccessful but may occasionally be worth attempting particularly in patients with cerebellar or brain stem symptomatology.

Static Images

One hour after the injection of the radiopharmaceutical, initial static images are performed. These routinely consist of 500,000 count views obtained in the anterior, posterior, and both right and left lateral positions. When technetium 99m pertechnetate is used, it is important to exclude any salivary gland activity; such activity may significantly reduce the statistical quality of the cerebral images.

Occasionally a vertex view may be employed to better define an abnormality present high in the cerebral hemispheres. True posterior and oblique posterior fossa views taken with a pinhole or converging collimator may greatly enhance visualization of a lesion in the posterior fossa.

Delayed Static Images

Images taken at 3 to 4 hours are usually obtained in those views in which a lesion is expected to be discovered or confirmed from the earlier study. Almost any type of lesion other than vascular malformations, which may diminish in intensity with time, will present more definitively on the delayed images because of the time allowed for enhanced target/nontarget ratios. Delayed images should be routinely obtained in patients in whom subdural hematoma is suspected, as this abnormality is best delineated on the delayed views. In addition, comparison of initial static images with delayed images may aid in distinguishing soft tissue or calvarial activity from a peripheral cortical cerebral abnormality. Generally, superficial lesions of the bone or soft tissue will become less apparent as time passes, whereas true cerebral lesions will become more evident. Finally, a suspected abnormality of any sort noted on the initial static images should be evaluated with delayed views to allow for substantiation or possible better delineation of the abnormality.

Clinical Applications

THE NORMAL BRAIN SCAN

Radionuclide Angiogram

Normally, prompt symmetric perfusion is noted to both cerebral hemispheres, with middle cerebral arterial distributions being clearly identified and with the anterior cerebral arterial distributions seen as a single midline area of activity. In both areas, perfusion should extend to the calvarial convexities bilaterally (Fig. 6–1). While symmetry is the hallmark of the arterial–capillary phase of a normal perfusion scan, asymmetry in the venous phase is common because of expected variation in venous anatomy. Care

should be taken not to overinterpret lack of symmetry in the venous phase in the absence of an arterial abnormality. Some causes of abnormal perfusion are listed in Table 6–2.

Static Images

The normal static brain images include a number of consistent landmarks (Fig. 6–2). Some aspect of the venous sinuses is always identifiable, prominent activity being found in the sagittal and transverse sinuses. On the posterior view, the transverse sinuses are generally symmetric, although it is not uncommon for the right sinus to be dominant. On the lateral views, activity in the suprasellar and sylvian regions is noted, although it is less constant and less well defined than in

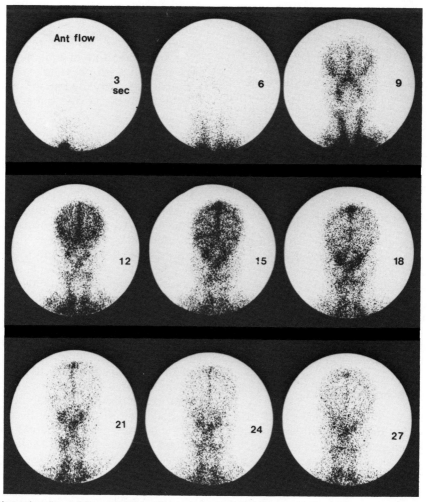

Figure 6–1. Normal radionuclide angiogram. The anterior and middle cerebral arteries are clearly visualized on the 9-second frame. The sagittal sinus is easily seen by 15 seconds.

Table 6–2. CAUSES OF ABNORMAL RADIONUCLIDE ANGIOGRAM

- Symmetrically delayed activity
  - Poor bolus injection
  - Atherosclerosis
  - Congestive heart failure
- Localized reduced perfusion
  - Occlusive disease
    - embolism
    - atherosclerosis
  - Low-grade neoplasm
  - Hematoma
    - intracranial
    - subdural
  - Cystic lesion
    - neoplasm
    - focal
    - atrophy
    - old infarct
  - Edema
    - traumatic
    - neoplastic
- Localized increased perfusion
  - Arteriovenous malformation
  - Vascular metastasis
  - Meningioma or high-grade glioma
  - Inflammatory lesion

the venous sinuses. Occasionally, activity in the soft tissues of the ears may be identified, overlapping or just anterior to the sigmoid sinus region. While little radionuclide is present in the cerebrum itself due to the integrity of the blood–brain barrier, activity may be seen outlining the periphery of the hemispheres, primarily within the subarachnoid space, calvaria, and soft tissues of the scalp.

THE ABNORMAL BRAIN SCAN

As discussed earlier, detection of a lesion on a brain scan depends primarily on its size, location, and the degree of breakdown of the blood–brain barrier or edematous reaction.

Neoplasms

Metastatic cerebral lesions are commonly encountered brain tumors. They classically present as multiple areas of focally increased activity in the cerebral hemispheres on the static brain views. At this time, the initial test of choice is contrast-enhanced computed tomography or magnetic resonance imaging. Tumors that most frequently metastasize to the brain include melanomas and those of the lung, breast, and gastrointestinal tract. With lesions that metastasize both to the calvaria and the brain, differential localization of these abnormalities may be difficult. A concurrent skull film is also often helpful. The radionuclide arteriogram is usually un-

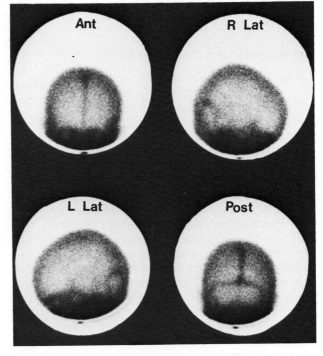

Figure 6–2. Normal static brain scan. A large amount of activity is normally seen in the face and base of the skull. The sagittal and transverse sinuses are prominent.

remarkable in patients with brain metastases, although very large or highly vascular metastatic lesions may be identified.

As might be expected, not all primary brain tumors display the same propensity for detection on radionuclide scanning. High-grade gliomas (Fig. 6–3) such as glioblastoma multiforme and meningioma are detected more than 90 percent of the time, whereas low-grade astrocytomas or oligodendrogliomas, pituitary adenomas, pinealomas, ependymomas, and even craniopharyngiomas frequently escape detection. With current imaging techniques, hemispherical lesions of 1 cm or greater can generally be visualized. Even smaller tumors are detectable if concomitant edema or hemorrhage is sufficient. Lesions at the base of the brain are more difficult to identify because of the interfering activity from the nasopharynx, salivary glands, and venous structures at the base of the skull. Various therapies, including corticosteroid treatment, radiation therapy, and chemotherapy, may make the lesions undetectable.

In scanning for primary brain lesions, it is important to remember that the lesions are distributed differently in adults than in children. In adults, more than 75 percent of primary lesions occur above the tentorium, whereas posterior fossa tumors comprise 75 percent of pediatric brain tumors. Therefore, detailed views of the posterior fossa are mandatory in children.

Cerebrovascular Occlusive Disease

The cerebral radionuclide angiogram can be used for patients with suspected vascular occlusive disease, as it is a convenient non-invasive method of evaluating the common carotid arteries and the intracerebral arterial distributions. Stenoses of greater than 80 percent of the common or internal carotid arteries are detected with a sensitivity of more than 75 percent. With stenoses of lesser degree, the study is significantly less sensitive, and it is uncommon to identify lesions with less than 50 percent occlusion. Because the detection of vascular occlusions is based heavily on the comparison of relative perfusion to both cerebral hemispheres, the diagnosis of bilateral disease is frequently not identified.

Severe stenosis and vascular occlusion present as regional areas of relatively diminished or absent activity distal to the site of the lesion during the arterial phase of the perfusion study. In large acute vascular occlusions, it is not uncommon to identify relatively increased activity in the region of occlusion during the venous phase of the examination. This "flip-flop" phenomenon represents collateral circulation to the involved region. It is most often found in patients with occlusion or high-grade obstruction of the internal carotid or middle cerebral arteries (Fig. 6–4).

The detection of ischemic cerebrovascular disease on static brain images depends on a number of factors, the most important of which is the interval between the infarction and the brain scan. In the first few days after the infarction, only 20 percent of patients show abnormal scans. Most ischemic infarctions detected by brain scans become positive 7 to 10 days after their occurrence. However, hemorrhagic infarctions may be positive considerably earlier than ischemic lesions. Furthermore, the size and position of the lesion greatly influence detectability; small infarcts and those occurring in the brain stem, for example, frequently go undiagnosed by static imaging. As with most cerebral lesions, delayed imaging increases the likelihood of visualizing a recent infarction. By the end of the third week after onset of clinical symptoms, over 75 percent of cerebral infarctions become positive. They remain positive for varying periods of time but generally decrease in activity after 1 month, with most infarcts returning to normal after 6 weeks.

In both thrombotic and embolic insults, the area of subsequent infarction involves a segment of tissue distal to the occlusion, thereby giving rise to a somewhat characteristic distribution on the brain scan (Fig. 6–5). The lesions are usually peripheral in the cerebral hemispheres, may be wedge-shaped, and are typically confined to a single arterial distribution. An appreciation of arterial territorial distributions on routine brain scan images as well as on the vertex view is of considerable importance in reaching a diagnosis. "Watershed" infarctions secondary to prolonged hypotension and cerebral hypoxia may also present a characteristic pattern on static brain imaging. Increased activity is noted in the watershed areas between two major cerebral artery distributions, most frequently parasagittally at the junction of the anterior and middle cerebral artery territories.

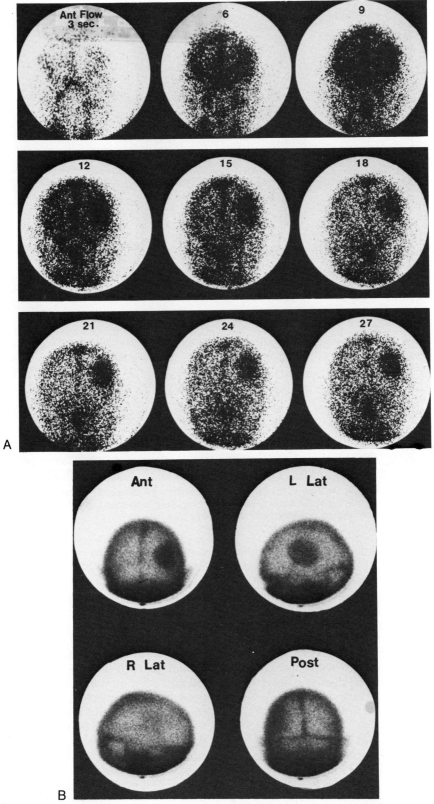

Figure 6–3. High-grade glioma. (A) The radionuclide angiogram demonstrates a very vascular lesion in the left hemisphere. The lesion has a large amount of activity even at the end of the angiogram. Such a lesion may also be a meningioma or a hypervascular metastasis. (B) The delayed images also clearly delineate the lesion.

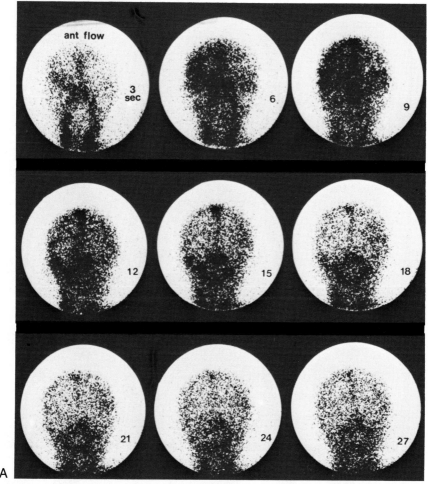

Figure 6–4. Cerebral infarction. (A) The radionuclide angiogram demonstrates early decreased flow in the distribution of the left middle cerebral artery. Later in the study there is delayed flow into this region, constituting a "flip-flop" phenomenon. *(Figure continues on next page.)*

In major carotid occlusions, marked delay or absence of activity in the carotid artery may be identified. Isolated obstruction of the internal carotid artery may produce strikingly increased activity in the nasal area during the arterial phase of the radionuclide arteriogram—the "hot nose" sign. This is caused by collateral flow through the external carotid artery and maxillary branches. This may also occur with a generalized decrease in cerebral perfusion.

Cerebral Death

The radionuclide arteriogram is a simple noninvasive method of determining the presence or absence of intracerebral perfusion. The study may be performed at the patient's bedside with the aid of a portable gamma camera. Blood flow to the superficial scalp vessels is occluded by an elastic band placed around the head just above the orbits. In the presence of cerebral death, the injected activity typically proceeds through the carotid artery to the base of the skull, where the radioactive bolus stops due to increased intracranial pressure without evidence of intracranial entry (Fig. 6–6). As with all radionuclide arteriograms, it is important that a good bolus be injected. If distinct activity in the common carotid artery is not identified, the injection should be repeated. Demonstration of the absence of intracerebral flow is strong corroborative evidence of cerebral demise. This appears to be valid whether or not sagittal venous sinus activity is detected. Although the "hot nose" sign cannot be used to specifically indicate brain death, it may be

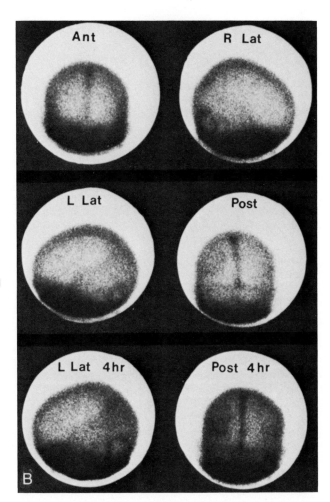

Figure 6–4 *Continued* (B) The static images show some activity posteriorly on the left side of the brain on the initial static images. The delayed static images at 4 hours show the lesion much more clearly, and the lesion is noted to be wedge-shaped on the left lateral view.

used as a strong secondary sign when intracerebral perfusion is absent. When ^{99m}Tc-labeled perfusion agents that cross the blood–brain barrier (^{99m}Tc HMPAO) are used to perform radionuclide angiography, subsequent static images fail to show localization in brain tissue in brain-dead patients.

Intracranial Inflammatory Disease

Static radionuclide brain imaging has proved a sensitive method of detecting suspected cerebral inflammatory disease in all of its manifestations from early cerebritis to localized pyogenic abscess. The radionuclide angiogram is frequently unremarkable but may demonstrate increased perfusion to the region of the abnormality. While the radionuclide findings in frank abscess are usually not distinguishable from cerebritis, the presentation of an area of increased activity with a central area of diminished activity (the "doughnut" sign) is suggestive of abscess. Initially, this sign was felt to be pathognomonic of cerebral abscess, but it is now known to be nonspecific and appears in numerous disease entities.

Brain scanning has proved very reliable in the investigation of herpes simplex encephalitis. Cerebral imaging is usually positive very early in the onset of the disease, frequently before computed tomography can demonstrate the abnormality. The lesion characteristically presents as an area of increased activity in one or both temporal lobe regions, with occasional involvement of the adjacent parietal or frontal lobes.

Trauma

Although computed tomography has largely supplanted radionuclide imaging for the investigation of acute cerebral injury, the more insidious effects of trauma, such as

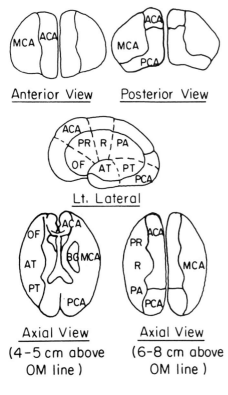

Anterior View   Posterior View

Lt. Lateral

Axial View
(4–5 cm above
OM line)

Axial View
(6–8 cm above
OM line)

Figure 6–5. Arterial distribution in the brain. Anterior (ACA), middle (MCA), and posterior (PCA) cerebral arteries. Branches of the middle cerebral artery are also indicated, including anterior temporal (AT), orbital frontal (OF), pre-Rolandic (PR), posterior temporal (PT), parietal angular (PA), and the basal ganglia (BG). (Reprinted with minor modification from Chiu LC, McWilliams FE, Christie JH: Comparison of radionuclide and computed tomography scanning in non-neoplastic intracranial disease. CT: J Comput Tomogr 2 (4):295–318, 1978. With permission.)

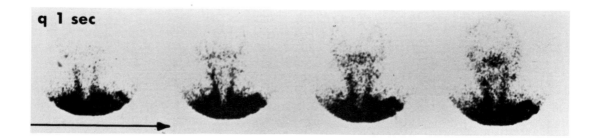

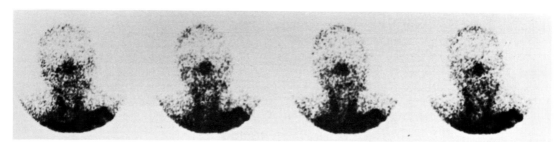

Figure 6–6. Brain death. The radionuclide angiogram demonstrates a good bolus of activity in the region of the carotids and the scalp. There is no evidence of activity in the anterior or middle cerebral distribution. A "hot nose" sign is present.

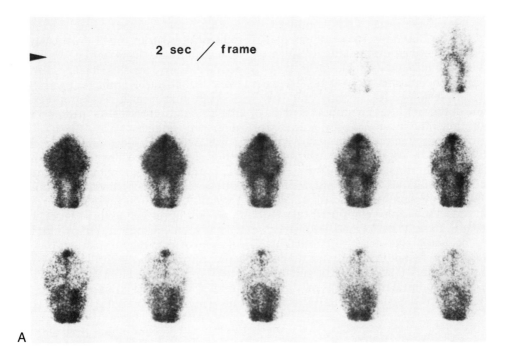

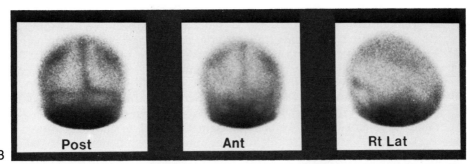

Figure 6–7. Bilateral subdural hematomas. (A) The radionuclide angiogram shows the classic "pointed head" sign of bilateral subdural hematoma. This is due to bilateral compression of the cerebral hemispheres. (B) The static images show bilateral areas of increased activity due to subdural hematomas. (Photographs courtesy of Russell Briggs, M.D.)

subdural hematoma, may be evaluated by radionuclide techniques. In acute lesions, detection ranges from approximately 50 percent to 80 percent, whereas in subacute or chronic lesions (10 days to 2 weeks in duration) sensitivity approaches 100 percent. In the acute phase of subdural hematoma, when the static images may well be unremarkable, radionuclide angiography can significantly increase the detection rate by demonstrating decreased or absent perfusion to one or both cerebral convexities or displacement of middle cerebral vasculature (Fig. 6–7). The dynamic study may also increase the specificity

of the examination in the chronic phase when the static images are positive. Three- to four-hour delayed static views likewise greatly enhance the sensitivity of the examination and should be routinely obtained when the diagnosis of subdural hematoma is suspected.

Typically, the static image appearance of subdural hematoma is that of a peripheral "crescent" of increased activity along the cerebral convexity. This is best seen in either the anterior or posterior view and is commonly not identified on the lateral views. This characteristic may be used to distinguish subdural hematoma from other conditions that may produce the crescent sign and that are generally identified on the lateral view as well. These abnormalities include cerebral infarction and neoplasms as well as various skull or scalp lesions. Occasionally only the membrane of the subdural hematoma is identifiable on the static images, as the so-called "rim sign"—a thin line of curvilinear activity in the region of the cerebral convexity with its concave margin directed laterally.

Other manifestations of cerebral trauma are not commonly identified on radionuclide imaging, possibly because computed tomography is now usually performed. However, it should be noted that cerebral contusions and intracerebral hematomas may present as focal areas of increased activity in the cerebral cortex and that epidural hematomas may give findings similar to those of subdural lesions.

Functional Brain Imaging

In the past, radionuclide imaging of the brain in the evaluation of cerebrovascular disorders was limited to compounds that only enter the brain substance when there is disruption of the normal blood–brain barrier. More recently, however, two groups of radiopharmaceuticals of clinical interest have been introduced that cross the intact blood–brain barrier and are retained by the cerebral cortex.

The first group includes gamma-emitting iodine 123 labeled amines and technetium 99m agents that may be imaged on standard gamma cameras using transaxial tomographic techniques. The second group consists of positron-emitting radiopharmaceuticals, the most notable of which is fluorine 18 deoxyglucose.

IODINATED RADIOPHARMACEUTICALS

Amine compounds are lipophilic substances that move across the blood–brain barrier with almost complete extraction during a single pass through the cerebral circulation. The distribution of these compounds in the brain reflects regional cerebral blood flow (rCBF). Once inside the brain substance, they are either bound to nonspecific receptors or are metabolized to nonlipophilic compounds. As a result, these tracers do not redistribute within the brain substance for at least 1 hour after intravenous administration. Because they can be labeled with gamma emitters, satisfactory images can be obtained by both planar and tomographic imaging, but lesions are better delineated on the tomographic images.

The two iodinated amines currently most widely investigated are the monoamine, N-isopropyl–123-I-p-iodoamphetamine (IMP), and the diamine, N-trimethyl-N-(2-hydroxyl–3-methyl–5-iodobenzyl)- 1,3-propanediamine (HIPDM). While there is much similarity between the two tracers, there are some differences that may impact on the choice of radiopharmaceuticals for brain perfusion images. For instance, HIPDM accumulates more rapidly within the brain substance after IV injection, while the ultimate peak concentrations within the brain substance with IMP are 30 to 40 percent higher than with HIPDM. Both tracers maintain a steady state in the brain over a sufficiently long period of time, however, to allow successful static imaging. Maximal brain activity is maintained with both tracers for 30 to 60 minutes after injection. For tomographic techniques, the higher concentrations of iodine 123 IMP (^{123}I-IMP) are more attractive due to the limited sensitivity of rotating gamma cameras.

The search for a technetium 99m labeled radiopharmaceutical for functional brain imaging has led to the development of ^{99m}Tc hexamethylpropyleneamine oxime (^{99m}Tc HMPAO or ^{99m}Tc hexametazime). It is a lipophilic agent that crosses the blood–brain barrier with rapid first pass uptake comparable to iodoamphetamine. Uptake in the brain is about 5 percent of the injected activity with no significant late redistribution. Activity of ^{99m}Tc HMPAO is highest in gray matter and is proportional to rCBF. Excretion during the first 48 hours is through the intestinal tract (50 percent) and kidneys (40 percent). The shorter half-life of ^{99m}Tc relative to ^{123}I allows higher administered activities, which is critical in SPECT imaging. Another ^{99m}Tc agent, L-ethyl cysteinate dimer (ECD), has uptake and redistribution properties similar to HMPAO.

TECHNIQUE

These agents are injected intravenously. Activities for radioiodinated amines range from 3 to 5 mCi (111 to 185 MBq), while 10 to 20 mCi (370 to 740 MBq) is given for the ^{99m}Tc agents. Images are obtained 15 to 20 minutes after injection. Because radioiodinated amines redistribute, the patient should be positioned prior to injection to avoid delay. When imaging suspected cerebrovascular accidents (CVAs), repeat imaging at 2 to 4 hours post-injection to assess redistribution may be desirable when iodinated agents are employed. Because external sensory stimuli such as noise and light affect rCBF, these should be minimized in the imaging area to prevent interfering activity in the appropriate sensory cortex.

NORMAL EXAMINATION

The normal distribution of these functional agents is proportional to blood flow with significantly greater activity seen in the cortical gray matter (Figs. 6–8 and 6–9). This is consistent with the fourfold greater blood flow in the gray matter compared with the white matter. Thus, activity is symmetric and greatest in the strip of cortex along the convexity of the frontal, parietal, temporal, and occipital lobes. Activity is also high in the regions corresponding to the basal ganglia and the thalamus. The cortical white matter has substantially less activity, and the border between white matter and ventricles is indistinct. However, the purpose of SPECT imaging is to evaluate rCBF and metabolic activity rather than structural detail.

PATHOLOGIC STATES

The assessment of regional or global distribution of cerebral perfusion is useful in a number of neurologic conditions. The cerebral perfusion images should be inspected for symmetry of radiopharmaceutical distribution as well as for continuity of perfusion in the rim of cortical gray matter.

Clinical indications for functional brain imaging include evaluation of cerebrovascular disease, dementia, and localization of seizure foci. Since cerebral perfusion radiopharmaceuticals are distributed in direct proportion to blood flow, it is not surprising that the major clinical setting for the use of such agents thus far has been in the realm of both acute and chronic cerebrovascular disease. Regions of decreased or absent blood flow secondary to cerebral vascular disease appear as photopenic areas on the scintigraphic image. Current studies have shown that SPECT imaging is as accurate as computed tomography (CT) for the diagnosis of acute cerebral infarction and has the advantage that a stroke can be diagnosed in the first 2 days after onset of symptoms when CT may be normal. Not only does emission tomography show the ischemic damage from a stroke earlier than CT, but the extent of the perfusion defect may be substantially greater than would be seen on CT. When imaging CVAs with iodinated amines, delayed imaging at 2 to 4 hours may allow differentiation of irreversibly infarcted tissue from areas of reversible ischemia by demonstrating the redistribution of IMP into areas of ischemia evident on early views.

In addition to the diagnosis and assessment of extent of cerebrovascular disease, the technique may be used to select patients who may benefit from neurovascular intervention as well as to judge the success of such procedures.

Alzheimer's disease may be differentiated from other causes of senile dementia by the characteristic bilateral decrease in rCBF in the parietotemporal cortex with preservation of uptake in the sensory-motor cortex, basal ganglia, visual cortex, and cerebellum (Fig. 6–10). Seizure foci may be localized using functional brain imaging and present as localized areas of increased activity. This can be used as a guide for surgical ablation.

POSITRON-EMITTING AGENTS

Although a variety of positron-emitting radionuclides have been employed in studies of cerebral blood flow and metabolism, the most widely applied of these is the glucose analog, deoxyglucose, labeled with fluorine 18. Fluorodeoxyglucose (FDG) is transported from the blood to the brain substance in a manner analogous to glucose. Unlike glucose, however, FDG is phosphorylated and trapped in the brain substance because it cannot be transported out through the cell membrane and thus is not metabolized farther along the glycolytic pathway. This limited metabolism, along with the half-life of 110 minutes for fluorine 18, allows adequate time for tomographic positron imaging. As might be surmised, the distribution of FDG in the brain is directly related to blood flow and metabolic rate. The cortical gray matter

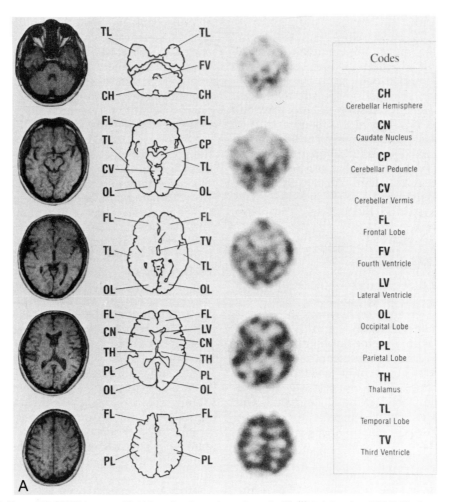

Figure 6–8. (A and B) SPECT images (right-hand columns) produced with [123]I Iofetamine HCl (IMP) shown with comparable magnetic resonance images (left-hand columns) and anatomic diagrams (middle columns). (Copyright 1988 by IMP Incorporated, Houston, Texas. All rights reserved.)

and the subcortical structures such as the basal ganglia and thalami have the greatest concentrations of activity.

Positron emission tomography (PET) with FDG permits the only noninvasive method of quantifying local cerebral metabolism in humans in vivo, and, unlike transmission CT, PET provides a physiologic tool that illustrates pathologic conditions *before* morphologic manifestations are discernible. There is also a more specific class of positron-emitting radiopharmaceuticals that have received recent attention. These are the receptor-specific agents such as the dopamine receptor–seeking radiopharmaceutical, carbon 11-*N*-methylpiperone. It is hoped that these agents will be able to map the distribution of neuromediators in normal and pathologic states.

Cerebrospinal Fluid Imaging

Cerebrospinal fluid (CSF) is formed largely in the choroid plexus of the cerebral ventricular system at a rate of approximately 400 to 500 ml/day in the normal adult. It is essentially an ultrafiltrate of plasma with an actively secreted component added by the choroid plexus. The total CSF volume ranges between 120 and 150 ml, of which approximately 40 ml are contained within the ventricular system. After exiting the ventricles by way of the fourth ventricular foramina,

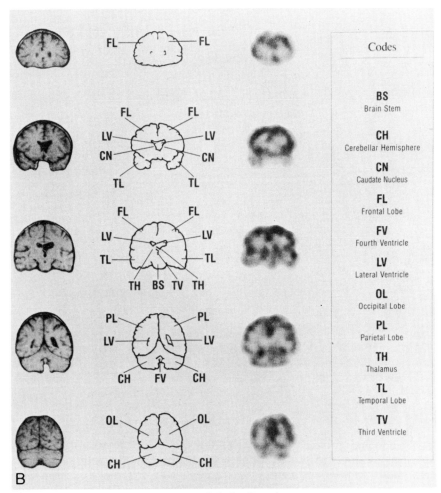

Codes	
BS	Brain Stem
CH	Cerebellar Hemisphere
CN	Caudate Nucleus
FL	Frontal Lobe
FV	Fourth Ventricle
LV	Lateral Ventricle
OL	Occipital Lobe
PL	Parietal Lobe
TH	Thalamus
TL	Temporal Lobe
TV	Third Ventricle

Figure 6–8 *Continued*

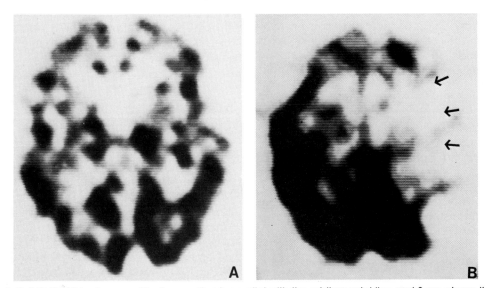

Figure 6–9. IMP SPECT brain scans. The image slice is parallel with the orbitomeatal line and 2 cm above it. (A) Normal study. (B) Patient with an acute left middle cerebral artery infarct. The infarction is seen as an area of decreased activity (arrows). This scan was obtained at a time when the CT scan was still normal. (Case courtesy of B. Leonard Holman, M. D.)

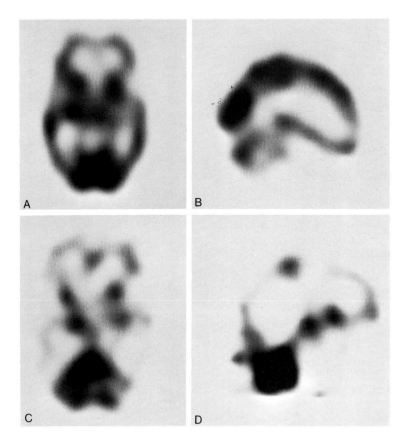

Figure 6–10. Iodine 123-IMP SPECT scan shown in a normal volunteer (A and B) and in a patient with Alzheimer's disease (C and D). Transaxial slice (C) and midsagittal slice (D). (Case courtesy of B. Leonard Holman, M.D.)

the CSF flows cephalad through the subarachnoid space to the level of the superior sagittal sinus, where primary resorption occurs in the arachnoid villi. Absorption also occurs across the meninges of both the brain and the spinal cord as well as through the ependymal lining of the ventricular system. These latter pathways are probably of great importance in pathologic states causing blockage of absorption through the arachnoid villi.

The principle involved in imaging the CSF consists of intrathecal administration of a substance that is miscible with and diffusable in the CSF and that remains in the CSF compartment until being absorbed through the normal pathways. Any such substance must, of course, be nontoxic and nonpyrogenic. Strict pyrogen testing of all intrathecally administered agents should be routinely performed.

RADIOPHARMACEUTICALS

Currently, the most widely employed agent for studies of CSF dynamics is indium 111 labeled DTPA with a physical half-life of 2.8 days and abundant gamma emissions. The short (6-hour) half-life of technetium 99m labeled agents renders them of limited use in CSF function studies. However, they may be of much value in the assessment of intraventricular shunt patency or in routine cisternography in children, who normally demonstrate more rapid CSF flow dynamics than adults.

TECHNIQUE

The administration of 500 μCi (18.5 MBq) of indium 111 DTPA is accomplished by lumbar puncture with a small-bore (22-gauge) needle into the subarachnoid space. To minimize leakage from the puncture site, it is wise to postpone such procedures for approximately a week after the most recent diagnostic lumbar puncture.

Gamma camera images are obtained at 6, 24, and 48 hours, and at 72 hours if necessary. Initial images over the thoracolumbar spine may be obtained at 2 to 4 hours to discern the success of injection.

NORMAL EXAMINATION

After injection of the radiopharmaceutical into the lumbar subarachnoid space, the activity ascends in the spinal canal and reaches the basal cisterns at approximately 4 hours in adults (Fig. 6–11). Subsequent images obtained over the next 24 hours demonstrate ascent of the radiopharmaceutical through the intracranial subarachnoid spaces, with identification of activity in the sylvian and interhemispheric cisterns. At 24 hours, complete ascent of activity over the convexities and the parasagittal region, with relative clearance from the basilar cisterns, is noted.

The presence of radioactivity in the lateral ventricles at any point in the examination should be considered abnormal. However, transient entry noted at 4 hours and disappearing by 24 hours is of questionable pathologic significance. Failure of the radionuclide to achieve complete ascent and activity in the ventricles at 24 hours are indications for further evaluation at 48 and/or 72 hours.

PATHOLOGIC STATES

The major indications for radionuclide imaging of the CSF are (1) communicating hydrocephalus (normal pressure hydrocephalus), (2) CSF leaks, and (3) diversionary CSF shunt patency.

Communicating Hydrocephalus

Normal pressure hydrocephalus characteristically presents as a clinical triad of ataxia, dementia, and urinary incontinence. By definition, hydrocephalus without significant atrophy is noted on CT scans with a normal CSF pressure determination. If the diagnosis of normal pressure hydrocephalus can be established, CSF shunting from the ventricular system may provide prompt relief of symptoms in selected patients. CSF imaging may provide corroborative evidence of the diagnosis as well as aid in selecting patients most likely to benefit from shunt therapy.

Hydrocephalus with normal lumbar pressures often presents a problem of differentiation between cerebral atrophy and normal pressure hydrocephalus. CT scanning can generally provide the answer. However, in some patients with mild degrees of atrophy and dilated ventricles, radionuclide CSF imaging provides more differential information

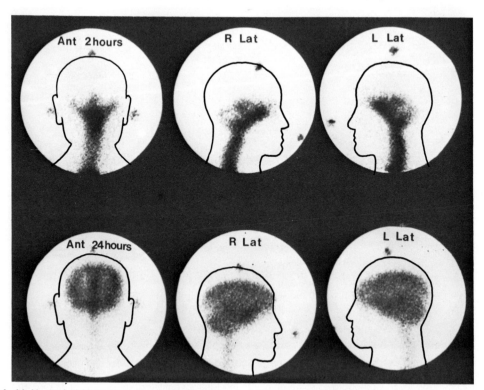

Figure 6–11. Normal cisternogram. The images obtained at 2 hours demonstrate activity in the basal cisterns as well as some activity in the sylvian and interhemispheric cisterns. The images obtained at 24 hours demonstrate that there has been normal ascent of activity over the convexities.

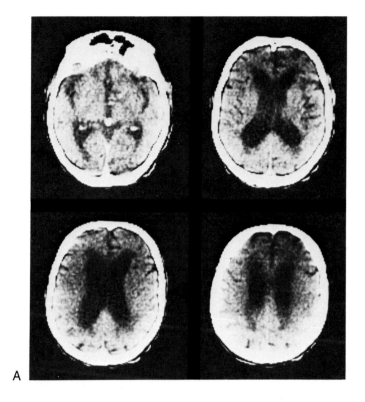

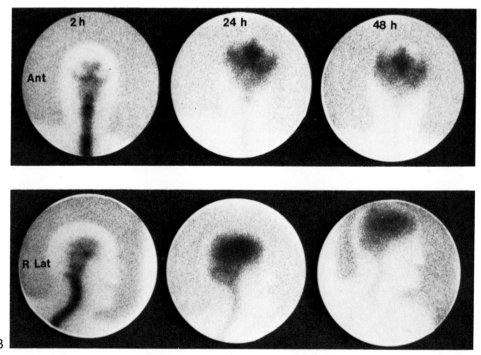

Figure 6–12. Normal pressure hydrocephalus. (A) The CT scans demonstrate ventricular dilatation without cerebral atrophy, suggesting the diagnosis of normal pressure hydrocephalus. This is confirmed by the cisternogram taken at 2 hours (B), which demonstrates some entry into the lateral ventricles that persists at 24 and 48 hours. Even at 48 hours, the anterior view indicates no activity over the hemispheres.

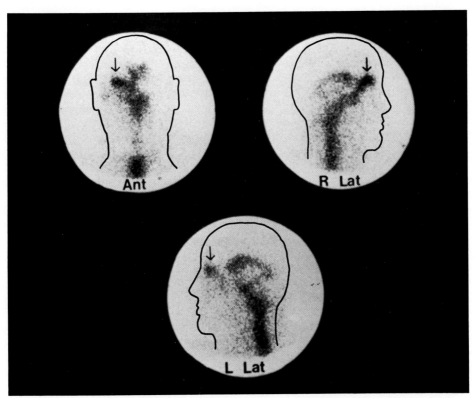

Figure 6–13. CSF leak. Three images of the head obtained during the sixth hour of an indium 111 DTPA cisternogram demonstrate ventricular entry of the radiopharmaceutical with a prominent area of increased activity in the right frontal sinus in a patient with post-traumatic CSF rhinorrhea.

than CT scanning. The classic pattern of scintigraphic findings in normal pressure hydrocephalus is that of early entry of the radiopharmaceutical into the lateral ventricles, with persistence at 24 and 48 hours but with considerable delay in the ascent to the parasagittal region (Fig. 6–12). In general, patients who demonstrate these characteristic findings are among those most likely to benefit from diversionary shunting. Although varying degrees of ventricular entry and persistence, with or without delay in convexity ascent, may be noted, these patterns are of questionable value in establishing a firm diagnosis of normal pressure hydrocephalus or in predicting therapeutic success.

Noncommunicating Hydrocephalus

Because the radiopharmaceuticals injected into the lumbar space normally do not enter the ventricular system, a radionuclide cisternogram cannot be used to distinguish communicating from noncommunicating hydrocephalus. However, by injecting the material directly into the lateral ventricles, communication between the ventricles and the subarachnoid space can be discerned. This method may be of value in the investigation of enlarged lateral ventricles noted on computed tomography when noncommunicating disease is suspected.

CSF Leaks

Radionuclide cisternography is frequently used to substantiate the presence of a CSF leak from the nose or ear or to more precisely localize the site of a leak. The most common sites of CSF fistulae occur in the region of the cribriform plate and ethmoid sinuses and from the sella turcica into the sphenoid sinus. Because such leaks are frequently intermittent, it is important to realize that the results of the radionuclide cisternogram are greatly dependent on whether or not the leak is active at the time of the examination (Fig. 6–13).

The radionuclide evaluation of CSF rhinorrhea should consist of (1) imaging the site of the leak and (2) measuring differential activity in pledgets placed deep into each nostril. It is important to image for a CSF leak at the time the radioactive bolus reaches the assumed site of origin of the leak. Since most such leaks develop near the basilar cisterns, imaging between 1 to 3 hours is typical. Following the bolus at half-hour intervals may better allow determination of the precise time of imaging. Likewise, if any position or activity is known by the patient to provoke or aggravate the flow of CSF, such should be accomplished immediately before or during imaging.

Pledgets placed in the nostrils prior to lumbar injection of the radiopharmaceutical are removed 4 to 6 hours after placement and counted in a well counter. Concurrent blood serum samples should be obtained and counted. Sample counts should be expressed in terms of counts per gram to normalize for differences in pledget size and amounts of absorbed fluid. Pledget/serum ratios of over 1.5 may be interpreted as evidence of CSF rhinorrhea.

Shunt Patency

Shunt obstruction is a common complication of ventriculoatrial or ventriculoperitoneal shunts used to treat obstructive communicating and noncommunicating hydrocephalus. A number of methods of determining shunt patency have been devised using radionuclide techniques. Because of the relatively short duration of the examination, technetium 99m labeled pharmaceuticals may be used. Injection of the radiopharmaceutical into the shunt reservoir or tubing is performed under strict antiseptic conditions. In the presence of shunt patency, serial gamma camera images demonstrate rapid passage of the radiopharmaceutical through the distal limb of the shunt, with activity noted in the peritoneal cavity or right atrium 30 minutes to 1 hour postinjection. If the distal limb of the shunt is manually occluded during injection of the reservoir, some reflux

of the radiopharmaceutical may be found in the ventricular system.

This procedure may give information regarding the patency of the proximal limb of the shunt as well as permit subsequent evaluation of rate of ventricular clearance of the radioactively labeled CSF from the ventricular system by employing serial images. Failure to obtain reflux into the ventricular system or failure of the radiopharmaceuticals to clear from the ventricles after several hours may be taken as evidence of proximal limb obstruction.

In ventriculoperitoneal shunts, the activity reaching the peritoneal cavity must be seen to diffuse throughout the abdomen. If the radiopharmaceutical collects focally in a pool at the tip of the catheter, obstruction of the distal limb by entrapment is likely. Because the CSF is not allowed to resorb properly in the abdomen under these circumstances, relative obstruction of the shunt flow develops. In examining ventriculoatrial or ventriculoperitoneal shunts, it is important to determine the type of shunt employed and understand the mechanics of its operation before proceeding with the shunt patency examination. In many cases, the technique can be tailored to the particular clinical problem suspected and to the type of shunt in place.

Suggested Readings

Alavi A, Kung HF: Imaging of the brain with SPECT: Is it coming of age? In: Hoffer PB (ed). Yearbook of Nuclear Medicine 1989. Chicago, Year Book Medical Publishers, 1989:xiii–xxvii

Di Chiro G: Positron emission tomography using fluorine 18 deoxyglucose in brain tumors: A powerful diagnostic and prognostic tool. Invest Radiol 22:360–371, 1987

Freeman LM, Blaufox MD (eds): Functional brain studies—Part I. Semin Nucl Med 15(4):324–394, 1985

Freeman LM, Blaufox MD (eds): Functional brain studies—Part II. Semin Nucl Med 16(1):2–73, 1986

Holman BL: Perfusion and receptor SPECT in the dementias: George Taplin Memorial Lecture. J Nucl Med 27:855–860, 1986

Porani D, DiPiero V, Vallar G, et al: Technetium 99m HMPAO-SPECT study of regional cerebral perfusion in early Alzheimer's disease. J Nucl Med 29:1507–1514, 1988

Thyroid and Parathyroid

The use of iodine 131 for measuring thyroid functional parameters and imaging the gland has historically served as the nucleus of the evolution of the field of nuclear imaging. Although significant changes have taken place in the radionuclide approach to thyroidology, the essential principles remain unchanged. Therefore, a basic understanding of these principles is necessary before attempting interpretation of the functional data.

Most current thyroid imaging techniques capitalize on some phase of hormone synthesis within the thyroid gland. Iodides or iodide analogs are actively transported *into* the thyroid gland, a process called "trapping." The iodides are then oxidized by thyroid peroxidase and originally bound to tyrosyl moieties (organification) to form mono- and di-iodinated tyrosine (MIT and DIT). These are then coupled to form triiodothyronine (T_3) and thyroxine (T_4) (see Fig. 7–1). Technetium 99m pertechnetate, however, does not undergo organification to form thyroid hormone; instead, after trapping it slowly "washes" from the gland.

Radiopharmaceuticals

The radioactive iodides (^{131}I, ^{123}I) and ^{99m}Tc constitute the radionuclides currently employed in imaging the thyroid gland.

IODINE 131

This iodine decays by beta emission and has a half-life of approximately 8 days. The principal gamma emission of 364 keV is considerably higher than the ideal for imaging with gamma cameras. A 1/2-inch-thick crystal has only a 30 percent efficiency for these photons.

The major advantages of ^{131}I are its low price and ready availability. Its major disadvantages are its long physical half-life and high beta emission, which cause a relatively high radiation dose to be delivered to the thyroid, although the whole-body dose is acceptable. It should be pointed out, however, that the high thyroid dose and relatively low whole-body dose make ^{131}I an ideal radiotherapeutic agent for treating certain thyroid disorders. Also, its long half-life is of advantage in scanning for the detection of functioning metastatic thyroid carcinoma because imaging can be done over several days to allow for optimum concentration by the metastatic deposits. Finally, its high-energy gamma emission is helpful in imaging substernal thyroid tissue; the lower-energy emissions of other radioisotopes may be absorbed by the sternum and chest wall.

IODINE 123

Radioactive iodine 123 has excellent physical properties for an imaging agent. Like ^{131}I, its biochemical behavior is identical to that of stable iodide. Iodine 123 decays by electron capture, with a photon energy of 159 keV and a half-life of 13 hours. The gamma emission of ^{123}I allows excellent imaging (80 percent efficiency) with low background activity. It provides a considerably lower dose of radiation to the thyroid with comparable activity than does ^{131}I.

The major disadvantages of ^{123}I are high cost due to the fact that it is produced by cyclotron, and problems with availability and delivery. In many parts of the United States ^{123}I is available only 1 day a week and must be specially ordered. In spite of these restrictions ^{123}I is the iodine of choice for thyroid imaging.

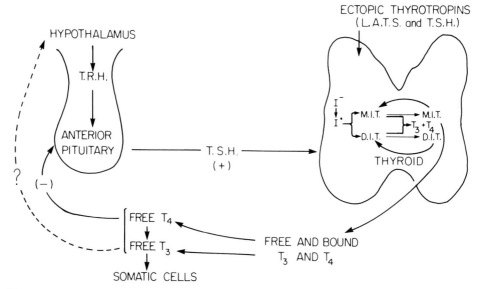

Figure 7–1. Schematic representation of thyroid hormonal stimulation, production, and feedback.

IODINE 125

The radioisotope of iodine ^{125}I is mentioned briefly for its historical significance in thyroid imaging and because it is a common agent for use in radioimmunoassay. Because of its long half-life of 60 days and its low energy emissions (27 to 35 keV), which allow for considerable absorption by overlying bony structures, ^{125}I has never gained popularity for in vivo usage. However, imaging with a gamma camera can produce diagnostic thyroid images.

TECHNETIUM 99m

Technetium 99m pertechnetate is trapped by the thyroid in the same manner as iodides but is not organified; therefore it is released over time as the pertechnetate (TcO$_4^-$) ion. Its short physical half-life of 6 hours and principal gamma energy of 140 keV are ideal for gamma camera imaging (greater than 90 percent efficiency with a 1/2-inch crystal). These physical characteristics and its ready availability in most nuclear imaging facilities are distinct advantages for thyroid scanning. In addition, the low absorbed dose to the thyroid permits administration of higher scanning doses and therefore allows for more rapid imaging of the gland with minimal motion artifact. Only 1 to 5 percent of administered ^{99m}Tc pertechnetate is normally

trapped by the thyroid so that image background levels are higher than with radioiodine. Technetium 99m pertechnetate is preferred over radioiodine when the patient has been receiving thyroid-blocking agents (such as propylthiouracil) or is unable to take medication orally, or the study must be completed in less than 2 hours.

Dosimetry

Radiation doses to the adult thyroid and whole body for the radioiodides and ^{99m}Tc pertechnetate are summarized in Table 7–1. With the usual scanning doses, the radiation to the thyroid gland is comparable for ^{123}I and ^{99m}Tc and the whole body dose is only slightly greater with ^{99m}Tc. Both agents provide considerably less radiation dose to the thyroid and to the total body than ^{131}I. The dose to the thyroid from ^{131}I is about 100 times greater than from ^{123}I for the same administered activity (about 1 rad/μCi vs 1 rad/100 μCi). The absorbed thyroid dose from ^{99m}Tc pertechnetate is about 1 rad/5000 μCi.

Because both ^{99m}Tc and the various radio-iodides cross the placenta, and as the fetal thyroid begins accumulation of iodine at about the 12th week of gestation, care must be taken when administering these radiopharmaceuticals during pregnancy. They are also secreted in breast milk in lactating

Table 7-1. RADIOPHARMACEUTICAL AGENTS FOR THYROID IMAGING

| RADIOPHARMA-CEUTICAL | USUAL DOSE | ROUTE OF ADMINIS-TRATION | PHYSICAL HALF-LIFE | TIME TO IMAGING | ABSORBED DOSE ESTIMATES (Rad/mCi)* | | |
					Whole Body	Gonads	Other
[99m]Tc pertechnetate (without perchlorate)	5–10 mCi (185–370 MBq)	IV	6 hr	0.3–1.0 hr	0.01	0.01–0.04	Thyroid† 0.12–0.20 Stomach 0.10–0.30 Colon 0.10–0.30
[123]I	10–20 μCi (0.4–0.7 MBq) (uptake) 100–400 μCi (3.7–14.8 MBq) (scan)	Oral	13 hr	4–24 hr

24 hr | 0.02–0.04 | 0.01–0.03 | Thyroid† 11.0–20.0

Stomach 0.22 |
| [131]I | 4–6 μCi (0.15–0.22 MBq) (uptake) 30–50 μCi (1.1–1.9 MBq) (scan) | Oral | 8.06 days | 4–24 hr

24 hr | 0.50–4.00 | 0.08–0.18 | Thyroid† 1100–1600 |

*To convert to mGy/MBq, divide values by 3.7.
†Indicates critical organ.

women, and so may be transferred to nursing infants. Nursing can usually be resumed 48 to 72 hours after the administration of ^{99m}Tc pertechnetate and approximately 2 to 3 weeks after the administration of [131]I.

On an administered activity basis, the dose to the thyroid is significantly greater in infants and children than in adults, and considerably smaller scanning and uptake doses should be administered to pediatric patients (see Appendix D). In addition, because the radiation dose to the pediatric thyroid from ^{131}I nears the level shown to increase the incidence of thyroid carcinoma, ^{131}I is not usually recommended for children or pregnant women.

Iodine Uptake Test

The thyroid uptake test for the study of thyroid function has remained a routine diagnostic tool even though more sophisticated procedures such as thyroid hormone and thyroid stimulating hormone (TSH) measurements are available. The procedure is simple and easily performed, and gives a useful clinical index of thyroid function.

PRINCIPLE AND TECHNIQUE

Thyroid uptake is based upon the principle that the administered radiopharmaceutical will be concentrated by the thyroid gland in a manner that reflects the gland's handling of stable dietary iodine and therefore the functional status of the gland. The higher the uptake of the radiopharmaceutical, the more active the thyroid, and conversely, the lower the uptake, the less functional the gland. Uptake is conventionally expressed as the percentage of the dose in the thyroid gland at a given time after administration.

PROCEDURE

To aid absorption, it is advisable for patients to be NPO beginning at midnight the day before oral administration of the radionuclide. It is also helpful to determine the functional status of the gastrointestinal tract before administering the radiopharmaceutical, because vomiting or diarrhea may hinder adequate absorption.

To begin the test, 5 to 10 μCi (0.4 to 0.7 MBq) of ^{131}I sodium in either liquid or capsule form are administered. An identical dose, called a "standard," is placed in a neck phantom, and the activity at 18 to 24 hours is compared with that in the patient's thyroid, using a single-crystal counting probe with a flat-field collimator. Such standards obviate the use of decay constants or geometrical corrections in calculating uptakes.

The distance from the face of the probe crystal to the anterior aspect of the neck and the method of counting the ^{131}I standard are the same for all patients. It is usually unnecessary to correct measurements for body blood pool activity in the neck at 24 hours, but this procedure is usual, especially when uptakes earlier than 24 hours are desired. Correction is approximated by measuring the activity in the patient's thigh in the same manner as the neck measurements are performed. The number of counts obtained may then be subtracted from the neck reading to estimate counts isolated in the thyroid gland.

All measurements are usually performed twice, for 1 to 2 minutes each, and are then averaged to calculate the percentage uptake, using the following formula:

$$\% \text{ Thyroid uptake} = \frac{\text{Counts in the neck} - \text{Counts in the thigh}}{\text{Counts in the standard}} \times 100$$

It is occasionally advantageous to perform a 6-hour ^{131}I uptake in addition to the 24-hour determination, particularly for those abnormalities in which the iodine turnover is rapid or in which organification of the trapped iodine is defective. In both of these instances, the uptake obtained at 6 hours may be significantly higher than that at 24 hours due to rapid uptake and secretion, or enhanced washout from the gland. Thyroid uptake procedures may also be performed using protocols for ^{123}I and ^{99m}Tc pertechnetate.

FACTORS AFFECTING UPTAKE

Over the past several decades, there has been an increase in dietary intake of iodides, causing a lower nomal range (approximately 10 to 30 percent) for 24-hour ^{131}I uptake determinations. Increased circulating iodides serve to compete with administered ^{131}I for trapping and binding by the thyroid gland. An increase in the body iodide pool is most frequently caused by an increase in dietary intake of iodine, which reduces significantly the uptake values obtained. Conversely, a decrease in ambient iodine produces an "iodide-starved gland," which traps and binds greater amounts of radioactive iodide producing elevated uptake values. In addition, regional differences in dietary iodide intake give rise to local variations in the normal range. These factors, along with differences in technical aspects of the procedure between laboratories, make it necessary for each facil-

ity to determine its own range of normal values.

Good renal function is essential to normal ^{131}I uptake. In patients with chronic renal failure, iodides usually excreted by the kidneys are retained, producing an increase in the iodide pool. This dilutes the percentage of radioiodine taken up by the gland, resulting in low uptake determinations.

Numerous medications also affect ^{131}I uptake (Table 7–2). In order to successfully perform ^{131}I uptakes, these medications must be withheld for appropriate periods of time before attempting the uptake procedure. Also careful interviewing of patients undergoing the ^{131}I uptake test is necessary to determine whether there is a history of antithyroid drugs, thyroid hormones, iodide preparations, or radiographic contrasts used in gallbladder, kidney, myelographic studies, and CT scans. Of note is the fact that beta-blockers such as propranolol, which are commonly used to combat the clinical manifestations of hyperthyroidism, do not affect the function of the gland and therefore do not interfere with thyroid uptake of the radioactive iodides.

CLINICAL CONSIDERATIONS

Iodine 131 uptake is employed to estimate the function of the thyroid gland by measuring its avidity for administered radioiodide. In the absence of exogenous influences, glands demonstrating a poor avidity for iodide are generally considered to be hypofunctioning, and vice versa for hyperfunctioning glands.

Elevated [131]I Uptake

Primary hyperthyroidism (Graves' disease) and secondary hyperthyroidism commonly produce elevated ^{131}I uptakes. In addition to providing information about the functional status of the gland, these uptakes are useful in determining the level of therapeutic ^{131}I doses for the treatment of Graves' disease. On the other hand, hyperthyroidism produced by toxic nodular goiters (Plummer's disease) frequently yields uptake values in the normal range. Therefore, a normal ^{131}I uptake alone cannot be used to exclude the diagnosis of hyperthyroidism when it is clinically suspected.

Elevated ^{131}I uptakes also may be produced

Table 7–2. COMPOUNDS THAT MAY DECREASE THYROID IODINE UPTAKE

MEDICATION		TIME
Adrenocorticosteroids	Perchlorate	
Amiodarone	Propylthiouracil	
Bromides	Salicylates (large doses)	
Butazolidine	Sulfonamides	1 week
Mercurials	Tapazole	
Nitrates	Thiocyanate	
Iodine solution (Lugol's)		
Kelp		2 weeks
Some cough medicines and vitamin preparations		
Triiodothyronine (Cytomel)		
Thyroid extract (Synthroid, Proloid)		3 weeks
Intravenous contrast agents		1–2 months
Oral cholecystographic agents		3–6 months
Oil-based iodinated contrast		
Bronchographic		6–12 months
Myelographic		2–10 years

by a variety of other conditions (Table 7–3), including any state of the gland characterized by increased avidity of the organ for iodide. The so-called "iodine rebound phenomenon" may result from the release of thyroid stimulating hormone (TSH) by the pituitary following sudden withdrawal from thyroid hormone suppression therapy. It may also result from hormone synthesis rebound after withdrawal of antithyroid drugs such as propylthiouracil.

Reduced ^{131}I Uptake

Primary or secondary hypothyroidism may produce decreased ^{131}I uptake. Primary hypothyroidism is a failure of the gland itself to respond to TSH, whereas secondary hy-

Table 7–3. FACTORS AFFECTING IODINE UPTAKE

* *Increased uptake*
  Hyperthyroidism (diffuse or nodular goiter)
  Early Hashimoto's thyroiditis
  Rebound after abrupt withdrawal of antithyroid medication
  Enzyme defects
  Iodine starvation
  Hypoalbuminemia
* *Decreased uptake*
  Hypothyroidism (primary or secondary)
  Iodine overload (especially radiographic contrast)
  Medications (see Table 7–2)
  Subacute thyroiditis
  Thyroid hormone therapy

pothyroidism is due to insufficient pituitary secretion of TSH. However, because of the recent decrease in the lower limits of normal for ^{131}I uptake due to increased dietary iodides, it has become increasingly difficult to use reduced ^{131}I uptake as an indicator of hypothyroidism.

Of note in considering the causes of decreased ^{131}I uptake are the numerous medications outlined in Table 7–2. Again, withdrawal of the medications for the time period given in the table is necessary to obtain accurate measures of thyroid function.

Special Tests of Thyroid Function

At times it may be advantageous to repeat thyroid uptake and imaging procedures after the administration of various hormonal preparations in order to assess their effect on the gland. The most common of these tests are the thyroid stimulation and thyroid suppression examinations. Each test has a specific purpose, and each requires the prior performance of a routine uptake and thyroid scan. Both of these examinations are primarily employed to evaluate functioning thyroid nodules (hot nodules) or diffuse toxic goiters.

THYROID SUPPRESSION TEST

The aim of the thyroid suppression test is to determine the autonomy of a functioning hot nodule or a diffusely enlarged gland. It consists of obtaining 24-hour ^{131}I uptakes and images, before and after attempted suppression of the nodule or gland with exogenous thyroid hormone (Fig. 7–2). The administration of thyroid hormones (T_3) produces a negative feedback to the pituitary axis, which results in cessation of TSH production and release. Since the stimulatory effect of TSH on normal thyroid tissue is no longer present, thyroid function as determined by ^{131}I uptake diminishes. Failure of uptake by the thyroid or a thyroid nodule to diminish under such decreased stimulation indicates that the tissue is not under the regulatory mechanism of the pituitary-hypothalamic axis; that is, it is functioning autonomously.

Upon completion of suppression therapy (100 mcg/day of Cytomel [liothyronine sodium] for 7 days), the 24-hour ^{131}I uptake in a normal thyroid gland falls to at least 50 percent of the presuppression value. If, however, the gland or nodule is autonomous, the uptake will not suppress to this level. Such autonomy can be found in patients with hyperthyroidism produced either by diffuse hyperplasia of the gland as in Graves' disease or by a toxic nodule as in Plummer's disease, or with euthyroid autonomous nodules.

Because nontoxic autonomously functioning nodules frequently do not subsequently become toxic, treatment of these entities varies considerably from toxic nodules. When the thyroid suppression test is employed to evaluate the possible autonomy of a hot nodule, imaging of the gland with radioiodine should also be performed. This permits not only the identification of the nodule but also assessment of the change in function of the nodule itself. In some cases, normally functioning tissue in the remainder of the thyroid gland may be suppressed sufficiently to allow a fall to 50 percent or less of the pre-T_3 value, even though regional uptake of radioiodine in the nodule has not changed significantly. In these cases, visual or computer region-of-interest assessment of the uptake change in the nodule during the examination gives evidence of autonomy in the presence of false-negative suppression.

The thyroid suppression test has largely been replaced by laboratory assessments of TSH response to thyroid releasing hormone (TRH) administration. This procedure allows assessment of gland autonomy without the administration of thyroid hormone in patients who may already be thyrotoxic.

TSH STIMULATION TEST

The current indications for TSH stimulation before thyroid imaging consist of (1) the identification of thyroid tissue suppressed by autonomously functioning thyroid nodules and (2) identification of functioning thyroid metastases. All other previous indications have largely been replaced by laboratory determinations of TSH response to TRH administration.

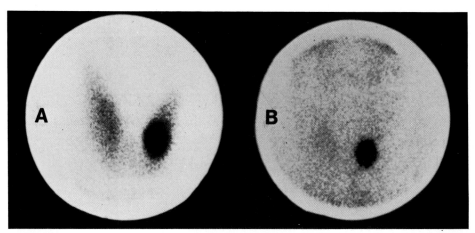

Figure 7–2. Thyroid suppression test. (A) A [99mTc] pertechnetate thyroid image in the anterior view demonstrates a solitary hot nodule in the midportion of the left lobe of the gland with mild suppression of activity in the remainder of the gland. (B) A repeat [99mTc] pertechnetate image obtained after 2 weeks of T_3 (Cytomel) suppression demonstrates suppression of the normal thyroid gland without suppression of the hot nodule. An ^{131}I uptake performed at the same time disclosed an insignificant decrease in ^{131}I uptake in the region of the hot nodule. The findings are compatible with an autonomous hyperfunctioning adenoma.

The TSH stimulation test requires subcutaneous administration of 10 U/day of TSH for 3 days. This is followed by routine imaging of the thyroid gland, or of the total body if metastatic foci are being sought.

A TSH stimulation test is most often used to further evaluate a scan with one or more focal areas of increased activity in the thyroid bed without imaging surrounding normal thyroid tissue. It is important to differentiate between localized functioning adenomas and residual islands of functioning tissue in a diseased gland, such as may be found in the late stages of thyroiditis or post-surgically when small quantities of residually functioning tissue may have been left in the neck. If any additional thyroid tissue is identified after the administration of TSH, this may be taken as evidence of suppression of normal tissue by autonomously functioning nodules. Based on clinical and laboratory findings, appropriate therapy may then be instituted.

PERCHLORATE WASHOUT TEST

This test is occasionally useful for identifying congenital or acquired organification defects in the thyroid gland. In such diseases as thyroiditis, an uncoupling of the trapping and organification mechanisms may occur, producing a thyroid gland that traps iodine but does not fix or organify it. In a patient with such a defect, the administration of sodium perchlorate successfully competes with radioiodine molecules for trapping sites in the thyroid gland. Because previously administered radioiodine is not bound within the gland, it is discharged from the thyroid by the perchlorate molecules, which supplant radioiodine at the trapping sites.

The procedure consists of the oral administration of ^{131}I or ^{123}I with a 2-hour uptake determination. At least 1 gm of potassium perchlorate or sodium perchlorate is then administered orally and thyroid uptakes are obtained every 1/2 hour for the next 2 hours. In normal patients, the radioiodine uptake obtained 2 hours after the administration of perchlorate is essentially unchanged from the initial determination. However, in patients with organification defects, the perchlorate causes a discharge of iodine from the thyroid gland, producing at least a 10 percent drop in the initial uptake value at 2 hours.

Clinical Applications

While ^{131}I may still be used for obtaining thyroid uptakes, ^{99m}Tc pertechnetate and ^{123}I sodium remain the agents of choice for obtaining maximum morphologic detail of the thyroid gland with the gamma camera. Technetium 99m pertechnetate is probably the most commonly used radiopharmaceutical for imaging the thyroid because of its cheaper cost and its ready availability. However, either radionuclide provides images of excellent quality, although ^{131}I is preferable for imaging ectopic tissue.

Imaging with ^{99m}Tc pertechnetate or radioiodine requires no prior preparation of the patient. However, as with uptake studies, a brief screening of patients for a possible history of recent medication or iodinated contrast administration is advisable. In addition, before imaging is begun, palpation of the thyroid gland, with the patient sitting upright, is recommended to assess any enlargement or nodules. The prior localization of palpable nodules within the gland makes it much easier to relocate these abnormalities with the patient in the supine scanning position, when marker localization may be required.

Even with a history of recent radioiodinated contrast or suppressive medications, it is frequently possible to obtain reasonably good anatomic assessment of the thyroid gland with ^{99m}Tc when it is not possible with radioiodine. This, in part, is related to the significantly greater allowable activity for pertechnetate scanning compared with radioiodine. However, when feasible, the patient should return after an appropriate interval of withdrawal from the interfering drug for a more definitive examination.

TECHNICAL CONSIDERATIONS

The thyroid is imaged 20 minutes after the intravenous administration of 2 to 5 mCi (74 to 185 MBq) of ^{99m}Tc pertechnetate, using a scintillation camera with a pinhole collimator. Anterior and left and right anterior oblique images are then obtained for 200,000 to 300,000 counts each with the patient supine and neck extended. In addition, the position of palpable nodules under investigation should be documented with a view obtained with a radioactive marker placed on the lesion. This aids in an accurate correlation of the physical and scan findings. The oblique images are essential for the identification of laterally and posteriorly placed nodules that might be missed with simple anterior imaging.

In some laboratories, the static images are preceded by a flow study of the thyroid. If this is to be done, at least 10 mCi (370 MBq) of ^{99m}Tc pertechnetate should be utilized, as should a parallel hole collimator. The field of view is from the level of the salivary glands to the upper sternum. An immediate static image of the blood pool distribution may be obtained, allowing for differentiation of cystic and solid masses. The initial static image also allows a relative measure of the size of the thyroid gland in comparison with the salivary glands as well as a relative measure of the uptake ratio between these glands.

Imaging with ^{123}I may be performed at 2 to 6 hours following the oral administration of 100 μCi (3.7 MBq), although imaging at 24 hours after 200 to 400 μCi (7.4 to 14.8 MBq) may give a more accurate indication of the distribution of organified iodine within the gland.

NORMAL THYROID IMAGES

The normal thyroid gland is a bilobed organ with reasonably homogeneous distribution of activity in both lobes. The normal gland weighs between 15 and 25 gm total, and each lobe measures approximately 2 × 5 cm. Slight asymmetry in the sizes of the lobes is common, with the right lobe generally dominating. The lobes are usually joined inferiorly and medially by the thyroid isthmus, which may demonstrate relatively decreased activity compared with the adjacent lobes. In some instances, complete absence of activity is noted in this region. In a small number of patients, a pyramidal lobe is identified arising from the isthmus or medial aspect of one lobe and extending superiorly and medially. Although this is a common variation, it may be accentuated in postsurgical patients and in patients with diffuse thyroid abnormalities such as Hashimoto's thyroiditis or Graves' disease. Less common variants of thyroid configuration include total congenital absence of one lobe, substernal extension of the gland, or a sublingual thyroid with functioning tissue at the base of the tongue.

The most common artifact of ^{99m}Tc pertechnetate studies of the thyroid is produced by activity secreted by the salivary glands and swallowed by the patient. This usually presents as a linear area of esophageal activity in the midline of the image. If this complicates interpretation or causes confusion with an enlarged pyramidal lobe, repeat imaging should be performed after clearing the esophagus with drinking water.

ABNORMAL IMAGES

Histologically Normal Ectopic Thyroid Tissue

This may occur in the neck (lingual thyroid) (Fig. 7–3), pelvis (struma ovarii), or retrosternally in the region of the mediastinum (substernal goiter). When such ectopic sites are suspected, 24-hour imaging with ^{131}I sodium is the method of choice. Because of interfering salivary gland activity in the neck and absorption of 140 keV gamma rays by the sternum or soft tissues of the abdomen and pelvis, ^{99m}Tc pertechnetate is generally not as useful for imaging these areas. In addition, the longer half-life of ^{131}I allows for delayed imaging at 24 and 48 hours, permitting higher target/nontarget ratios and clearance of the radiopharmaceutical from the kidneys and urinary bladder.

Identification of an anterior mediastinal mass on chest radiographs is the most frequent indication for ^{131}I imaging of the chest. Intrathoracic thyroid tissue most commonly presents as a substernal extension of a cervical thyroid goiter. Less commonly it presents as a mediastinal mass anatomically unrelated to the thyroid gland. Thoracic thyroid tissue is most frequently found in middle-aged females but may occur in either sex at any age. Thyroid tissue in the chest may not demonstrate ^{131}I uptake as intensely as that in the neck, and some mediastinal thyroid tissue may not function at all. Therefore, while uptake in a mediastinal or substernal mass indicates the tissue to be thyroid-related, lack of concentration of ^{131}I does not necessarily exclude that diagnosis.

Aberrant functioning thyroid tissue known as struma ovarii is rarely identified in some ovarian teratomas. Even more rarely this tissue may hyperfunction, producing symptoms of hyperthyroidism with suppression of function in the normal thyroid.

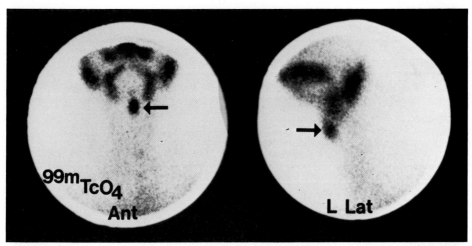

Figure 7–3. Lingual thyroid. Anterior and lateral views of the cervical region from a ^{99m}Tc pertechnetate study demonstrate no activity in the region of the thyroid bed, but a focal area of increased activity is seen high in the midline of the neck near the base of the tongue (arrow), compatible with a lingual thyroid. The patient was clinically hypothyroid.

Thyroid Nodules

The most common indication for radio-nuclide thyroid imaging is for the evaluation of a palpable nodule in the thyroid bed. Imaging provides information regarding the functional status of the nodule and may indicate the presence of additional nodules. Conventionally, nodules are classified at imaging with respect to the relative amount of activity present. Cold nodules demonstrate an essential absence of activity, whereas hot nodules are identified by focally increased activity compared with the normal thyroid parenchyma. Nodules that are neither hot nor cold but contain activity comparable to that of the surrounding gland are frequently termed "warm" nodules.

Cold Nodule. A nonfunctioning thyroid nodule is essentially a nonspecific finding and may be due to any of numerous pathologies (Table 7–4). While the overwhelming majority of "cold" nodules are benign, the small percentage that prove to be cancerous is sufficient to warrant further investigation and/or therapy, depending on the clinical circumstances. The reported percentage of solitary cold nodules harboring thyroid cancer varies depending on the clinical bias of the particular study but is generally felt to be within the range of 15 to 25 percent. The likelihood of carcinoma significantly increases if the patient is a young female or a male of any age. Suspicion is further in-creased if associated lymphadenopathy is identified or if the nodule fails to decrease in size after a trial of thyroid hormone suppression. If a history of previous head and neck radiation therapy is elicited, a cold nodule has about a 40 percent chance of being malignant (Table 7–5).

Ultrasound may frequently be of value in distinguishing between a benign cystic abnormality and a solid lesion, which may harbor a neoplasm (Fig. 7–4). In addition, anterior radionuclide thyroid angiography performed with ^{99m}Tc pertechnetate and a gamma camera may also provide information regarding the perfusion status of the lesion. Definite evidence of perfusion in the region of a cold nodule is compatible with a solid lesion in need of further investigation.

Hot Nodule. The vast majority of nodules demonstrating increased radionuclide con-

Table 7–4. PATHOLOGIES OF SOLITARY COLD THYROID NODULE

Colloid cyst Adenoma	70–75 percent
Carcinoma	15–25 percent
Focal area of thyroiditis Abscess Hemorrhage Lymphoma, metastases Parathyroid adenoma Lymph nodes	

Table 7–5. CLINICAL FACTORS INFLUENCING TREATMENT OF COLD THYROID NODULE*

FACTORS TENDING TOWARD BENIGN	FACTORS TENDING TOWARD MALIGNANT
• Older patients	• Young patients
• Females	• Males
• Sudden onset	• History of radiation to head or neck
• Tender or soft lesion	• Hard lesion
• Multiple nodules	• Other masses in neck
• Shrinkage on thyroid hormone	• No shrinkage on thyroid hormone
	• Familial history of thyroid carcinoma

*None of these factors is absolute.

centration are benign, although thyroid carcinoma has been described in a small percentage (less than 1 percent). These nodules almost always represent hyperfunctioning adenomas, of which up to half are autonomous. Autonomous functioning nodules function independently of the thyroid pituitary axis feedback mechanism; thus, they are not suppressible with exogenous thyroid hormone. Whether a nodule is autonomous or not may be determined by the thyroid suppression test. (See Special Tests of Thyroid Function.) Autonomous hyperfunctioning nodules may produce enough thyroid hormone to inhibit pituitary secretion of TSH and secondarily suppress function in the surrounding normal thyroid tissue, which still responds to appropriate feedback mechanisms. Demonstration of this suppressed tissue may be identified using a TSH stimulation test.

Discordant Thyroid Nodule. By using iodine imaging, a small number of cases of hot nodules on ^{99m}Tc pertechnetate imaging have subsequently proven to be cold, and some of those lesions have been shown to be thyroid carcinoma. Theoretically, the discordant images are produced by the preservation of technetium trapping, but not of organification of iodine within the nodules. Since the ^{99m}Tc pertechnetate scan is performed at 20 minutes, the avid trapping of pertechnetate by the nodules renders a focal area of increased activity. However, with radioiodine imaging, which is normally performed at 24 hours, the trapped radiopharmaceutical has not been organified and has thus washed out of the nodule, giving rise to a cold area on the scan (Fig. 7–5). It has been recommended that patients demonstrating solitary hot nodules on pertechnetate scans be reimaged using an iodine agent to determine whether the lesion represents a discordant nodule or a true hyperfunctioning adenoma. If the lesion proves to be discordant, further investigation is warranted, depending on the clinical status of the patient.

Warm Nodule. Although some warm nodules do function normally, many are actually cold nodules deep within the thyroid gland with overlying normally functioning tissue. Oblique views may often disclose the true nature of these abnormalities. However, frequently the abnormality can only be classified as warm even after thorough imaging. Because of the risk of carcinoma in a cold nodule obscured by overlying tissue, it is probably prudent to classify these abnormalities as "cold" and in need of further investigation.

Multinodular Gland

Multinodular goiter typically presents as an enlarged gland with multiple cold, warm, and hot areas, which give the gland a coarsely patchy appearance (Fig. 7–6). These nodules generally constitute a spectrum of thyroid adenomas ranging from hyperfunctioning to cystic or degenerating lesions. This type of gland is most frequent in middle-aged females but may occur in younger individuals, usually females. In adults, the cold lesions identified in a multinodular goiter are significantly less likely to represent carcinoma than are solitary cold nodules. However, dominant or otherwise suspicious cold nodules in a multinodular goiter warrant further characterization. In children, however, multinodular goiters with cold lesions are somewhat more likely to harbor malignant neoplasms than they are in adults, although the incidence is still low. In addition, any patient with a previous history of head

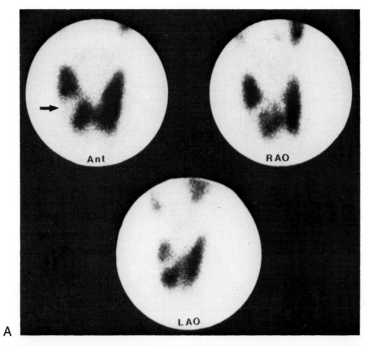

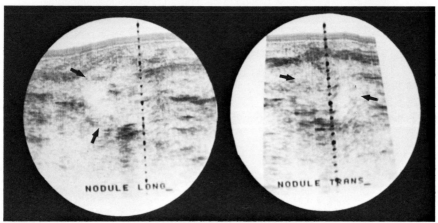

Figure 7–4. Nonfunctioning thyroid adenoma presenting as a cold nodule (arrow) in the right lobe of the thyroid. (A) The ⁹⁹ᵐTc pertechnetate scan also demonstrates normal salivary gland activity at the top of the images. (B) Ultrasound images in the region of the nodule demonstrate a solid-appearing lesion.

and neck radiation is also at higher risk for carcinoma.

Occasionally, multinodular goiter may be mimicked by thyroiditis with multifocal involvement of the gland. This, however, is an unusual occurrence, and differentiation on clinical and laboratory grounds is usually possible.

Diffuse Toxic Goiter

This disease, also known as Graves' disease, usually presents with varying degrees of thyromegaly, with notably uniform distribution of increased activity throughout the thyroid gland and frequently with a prominent pyramidal lobe (Fig. 7–7). Significantly, in these patients, the ⁹⁹ᵐTc perfusion study generally shows increased perfusion to the gland, with rapid accumulation of the radionuclide in the organ compatible with the increased avidity of the gland for iodine (Fig. 7–8). This finding, in conjunction with diffusely increased activity in an enlarged gland, may be taken as supportive evidence for hyperthyroidism.

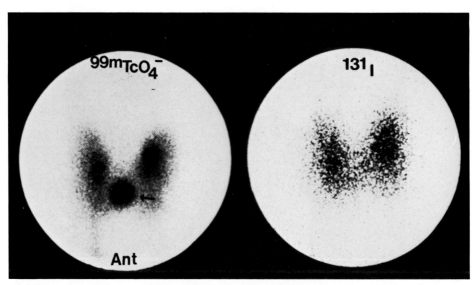

Figure 7–5. Discordant nodule. Two images obtained in a patient with a prominent nodule in the thyroid isthmus demonstrate increased ^{99m}Tc pertechnetate activity in the region of the nodule (arrow) but no significant activity when imaged with ^{131}I. At surgery, this lesion proved to be a mixed papillary follicular carcinoma.

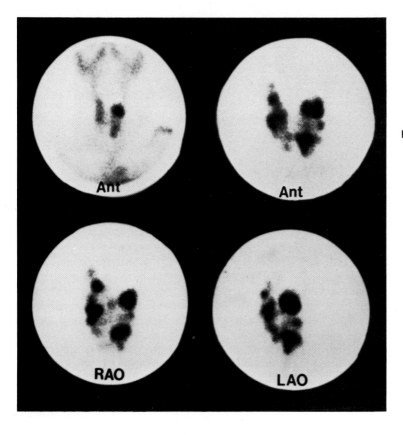

Figure 7–6. Multinodular goiter. An immediate postinjection image obtained with a parallel-hole collimator demonstrates mottled ^{99m}Tc pertechnetate activity in the region of an enlarged thyroid gland. Subsequent detailed pinhole views in anterior and oblique projections show multiple hot and cold areas in the gland compatible with the typical appearance of multinodular goiter.

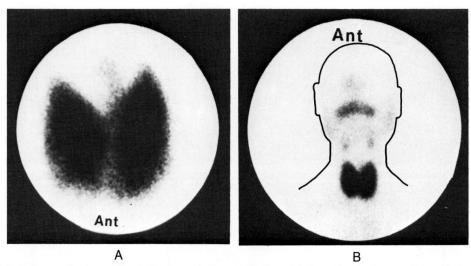

Figure 7–7. Diffuse goiter in a patient with Graves' disease. (A) The pinhole collimator image demonstrates a large gland with increased activity and a pyramidal lobe arising from the superior aspect of the left lobe. (B) An image obtained with the parallel-hole collimator demonstrates the relatively increased trapping of ^{99m}Tc pertechnetate in the thyroid compared with the salivary gland activity.

Although cold nodules are sometimes found in patients with diffuse toxic goiter, carcinoma under these circumstances is exceedingly uncommon. However, it is still prudent to further evaluate any solitary cold nodules occurring in this setting.

Thyroiditis

Chronic thyroiditis (Hashimoto's thyroiditis) is the most common form of inflammatory disease of the thyroid. The disease is thought to be autoimmune in origin and is much more common in females. Thyromegaly is usually the presenting finding, although occasionally symptoms of mild hyperthyroidism or hypothyroidism may be present, depending on the stage and severity of the disease.

The scan appearance of the thyroid varies from diffusely uniform increased activity in the gland (which may resemble Graves' disease) to a coarse patchy distribution or focal or diffuse absence of activity within the gland (which may mimic multinodular goiter).

The more uncommon diseases of acute (bacterial) and subacute (viral) thyroiditis have such typical clinical features that they are usually diagnosed on physical and clinical grounds, and scanning generally plays little role in their evaluation. Subacute thyroiditis usually presents as a painful swollen gland with elevated circulating thyroid hormone levels but with markedly depressed ^{131}I uptake. Attempts at imaging usually show little or no localization of radiopharmaceutical in the gland.

Thyroid Carcinoma

Well-differentiated papillary, follicular, and mixed carcinomas represent about 75 percent of all primary thyroid malignancies. Rarely are these lesions strictly the single-cell type, and the papillary or follicular term refers to the predominant histology. The overall prognosis of patients with these well-differentiated types of thyroid cancer is quite good, with a 5-year survival rate of over 95 percent in properly treated patients. Well-differentiated papillary carcinomas tend to metastasize to local neck nodes, whereas follicular lesions tend to hematogenously metastasize with a predilection for lungs and skeleton. The metastases of either lesion may histologically present the characteristics of the other; i.e., primary follicular lesions may give predominantly papillary metastases or vice versa.

The remaining thyroid malignancies are primarily anaplastic or poorly differentiated carcinomas (20 percent) and occur primarily in older patients. The prognosis is generally poor. Finally, medullary carcinoma of the thyroid parenchyma composes about 5 percent of malignant thyroid lesions. This cancer may be associated with other endocrine lesions such as pheochromocytoma, may ac-

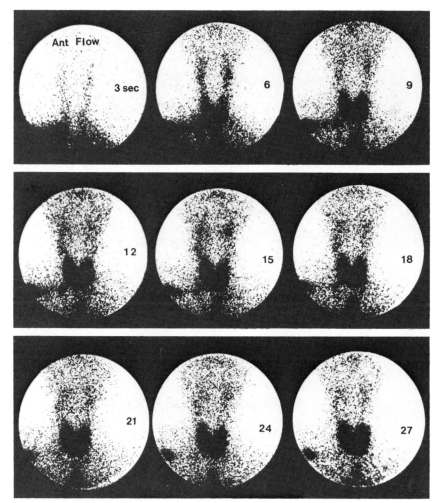

Figure 7–8. Graves' disease. The flow study performed with ^{99m}Tc pertechnetate demonstrates extremely rapid trapping (within 30 seconds).

tively secrete hormones (most notably thyrocalcitonin), and may be familial.

Clinically and scintigraphically, primary carcinomas of the thyroid may initially present as discrete thyroid nodules, or as enlargement of one lobe with or without cervical nodal, or distant metastases. When discrete, the lesions are almost invariably demonstrated as cold areas on the radionuclide images. Using a gamma camera, ^{99m}Tc, and a pinhole collimator, 80 percent of lesions 8 mm in diameter are detected.

Because the metastatic lesions of well-differentiated thyroid carcinomas with follicular elements frequently concentrate radioiodine, total body imaging with ^{131}I may be of value in following post-thyroidectomy patients to detect possible metastases or assess the re-

sults of treatment of known metastatic lesions (Fig. 7–9). Because medullary and anaplastic carcinomas rarely concentrate ^{131}I, the procedure generally is of no use in following these patients, nor is ^{131}I useful in a therapeutic capacity.

Whole-body evaluation for metastatic thyroid disease is first performed within 1 to 2 months after total or subtotal thyroidectomy. Thyroid hormone replacement is withheld during this period to allow for endogenous TSH stimulation of any remaining normal tissue in the thyroid bed and any functioning metastatic lesions. This stimulation allows even poorly functioning or small amounts of tissue to be maximally visualized. After the oral administration of approximately 3 to 5 mCi (111 to 185 MBq) of ^{131}I sodium, sequen-

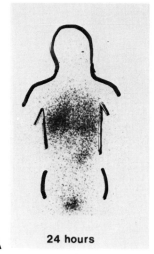 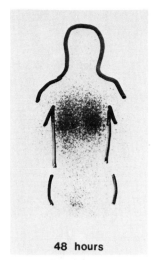

A **24 hours**   **48 hours**

Figure 7–9. Metastatic disease from thyroid carcinoma. (A) The anterior whole-body images obtained at 24 and 48 hours demonstrate a large amount of lung activity. The 24-hour image also shows some activity in the bowel and bladder. In many cases, it is necessary to image the patient again at 72 or 96 hours. (B) A chest radiograph demonstrates multiple hematogenous metastases, in this case due to a mixed papillary-follicular carcinoma.

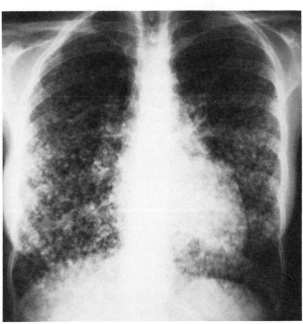

B

tial whole-body images are obtained for the next several days, generally at 48, 72, and, if necessary, 96 hours. A whole-body imaging device or large-field-of-view gamma camera may be used. If gamma camera spot images are the method of imaging, it is important to include adequate neck, chest, abdominal, and pelvic views in the anterior position as well as appropriate posterior images. Imaging is usually not performed in the first 24 hours because of high background body radiation, and frequently the best images are obtained at 72 to 96 hours. Knowledge of the normal distribution of ^{131}I before and after thyroid ablation is essential (Fig. 7–10).

If significant functioning thyroid tissue remains in the neck—as is frequently the case even after "total" thyroidectomy—ablation of the remaining tissue is urged with high-dose ^{131}I therapy. Because metastatic lesions are only infrequently visualized with ^{131}I whole-body imaging when there is functioning thyroid in the neck, ablation of residual tissue allows for sufficient TSH stimulation by the pituitary to permit functioning of distant metastatic sites and therefore allows their detection on follow-up ^{131}I imaging. Adequate endogenous TSH stimulation usually takes 4 to 6 weeks. This method is in most cases preferable to the exogenous administra-

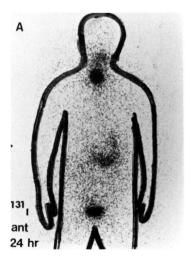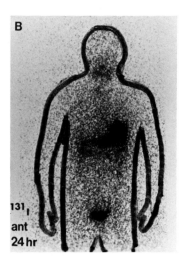

Figure 7–10. Whole-body distribution of ^{131}I displayed at 24 hours after oral administration. (A) Activity is present in the thyroid and salivary glands, stomach, and bladder of a patient who has residual thyroid tissue. After ablation or total thyroidectomy (B), activity is present in salivary glands, stomach, and bladder as well as much greater background activity.

tion of TSH. However, in some laboratories, intramuscular TSH administration is routinely employed before imaging. Once all residual thyroid tissue in the neck has been ablated, follow-up whole-body imaging with ^{131}I may be performed at 6-month to 1-year intervals as needed to survey for possible metastases. For maximum sensitivity in detecting functioning lesions, the patient's hormone replacement should be withheld for approximately 4 to 6 weeks before each follow-up scan, with or without concomitant administration of exogenous TSH.

In patients with suspected metastatic lesions to the skeleton, a radionuclide bone scan before the administration of a whole-body ^{131}I scanning dose may be done, although thyroid metastases to bone are not uncommonly "cold" and may go undetected on phosphate bone scans.

^{131}I Therapy in Thyroid Disease

While this introduction to diagnostic radionuclide techniques is primarily restricted to in vivo imaging methods, a brief discussion of the use of ^{131}I in the treatment of thyroid disease is appropriate, because it plays an important role in the control and cure of certain thyroid diseases. Each institution should develop a protocol for patient care and personnel safety when patients are hospitalized for radioiodine therapy. This needs to comply with relevant local, state, and/or Nuclear Regulatory Commission require-

ments. A sample protocol is provided in Appendix G. The primary therapeutic uses of ^{131}I lie in (1) the treatment of hyperthyroidism caused by either diffuse or nodular goiter, (2) the treatment of functioning thyroid metastases, and (3) the ablation of the thyroid gland in certain clinical circumstances.

PRINCIPLE

Whether benign or neoplastic, any thyroid tissue that demonstrates the capability of producing thyroid hormone will trap and organify stable iodine or its radioactive isotopes. Once a radioactive form of iodine has been taken up by the functioning tissue, therapeutic effects are made possible by the delivery of destructive ionizing radiation, primarily in the form of relatively high-energy beta emissions. Subsequent to irradiation, cell death occurs over a period of weeks to months. The beta-emitting properties of ^{131}I have made this radioisotope the most useful for the elimination of unwanted benign or malignant thyroid tissue.

Several factors influence the dose of radiation delivered to functioning thyroid tissue by ^{131}I and therefore govern its effectiveness as a therapeutic agent. These include (1) the degree of uptake of ^{131}I, (2) the bulk of tissue to be destroyed, (3) the length of residence of ^{131}I within the gland, (4) the distribution of ^{131}I within the tissue, and (5) the radiosensitivity of the particular thyroid cells. A serum pregnancy test should be performed on any woman of childbearing age for whom there may be a question of adequate birth control.

HYPERTHYROIDISM

The three basic approaches to the therapy of hyperthyroidism are (1) antithyroid drugs such as propylthiouracil, (2) surgery, and (3) [131]I therapy. Iodine 131 is currently regarded by many as the treatment of choice for hyperthyroidism in patients over age 30 and in patients of any age when hyperthyroidism is accompanied by medical complications or when other treatments have failed. Although antithyroid drugs are frequently used as an initial approach to the control of diffuse toxic goiter (Graves' disease), such drugs are generally not employed in the treatment of toxic nodules or multinodular goiter. In a significant number of patients with Graves' disease, conventional drug therapy either produces intolerable side effects or does not adequately control the disease. In these patients and in those with toxic nodular disease,[131]I therapy should be considered as an alternative to surgery. [131]I therapy is also of value (1) in patients with recurrent hyperthyroidism after previous thyroidectomy when repeat surgery would cause enhanced risks, (2) in children who have experienced toxicity to antithyroid drugs, and (3) for patients who refuse thyroidectomy.

While there is a certain amount of controversy regarding the treatment of children and adolescents with ^{131}I, it should be pointed out that the complication rate in children undergoing thyroid surgery is significantly higher than in adults and that antithyroid therapy in children carries a significantly higher risk of toxicity and relapse compared with that experienced in adults. As many as 80 percent of children and adolescents treated for Graves' disease with antithyroid drugs will eventually require ^{131}I therapy. On the other hand, there is little evidence to indicate significant radiation carcinogenesis from therapeutic doses of ^{131}I in these patients. Still, some physicians choose not to employ ^{131}I therapy routinely in children or even in adults under age 40.

Proposed methods of calculating doses for treating hyperthyroidism are numerous and varied. Determination of dose follows one of two basic philosophies, which are referred to as low-dose and high-dose therapy. The difference in approaches is predicated on the likelihood of the induction of hypothyroidism. In low-dose therapy there is an emphasis on reducing the resulting hypothyroidism in the first year after therapy and acceptance of any morbidity associated with the prolonged presence of hyperthyroidism. However, this method does not appear to alter the incidence of hypothyroidism after one year. High-dose therapy considers that hypothyroidism is an acceptable risk and, indeed, almost an inevitability of ^{131}I therapy or Graves' disease itself and that rapid reduction in thyroid function is the most important objective of therapy.

In both cases, formulas for the calculation of actual doses generally take into account one or more of the following: the size of the gland, the presence or absence of nodularity in the gland, and the results of the 24-hour[131]I uptake test. Of necessity, palpation, which is used to estimate the mass of the thyroid gland, often introduces a substantial subjective error into the calculation of dose, although assessment of thyroid images and the occasional use of sonography may aid in improving the estimate of gland size. However, with experience, a reasonable estimate can be made by palpation alone.

In general, for treatment of diffuse goiter, low-dose therapy may be in the range of 3 to 6 mCi (111 to 222 MBq) of ^{131}I in patients with no evidence of thyroid nodularity. This represents approximately 50 to 80 μCi (1.85 to 2.96 MBq) of ^{131}I per gram of thyroid tissue, resulting in an absorbed dose of at least 5000 rad (50 Gy). These doses may be repeated at 3- to 6-month intervals as necessary for the control of hyperthyroidism. In the case of high-dose therapy, doses in the range of 8 to 20 mCi (296 to 740 MBq) or higher may be initially administered to allow for definitive therapy.

Administered doses are frequently selected at the higher end of the dose range if the patients are severely hyperthyroid or have large glands or significant cardiac disease aggravated by their thyrotoxic state. With high-dose therapy, retreatment is usually unnecessary.

Hyperthyroidism related to toxic nodular goiter (Plummer's disease) is particularly resistant to radioactive iodine therapy and frequently requires doses 2 to 3 times larger than those applicable in diffuse toxic goiter. Thus, in addition to ^{131}I uptakes, thyroid imaging is usually employed before ^{131}I therapy to distinguish toxic nodular goiter from Graves' disease. Large multinodular goiters may require doses in excess of 30 mCi (1.11 GBq), and multiple treatments may be needed. Solitary toxic nodules may generally be successfully treated with administered doses in the 15 to 25 mCi (555 to 925 MBq) range. Even with such large doses, it is not usual to induce hypothyroidism.

Regardless of the type of dose regimen employed, it is often difficult to accurately predict the outcome of radioactive iodine therapy in a given patient. Results are frequently significantly affected by a number of variables: (1) nodular thyroids (including those of nodular Graves' disease) are usually more resistant and require larger doses; (2) blacks appear more resistant than whites; (3) bulkier thyroid glands demonstrate diminished response; (4) prior administration of antithyroid drugs increases resistance; and (5) patients with severe hyperthyroidism may likewise be less responsive, possibly based upon the rapid turnover of ^{131}I within the gland.

Although there is a clear correlation between the dose of radioiodine used and the onset of hypothyroidism in the first year after therapy, the incidence of hypothyroidism after that time shows less correlation with the dose employed. At least 50 percent of patients exhibit hypothyroidism ten years after therapy regardless of the ^{131}I dose regimen chosen. Therefore, careful follow-up is necessary in all patients who become initially euthyroid, to watch for the development of late hypothyroidism. Aside from latent hypothyroidism, other complications of radioiodine therapy for hyperthyroidism are rare. No evidence exists of increased incidence of radiation-induced malignancies, including thyroid cancer and leukemia after radioiodine therapy. No change in fertility rates or genetic damage in offspring has been found. Thyroid storm and clinically significant radiation thyroiditis are very uncommon.

Patient Preparation

Prior to the oral administration of a therapeutic dose of ^{131}I, the diagnosis of toxic goiter must have been firmly established on the basis of physical examination, history, and circulating serum thyroid hormone levels. An ^{131}I uptake to exclude hyperthyroidism due to such diseases as silent, painless acute thyroiditis and to gauge the dose required should be routinely performed. The patient should remain NPO after midnight the evening before the therapy. Female patients should be carefully screened for possible pregnancy. Pregnancy is a contraindication for radioiodine therapy because of possible somatic or genetic injury to the fetus or the risk of injury to the fetal thyroid gland after the first trimester. In lactating mothers, therapy should be instituted only if the patient is willing to forgo breast-feeding, since the iodine is secreted in breast milk.

Although pretreatment with antithyroid drugs remains somewhat controversial in hyperthyroid patients who are awaiting radioiodine therapy, certain patients with severe thyrotoxicity should probably be pretreated to avoid worsening the clinical status or causing thyroid storm (a remote possibility), which results from the sudden release of hormone from the gland following radiation destruction of thyroid follicles.

If antithyroid drugs are already in use, they should be discontinued for 5 to 7 days before the ^{131}I treatment is administered, depending on the clinical status of the patient. If clinically necessary, these drugs may be readministered 7 to 10 days after therapy. As an alternative, beta-adrenergic blocking agents such as propranolol may be employed throughout the therapy period, because they do not affect thyroid function and therefore permit recirculation of ^{131}I in the gland for maximum radiation effect.

In the first week after a therapeutic dose of radioiodine, a patient may experience several symptoms, including sore throat, dysphagia, and an increase in hyperthyroid symptoms due to increased release of hormone. Whichever dose regimen is used, there is generally no significant improvement in hyperthyroid symptomatology for approximately 3 to 6 weeks after treatment, with maximum effects evidenced at 3 to 4 months. However, in adequately treated patients with diffuse toxic goiter, a significant shrinkage in the size of the gland is usually identified in the first month after therapy. If after 3 to 4 months the patient still has signs, symptoms, or laboratory evidence of hyperthyroidism, a repeat dose of ^{131}I may be administered. A second treatment is necessary in less than about 15 percent of patients. Women should be advised to refrain from conceiving children for 6 months after therapy so that the full effects of treatment can be assessed and, thus, the need for any retreatment can be determined.

^{131}I In Treatment of Thyroid Carcinoma

^{131}I therapy remains a valuable adjunct in thyroid carcinoma therapy for (1) ablation of post-surgical residual thyroid tissue in the neck and (2) eradication of functioning local and distant thyroid metastases.

POSTSURGICAL ABLATION

Surgery is seldom able to effect removal of all of the functioning thyroid tissue, even in the best hands. Residual tissue may be confused with local nodal metastatic disease when post-surgical scanning is performed. In addition, through suppression of TSH, residual thyroid tissue in the neck significantly reduces the likelihood that distant metastatic lesions will be visualized with follow-up whole-body ^{131}I scanning techniques. Therefore, ^{131}I ablation of remaining thyroid tissue in the neck is a convenient and relatively inexpensive method for obtaining the desired results of total thyroidectomy.

Generally, whole-body thyroid imaging is performed 4 to 6 weeks after thyroidectomy in order to detect residual functioning tissue in the thyroid bed and any possible distant metastases. Residual tissue is ablated using a dose in the range of 30 to 150 mCi (1.1 to 5.5 GBq).

Alternatively, some clinicians feel that ^{131}I ablation may be desirable whether or not residual thyroid tissue or metastases are identified—the rationale being that such therapy may destroy undetectable, functioning micrometastases. Using this approach, pre-ablation imaging is not necessary. Imaging may be performed 4 to 6 days post-treatment using the residual ^{131}I activity. Thyroid replacement may be instituted 5 to 7 days after the administration of therapy.

Re-examination post-ablation in 3 to 6 months is typical, and therapy is repeated if residual thyroid tissue is found.

Prior to rescanning, the patient should be off T$_4$ supplements for at least 4 to 6 weeks. If T$_3$ supplement is used in the interval for patient comfort, it should be withheld for 2 weeks prior to imaging. TSH serum levels (elevated) obtained immediately before im-

aging may provide evidence of adequate stimulation of functioning tissue. After all functioning tissue within the thyroid bed has been ablated, subsequent identification of functioning tissue in the neck should be considered to be tumor recurrence and treated appropriately.

FUNCTIONING METASTASES

Doses for the eradication of well-differentiated thyroid metastases are high, usually 100 to 200 mCi (3.7 to 7.4 GBq). ^{131}I may be administered as needed at 3- to 6-month intervals for as many as 5 to 10 times. In some institutions, increased dose of ^{131}I to the functioning tissue is achieved by depleting the extracellular iodide pool using pre-therapy low-iodine diets and/or drug-induced diuresis.

In patients with extensive metastatic lesions or in whom repeat therapeutic administrations are contemplated, monitoring of the patient's hematologic status is desirable since bone marrow suppression may occur in patients with large absorbed doses. In addition, because of the high doses employed, strict radiation protection procedures must be outlined and carefully followed. Any patient treated with ^{131}I in doses of 30 mCi (1.1 GBq) or greater must be hospitalized until body burdens fall below 30 mCi (1.1 GBq), which usually occurs after 2 to 3 days, with the major portion of the radioactive dose being excreted in the urine. This yields an exposure of less than 7 mR/hr (2×10^{-6} Ckg^{-1}) at 1 meter from the patient. At the time of discharge, patients are usually given thyroid hormone replacement. Follow-up scanning is then done at 6-month intervals with therapy repeated as needed until the disease is eradicated, after which scanning follow-ups may be performed at 3- to 5-year intervals.

Parathyroid Imaging

Because of the small size and topographic location of the parathyroid glands and the absence of a suitable specific radiopharmaceutical, previous attempts at imaging the parathyroid glands have not proved satisfactory. Selenium 75 methionine, gallium 67 citrate, and thallium 201 chloride all have been used in an attempt to visualize parathy-

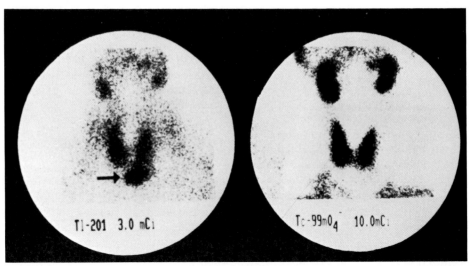

Figure 7–11. Parathyroid adenoma. Simultaneous thallium 201 and ^{99m}Tc pertechnetate imaging of the anterior cervical region demonstrates a focal area of increased thallium activity adjacent to the inferior pole of the left lobe of the thyroid gland (arrow) that is not seen on the ^{99m}Tc pertechnetate–only images. This is characteristic of a parathyroid adenoma. Computer subtraction techniques are sometimes necessary in more subtle lesions. (Case courtesy of Michael Hartshorne, M.D.)

roid adenomas. Particular interest has developed in thallium 201 chloride because of its better energy characteristics for imaging. Unfortunately, its significant uptake in the thyroid gland itself has made identification of the parathyroid glands difficult, if not impossible, on most occasions. Recently, a double isotope technique employing both thallium 201 chloride and ^{99m}Tc pertechnetate has yielded some encouraging results. The theoretical basis of the examination is predicated on the selective uptake of ^{99m}Tc by the thyroid gland and the concentration of thallium by both the thyroid and parathyroid organs (Fig.

7–11). After obtaining images of the distribution of both radionuclides in the neck at appropriate energy settings, computer subtraction of the ^{99m}Tc image from the thallium image is performed. Any activity remaining in the neck then theoretically represents activity in the parathyroid glands. Other considerations are listed in Table 7–6. While some success in the identification of parathyroid adenomas has been documented, the method is still unable to consistently image the normal parathyroid glands. Since up to 5 percent of hyperfunctional parathyroid lesions are missed at the initial operation, the parathyroid imaging is especially useful in patients with negative neck explorations and recurrent or persistent hypercalcemia.

Table 7–6. CAUSES OF FALSE POSITIVE ^{99m}Tc/ ^{201}Tl SCANS FOR PARATHYROID ADENOMAS

Common
  Thyroid neoplasms
  Colloid goiter
  Focal Hashimoto's thyroiditis
Uncommon
  Metastatic carcinomas
  Lymphoma
  Sarcoidosis

Suggested Readings

Fine EF: Parathyroid imaging: Its current status and future role. Semin Nucl Med 17(4):350–359, 1987
Freeman LM, Blaufox MD (eds): Nuclear oncology—Part III. Semin Nucl Med 15(2):106–131, 1985
Harbert JC: Nuclear Medicine Therapy. New York, Thieme Medical Publishers, 1987

CHAPTER 8

Cardiovascular System

Advances in radionuclide techniques brought about by significant developments in instrumentation, radiopharmaceuticals, and computer applications have revolutionized the noninvasive evaluation of cardiovascular physiology and function. Nuclear cardiovascular examinations now permit the sensitive detection and diagnosis of numerous cardiac abnormalities as well as the determination of the functional consequences of these diseases. In most institutions, the best results from both a technical and clinical viewpoint are obtained when the nuclear medicine physician and the cardiologist work in a cooperative fashion.

Currently, three types of procedures constitute the diagnostic thrust of cardiovascular nuclear imaging: (1) acute myocardial infarction imaging with ^{99m}Tc pyrophosphate; (2) evaluation of coronary artery perfusion with thallium 201; and (3) tests of ventricular pump performance employing gated equilibrium blood pool or first-transit methodology. Extensive experience with these procedures in their appropriate clinical settings has proved them to be valuable noninvasive adjuncts to the investigation of cardiac disease, with application to a broad class of both ambulatory and critically ill patients.

Anatomy and Physiology

Since the heart predominantly functions as a pump, it is important to examine the physiology and anatomy related to this function. Under normal circumstances, the flow through the cardiac chambers must be equal; therefore there is a relationship between the size of each valve and the pressure sustained by it. The smallest of the cardiac valves is the aortic valve, and the pressure generated during systole in the left ventricle is the highest of any chamber. The pulmonary valve is slightly larger than the aortic valve, the mitral valve is somewhat larger still, and the tricuspid valve is the largest.

The volume of each chamber may be expressed as end-diastolic volume (EDV)—the volume of the chamber after it is completely filled with blood at the end of diastole. Typical values for EDV for each chamber are given in Table 8–1. More precise values may be obtained by using a nomogram based on patient size. Although it can be seen that end-diastolic volumes of the chambers are different, the stroke volumes (volume of blood ejected by each ventricle during systole) must be equal and normally range from 80 to 100 ml. Cardiac output is the volume of blood pumped by either ventricle over a period of 1 minute; it can be obtained by multiplying stroke volume by heart rate. However, the ejection fraction of a chamber is the measurement normally used clinically, since it takes into account the end-diastolic volume and the stroke volume. The ejection fraction is the percentage of end-diastolic volume that is ejected by a ventricle during systole.

Table 8–1. TYPICAL END-DIASTOLIC VOLUME (EDV) FOR EACH HEART CHAMBER

	EDV	WALL THICKNESS	EJECTION FRACTION
Right atrium	57 ml	2 mm	
Right ventricle	165 ml	5 mm	45–60%
Left atrium	50 ml	3 mm	
Left ventricle	150 ml	15 mm	50–65%

During systole, the various walls of the left ventricle move inward. The apical portion of the left ventricle moves inward the least amount, and the anterior wall the most. The left ventricle normally shortens at least 20 percent along its long axis and 40 percent along the short axis. Septal motion is particularly important; on a left anterior oblique view taken during systole the septum should thicken and move slightly toward the center of the left ventricle. Assessment of wall motion by nuclear medicine techniques depends largely on viewing ventricular wall segments in tangent. When identified, regional wall motion abnormalities are generally classified as hypokinetic, akinetic, or dyskinetic. Dyskinesia indicates that a particular segment moves paradoxically outward rather than contracting inward during systole.

In the diastolic phase of the cardiac cycle, the myocardium first relaxes without a change in volume but with an exponential decline in left ventricular pressure. This is referred to as *isovolumic relaxation*. As the ventricular pressure falls below that of the left atrium, the mitral valve opens and the *early rapid filling phase* is initiated. This is followed by *diastasis,* the third phase of diastole, which begins with the decline of passive filling (abatement of the transmitral pressure gradient) and ends with the onset of an atrial kick that concludes diastole (Fig. 8–1).

The heart muscle is supplied by the right and left coronary arteries. The major branches of the left coronary artery are the left anterior descending, circumflex, and obtuse marginal branches (Fig. 8–2). The left anterior descending branch supplies the interventricular septum anteriorly and the anterolateral wall of the left ventricle. The left circumflex branch supplies the left atrium and the posterolateral wall of the left ventricle. The right coronary artery has an acute marginal branch and often terminates as the posterior descending artery. It supplies the right atrium, right ventricle, and inferior wall of the left ventricle and a variable portion of the interventricular septum. In 80 percent of people, the right coronary artery is dominant even though it is usually smaller. Dominance refers only to the origin of the blood supply to the posterior descending artery.

The normal coronary blood flow is approximately 224 ml/min. With exercise, however, both the coronary flow and the cardiac output may increase 4- to 6-fold. Myocardial blood flow is greatest during diastole because at this time the blood flows fastest through vessels that are not being constricted by the surrounding cardiac muscle. These flow changes with the cardiac cycle are much more prominent in the left coronary artery than in the right, due to the larger mass and higher pressure achieved by the left ventricular muscle.

When the narrowing of a coronary vessel is less than 50 percent of the diameter of the vessel, the effect on blood flow is in general clinically insignificant. As narrowing approaches 70 percent, the lesions become much more hemodynamically significant, particularly during exercise. Experiments in dogs show that resting coronary artery flow is not greatly reduced until the stenosis reaches 80 to 85 percent, but with exercise 50 percent narrowing may be identified with radionuclide imaging techniques.

Myocardial Infarct Imaging (Pyrophosphate Imaging)

Imaging the myocardium for acute injury is based upon the principle that the radiopharmaceutical will concentrate in the areas of acute myocardial damage. Thus, this type of study has also been termed "infarct avid" or "hot spot" imaging. Since the introduction of ^{99m}Tc pyrophosphate in 1975, infarct imaging has become a procedure of significant

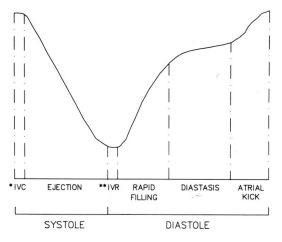

* IVC EJECTION **IVR RAPID FILLING DIASTASIS ATRIAL KICK

SYSTOLE DIASTOLE

* ISOVOLUMIC CONTRACTION
** ISOVOLUMIC RELAXATION

Figure 8–1. Time–activity curve obtained over left ventricle.

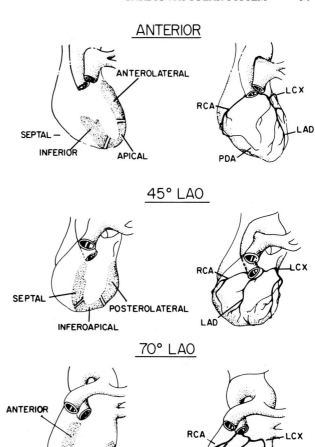

Figure 8–2. Schematic representation of the left ventricular wall and the associated blood supply. The coronary circulation is abbreviated as follows: Right coronary artery (RCA), posterior descending artery (PDA), left circumflex (LCX), left anterior descending artery (LAD).

diagnostic importance in selected patients. The radiopharmaceuticals for most cardiac imaging studies and their absorbed doses are given in Table 8–2.

PATHOPHYSIOLOGY

Prior to its recognition as the agent of choice in infarct avid imaging, ^{99m}Tc pyrophosphate was widely employed as a bone-seeking agent for skeletal imaging. Initially, it was felt that the avidity of pyrophosphate for complexing with calcium in the hydroxyapatite matrix was also the primary reason for its concentration in irreversibly damaged myocardial cells. Although detailed pathologic studies have substantiated the deposition of crystalline and subcrystalline forms of calcium in the mitochondria and cytoplasm of irreversibly injured myocardial cells, other

possible mechanisms have more recently been cited, including pyrophosphate binding to denatured proteins or other macromolecules at infarction sites. However, the deposition of pyrophosphate in acute myocardial infarction parallels closely the accumulation of calcium in the damaged tissue so that the pyrophosphate images are most likely to be positive during the time period over which calcium deposition is most active. Therefore, the timing of the examination is crucial.

In order for pyrophosphate or any similar agent to accumulate at the site of an acute infarction, perfusion to at least the periphery of the injury site must be preserved or reestablished. The area of maximal calcium and pyrophosphate uptake is in the periphery of the infarct and may well be due to residual collateral coronary blood flow at the edges of the infarct site.

/ mCi = 37 MBq

Table 8–2. RADIOPHARMACEUTICAL AGENTS FOR CARDIAC IMAGING

RADIO-PHARMA-CEUTICAL	USUAL DOSE	ROUTE OF ADMINIS-TRATION	PHYSICAL HALF-LIFE	TIME TO IMAGING	ABSORBED DOSE ESTIMATE (rad/mCi)*			REMARKS
					Whole Body	Gonads	Other	
^{99m}Tc pyro-phos-phate	10–20 mCi (370–740 MBq)	IV	6 hr	2–4 hr	0.01	0.01–0.03	Bone 0.02–0.07 Bladder† 0.1–0.2 Marrow 0.01	Forcing fluids and frequent voiding reduce bladder dose
^{99m}Tc red cells (in vivo labeling)	15–30 mCi (555 MBq–1.11 GBq)	IV	6 hr	0.3–2 hr	0.015–0.057		Heart 0.06–0.08 Lungs 0.03–0.13 Spleen 0.03–0.23	
^{201}Tl chlo-ride	1–3 mCi (37–111 MBq)	IV	73 hr	Immedi-ate—4 hr	0.06–0.3	Testes 0.2–1.4 Ovary 0.3	Kidneys† 0.4–0.9 Heart 0.2 Colon 0.6–0.8 Thyroid 0.43–0.93	

*To obtain absorbed dose in mGy/MBq, divide values by 3.7.
†Indicates critical organ.

RADIOPHARMACEUTICALS

As with all radiopharmaceuticals, careful quality control of ^{99m}Tc pyrophosphate is required to ensure accurate results in imaging for acute myocardial infarction. Normally, over half of the injected dose is deposited in the skeleton, with the remainder being rapidly excreted through the kidneys. In the presence of good renal function and adequate cardiac output, less than 5 percent of the injected dose remains in the blood 1 1/2 hours after injection. Because significant activity within the cardiac blood pool may be misinterpreted as myocardial activity or may obscure true myocardial uptake, it is important to ensure that the binding of pyrophosphate in the radiopharmaceutical is as complete as possible. Any free ^{99m}Tc pertechnetate injected with the tagged pyrophosphate will persist in the blood pool significantly longer because of its slower renal excretion and possible tagging to red blood cells; therefore the free agent may interfere with scan interpretation. For this reason, only freshly prepared ^{99m}Tc pyrophosphate with proper quality control (less than 1 percent free technetium) should be employed.

It is also important that ^{99m}Tc pyrophosphate be injected directly into a vein rather than through IV tubing, because the radiopharmaceutical may adhere to the sides of the tube and prevent adequate radionuclide administration.

IMAGING TECHNIQUE

Imaging is performed 2 to 4 hours after the intravenous administration of 10 to 20 mCi (370 to 740 MBq) of ^{99m}Tc pyrophosphate. Planar gamma camera images of 500 to 1000 K counts each are obtained with a LEAP or high-resolution collimator in multiple projections to allow for adequate surveying of the left ventricular region as well as to permit separation of the ventricle from overlying bony structures. This series of images should include anterior, 30° and 60° left anterior oblique, and left lateral views of the thorax. Care should be taken to include the entire cardiac area on each image. If initial images disclose persistent blood pool activity, further delayed imaging must be performed.

Experimentally and clinically, the conditions necessary for a positive scan occur within 10 to 12 hours after acute infarction in most patients, and scans generally become increasingly positive until about 72 hours after the insult. Subsequently in a majority of patients, the scintigrams become significantly less positive or revert to negative 10 days to 2 weeks or more after infarction occurs.

An appreciation of the temporal relationship between the pathologic lesion and the development of a positive ^{99m}Tc pyrophosphate scan is crucial to successful use of the procedure and the accurate interpretation of the images. Because there is not uncommonly an imprecise association between the onset of clinical symptoms of myocardial infarction and the actual event, post-event timing may not be precisely established in any given patient. For this reason, a negative scan result obtained in the first 12 to 24 hours after the onset of symptoms may not be used to exclude an acute myocardial infarction in the face of supporting clinical or laboratory data. In these instances, a repeat examination in 24 to 48 hours may be necessary to allow for the development of a positive scintigram. Rarely, a patient may not develop a positive scan until 4 or 5 days after the onset of symptoms. This, however, is clearly an exception to the norm.

Optimally, scanning for acute myocardial infarction should be performed between 24 and 72 hours after the onset of symptoms. A negative scan performed between 12 and 24 hours or more than 72 hours after onset does not necessarily exclude acute injury.

NEW INFARCT-AVID RADIOPHARMACEUTICALS

Monoclonal antibodies to the cardiac contractile protein (myosin) are currently undergoing investigation for clinical application. During myocardial infarction, the myocyte cell membrane is disrupted and the the myosin molecule becomes exposed to the extracellular space. Monoclonal antibodies (or antibody fragments) labeled with indium 111 or technetium 99m may thus be used to detect the presence of myocardial injury, either from acute myocardial infarction or from other injuries such as myocarditis. This technique may also be used to evaluate acute cardiac allograft rejection or to quantitate myocardial infarct size. Further investigation is needed before the efficacy of such radiopharmaceuticals is fully elucidated.

Although in most cases conventional planar imaging with ^{99m}Tc pyrophosphate provides adequate, sensitive diagnostic information, SPECT imaging may add an increased accuracy in infarct localization and sizing. In addition, separation of interfering bony activity and residual blood pool activity from the myocardium may be achieved. There is also evidence that SPECT imaging using ^{99m}Tc pyrophosphate is a more sensitive and accurate means of detecting nontransmural infarctions than is planar imaging.

SPECT pyrophosphate images are usually obtained 6 hours after the intravenous injection of 25 mCi (925 MBq) of technetium 99m labeled pyrophosphate. The additional delay allows more time for interfering soft tissue and residual blood pool activity to abate. Acquisition may use either a 360° or a 180° rotation. Typically, 64 views obtained at 20 seconds per view over 360° will provide images of adequate quality. The images are reformatted in the standard, transverse, sagittal, and coronal planes. Because normal myocardium is not imaged, the multiple reconstructions allow definition of sufficient bony reference points to aid in the location and sizing of infarcts.

SCAN INTERPRETATION

Normally, only activity in the thoracic cage and spine is identified. No activity should be identified in the region of the left ventricle. However, in patients with reduced renal function or diminished cardiac output, varying degrees of blood pool activity in the left ventricle may be identified due to delayed renal clearance.

Abnormal scan findings may be categorized as focal or diffuse. In either category, the abnormality is graded according to its intensity relative to the activity in the ribs or sternum as seen on the same image. The image demonstrating the most intense myocardial activity should be used. In one grading system developed by Parkey and colleagues, myocardial activity is rated from 0 to 4+ (Table 8–3). Scans with a rating of 2+ to 4+ are considered positive. In addition, when the increased myocardial activity is focal, that area should be localized to a particular wall of the left ventricle as accurately as can be determined.

Several other grading systems have been proposed that take into consideration the difference in diagnostic accuracy between focal and diffuse myocardial activity. One such system is that described by Holman, Chisholm, and Braunwald (Table 8–3 and Fig. 8–3).

Regardless of which grading method is employed, it is most practical to adhere to a particular system that has proved useful in an individual laboratory. It is also imperative that the diagnostic and clinical implications of a particular rating system be understood by the referring physicians.

Table 8–3. TWO CLASSIFICATION METHODS FOR INTERPRETATION OF THE ⁹⁹ᵐTc PYROPHOSPHATE MYOCARDIAL IMAGE

HOLMAN AND WYNNE*	PARKEY ET AL.†
0 Normal	0 Normal
1+ Less than rib (mild diffuse)	1+ Questionable activity
2+ Equal to or greater than rib (moderate diffuse)	2+ Definite activity, less than rib
3+ Equal to or greater than sternum (focal massive)	3+ Equal to rib
	4+ Greater than rib

*Holman BL, Wyme J: Infarct avid (hot spot) myocardial scintigraphy. Radiol Clin North Am 18:487–499, 1980.
†Parkey RW, Bonte FJ, Meyer SL, et al: A new method for radionuclide imaging of acute myocardial infarction in humans. Circulation 50:540–546, 1974.

Diffuse Uptake

In the absence of acute myocardial infarction, the pattern of diffuse uptake in the region of the left ventricle may be produced by a number of entities. This may be mimicked by persistence of activity in the ventricular cavity blood pool, especially when the ventricular chambers are enlarged. Because of the problems associated with the determination of the diagnostic significance of the diffuse uptake pattern, some authors have suggested that such a pattern be considered significant only if it is of such intensity as to be graded 3+ or 4+ in the Parkey system or equal to or greater than rib activity in the classification proposed by Holman. In general, the more intense the diffuse activity within the myocardium, the more likely that the finding will have clinical significance.

Acute myocardial infarctions presenting with diffuse myocardial uptake are generally the subendocardial or nontransmural type, although nontransmural infarctions may appear as a focal abnormality in 40 to 50 percent of patients. Numerous other pathologic processes have been reported to produce a diffuse uptake pattern. The most common of these are marked with an asterisk in Table 8–4.

The scintigraphic differentiation of diffuse

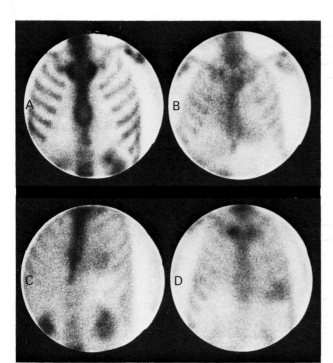

Figure 8–3. Grading system for pyrophosphate infarct imaging. (A) No activity in the region of the heart, which is a normal pattern graded 0. (B) Activity in the cardiac region less than the rib, graded 1+. (C) Activity equal to or greater than rib activity, graded 2+. (D) Activity equal to or greater than the sternum, graded 3+.

Table 8–4. THORACIC SOFT TISSUE LOCALIZATION OF ^{99m}Tc PYROPHOSPHATE

- Acute myocardial infarction
- Myocardial contusion
- Extending infarction
- Aneurysm formation
- Calcification
    dystrophic
    valvular
    costal cartilage
- Tissue necrosis—cardioversion
- Trauma
    soft tissue
    skeletal
- Unstable angina*
- Cardiomyopathy and myocarditis*
- Adriamycin cardiotoxicity
- Breast tumors
- Extensive subendocardial infarction*
- Blood pool activity*
- Pericarditis
- Cardiac
    amyloidosis

*May present as diffuse cardiac activity.

myocardial uptake from persistent blood pool activity may at times be accomplished by obtaining further delayed images to discern if the activity in the region of the heart decreases with time, as would be expected with blood pool activity. True myocardial uptake secondary to acute myocardial infarction would be expected to increase in intensity.

Focal Uptake

The most common causes for focal uptake within the myocardium are acute myocardial infarction and, much less frequently, myocardial damage accompanying unstable angina pectoris. When such focal activity is identified, it can usually be localized to one or more ventricular wall segments by examination of the abnormality in the multiple projections obtained. Occasionally, an extensive transmural infarction may present as a large area of increased activity with a central zone of relatively decreased intensity. This so-called "doughnut" pattern has been explained by the absence of blood flow to the central region of the infarct (Fig. 8–4). Such a pattern is associated with a higher degree of morbidity and mortality than with less extensive lesions.

Activity within the thoracic cage and overlying soft tissues may mimic a positive examination: rib fractures, calcified costochondral cartilage, and calcified skin lesions or breast tumors have all been reported to cause focal accumulations of pyrophosphate (see Table 8–4). However, in a majority of these instances, such activity may be separated from myocardial activity through analysis of

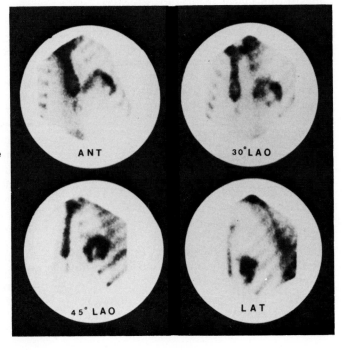

Figure 8–4. Extensive transmural infarct. The intense activity is clearly identified. A large central cold area represents absence of blood flow to the central region of the infarct. This area should not be mistaken for the ventricular cavity.

ANT   30°LAO

45°LAO   LAT

the multiple scintigraphic projections or SPECT imaging.

Persistent Uptake

In a minority of patients with acute myocardial infarction, the scintigrams may remain positive for weeks, months, or even years, rather than returning to normal in the usual 10 to 14 days. In most of these patients, the persistent activity is of a diffuse type, although approximately 20 percent may demonstrate persistent focal activity. In patients with prolonged focal activity, ongoing myocardial necrosis or, less commonly, ventricular aneurysm formation must be considered since they are well-documented causes of a persistently positive scan. Both diffuse and focal persistent activity has been found to correlate with considerably higher rates of complications, including death due to cardiac causes (cardiac death). In addition, prolonged abnormal activity at the site of an infarction may substantially complicate repeat scanning for possible reinfarction.

Sensitivity and Specificity

In general, both sensitivity and specificity are best for transmural (Q wave) lesions with about 90 percent sensitivity and 60 to 80 percent specificity. For nontransmural (non–Q wave) infarctions, reported sensitivity varies considerably, undoubtedly related to significant differences in diagnostic criteria, especially regarding diffuse uptake patterns. Recent series employing rigid focal criteria and dismissing faint diffuse uptake patterns as insignificant indicate the sensitivity for nontransmural lesions to be in the 90 percent range. Using these criteria, specificity approaches that for transmural infarction.

CLINICAL APPLICATIONS

Diagnosis of Acute Myocardial Infarction

Under the proper circumstances, ^{99m}Tc pyrophosphate imaging is a useful adjunct to the standard diagnostic regimen in diagnosis of acute myocardial infarction, particularly when clinical and laboratory findings are nondiagnostic. It is particularly useful in the following clinical situations:

- When the diagnosis of acute infarction is not established by nonscintigraphic studies
- To evaluate unstable angina pectoris
- To establish the presence of reinfarction or extension of a previously existing infarct
- To investigate suspected infarction following cardiac surgery
- To evaluate suspected right ventricular infarction

In the overwhelming majority of patients presenting with signs and symptoms of acute myocardial infarction, the diagnosis may be established without the use of ^{99m}Tc pyrophosphate imaging. However, in selected patients, a pyrophosphate scan may reinforce or establish a suspected diagnosis of acute myocardial injury, especially when electrocardiogram (ECG) and enzyme results are equivocal or rendered unreliable by intervening circumstances. This may be the case: (1) several days (more than 48 hours) after the acute injury when serum CK-MB has returned to normal, (2) after cardioversion, (3) just after cardiac surgery, or (4) in the presence of ECG abnormalities such as left bundle branch block or those caused by a previous infarction.

Following cardiac surgery, the diagnosis of perioperative myocardial infarction may be difficult due to accompanying chest discomfort as well as alterations in enzyme levels and post-surgical ECG changes. In this clinical situation, the diagnosis may be established by pyrophosphate scintigraphy. In patients who have had a previous myocardial infarction, diagnosis is made easier and more specific by obtaining a baseline preoperative examination. Because the surgery itself may produce some degree of diffuse activity, care must be taken not to overinterpret faint diffuse activity identified on the post-surgical images.

In order to adequately demonstrate the extension of an acute myocardial infarction or reinfarction in the area of a previous insult, serial images are required. In patients with pyrophosphate scan documentation of the initial insult and its course, extension of an acute infarction may appear as a noticeable increase in the size of the existing lesion or as a reappearance of activity at the site of a previously resolving infarct. In addition, the identification of increased activity in an area different from the original insult may be used to diagnose reinfarction. In those patients with recent infarction and recurrence of symptoms but without a baseline scan, a negative scan may be used as evidence against extension of the insult or a new infarction. A positive study may be of value if multiple serial images disclose increasing intensity of the abnormality over 2 to 3 days, followed by progressive decrease—the classic findings of acute injury. However, without a baseline study, reinfarction cannot be established without demonstration of this typical course of events.

Acute myocardial infarction scanning may be useful in better localizing and estimating the extent of infarctions of either ventricle identified on ECG. This method is particularly accurate in the mapping of left ventricular transmural infarctions, which present as discrete abnormalities on the pyrophosphate images. Furthermore, pyrophosphate imaging may be of value in defining the location of ST-T wave (subendocardial) infarctions. Infarctions of the right ventricle, especially in patients with suspected extension of inferior wall infarctions, may also be accurately localized. Such a diagnosis is frequently difficult or impossible when attempted on clinical or laboratory evidence alone.

Recent clinical interest in interventional therapy to reduce or limit infarction has placed considerable emphasis on the estimation of infarct size. Technetium 99m pyrophosphate imaging has considerable potential in the accurate sizing of infarcts, especially anterior wall lesions. SPECT imaging may provide even greater accuracy, particularly in posterior or inferior wall infarctions.

Prognosis and Risk Stratification

In general, ^{99m}Tc pyrophosphate imaging appears to predict morbidity and mortality by confirming the direct relationship between infarct size and the likelihood of acute complications. More specifically, patients with extensive local infarcts (especially a doughnut pattern) on pyrophosphate imaging and those with serial scans showing enlarging infarcts with increasing scan intensity are found to have poor prognoses with high risk of complications and mortality. Furthermore, scans remaining persistently positive for more than 3 months are associated with an increased risk of future ischemic events. Pyrophosphate scanning also provides useful prognostic information in patients with unstable angina. The demonstration of a positive ^{99m}Tc pyrophosphate examination without clinical or laboratory evidence of infarction correlates positively with a high incidence of subsequent myocardial infarction and with increased mortality rates. Approximately one-third of hospitalized patients with unstable angina will exhibit abnormalities on pyrophosphate imaging, generally diffusely increased activity. This has been explained by a number of mechanisms, including recent silent or remote myocardial infarction and diffuse areas of myocardial necrosis. Such patients are at higher risk for significant cardiac complications, including nonfatal myocardial infarction and death, compared with patients with negative images.

Myocardial Perfusion Scintigraphy

In the past decade, thallium 201 has essentially dominated all other radiopharmaceuticals in the clinical nuclear imaging laboratory as the agent of choice in evaluating the physiologic status of coronary perfusion. Stress-redistribution thallium 201 imaging has become a major noninvasive test for the detection of coronary artery disease and for estimating its extent and severity.

PHYSICAL CHARACTERISTICS

Thallium 201 is a cyclotron-produced radionuclide that decays by electron capture, with a half-life of approximately 73 hours. On decay, the major emissions are characteristic x-rays of the daughter product, mercury 201, with an energy range of 69 to 81 keV (98 percent abundance). Thallium 201 does emit smaller numbers of gamma rays at energies of 167 keV (8 percent) and 135 keV (2 percent).

The relatively long physical half-life of thallium 201 is advantageous in that it provides somewhat convenient shelf storage and allows for successful imaging over a period of hours.

BIOKINETICS

Thallium is a group IIIA metallic element with biokinetic properties similar to but not identical with potassium. Like potassium, thallium crosses the cell membrane via active transport mechanisms, and it ultimately has a mainly intracellular distribution after intravenous administration. When introduced into the bloodstream by intravenous injection, thallium localizes in the myocardium in two phases: (1) initial distribution based on cellular extraction by the myocardium and (2) redistribution or equilibrium based on the continued myocardial extraction of thallium from the blood and ongoing washout of previously extracted thallium from the cells.

The initial distribution of thallium in the myocardium is dependent on coronary blood flow and the extraction of blood-borne thallium by viable myocardial cells. Under resting and normal stress conditions, regional myocardial uptake of thallium 201 is linearly related to the regional coronary perfusion. Decreased perfusion to an area of myocardium results in a decrease in thallium accumulation in that region, with opposite results at normal or slightly elevated levels of perfusion. Animal studies have shown that a flow differential between a normal and a stenotic coronary artery of approximately 2 to 1 is required before a definite defect is noted on a planar thallium image. At maximum exercise, a 50 percent stenosis is generally sufficient to consistently present as a defect.

Once the blood-borne thallium is presented to viable myocardial cells, its extraction is quite rapid, approaching 90 percent extraction efficiency. However, the total amount of thallium ultimately accumulating in the normal heart is limited by the concentration of thallium circulating through the coronary blood supply. Therefore, only approximately 3 to 5 percent of the total injected dose is localized in the heart. Although the exact mechanism of extraction of thallium by the myocardial cells has not been definitely illuminated, it is clear that it is related to some extent to the sodium-potassium pump.

Besides the myocardium, thallium is initially distributed in other tissues, especially those of the gastrointestinal tract, skeletal muscle, and kidneys, with only about 5 percent of the injected dose persisting in the blood at 5 minutes after intravenous injection. This provides for myocardium-to-background ratios adequate for scintigraphic imaging. Exercise diminishes the activity within the gastrointestinal tract, particularly the liver, by reducing splanchnic blood flow. Thallium clearance from the body is mostly

via urinary excretion with only 4 to 8 percent cleared in 24 hours. In addition to the biologic clearance, there is physical decay of the radionuclide, and the effective half-life in the body is 56 hours.

After the initial uptake of thallium 201 by the normal myocardium, there begins a slow process of washout of the thallous ion from the myocardial intracellular compartment back into the vascular compartment, and simultaneous representation of additional thallium to the myocardial cells for extraction. This thallium is provided by the large percentage of the injected radioisotope that was initially held by other organs of the body. The large reservoir of extracardiac thallium, therefore, provides a means for equilibrium between thallium slowly washing out from the myocardial cells and the re-extraction of thallium continuously presented by blood from remote organs. Unlike the re-extraction fraction of thallium 201 by the myocardium from the circulating blood pool, the washout component of redistribution is strongly dependent upon coronary perfusion with ischemic areas demonstrating much slower washout than normal regions. These simultaneous processes of thallium washout and re-extraction define the phenomenon of redistribution. This concept of redistribution equilibrium is very important for understanding the theoretical basis of thallium exercise imaging in the diagnosis and evaluation of coronary artery disease.

Thallium Exercise Imaging

PLANAR TECHNIQUE

Because relatively low-energy mercury 201 x-rays are used to image thallium 201 in the evaluation of myocardial perfusion, gamma cameras with thinner sodium iodide crystals (1/4 inch thick) allow adequate resolution without significant loss of sensitivity. While LEAP collimators may provide acceptable images, further resolution enhancement may be obtained with the use of high-resolution, thin septa collimators. Normally, a 15 to 20 percent window centered on the mercury x-ray photopeak provides acceptable count rates. If, however, a camera system with multiple pulse height analyzers is used, sensitivity may be increased by including the less abundant 167- and 135-keV gamma photopeaks.

Thallium studies may be performed as exercise examinations or less frequently as resting determinations of coronary perfusion. In either case, strict compliance with the protocol established in each laboratory is paramount for the standardization of the procedure and for the accurate interpretation of scan results.

The thallium exercise test consists of an initial post-exercise set of myocardial images and an identical set of delayed redistribution images. Patients should remain NPO for 4 to 6 hours before the exercise test. This allows for a decrease in splanchnic blood flow and, therefore, diminished thallium uptake in the bowel and liver. It has also been recommended that calcium antagonists and beta-blocker drugs such as propranolol be discontinued, if possible, for a sufficient length of time before the examination to avoid any interference with obtaining an adequate stress examination. Long-acting nitrates should also be withheld on the day of testing.

The most common mode of stress employed in exercise thallium studies is a multistage treadmill test based on a Bruce or modified Bruce protocol. Although bicycle ergometer exercise may be used, it generally results in less optimal exertion levels that may compromise the sensitivity of the study. Once exercise has begun, timing is critical. Ideally, approximately 2 mCi (74 MBq) of thallium 201 is injected at peak stress through a working intravenous line or heparin lock with the patient continuing to exercise for approximately 30 seconds to 1 minute after the injection. The determination of peak stress varies with the institution, but it is generally considered to be maximal (terminated with appearance of chest pain, significant ECG changes, or exhaustion), near-maximal (usually defined as reaching 85 percent of maximum predicted heart rate), or submaximal (less than 85 percent of maximal predicted heart rate). Maximal or near-maximal stress provides for optimal myocardial to background ratios, as well as for the most sensitive evaluation of myocardial perfusion. In patients who have recently sustained acute myocardial infarction, an intentionally submaximal thallium exercise test may be performed as part of the patient's predischarge evaluation.

Because redistribution of thallium within the myocardium begins immediately at the termination of exercise and may be very rapid in some patients, gamma camera imaging should commence as soon as possible, ideally within the first 5 to 10 minutes post-exercise. This helps to ensure that the initial images reflect as nearly as possible the distribution of coronary perfusion at peak stress.

The initial set of thallium images consists of an anterior view, a left anterior oblique (LAO) view, usually at 45°, and a left lateral or steep LAO view, usually obtained at 70°. Each image is obtained for 10 minutes or 300,000 counts, whichever occurs first. After the completion of these views and before the redistribution images, the patient is instructed to eat sparingly and to avoid strenuous exercise, even climbing stairs.

Redistribution images are obtained 3 to 4 hours after the initial set. Ideally, these are performed on the same instrument that was used to collect the post-exercise images. Care is taken to reproduce the positioning and degree of obliquity of the camera as precisely as possible so that the images will be comparable. Oblique and even anterior views are obtained with the patient's right side dependent in order to minimize the attenuation of thallium activity in the inferior ventricular wall by the left hemidiaphragm. This also aids in excluding overlying breast tissue, which may significantly attenuate the low-energy mercury x-rays. In some laboratories, 24-hour repeat images are obtained in patients who exhibit nonreversible defects on the 4-hour redistribution images. This is done to determine with greater certainty any degree of reversibility of the post-exercise defects. Some technical sources of error are listed in Table 8–5.

The quality of thallium 201 images is greatly enhanced by computer processing and display. In fact, computer acquisition and display of thallium images has become the standard for producing the final images for interpretation. The most frequent maneuvers applied to the thallium raw data are background subtraction, contrast enhancement, and image filtering. The most commonly used, background subtraction, can be performed by various approaches, but the goal is to clear the image of unwanted activity, thereby improving contrast and correcting for background nonuniformity, which may produce spurious differences in intensity in the myocardial perfusion pattern. High-frequency filtering techniques are primarily employed to improve images by removing unwanted statistical noise.

Table 8–5. SOURCES OF TECHNICAL ERROR IN THALLIUM 201 PERFUSION STRESS TESTS

- Failure to obtain adequate stress before thallium injection (submaximal exercise)
- Failure to obtain 85 percent of maximum heart rate because of interfering drugs such as propranolol
- Too long a delay in obtaining the initial post-stress images
- Breast or diaphragmatic attenuation producing an area of diminished thallium activity
- Camera field nonuniformity producing false areas of diminished activity
- Oversubtraction of background, producing falsely diminished areas of thallium distribution
- Dose infiltration or premature thallium administration
- Positioning variation causing noncomparable images
- Exercise or eating between stress images and delayed images

Some investigators have felt that by using ECG synchronized or "gated" collection of images by the computer, the degrading effect of ventricular wall motion can be eliminated or reduced. When gated acquisition is used, actual cinematic display of the thallium images is possible over the entire cardiac cycle, allowing for evaluation of wall motion. While resolution may be improved, imaging times are lengthened with no apparent increase in sensitivity or specificity for diagnosing coronary artery disease.

In addition to visual inspection of images, computer quantitative analysis of thallium images, primarily with the goal of expressing the relative distribution of thallium 201 in the myocardium as a function of space and/or time, is frequently employed. This allows a more accurate comparison of relative thallium distribution over the various segments of the myocardium in a given projection. In addition, these techniques should permit a more objective assessment of the change in activity within a given segment of myocardium at different imaging times as a reflection of redistribution. This can be quite helpful in the evaluation of perfusion by allowing for the documentation of subtle areas of ischemia or abnormal washout.

PLANAR IMAGE INTERPRETATION

Evaluation of a set of initial post-exercise and redistribution images should begin with an overall assessment of the technical quality of the images. It is imperative that positioning of the heart in the initial views be meticulously repeated in the corresponding redistribution images so that comparable myocardial segments can be accurately correlated. In addition, an assessment of the degree of myocardial uptake compared with background, as well as liver and spleen activity, may be used to estimate the adequacy of exercise. In patients who have exercised maximally, only spare activity in the region of the liver and spleen should be seen, and a good myocardial-to-background activity differential is generally noted.

Next, attention should be focused on the lungs, primarily in the anterior view, to determine the presence of abnormal pulmonary thallium concentration. Normally, no significant pulmonary activity is identified. Finally, thallium activity in the myocardium should be detailed. Once categorized, thallium distribution abnormalities should be localized to a specific ventricular wall segment or coronary vascular distribution.

Normal thallium scintigrams (Fig. 8–5) are characterized by uniform distribution of radioactivity throughout most of the left ventricular myocardium. However, several normal variations should be recognized. These include (1) decreased activity in the region of the cardiac apex—so-called apical thinning; (2) occasional decreased activity along the posterior basal portion of the myocardium; (3) nonuniform activity in the proximal portions of the septum and posterior lateral wall as seen in the 45° image; and (4) focal areas of increased activity corresponding to papillary muscles (at approximately 2 o'clock and 7 o'clock on 45° LAO images). Persistence of these regional variations on the redistribution images generally aids in differentiation from areas of stress-induced ischemia. Normally, the most superior aspects of the images, corresponding to the cardiac valve planes, demonstrate decreased or absent activity compared with the remainder of the myocardium. Of course, the large central area of decreased activity is the left ventricular cavity.

Some normal variation between the stress and resting images should also be appreciated. This includes the frequent visualization of the right ventricle on the stress images, with little or no activity seen in that area on the redistribution views. When the thallium

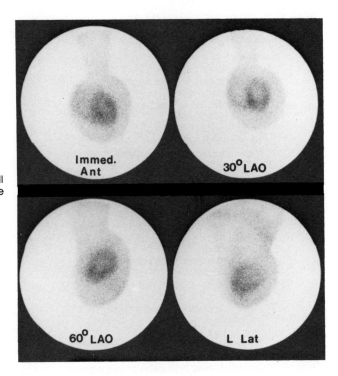

Figure 8–5. Normal planar thallium scan. The left ventricular myocardium is clearly identified. Since this is a stress examination, a small amount of activity is seen in the region of the right ventricle. In this particular instance, the patient has been fitted with a lead apron mask to reduce extraneous activity.

study is *initiated* at rest, no right ventricular activity should be identified and, when present, usually indicates hypertrophy of the right ventricular myocardium. Some points to keep in mind when interpreting these examinations are listed in Tables 8–6, 8–7, and 8–8. In many laboratories, computer-assisted circumferential analysis of stress and delayed images, along with thallium washout curves, is performed in hopes of improving accuracy and to quantitate the results of therapy on serial studies. Protocols for quantitative analysis and washout assessment as well as the display of the derived information vary

from laboratory to laboratory and with different manufacturer computer software. In general, however, the principles underlying such programs are the same.

THE ABNORMAL SCAN

Three distinct patterns of abnormal thallium distribution provide the basis for the detection and differential diagnosis of stress-induced ischemia and permanent myocardial damage. These patterns are referred to as (1) reversible abnormalities, (2) nonreversible (fixed) abnormalities, and (3) rapid washout or reverse redistribution. True defects are usually visible on at least two of the three standard views.

Reversible Abnormalities

Generally speaking, a reversible abnormality is virtually synonymous with stress-induced ischemia in patients with coronary artery disease. The abnormality is identified on the initial post-stress images as an area of relatively decreased thallium activity, but is seen to disappear or significantly improve on the later redistribution views (Fig. 8–6). Thallium is initially distributed in the myocardium in a manner that reflects relative per-

Table 8–6. EFFECT OF DRUGS ON THALLIUM 201 EXERCISE SCINTIGRAPHY

CARDIAC EXTRACTION	
Increased	*Decreased*
Dipyridamole*	Adriamycin
Dexamethasone	Beta-blockers (propranolol)
Isoproteranol	Digitalis
	Furosemide without potassium supplements
	Lidocaine
	Nifedipine
	Ouabain

*Also causes delayed redistribution.

Table 8–7. EXERCISE THALLIUM 201 SCINTIGRAPHY

- **Sources of false positive examinations**

  True defects
    Coronary anomaly
    Coronary spasm (variant angina)
    Noncoronary disease
      Mitral valve prosthesis
      Cardiomyopathies
      Aortic stenosis
      Myocardial bridge
      Idiopathic hypertrophic subaortic stenosis
    Conduction defects (LBBB)
    Miscellaneous
      Long-distance runners
      Young females
      Ischemia of noncoronary origin
  Apparent defects
    Artifacts
      Chest wall artifacts
        Breast tissue or pectoral muscles
        Breast prosthesis
        ECG leads
        Braces
        Items in pockets, pendants, etc.
        Obesity
      High left hemidiaphragm
      Excess patient motion (deep respiration)
  Misinterpretation of normal variants
    Over- or underappreciation of inferoapical
      defects
    Variant activity at cardiac base, proximal
      septal area, and posterolateral walls
    Papillary muscle attachments
    Small ventricular cavity

- **Sources of false negative examinations**

  Early or delayed redistribution
  Submaximal exercise
  Noncritical stenoses (30 to 45 percent)
  Small ischemic area
  Isolated right coronary lesion
  Coronary collaterals
  Multivessel disease
  Overestimation of stenosis on
    angiogram
  Interfering medications

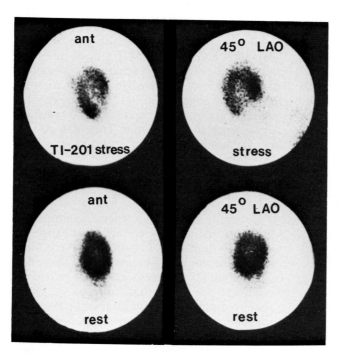

Figure 8–6. Stress-induced myocardial ischemia. The two top images, performed immediately after stress, demonstrate marked decrease of activity in the apical and inferoapical regions. Following redistribution, images (bottom row) demonstrate significant reversibility of the defect.

Table 8–8. APPROACH TO INTERPRETATION OF THALLIUM 201 STRESS-REDISTRIBUTION IMAGES

IMAGE	INTERPRETATION
Splanchnic activity (liver/spleen) on initial images	Inversely proportional to adequacy of exercise
Lung activity	Increased activity post-exercise that decreases on delayed images correlates with left ventricular dysfunction at stress and the presence and severity of coronary artery disease.
Degree of myocardial activity relative to background	Generally relates to adequacy of exercise
Ventricular cavity size	Enlargement on initial images may indicate transient failure.
Cardiac positioning	Must be comparable from initial to redistribution in each view
Right ventricular activity	Expected on both initial and redistribution images with adequate exercise
Homogeneity of left ventricular activity	Patchy activity may be seen in some cardiomyopathies, coronary heart disease, infiltrative disorders, and inadequate exercise.
Left ventricular myocardial defects	
Fixed	Usually indicates previous myocardial infarction
Reversible	Indicator of stress-induced ischemia
Left ventricular myocardial washout	Abnormally slow washout may be indirect evidence of regional coronary heart disease. Scars have normal washout.
Left ventricular wall thickness	May be increased in left ventricular hypertrophy or diminished on post-exercise images in subendocardial ischemia

fusion. Ischemic or scarred areas appear as defects compared with normal tissue. After this early deposition, thallium begins to leave or "washout" from the myocardium in direct relation to its initial concentration. Since the concentration of thallium is greater in areas of normal perfusion, the loss of thallium from these regions is greater than from zones of ischemia so that on delayed images the relative thallium distributions become similar. This allows for relative "equalization" of activity in the normal and previous ischemic areas, so that a differential of activity or "defect" is "filled in" and becomes less apparent or no longer identifiable. Because of the difference in thallium washout over time between normally perfused and ischemic regions of myocardium, computer-generated washout curves may demonstrate an abnormality in ischemic regions that appear as areas of relatively diminished or slow washout.

Nonreversible Abnormalities

Typically, this pattern is in most instances compatible with acute or remote myocardial infarction with subsequent scarring. The abnormality is termed "nonreversible" since there is no significant change in the perfusion defect between the post-stress and redistribution studies (Fig. 8–7). Because there are no or few viable cells left in this region of the ventricular wall, no redistribution is possible and the defect persists.

Because thallium in areas of scarring or fibrosis washes out over time at the same rate as from normal tissue, the initial differential activity with normal tissue in the post-stressed images is maintained over time and the defects produced on the initial images persist. Thus, computer-generated washout curves will identify no significant abnormality in regions of pure scarring. This may further aid in the differentiation of abnor-

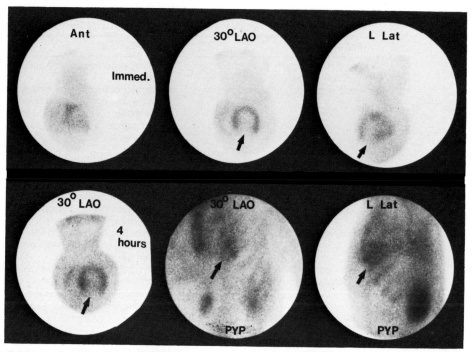

Figure 8–7. Myocardial infarction. Post-stress thallium images obtained in three different projections demonstrate a large defect in the apical portion of the left ventricle. A single 30° LAO view obtained 4 hours later shows no evidence of redistribution. A pyrophosphate scan shows increased activity at the apex consistent with acute infarction.

malities produced by ischemia from those produced by scarred myocardium.

Nonreversible defects are significantly less specific than reversible abnormalities and have been reported in patients with sarcoid myocardial disease, various cardiomyopathies, idiopathic hypertrophic subaortic stenosis, infiltrative or metastatic lesions, coronary spasm, and the syndrome of myocardial infarction without detectable coronary artery disease.

Some lesions identified on the initial post-stress images may be partially reversible, such as those seen around the edges of previous infarctions (peri-infact ischemia).

This straightforward approach to exercise-redistribution thallium scan interpretation is complicated by the recognition that up to 30 percent of patients with nonreversible (fixed) defects on 3- to 4-hour delayed images actually have ischemia in viable myocardium rather than fibrosis. The lack of redistribution is particularly evident in patients who eat between the initial and the redistribution images. The resultant release of insulin may alter potassium and therefore thallium redistribution kinetics by stimulation of the Na^+–K^+ ATPase transport system, acceler-

ating the clearance of these cations from the myocardial intracellular space. This in turn results in less reversibility of the initial thallium 201 defect and increases the likelihood that such a defect will be perceived as "fixed."

In order to differentiate ischemia from scar in patients with fixed thallium defects on 4-hour redistribution images, 24-hour images to allow more time for possible equilibration in ischemic myocardium or reinjection of patients with thallium at rest may be employed as necessary. Unfortunately, 24-hour images require a delay in diagnosis and may be difficult to interpret given the low myocardial thallium activity at 24 hours. A reinjection study at 4 hours post-exercise requires a smaller dose of thallium than initially used (about 1 mCi) and provides diagnostic information sooner but does involve an added expense for the second thallium dose.

Reverse Redistribution

In some instances, a scan appears normal on the stress views and becomes abnormal only on the delayed images, demonstrating relative defects not present on the initial views. While several authors have asserted that this finding correlates positively with coronary artery disease, recent studies have cast some doubt on this correlation and have described the occurrence of reverse distribution in patients with normal coronary arteries at angiography and in cardiomyopathies.

Lung Activity

Accumulation of thallium 201 in the lung is variable, with a normal lung-to-heart activity ratio of about 30 percent. This normal lung-to-heart thallium index does not change significantly from the initial image to redistribution images. The presence of excessive thallium 201 in the lungs should be noted as part of the routine interpretation of post-exercise and redistribution myocardial images. Abnormally increased lung activity (lung-to-heart ratio greater than approximately 50 percent) on post-stress images has been consistently shown to be a marker of transient left ventricular dysfunction at exercise. The mechanism appears to be related to transient interstitial pulmonary edema caused by a rise in left ventricular end-diastolic pressure secondary to stress-induced myocardial ischemia.

Circulating thallium 201 present at the point of peak stress serves as a marker of elevated pulmonary capillary pressure and interstitial lung fluid, manifested as increased lung activity on the immediate post-exercise images. As pulmonary pressure returns to normal and pulmonary edema subsides, the scintigram approaches normal on the delayed image as thallium washes out of the lungs. Whether determined by qualitative or quantitative methodology, abnormally increased thallium uptake in the lungs correlates anatomically with multi-vessel coronary artery disease or single-vessel disease involving either a dominant left circumflex artery or a high-grade proximal LAD lesion and clinically with increased morbidity and mortality rates.

Quantitation of thallium activity in the lungs may be performed by calculating the lung-to-heart thallium index. This is essentially a ratio of activity in a region of interest over the left upper lung field on the anterior view and a second region of interest of the same size over the myocardial segment with the highest count density in the same view.

Right Ventricular Activity

As previously noted, right ventricular activity is a common finding on post-stress images, and it usually fades considerably by the time of the redistribution views. Furthermore, the absence of right ventricular thallium activity post-exercise or a transient right ventricular defect should raise a strong suspicion of right coronary artery disease. On the contrary, significant right ventricular activity noted on studies done only at rest should be considered abnormal. Most commonly, this activity is attributed to right ventricular wall hypertrophy or to increased work load of the right ventricle in response to increased pulmonary vascular resistance with a subsequent increase in right ventricular myocardial perfusion.

DIPYRIDAMOLE THALLIUM IMAGING

In patients who cannot perform or tolerate adequate exercise, non-nitrate vasodilators such as dipyridamole (Persantine) and adenosine have been employed as a means to simulate the physiologic effects of exercise. The most widely used of these, dipyridamole, is an adenosine deaminase inhibitor that allows the accumulation of the potent vasodilator adenosine in the coronary bed. This produces selective vasodilatation of normal coronary arteries, predominantly in the small, resistant vessels of the coronary bed. At the usual dosages used, intravenous dipyridamole increases coronary blood flow by three to five times resting levels compared with a one- to three-fold increase with exercise. In addition to coronary vasodilatation, intravenous dipyridamole infusion typically produces a mild reduction in systemic blood pressure and increases heart rate and cardiac output with no significant effect on left ventricular ejection fraction.

Unlike normal coronary vessels, diseased stenosed vessels demonstrate no further dilatation because they are already maximally dilated secondary to autoregulatory mechanisms in the myocardium. Therefore, whereas there is proportionally increased flow to the normal vessels supplying the myocardium, blood flow in the distribution of abnormal vessels is not increased. Thus, when dipyridamole is used in conjunction with thallium 201 imaging, there is a radionuclide mapping of this discrepancy in perfusion with a consequent accentuation of normal to abnormal thallium concentrations in the heart. For purposes of imaging, this accomplishes the effect of exercise on the coronary arteries with one important exception: there is minimal effect on cardiac work or myocardial oxygen demand, thus providing an additional margin in safety in patients with significant coronary stenosis.

It should be noted that as with many interventional pharmaceuticals, significant undesirable side effects may occur. In the case of dipyridamole, the drug may cause angina, headaches, dizziness, flushing, and nausea. These side effects may be rapidly reduced by the intravenous administration of aminophylline (100 to 200 mg/min). This antidote should be readily available during the procedure.

Because excretion of dipyridamole is primarily biliary, caution should be exercised with marked hepatic dysfunction. In addition, care should be taken in patients with respiratory distress or those recently recovering from respiratory failure because dipyridamole may occasionally induce acute bronchospasm. It is also prudent to avoid intravenous dipyridamole in patients with acute unstable angina or recent myocardial infarction. Generally, it is a good idea to employ intravenous type dipyridamole thallium imaging only in patients who would otherwise be candidates for an exercise study if it were not for their physical limitations.

Technique

Techniques described in the literature have involved either oral or intravenous administration of dipyridamole. In either case, patients should be fasting or NPO for 4 to 6 hours. Stopping or altering any preexisting oral dipyridamole therapy does not appear necessary.

Xanthine medications, including theophylline (aminophylline) and caffeine, reverse the cardiovascular effects of dipyridamole and thus should be avoided, when possible, prior to the examination. Xanthine-containing medication should be withheld for 36 hours and caffeine-containing beverages for 12 to 24 hours prior to the study. Patients dependent upon theophylline because of respiratory illnesses may not tolerate cessation of therapy.

Dipyridamole may be administered orally or intravenously, although the intravenous route is preferred because of its more reliable, predictable blood levels. Intravenous infusion through a large (antecubital) arm vein is performed over 4 minutes at a concentration of about 0.5 mg per kg in 20 to 40 ml of normal saline (an infusion rate of 0.142 mg/kg/min). ECG and blood pressure should be monitored for the first 15 minutes.

Patients may be supine, standing, or sitting, and low levels of exercise, including walking or isometric hand grip, may be employed adjunctively if desired. A dose of 2 to 3 mCi (74 to 111 MBq) of thallium 201 chloride is administered intravenously 3 to 4 minutes after the dipyridamole infusion is completed, with initial imaging begun approximately 5 to 15 minutes later. If desired, 50 mg of aminophylline may be administered intravenously at 20 minutes into the study to prevent adverse side effects or with any earlier occurrence of angina. In oral dipyridamole studies, thallium is administered 45 minutes after an oral dose of 300 mg.

Dipyridamole Thallium Image Interpretation

Myocardial uptake of thallium 201 is greater with dipyridamole than with exercise stress, although there is no significant difference in lung activity. Washout rates from heart and lung do not differ from post-exercise studies. The pattern of liver, spleen, and splanchnic activity is the reverse of that noted with maximal exercise; that is, increased activity in these regions is seen on initial images, which decreases on the delayed views.

The cardiac findings are interpreted identical to exercise examinations with comparable sensitivity and specificity. As expected, however, the additional information such as ECG response, exercise capacity, and heart rate–blood pressure product obtained during conventional physical stress is not available. Increased lung activity correlates with the presence of coronary artery disease but does not predict severity or extent.

QUANTITATIVE ANALYSIS OF THALLIUM

Visual interpretation of thallium 201 planar or SPECT images is subject to considerable inter-observer variability and is markedly dependent on the quality of the visual display. Furthermore, regional thallium washout provides crucial diagnostic information that is difficult to detect by visual inspection. Thus, a number of approaches have been devised to permit quantitative and semiquantitative evaluation of the distribution and washout information available in thallium 201 exercise stress studies. Typically, such programs produce circumferential profiles displayed as curves of relative thallium activity in the myocardium at both exercise and stress. Subsequently, a washout circumferential profile is calculated, which presents a curve of percent washout from the initial stress images to the 4-hour redistribution views (Fig. 8–8). Normally, percent washout rates of thallium 201 from the myocardium are roughly uniform from all myocardial regions. Such efforts may be further enhanced by comparison of the resultant profiles with a pooled file of normal controls with a deviation of more than 2.5 standard deviations below the mean normal usually considered abnormal.

For the overall detection of coronary artery disease (CAD), the quantitative method is similar in sensitivity and specificity to visual interpretation. However, in addition to being objective and reproducible, quantitation presents significant advantages in certain situations. Specifically, quantitation allows improvement in the sensitivity for the detection of individual coronary stenoses, the detection of coronary stenosis of only moderate (50 to 75 percent) degree, and the identification of triple-vessel coronary disease. Although the quantitative method does aid somewhat in detecting myocardial defects that may be

difficult to detect visually, the major contribution to the sensitivity of the test is in the identification of areas of slower than normal regional washout rate as a marker for areas of less than normal perfusion (Fig. 8–9). This may be seen as a localized area of reduced washout rate or, in extensive coronary artery disease, as a diffuse, slow washout pattern throughout all myocardial regions. It should be noted that like visual interpretation, the quantitative method is dependent on the degree of exercise attained during the study. The specificity of washout rate analysis for the detection of regional myocardial hypoperfusion has been shown to be reduced in patients who achieve less than 85 percent maximal predicted heart rate, although to a lesser degree than originally thought.

CLINICAL APPLICATIONS OF THALLIUM EXERCISE IMAGING

Coronary Artery Disease

Even in the presence of high-grade coronary artery stenosis, perfusion to the myocardium distal to the stenosis is generally normal or near normal when a patient is at rest. However, under stress, the increased demands placed on the myocardium are reflected by need for increased oxygen supply and, therefore, for increased perfusion. Under these circumstances, there may be diminished coronary vascular reserve if sufficient blood flow is not permitted through the stenotic area to supply the increased demands

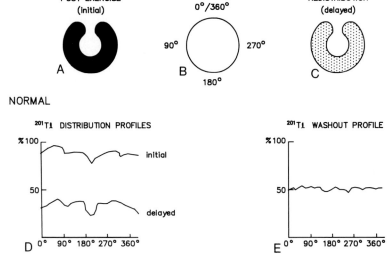

Figure 8–8. Circumferential analysis of thallium distribution in the left ventricle. Initial post-stress image (A) is analyzed by computer (B), in this case beginning at the 12 o'clock position and proceeding counterclockwise. (This progression may vary with computer program.) The activity is compared with the delayed redistribution image (C) and plotted graphically (D). The washout profile is shown in (E).

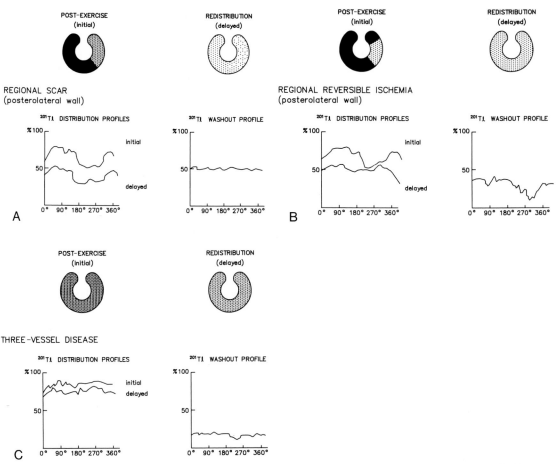

Figure 8–9. Circumferential thallium analysis in pathologic states. (A) A regional scar shows decreased thallium at about 270° on both initial and delayed plots but a normal washout profile. (B) Regional reversible ischemia shows decreased thallium at 270° initially but near normal activity on delayed plot and a focal decrease in thallium washout profile. (C) Three-vessel disease shows no focal defects but a markedly reduced thallium washout profile.

of the stressed myocardium. Such an occurrence results in the induction of stress-induced ischemia in the tissues distal to the stenosis. This principle is the underlying basis for all stress examinations designed for the detection and evaluation of coronary artery disease, whether the patient is monitored with a myocardial perfusion imaging agent such as thallium or with gated radionuclide ventriculography. When thallium 201 is injected at peak stress, it localizes in the myocardium in a fashion that reflects regional perfusion and, if present, regional ischemia. Ischemic areas are perceived as regions of diminished thallium uptake. In addition, those areas of the myocardium that experience normally augmented perfusion at stress will have increased thallium deposition over that which they experience at rest. Therefore, a maximum contrast is produced by the differences in decreased regional thallium deposition in ischemic areas and the augmented deposition in adjacent normal regions.

Thallium stress imaging has proved to be an examination of high sensitivity and specificity for the detection of coronary artery disease when post-exercise and subsequent redistribution images are obtained. Its sensitivity for the detection of coronary artery stenosis increases with the severity of the stenoses and the extent of the disease (number of vessels involved). The overall sensitivity in the detection of stress-induced ischemia is approximately 80 to 90 percent and specificity is 90 percent. This represents a considerable increase in sensitivity over exercise electrocardiography (60 to 70 percent sensitivity), with a comparable or slightly increased specificity. The significantly greater sensitivity of thallium 201 imaging over exercise electrocardiography is probably in large part due to the great number of patients with nondiagnostic exercise tests because of baseline electrocardiographic abnormalities or inadequate stress. It should be noted that sensitivity for planar imaging in the detection of individual stenoses varies with the vessel involved. Sensitivity is greatest for left anterior descending coronary artery disease (80 percent), followed by right coronary artery disease (75 percent), with sensitivity being least in left circumflex stenosis (50 percent).

Despite its superiority for the detection of coronary perfusion abnormalities, the thallium examination has not and should not replace routine stress ECG examinations for the general screening of patients for coronary lesions. Thallium 201 imaging is most useful when it is applied to two broad groups of patients with coronary artery disease: those in whom exercise electrocardiography is nondiagnostic and those with an intermediate probability of disease. The latter group includes both patients with high suspicion of coronary artery disease but with negative exercise electrocardiograms and those with a low likelihood of coronary artery disease but with a suggestive or positive ECG at stress. Patients with underlying ECG abnormalities such as from left bundle branch block, pacemakers, or left ventricular hypertrophy may also be successfully studied by this method. While radionuclide stress ventriculography may also be used to detect the presence of coronary insufficiency, thallium imaging may be preferable or more practical (1) in the presence of resting or exercise-induced arrythmias, (2) in patients with valvular myocardial heart disease who may give abnormal ejection fraction responses, (3) in patients who have sympathetic augmentation of the left ventricular performance due to accompanying high anxiety states, (4) when particular coronary artery distributions are to be evaluated, and (5) in patients in whom coronary artery disease is still suspected after a normal or nondiagnostic radionuclide ventriculogram.

While thallium stress-redistribution imaging is a sensitive and specific means for determining the presence of coronary artery disease, it is less sensitive in determining the *extent* of disease in many patients, although the sensitivity for the detection of coronary artery disease by thallium stress imaging increases directly with the number of vessels involved. The presence of perfusion defects in more than one vessel distribution strongly indicates the presence of two- or three-vessel disease; however, a perfusion defect present in the distribution of only one vessel cannot be used to exclude the involvement of other vessels. Contrary to previous belief, patients with relatively symmetric three-vessel disease uncommonly demonstrate normal thallium imaging due to proportionally reduced flow through each artery.

Experimental evidence suggests that coronary artery diameter narrowing greater than 50 percent as determined by arteriography is likely to be hemodynamically significant. However, in many instances, the exact percentage of narrowing is difficult to ascertain on routine arteriography, and thallium stress imaging can be useful in determining the hemodynamic significance of an angiographically demonstrated stenosis. Stress-induced ischemia in the distribution of a stenosis may be interpreted as strong evidence of physiologic significance. But because the thallium test is not 100 percent sensitive, a stress test demonstrating normal regional thallium accumulation in a particular arterial distribution is less definitive in predicting the absence of a significant narrowing. This problem may be further complicated in patients with multiple stenoses, in whom exercise performance may be limited by the more severe lesions so that an exercise level sufficient to induce ischemia in the distribution of the questionable stenosis may not be reached.

The functional significance of collateral vessels identified at coronary arteriography may be similarly evaluated. There is some evidence to suggest that while collaterals may maintain adequate rest perfusion to the myocardium distal to a stenosis, they may not be able to meet the oxygen demands of this tissue during exercise. Therefore, thallium stress imaging may be able to give a clearer idea of the reserve perfusion potential of such collaterals.

Thallium may also be used to assess the viability of myocardium in regions of asynergy demonstrated with contrast or radionuclide ventriculography. Such segments may be determined to be viable tissue if exercise-delayed thallium images demonstrate activity within the region. Such information may be useful in planning bypass surgery by determining the practicality of reestablishing blood flow to questionably viable tissue.

Chest pain after cardiac bypass surgery may or may not have a cardiac origin, but the ability to distinguish between the two is of significance. Postoperative pain from a cardiac etiology may be related to occlusion of the bypass grafts or to the progression of disease in indigenous vessels. Postoperative exercise thallium imaging gives information regarding the hemodynamic success of bypass surgery by comparing preoperative and postoperative stress images. The return of a normal perfusion appearance to areas that preoperatively demonstrated stress-induced ischemia correlates not only with the technical success of the surgery but also with an improvement in symptomatology. The persistence of defects on postoperative images shows a positive correlation with vein graft closure and may further demonstrate lesions not identified on the preoperative study, indicating progression of disease in indigenous vessels. In addition, new fixed defects may indicate perioperative myocardial injury.

Because of the ability to evaluate specific regions of the left ventricular myocardium as defined by coronary artery vascular distributions, thallium stress imaging may be used to evaluate the success of percutaneous transluminal coronary angioplasty in improving perfusion to the myocardium distal to a treated stenosis. In this setting, the added anatomic localization and sensitivity provided by SPECT imaging and associated quantitative protocols provide additional advantages.

Prognostication and Risk Stratification in Coronary Artery Disease

As a direct measure of the degree and distribution of impaired myocardial perfusion at stress, thallium 201 imaging has been shown to be effective for assessing risk of future cardiac events in patients with presumed chronic or known coronary artery disease. Findings on abnormal thallium 201 stress imaging that have been found to represent potent prognosticators of future cardiac events include

1. The number of reversible thallium defects (an indicator of multi-vessel disease)
2. Initial size and severity of the reversible defect
3. Reversible defects in the left main coronary artery distribution
4. Abnormal lung accumulation of thallium 201

In the post-myocardial infarction patient, exercise redistribution thallium 201 imaging permits future risk stratification through the identification of significant residual peri-infarct ischemia (myocardium at risk) and/or ischemia remote from the acute injury (multi-vessel disease). Conversely, a normal exercise thallium 201 study or a small fixed defect in a single vascular territory allows low-risk classification.

Noncoronary Disease States

Valvular Lesions

A variety of abnormalities may produce positive thallium stress tests in the absence of coronary artery disease. Perhaps the most controversial is mitral valve prolapse syndrome. Although exercise perfusion defects may be identified in patients with mitral valve prolapse and without angiographic evidence of coronary artery disease, this is an uncommon occurrence. At the moment, the etiology and significance of such defects remain uncertain. However, a normal exercise thallium study in a patient with suspected mitral valve prolapse serves as evidence against superimposed coronary artery disease.

Patients with valvular aortic stenosis may present with angina-like symptoms without the presence of coronary artery disease at angiography. Such patients may demonstrate reversible perfusion defects on thallium imaging, which is thought to be related to a reduced perfusion gradient in the coronary arteries associated with tight aortic stenosis. In addition, apparent thinning of the walls of the left ventricle may be identified after stress, again possibly related to diffuse subendocardial ischemia accompanying massive hypertrophy. Thus, thallium imaging defects after exercise in patients with aortic stenosis cannot be used to successfully predict the presence of superimposed coronary artery disease, since 40 to 60 percent of such patients without significant coronary lesions show such defects.

Patients with aortic regurgitation and normal coronary arteries may demonstrate reversible thallium defects in the apical segment of the left ventricular myocardium. The mechanism of this observation is uncertain, but may be secondary to marked left ventricular volume overload at exercise. Although apical reversible defects in this setting are thus equivocal, reversible perfusion deficits elsewhere in the left ventricle of a patient with aortic regurgitation should be considered as evidence of superimposed coronary artery disease.

Left Bundle Branch Block

Because left bundle branch block renders ECG stress testing nondiagnostic, a noninvasive diagnosis of coronary artery disease is often sought using thallium 201 imaging. Patients with left bundle branch block, however, may demonstrate reversible septal perfusion abnormalities in the absence of demonstrable coronary artery disease. Diminished coronary flow at exercise due to altered septal relaxation has been proposed as the mechanism for this phenomenon. Thus, reversible perfusion defects in the septal region of patients with left bundle branch block are an indeterminate finding. However, reversible defects elsewhere in the left ventricular myocardium retain their specificity for the diagnosis of transient ischemia.

Idiopathic Hypertrophic Subaortic Stenosis (IHSS)

Asymmetric septal hypertrophy, a hallmark of IHSS, may present as increased count density in the region of the thickened septum, compared with the lateral or free ventricular wall. This alteration of thallium distribution must be taken into consideration when evaluating patients with IHSS and angina for the presence of coronary artery disease. Although such patients frequently may present with significant ECG abnormalities at exercise, thallium 201 imaging appears to be useful and accurate in excluding coronary artery disease in patients with IHSS and angina because significant false positive perfusion defects do not appear to be a problem.

Cardiomyopathy

Attempts have been made to use thallium stress scintigraphy to differentiate ischemic from idiopathic congestive cardiomyopathy. Unfortunately, a great deal of overlap of abnormal findings has been described with significant reversible defects identified in both groups of patients. There is some evidence, however, that when severe focal defects of essentially absent thallium activity are identified, ischemic cardiomyopathy is more likely.

Hypertensive Myocardial Hypertrophy

In patients with myocardial hypertrophy resulting from long-standing hypertension, thallium 201 myocardial count density both on stress and redistribution images may demonstrate a relative increase in the septal wall that is not necessarily indicative of selective septal hypertrophy. However, this increased count density leads to a relative decrease in activity in the lateral wall, which is especially apparent on horizontal long axis SPECT images. This may lead to the false impression of a fixed lateral wall defect indicative of a myocardial infarction. Because hypertension is a major risk factor for coronary artery disease, hypertensive patients are often referred for thallium 201 myocardial perfusion scintigraphy. Thus, a history of possible hypertension should be elicited in patients undergoing these studies.

SPECT THALLIUM IMAGING

In spite of its acceptable sensitivity and specificity for the detection of coronary artery disease, qualitative planar imaging is limited in its detection of localized perfusion deficits because of the reduced contrast resolution largely due to superimposed areas of normally perfused myocardium. This leads to a lower sensitivity than with SPECT for moderate coronary artery disease (50 to 70 percent stenosis) as well as to difficulty in specifically localizing the visualized defect to a particular coronary distribution.

Experience with qualitative SPECT imaging has established that the technique is superior to planar imaging for the detection of specific vessel disease and thus for the identification of multi-vessel involvement. The most dramatic improvement is in detecting left circumflex coronary artery disease. Although qualitative SPECT imaging permits better detection of moderate stenoses, quantitative SPECT thallium imaging with washout analysis appears to be an additional improvement with about 80 percent sensitivity for such lesions. Overall, it is apparent that SPECT thallium imaging with or without quantitation provides improved specificity and sensitivity for defining the extent and severity of coronary artery disease.

Technique

Commonly, SPECT exercise-redistribution thallium imaging is performed subsequent to the intravenous injection of 2 to 3 mCi (74.0 to 111 MBq) of thallium 201 chloride at peak stress, with the patient being imaged as soon as possible after injection. The patient is placed on the imaging table with the arms over the head and with significant interfering breast tissue being uniformly compressed over the chest or elevated. A rotational arc of 180° is used beginning at the 45° RAO position and ending at 45° LPO. Using a 64 × 64 computer matrix, 64 images are obtained over the 180° arc for a total study recording time of approximately 30 minutes. A low-energy, all-purpose collimator provides an adequate compromise between sensitivity and image resolution.

After acquisition, the images are reconstructed in oblique planes using the reconstruction parameters selected by the operator (Fig. 8–10). Standard reconstruction planes offer appropriate transsectional views for anatomic structures with axes of symmetry parallel with or perpendicular to the axis of rotation; however, for structures such as the heart, whose axis of symmetry is not so oriented, the standard reconstructed views are inadequate. Thus, image reconstruction of cardiac tomograms is performed in planes that are perpendicular to or parallel with the long axis of the heart and oblique to the axis of the body and, thus, to the standard reconstruction views, (Figs. 8–11, 8–12, and 8–13). Generally, the only operator input required for reconstruction is the identification of the long axis of the heart. This allows the computer to reconstruct tomographic images in three oblique orthogonal planes relative to the orientation of the heart in the chest. Typically, the reconstructed slices are 1 to 2 pixels in thickness when a 64 × 64 matrix is used.

After processing is completed, the images must be displayed in a fashion that facilitates comparison. Whereas each computer system software has a display algorithm for the tomographic images, it is attendant upon the interpreter to ensure that comparable sections are displayed so that an accurate comparison can be made. Generally, only tomographic sections that represent slices through both the myocardium *and* the cavity of the heart are of value. Subsequent interpretation is best performed by manipulation of the images on the computer screen, with filming (hard copy) used primarily for permanent image storage (Fig. 8–14).

The theoretical basis for image interpretation is essentially identical with that of planar images. However, a knowledge of SPECT imaging artifacts and normal anatomy is critical in SPECT image interpretation (Table 8–9). Since tomographic images are composed of highly processed data, the interpreter must first ascertain that the acquisition and resulting processed images are artifact-free. Careful but rapid examination of the raw data as displayed in the rotating planar format will aid in detecting gross patient motion, areas of significant soft tissue attenuation, and any superimposed liver or spleen activity. If the imaging system provides other means for detecting patient motion, such as a "sinogram," this should also be viewed. After determining the validity of the images, the interpreter should next assess the processed data rapidly by checking the short axis views to ensure that they are aligned and free of significant artifacts.

Accurate interpretation of thallium 201

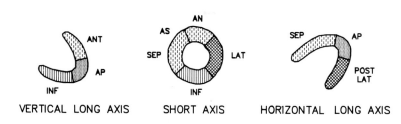

Figure 8–10. SPECT thallium images: mid-ventricular sections in the three common oblique projections showing ventricular wall anatomy with vascular supplies approximated by shading.

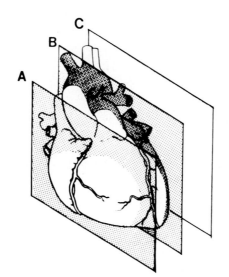

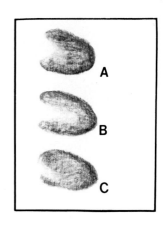

Figure 8–11. Vertical long axis sections through the left ventricle from septum to free wall are shown with corresponding thallium 201 myocardial images.

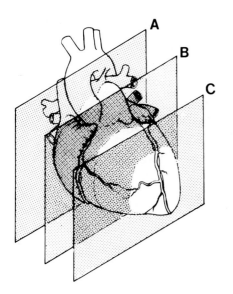

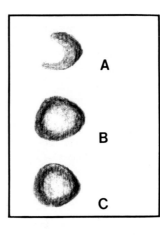

Figure 8–12. Short axis slices through the left ventricle from the base of the heart to apex are shown with corresponding thallium 201 images. Note the considerable thinning of the upper septal wall.

Figure 8–13. Horizontal axis sections are shown through the left ventricle from anterior to inferior with corresponding thallium 201 myocardial images.

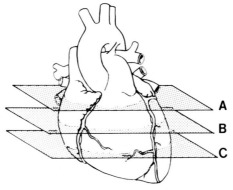

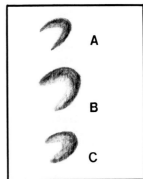

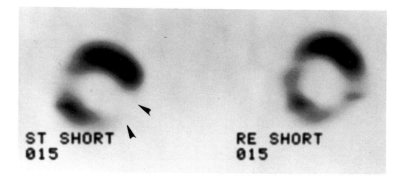

Figure 8–14. Stress and redistribution thallium 201 SPECT short axis views, demonstrating an inferolateral wall defect at stress, which partially redistributes. This indicates an ischemic component.

Table 8–9. THALLIUM 201 SPECT IMAGE ARTIFACTS AND VARIANTS

CAUSE	RESULT	RECOGNITION/CORRECTION
Acquisition		
Soft tissue attenuation		
Breast/obesity	Anterior or lateral wall defect	Bind or elevate breast; view rotating planar image
Elevated left hemidiaphragm	Inferior wall defect	View rotating planar image
Abdominal visceral activity (liver/spleen)	Relative increased inferior wall activity	
Patient motion	Myocardial defects (depend on type and direction of motion)	View rotating planar images or image sinogram; use computer motion correction algorithm
Post-exercise respiratory motion	Reversible inferior wall defect	Delay immediate post-exercise images 10–15 minutes
Processing		
Oblique axis reconstruction: incorrect selection of LV long axis	Myocardial defects—frequently basal	Review long axis selection
Instrumentation		
COR* errors		
Rightward (+)	Posteroapical defect	Misaligned anteroposterior walls in horizontal axis view
Leftward (−)	Anteroapical defect	Strict quality control and COR correction
Marked flood field nonuniformity	Ring artifacts	Strict quality control and field uniformity correction
Normal Variant		
Variable septal and apical thinning	Myocardial defects	Typical location
Papillary muscles	Focal myocardial hot spots	Typical location (2 and 7 o'clock in transverse images)
Cardiac rotation		
Dextrorotation	Fixed relative lateral wall defect	History of congenital heart disease; hyperexpanded lungs; marked right or left selective chamber enlargement. Inspect ECG/transaxial slices
Levorotation	Fixed relative septal defect	
Noncoronary Disease		
Left bundle branch block	Reversible septal defect	Review ECG
Myocardial hypertrophy	Fixed relative lateral wall defect (lower lateral/septal count ratio)	Review ECG; history or hypertension or valvular heart disease

*COR = center of rotation.

SPECT images requires an understanding and awareness of common artifacts. Significant soft tissue attenuation in patients with large breasts or breast implants or obese patients with considerable accumulation of adipose tissue in the lateral chest wall may produce fixed anterior or lateral wall defects if the patient is imaged identically in the post-exercise and subsequent redistribution studies. Changes in positioning of the patient or of the patient's breasts in the redistribution images, however, may give rise to apparent reversible abnormalities.

In addition, patients with abdominal protuberances or left hemidiaphragmatic elevation may have spurious inferior wall defects due to focal attenuation. Liver or spleen activity overlying the inferior wall of the left ventricle, especially on the redistribution images, may produce a relative increase in activity in the inferior wall, with the resultant appearance of reverse redistribution on exercise studies and the reverse effect noted on dipyridamole studies suggesting inferior wall myocardial ischemia.

Patient motion is a significant cause of spurious myocardial defects, with the appearance of the scan artifact depending on the direction of motion (when it occurs during acquisition) and whether the motion is abrupt or gradual. Exaggerated diaphragmatic motion due to rapid respiration immediately post-exercise that subsequently returns to normal may produce an artifact that mimics inferior wall ischemia. To avoid the "diaphragmatic creep" artifact, some have advocated the delay of immediate post-exercise images for approximately 15 minutes to allow for hyperventilation to subside and the depth of respiration to return to normal.

Artifacts in oblique axis image reconstruction may occur if the long axis of the left ventricle is incorrectly selected from either the mid-transaxial or mid-ventricle long axis slice. This generally results in over- or underestimation of activity at the apex. As expected, breaches in quality control of the imaging system, such as center of rotation malalignment and flood-field nonuniformity, may produce significant image artifacts.

After the thallium images have been determined to be free of significant artifacts, visual interpretation proceeds in essentially the same manner as with planar imaging. In the normal study, there is typically diminished activity in the membranous portion of the intraventricular septum and to a varying degree in the apicoinferior wall. These should not be mistaken for areas of scarring. Furthermore, the lateral myocardium generally demonstrates more activity than other myocardial territories, especially when compared with the septum in the short axis slices. This likely results from the lateral wall being closest to the camera during much of the 180° acquisition. Areas of focally increased activity in and at the insertions of the anterior and posterior papillary muscles may frequently be seen at approximately 2 o'clock and 7 o'clock in the short axis images.

In addition to inspecting the set of images for fixed and transient defects in the myocardium, quantitative methods may be applied to SPECT images, which, importantly, permit the detection of significant washout abnormalities. This is frequently performed by comparing thallium distribution with gender-matched normal files.

In addition to the conventional display of multiple slices, a set of images may be condensed into one image by using a so-called *bull's eye plot* (Fig. 8–15). This is simply a polar map or representation of the entire myocardium in multiple concentric circles forming a single image that represents thallium distribution at exercise or stress. For

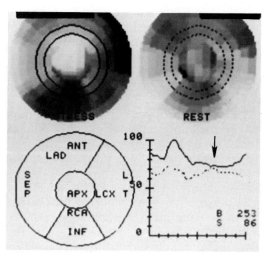

Figure 8–15. Black and white display of color bull's-eye polar plots of thallium 201 activity in the myocardium, at post-exercise and redistribution, demonstrates a septal defect (arrow) that partially redistributes and is compatible with ischemia. The corresponding curves represent activity distributions in each image progressing clockwise from 3 o'clock (0 degrees).

many, this is a convenient solution to reviewing a large number of images, or, alternatively, it can be used as an adjunct to the standard interpretative approach.

Resting Thallium Scintigraphy

When thallium 201 chloride is injected intravenously at rest, the subsequent distribution of activity in the myocardium reflects coronary artery perfusion at rest. Since resting-state coronary blood flow may remain adequate in spite of severe stenotic disease, such examinations are of limited, but occasional value in the detection of transient ischemia. Most commonly, the identification of a thallium perfusion defect at rest reflects the presence of scarred tissue associated with previous myocardial infarction, either acute or chronic. However, as previously mentioned, the defects are nonspecific and may be occasionally produced by a number of other entities. When performing resting thallium scintigraphy, it is nevertheless important to obtain both immediate post-injection images and 2- to 4-hour redistribution views so that the fixed defects of scarring may be differentiated from any transient ischemic component.

Resting thallium studies may be useful in the detection and evaluation of acute myocardial infarcts. The most practical applications of this technique are for ruling out myocardial infarctions and for early recognition of patients at high risk for post-infarction complications.

The detection of acute myocardial infarction by thallium scanning is highly reliable in the first 24 hours after an infarct. In fact, the sooner imaging is performed after the onset of symptoms, the more likely is the thallium study to be positive. A sensitivity of 96 percent has been reported for the detection of acute infarcts when scans are obtained within the first 6 hours following the onset of symptoms. Sensitivity decreases thereafter with time, possibly related to the resolution of associated acute reversible ischemia in the region of infarction. An entirely normal study performed within the first few hours after the onset of symptoms provides significant evidence against the likelihood of acute myocardial infarction. This is in contrast to ^{99m}Tc pyrophosphate imaging, which is frequently negative in the first 12 hours. Unfortunately, thallium imaging does not distinguish between old and new myocardial infarctions and is, therefore, most useful in patients without ECG or historical evidence of previous infarction as well as in patients with previous baseline thallium studies.

Thallium images may also serve as an indicator of the location and extent of damaged myocardium and, therefore, may provide prognostic information. Thallium data correlate well with enzymatic and autopsy estimates of infarct size. In general, the larger the perfusion defect, the poorer the prognosis and the more likely reinfarction or sudden death. Clinical studies have also shown that thallium defects representing acute myocardial infarction on the initial resting images may indeed diminish in size with further delayed imaging. Such delayed imaging may allow for differentiation between permanently damaged and reversible myocardium. Demonstration of the degree of reversibility of a resting thallium defect early in the course of myocardial infarction may be employed to determine therapy in patients with large areas of potentially salvageable myocardium.

Thallium 201 imaging at rest has also been used to differentiate unstable angina pectoris from acute myocardial infarction. When the study is performed during an episode of pain, approximately 50 percent of patients with unstable angina demonstrate perfusion defects on initial resting images. Delayed images obtained after the pain has subsided demonstrate that these defects are usually reversible, as opposed to those associated with completed infarction.

NEW MYOCARDIAL PERFUSION AGENTS

Several classes of technetium 99m complexes for myocardial perfusion imaging are currently undergoing clinical testing. The two most prominent of these are the family of technetium 99m labeled isonitriles and the technetium 99m boronic adducts of technetium oxine (BATOs).

The isonitriles demonstrate good myocardial uptake with variable liver and lung activity that generally subsides over time. BATOs have also shown good myocardial uptake, which is followed, however, by rapid myocardial clearance and relatively low liver and lung uptake that clears quickly. Thus imaging with BATOs must be initiated as early as 2 to 3 minutes post-injection and completed within 15 to 20 minutes.

A major distinction between these new technetium 99m agents and thallium 201 is that, unlike thallium, these agents do not undergo significant myocardial redistribution in transiently ischemic areas on delayed images. Thus, diagnostic evaluation using post-stress and subsequent delayed imaging requires two separate injections. The ultimate role of new technetium 99m myocardial perfusion agents in the clinical setting awaits further evaluation.

Tests of Cardiac Function

Examinations providing information about ventricular function play a decisive role in the detection and diagnosis of a variety of cardiac problems and in the management of patients with known heart disease. In this respect, radionuclide methods provide a non-invasive means to assess both right and left ventricular pump performance at rest and during exercise and allow valuable insight into intracardiac and cardiopulmonary dynamics.

Radionuclide tests of ventricular function are generally accomplished by two discrete methods: (1) the first-transit or first-pass technique, in which imaging is undertaken during the initial pass of an intravenously administered radioactive bolus through the heart, lungs, and great vessels; and (2) the equilibrium technique, in which images of the cardiac blood pool are obtained after the radiopharmaceutical has equilibrated within the intravascular space.

Although equilibrium and first-pass methods require different procedural approaches, both are valid for qualitative and quantitative assessment of left ventricular function and provide essentially identical information. Both techniques are accurate and reproducible when compared with cardiac catheterization results. Therefore, although there are specific advantages and limitations to each, either method may be employed for the evaluation of ventricular function at rest or at exercise. Whichever technique is used, complete familiarity with the type of procedure employed and confidence in the performance of the technique provide the best approach for successful application.

COMPUTER METHODS

Among routine nuclear medicine procedures, those measuring cardiac function are perhaps the most dependent on computer methodology for the collection and processing of scintigraphic data. A basic knowledge of some specific computer methods is crucial to an understanding of cardiovascular nuclear medicine.

An important advantage of radioisotope methodology over that of conventional contrast radiography is the readiness with which the statistical information obtained by the gamma camera can be digitalized employing a computer. When a computer system coupled with a gamma camera is used to acquire, analyze, and display the data obtained from nuclear cardiac studies, two types of information result: (1) qualitative data displayed as images and (2) quantitative data expressed as numbers or curves.

Data can be acquired by a computer in a "list mode" or a "frame mode." Basically, list mode consists of digitalizing and filing data in the time sequence in which it occurs, permitting later retrieval and manipulation of the data. In this manner, decisions concerning the sorting and formatting of the filed information and the discarding of unwanted information may be made at any time after the information is acquired. This flexibility allows the computer operator to format the data in varying time sequences as may be dictated by the specific goals in mind. For instance, the data of a first-pass study may be formatted such that frames of several seconds' duration are generated and visual inspection of cardiac anatomy is possible. Alternatively, the data may be reformatted in frames of a fraction of a second's duration so that ventricular time-activity curves may be derived, allowing for quantification of ventricular function indices. Such flexibility necessarily has a price—the need for a relatively expensive hard disk system.

Frame mode acquisition requires formatting decisions to be made prior to the beginning of the study. After the information is collected, it cannot be reformatted to allow manipulation in varying time sequences. A major advantage is that frame mode requires substantially less computer memory.

Qualitative Data Display

Computer-generated images are generally better than their analog counterparts obtained directly from the gamma camera. Such images can be processed to allow for edge or contrast enhancement, background subtraction, smoothing, filtering, or other manipulations to produce improved images. In addition, these procedures may be performed as many times as necessary to provide for optimization of image quality. After images have been processed, they may be displayed as static images or in an "endless-loop" cine format that allows visual inspection of the ventricular walls during cardiac contraction and thus permits qualitative assessment of ventricular segmental wall motion.

Using various computer algorithms, "functional" images may also be generated from the data acquired from either first-pass or gated equilibrium blood pool studies. Rather than emphasizing spatial resolution, these images display global or regional changes in radioactivity, reflecting proportional volume changes within the ventricles.

Functional (Parametric) Images

As the name implies, functional images are generated for the isolation and evaluation of specific functional cardiac parameters. The images may be produced from data obtained by either gated equilibrium or first-pass techniques. Although a number of functional images may be derived, those in common use are the conventional functional images—stroke volume, paradox, and ejection fraction images—and phase and amplitude images.

The *stroke volume* image may be obtained by subtracting the end-systolic frame of the ventriculogram from the end-diastolic frame and displaying the resultant distribution of activity in a gray scale or color format (Fig. 8–16). This image presents the distribution of relative regional volume changes. Thus, the stroke volume image is an aid to the qualitative assessment of regional ventricular function and, indirectly, of wall motion. Because the image presents only positive values, only those areas that contain more blood activity in diastole than in systole will be seen. Thus, under usual circumstances, only the two ventricles will appear in the image. Regional wall motion abnormalities will, of course, alter the appearance of the stroke

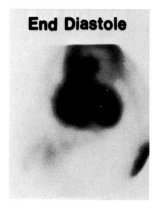

End Diastole

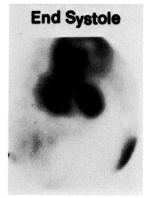

End Systole

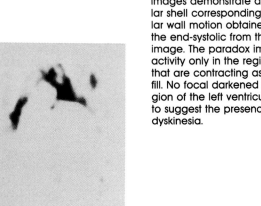

Figure 8–16. Normal gated radionuclide ventriculogram with functional images. End-diastolic and end-systolic images of the heart in the 45° LAO projection are shown with subsequent computer manipulation of the data to produce functional images. The stroke volume images demonstrate a darkened circular shell corresponding to left ventricular wall motion obtained by subtracting the end-systolic from the end-diastolic image. The paradox image displays activity only in the regions of the atria that are contracting as the ventricles fill. No focal darkened area in the region of the left ventricular wall is seen to suggest the presence of localized dyskinesia.

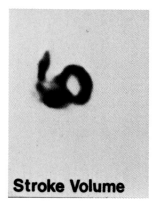

Stroke Volume

Paradox

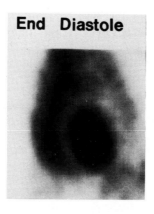 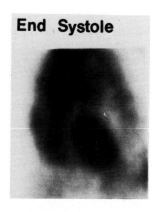

End Diastole   **End Systole**

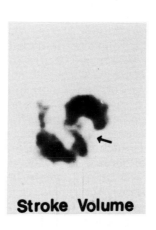 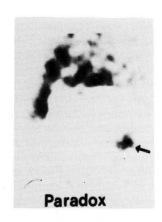

Stroke Volume   **Paradox**

Figure 8–17. Left ventricular aneurysm. The end-diastolic and end-systolic frames from the radionuclide ventriculogram are displayed with the functional paradox and stroke volume images. The stroke volume image demonstrates a break in the stroke volume shell seen in the region of the left ventricular apex (arrow), which could be interpreted as akinesia in this patient. However, the paradox image shows a focal darkened area at the left ventricular apex (arrow) compatible with focal dyskinesia and consistent with a left ventricular apical aneurysm.

volume image. In the case of marked focal hypokinesia, localized negative values will be generated, which will appear as an area of diminished activity. Likewise, an area of dyskinesia will also appear as a localized defect in the image due to the fact that negative values are not displayed.

The *ejection fraction images* are obtained through computer manipulation of the end-systolic and end-diastolic images to provide a static representation of the ejection fraction equation, that is, the stroke volume image divided by the end-diastolic image. In the stroke volume image, no quantitative parameters are derived, but the ejection fraction image allows qualitative and quantitative assessment of regional ejection fraction values as relative measures of local wall motion.

Typically, both the ejection fraction and stroke volume images obtained in the 45° LAO projection appear similar. The images frequently resemble a horseshoe or incomplete doughnut since most of the volume and ejection fraction changes occur at the apex, posterior wall, and distal septal walls in this projection. The basal portion of the heart,

which constitutes the membranous portion of the interventricular septum and the aortic outflow tract, contributes little to ventricular function and may, therefore, present as a relative defect in the activity distribution. The central portion of the left ventricular chamber also represents an area of decreased activity because the relative count changes in the center of the ventricle are small during systole.

Defects in the horseshoe or doughnut distribution of the "ejection shell" indicate areas of diminished stroke volume and/or ejection fraction as may be found in regional hypokinesis and/or akinesis (Fig. 8–17). Dyskinetic segments are not evaluated in these images since negative changes are given a zero value by the functional image program.

Dyskinetic segments, however, may be identified by employing another type of functional image called the *paradox image*. The paradox image is essentially an inverse stroke volume image in that the diastolic frame of the ventriculogram is subtracted from the systolic frame. With normal left ventricular contraction, no areas of activity (positive values) should be identified in the region of the left ventricular wall. Thus, in normals, only the atria and the great vessels are seen. However, in the presence of regional dyskinesia, a focal area of increased activity will appear in the image since the regional end-systolic volume is larger than the end-diastolic volume. Thus, subtraction of the two volumes gives a net positive value focally. Because maximum paradoxic motion in a region of dyskinesia does not always occur at end-systole, but may occur earlier in the cardiac cycle, paradox images may underestimate the magnitude of dyskinetic wall motion or even fail to represent it if dyskinesia is mild.

By applying *amplitude* and *phase analysis* (often called Fourier) techniques to digital images, information regarding the sequence of contraction of the cardiac chambers as well as individual wall segments of the left or right ventricle may be derived. Such analysis permits sensitive evaluation of regional wall motion and the detection and assessment of ventricular conduction abnormalities such as bundle branch block. Furthermore, because more precise differentiation between atrial and ventricular contraction is possible, the identification and exclusion of atrial activity from regions of interest for ejection fraction determinations are possible, allowing greater accuracy.

In this method, each pixel of the ventriculogram is presumed to represent a volume element with its own characteristic magnitude (amplitude) of contraction and a unique time of contraction (phase). By describing the count changes in each pixel during the cardiac cycle in terms of sinusoidal curves, a summary of the parameters of heart motion is determined. Essentially, each myocardial segment in the LAO projection is assigned a phase angle that categorizes the motion of that segment of myocardium. For example, a dyskinetic segment would be assigned a phase angle of 180°, indicating that it is out of phase with the normal motion of the surrounding myocardium. These parameters of phase and amplitude are then displayed as functional images that allow the evaluation of magnitude of regional wall motion and sequence of contraction. The phase image represents only the information related to *synchrony* or *asynchrony* of wall motion and is independent of the magnitude of that motion. The amplitude image represents the

extent of regional wall motion regardless of the time of occurrence within the cardiac cycle. The appearance of the amplitude image is generally similar to the sum of the stroke volume and the paradox functional images.

Different formats may be used for phase and amplitude image display, including static gray or color scales or histogram format showing the regional distribution of phase within the heart. However, the most easily interpretable display consists of a functional image of the entire multigated study using different colors to highlight pixels and/or wall segments in the frame in which they contract. This is performed on a frame-by-frame basis and, when played in a cine mode, displays a dynamic wave of contraction sweeping across the heart, demonstrating both various conduction abnormalities and segmental wall motion abnormalities.

In a normal phase analysis, the contraction pattern is expected to follow a standard sequence: atrial contraction fills the ventricular chambers followed by contraction of the ventricles. Since the atria are filling when the ventricles are emptying and vice versa, they can be thought of as contracting with the phase difference of 180°. The normal phase pattern, as seen in the functional image, will show the ventricles at one value of phase and the atria at 180° phase relative to the ventricles. Background regions around the heart will have random phases. Abnormal phase patterns may be found in patients with cardiac pacemakers, either right or left bundle branch block, Wolff-Parkinson-White syndrome, and ventricular tachycardia. Thus, the information obtained from phase analysis gives a demonstration of the mechanical (wall motion) manifestations of underlying conduction abnormalities, showing clearly the relationships between the electrical and mechanical sequences.

A normal phase analysis is shown in Figure 8–18. The normal images have both a histogram located on the left and static representation image on the right. The histogram demonstrates the number or pixels with a given phase angle, which describes their contraction. On the left of the histogram is a gray scale that corresponds to the gray scale in the static image. For instance, in a phase image on a normal study, the atria are relatively light gray, whereas the ventricle is dark gray. When the gray on the static image is

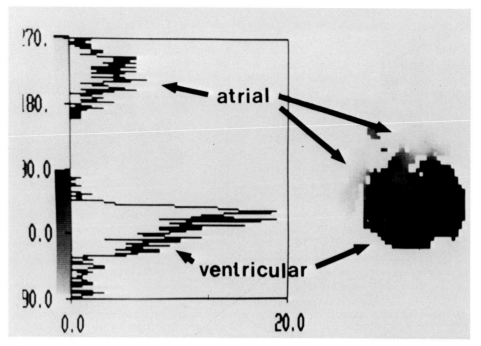

Figure 8–18. Phase analysis of a normal gated ventriculogram in the LAO projection. The phase information is displayed as a histogram on the left and as a gray scale image on the right. Clearly separated are the ventricular and atrial contraction peaks with differentiation of ventricular and atrial contraction on the gray scale image.

compared with the histogram, it is revealed that the upper portion of the histogram represents the atria, which are 180° out of phase with the lower portion of the histogram, which represents the ventricles. The uniformity of gray in the ventricular portion demonstrates a normal sequence of contraction. This may be compared with the abnormal image seen in Figure 8–19. In this figure, the static representation shows an area of light gray located in the apex of the ventricle. This is identified as a broadening of the atrial peak on the histogram due to the contribution of the dyskinetic segment of the ventricle. This broadens the apical peak of the histogram because the segment in the ventricle is 180° out of phase with the remainder of ventricular contraction.

Quantitative Data Display

Computer manipulation of the numerical information contained within digitalized images permits the quantitation of various indices of cardiac performance. Current computer programs allow access to several basic approaches including the classical or geo-

metric approach, and the count-volume or time–activity method.

The geometric approach is used infrequently. This technique is essentially identical with the contrast angiographic method of determining the ventricular borders at end-systole and end-diastole and using geometric assumptions of three-dimensional ventricular shape to calculate chamber volumes and hence ejection fractions. This method is fraught with the same errors inherent in the angiographic technique and is particularly unreliable when unusual ventricular shapes are encountered.

The count-volume or time–activity method of quantifying ventricular function solves many of the problems associated with geometric methods. The basic principle underlying this approach is the assumed proportionality between recorded activity and the volume of blood in which it is contained. That is, after the administered radioactive agent has thoroughly mixed with the blood in the cardiac chambers, any change in the count rate obtained from a particular chamber will reflect a proportional change in the volume of blood within that chamber. By

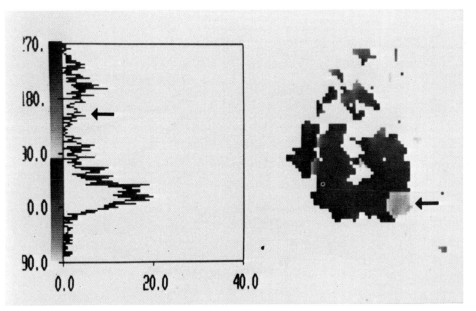

Figure 8–19. Phase analysis of a gated ventriculogram demonstrating a left ventricular apical aneurysm. The phase information is displayed as a histogram on the left and as a gray scale image on the right. On the histogram, a discrete peak for the ventricular contraction is seen, but there is significant broadening of the atrial peak compatible with a dyskinetic (out-of-phase) segment of left ventricular myocardium appearing during atrial contraction (arrow). The gray scale image on the right clearly depicts the focal apical aneurysm as a lighter shade of gray.

choosing a region of interest over the left ventricular blood pool and a periventricular area of background to allow for subtraction of counts from structures overlying the ventricular area of interest, a time–activity curve is generated, which represents changes in ventricular activity and therefore in relative ventricular volume during the cardiac cycle. This curve is analogous to the time–volume curves derived from the data acquired at contrast ventriculography and allows the calculation of perhaps the most important ventricular functional parameter: the global ejection fraction. By determining the number of counts present at end-systole and end-diastole (Fig. 8–20), the difference, expressed as a percentage of the counts at end-diastole, gives the ejection fraction:

Ejection fraction =

$$\frac{\text{end-diastolic counts} - \text{end-systolic counts}}{\text{end-diastolic counts} - \text{background counts}}$$

In most laboratories, a normal left ventricular ejection fraction is greater than 0.55. By mathematically differentiating the time–activity curves, ventricular ejection and filling rates may also be calculated.

One of the considerable advantages of ejection fractions calculated from count-volume techniques is their relative independence from geometric assumptions regarding the shape of the ventricle. Because these determinations are based solely on the change of counts within the ventricle over the cardiac cycle, the effect of geometry is minimized. As with any time–activity analysis of digitalized images, the accuracy of the calculations is largely dependent on the precision of selection of the region of interest. Because it is important to accurately determine the edges of the left ventricle and to exclude any activity in great vessels, lungs, and adjacent chambers, many computers are now equipped with algorithms for the detection of edges of the left ventricle as they change throughout the cardiac cycle. Such semi-automatic edge detection programs are accurate in a majority of patients. However, it is important that the physician analyzing the visual data correlate the calculated ejection fraction based on the computer selection of left ventricular edges with his or her qualitative impression of left ventricular function. Inaccurate definition of the aortic or mitral valve planes with resultant inclusion of por-

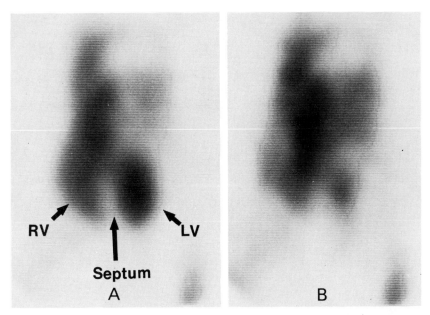

Figure 8–20. Normal blood pool ventriculogram. The views obtained in the LAO projection demonstrate (A) end-diastole and (B) end-systole. The right ventricle, left ventricle, and septum are easily identified.

tions of either the ascending aorta or the left atrium in the left ventricular region of interest leads to underestimation of the left ventricular ejection fraction. An artificially elevated left ventricular ejection fraction may occur when a portion of the left ventricle is excluded from the left ventricular region of interest at end-systole. In some cases, manual selection of left ventricular edges must be performed in order to ensure accurate ejection fraction determination.

Selection of the background region of interest is also of considerable importance so that the ejection fraction will not be under- or overestimated. Overestimation and oversubtraction of background artificially elevate ejection fraction, whereas underestimation erroneously reduces ejection fraction values. There are various standard areas for placement of such regions (usually periventricular); whichever method is employed, it should be consistently used for all such determinations to ensure consistency of technique.

FIRST-TRANSIT STUDIES

Principle

In first-pass radionuclide angiocardiography, a bolus of radioactivity is injected into a peripheral vein, and the initial transit of the bolus through the heart, lungs, and great vessels is imaged in rapid sequence using a gamma camera (Fig. 8–21). The output is fed into a digital computer, from which subsequent anatomic images can be obtained for visual interpretation. In addition, computer collection of the data allows for the quantitative analysis of the images and can provide a number of hemodynamic indices, the most notable of which are left and right ventricular ejection fractions.

Radiopharmaceutical

Because the time for imaging of the first-pass study is necessarily limited, images of adequate statistical quality can be obtained only by administering a sufficient bolus of radioactivity, usually a minimum of 10 mCi (370 MBq). In addition, because each study requires a separate injection of radioisotope, a radiopharmaceutical that clears rapidly from the blood is necessary if multiple determinations are to be performed. Because of their rapid clearance by the liver and kidneys, respectively, technetium 99m labeled sulfur colloid and technetium 99m labeled DTPA are frequently employed. However, any technetium 99m labeled pharmaceutical may be used if a repeat determination is not immediately contemplated. In fact, many labora-

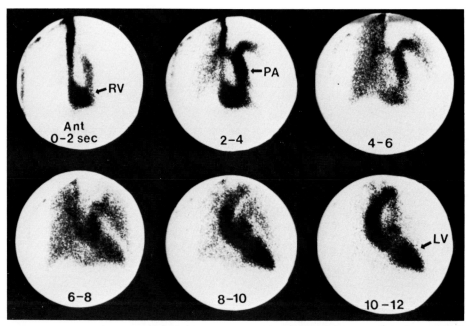

Figure 8–21. Selected images from a normal first-pass radionuclide angiogram demonstrate the sequential identification of right ventricle (RV), pulmonary artery (PA), and left ventricle (LV). Such temporal separation of chamber activity allows selective evaluation of both right and left ventricular function.

tories employ technetium 99m blood pool agents to obtain a first-pass study immediately prior to gated equilibrium imaging, so that both examinations are performed with only one radionuclide injection.

Technique

Either a single-crystal or multiple-crystal gamma camera connected to a computer may be employed for first-pass studies. An important consideration in selecting an imaging device is the inherent low statistical nature of the first-pass approach. Multiple-crystal imaging devices are ideal in that they allow for efficient collection of the brief but high count rates characteristic of first-pass studies but do not cause significant data distortion. However, adequate examinations can be accomplished with single-crystal instruments. The uniqueness of the first-pass examination is that with bolus injection, the activity progresses through the heart in such a manner that each chamber is visualized separately in temporal sequence, and problems with interfering activity in overlapping chambers such as may be encountered with equilibrium imaging are avoided.

The examination may be performed in any view that places the ventricles reasonably near the camera face. The 30° right anterior oblique projection is most frequently employed as it best allows separation of ventricular from any atrial or aortic activity. Other projections may be used depending on the particular aim of the study. Because only one projection may be obtained with each radionuclide bolus injection, multiple injections may be needed if several projections are required. Only a few injections should be performed over 24 hours, to avoid administering a large dose of radiation to the patient.

The collection of data in first-pass studies begins just prior to the injection of the radioactive bolus and is terminated after the activity traverses the left heart and is seen in the great arterial vessels. The entire study is normally completed in less than 60 seconds. Data are usually acquired by the computer in the standard list mode as a sequence of images, and gated acquisition may also be employed in synchrony with the patient's ECG (gated acquisition). Although quantitative data are not as complete as with standard list mode collection, gated first-pass studies allow for much more rapid processing of the information obtained and permit the evaluation of regional wall motion by the cine display of gated images. After the study has been entered into the computer, the data may be replayed and analyzed at the workstation.

Interpretation

As previously mentioned, first-transit studies may be formatted to allow visual and quantitative analysis of the initial passage of radionuclide through the heart and lungs, thereby providing considerable functional information regarding the integrity of the intracardiac and cardiopulmonary circulations. This includes the calculation of pulmonary transit times and the quantitation of left-to-right intracardiac shunts.

Because the first pass of the radioactive bolus through the heart and lungs takes place over many cardiac cycles (Fig. 8–22), the data from several of these cycles can be analyzed or summed to form a single cycle of sufficient statistical nature for detailed visual and quantitative inspection. Although first-transit images of ventricular contraction are not of the statistical quality of equilibrium blood pool images and are usually limited to only one projection, the results are similar. When viewed in "endless loop" cine display, assessment of regional ventricular wall motion is possible. Wall motion also may be inferred by simply superimposing end-systolic and end-diastolic images.

Quantitative assessment of the data presented in these digital images provides infor-

mation regarding ventricular ejection fractions, ejection rates, cardiac output, and stroke volume as well as end-diastolic and end-systolic volumes.

EQUILIBRIUM OR BLOOD POOL RADIONUCLIDE VENTRICULOGRAPHY

Principle

Gated blood pool ventriculography is an alternative method of imaging and quantifying ventricular function. This technique consists of imaging the cardiac blood pool after the injected tracer has mixed thoroughly with the intravascular space. Images are obtained during contraction by synchronizing the camera collection of data with the electrocardiographic signals from the patient. Since the data are acquired and processed by a computer, information regarding the size and configuration of the cardiac chambers as well as quantitative functional parameters of global and regional ventricular performance can be obtained.

Radiopharmaceutical

Basically, any radiopharmaceutical that is compartmentalized to the intravascular space for the time period required to obtain the study may be used. Technetium 99m labeled autologous red blood cells are the agent of choice, although technetium 99m tagged human serum albumin may also be used.

Various methods of labeling autologous red blood cells with technetium 99m have been described (see Appendix E), including in vivo, modified in vivo, and in vitro techniques. All methods employ the initial addition of stannous ion as a reducing agent (commonly stannous pyrophosphate) to "pre-tin" the red blood cells. The intracellular stannous ion permits the binding of the subsequently introduced ^{99m}Tc pertechnetate to the beta chain of the hemoglobin molecule. Although superior labeling efficiency is obtained using in vitro methods in which the patient's blood sample is labeled externally and then reinjected, the relative complexity and time-consuming nature of this technique make it somewhat impractical in most clinical settings.

In a majority of patients, adequate tagging of the red blood cells can be obtained using in vivo methods. The procedure essentially

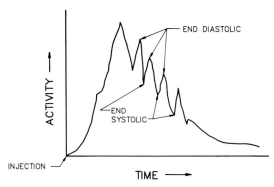

Figure 8–22. A first-pass curve depicting the passage of a radioactive bolus through a left ventricular region of interest. The saw-tooth peaks and valleys represent individual left ventricular contractions and thus represent discrete left ventricular volume curves. The overall shape of the curve indicates the passage of the activity as a discrete bolus through the ventricle.

consists of intravenous injection of 0.5 to 1.0 mg of stannous ion in the form of "cold" stannous pyrophosphate. After allowing the tin ion to equilibrate in the blood for 20 minutes, approximately 20 mCi (740 MBq) of ^{99m}Tc pertechnetate are injected. With the tin acting as a complexing agent, a sufficient number of red blood cells are tagged in vivo to allow for labeling of the intravascular space. While this technique will provide sufficient tagging in a majority of patients, a certain amount of injected technetium 99m will be rapidly lost from the intravascular space and will not participate in the labeling process. The exact percentage of injected technetium that remains intravascularly and labels red cells is difficult to quantitate but probably is about 75 percent. The radioisotope in the extravascular space contributes to longer imaging times as well as background and thus to the degradation of images.

A modified in vivo technique provides for a combination of both in vivo and in vitro labeling procedures, giving a labeling efficiency of approximately 90 percent. This results in an increased intravascular concentration of technetium 99m, with subsequent improvement in the quality of radionuclide images.

Because the technetium red blood cell bond lasts considerably longer than the 6-hour half-life of technetium 99m, the physical half-life of the radiopharmaceutical determines the length of time over which serial imaging is possible. With the use of 20 to 30 mCi (740 MBq to 1.11 GBq) of ^{99m}Tc pertechnetate, delayed imaging is possible for up to 10 to 12 hours after injection.

Technique

After the cardiac blood pool has been labeled, gated images of the heart are obtained. Gating is performed employing a computer coupled with an "R-wave trigger," which signals the computer to begin recording data in the computer memory at the onset of the electrocardiographic R wave. This synchronizes the collection of data from the gamma camera with the onset of cardiac cycle within the patient. The computer divides the R-R interval of each cardiac cycle into equal subdivisions, numbering between 16 to 32, depending upon the patient's heart rate. Data collected from the scintillation camera are sorted during each cardiac contraction so that

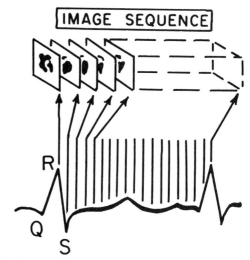

Figure 8–23. Computer imaging sequence for gated blood pool ventriculography. The sequence is normally triggered by the R wave, with the cardiac cycle divided into discrete components. Counts arriving during any division are placed in the computer matrix relevant to that division. After several hundred cardiac cycles, there is enough information on each frame to form a useful image.

corresponding statistical information is filed temporally into one of the R-R interval segments, depending on its displacement in time from the initial R wave (Fig. 8–23). Such sorting of data over numerous cardiac cycles allows for the accumulation of enough statistical data in each interval subdivision to allow for creation of a single composite image of cardiac contraction. This process is the basis of all equilibrium blood pool ventriculography and may be employed in the collection of data from first-pass examinations as well.

Because of the inherent reliance of gated methodology on electrocardiographic input, the success of the technique is necessarily related to the consistency of cardiac rate and rhythm in a given patient. Ordinarily, because the length of systole does not change proportionally as the length of the cardiac cycle increases or decreases, minimal variations in heart rate during acquisition will not significantly affect the study. However, severe disturbances in rhythm will cause distortion of the data obtained. Although a small number of aberrant cardiac cycles may be tolerated (less than 10 percent), as the number of such beats increases there is a progressive degradation of the recorded data, which may give false information regarding such measurements as regional wall motion.

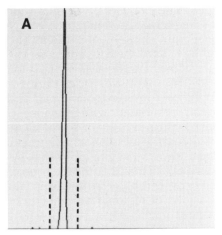 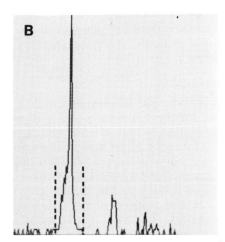

Figure 8–24. Histogram display of R-R interval distribution of two-gated ventriculograms. (A) A normal histogram demonstrates a single narrow peak in a patient with normal sinus rhythm with no aberrant beats falling beyond the desired R-R length. (B) Histogram display of R-R intervals in a patient with a significant arrhythmia demonstrates multiple peaks corresponding to aberrant beats with R-R intervals falling outside the desired length. Such histogram analysis constitutes good quality control of the nuclide ventriculograms.

Many computer programs have software that provide the operator with a histogram of distribution of the lengths of R-R intervals over the acquisition time of the study. Such histograms allow for easy recognition of aberrant beats (Fig. 8–24). In a patient with normal rhythm, the histogram demonstrates a single well-defined peak, whereas, with aberrant beats, there are many smaller peaks.

In patients with occasional aberrant beats, the validity of the data may be preserved by "arrhythmia filtering." This process allows for the rejection of cardiac cycles that do not conform to the average length of a cardiac cycle in a particular patient. However, because such arrhythmic information is excluded from the study, the time of acquisition for the examination will increase.

This is usually accomplished in one of two ways: gated-list-mode collection or "on-the-fly" (real-time) bad beat rejection. In the gated-list-mode collection method, all the beats are recorded in list mode as are the R waves. Following this, there is analysis of the data, which allows the exclusion of data from beats occurring outside a given R-R interval length. This method, though effective, takes longer than processing on the fly. Real-time list mode allows the data to be held for an instant in a buffer while the R-R interval is measured. If the R-R interval is outside accepted limits, the data are rejected on the fly and thus do not require lengthy post-acquisition processing in order to exclude the abnormal beats.

A high-resolution parallel-hole collimator may be used when performing left ventriculography, provided that the counting rates are adequate. This method provides the best spatial resolution for evaluation of regional wall motion. However, general low-energy, all-purpose, parallel-hole collimators may also be used at rest and provide a good compromise between sensitivity and resolution. General all-purpose and high-sensitivity collimators are generally desirable for exercise studies, because they provide increased sensitivity for the collection of images during the necessarily short intervals of exercise.

After the intravascular space has been labeled, resting studies usually require approximately 5 to 10 minutes per view, whereas exercise images are generally collected over several minutes. In resting studies, three views are normally obtained to allow for adequate visualization of the cardiac chambers and great vessels. These include (1) an anterior view, (2) a left anterior oblique ("best septal") view at approximately 45° to visualize the septum and allow separation of the ventricles, and (3) left lateral or 70° left anterior oblique view. During exercise, usually only the 45° LAO view is imaged, to permit calculation of left ventricular ejection fraction changes at various levels of stress.

Interpretation

When multigated equilibrium images are viewed cinematically in an endless loop display, they present the image of a beating heart, which can then be qualitatively and quantitatively analyzed using various computer programs.

Qualitative Data

Cinematic computer display of gated images allows for the visual assessment of regional wall motion of both the left and right ventricles. Optimally, pixel size in the computer should be less than 5 mm for this purpose. In addition to ventricular wall excursion, relative sizes of the cardiac chambers, the size and position of the great vessels, the relative thickness of ventricular walls (particularly the septum) and the pericardial space, and any filling defects within the cardiac blood pool should be noted (Table 8–10).

Since it is the blood pool within the cardiac chambers that is actually displayed, ventricular wall excursion is inferred by the impact of wall motion on the immediately adjacent portion of the blood-filled cavity. Once contraction begins, all ventricular wall segments should contract simultaneously, although some walls demonstrate greater absolute excursion than others. Generally, the anterior, posterior, and lateral walls appear to move to a greater degree than the septum, apex, and frequently the inferior wall.

Segmental wall motion abnormalities are usually described as *hypokinesis* (relatively diminished wall motion), *akinesis* (no wall motion), and *dyskinesis* (paradoxical wall motion). Areas of injured or scarred myocardium usually present as regions of hypokinesis or akinesis, while ventricular aneurysms appear as focal areas of dyskinesis. Lesions are localized as nearly as possible to particular segments of the left ventricular wall by correlating the multiple views obtained. The evaluation of septal wall motion may frequently present a problem. Normally the septum shortens or thickens and moves slightly toward the left ventricular cavity during systole. Paradoxical septal motion (toward the right ventricle during systole) should be considered abnormal and is frequently associated with previous coronary artery bypass surgery or septal infarction.

Although wall motion abnormalities are almost always evident on visual inspection of standard images, functional images generated by computer software to aid in the evaluation of regional wall motion are available and may help in substantiating a suspected abnormality.

Quantitative Data

SYSTOLIC FUNCTION

In addition to left ventricular ejection fractions and ejection rates, various other indices of left ventricular function may be calculated as needed, including left ventricular volumes and regional ejection fractions.

Because the left ventricle is not temporally segregated from the other cardiac chambers as in first-transit studies, a common problem in choosing a region of interest for left ventricular ejection fraction determination is the inclusion of a small amount of left atrium or left atrial appendage in the selected region of interest. Normally, the left atrium lies sufficiently posterior to the left ventricle so that counts within this chamber do not contribute significantly to left ventricular activity. However, when the left atrium is enlarged, a portion of this structure may be included in the determination and falsely lower the ejection fraction. As previously discussed, phase analysis may aid in excluding any left atrial activity from the desired region of interest.

Unlike first-transit studies, right ventricular ejection fractions are not as reliably calculated from the equilibrium study, because the right ventricle is not easily separated from the right atrium or left ventricle. If a right ventricular ejection fraction is desired, it may be obtained by performing a first-pass examination during the initial transit of the bolus at the beginning of the study. Furthermore, because data are obtained at equilibrium of the injected dose, shunt quantification is not possible with the gated blood pool technique.

Table 8–10. GATED CARDIAC EQUILIBRIUM BLOOD POOL IMAGING VISUAL DATA ANALYSIS

- Quality of red cell labeling
- Overall distribution of labeled red cells
- Course and caliber of great vessels
- Relative pulmonary blood pool activity
- Thickness of pericardial-myocardial space
- Shape and thickness of interventricular septum
- Clot or mass within the cardiac chambers
- Size of each chamber
- Chamber wall motion
- Sequence of chamber contraction

DIASTOLIC FUNCTION

Because diastolic dysfunction may precede abnormalities of systolic function, i.e., ejection fraction in a variety of cardiac disease states including coronary artery disease, quantitation of diastolic parameters may permit the early detection of left ventricular functional impairment. The diastolic parameters available from the radionuclide data (left ventricular time–activity curve) include ventricular filling rates and indices derived from temporal analysis.

Ventricular Filling Rates. The most frequently derived diastolic parameter, *peak filling rate* (PFR) reflects the early rapid filling phase of diastole and is commonly seen as a measure of left ventricular compliance. PFR is obtained by differential analysis of the ventricular time–activity curves generated during gated blood pool or first-pass imaging. High temporal resolution is necessary for such analysis, requiring a minimal framing rate of 32 frames per cycle. *Average filling rate* (AFR) is an alternative index of early filling.

Temporal Analysis. Filling fractions quantify changes in left ventricular activity (volume) during specific time intervals as a percentage of stroke counts (e.g., first-third filling fraction as an index of early filling). Absolute time interval measurements include the calculation of time to *peak filling rate* (TPFR), the interval between end-systole and the occurrence of PFR, and is often viewed as an index of the rate of left ventricular relaxation.

Diastolic dysfunction as defined by parameters such as subnormal PFR has been shown to occur in patients with coronary artery disease who have preserved systolic function as measured by left ventricular ejection fraction and no evidence of active ischemia or previous infarction, regardless of the severity or extent of disease. Deterioration of PFR at exercise can be a significant discriminant between normals and patients with coronary artery disease. Assessment of diastolic function parameters may also play an important role in the evaluation of congestive heart failure. Approximately 40 percent of patients with a diagnosis of congestive heart failure demonstrate normal left ventricular systolic function but impaired diastolic filling. In about half of these patients, systemic hypertension is the underlying etiology.

It should be noted that filling rate indices may be influenced by unrelated parameters such as systolic ejection fraction and length of cardiac cycle, as well as noncoronary diseases of the heart including systemic hypertension, age-related decline in PFR, and anti-ischemic therapy. Some of the temporal indices can be difficult to derive precisely, so their values may vary in specific clinical settings.

Clinical Applications

Coronary Artery Disease

Because exercise radionuclide ventriculography is somewhat more quantitative than thallium imaging, it is frequently recommended in the evaluation of coronary artery disease. As with thallium imaging, a significant number of patients with suspected or known coronary artery disease demonstrate normal ventricular function at rest. Therefore, studies for the detection of suspected coronary artery disease or for the evaluation of known disease are better performed during exercise. Although pharmacologically induced stress examinations have been described, physical exercise studies are more commonly employed. Exercise ventriculography may be accomplished using either the first-transit or gated equilibrium techniques.

Although a number of stress protocols have been described, most involve an initial resting baseline determination of ventricular wall motion and ejection fraction, with subsequent serial images being obtained over a period of stepwise increases in stress. Since first-pass acquisition requires only 20 to 30 seconds and since patient motion is less of a problem during that period, upright treadmill testing may be employed. Equilibrium examinations generally take 2 to 3 minutes at each level of stress; therefore, supine or semisupine graduated bicycle exercise to minimize patient motion is preferable. Protocols for hand-grip isometric exercise have also been used and may be appropriate in patients who, for various reasons, cannot exercise adequately by means of standard techniques.

Since the sensitivity of detecting coronary artery disease is directly proportional to the degree of exercise achieved, effort should be made to obtain maximal stress: 85 percent of predicted heart rate or the induction of ECG abnormalities, chest pain, hypotension, dyspnea, or exhaustion. It should be noted that leg cramps or leg muscle fatigue may preclude adequate maximal cardiac stress when a bicycle is used.

Patients receiving beta-blocking agents such as propranolol have limited heart rate response to exercise, and submaximal studies are frequently obtained in these patients. These and other drugs such as nitrates and calcium channel blockers may reduce or prevent the induction of left ventricular dysfunction at exercise. If possible, such medication should be discontinued 24 to 48 hours prior to performing the exercise ventriculogram in order to improve test sensitivity.

Criteria for an abnormal study have been established through the detection of stress-induced changes in global or regional left ventricular function as manifested by left ventricular ejection fraction and left ventricular wall motion. The physiologic basis underlying exercise-induced abnormalities assumes that the hypoperfused areas of myocardium distal to significant stenotic lesions do not respond with effective contraction under stress, thereby giving rise to wall motion abnormalities and regionally or globally decreased ejection fractions.

In normal subjects, the left ventricular ejection fraction increases during maximal exercise, usually by more than 5 percent (0.05) above resting levels (Fig. 8–25). However, it should be noted that in some patients, particularly young females, the elderly (over 60 years), and patients with high resting ejection fractions (> 70 percent), a significant increase in ejection fraction with exercise may not occur. On the contrary, up to 90 percent of patients with significant coronary artery disease will have evidence of abnormal left

ventricular reserve, as indicated by the failure of the ejection fraction to rise or by a definite decrease. Essentially every patient with ECG evidence of significant myocardial ischemia will demonstrate an abnormal ejection fraction response. The ischemia induced at exercise may also result in the development of generalized wall motion abnormalities or in significant worsening of a lesion present on the resting examination. Although segmental wall motion abnormalities during exercise occur less frequently than changes in ejection fraction, many investigators feel that they are a more sensitive and specific indicator of the presence of significant coronary artery disease. However, ejection fraction alteration during stress may be the only indicator of an abnormal ventricular response in patients who may not demonstrate detectable segmental contraction abnormalities. In any case, ejection fraction response is clearly valuable supporting evidence in making or excluding the diagnosis of coronary artery disease.

Dilation of the left ventricular cavity and an acute increase in pulmonary blood volume during exercise should also be regarded as abnormal ventricular responses to stress. Pulmonary blood volume can be estimated from the product of pulmonary transit time and cardiac output, and this determination has been used to increase the sensitivity of the technique.

Evaluation of left ventricular function in the setting of chronic coronary artery disease primarily provides a measure of fibrosis (lost myocardium) when ventriculography is performed at rest and is an indicator of both fibrosis and ischemia (myocardium at risk) when performed with adequate exercise

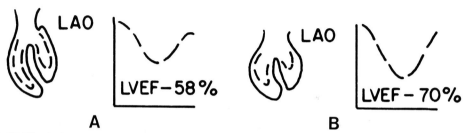

Figure 8–25. Effect of exercise on the left ventricular ejection fraction in a normal individual. With exercise, the ejection fraction normally rises at least 5 percent (0.05). The schematic cardiac diaphragm is shown for both rest (A) and exercise (B) in the left anterior oblique projection, with both the systolic and diastolic outlines. The computer-generated time–activity curve over the cardiac cycle begins with diastole and shows that during systole (represented by the lowest portion of the curve) there is relatively less activity in the left ventricle in the exercise state as the ejection fraction rises.

stress. Resting left ventricular ejection fraction is used as a measurement of any permanent damage to the left ventricular myocardium that is unlikely to be reversed by revascularization procedures. Ventricular ejection fraction response to exercise indicates any ischemic myocardium salvageable by such procedures. This may serve as the basis for a rational approach to therapeutic decision making.

Sensitivity and Specificity in Coronary Artery Disease. Radionuclide stress ventriculography has been demonstrated to be a sensitive tool in the detection of coronary artery disease. Clinical studies have demonstrated a significantly greater sensitivity with this technique than with routine exercise electrocardiography. Sensitivities approaching 90 percent have been reported for exercise ventriculography, compared with 60 to 70 percent sensitivity with electrocardiographic techniques. However, because a variety of cardiac diseases, including valvular lesions and cardiomyopathies, may produce abnormal ventricular responses to stress, an abnormal radionuclide ventriculogram (as low as 60 percent specificity) is not equally specific (Table 8–11). This is particularly true with respect to ejection fraction changes. However, abnormal segmental or regional wall motion responses are relatively specific for coronary artery disease and, when present, help to pinpoint this condition.

Acute Myocardial Infarction. Radionuclide ventriculography at rest may be performed at the patient's bedside to obtain parameters regarding right and left ventricular dysfunction, define the location and extent of re-

gional wall motion abnormalities, and detect complications such as aneurysm formation or intracardiac thrombosis. Such information reflects the extent of myocardial damage and has both management and prognostic implications.

Prognosis in myocardial infarction is related to infarct size as reflected by global left ventricular ejection fraction and extent and degree of wall motion abnormalities. Large infarcts may produce extensive wall motion abnormalities with significantly decreased left ventricular ejection fractions whereas smaller injuries may produce only focal wall motion impairment with a normal or slightly decreased left ventricular ejection fraction or no abnormality at all. Anterior infarcts generally lower left ventricular ejection fraction to a greater degree than inferior wall lesions.

Both ejection fraction and wall motion abnormalities may change significantly in the acute phase of the insult, especially in the first week post-infarct, and then generally stabilize by 2 weeks. After approximately 12 weeks, the findings are fully evolved. Any improvement in ejection fraction or wall motion over the evolutionary course of the myocardial infarction may result from recovery of initially stunned myocardium and/or therapeutic or spontaneous reperfusion that rescues local tissue and hence myocardial function. In assessing the impact of a myocardial infarction on left ventricular function using radionuclide ventriculography, especially for therapeutic decision making, consideration should be given to the dynamic evolution of myocardial injury.

The resting left ventricular ejection fraction as determined by gated radionuclide ventriculography has proved to be a reliable measure of the impact of coronary occlusion on left ventricular function in early myocardial infarction and, as such, has shown to be an important predictor of prognosis. In this setting, an ejection fraction of 0.30 during the first 24 hours post-infarction appears to represent a watershed with approximately 50 percent of the patients with values at or below this level succumbing to left ventricular failure and/or death. This represents a nearly nine-fold higher mortality than patients with a left ventricular ejection fraction greater than 0.30. Conversely, only about 2 percent of patients with higher ejection fractions will die acutely.

Table 8–11. EXERCISE RADIONUCLIDE VENTRICULOGRAPHY FOR CORONARY ARTERY DISEASE: CAUSES OF FALSE POSITIVE EXAMINATIONS

Nonischemic cardiomyopathies
Prior myocarditis
Valvular heart disease
Mitral valve prosthesis
Hypertensive patients
Elderly patients and young females
Atrial fibrillation
Left bundle branch block

After early recovery from the initial insult, a predischarge resting left ventricular ejection fraction of 0.40 or less remains a potent predictor of future events and death, with the 1-year mortality rate increasing exponentially as the resting left ventricular ejection fraction falls below 0.40. In addition to resting left ventricular ejection fraction, a post-myocardial infarction exercise radionuclide ventriculogram may provide further risk stratification in patients with left ventricular ejection fractions greater than 0.30. Near-term mortality rate appears to be significantly lower in patients with a normal left ventricular ejection fraction response to exercise.

Although it is frequently a difficult clinical diagnosis, the differentiation of predominantly right from left ventricular infarction may be important in the determination of therapy. Radionuclide imaging of ventricular wall motion will often provide the distinction as well as discern the extent of the injury.

Noncoronary Disease States

Characteristic findings on gated blood pool imaging in patients with noncoronary heart disease are shown in Table 8–12.

Evaluating Dyspnea. Radionuclide ventriculography may aid in the differential diagnosis of cardiopulmonary disease by helping distinguish between the dyspnea related to primary left ventricular failure and chronic pulmonary disease, when differentiation on clinical grounds is not possible. For instance, right ventricular dysfunction and cardiac chamber dilation with a normal left ventricle are associated with chronic obstructive pulmonary disease, while pulmonary vascular congestion related to left ventricular failure is accompanied by left ventricular enlargement and/or functional abnormalities. In patients with known chronic obstructive pulmonary disease, a resting right ventricular ejection fraction of less than 0.40 is a rela-

Table 8–12. CHARACTERISTIC FINDINGS ON GATED BLOOD POOL IMAGING IN PATIENTS WITH NONCORONARY HEART DISEASE

LESION	FINDINGS
Valvular	
Aortic regurgitation	Dilated LV cavity with hypertrophy; normal or decreased LVEF
Aortic stenosis	Normal LV cavity and LVEF; LV hypertrophy; dilated LA
Mitral regurgitation	Dilated LV cavity and normal or decreased LVEF; normal LV wall thickness; dilated LA
Mitral stenosis	Normal left and right cavity size and EF; severely dilated LA
Tricuspid regurgitation	Dilated RV cavity and decreased RVEF; dilated RA
Hypertensive	LV concentric hypertrophy; normal or supranormal LVEF; diastolic dysfunction
Cardiomyopathy	
Dilated (congestive)	Dilatation of all four chambers; decreased LVEF and RVEF; decreased LV wall thickness
Ischemic	Normal or dilated LV cavity and decreased LVEF; decreased LV wall thickness; normal or dilated LA
Hypertrophic	Normal or small LV cavity; normal or supranormal LVEF; severe LV hypertrophy; normal or dilated LA
Restrictive	Normal LV cavity and normal or decreased LVEF; normal or increased RV cavity and normal or decreased RVEF
	Normal or increased LV wall thickness; dilated LA
Septal Defect	
Atrial	Dilated RV cavity and decreased RVEF; dilated RA with normal or dilated LA
Ventricular	Normal or increased LV cavity and normal or increased LVEF; dilated RV and normal or decreased RVEF; dilated LA

LV = left ventricle; RV = right ventricle; LA = left atrium; RA = right atrium; EF = ejection fraction.
Adapted from Dilsizian V, Rocco TP, Bonow RO, et al: Cardiac blood-pool imaging II: Applications in noncoronary heart disease. J Nucl Med 31(1):10–22, 1990.

tively sensitive predictor of pulmonary artery hypertension. In addition, abnormal right ventricular functional parameters in the presence of chronic obstructive pulmonary disease may have important therapeutic implications.

Monitoring Left Ventricular Function. Nuclear medicine techniques have become important in assessing and monitoring left and right ventricular function in patients with a variety of known cardiac or systemic diseases as well as in those receiving cardiotoxic chemotherapy agents. Because the results are reproducible and readily obtained at the patient's bedside, the technique is useful in both chronic and acute clinical situations.

The serial assessment of ejection fractions has gained in popularity with the use of cardiotoxic chemotherapeutic agents such as doxorubicin. The study is of use in selecting patients who may best tolerate the medication and in monitoring those who receive it in order to determine the onset of cardiac toxicity. Patients receiving doxorubicin usually do not have toxic cardiac responses below doses of 550 mg/m². Many clinicians allow the ejection fraction to fall to 0.45 before discontinuing therapy.

Cardiomyopathy. Cardiomyopathies constitute a group of heterogeneous primary myocardial diseases usually classified as dilated, hypertrophic, or restrictive. Gated blood pool imaging has proved useful in not only detecting cardiomyopathies, but also in evaluating the degree of systolic and/or diastolic functional impairment and in assessing the effects of medical therapy.

On gated blood pool imaging, hypertrophic cardiomyopathy typically presents with a normal or elevated left ventricular ejection fraction and hyperdynamic systolic function with evidence of ventricular wall thickening and a concomitantly small left ventricular cavity. Eighty percent or more of these patients exhibit impaired diastolic function (Fig. 8–26). A small subset of these patients may progress to a dilated, poorly contracting ventricle with a reduced left ventricular ejection fraction. Since treatment differs significantly in these two groups, radionuclide blood pool imaging is of value in distinguishing between them.

Dilated cardiomyopathies typically present with four-chamber dilatation and diffuse hypokinesis with a reduced left ventricular ejection fraction. Since marked focal wall motion

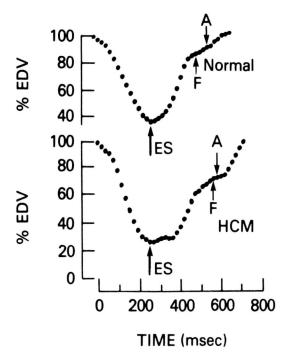

Figure 8–26. Left ventricular (LV) time–activity curves from a normal subject and a patient with hypertrophic cardiomyopathy (HCM). Despite normal systolic function, the patient with HCM has impaired LV diastolic filling with reduced peak filling rate, prolongation of the time-to-peak-filling rate, and increased contribution of atrial systole to total left ventricular filling. EDV = end-diastolic volume; ES = end-systole; F = end of rapid filling; and A = onset of atrial systole. (Dilsian V, Rocco TP, Bonow RO, et al: Cardiac blood-pooling imaging II: Applications in noncoronary heart disease. J Nucl Med 31(1):16, 1990)

abnormalities are usually not present, this may allow differentiation from end-stage coronary artery disease, which may present with superimposed focal wall motion abnormalities.

Valvular Heart Disease. While echocardiography is generally the procedure of choice in noninvasive evaluation of suspected valvular cardiac disease, nuclear methods may be useful to assess the ventricular functional consequences at rest or during exercise. Most clinical experience has centered around the investigation of valvular insufficiency, particularly aortic regurgitation. Computer programs are available to allow for quantification of regurgitant fractions in such patients, and results correlate well with catheterization data. Exercise evaluation of patients with known valvular heart disease has been used to predict the appropriateness of valvular surgery and to monitor the results of any surgery performed.

Of interest is the use of gated blood pool studies in the diagnosis of idiopathic hypertrophic subaortic stenosis. Radionuclide findings have been well defined and include a "super-elevated" left ventricular ejection fraction in patients with small left ventricular cavities, which appear best defined toward the apex of the heart and show asymmetric thickening of the upper portion of the ventricular septum.

Intracardiac Shunts. First-pass studies are a valuable adjunct in the evaluation of congenital heart disease, particularly with respect to the diagnosis and quantification of left-to-right intracardiac shunts. This is made possible by analysis of time–activity curves obtained from pulmonary regions of interest. Early pulmonary recirculation of the radiopharmaceutical through a left-to-right shunt may be detected as an alteration in the normal curve; however, a compact bolus of activity is essential to an accurate study. Various methods of analysis allow for shunt quantification with an accuracy equal to that of contrast arteriography. Although various mathematical approaches are available for the calculation of shunt size, the *gamma variate function method* provides the most accurate and reproducible technique. Using this method, pulmonary to systemic flow ratios of 1.2:1 or greater are considered evidence of left-to-right shunting. While right-to-left shunts may occasionally be defined by the first-pass method, this method is neither sensitive for the detection of such shunts nor does it allow for accurate quantitation.

Suggested Readings

Depasquale EE, Nody AC, DePuey EG, et al: Quantitative rotational thallium 201 tomography for identifying and localizing coronary artery disease. Circulation 77:316–327, 1988

DePuey EG, Garcia EV: Optimal specificity of thallium 201 SPECT through recognition of imaging artifacts. J Nucl Med 30:441–449, 1989

Dilsizian V, Rocco TP, Bonow RO, et al: Cardiac blood-pool imaging II: Applications in noncoronary heart disease. J Nucl Med 31:10–22, 1990

Guiberteau MJ: Nuclear Cardiovascular Imaging: Current Clinical Practice. New York, Churchill Livingstone, 1990

Iskandrian AS, Heo J, Mostel E: The role of radionuclide cardiac imaging in coronary artery bypass surgery. Am Heart J 113:163–170, 1987

Kaul S, Newell JB, Chesler DA: Quantitative thallium imaging findings in patients with normal coronary angiographic findings and in clinically normal subject. Am J Cardiol 57:509–512, 1986

Klaw BA, Yasuda T, Gold HK, et al: Acute myocardial infarct imaging with indium 111 labeled monoclonal antimyosin Fab. J Nucl Med 28:1671–1678, 1987

Nichols AB, Brown C, Han J, et al: Effect of coronary stenotic lesions on region myocardial blood flow at rest. Circulation 74:746–757, 1986

Rocco TP, Dilsizian V, Fischman AJ, Strauss HW: Evaluation of ventricular function in patients with coronary artery disease. J Nucl Med 30:1149–1165, 1989

Wackers FJ, Russo DJ, Russo D, et al: Prognostic significance of normal quantitative planar thallium 201 stress scintigraphy in patients with chest pain. J Am Coll Cardiol 6:27–30, 1985

CHAPTER 9

Respiratory System

Radionuclide lung imaging most commonly involves the demonstration of pulmonary perfusion employing limited capillary blockade as well as the assessment of ventilation using inspired inert gas, usually xenon. While these studies are essentially qualitative, they have an advantage over most quantitative tests of global lung function in distinguishing between diffuse and regional pulmonary disease. The information gained from radionuclide lung imaging may be used to diagnose such disease and to determine treatment. In addition, the display of regional airway and vascular integrity forms the basis for the noninvasive diagnosis of pulmonary emboli.

Anatomy and Physiology

The trachea divides into the right and left mainstem bronchi, and these in turn divide to form lobar bronchi. The lobar divisions on the right are the upper, middle, and lower lobe bronchi; on the left there are only upper and lower lobe bronchi. The lobes are further divided into segments, which are shown in Figure 9–1. Knowledge of the anatomy of the lobes and segments of the lungs is essential for accurate interpretation of radionuclide pulmonary images.

Inspiration produces a negative intrapleural pressure, which is generated by action of the thoracic cage musculature and the diaphragm. Each terminal respiratory unit or alveolus is quite elastic, and this elasticity provides the major impetus for expiration. In an adult there are approximately 250 to 300 million alveoli, with an average diameter of 150 μ per alveolus. It is important to remember that the direct anatomic pathway is not the only means by which air can enter the alveoli. If a bronchiole is blocked, air may get into the distal alveoli through the pores of Kohn, which provide direct communication between neighboring alveoli. In addi-

tion, the canals of Lambert connect the respiratory bronchioles and alveolar ducts. Both of these indirect pathways allow collateral ventilation in the peripheral lung and often prevent collapse of an obstructed pulmonary segment or segments.

The main pulmonary arteries divide in each lung to follow the divisions of the bronchi and bronchioles to the level of the alveoli. Each alveolus is supplied by a terminal pulmonary arteriole, which in turn gives rise to capillaries. The capillaries that surround the alveoli are between 7 and 10 μ in diameter. The lungs also receive blood from the aorta via the bronchial arteries, which follow the bronchial tree as far as the respiratory bronchioles. The bronchial arteries anastomose at the capillary level with the pulmonary circulation, and most of the blood from the bronchial arteries returns to the left atrium via the pulmonary veins. The bronchial circulation supplies approximately 5 percent of the blood flow to the lung under normal circumstances.

Gravity and patient position have a significant impact on both ventilation and perfusion. However, the alteration of blood flow throughout the lungs with positional change is much more marked than accompanying changes in ventilation. In the upright position, intrapleural pressure is significantly more negative at the apices than at the lung bases. This negative pressure difference causes the upper lung zone alveoli to be held more open in expiration than the lower lung alveoli, which are relatively collapsed. The increased potential volume in the lung bases provides a greater change in alveolus size during inspiration than at the apices, with the net effect that ventilation (air exchange) is greater in the lower lungs. Normally, ventilation in the lower portion of the lung is about 150 percent of that in the apex. Pulmonary perfusion is also unevenly distributed throughout the lungs. Maximal pulmo-

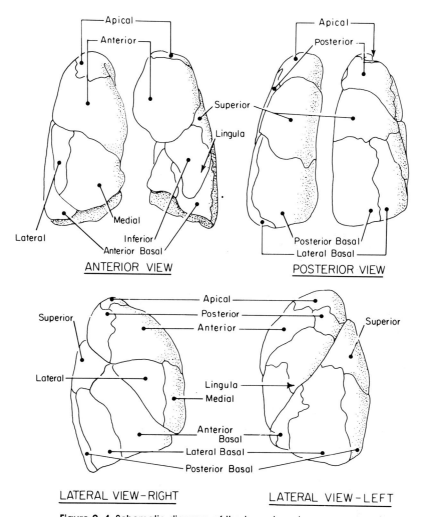

Figure 9–1. Schematic diagram of the bronchopulmonary segments.

nary blood flow normally occurs in the lung zone bracketing the junction of the lower third and upper two-thirds of the lungs. In the upright position, the apex receives only about one-third of the blood flow per unit volume as compared with the bases. In the supine position, however, perfusion is more uniform, although again there is relatively increased blood flow in the dependent portions of the lung. In patients who demonstrate more flow to the upper lobes, congestive failure with increased left atrial pressure, and alpha-1-antitrypsin deficiency should be considered.

Thus, in the normal upright patient, both ventilation and perfusion increase progressively from the lung apex to the bases, although this gradient is more pronounced for perfusion. Because ventilation increases much less rapidly from apex to base, the ventilation/perfusion ratio changes in the reverse direction, increasing from base to apex. However, in the supine position, both ventilation and perfusion gradients are less pronounced, resulting in more even ventilation and perfusion throughout the lungs.

Uncommonly, acute changes in perfusion affect ventilation; local ischemia and hypoxia can cause reflex bronchoconstriction, with a resulting shift of ventilation away from the hypoperfused areas. However, this phenomenon appears to be transient and is uncommonly demonstrated in humans. Conversely, abnormalities of ventilation commonly cause redistribution of pulmonary perfusion; hypoventilation leads to regional hypoxia and reflex redistribution of perfusion away from the hypoventilated regions.

Radiopharmaceuticals

PERFUSION AGENTS

The radiopharmaceutical used for pulmonary perfusion imaging is technetium 99m macroaggregated albumin (MAA). It localizes by the mechanism of capillary blockade. In general, less than 1 in 1000 (less than 0.1 percent) of the capillaries are blocked. In the absence of shunts, 95 percent of the particles are removed from the circulation on the first pass through the pulmonary capillary bed. Approximately 5 percent of particles measure less than 5 μ in diameter and will pass through the capillary system. For purposes of pulmonary perfusion imaging, it is important to employ a sufficient number of particles to allow for good statistical distribution. In general, injection of a minimum of 100,000 particles and optimally between 200,000 and 400,000 particles is required.

The production of ^{99m}Tc MAA entails aggregation of human serum albumin using heat and a reducing agent to form the particles. Visual inspection of the preparations through the use of a microscope and hemocytometer will demonstrate whether the MAA particles are too large or have clumped. The particle size of ^{99m}Tc MAA generally ranges from 5 to 100 μ. MAA has a biologic half-life in the lung of 2 to 9 hours, depending upon the kit manufacturer and preparation. Some preparations begin to break down as early as 30 minutes post-injection. The particle fragments enter the general circulation as smaller particles, which are usually removed from the circulation by the liver and spleen. The normal administered activity is 3 mCi (111 MBq) and the lung is the critical organ. The absorbed dose to the lung is variable but is approximately 0.5 rad (50 mGy) for a 3-mCi (111 MBq) dose (see Table 9–1).

In addition to capillary blockade, the intravenous injection of soluble gases has been used to examine pulmonary perfusion. Since the gases are rapidly washed out of the circulation into the lungs during respiration, it is difficult to obtain multiple images in different projections, and this method is not commonly used.

VENTILATION AGENTS

Xenon 133 is the primary isotope used for assessment of ventilation. It is relatively inexpensive and has a half-life of 5.3 days and a principal gamma ray energy of 81 keV. The low energy of these photons causes about half of them to be attenuated by 10 cm of inflated lung tissue. Thus, overlying soft tissues such as breasts can produce substantial artifacts, which are usually avoided by performing ventilation scans in the posterior

Table 9–1. RADIOPHARMACEUTICAL AGENTS FOR LUNG IMAGING

RADIOPHAR-MACEUTICAL	USUAL DOSE	ROUTE OF ADMINIS-TRATION	PHYSICAL HALF-LIFE	TIME TO IMAGING	ABSORBED DOSE ESTIMATE (rad/mCi)* Whole Body	Gonads	Other	REMARKS
^{99m}Tc MAA	2–4 mCi (74–148 MBq)	IV	6 hr	Immediate	0.013–0.050	0.015	0.15–0.48 (lungs)† 0.07 (thyroid)	Biologic half-life 2–9 hr Particle size 5–100 μ (90%) Administer within 8 hr of preparation.
^{127}Xe gas	8–15 mCi (296–555 MBq)	Inhalation	36.4 days	Immediate	0.001	0.001	0.003–0.012 (lungs) 0.04 (bronchus)	
^{133}Xe gas	8–15 mCi (296–555 MBq)	Inhalation	5.3 days	Immediate	0.001	0.001	0.017–0.040 (lungs) 0.640 (trachea)† 0.1 (bronchus)	Biologic half-life 30 sec
^{81m}Kr gas	8–10 mCi/min (296–370 MBq)	Inhalation	13 sec	Immediate			0.0007 (lungs)	Doses usually include 3 min rebreathing.
^{99m}Tc DTPA aerosol	10–20 mCi (370–740 MBq)	Inhalation	6 hr	Immediate	0.008	0.009	0.07 (lungs) 0.18 (bladder)	—

*To obtain absorbed dose in mGy in MBq, divide values by 3.7.
†Indicates critical organ.

position. The critical organ for xenon 133 is the trachea, which receives approximately 100 mrad/mCi/liter/min (0.03 mGy/MBq/liter/min). Xenon 133 allows for the assessment of all phases of regional ventilation: initial single breath, washin, equilibrium, and washout. Single breath images represent instant ventilation, washin and equilibrium images are proportional to aerated lung volume, and washout phases show regional clearance of activity from the lungs.

Ventilation imaging with xenon 133 requires a considerable amount of patient cooperation because the patient must be able to tolerate breathing on a closed spirometer system for several minutes in order to reach equilibrium. Use of xenon 133 also requires special considerations in room design. The camera room should be maintained at a negative pressure relative to outside hallways, and a dedicated xenon trap or exhaust vent must be used to remove the xenon gas. Xenon gas is heavier than air, and exhaust vents should be placed at a low level. Details of xenon production and decay are discussed in Chapter 1.

Xenon 127 and krypton 81m have also been advocated for use in ventilation imaging. Xenon 127 has a half-life of 36.4 days, and its higher major photon energy (203 keV) allows the perfusion study to be performed first. However, it is expensive and availability is limited by the requirement of a high-energy linear accelerator for production. Krypton 81m has a half-life of 13 seconds, with photon emissions between 176 and 192 keV. Krypton generators employing the parent isotope ^{81}Rb are available; but they have a short shelf life (half-life 4.6 hours) and are therefore somewhat inconvenient to use. Unlike xenon 133, krypton 81m can be used in a continuous steady state inhalation technique that is proportional to regional ventilatory rate rather than to lung volume; thus, multiple images with good statistical information can be obtained. However, the short half-life of krypton 81m precludes single-breath and washout images. In addition, krypton 81m is very expensive.

Ventilation can also be examined in a steady-state fashion by the administration of technetium-labeled radioactive aerosols. An ultrasonic nebulizer is used to form the aerosol, which is then inhaled by the patient. The aerosols usually have a mean aerodynamic diameter of about 0.5 μ. The half-life clearance time from the lungs is 45 to 60 minutes in nonsmokers and 20 minutes in smokers. The larger the particle size, the more central is its deposition in the bronchial tree. Central deposition is also quite common in patients with chronic obstructive pulmonary disease (COPD), probably due to turbulent flow in the central airways compared with that of normal persons (Fig. 9–2).

Technetium 99m DTPA aerosol for ventilation imaging has several advantages, the most notable of which are the ready availability of technetium 99m and its ideal imaging energy. Very little patient cooperation is required. The aerosol may be delivered in a room separate from the camera room (or at the patient's bedside) and can easily be delivered through mechanical ventilators or during normal tidal breathing. There is no need for special exhaust systems or traps.

DTPA aerosol particles cross the alveolar-capillary membrane with a half-time of about 1 hour, enter the pulmonary circulation, and from there are rapidly cleared by the kidneys.

One of the major disadvantages in the use of technetium 99m DTPA aerosols is the small amount of activity actually delivered to the patient (2 to 10 percent) compared with that available in the aerosol generator. Usually about 30 mCi (1.11 GBq) is placed in the system nebulizer with only 1 or 2 mCi (37 to 74 MBq) actually being delivered to the patient. Unlike xenon 133, aerosol studies do not allow for single breath or washout phase imaging but do permit imaging in multiple projections.

Figure 9–2. Functional right-to-left shunt demonstrated using ^{99m}Tc DTPA aerosol ventilation scan. (A) Portable chest radiograph demonstrates bilateral (right greater than left) diffuse infiltrates and cardiomegaly. (B) The anterior and posterior aerosol images show aerosol deposition in the trachea, left main stem bronchus, and left lung. There is reduced ventilation to the right lung and patchy ventilation on the left. Some absorbed aerosol is seen in the renal pelvis on the anterior view. (C) Anterior and posterior perfusion images done immediately after the scan show persistent aerosol in the upper trachea and some DTPA in the right and left renal pelvis. The perfusion in both lungs is nearly normal, excluding a pulmonary embolus. The cause of the patient's medical deterioration was a functional right-to-left shunt through the hypoventilated right lung. (Case courtesy of Barry Siegel, M.D.).

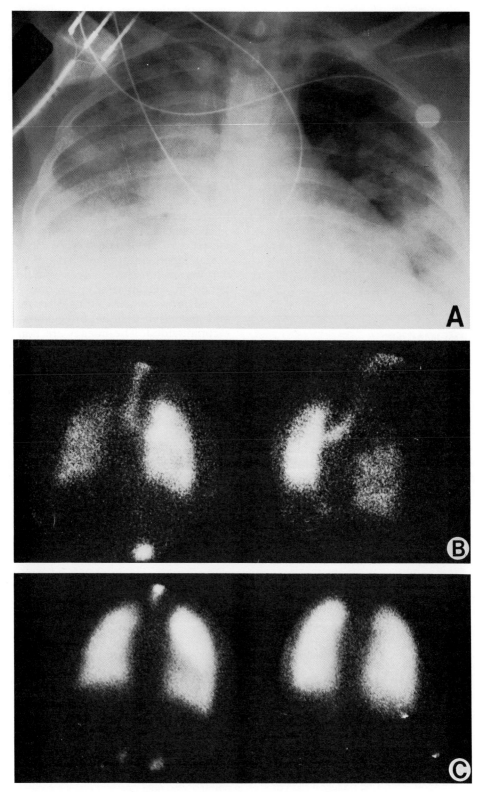

Figure 9–2 *See legend on opposite page*

Technique

Since most clinical situations dictate the performance of both ventilation and perfusion studies, the question may frequently arise as to which study to perform first. Most laboratories begin with the xenon 133 ventilation study because of xenon's lower photon energy. The disadvantage of this order is that the ventilation study may not have been performed in the projection that best evaluates the region of a subsequently demonstrated perfusion defect. If the technetium perfusion study is done first and followed by the ventilation examination, it is helpful to decrease the technetium dose and increase the dose of xenon to overcome the effect of any Compton scatter from the technetium 99m that may occur in the xenon window of the pulse height analyzer and degrade the ventilation images.

PERFUSION IMAGING

Particulate radiopharmaceuticals for perfusion studies should be injected during quiet respiration, with the patient supine to minimize the normal perfusion gradient between the apex and lung base. The particles should be thoroughly agitated prior to injection to ensure even mixing. To assist in homogeneous pulmonary distribution of the particles, injection should be made slowly, usually over 30 seconds or more, and the injected volume should be at least 1 to 2 ml. If blood is drawn into the syringe to confirm an intravascular needle location, it is important not to let the blood sit long in the syringe, because this may allow the formation of small labeled clots, which, when injected, result in focal hot spots on the perfusion scan (Fig. 9–3). When this occurs, a statistical skew in the images may result from the large concentrations of radioactivity within the clots, and significant abnormalities elsewhere in the lungs thus may be missed. It is best to interpret such an examination with caution and to repeat it in 12 to 24 hours, if necessary.

The perfusion images are normally obtained on a large-field-of-view camera or on a standard-field-of-view camera with a diverging collimator. Images should be obtained in the anterior, posterior, and both lateral projections. Routine bilateral anterior and posterior oblique projections are also recommended. The images are normally accumulated for 2000 counts per sq centimeter. If this mode is not available, at least 500,000 counts should be obtained in the anterior and posterior views and in one lateral view, with the other lateral view taken for the same length of time as the first.

A relative contraindication to performing particulate perfusion lung scans is severe pulmonary hypertension. Some authors recommend avoiding particulate perfusion scans in patients with known right-to-left

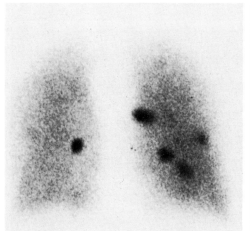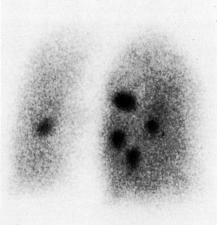

Figure 9–3. "Hot spots" on a lung perfusion scan as seen in posterior and right posterior oblique projections. These represent injected blood clots inadvertently formed and labeled in the syringe containing ^{99m}Tc MAA. Note the relative decrease in activity in the remainder of the lungs, which could hamper detection of perfusion abnormalities.

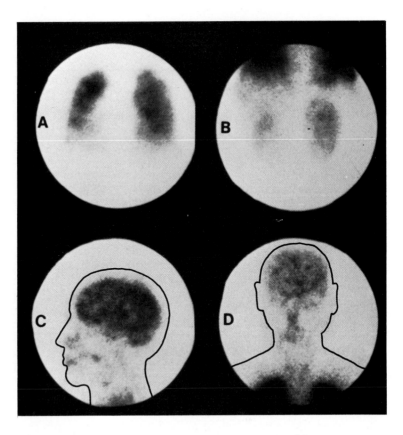

Figure 9–4. Right-to-left shunting of pulmonary perfusion agent. (A) A posterior image from a perfusion lung scan obtained with technetium 99m labeled MAA shows mottled activity in this patient with a right-to-left intracardiac shunt. Such shunting is characterized by the appearance of the radiopharmaceutical in the capillary bed of the kidneys (B) and the brain (C and D).

shunts for fear that the particles may have an impact on the coronary or cerebral circulation, although such problems have rarely, if ever, been observed. However, in such patients it probably is prudent to reduce the number of injected particles to 100,000. The presence of a right-to-left shunt can be easily recognized on posterior images by the immediate presence of renal activity and can be confirmed by the demonstration of activity in the brain (Fig. 9–4).

VENTILATION IMAGING

Ventilation examinations are generally performed either to assess regional ventilation or to improve the specificity of a perfusion scan. Ventilation imaging utilizing xenon 133 is limited in that images are usually obtained in only one projection and are performed before the perfusion study. The use of a single projection image ensures that some regional ventilation abnormalities will be missed, since the lungs are not entirely imaged. The xenon is usually administered employing a number of commercially available delivery and rebreathing units. These generally allow the disposal of expired xenon by one of two methods. The simplest way is to exhaust-vent the xenon to the atmosphere, remembering that the Nuclear Regulatory Commission requires the average yearly concentration of xenon emission to be less than 3×10^{-7} mCi/ml (1 Bq/ml). Another satisfactory method is to use an activated charcoal xenon trap to accumulate the exhaled gas until it has decayed to background.

The ventilation study is normally performed in the posterior view with the patient in the upright position. The posterior view is selected because it is technically convenient and allows a ventilation survey of the greatest number of pulmonary segments. While there are several common methods of performing ventilation imaging, the most complete involves three phases: (1) single or initial breath, (2) equilibrium, and (3) washout phases. In some laboratories only a single-breath or equilibrium phase followed by washout images is performed. The single-breath phase involves having the patient exhale as deeply as possible and then inhale 10 to 20 mCi (370 to 740 MBq) of xenon 133, holding his or her breath for approximately

Table 9–2. CHARACTERISTICS OF AGENTS FOR VENTILATION IMAGING

CHARACTERISTICS	^{133}Xe	^{127}Xe	^{81m}Kr	^{99m}Tc-DTPA AEROSOL
Energy (keV)	81	203	126–192	140
Pulmonary radiation dose	High	Moderate	Low	Low
Spatial resolution	Low	Good	Good	Good
Sensitivity for obstructive air-ways disease detection	Excellent	Excellent	Good	Good
Portability	Difficult	Difficult	Easy	Easy
Disposal	Vent or trap Negative pressure room	Vent or trap Negative pressure room	Easy	Easy
Cost	Low	Moderate	High	Low

15 seconds while a static image is taken. The equilibrium phase constitutes the rebreathing of the expired xenon diluted by approximately 2 liters of oxygen contained in a closed system. The patient usually rebreathes this mixture for 2 to 3 minutes while a static image is taken. Thus, the xenon 133 image obtained at equilibrium essentially represents the distribution of aerated lung volume. After equilibrium is reached, fresh air is then breathed during the washout phase while serial 15-second images are obtained for 2 to 3 minutes as the xenon clears from the lungs. In patients with chronic obstructive pulmonary disease (COPD), the washout phase may be prolonged to 3 to 5 minutes if necessary to assess areas of regional airway trapping.

Preparation of technetium 99m DTPA aerosol begins with the injection of approximately 30 mCi (1.1 GBq) of technetium 99m DTPA in a volume of 2 ml into the nebulizer of an aerosol delivery system. Oxygen tubing is then connected to the side port and oxygen is supplied through a flow meter. Flow rates are in the range of 7 to 10 liters per minute. A mouthpiece with a nose clip is then used to administer the aerosol. If necessary, this can be connected to an endotracheal tube. The patient is usually in a supine position (which allows for an even distribution of aerosol) and breathes at tidal volume for 3 to 5 minutes.

Initial images are taken for approximately 200,000 counts, or about 3 minutes, with the patient in the erect position, if possible. If the patient is unable to sit, a posterior image with the patient in the lateral decubitus position is acceptable. Other views may include posterior oblique, anterior, and lateral views.

Because lung perfusion imaging is also performed using a technetium 99m agent, a 3 to 5 times count rate differential must be used when using technetium 99m aerosol to prevent interference of the two radiopharmaceuticals. The order in which the procedures are performed dictates the relative administered doses. Performing the aerosol ventilation study after perfusion imaging has the advantage of allowing the ventilation scan to be avoided if perfusion is normal. Characteristics of different ventilation imaging agents are shown in Table 9–2.

Normal Lung Scan

PERFUSION SCAN

A normal perfusion scan is shown in Fig. 9–5. In the posterior projection there is some tapering of activity toward the bases due to the thinning of the lungs in the region of the posterior sulci. In the anterior view, the cardiac silhouette and the aortic knob are commonly identified. The left lateral view may show a substantial anterior defect due to the heart. It should be remembered that in the lateral gamma camera views approximately one-third of the image statistics (or counts) come from the contralateral lung. This so-called "shine through" may frequently allow enough photons to be collected from the opposite lung to render a normal lateral image, even in the presence of a prominent defect seen in one lung on the anterior or posterior view. Oblique projections are often helpful but may be confusing to the uninitiated observer and frequently demonstrate prominent hilar defects. In general, defects

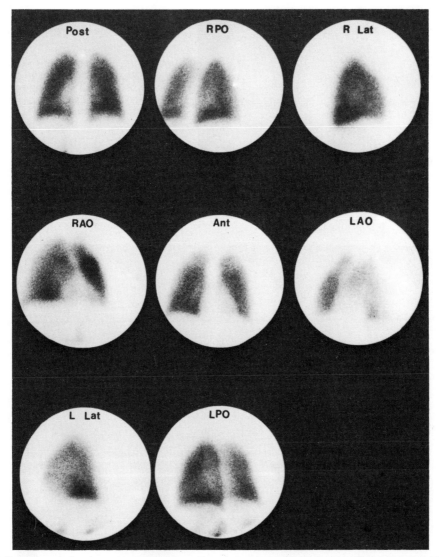

Figure 9–5. Normal perfusion lung scan. Normal cardiac defect is most prominent in the anterior and left lateral views. A small amount of activity is seen in the kidneys on the images performed at the end of the study from breakdown of the radiopharmaceutical.

suspected on the oblique projections should be confirmed on one of the four standard views.

Pleural disease may produce distinctive changes on an otherwise normal perfusion scan. Small pleural effusions may best be seen on the lateral or oblique views as posterior sulcus blunting or as a "fissure sign," a linear defect caused by fluid in a fissure separating lobes (Fig. 9–6). The fissure sign may also be produced by pleural scarring or thickening (even when not apparent on chest radiographs), COPD, or rarely by multiple pulmonary microemboli. Moderate-sized pleural effusions may occasionally simulate segmental defects: if scanning is performed in the supine position in a patient with a pleural effusion, the fluid may collect in the superior part of the major fissure and mimic a superior segment lower lobe defect. However, the defect frequently disappears in the upright position. If an effusion is large, it may compress an entire lung and decrease the blood flow to that side generally or may surround the lung, producing the appearance of a small lung.

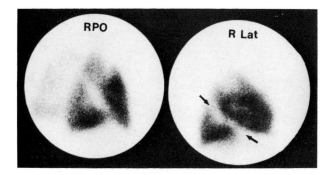

Figure 9–6. "Fissure sign." The arrows indicate a negative defect in the region of the major fissure on the right. In this case, it is due to fluid within the fissure in a patient with congestive heart failure.

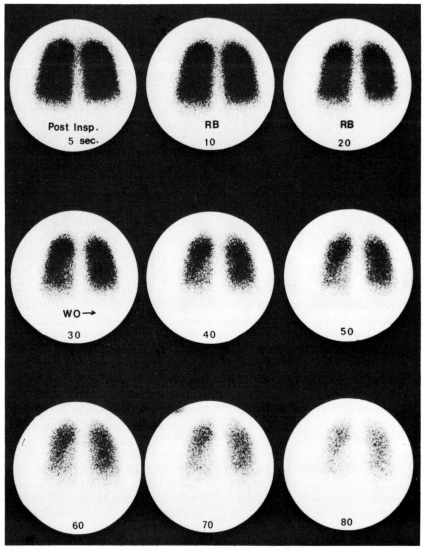

Figure 9–7. Normal ventilation lung scan performed in a posterior projection with xenon 133. An initial inspiratory image was obtained, followed by rebreathing. At 30 seconds, the washout phase began, with approximately half of the xenon activity gone each 30 to 45 seconds.

It is worth noting that perfusion defects may occur incidentally in asymptomatic people with normal chest x-rays and without a clinical history of pulmonary emboli. Among young nonsmokers about 7 percent may demonstrate subsegmental defects and 3 to 4 percent have lobular or segmental defects. If smokers are added to this population, as many as 10 percent may exhibit some type of perfusion defect.

VENTILATION SCAN

A normal xenon 133 ventilation study performed in the posterior projection is shown in Fig. 9–7. After the initial breath, a relatively homogeneous distribution of activity should be seen throughout both lungs; the initial breath image reflects regional ventilatory rate if there is maximum inspiratory effort. The equilibrium-phase image indicates the aerated volume of lung and may be thought of as the "scintigraphic chest x-ray." Even in patients with abnormal single-breath and washout images the equilibrium phase frequently is normal, particularly if rebreathing is performed for several minutes. During the washout phase, activity clears from the lower portions of the lung at a faster rate than from the apices because the air exchange is greater. However, activity is frequently seen for longer at the bases due to the relatively larger volume of lung present in that region. In most normal studies, the lungs are almost completely clear of xenon within 2 to 3 minutes of beginning the washout phase, the normal half-time for xenon washout being approximately 30 to 45 seconds. While washout is the most sensitive phase for the detection of trapping caused by airway obstruction, it must be noted that if xenon gas does not enter an area during equilibrium, washout cannot be evaluated. Thus, the sensitivity of the washout phase is to a large extent dependent on performing sufficient rebreathing to obtain adequate equilibrium in as much of the lung volume as possible as well as on the length of the washout phase.

Since xenon is soluble in fat and somewhat soluble in blood, it may be deposited in the liver, resulting in increased activity in the right upper quadrant. This becomes apparent near the end of the xenon washout study and should not be mistaken for trapping of xenon in the right lower lung. The finding is particularly prominent in patients with disorders producing a fatty liver.

Normal DTPA aerosol ventilation images demonstrate homogeneous symmetric aerosol deposition from apex to base. Areas in which there is no activity represent nonventilated regions. Normal aerosol scans resemble perfusion scans, except that the trachea and the bronchi are visualized. In addition, swallowed activity can sometimes be seen in the esophagus and stomach (Fig. 9–8 A, B).

Clinical Applications

Regardless of the reason for performing pulmonary ventilation–perfusion imaging, it cannot be overemphasized that a high-quality recent chest radiograph and pertinent clinical and laboratory findings should be fully utilized when interpreting lung scans. Use of poor-quality portable supine films can lead to mistakes in interpretation. Ideally, full-inspiration upright posterior-anterior and lateral chest radiographs should be obtained as near as possible to the time the lung images are performed, certainly within 12 to 24 hours before or after the completion of the scan.

PULMONARY EMBOLISM

The clinical diagnosis of pulmonary embolism is often difficult. Less than one-fourth of patients with pulmonary emboli show the classic signs or symptoms of the disease; hemoptysis is seldom observed and blood enzyme determinations are often not reliable. Clinical presentations are frequently vague and may be mimicked by a variety of thoracic and abdominal disorders. Although pulmonary arteriography offers the only definitive means of establishing a diagnosis of pulmonary embolus, it is not practical to employ such an invasive and expensive technique as a screening test. Interposed between clinical suspicion and angiography is radionuclide ventilation–perfusion imaging, which when properly performed and interpreted is a highly sensitive and often accurate procedure for the detection of pulmonary emboli. In addition, a normal scan essentially excludes the diagnosis. It must be emphasized that even in the small percentage of patients in whom the studies may be nondiagnostic, radionuclide imaging may be used to guide selective pulmonary arteriography, thereby increasing the sensitivity of that examination.

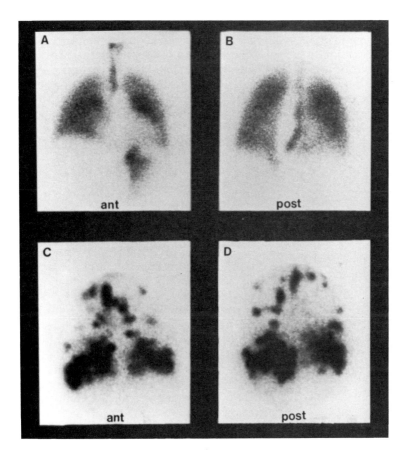

Figure 9–8. (A and B) Normal technetium 99m DTPA aerosol ventilation images show relatively homogeneous activity throughout the lungs. Activity is also present in the esophagus and stomach from swallowed aerosol. (C and D) A patient with COPD shows central and basilar nonuniform deposition.

Ventilation–Perfusion (V/Q) Scan Findings

The classic presentation of pulmonary emboli on ventilation–perfusion lung images is as multiple peripherally based focal areas of decreased or absent perfusion that ventilate normally—the so-called *ventilation–perfusion mismatch* (Figs. 9–9 and 9–10). The perfusion defects characteristically correspond to anatomic divisions of the lung: lobes, segments, or subsegments. It is therefore of paramount importance to acquire a thorough appreciation of segmental lung anatomy as displayed on routine scintigraphic perfusion images. Figure 9–11 shows the individual pulmonary segments in the projection that best visualizes each segment.

Of patients with pulmonary emboli, approximately 75 percent have segmental or lobar perfusion defects, whereas the remaining 25 percent have only subsegmental defects. Pulmonary emboli are multiple in 90 percent of cases, bilateral in 85 percent of cases, and more frequent in the lower lobes, where the blood flow is greater. The presence

of defects in the upper lobes only, however, does not in itself exclude the presence of emboli. While segmental perfusion defects are quite sensitive for and suggestive of pulmonary emboli, especially in the presence of a normal chest x-ray, it should be emphasized that they may be produced by a number of other diseases (see Tables 9–3 and 9–4). However, the specificity of such defects is greatly enhanced by correlation with a ventilation study and appropriate clinical and physical data.

In addition to the classic appearance just described, other perfusion scan presentations have been associated with pulmonary emboli. The fissure sign has been described with multiple pulmonary microemboli but is not specific and most commonly represents fluid within the fissure or thickening of the adjacent pleural surfaces. Occasionally, massive pulmonary emboli may cause absent perfusion to an entire lung, although hilar masses or adenopathy, a hypoplastic pulmonary artery (Fig. 9–12), and mediastinal fibrosis may also cause significantly diminished blood flow to one lung. Another sign that has

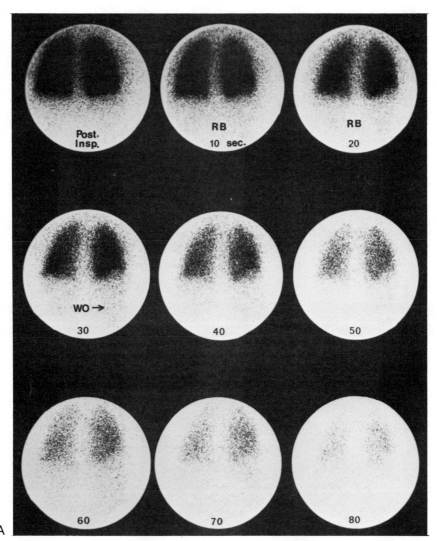

Figure 9–9. Multiple pulmonary emboli. (A) The ventilation scan demonstrates normal ventilation bilaterally, with good washout and no areas of trapping.

Illustration continued on following page

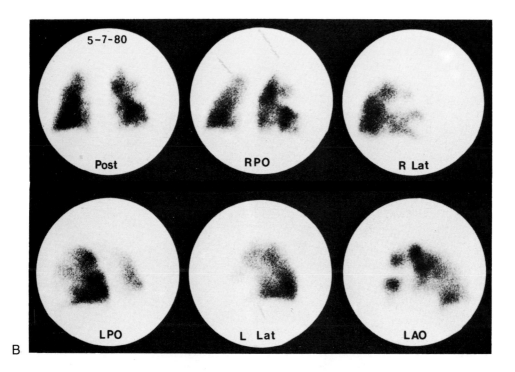

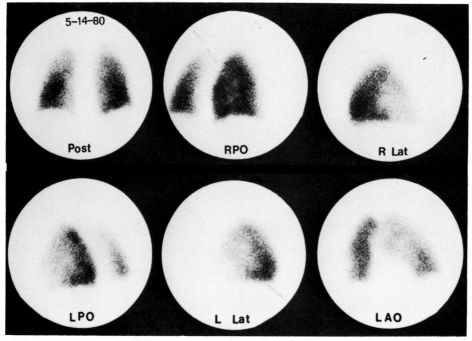

Figure 9–9 *Continued* (B) A perfusion scan demonstrates multiple segmental and subsegmental defects. (C) A follow-up perfusion scan performed 7 days later reveals almost complete resolution of the pulmonary emboli.

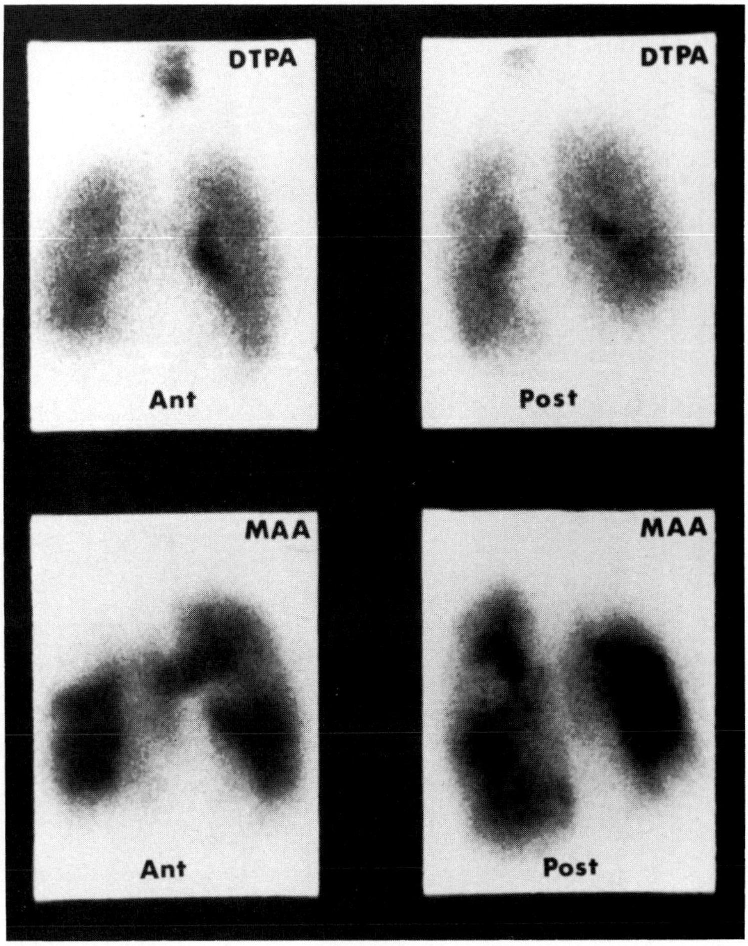

Figure 9–10. Technetium used to detect pulmonary emboli. The ^{99m}Tc DTPA aerosol scans (top row) are normal except for some central deposition. The ^{99m}Tc MAA perfusion images (bottom row) show significant defects particularly at the right lung apex. (Case courtesy of Henry D. Royal, M.D.)

Table 9–3. CAUSES OF DEFECTS ON PERFUSION LUNG SCANS

Pulmonary embolism (thrombotic, septic, marrow, or air)*
Bulla or cyst
Localized hypoxia due to asthma, bronchitis, emphysema
Surgery (e.g., pneumonectomy)
Pleural effusion*
Tumor (hilar or mediastinal)*
Metastases (hematogenous or lymphangitic)
Hilar adenopathy (lymphoma, sarcoid)
Pulmonary artery atresia or hypoplasia*
Fibrosing mediastinitis*
Radiation therapy*
Pneumonia
Pulmonary edema
Atelectasis
Fibrosis (post-inflammatory, post-radiation, pleural thickening)
Vasculitis*

*Entity may cause a V/Q mismatch.

proved useful in characterizing perfusion defects but that has a negative correlation with pulmonary emboli is the so-called "stripe sign." The stripe sign is a thin line or stripe of activity at the periphery or pleural surface of a perfusion defect, presumed to represent perfused parenchyma. Such a defect is unlikely to represent a pulmonary embolus,
Text continued on page 164

Table 9–4. CAUSES OF DECREASED PERFUSION TO ONE LUNG

Pulmonary agenesis or stenosis
Swyer-James syndrome
Embolus
Pneumothorax
Massive effusion
Mediastinal fibrosis
Tumor

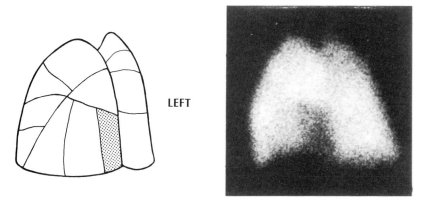

LEFT

RIGHT

L. POSTERIOR OBLIQUE

Figure 9–11A. Left lower lobe—posterior basal segment.

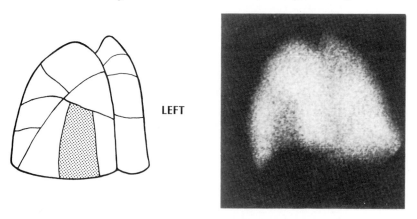

LEFT

RIGHT

L. POSTERIOR OBLIQUE

Figure 9–11B. Left lower lobe—lateral basal segment.

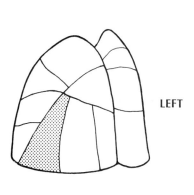

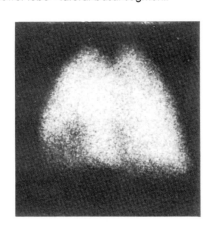

LEFT

RIGHT

L. POSTERIOR OBLIQUE

Figure 9–11C. Left lower lobe—anterior medial basal segment.

Figure 9–11. Segmental perfusion defects. Each is shown diagramatically and in the position that best demonstrates the defect on the perfusion scan. **Right** and **Left** and **Posterior** and **Anterior** refer to the scintigrams. (Reprinted with permission from Mandell CH: Scintillation Camera Lung Imaging. New York, Grune & Stratton, 1976, pp 10–17, 20–27, 30–38, 42–51.)

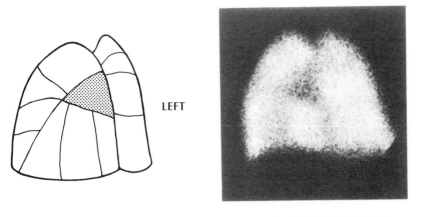

LEFT   RIGHT

L. POSTERIOR OBLIQUE

Figure 9–11D. Left lower lobe—superior segment.

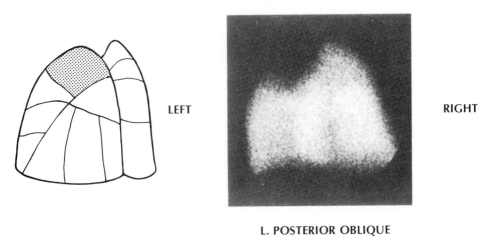

LEFT   RIGHT

L. POSTERIOR OBLIQUE

Figure 9–11E. Left upper lobe—posterior apical segment.

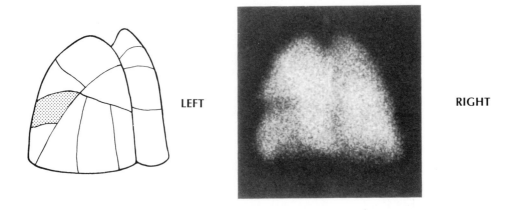

LEFT   RIGHT

L. POSTERIOR OBLIQUE

Figure 9–11F. Left upper lobe—superior lingular segment. The lingular segment is difficult to identify because of the normal cardiac defect.

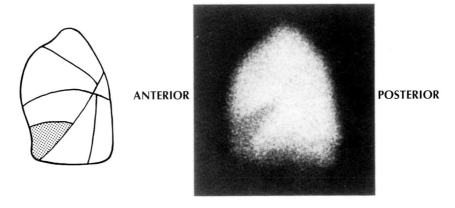

L. LATERAL

Figure 9–11G. Left upper lobe—inferior lingular segment. The lingular segment is difficult to identify because of the normal cardiac defect.

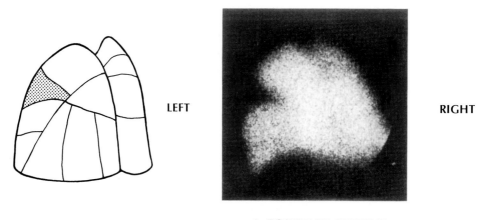

L. POSTERIOR OBLIQUE

Figure 9–11H. Left upper lobe—anterior segment.

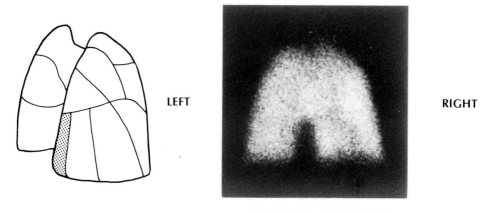

R. POSTERIOR OBLIQUE

Figure 9–11I. Right lower lobe—posterior basal segment.

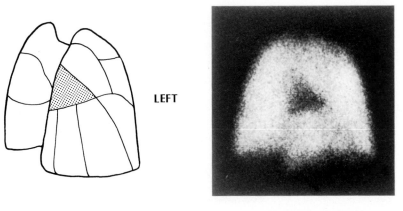

LEFT   RIGHT

R. POSTERIOR OBLIQUE
Figure 9–11J. Right lower lobe—superior segment.

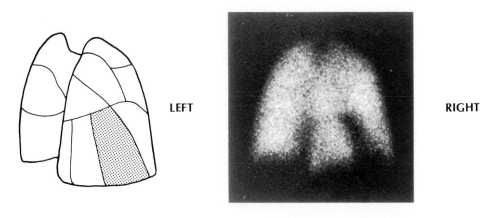

LEFT   RIGHT

R. POSTERIOR OBLIQUE
Figure 9–11K. Right lower lobe—anterior basal segment.

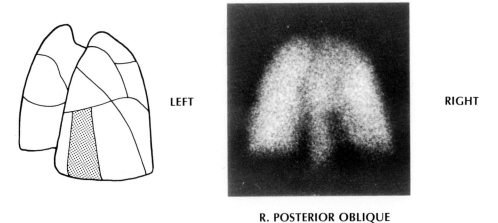

LEFT   RIGHT

R. POSTERIOR OBLIQUE
Figure 9–11L. Right lower lobe—lateral basal segment.

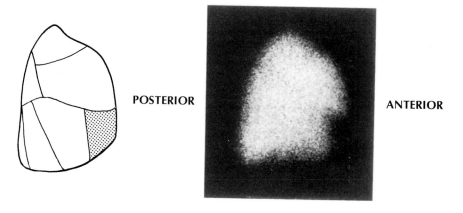

POSTERIOR   ANTERIOR

R. LATERAL

Figure 9–11M. Right middle lobe—medial segment.

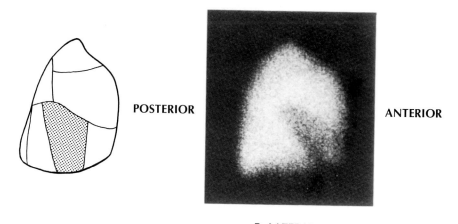

POSTERIOR   ANTERIOR

R. LATERAL

Figure 9–11N. Right middle lobe—lateral segment.

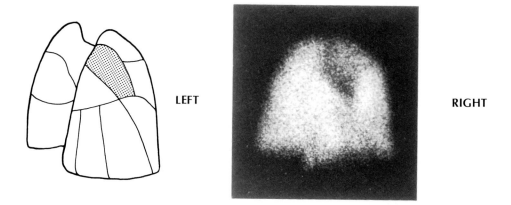

LEFT   RIGHT

R. POSTERIOR OBLIQUE

Figure 9–11O. Right upper lobe—posterior segment.

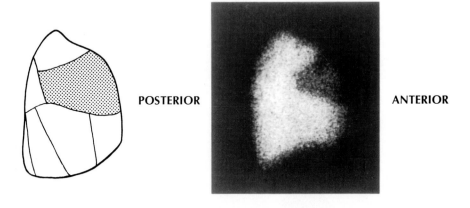

POSTERIOR   ANTERIOR

R. LATERAL

Figure 9–11P. Right upper lobe—anterior segment.

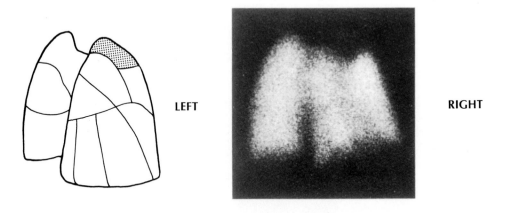

LEFT   RIGHT

R. POSTERIOR OBLIQUE

Figure 9–11Q. Right upper lobe—apical segment.

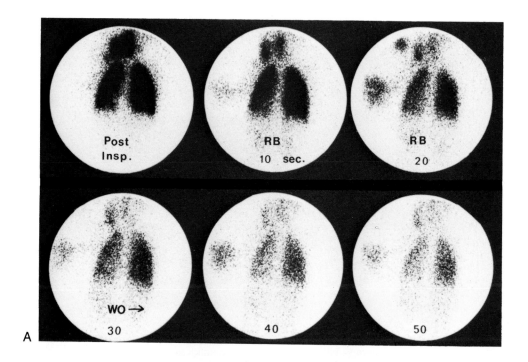

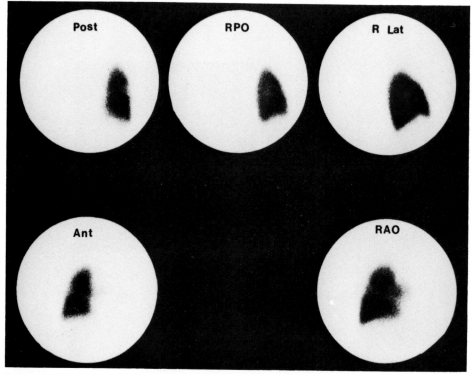

Figure 9–12. Hypoplastic or absent left pulmonary artery. (A) The ventilation scan demonstrates good ventilation in both lungs, with slightly more rapid washout on the left. (B) The perfusion scan demonstrates completely absent perfusion to the left lung.

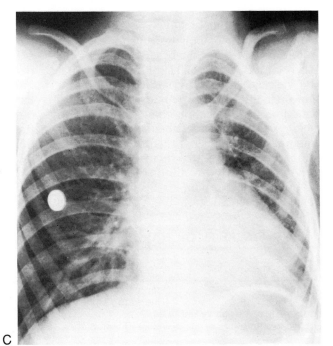

Figure 9–12 *Continued* (C) The chest radiograph demonstrates the classic findings compatible with this entity, including volume loss and bronchial vascularity.

C

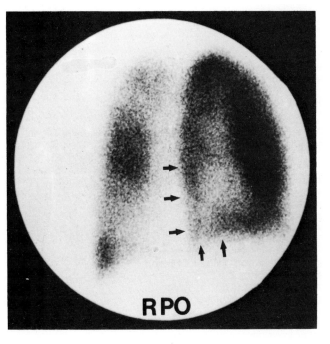

Figure 9–13. Perfusion defect demonstrating a central negative defect that does not extend to the periphery, with a rim of activity at the edge of the pleura—the stripe sign (arrows). This indicates a low probability of pulmonary embolus.

based on the assumption that nonpleural-based lesions are not emboli (Fig. 9–13).

In the absence of underlying primary airway disease, ventilation lung imaging is normal in approximately 80 percent of patients with pulmonary emboli; however, if the scan is performed immediately after an embolus has occurred, there is a slight possibility that the vascular insult may induce reflex bronchoconstriction, which would usually be detected on the ventilation scan. Although this phenomenon has been demonstrated experimentally in animals, it is rarely demonstrated clinically, and when it occurs it is generally restricted to the first 4 or 6 hours following embolization. Possible mechanisms that have been suggested as a cause for this bronchoconstriction include release of transient vasoactive substances by the platelets and local hypocarbia.

Approaches to Scan Interpretation

In the clinical setting of suspected pulmonary emboli, the proper interpretation of lung scans is one of the most difficult tasks facing the nuclear medicine physician. It requires meticulous review and comparison of three separate sets of images: the perfusion images, the ventilation images, and the chest radiographs.

Interpretation of the perfusion scans first entails the identification and classification of any defects according to their appearance.

Table 9–5. SCHEME FOR INTERPRETATION OF V/Q IMAGING

INTERPRETATION*	PATTERN†	PULMONARY EMBOLISM (%)
Normal	Normal perfusion conforming to the shape of the lungs	0
Probability of Pulmonary Embolism		
Low	Small V/Q mismatches	<10
	Small focal V/Q matches with no corresponding radiographic abnormalities	
	Any perfusion defects substantially smaller than associated radiographic abnormalities	
Intermediate	Widespread severe COPD	<20–40
	Perfusion defects and radiographic abnormalities of same size and location	
	Single moderate or large V/Q mismatch without corresponding radiographic abnormality	
	Not falling into other categories	
High‡	Perfusion defects substantially larger than radiographic abnormalities in the same location	>85
	Two moderate and one large mismatches without corresponding radiographic abnormality in that area	
	Two large V/Q mismatches without corresponding radiographic abnormalities	

*Highest applicable criteria apply. Thus, a patient with widespread diffuse COPD and two segmental mismatches should be interpreted as high probability.
†Small defect = less than 25 percent of a pulmonary segment (e.g., a "rat bite"); moderate defect = between 25 and 75 percent of a segment; large defect = greater than 75 percent of a segment.
‡Defects in this category are usually wedge-shaped and extend to the lung periphery.
Adapted from Biello DR, Mattar AG, Osei-Wusu A, et al: Interpretation of indeterminate lung scintigrams. Radiology 133:189–194, 1979; and Saltzman HA, et al: Value of ventilation/perfusion scan in acute pulmonary embolism: Results of the Prospective Investigation of Pulmonary Embolism Diagnosis (PIOPED). JAMA 263(20):2753–2759, 1990.

Defects corresponding to anatomic divisions should be classified as lobar, segmental, or subsegmental. Those that are not anatomic or do not respect segmental boundaries may be considered nonsegmental and unlikely to represent pulmonary emboli. One scheme (Table 9–5) classifies patients as having high, intermediate, or low probability of pulmonary embolus based on the size and number of perfusion defects along with careful comparison of these defects with ventilatory and radiographic findings. Additional data are shown in Table 9–6.

The accuracy of any test is dependent upon the number of patients in the test population who actually have the disease (pre-test probability). In general, when a V/Q scan is interpreted as "high probability or likelihood," there is an excellent chance that pulmonary emboli are present regardless of the pre-test probability in the patient population. The same is true of "low probability" interpretations; that is, there is a relatively low chance of pulmonary emboli. In contrast, when the "intermediate" category is determined, there is a significant impact of the pre-test probability. Thus, when an intermediate interpretation is rendered, careful attention should be paid to the type of patient, the history, and the clinician's suspicion level in arriving at a conclusion regarding patient therapy.

Although lung scan interpretation is easiest in the presence of a clear chest x-ray, the presence of either a localized infiltrate or diffuse lung disease should not be seen as an insurmountable problem. Any approach that does not attempt to interpret pulmonary emboli in the presence of infiltrates or diffuse lung disease will result in a large number of scans being read as indeterminate and will unnecessarily subject a large number of patients to pulmonary angiography. One of the most common situations involves the presence of one or more localized pulmonary infiltrates on the chest x-ray of a patient suspected of having pulmonary emboli. Certainly, the infiltrate or infiltrates could represent either inflammatory disease or pulmonary emboli, with or without infarction. However, since pulmonary emboli are generally multiple and since only about 25 percent of such lesions progress to infarction, the likelihood is excellent that V/Q mismatches suggesting pulmonary embolus may be found elsewhere, in areas of otherwise radiographically normal lung. In the absence of such findings, some diagnostic probability information can nevertheless be obtained by comparing the size of the radiographic infiltrate with the size of the corresponding perfusion deficit. It has been suggested that when a perfusion defect is substantially smaller than the corresponding x-ray abnormality, the probability of pulmonary embolus is low. Conversely, if the perfusion defect is substantially larger than the radiographic infiltrate, the probability of such an occurrence is high (Table 9–7). A perfusion defect that corresponds closely in size to an infiltrate carries an intermediate probability of embolus. In this latter case if clinical suspicion is high, angiography is probably indicated.

Normal or near-normal perfusion lung scans may occur in a large percentage of patients with a diffusely abnormal chest x-ray. While the presence of perfusion abnormalities in such patients may cause difficulty in interpretation, the surprising number of normal or near-normal scans obtained indicates that pulmonary emboli can be effectively excluded in many patients with underlying lung diseases. This is of great clinical and economic significance in that angiography can be avoided in the majority of cases. It should be re-emphasized that a normal ventilation–perfusion lung scan in any patient essentially excludes the possibility of recent significant pulmonary embolization.

With or without a normal chest radiograph, careful correlation of any perfusion

Table 9–6. COMPARISON OF SCAN CATEGORY WITH ANGIOGRAM FINDINGS, SENSITIVITY, AND SPECIFICITY

SCAN CATEGORY	SENSITIVITY, %	SPECIFICITY, %
High probability	41	97
High or intermediate probability	82	52
High, intermediate, or low probability	98	10

Saltzman HA et al: Value of ventilation/perfusion scan in acute pulmonary embolism: Results of the Prospective Investigation of Pulmonary Embolism Diagnosis (PIOPED). JAMA 263(20):2753–2759, 1990. Copyright 1990, American Medical Association.

**Table 9–7. ANGIOGRAPHIC FINDINGS IN REGIONS
WITH SCINTIGRAPHIC PERFUSION DEFECTS
AND RADIOGRAPHIC ABNORMALITIES**

SIZE OF DEFECT COMPARED WITH RADIOGRAPHIC ABNORMALITY	PATIENTS (NO.)	PULMONARY EMBOLISM
Smaller	14	1 (7%)
Equal	77	20 (26%)
Larger		
V/Q mismatch	18	16 (89%)
V/Q match	2	0 (0%)
Total	111	37 (33%)

Reprinted with minor modifications from Biello DR, Mattar AG, Osei-Wusu A, et al: Interpretation of indeterminate lung scintigrams. Radiology 133(1):189–194, 1979. With permission.

abnormalities with the corresponding regions on the ventilation study should be undertaken to exclude airway disease as a cause for a perfusion defect. Matched ventilation–perfusion abnormalities in a radiographically normal area demonstrate a very low probability of pulmonary embolus. Since the ventilation examination is usually performed in the posterior position, it is best compared with the posterior perfusion image. If perfusion defects are best seen or only seen on another projection, a repeat ventilation study in the view that best demonstrates the lesion may be undertaken on the same or the following day to evaluate airway patency in that region. If the perfusion defect corresponds to a prominent chest radiograph infiltrate, however, a ventilation defect is to be expected and a repeat study usually will not be of value.

One of the more common clinical situations involves patients with underlying COPD and suspected pulmonary emboli. In COPD both nonsegmental and segmental perfusion defects may occur, making differentiation from superimposed pulmonary emboli impossible without an accompanying ventilation study. When COPD is severe and diffuse, even the combined ventilation–perfusion study may not provide an answer, and pulmonary angiography may be indicated if emboli are strongly suspected. However, in the presence of severe COPD, even angiography may be fraught with interpretive error.

Lung Scan Versus Pulmonary Angiography

There is excellent correlation between the angiographic demonstration of pulmonary emboli and the identification of defects on perfusion scan. However, because of the essential nonspecificity of perfusion defects, the pulmonary angiogram is probably still the "gold standard" for diagnosis of pulmonary emboli. Angiography may even be more sensitive than the perfusion scan in the diagnosis of a nonoccluding embolus of a major artery. The only pathognomonic finding of pulmonary embolism by arteriography is an intraluminal defect, with a sharp cutoff of a vessel being indicative but less specific. Areas of avascularity, hypoperfusion, and delayed filling are nonspecific and may be due to other pulmonary diseases. Pulmonary arteriography is best reserved for patients with an intermediate probability of emboli based upon the scan criteria previously discussed and those in whom definitive diagnosis is required before any contemplated interventional treatment such as inferior vena cava ligation is undertaken. When angiography is indicated, the ventilation–perfusion study may be quite valuable in directing a selective or subselective angiogram to a particular suspicious region. This is often important in patients with chronic pulmonary abnormalities, such as emphysema or pulmonary hypertension, who may poorly tolerate a bilateral pulmonary angiogram.

Obviously, the decision to subject a patient to pulmonary arteriography cannot be fully determined by a set formula since no group of criteria will be satisfactory in all clinical situations. In every case, the relative risks of pulmonary arteriography and anticoagulation therapy and the confidence in the radionuclide diagnosis must be carefully considered.

Follow-Up

Once the diagnosis of pulmonary embolus has been established, perfusion imaging may be used to follow the course of the disease. Typically, there is some evidence of change in the pattern of perfusion defects in the first few days after the embolism. Defects may become smaller or disappear altogether, and new defects may appear. New defects may result from fragmentation of larger centrally placed clots that pass to the lung periphery or from altered regional perfusion pressure in the lung, which may convert a partially obstructing clot to a complete obstruction. Of course, recurrent emboli also produce new defects, but the mere presence of new defects per se cannot be used to establish recurrent embolization during this period.

The ultimate fate of pulmonary emboli is quite variable and to some extent dependent on the size of the emboli and the age of the patient. The larger the initial defect and the older the patient, the less likely is the pulmonary perfusion scan to return to normal. About half of patients less than 40 years old with pulmonary emboli have complete resolution of defects, and very few patients over 60 years of age with pulmonary emboli ever show complete resolution. Emboli occurring in the presence of underlying diffuse diseases are also less likely to show complete resolution, as are those that produce actual infarction of lung.

COPD

Emphysema and chronic bronchitis are the most common forms of COPD. A large number of older patients referred for pulmonary imaging have emphysema or chronic bronchitis, frequently related to cigarette smoking. Both diseases are associated with patchy, uneven ventilation, reduced lung compliance, and increased peripheral resistance. In emphysema there is parenchymal destruction distal to the terminal bronchioles, causing damage in the secondary pulmonary lobule; this includes damage to the alveoli as well as the pulmonary capillaries. The destruction in the secondary lobule may be central (centrilobular) or may involve the whole secondary lobule (panlobular). Panlobular emphysema is seen more frequently in the lower lungs, whereas centrilobular emphysema is more common in the lung apex.

In either case, extensive destruction may result in the formation of bullae.

The best tests for early detection of emphysema are spirometry and blood gas measurements. Pulmonary ventilation imaging is most helpful in characterizing the regional distribution of abnormalities and to a lesser extent in delineating the clinical severity of the disease. It is not uncommon for patients to have rather marked changes on the ventilation scan but a relatively normal chest x-ray. The typical x-ray changes of an increased diameter of the chest and flattening of the diaphragm are often late manifestations of emphysema.

The sensitivity of the ventilation scan for detection of chronic obstructive airway disease varies with the imaging phase of the examination. The xenon 133 single-breath image detects approximately 66 percent of matched ventilation–perfusion abnormalities whereas the equilibrium images detect only 20 percent of such defects. The washout or clearance phase, however, is much more sensitive, detecting over 90 percent of matched ventilation–perfusion lesions. Because the late phase is most sensitive, particular care should be given to this part of the examination. A xenon 133 washout study in patients with suspected COPD should continue for at least 3 to 5 minutes since single-breath and equilibrium images may be normal in such patients. Because they do not permit washout imaging, short-lived isotopes such as krypton 81m are of less value than xenon 133 in assessing subtle obstructive changes. When using ^{99m}Tc DTPA aerosol ventilation imaging in patients with COPD, little or no peripheral activity may be seen in the lungs, since increased turbulence in the large airways causes marked deposition in the trachea and bronchi (see Fig. 9–8C, D).

In patients with early or mild COPD, the perfusion scan may be normal or near normal. However, as the destruction of lung parenchyma progresses it characteristically produces multiple nonsegmental perfusion defects, which may be relatively focal and discrete or diffusely scattered throughout the lungs, giving a coarsely mottled pattern. Perfusion defects may also be caused by regional hypoxia producing reflex vasoconstriction and by bullae themselves or their compression of adjacent lung. Large apical bullae may render strikingly reduced or absent perfusion to the upper lung zones.

In the presence of COPD, the perfusion scan is nonspecific unless accompanied by a ventilation study. Ventilation scans characteristically reveal defects in activity in the involved areas on the single-breath images and less frequently on the equilibrium views. Washout images usually demonstrate areas of delayed clearance (trapping) that may correspond to the initial defects seen on the single-breath views. Ventilation abnormalities that correlate with defects seen on the perfusion scan constitute a so-called ventilation–perfusion match, a hallmark of primary airway disease (Fig. 9–14). This finding may be of great value in distinguishing between chronic obstructive pulmonary disease and superimposed pulmonary emboli when the latter are suspected. Many patients who present for ventilation–perfusion imaging for evaluation of pulmonary emboli have COPD. Thus, it is important to carefully correlate the ventilation and perfusion scans. If all the defects are small and subsegmental, and have matched ventilation defects, emphysema is likely. The diagnosis of pulmonary embolism usually is not made unless there are at least two superimposed unmatched segmental defects (Fig. 9–15).

Ventilation–perfusion scintigraphy has also been used to investigate less common forms of COPD, such as alpha-1-antitrypsin deficiency and cystic fibrosis. Alpha-1-antitrypsin deficiency is a recessive inherited form of panlobular emphysema in which

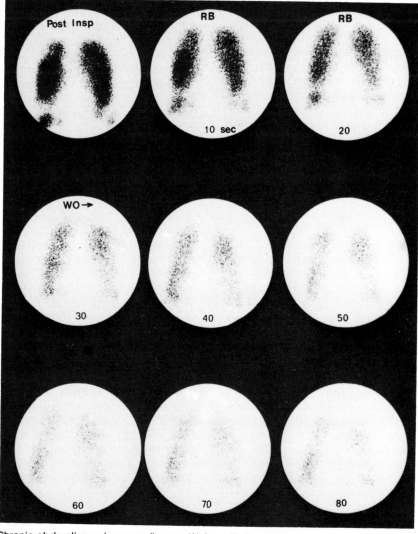

Figure 9–14. Chronic obstructive pulmonary disease. (A) A ventilation scan demonstrates prominent defects at both bases on the inspiration views. On the washout views there is trapping at both bases.

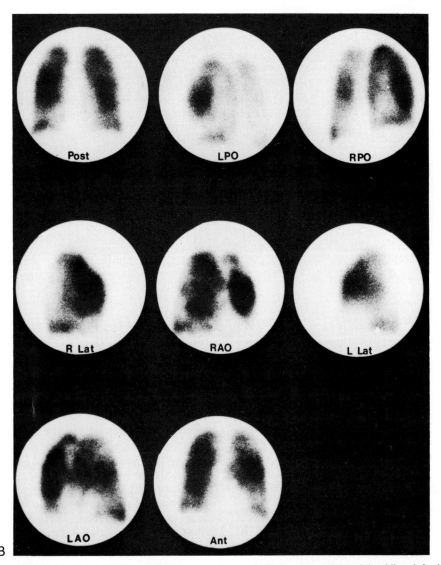

B

Figure 9–14 *Continued* (B) The perfusion scan demonstrates a complete match of the defects.

Illustration continued on following page

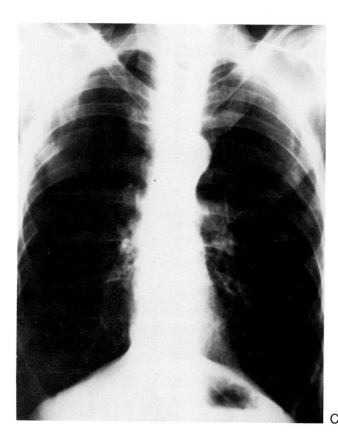

Figure 9–14 *Continued* (C) The chest radiograph demonstrates hyperlucent lungs, which are hyperexpanded, with flattening of both hemidiaphragms.

C

homozygotes demonstrate marked abnormalities of ventilation and perfusion in the lower lungs, and even heterozygotes may show delayed clearance of xenon from these zones. V/Q studies performed in patients with cystic fibrosis demonstrate patchy segmental defects in perfusion and markedly disturbed ventilation, particularly in the washout phase.

ASTHMA, BRONCHIECTASIS, AND BRONCHITIS

Asthma, bronchiectasis, and bronchitis all cause airway obstruction by different but often overlapping mechanisms. *Asthma* is primarily related to acute spastic narrowing of the bronchi. *Bronchiectasis* destroys the elastic and muscular tissue in the bronchial walls, causing dilation and sometimes collapse, usually with associated infection. *Bronchitis* results in large amounts of viscous mucus in the bronchi and the trachea. Often all three disorders are present in the same patient (usually a smoker) and may ultimately lead to emphysema. These diseases are character-

ized by acute episodic exacerbation, during which ventilation and accompanying perfusion abnormalities are found on pulmonary V/Q scans. In spite of the clinical symptoms, chest x-rays are often negative, and excluding the presence of superimposed diseases such as pulmonary emboli may be difficult.

Scattered nonsegmental perfusion defects are generally present during an acute asthma attack, probably related to localized hypoxia. Corresponding ventilation defects are frequently noted during the single-breath xenon study but may become less apparent with rebreathing, and regional areas of delayed washout are also usually identified. The geographic location of these abnormalities within the lungs may characteristically change during the same or subsequent attacks, giving an altered pattern of V/Q abnormalities on the lung scan. This provides a scintigraphic distinction from chronic emphysema, which results in a fixed location of the abnormalities. In asthmatics without COPD, V/Q scans frequently return to normal within 24 hours after treatment with bronchodilators. This may be used to distinguish between pulmo-

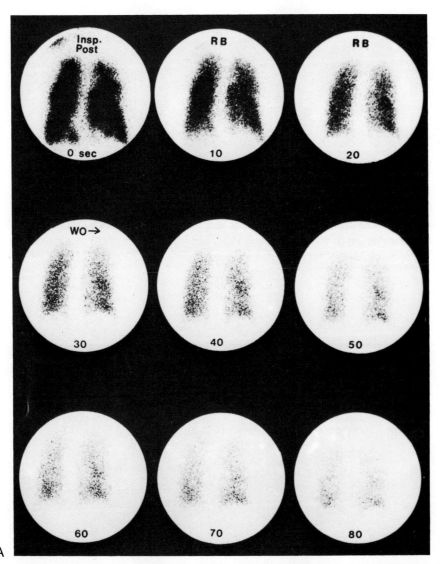

Figure 9–15. Pulmonary embolism in a patient with chronic obstructive pulmonary disease. (A) The ventilation scan demonstrates marked areas of abnormality with trapping at both bases.

Illustration continued on following page

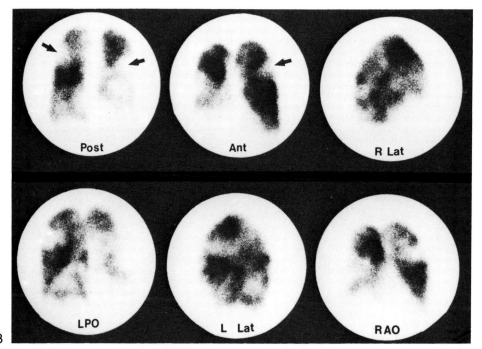

B

Figure 9–15 *Continued* (B) The perfusion scan shows many additional defects, some of which are segmental (arrows) and do not have a rim of peripheral activity. In this case, even though the patient has COPD, there is a very high probability of pulmonary emboli.

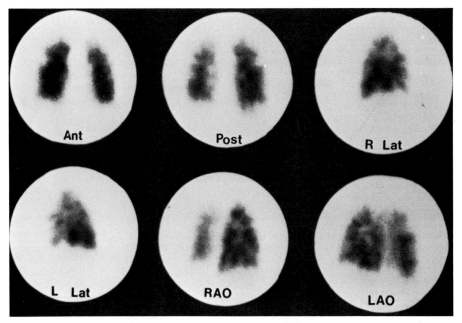

Figure 9–16. Pulmonary lymphangitic spread of breast carcinoma. Multiple perfusion images obtained with technetium 99m labeled MAA show multiple discrete linear defects in both lungs, which actually outline the margins of the bronchopulmonary segments in a patient with a normal chest radiograph and normal ventilation study. This appearance is typical of that described in patients with lymphangitic spread of tumor to the lung.

nary emboli and asthma if they cannot be differentiated on the basis of initial clinical and scintigraphic assessment. The detection of wheezing and/or ascertaining any prior history of asthma in a patient undergoing imaging for suspected pulmonary emboli may greatly aid in the interpretation of the images and in determining the need for repeat imaging after bronchodilator administration.

Unlike asthma, the perfusion defects produced by bronchiectasis are constant in location (generally restricted to the lung bases) and are in large part related to reflex vasoconstriction secondary to local hypoxia. Regional ventilation defects with or without associated trapping are the expected findings on the xenon study.

LUNG NEOPLASMS

If large enough, any lung neoplasm, whether benign, malignant, or metastatic, may produce localized ventilation–perfusion defects corresponding to the lesion on a lung scan. If there is secondary pulmonary arterial or bronchial obstruction, then larger V/Q defects in the lung distal to the lesion may occur, with possible delayed washout of xenon. If the lesion is bronchial (such as an adenoma), there may be distal hypoxia with reflex decreased perfusion. With lesions that cause arterial compression, the perfusion abnormality is generally more striking than the ventilatory impairment. In general, however, the value of ventilation–perfusion lung scanning in detecting or evaluating early stage lung tumors is limited.

In staging bronchogenic carcinoma, it is frequently important to know the extent of the tumor invasion into the hilum, pulmonary vasculature, or mediastinum. In the last decade, preoperative perfusion lung scans were often performed to determine whether the tumor significantly impinged or invaded the main pulmonary artery. If the involved lung received less than 25 percent of total pulmonary blood flow, a successful resection of the tumor was felt to be unlikely. At the present time, a more accurate assessment of tumor size and extent, particularly in relation to the mediastinum, can be made using computed tomography (CT) of the chest. The emphasis of preoperative lung imaging now rests on the assessment of regional lung function to predict expected residual function after surgery, which is usually done in con-junction with standard spirometry. These evaluations are particularly important because coexistent chronic lung disease is common in these patients.

In patients with multiple tumor microemboli or lymphangitic carcinomatosis, there may be multiple small linear perfusion defects that outline the bronchopulmonary segments, a finding known as "contour mapping" (Fig. 9–16). Contour mapping may be present even when the chest radiograph and ventilation scans are normal. The sign may be of value in differentiating these conditions from suspected pulmonary embolism, in which the perfusion defects usually occupy entire segments or subsegments. Although routine V/Q lung scanning is of no real value in the detection or assessment of pulmonary metastases, specific types of metastases may occasionally be visualized by other scanning methods; for instance, hepatobiliary scans may demonstrate functional metastases from a hepatoma, and bone agents sometimes visualize metastases from osteogenic sarcomas.

INFLAMMATORY DISEASE

When a localized infiltrate is identified on the chest radiograph of a patient with thoracic symptoms, pneumonitis is frequently the foremost consideration, although in certain patients other causes such as pulmonary emboli may need to be excluded. In the presence of any radiographic infiltrate, regardless of etiology, both ventilation and perfusion are expected to be markedly decreased or absent in the involved area on lung imaging. The areas of infiltration usually do not ventilate on the initial or rebreathing studies and do not retain xenon during the washout procedure unless there is associated obstruction. With pneumonic infiltrates, the ventilation defects are normally larger than the perfusion defects (Fig. 9–17), and ventilation and perfusion abnormalities often persist for some time after an infiltrate has resolved on the chest radiograph.

When the cause of an infiltrate is in doubt, the size of the perfusion defect in relation to that of the radiographic infiltrate may provide a clue to its etiology. In small or early pneumonias, there is almost always a perfusion defect that is smaller than or equal in size to the corresponding radiographic infiltrate. With large pneumonias (such as lobar pneumonia), the perfusion deficit is usually the same size as the radiographic infiltrate.

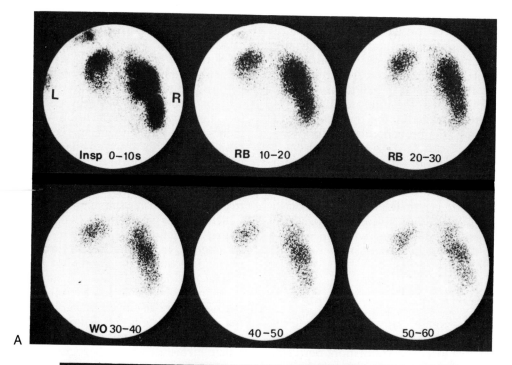

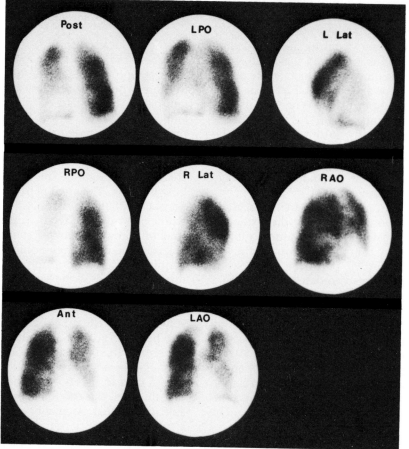

Figure 9–17. Pneumonia. (A) The ventilation scan demonstrates a rather marked area of nonventilation in the left base. (B) The perfusion scan shows a defect that is smaller than the ventilation defects, in the area where an infiltrate was identified on a chest radiograph. Note the presence of the "stripe sign."

Perfusion defects that appear significantly larger than the radiographic abnormality or are out of proportion to the ventilatory defect may raise a serious suspicion of pulmonary embolus. Frequently, such a suspicion may be substantiated by the presence of segmental V/Q mismatches in areas of radiographically normal lung. In the absence of corroborating perfusion defects elsewhere in the lungs, pulmonary arteriography may be needed to exclude the diagnosis.

CARDIOVASCULAR ABNORMALITIES

Normal cardiovascular structures commonly cause significant defects on the V/Q images, which may be accentuated in disease. Thus, it is important to examine the chest radiograph for cardiovascular abnormalities, particularly structural enlargement, abnormal contours, aneurysmal dilations, and changes due to either congestive failure or pulmonary hypertension.

Uncomplicated congestive heart failure is typically characterized by nonsegmental perfusion defects, which are usually diffuse and scattered throughout both lungs but which may occasionally be focal. Fissure signs may be present as well as other abnormalities due to pleural effusions, cardiac enlargement, redistribution of pulmonary blood flow to the upper lung zones, or pulmonary edema (Table 9–8). Occasionally, patients with congestive heart failure may be suspect for superimposed pulmonary emboli, and differentiation of the two entities by scintigraphic techniques may be difficult, especially when congestive heart failure is manifested by pulmonary edema or pleural effusions. Diffuse interstitial edema is frequently not a problem since a relatively normal perfusion scan may be obtained in the absence of emboli. However, when alveolar edema is present focal perfusion defects often result, usually corresponding to localized alveolar densities seen on the chest radiographs. In such cases, congestive heart failure may be distinguished from pulmonary emboli if segmental V/Q mismatches are identified in areas of relatively normal lung, a finding that renders a high probability of emboli. Such a presentation can frequently obviate the need for angiographic evaluation. However, if a distinction cannot be made, angiography may be mandatory to establish the diagnosis.

Loculated pleural effusions accompanying congestive heart failure may cause peripheral defects in the lungs, but these are usually easily discernible on the chest radiograph and rarely appear segmental or multiple on upright views. To minimize the imaging problems, patients with pleural effusions are normally injected supine and imaged in the upright position.

Pulmonary hypertension results in a reversal of the perfusion gradient in the lungs, producing a redistribution of pulmonary blood flow to the upper lung zones. Because of accompanying perivascular fibrosis in patients with chronic pulmonary hypertension from various etiologies, the lung bases generally remain poorly perfused, regardless of the position in which the patient is injected. In addition, focal and segmental basilar perfusion defects may also be present.

A multitude of other diseases related to the cardiovascular system can cause abnormalities on the ventilation and perfusion scans. However, such scan abnormalities can frequently be sorted out when reviewed with the benefit of clinical history and recent chest radiographs.

DEEP VENOUS IMAGING AND THROMBUS DETECTION

While the majority of pulmonary emboli originate in the deep venous systems of the pelvis and legs, the clinical signs of venous thrombosis are absent in about half of patients with demonstrable thrombi. When performing a V/Q lung scan in patients with possible pulmonary emboli and suspected deep venous thrombosis of the lower extremities, it is therefore frequently helpful to inject the ^{99m}Tc MAA into the veins of both feet to obtain a lower-extremity radionuclide venogram. Normally, the technique is most useful for the detection of venous thrombi in the deep venous system above the knee. When deep venous thrombosis is present, the

Table 9–8. PERFUSION SCAN FINDINGS IN CONGESTIVE HEART FAILURE

Cardiomegaly
Fissure sign secondary to effusion
Basilar defects secondary to effusion
Redistribution of flow to upper lobes
Diffuse irregular perfusion due to interstitial edema
Focal nonsegmental defects due to alveolar edema

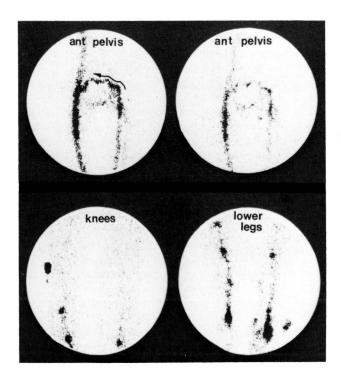

Figure 9–18. Deep venous thrombosis demonstrated by a radionuclide venogram. In this instance, there were bilateral pedal injections of technetium 99m MAA. Obstruction is present in the left iliac region, with collateral flow to the right (arrow). Views of the legs below the knees show multiple areas of increased activity; however, these are not pathognomonic of thrombi and may be due to valves or other causes.

radionuclide images may demonstrate obstruction or collateral flow on the initial views and sometimes focal areas of increased activity on post-exercise images (Fig. 9–18). Whether the areas of increased activity are due to accumulation of the injected particles on formed thrombi or localization at sites of anatomic valves makes this latter finding difficult to interpret in the superficial venous system and below the knee, and in the absence of frank obstruction or well-defined collaterals contrast venography may be indicated.

Radiolabeled fibrinogen, usually with ^{125}I, has also been used for detection of thrombi. This nonimaging procedure usually involves tedious counting with an external probe over multiple sites in the lower extremities, repeated daily for several days to a week. The mechanism of localization of labeled fibrinogen is unclear and it may simply represent deposition at the site of endothelial damage in some cases rather than true incorporation into forming thrombi. In addition, the fibrinogen test is not very sensitive in detecting already formed clots in which the clotting mechanism is no longer active, and sensitivity may be further reduced in the larger veins of the upper thigh and pelvis by soft tissue and bladder background activity. The same limitations may apply to the utilization of labeled platelets and white cells for clot detection.

Suggested Readings

Alderson PO, Martin EC: Pulmonary embolism: Diagnosis with multiple imaging modalities. Radiology 164:297–312, 1987

Frankel N, Coleman RE, Pryor DP, et al: Utilization of lung scans by clinicians. J Nucl Med 27:366–369, 1986

Freeman LM, Blaufox MD (eds): An update on pulmonary nuclear medicine. Semin Nucl Med 16(4):236–337, 1986

Rosen JM, Biello DR, Siegel BA, et al: Kr–81m ventilation imaging: Clinical utility in suspected pulmonary embolism. Radiology 154:787–790, 1985

Smith R, Maher JM, Miller RI, et al: Clinical outcomes of patients with suspected pulmonary embolism and low probability aerosol-perfusion scintigrams. Radiology 164:731–733, 1987

Sostman HD, Rapoport S, Gottschalk A, et al: Imaging of pulmonary embolism. Invest Radiol 21:443–454, 1986

Webber MM, Gomes AS, Roe D, et al: Comparison of Biello, McNeil, and PIOPED criteria for the diagnosis of pulmonary emboli on lung scans. AJR 154:975–981, 1990

Gastrointestinal Tract

Liver–Spleen Imaging

Although computed tomography and ultrasound offer better anatomic display of liver and spleen architecture, radionuclide imaging provides a sensitive, simply performed assessment of these organs for purposes of identifying both space-occupying and functional pathology. In addition, it is the only technique that displays the organs in their entirety rather than in cross-section. In the sometimes confusing hierarchy of current medical imaging modalities, radionuclide liver–spleen scanning ranks high in terms of reliability, convenience, low cost, and availability. Furthermore, unlike ultrasound, radionuclide liver–spleen studies are unaffected by bowel gas or abdominal appliances and are less dependent on technician expertise.

There are numerous indications for liver–spleen scanning, the most frequent of which are the confirmation or evaluation of suspected hepatomegaly or hepatocellular diseases and the detection of space-occupying lesions.

RADIOPHARMACEUTICAL

The liver and spleen are organs of widely differing functions, but radionuclide imaging capitalizes on a function common to both: phagocytosis. The most commonly used agent is technetium 99m sulfur colloid, which is administered in a dose of 4 to 6 mCi (148 to 222 MBq) (Table 10–1). The average particle is 0.3 to 1.0 μm in size and is thus larger than a true colloid.

The uptake and distribution of ^{99m}Tc sulfur colloid in the liver reflects both the distribution of functioning reticuloendothelial cells and the distribution of hepatic perfusion. In normal patients, the majority of particles are rapidly accumulated by the phagocytes of the reticuloendothelial system of both the liver (Kupffer cells) and the spleen, allowing simultaneous imaging of both organs. Sulfur colloid is cleared from the bloodstream with a half-time of 2 to 3 minutes. Under usual circumstances, 80 to 90 percent of the injected particles are sequestered by the liver, and 5 to 10 percent localize in the spleen. A small percentage of particles appears in other reticuloendothelial sites, particularly the bone marrow, but usually in amounts insufficient to permit imaging. In theory, there is some correlation between particle size and organ avidity for colloid: the larger particles are favored by the spleen, smaller particles go to the liver, and the smallest particles are sequestered by the bone marrow. A significant alteration in particle size of the radiocolloid may affect relative distribution among the organs. Gelatin, a stabilizing component in the radiopharmaceutical kit, affects particle size; the more gelatin used, the smaller the particle size. As will be discussed later, visualization of uptake in the bone marrow on a technically satisfactory sulfur colloid liver–spleen scan is an abnormal finding. However, when amounts of ^{99m}Tc sulfur colloid significantly higher than the usual liver–spleen scanning dose are employed, routine bone marrow imaging is possible.

TECHNIQUE

Adequate accumulation of ^{99m}Tc sulfur colloid for imaging the liver requires approximately 5 to 10 minutes in normal patients. This allows for an optimum target (liver–spleen) to background (blood pool) ratio. In patients with compromised hepatic function and/or portal hypertension, optimum liver concentration of the radiopharmaceutical may take considerably longer. In such patients, it is wise to wait 20 to 30 minutes before imaging.

Routine gamma camera images for liver–spleen scanning consist of anterior and pos-

Table 10–1. RADIOPHARMACEUTICAL AGENTS FOR GASTROINTESTINAL IMAGING

| RADIOPHARMA-CEUTICAL | USUAL DOSE | ROUTE OF AD-MINISTRATION | PHYSICAL HALF-LIFE | TIME TO IMAGING | ABSORBED DOSE ESTIMATES (rad/mCi)* | | | REMARKS |
					Whole Body	Gonads	Other	
99mTc sulfur colloid	4–6 mCi (148–222 MBq)	IV	6 hr	0.3–2.0 hr	0.01–0.02	0.01–0.02	Liver 0.2–0.4† Marrow 0.02–0.03 Spleen 0.1–0.4	Localization: 80–90% liver, 5–10% spleen, remainder bone marrow. Particle size 0.3–1.0 μm. Do not use more than 6 hr after preparation.
99mTc pertechnetate (without perchlorate)	2–10 mCi (74–370 MBq)	IV	6 hr	0.2 hr	0.01	0.01–0.04	Thyroid 0.12–0.20† Stomach 0.20 Colon 0.10–0.30	Meckel's imaging.
99mTc IDA (iminodiacetate complexes)	5–10 mCi (185–370 MBq)	IV	6 hr	0–24 hr	0.01	0.01–0.03	Gallbladder 0.12–0.18† Liver 0.04–0.17 Small bowel 0.10 Colon 0.27	6 hr shelf life after preparation.
99mTc red blood cells (in vivo labeling)	15–20 mCi (555–740 MBq)	IV	6 hr	0–24 hr	0.015–0.57	—	Heart 0.06–0.08 Lungs 0.03–0.13 Spleen 0.03–0.23	

*To obtain absorbed dose in mGy/MBq, divide values by 3.7.
†Indicates critical organ.

terior views as well as both laterals. Each image is obtained for 500 K to 1000 K counts using a low-energy parallel-hole collimator. Various oblique images may be routinely obtained or performed as needed for further evaluation of a suspected abnormality in either organ. Because excessive respiratory motion may degrade the quality of liver images, breath holding or upright imaging may aid in reducing the effects of diaphragmatic excursion on the liver scan. One anterior view with a lead marker identifying the right inferior costal margin is usually obtained as well. The marker should be of a known size so that hepatic and splenic measurements may be obtained. Tomographic scanning of the liver using a rotating gamma camera occasionally adds additional information, although focal areas of decreased activity due to normal biliary and vascular structures often make interpretation difficult.

By collecting multiple rapid-sequence images at a rate of 1 image every 2 to 3 seconds for 30 to 60 seconds, an abdominal perfusion study may be obtained during the initial pass of the injected bolus of the radiopharmaceutical through the abdomen. This procedure is performed routinely in some nuclear medicine laboratories to assess hepatic perfusion. In the normal state, only 20 to 25 percent of liver blood flow is derived from the hepatic artery, with 75 to 85 percent supplied by the portal circulation. Thus, activity in the hepatic bed is minimal during the arterial phase of abdominal perfusion when blood flow to the spleen, kidneys, and bowel is most noticeable. Liver activity is seen 4 to 8 seconds later, when the bolus reaches the portal vein. Prominent early liver perfusion should be considered abnormal and has been associated with diffuse hepatic diseases such as infiltrative neoplasm and cirrhosis. Because such a pattern is noted in a number of generalized hepatic processes, it may help in their detection but is of little value in differential diagnosis.

SINGLE-PHOTON EMISSION COMPUTED TOMOGRAPHY (SPECT) IMAGING

Tomographic imaging using 99mTc sulfur colloid requires a fundamental knowledge of cross-sectional anatomy of the liver and spleen as well as of surrounding unimaged structures. Transaxial images are displayed in the conventional transmission computed tomography (CT) format along with coronal and sagittal reconstructions. In general, defects felt to represent significant pathology should be seen in at least two orthogonal planes in order to be described with confidence.

SPECT is most frequently employed to evaluate known or suspected focal or multifocal space-occupying disease. In this setting, SPECT sensitivity and accuracy of localization have been shown to be superior to planar imaging. In the presence of diffuse or infiltrative disease, emission tomography may provide an assessment of Kupffer cell distribution but generally is less useful.

Additionally, SPECT has proved valuable in ^{99m}Tc red blood cell blood pool imaging for suspected liver hemangiomas using the same technique parameters as for ^{99m}Tc sulfur colloid. Vascular structures appearing as characteristic defects on sulfur colloid SPECT images are usually identifiable as areas of increased activity. These include the inferior vena cava, abdominal aorta, portal and splenic veins, and some mesenteric veins.

A specific sample protocol for SPECT liver imaging is provided in Appendix E.

Clinical Applications

NORMAL LIVER SCAN

In the normal liver, there is a homogeneous distribution of activity throughout the organ. The liver usually consists of a dominant right and a smaller left lobe, which may occasionally be absent (Fig. 10–1). Numerous variant liver shapes have been described, the most notable of which are a long thin right lobe (Riedel's lobe) and a prominent quadrate lobe. The porta hepatis is frequently identifiable as an area of decreased activity in the inferomedial aspect of the right lobe; this should not be mistaken for a lesion. Peripheral marginal indentations in the liver may normally be produced by the lateral rib margins, the xiphoid, the gallbladder, the right kidney, the suprahepatic veins, the heart, and intrathoracic abnormalities that affect the diaphragmatic configuration. A defect is commonly seen in many anterior scans due to attenuation of the photons by overlying breast tissue (Fig. 10–2).

The normal liver is quite pliable and changes shape from deep inspiration to expiration as well as from upright to supine position. In fact, the lack of change in shape

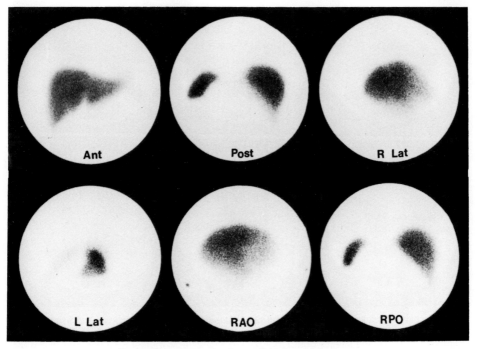

Figure 10–1. Normal sulfur colloid liver–spleen scan.

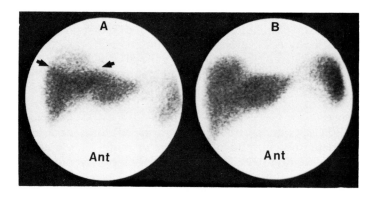

Figure 10-2. Normal anterior liver–spleen scan. (A) A defect is seen in the upper aspect of the right lobe due to attenuation by overlying breast tissue. In (B) the breast has been raised.

of the liver from one position to the other may be used as a test for diffuse disease, which may reduce pliability of the organ. Normal measurement for the right lobe of the liver is generally taken to be 17 to 18 cm in length on the anterior view. Patients with chronic obstructive pulmonary disease are often referred for liver scans because of suspected hepatomegaly. Usually in these patients, the liver is low and flattened superiorly due to the hyperinflated lungs (Fig. 10-3). The low position often makes the liver palpable below the costal margin even though it is not enlarged.

Evaluation of a liver scan should include (1) the size, shape, and position of the liver and spleen; (2) the homogeneity of activity within the organs; (3) the presence of any focal defects in activity; and (4) the relative distribution of colloid among the liver, spleen, and bone marrow.

ABNORMAL LIVER SCAN

Any localized space-occupying process in the liver may present as a focal area of decreased activity (commonly referred to as a defect), provided that it is of sufficient size

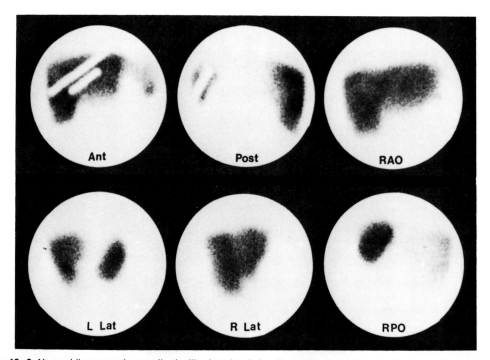

Figure 10-3. Normal liver scan in a patient with chronic obstructive pulmonary disease. The scan demonstrates marked inferior displacement of the liver and flattening of the superior margins of the liver on all views. The long lead marker indicates the inferior costal margin. The shorter lead marker is 10 cm long and is used for measurement.

Table 10–2. CAUSES OF SOLITARY COLD HEPATIC LESIONS

Metastasis (especially colon)
Cyst
Hepatoma (especially in cirrhosis)
Hematoma
Hemangioma
Abscess
Pseudotumor (cirrhosis)

to be detected. Radionuclide imaging is a sensitive method for the detection of localized lesions in the liver, identifying the presence or anatomic location of disease rather than providing a definitive histologic diagnosis. The size and location of a lesion are of paramount importance in determining whether it will be detected by gamma camera techniques. Using present technology, lesions as small as 8 mm may be identified and those 2 to 2.5 cm in size are routinely imaged. The nearer these lesions are to the surface of the organ, and therefore to the camera collimator surface, the more readily they may be detected and the smaller they need be before detection is possible.

Defects in the hepatic parenchyma are non-specific. Solitary intrahepatic defects may be produced by various lesions, any of which may be multiple (Table 10–2). In any patient with several liver defects, however, metastatic disease must be a prime consideration, particularly when accompanied by hepatomegaly or a known primary lesion. In many instances, particularly in cases of equivocal liver scan findings, ultrasonography may be an extremely useful adjunct.

A large area of decreased activity in the liver may be produced by the inclusion of part of that organ in a radiation therapy portal. However, this type of defect is usually readily recognized by its sharp linear edges, which correspond to the sides of the portal (Fig. 10–4).

In addition to primarily intrahepatic lesions, peripheral defects in the liver are frequently produced by adjacent extraparenchymal pathology, including subdiaphragmatic fluid accumulations or renal tumors, or by peripheral lesions of a primary hepatic origin.

Increased sulfur colloid concentration by the spleen and bone marrow compared with the liver ("colloid shift") may be found in

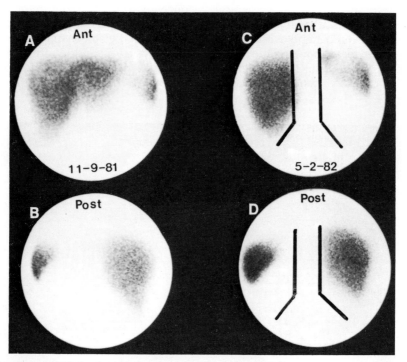

Figure 10–4. Negative defect due to radiation therapy. Prior to radiation therapy, the anterior (A) and posterior (B) views of the liver were normal. With an inverted Y radiation therapy port, a geometric defect (C, D) has been produced in the left lobe of the liver.

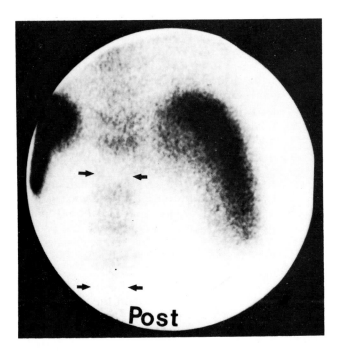

Post

Figure 10–5. Hepatocellular dysfunction with osseous metastases. The posterior liver–spleen scan demonstrates a colloid shift and bone marrow activity. Careful inspection reveals a negative defect in at least two vertebral bodies due to metastatic disease. This was confirmed by increased activity on the bone scan at the identical levels.

patients with diseases that cause derangement of hepatic function and/or portal hypertension. Among diffuse hepatocellular diseases, hepatic cirrhosis is the most common abnormality presenting in this fashion. Colloid shift accompanied by other typical scintigraphic findings is a hallmark of this disease. However, even patients with diffuse hepatic metastases may show colloid shift. The distribution of colloid in the bone marrow should be carefully examined in such patients, since localized defects in colloid activity indicating marrow involvement by tumor may be identified (Fig. 10–5).

The mechanisms governing colloid shift have variously been attributed to (1) the consequences of portal hypertension with shunting of colloid-laden blood away from the liver to the spleen and bone marrow and/or (2) a decrease in the number or functional capability of hepatic Kupffer cells, thereby decreasing liver clearance of sulfur colloid.

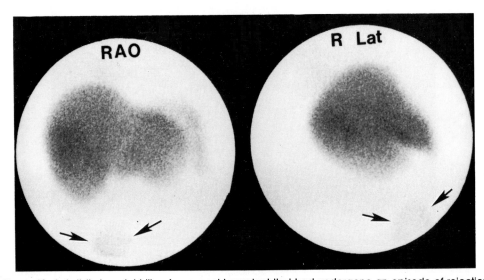

Figure 10–6. Activity in a right iliac fossa renal transplant that had undergone an episode of rejection.

In various liver diseases, either or both of these principles may play a role. However, the observation that alleviation of portal hypertension does not necessarily result in a return to a normal radiocolloid distribution has led some investigators to postulate that intrahepatic shunting, not portal hypertension per se, plays the major role in producing the phenomenon of colloid shift, especially in cirrhotic patients. Such shunting would allow portal blood to bypass hepatic sinusoids, making more colloid available to the spleen and bone marrow. Indeed, there is good experimental evidence for such a mechanism.

Other abnormal distributions of colloid that the reader should be aware of include activity in renal transplants, diffuse lung activity, and focal hot spots in the liver. In patients with renal transplants that are undergoing rejection, the transplant may be visualized (Fig. 10–6). This may occur long after the episode of rejection and does not necessarily indicate acute rejection. Diffuse pulmonary activity may be noted occasionally in cirrhosis, infection, and many other entities (Table 10–3). For patients with cirrhosis, the mechanisms postulated involve increased pulmonary phagocytosis and/or altered pulmonary endothelium. In the presence of superior vena cava or innominate venous obstruction, a bolus of activity injected into the basilic vein can travel via collaterals and deliver a large amount of activity to the anterior midportion of the liver, which causes a focal hot spot (Fig. 10–7), usually as a result of recanalization of umbilical vessels. Other entities that may cause apparent focal areas of increased hepatic activity are Budd-Chiari syndrome (hepatic vein obstruction), focal nodular hyperplasia, and cirrhosis.

SPECIFIC DISEASE ENTITIES

Alcoholic Liver Disease

A spectrum of scan findings are presented by alcoholic liver disease. In its early phases, alcoholic hepatitis or fatty infiltration may present as a normal-sized or enlarged liver with diffusely diminished activity. As the disease progresses and parenchymal scarring becomes more prevalent, the liver may become smaller than normal. An oddity of this disease is that the right lobe is frequently more affected, giving a typical pattern of a small right lobe and a relatively enlarged left lobe. As the process of injury, scarring, and regeneration continues, activity within the organ becomes less homogeneous, and is sometimes so coarsely mottled as to be confused with space-occupying lesions. In cirrhotic patients with this mottled pattern or with a large dominant defect, especially those who have demonstrated sudden unexplained clinical decompensation, superimposed hepatoma must be considered.

Colloid shift to the spleen and bone marrow is another prominent feature of all phases of alcoholic liver disease. When hepatocyte function is severely depressed, persistence of sulfur colloid in the blood pool may also be identified, especially in the cardiac area on static images. In the advanced stages of disease, the spleen is frequently enlarged, a finding that may correlate with portal hypertension. In some patients, ascites may be imaged on the anterior view as displacement of the right lobe of the liver from the lateral abdominal wall and diaphragm, producing indistinctness of the liver margin (Fig. 10–8).

Irrespective of etiology, hepatic cirrhosis may present with any of the findings described above for alcohol-induced disease. The particular scintigraphic appearance of the organ depends primarily upon the stage and severity of the disease.

Diffuse and Infiltrative Disorders

Any disease that secondarily invades the liver may produce a pattern of hepatomegaly,

Table 10–3. DIFFUSE PULMONARY UPTAKE OF TECHNETIUM 99m SULFUR COLLOID

Hepatic cirrhosis
COPD with superimposed infection
Estrogen therapy
Neoplasms (various primary tumors and metastases including hepatoma)
Disseminated intravascular coagulopathy
Mucopolysaccharidosis type II (Hunter's)
Histiocytosis X
Faulty colloid preparation (excess aluminum)
Children (normal minimal uptake)
Transplant patients

Adapted from Stadalnik RC: Gamuts: Diffuse lung uptake of Tc-99m sulfur colloid. Semin Nucl Med 10(1):106–107, 1980.

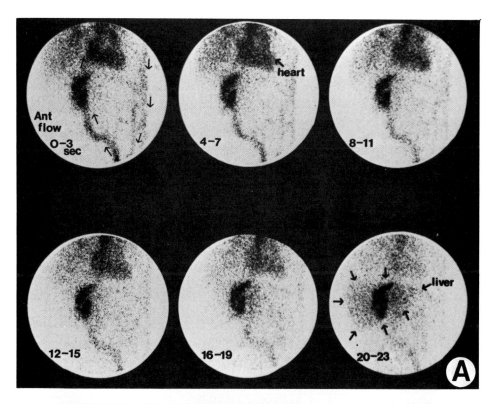

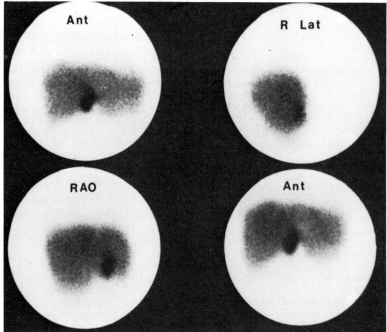

Figure 10–7. Superior vena caval obstruction. (A) The flow study was performed with a left antecubital injection of ⁹⁹ᵐTc sulfur colloid. The activity traverses down the lateral thoracic veins, up a recanalized umbilical vein, through a focal area of liver, and then to the inferior vena cava. (B) On the static images, an anterior focal area of increased activity can be seen in the quadrate lobe.

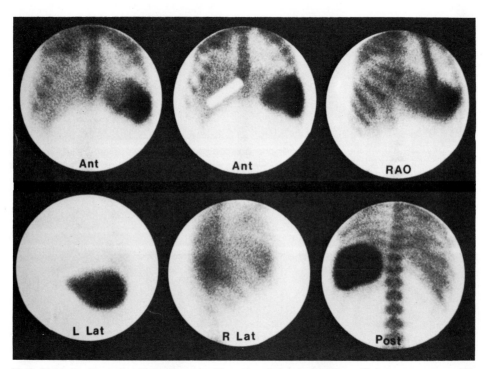

Figure 10–8. Cirrhosis with ascites. There is marked hepatocellular dysfunction, with bone marrow activity and some pulmonary parenchymal activity. The liver is small and displaced medially by ascites. The colloid shift is also evident, with a marked increase in splenic activity.

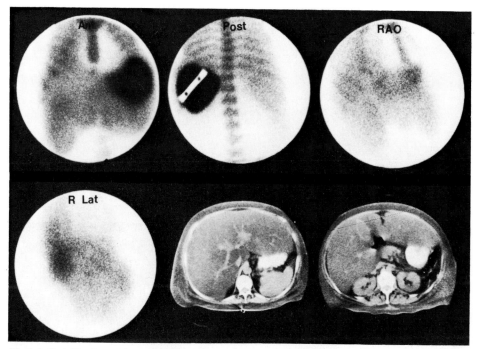

Figure 10–9. Fatty infiltration of the liver. The radionuclide scan demonstrates an enlarged liver with marked colloid shift. The CT scans demonstrate the characteristic "pseudoenhancement" in which the portal venous system is clearly visualized although no intravenous contrast has been given.

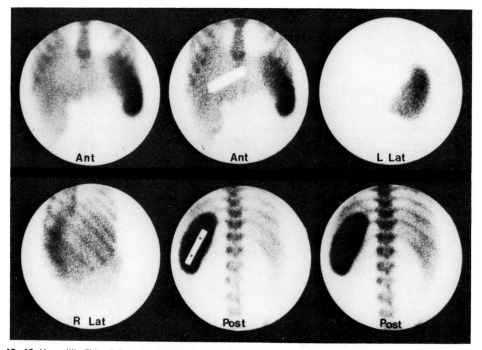

Figure 10–10. Hepatitis. This picture is very similar to fatty infiltration of the liver, although in this case there is splenomegaly as well. The basic findings are marked colloid shift, splenomegaly, and an enlarged liver.

Table 10-4. CAUSES OF HEPATOMEGALY WITH SLIGHTLY DECREASED ACTIVITY

Normal variant (i.e., large patient)
Diffuse hepatocellular disease (e.g., hepatitis)
Metastases
Diabetes mellitus
Fatty infiltration
Hemochromatosis
Amyloidosis
Lymphoma
Leukemia
Sarcoidosis
Lipid storage disorders
Passive congestion

with or without focal defects, and commonly with diffusely diminished activity (Fig. 10–9). Disease entities that may produce this pattern are listed in Table 10–4. Hepatitis may present in this fashion, reflecting diffuse parenchymal edema. If hepatic function is compromised, colloid shift may also be seen (Fig. 10–10). Passive congestion of the liver, a finding associated with acute or chronic cardiac decompensation, can produce an enlarged liver with patchy colloid distribution, mimicking diffuse intrinsic liver disease. However, correlation of findings with cardiac status and resolution of the scan abnormalities upon control of acute cardiac failure may suggest the diagnosis.

Metastatic Disease

The most nearly specific presentation of liver metastasis is as multiple focal defects (Fig. 10–11), although the lesions may present as coarsely inhomogeneous activity or simply as hepatomegaly. Using discrete hepatic defects as the diagnostic criterion for metastatic disease, the liver scan demonstrates a detection sensitivity of approxi-

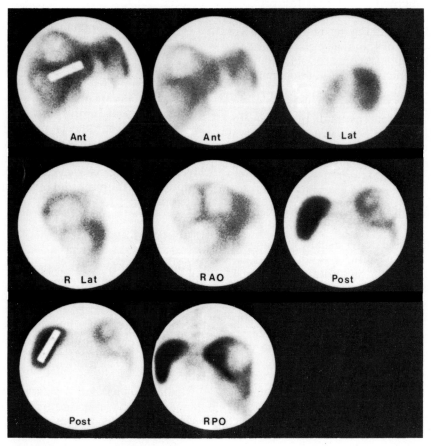

Figure 10-11. Metastatic colon carcinoma. Multiple large focal defects are identified throughout the liver. In this particular instance the metastatic disease is extensive enough that some colloid shift can be identified on the right posterior oblique view.

mately 75 to 80 percent for all types of primary lesions, especially when scintigraphic data are integrated with available clinical information. Individual sensitivity, of course, varies with the particular primary lesion. In colon and renal cell carcinomas, for example, which classically produce large round "cannonball" lesions in the liver, sensitivity is greater. For less discrete and more infiltrative carcinomas, such as those of the breast or lung, sensitivity is somewhat less. As discussed above, multiple focal defects are not specific for metastatic disease, and benign abnormalities may occasionally present in this fashion. Contrarily, a solitary liver defect may be produced by a metastatic lesion, and in any patient with a known primary neoplasm, such a single lesion should be further evaluated by ultrasound. If found to be solid, the abnormality should be considered a metastasis in the absence of evidence to the contrary. Once a diagnosis of metastatic disease to the liver is made, liver imaging is a convenient method to monitor the progression of disease or its response to therapy.

Use of chemotherapeutic agents can affect the appearance of the liver–spleen scan, resulting in findings such as colloid shift with increased splenic activity, heterogeneity of colloid distribution in the liver, and minimal hepatomegaly. Drugs that have been implicated are nitrosoureas and methotrexate. These findings usually resolve within several months of termination of therapy. Focal areas of decreased activity have not been associated with chemotherapy.

Primary Liver Neoplasms

Hepatoma. Hepatoma usually presents as a focal defect on sulfur colloid images, although uncommon multifocal forms exist. The lesions frequently occur in association with preexisting diffuse hepatic diseases, most notably alcoholic or postnecrotic cirrhosis. Other associations with hepatoma include type 1 glycogen storage disease (von Gierke's), hemochromatosis, thorotrast administration, schistosomiasis, and hepatic toxins (alpha toxins). The appearance of a prominent localized colloid deficit in a patient with one of these associations should alert the physician to the possibility of hepatoma. In these instances, gallium 67 imaging may aid in the differential diagnosis.

Focal Nodular Hyperplasia. The benign neoplasm of focal nodular hyperplasia generally occurs as an asymptomatic mass or as a serendipitously discovered lesion found predominantly in females. The lesions are unique in containing adequate numbers of Kupffer cells so that they normally concentrate and occasionally hyperconcentrate radiocolloid. Thus, in a majority of cases, they appear indistinguishable from normal hepatic parenchyma (Fig. 10–12); infrequently they present as regions of increased activity on liver scans. When lesions discovered by other imaging modalities are of sufficient size to be detected by the liver scintigraphy, yet appear normal on the liver scan, the diagnosis of focal nodular hyperplasia may be presumed in the proper clinical setting. In a minority of cases insufficient colloid is concentrated by the lesions, so that they are perceived as photopenic areas on the scan. When this occurs, the mass cannot be differentiated from other causes of parenchymal defects.

Hepatic Cell Adenomas. Hepatic cell adenomas are usually encountered in young women who have used birth control pills. Although the disease is asymptomatic, hemorrhage, often of massive degree, occasionally occurs. Because Kupffer cells are not a prominent feature of these lesions, adenomas present as focal defects on sulfur colloid images. When birth control pills are withheld, these lesions may rapidly regress. Liver–spleen scans may be used in such instances to monitor the regression of the adenomas.

Miscellaneous

Focal Lesions. Abscess or hematoma may commonly present as nonspecific solitary focal defects on liver scans, although multiple lesions may occur. Both diagnoses are frequently suggested by history. In the case of pyogenic or amebic abscess, gallium or indium leukocyte images may be useful in supporting the clinical suspicion.

Hemangiomas and Cysts. Although hemangiomas and cysts are usually occult and asymptomatic lesions, ultrasound can reliably establish the diagnosis of cysts and hemangiomas, and computed tomography with contrast may demonstrate progressive en-

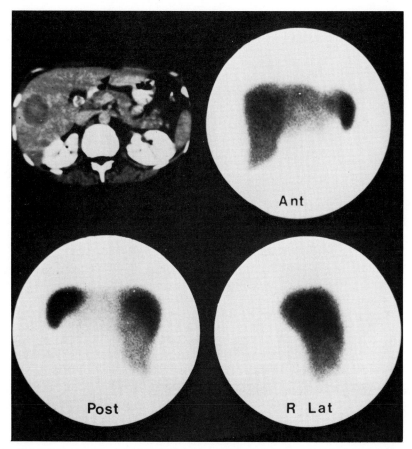

Figure 10–12. Focal nodular hyperplasia. A post-contrast abdominal CT scan of the liver in a young female with right upper quadrant pain demonstrated a well-defined focal low-density lesion in the right lobe of the liver. A liver–spleen scan obtained in the same patient demonstrated a normal sulfur colloid distribution in the region of the lesion. When this discrepancy occurs, focal nodular hyperplasia is a prime consideration.

hancement toward the center of the lesion suggestive of hemangioma. Hemangioma is also suggested when defect seen with ^{99m}Tc sulfur colloid imaging shows increased activity after administration of a ^{99m}Tc blood pool agent due to labeling of the blood pool in the lesion. In order to allow equilibration of the hemangioma blood pool with the labeled red blood cells, delayed imaging (sometimes over several hours) may be necessary when planar imaging is employed. Dynamic or blood flow images frequently show normal or decreased perfusion of the lesions.

Utilization of SPECT in the setting of suspected hepatic hemangioma increases the sensitivity of the study, especially when lesions are deep or less than 5 cm in diameter (Fig. 10–13). Furthermore, tomographic imaging may be diagnostic earlier after injection than with planar views due to improved image contrast.

Trauma. Because of the bulk of the liver, the effects of blunt trauma are usually less extensive than in the spleen. Scan findings are most frequently (1) peripheral impressions caused by subcapsular hematoma or (2) defects within the hepatic parenchyma produced by localized hemorrhage. The sensitivity of the liver–spleen scan for detecting such lesions is greatly dependent on the thoroughness of the study, but in general it is superior to ultrasound evaluation and inferior to CT.

Budd-Chiari Syndrome (Hepatic Vein Thrombosis). Hepatic vein thrombosis may occur secondary to tumor invasion or hypercoagulation syndromes, but frequently no underlying etiology is identified. The disease usually presents as an enlarged congested tender liver accompanied by ascites. With early or partial hepatic vein obstruction, activity in the liver becomes diffusely mottled.

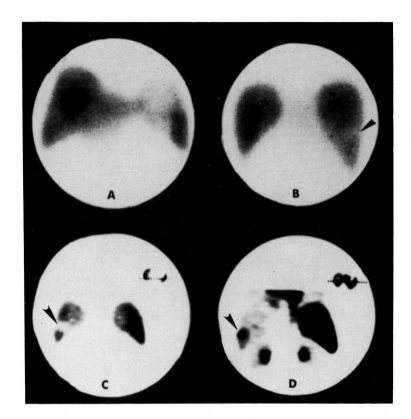

Figure 10–13. Hepatic hemangioma. A small defect is seen in the lateral portion of the right lobe on the anterior (A) and posterior (B) sulfur colloid planar views. A coronal SPECT image of the sulfur colloid study (C) clearly shows the "cold" defect. On a SPECT labeled red blood cell study done in the same projection (D), the area is seen to have significant blood pool.

As thrombosis progresses, activity in both lobes steadily decreases. Typically, the caudate lobe simultaneously enlarges and shows relatively increased activity. This latter phenomenon has been explained by the presence of separate venous drainage directly into the vena cava for the caudate lobe, which is unaffected by thrombosis of the major hepatic veins.

NORMAL SPLEEN IMAGING

The normal spleen exhibits homogeneous activity equal to or less than that of the liver. The organ is ovoid in configuration with occasional thinning of the anterior aspect. The normal length of the spleen on a posterior scan is about 10 ± 1.5 cm.

Routine imaging of the spleen and liver employs ^{99m}Tc sulfur colloid. Isolated imaging of the spleen is also possible with ^{99m}Tc or chromium 51 heat-damaged red blood cells, which are sequestered by the spleen; however, such scans are rarely necessary for clinical diagnosis. When imaging the spleen with sulfur colloid, routine liver–spleen scan views are obtained. Left anterior oblique and left posterior oblique views at varying degrees of obliquity also may be useful, especially when traumatic lesions are suspected. Occasionally, a right posterior oblique view may be needed to separate the left lobe of the liver from the spleen.

Two normal variants of splenic contour are worthy of note. The first of these is the "upside down" spleen, in which the splenic hilum presents on the upper margin of the organ as a concave defect, causing a crescent appearance (Fig. 10–14). The second configuration is the splenic lobule, in which a small appendage of normally functioning splenic tissue rests adjacent to the main body of the spleen, usually at the anterior or inferior margin. It is necessary to recognize such variant configurations so as not to confuse them with any suspected abnormalities.

ABNORMAL SPLEEN IMAGING

Focal Lesions

Solitary or multiple splenic defects are nonspecific and may be produced by a number of abnormalities. Careful correlation with

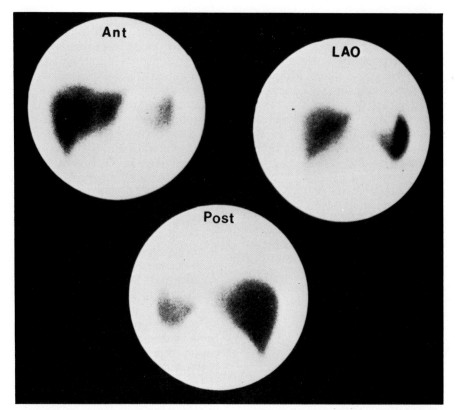

Figure 10–14. "Upside-down" spleen. A single posterior sulfur colloid image shows the typical appearance of an upside-down spleen with the hilus of the spleen presenting as a crescentic defect in the superior margin of the spleen. This is a common normal variant configuration.

pertinent clinical history is necessary to distinguish among these. More common abnormalities that may present as defects within the organ are cysts, hematoma, abscess, infarction, and neoplasm. Peripheral wedge-shaped defects may often be correlated with infarcts, especially when a pertinent history such as hemoglobinopathy is obtained.

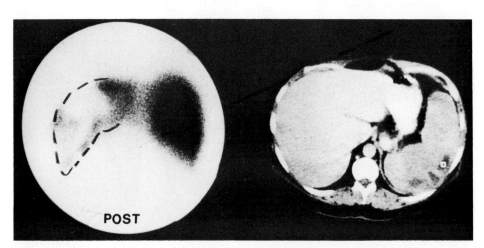

Figure 10–15. Lymphoma of the spleen. The left anterior oblique view demonstrates massive replacement of the spleen with very little remaining reticuloendothelial activity. The spleen has been outlined. The amount of replacement is much greater than would be suggested by the CT scan.

Metastatic lesions to the spleen are uncommon, although tumors such as lymphoma (Fig. 10–15), melanoma, chorioepithelioma, or soft tissue sarcoma may present with splenic lesions. Primary splenic neoplasms are extremely rare. Focal areas of decreased activity in the spleen occur in less than 1 percent of liver–spleen scans. If trauma is excluded, one-third of such defects are due to splenic infarcts, one-third to lymphoma, and one-third to metastatic disease.

Splenomegaly

Liver–spleen scans are frequently ordered to confirm clinical suspicion of splenomegaly (Fig. 10–16). The causes of splenomegaly are numerous (Table 10–5), and unless focal space-occupying disease is identified, scans are generally unhelpful in determining the etiology. Infiltrative disorders produce varying degrees of splenomegaly, with or without alterations in splenic activity. The findings are largely nonspecific and are best interpreted in light of clinical observations.

Trauma

The effects of trauma to the spleen may be readily identified on spleen imaging. Presentations range from frank rupture and disorganization to small intrapulp or subcapsular hematomas. Ruptures appear as linear or stellate defects within the parenchyma; intrasplenic hematomas as localized defects; and subcapsular bleeds as semilunar or "thumbprint" indentations on the periphery. Large hematomas may displace the spleen downward or away from the lateral abdominal wall, so attention to the position of the organ is often crucial. In severe injury, multiple fragments may be noted or the spleen may appear small.

Even with recent advances in ultrasound imaging, radionuclide spleen scanning is a useful diagnostic tool in cases of trauma. Accuracy in excess of 90 percent with a low false negative rate (up to 2 percent) has been documented in several series. Defects as small as 2 to 3 cm can be reliably detected. The accuracy of the examination is increased by recognition of normal variant configurations as discussed above and by the identification of possible preexisting conditions that may cause false positive results.

Technique is of utmost importance in examining the spleen for trauma. In addition to the standard views, at least two slightly different anterior and two different posterior

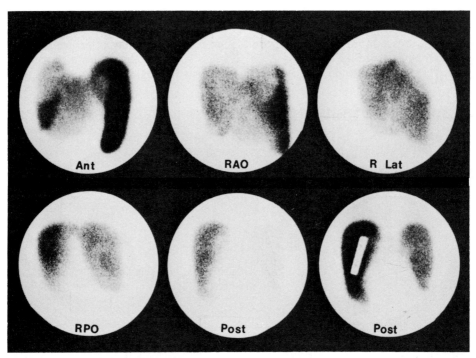

Figure 10–16. Chronic active hepatitis. The liver is enlarged and the activity is inhomogeneous. The spleen is massively enlarged and shows significantly more activity than the liver.

Table 10–5. DISEASES AFFECTING SPLENIC SIZE AND ACTIVITY

Massive enlargement
  Chronic leukemia
  Myelofibrosis
  Glycogen storage diseases
  Thalassemia major
Moderate enlargement
  Cirrhosis with portal hypertension
  Hepatitis, acute or chronic
  Hemolytic anemia
  Mononucleosis
  Lymphoma
Minimal enlargement
  Congestive heart failure
  Metastatic disease
  Collagen disease
  Infections
  Increased activity
  Portal hypertension
  Anemia
  Leukemia
  Lymphoma*
  Sepsis
  Melanoma*
  Stress (recent surgery or chemotherapy)
  Hepatocellular dysfunction (colloid shift)

*Depending upon disease stage, these entities may also cause decreased activity.

left oblique views should be obtained. Not only does this give a thorough survey of the organ distinct from the left lobe of the liver, but the oblique views may be the only ones to disclose the abnormalities. Following abdominal trauma, splenic tissue may seed to other locations (splenosis) such as the lung and peritoneal cavity. Such tissue fragments will accumulate colloid.

Nonvisualization of the Spleen

In certain instances, the spleen may not be visualized on a technetium 99m sulfur colloid scan even in the absence of a history of splenectomy (Table 10–6). Congenital asplenia may be associated with a number of cardiovascular, pulmonary, and abdominal anomalies. In sickle cell anemia, the spleen may not be seen because of atrophy related to repeated infarctions ("autosplenectomy"); in some of these patients, the spleen remains anatomically intact but with depressed or absent reticuloendothelial function due to mechanical obstruction of blood flow by the abnormal configuration of the red cells (functional asplenia). Transfusions with normal red cells may produce resumption of normal phagocytosis and subsequent visualization of

the spleen. Functional asplenia may also be due to postoperative splenic hypoxia, graft versus host disease, aggressive chronic hepatitis, and systemic lupus erythematosus.

Gastrointestinal Bleeding

LOWER GASTROINTESTINAL HEMORRHAGE

Attempts have been made for some time to detect and localize gastrointestinal (GI) bleeding using radionuclides. The nonimaging procedures used in the past have met with limited success, but recent interest in nuclear imaging as a diagnostic tool has spawned a body of clinical experience with a variety of ^{99m}Tc radiopharmaceuticals. The two most common of these are ^{99m}Tc red blood cells and ^{99m}Tc sulfur colloid. Both radiopharmaceuticals provide similar information, and sensitivity with both appears to be significantly greater than with angiography for the detection of lower GI bleeding (with the added advantage of being noninvasive). Because of significant background activity in the upper abdomen and the diagnostic efficacy of endoscopy in the GI tract, nuclear imaging techniques are primarily limited to lower GI bleeding, although active duodenal and distal gastric hemorrhage may be detected.

The common causes of lower GI bleeding in adults are diverticular disease, angiodysplasia, neoplasms, and inflammatory bowel disease. Preoperative localization of a bleed-

Table 10–6. CAUSES OF SPLENIC DEFECTS ON ^{99m}Tc SULFUR COLLOID SCAN

Focal defects
  Infarct
  Lymphoma
  Metastasis
  Cyst
  Abscess
  Hematoma or splenic artery aneurysm
  Anatomic variation
  Artifact
Nonvisualization
  Splenectomy
  Sickle cell disease (functional or autosplenectomy)
  Congenital absence of spleen (isolated or Ivemark syndrome)
  Tumor replacement
  Infarction
  Traumatic avulsion or volvulus
  Functional asplenia

ing site permits a more rational, tailored approach to surgical intervention. Since bleeding from these causes frequently is intermittent, chances of detecting the site of hemorrhage are enhanced by a radiopharmaceutical with a long vascular half-life, such as labeled red blood cells. Angiography may be negative in patients with intermittent bleeding or bleeding rates below 1.0 ml/min. With radionuclide techniques, bleeding rates on the order of 0.2 ml/min are reliably detected. These techniques are best applied to patients who are bleeding acutely. Patients with chronic, low-volume blood loss presenting with guaiac positive stools or chronic anemias seldom benefit from the examination.

Intravascular blood pool agents such as ^{99m}Tc red blood cells are the agents of choice in the investigation of GI hemorrhage, especially in cases of intermittent or slow bleeding with a sensitivity of greater than 90 percent. Because the agent remains in the intravascular space for up to 48 hours, imaging may be performed over a period of 24 hours. Any free technetium in the radiopharmaceutical is excreted by the gastric mucosa and passes into the small bowel and colon. This latter problem is obviated by use of in vitro or modified in vivo labeling techniques, which allow for a higher degree of red cell tagging and therefore a lower percentage of free technetium. With red blood cells, most bleeding sites will show increased activity with time and will change configuration. If the activity remains in the same location, vascular abnormalities such as an aneurysm or angiodysplasia should be suspected. When delayed imaging is necessary to identify a bleeding site, there may be uncertainty with respect to location. If the extravasated intraluminal agent is not identified shortly after its deposition, it may move to a more proximal or distal site during any prolonged intervals between images, especially with the increased peristalsis present in most patients with GI bleeding. However, establishing the mere presence of slow bleeding into the bowel remains possible, and therefore the study is undoubtedly of value in many patients.

^{99m}Tc sulfur colloid has a few advantages for the investigation of acute bleeding. Sulfur colloid is readily available, inexpensive, and easy to prepare. Sulfur colloid clears rapidly from the intravascular space via the reticuloendothelial system, providing excellent contrast between background and extravasated isotope at the bleeding site, and the material is not absorbed by the bowel. Because sulfur colloid is sequestered primarily by the liver and spleen, repeat and follow-up studies can be performed as needed with reinjection of additional sulfur colloid.

The rapid blood clearance is also a disadvantage in that the patient must be actively bleeding during the short time that the sulfur colloid is intravascular (vascular half-time = 2.5 to 3.5 minutes); thus significant intermittent hemorrhage may be missed. In addition, liver and spleen activity may interfere with detection of bleeding sites in the upper abdomen. This leads to a relatively lower overall sensitivity for bleeding detection with sulfur colloid.

TECHNIQUE

After intravenous reinjection of the autologous labeled red blood cells as a bolus (in vitro or modified in vivo preparation—see end of Appendix E), imaging may commence with a rapid sequence of 2- to 3-second abdominal/pelvic images obtained over 30 to 60 seconds. Static images (500 to 1000 K) are then performed at 5-minute intervals for 45 minutes, with images taken thereafter at intervals of 15 to 60 minutes depending on the clinical setting. Continuous computer acquisition may also be used. As discussed, 24-hour delayed images may substantiate an interval bleed but frequently do not accurately disclose the actual site of hemorrhage.

Detecting GI bleeding with ^{99m}Tc labeled sulfur colloid requires careful attention to technique. First, 10 mCi (370 MBq) of recently prepared ^{99m}Tc sulfur colloid with at least 97 percent binding efficiency is administered intravenously. The patient is immediately placed under the large-field-of-view camera with a low-energy collimator, and serial 500,000 count images are obtained every 1 to 2 minutes for 15 minutes. If a bleeding site has still not been identified, anterior oblique images may help to visualize the areas obscured by liver and spleen activity. If even then no bleeding site is identified, the examination may be extended for 15 minutes more to allow for activity hidden by the liver or spleen to move distally to an area where it may be imaged. If the initial study is negative, the examination may be repeated as needed.

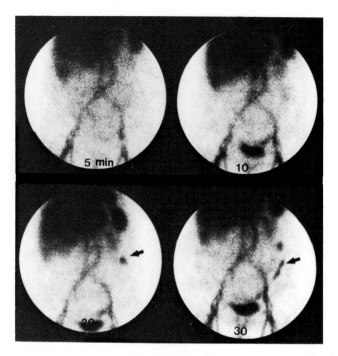

Figure 10–17. Gastrointestinal bleeding. This study was performed with labeled red cells and at 15 minutes demonstrates a very small focus of active colonic bleeding (arrow), which on the later views can be seen in the bowel distally.

INTERPRETATION

A positive scan shows a focal site of increased activity within the abdomen, which progresses distally in the bowel (Fig. 10–17). Once bleeding is identified, multiple subsequent images aid greatly in establishing its origin by recording the pattern of progression of the radionuclide within the bowel. Occasional confusion of bladder activity with a rectosigmoid bleed can usually be resolved on post-void views or lateral pelvic images. Interfering genital activity is usually identified by its location on anterior oblique or lateral pelvic views. Carefully performed studies show a high degree of sensitivity with a low false negative rate. In addition to providing evidence of active GI bleeding and its location, the examination may also be used as a guide for selective abdominal arteriography and to assess the results of any interventional therapy.

MECKEL'S DIVERTICULUM

Meckel's diverticulum occurs in approximately 2 percent of the population and affects males predominantly. While the overwhelming majority of the lesions remain asymptomatic throughout life, complications—primarily hemorrhage, intussusception, and volvulus—occur in a small percentage of patients. In virtually all cases accompanied by bleeding, ectopic gastric mucosa with or without associated ileal ulceration can be demonstrated in the diverticulum. The traditional method of radionuclide investigation of a patient with bleeding from suspected Meckel's diverticulum is based on visualization of the ectopic mucosa with intravenously administered ^{99m}Tc pertechnetate. Negative results are common in patients whose diverticula do not contain ectopic gastric tissue.

The study consists of intravenous injection of 10 to 15 mCi (370 to 555 MBq) of ^{99m}Tc pertechnetate in adults or approximately 200 to 300 μCi/kg (7.4 to 11.1 MBq/kg) in children. Sequential anterior abdominal images are then obtained for 45 to 60 minutes. A typical positive scan consists of a focal area of increased activity in the right lower quadrant, which, on a lateral view, is seen to be anterior and unrelated to ureteral activity (Fig. 10–18). This finding generally appears in the first 30 minutes of the study but may take up to 1 hour to appear, depending on the amount of gastric mucosa present. False positive results have been reported secondary to intussusception (possibly related to the associated hyperemia), urinary tract activity (often secondary to obstruction), various small bowel lesions, inflammatory bowel disease, and rarely, intestinal duplication cysts containing gastric mucosa. False negative

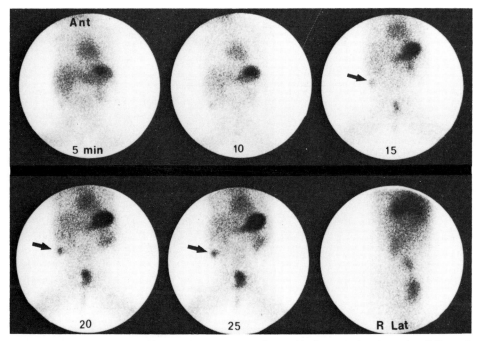

Figure 10–18. Meckel's diverticulum. This examination was performed in the anterior view using ^{99m}Tc pertechnetate. At 15 minutes and on subsequent views, the ectopic gastric mucosa is demonstrated (arrows). Activity is also identified in the stomach and the bladder.

scans have been reported in patients with malrotation of the ileum, small amounts of ectopic mucosa, and localized bowel irritability which causes rapid clearance of the pertechnetate from the area. However, the overall specificity and sensitivity for the examination are approximately 90 percent.

Several pharmacologic interventions have been proposed to increase the sensitivity of Meckel's imaging with varying degrees of success. These include the use of cimetidine to block release of pertechnetate from the ectopic mucosa, pentagastrin to enhance mucosal uptake of ^{99m}TcO$_4$, and glucagon to decrease small bowel (diverticular) motility.

Recently it has been suggested that actively hemorrhaging patients with suspected Meckel's diverticulum be initially investigated with radionuclide techniques intended to detect the bleeding site rather than the ectopic mucosa. When sulfur colloid is used for this purpose, a negative bleeding examination may be immediately followed by a gastric mucosa imaging study.

Hepatobiliary Imaging

Development of ^{99m}Tc labeled hepatobiliary agents enables accurate and convenient im-

aging in acute and chronic biliary disease. Considerable clinical experience has been obtained in the past using iodine 131 labeled rose bengal, but the relatively large absorbed radiation dose to the patient and the poor imaging characteristics of ^{131}I have dampened enthusiasm for this procedure.

A number of ^{99m}Tc IDA (iminodiacetic acid) analogs are now available, providing excellent-quality routine imaging of the biliary system.

RADIOPHARMACEUTICALS

The IDA imaging agents (Table 10–7) have excellent chelating properties and, therefore, bind readily to ^{99m}Tc, forming a stable complex. By forming N-substitutions, various IDA derivatives have been created with different excretion properties. In general, in-

Table 10–7. TECHNETIUM 99m IDA DERIVATIVES

HIDA—dimethyl
PIPIDA—paraisopropyl
BIDA—parabutyl
DISIDA—diisopropyl
DIEDA—diethyl

creasing the length of the alkyl chain substituted on the benzene ring of IDA increases the biliary excretion of the radiopharmaceutical and reduces renal clearance. This added biliary excretion can be of great value in imaging patients with elevated bilirubin levels.·

The first widely used IDA complex was the dimethyl derivative (HIDA). With the short length of the substitution, approximately 85 percent of this compound is excreted by the liver and approximately 15 percent by the kidneys. It provides successful visualization of the hepatobiliary system at bilirubin levels of approximately 5 to 7 mg/dl. The ratio of liver to renal excretion decreases significantly as hepatobiliary function is compromised. Currently, perhaps the most widely used IDA compound is DISIDA (diisopropyl IDA or disofenin), which, with its longer substituted chain, allows for increased biliary excretion and visualization of the hepatobiliary system at serum bilirubin levels approaching 20 mg/dl. The radiopharmaceutical is rapidly removed from the circulation by active transport into the hepatocytes.

TECHNIQUE

For elective studies, patients are given nothing by mouth beginning at midnight the night before the examination. In other pa-

tients, a minimum of 2 hours' fasting is suggested. Fortunately, in emergency patients with suspected acute cholecystitis, fasting has generally been self-imposed. In patients whose gallbladders are being stimulated by the presence of food in the upper gastrointestinal tract, the intermittent contraction of the gallbladder interferes with biliary filling and therefore may render a false positive study. It should also be mentioned that prolonged fasting in some patients has been implicated as a source of false positive examinations.

Subsequent to the intravenous injection of 3 to 10 mCi (111 to 370 MBq) of ^{99m}Tc labeled IDA, sequential anterior gamma camera images of the abdomen are obtained with the patient in the supine position. Images of 500 to 1000 K counts are obtained at 5-minute intervals for the first half-hour of the study. Similar images are then obtained at 10-minute intervals. Normally, the gallbladder is visualized within the first half-hour of the study, as are the common bile duct and duodenum. If these structures are not identified at 1 hour, delayed images should be obtained hourly up to 4 hours after injection.

In jaundiced patients, increased renal excretion of the radiopharmaceutical may be confused with gallbladder activity (Fig. 10–19). Activity in the right renal pelvis may be

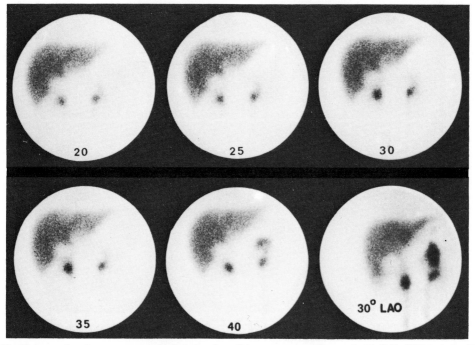

Figure 10–19. Long-standing common duct obstruction. This scan was performed with ^{99m}Tc PIPIDA. A significant amount of renal excretion and a negative defect are seen in the region of the gallbladder bed.

differentiated from gallbladder activity by obtaining a right lateral scintiphoto, on which the characteristic anterior abdominal location of the gallbladder can be identified. At times, the gallbladder activity may be obscured by activity collecting in the adjacent duodenal loop. In this case, an additional view in the left anterior oblique position can be used to distinguish the two structures. If this fails to provide the answer, a right lateral view may again be helpful.

THE NORMAL SCAN

In the normal patient, sufficient ^{99m}Tc IDA is present in the liver in 5 minutes to allow good visualization of that organ (Fig. 10–20). If for any reason additional views of the liver are sought, they should be obtained in the first 10 to 15 minutes of the examination. Following this time, there is progressive

clearance of the radiopharmaceutical from the liver and it will become less apparent. As the radiopharmaceutical is excreted into the biliary tree, the major hepatic ducts and gallbladder will be visualized. In the presence of a patent common duct, activity will flow promptly into the duodenal sweep and proximal small bowel. Normally, visualization of these structures is complete by 1 hour.

CLINICAL MANIFESTATIONS
Acute Cholecystitis

Hepatobiliary imaging has proved to be of greatest value in the diagnosis of acute cholecystitis. If one were to pathologically examine the gallbladders from patients with acute cholecystitis, over 95 percent would have cystic duct obstruction. In this group of patients, radiopharmaceuticals secreted into the bile by the liver cannot enter the inflamed

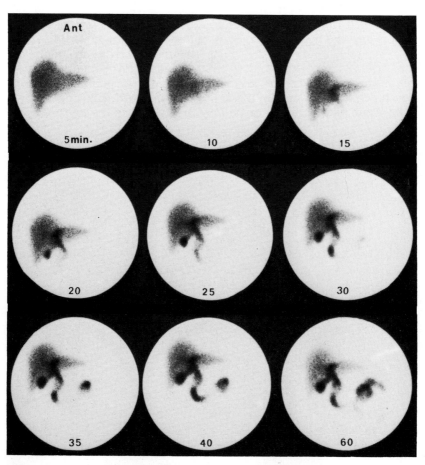

Figure 10–20. Normal hepatobiliary scan. Activity is seen within the gallbladder and common duct by 20 minutes. The small bowel activity is clearly identified at 35 minutes.

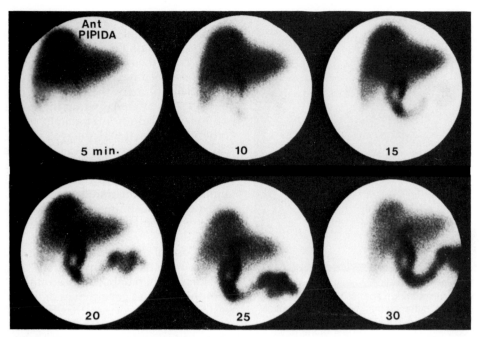

Figure 10–21. Acute cholecystitis. There is activity in the small bowel and common duct at 15 minutes as well as some reflux into the proximal duodenum. This study was continued for 4 hours and there was no visualization of the gallbladder.

gallbladder. This fact provides the theoretical basis for employing ^{99m}Tc hepatobiliary agents to diagnose the disease.

In the proper clinical setting, the diagnosis of acute (calculous or acalculous) cholecystitis in a fasting patient may be reliably made in the presence of hepatic uptake and excretion of the radiopharmaceutical through the common duct but without visualization of the gallbladder over a period of 4 hours after injection (Fig. 10–21). In several large series, accuracy has been greater than 95 percent. Additionally, this imaging modality is usually unaffected by modest levels of jaundice.

Occasionally the gallbladder may not be seen in a patient with chronic cholecystitis, but this is uncommon. Usually the gallbladder is visualized within 4 hours post-injection. Visualization of the gallbladder during this period of time effectively excludes the diagnosis of acute gallbladder disease. Thus, it is essential that this delayed sequence of images be a routine part of IDA imaging for acute cholecystitis. Table 10–8 lists some sources of error in interpretation when considering a diagnosis of acute cholecystitis.

Occasionally, the hepatobiliary imaging procedure results in nonvisualization of the gallbladder and an absence or marked delay in small bowel visualization in a patient suspected of acute biliary disease. When adequate hepatic uptake of the radiopharmaceutical is noted in this instance, a diagnosis of common bile duct obstruction must be considered. However, while mechanical obstruction is most likely in these instances, functional common duct obstruction accompanying ascending cholangitis cannot be excluded and further investigation is warranted.

A "rim sign" has been described in patients with acute cholecystitis. This has also

Table 10–8. INTERPRETATIVE DIFFICULTIES IN DIAGNOSIS OF ACUTE CHOLECYSTITIS BY HEPATOBILIARY SCAN

False positive
  Recent meal
  Alcoholism
  Pancreatitis (in at least some cases)
  Hepatocellular dysfunction
  Cholangiocarcinoma of cystic duct
  Prolonged fasting or hyperalimentation
False negative
  Acalculous cholecystitis
  Duodenal diverticulum simulating gallbladder
  Accessory cystic duct

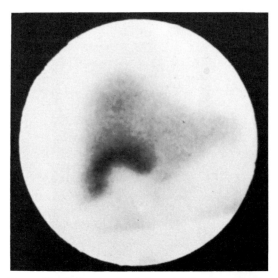

Figure 10–22. The rim sign in hepatobiliary imaging. A 90-minute anterior image from a ^{99m}Tc DISIDA study shows a patent common duct with nonvisualization of the gallbladder. A thin faint line of increased activity outlining the superior aspect of the gallbladder fossa is noted and constitutes the rim sign. This has been described in patients with acute cholecystitis. This sign should alert the clinician to the possibility of a gangrenous or perforated gallbladder.

been called the "pericholecystic hepatic activity (PCHA) sign," and it refers to a curvilinear band of increased activity along the right inferior hepatic edge above the gallbladder fossa (Fig. 10–22). This sign is seen in about 20 percent of all patients whose gallbladder is not visualized on DISIDA scans. This sign should alert the nuclear medicine physician, since about 40 percent of patients with this sign have either a perforated or gangrenous gallbladder.

Various pharmacologic adjuncts have been suggested to increase the sensitivity of hepatobiliary imaging in the evaluation of patients for acute cholecystitis. It has been noted that the sensitivity of the hepatobiliary scan may be increased by emptying the gallbladder prior to the administration of the radiopharmaceutical; this, theoretically, will reduce the false positive rate of the test in patients with chronic cholecystitis or viscous bile. Initially, fatty meals were employed but proved variable in their ability to produce gallbladder contraction. Consequently, cholecystokinin (CCK) or its synthetic derivative, sincalide, have been used. In normal patients there is prompt gallbladder contraction, reaching a maximum effect at 5 to 15 minutes

after slow (over 5 to 10 minutes) intravenous administration of sincalide. The standard dose is 0.02 µg/kg of body weight.

Although these maneuvers may reduce the false positive rate, such premedication may potentially obscure the diagnosis of chronic cholecystitis by speeding up the visualization of the gallbladder in patients who would otherwise present with delayed visualization. This problem may be obviated by reserving the administration of CCK or sincalide until failure to visualize the gallbladder at 30 to 60 minutes is demonstrated. At this time there can be administration of intravenous CCK along with reinjection of the IDA radiopharmaceutical.

The use of intravenous morphine has also been suggested to improve the diagnostic accuracy of hepatobiliary scanning. Because morphine causes constriction of the sphincter of Oddi, it is theorized that the subsequent rise in common duct pressure will produce increased flow of the radiopharmaceutical into the gallbladder. Thus, if after passage of the radiopharmaceutical into the common duct and small bowel there is no gallbladder visualization, intravenous morphine can be administered. The typical dose is 0.04 mg/kg of body weight. This is usually well tolerated by patients without significant aggravation of symptoms.

Chronic Cholecystitis

Although delayed gallbladder visualization correlates well with chronic gallbladder disease, it also occurs in a very small number of patients with acute cholecystitis. Thus, although late visualization strongly suggests chronic cholecystitis, acute disease cannot be definitely excluded. In those patients in whom the gallbladder is visualized after 1 hour and in whom acute disease is strongly suggested on clinical grounds, the contractile response of the gallbladder to administered cholecystokinin (CCK) may provide a clue to the true nature of the disease. A gallbladder that fails to contract upon stimulation with CCK should be held in suspicion for acute gallbladder disease until excluded by other modalities such as ultrasonography. If the gallbladder does respond, then continued investigation of presumed chronic cholecystitis is indicated.

Computer acquisition of a CCK gallbladder stimulation study allows calculation of a gallbladder ejection fraction obtained over the first 30 minutes of the examination. Generally, ejection fractions of less than 30 percent are considered abnormal and ejection fractions in the 30 percent to 50 percent range are considered equivocal. Expected normal ejection fractions are greater than 50 percent. An abnormal ejection fraction can be used along with clinical information to suggest the presence of gallbladder dysfunction.

Aside from delayed gallbladder visualization, several other scintigraphic patterns demonstrate good correlation with the diagnosis of chronic cholecystitis. Delayed biliary-to-bowel transit time in the presence of normal gallbladder and common duct visualization has been reported in chronic gallbladder disease. In addition, the longer intestinal visualization is delayed, the more likely is a diagnosis of chronic cholecystitis; however, this finding alone is by no means diagnostic.

Finally, poor but definite visualization of the gallbladder, filling defects within the gallbladder or common duct, and a less-than-optimal contractile response to CCK stimulation have all been reported in patients who have subsequently proved to have chronic cholecystitis. Identification of cholelithiasis is extremely poor unless the stones are quite large. However, none of these correlates as well with the disease as does delayed gallbladder visualization.

Biliary Obstruction

Lack of visualization of the biliary tree with good visualization of the liver is usual with complete obstruction of the common bile duct. With partial bile duct obstruction, the biliary tree is visualized to the level of obstruction, and occasionally a filling defect is identified at that point. Intrahepatic cholestasis, such as that produced by obstruction of the canaliculi by certain drugs, may also yield a pattern indistinguishable from complete common duct obstruction.

All of the above patterns are dependent upon good hepatocyte function. In the past, severe hepatocellular disease or dysfunction has precluded a diagnostic study because insufficient excretion of the radiopharmaceutical into the major biliary ducts rendered it impossible to distinguish between nonvisualization of the ducts secondary to primary liver disease and high-grade obstruction of the common duct. However, the use of longer-chain IDA analogs that allow good hepatic concentration and excretion even in the presence of marked jaundice should make this diagnostic problem considerably less frequent.

The sequence of events following acute complete biliary obstruction is as follows: 0 to 24 hours, hepatocyte function is normal and there will be good hepatic and bile duct visualization (ultrasound at this time will be normal); 24 to 96 hours, mild to moderate reduction in hepatic and bile duct visualization (ultrasound will show enlargement of the common bile and hepatic ducts); after 96 hours, poor hepatic uptake with no activity in bile ducts or gallbladder (ultrasound will show beginning dilatation of intrahepatic ducts). In all of these there will be no visualization of intestinal activity unless there is only partial obstruction. In the late stage (after 96 hours), differentiation of obstruction from hepatitis can be difficult or impossible without the use of ultrasound.

Post-traumatic and Post-surgical Scans

The confirmation and localization of biliary leaks after abdominal surgery or trauma using ^{99m}Tc IDA agents may lead to early definition and correction of the problem. This technique presents several advantages and overcomes several of the disadvantages of using conventional radiographic methods for the evaluation of suspected biliary fistula.

Hepatobiliary scintigraphy has also proved of use in the post-cholecystectomy patient by allowing the identification of persistent cystic duct remnants and retained stones as well as the assessment of biliary patency. In attempting to detect a remnant of the cystic duct, it is of the utmost importance to obtain delayed images to permit sufficient time for such a structure to visualize. Occasionally, retained common duct stones may be identified on the IDA scan as photon-deficient areas in the visualized common duct. Such a finding should be followed by ultrasonography, although stones may be missed in the presence of a normal-caliber common bile duct. Finally, the functional significance of a dilated common duct on ultrasound after gallbladder surgery may be clarified with cholescintigraphy by determining the patency or obstruction of the duct.

On occasion, cholescintigraphy may be

used to investigate surgically altered biliary and gastrointestinal anatomy by providing appropriate functional information. As with all post-surgical studies, it is important to obtain a precise understanding of the type of surgical procedure performed before proceeding with the examination.

Biliary Atresia

Radionuclide techniques have traditionally been used to differentiate between biliary atresia and neonatal hepatitis in the jaundiced infant. Because the successful surgical treatment of biliary atresia is greatly dependent on early intervention, prompt diagnosis is of the utmost importance. Frequently, the diagnosis cannot be made on clinical, laboratory, or even needle biopsy grounds, and cholescintigraphy may provide the only clue to the proper diagnosis.

Before the availability of IDA complexes, the radioisotope diagnosis of biliary atresia was made by the qualification of the amount of intravenously administered ^{131}I rose bengal excreted in the feces over a period of 72 hours. Patients with less than 5 percent of the administered dose present in the feces could be presumed to have biliary atresia. Patients with greater than 10 percent excretion of the administered dose were considered to have neonatal hepatitis. Both the inconvenience and the difficulty of the technique—particularly the risk of urinary contamination of the stool specimens and the diagnostic gray area between 5 and 10 percent excretion—have made the procedure unpopular.

More recently, imaging with ^{99m}Tc IDA analogs has been used to exclude a diagnosis of biliary atresia by demonstrating patent extrahepatic biliary systems in jaundiced neonates. However, in the absence of visualization of the biliary tree, atresia may not be successfully differentiated from severe hepatocellular disease. The relatively short physical half-life of ^{99m}Tc is disadvantageous in that imaging beyond 24 hours is not practical and therefore biliary flow into the small bowel more than 24 hours after injection may not be detected. If prolonged imaging is anticipated, the use of iodine 131 rose bengal may be indicated. There is some evidence that the examination using ^{99m}Tc IDA analogs is more diagnostic when the liver is primed first with 5 to 7 days of phenobarbital therapy

(2.5 mg/kg orally twice a day), which provides for better excretion of the radiopharmaceutical and therefore earlier identification of a patent biliary tree. In addition to biliary atresia, other anomalies of the biliary tract such as choledochal cysts and Caroli's disease (Fig. 10–23) have been identified successfully using ^{99m}Tc IDA imaging.

Evaluation of Defects on Sulfur Colloid Scans

When routine sulfur colloid imaging presents the diagnostic problem of a prominent gallbladder fossa, prominent porta hepatis, or possible intrahepatic gallbladder, ^{99m}Tc IDA cholescintigraphy may be conveniently employed to determine the true nature of the suspected abnormality. The study may be performed immediately after the sulfur colloid study. "Filling in" of the defect noted on routine liver imaging with the cholecystographic agent may be seen if the abnormality is indeed related to the biliary tract (Table 10–9).

Gastroesophageal Function

Radionuclide techniques provide a convenient, noninvasive, and direct method to assess GI motility. Using imaging and computer-assisted quantitation, numerous physiologic parameters of upper GI function may be evaluated. These include (1) gastric emptying rates, (2) esophageal transit, and (3) the detection and quantitation of gastroesophageal and enterogastric reflux.

Esophageal Transit

Scintigraphic methods are useful to quantitate esophageal transit. Other methods that have been used are the acid-clearance test, esophageal manometry, and barium esophograms. Several methods are currently utilized, and most of these use an orally administered liquid bolus and measure the time to esophageal clearance. Although the scintigraphic study is useful as a quantitative measure, it has very limited anatomic resolution, and therefore it is not a replacement for a barium study. The initial evaluation of a patient with esophageal symptoms should include a barium study.

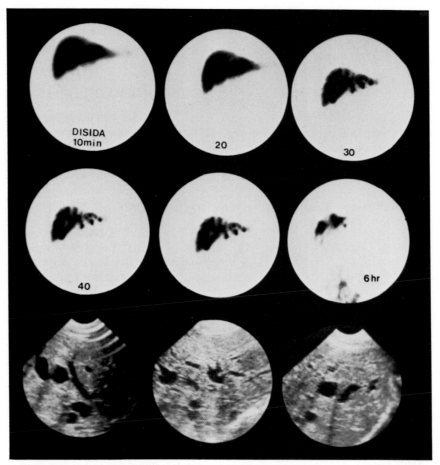

Figure 10–23. Caroli's disease. The hepatobiliary scan shows normal early activity; however, the subsequent images show accumulation of activity in focally dilated biliary radicals. Ultrasound (lower row) images confirm this finding. (Case courtesy of Barry Siegel, M.D.)

RADIOPHARMACEUTICALS

A number of radiopharmaceuticals can be used with success; however, ^{99m}Tc sulfur colloid is used most often. It has the advantages of being readily available, nonabsorbable, and inexpensive. The radiation absorbed dose from this procedure is about 20 mrad (0.2 mGy) compared with several rads for a barium esophagram.

TECHNIQUE

The patient should fast for at least 6 hours prior to the procedure. He or she is placed

Table 10–9. RADIONUCLIDE DIFFERENTIAL DIAGNOSIS OF SOLID HEPATIC LESIONS

LESION	^{99m}Tc SULFUR COLLOID	HEPATOBILIARY AGENTS			
		Perfusion	Parenchymal	Washout	RBCs
Adenoma/cancer	Cold	Normal	Decreased	Delayed	Normal
Focal nodular hyperplasia	Cold or normal	Increased	Normal	Delayed	Normal
Hemangioma	Cold	Normal	Decreased	—	Increased
Metastasis	Cold	Normal	Decreased	—	Normal

Adapted from Creutzig H, Gratz KF, Mueller ST, et al: Classification of liver tumors by radionuclide imaging. J Nucl Med 25(3):402, 1984.

supine under a gamma camera with the field of view including the entire esophagus and proximal stomach. The patient is instructed to swallow 300 microcuries (11.1 MBq) of ^{99m}Tc sulfur colloid in 15 ml of water at the same time that acquisition by the camera and computer is begun. The patient then "dry" swallows every 15 seconds for 5 to 10 minutes. After the acquisition is complete, regions of interest are outlined on the computer image. Some physicians divide the esophagus into thirds with each as a region of interest.

Esophageal transit is measured using the following formula:

$$C_t = \frac{E_{max} - E_t}{E_{max}} \times 100$$

In this formula, C_t is the percentage of esophageal transit at time t; E_{max} is the maximal esophageal activity in counts; and E_t is the number of counts in the esophagus at time t. In this single-swallow method, esophageal activity is measured at 1-second intervals for the first 15 seconds after maximal esophageal activity is obtained. Another method uses successive swallows primarily to compare with the acid-clearance test.

NORMAL AND ABNORMAL ESOPHAGEAL TRANSIT

In the normal person, at least 90 percent of the activity should have traversed the esophagus by the end of 15 seconds. In patients with scleroderma and achalasia, transit may be reduced to levels as low as 20 to 40 percent. Patients with various other motor disorders of the esophagus usually have intermediate values.

Gastroesophageal Reflux Studies

In those patients with symptoms of heartburn, regurgitation, or bilious vomiting, computer-assisted scintigraphic studies provide a sensitive and useful method for reflux determination and quantitation. Alternative methods are limited in usefulness. Fluoroscopic barium studies are not very sensitive and are very dependent upon the expertise and persistence of the fluoroscopist. Acid reflux testing is the standard that is used for comparison but it requires intubation. Esoph-

ageal manometry is sometimes used but it also requires intubation to measure the decreased resistance of the lower esophageal sphincter in cases of reflux.

RADIOPHARMACEUTICALS

^{99m}Tc sulfur colloid is the radiopharmaceutical of choice. The procedure calls for the oral administration of 300 μCi (11.1 MBq) in 150 ml of orange juice combined with 150 ml of 0.1 normal hydrochloric acid.

TECHNIQUE

The patient should fast overnight or for at least 2 hours after a liquid meal. An abdominal binder is placed about the upper abdomen. While in a sitting position, the patient drinks the 300 ml of solution, and after 30 seconds a single image is obtained to see that all the liquid is in the stomach. An additional 30 ml of water is then given, and the patient is placed in the supine position. The field of view of the gamma camera should include the esophagus and stomach. A 30-second image is obtained with the abdominal binder at 0, 20, 40, 60, 80, and 100 mm of mercury. In this method, position, pressure, and the presence of acid are all used to aggravate reflux. Gastroesophageal reflux is computed according to the following formula:

$$R = \frac{(E_t - E_b)}{G_0} \times 100$$

where R is the percentage of gastroesophageal reflux, E_t is the number of counts in the esophagus at time t, E_b represents the esophageal background counts at the beginning of the study, and G_0 represents the counts in the stomach at the beginning of the study. The study must be acquired on a computer, and regions of interest are outlined to include the stomach, esophagus, and a suitable area for background.

Some investigators have used a variation of this scintigraphic method to study gastroesophageal reflux and pulmonary aspiration of gastric contents in children. In this case an abdominal binder is not used, and the patient position should be left anterior oblique rather than supine.

NORMAL AND ABNORMAL STUDIES

The upper limit for gastroesophageal reflux in normals is 3 percent. Between 3 and 4

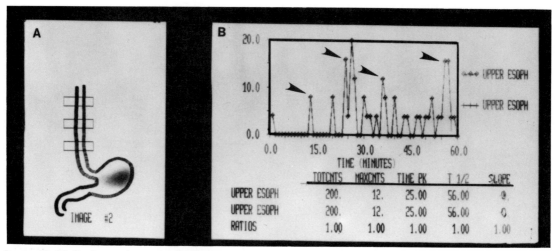

Figure 10–24. Gastroesophageal reflux. (A) Anterior view of the chest and upper abdomen shows activity within the stomach and three computer regions of interest. (B) A computer-generated graph of activity over the upper esophagus shows multiple spikes indicating significant reflux.

percent is considered indeterminate, and over 4 percent reflux is abnormal (Fig. 10–24). The sensitivity of this study is in excess of 90 percent; however, if the acid, abdominal binder, and supine position are not utilized, the sensitivity of the study will decrease. The study can be utilized in the initial diagnosis of reflux as well as in the evaluation of various therapeutic modalities.

Gastric Emptying

Scintigraphic studies of gastric emptying have been complicated by the fact that liquid and solid contents empty from the stomach at different rates; there are a host of factors that regulate this process. Liquids empty from the stomach in an exponential fashion, whereas solid foods empty in a more linear manner. Osmolality, pH, volume, and caloric content as well as the amount of protein, carbohydrate, and fat all affect emptying rate. For example, distention of the stomach accelerates gastric emptying, whereas lipids are potent inhibitors.

RADIOPHARMACEUTICALS

A wide variety of radiopharmaceuticals have been used for the test for gastric emptying. Two main classes are used: those for the solid phase and those for the liquid phase. The solid phase may use ^{99m}Tc sulfur colloid to label chicken liver, whole eggs, or egg whites. Iodinated alphamethylcellulose can be used to measure emptying rates of fiber. Perhaps the most widely used method is to mix 0.5 to 3 mCi (18.5 to 111 MBq) of ^{99m}Tc sulfur colloid with scrambled eggs as they are being cooked. If a liquid phase study is desired, this can be performed simultaneously by utilizing another radionuclide, such as indium 111 DTPA (125 μCi [4.6 MBq] in 300 ml of water) and doing computer analysis of different photopeaks.

TECHNIQUE

The patient should consume both the solid and liquid phases of a 300 gm meal within 10 minutes. The patient is placed under the gamma camera in the supine position, and images are obtained every 15 minutes for 3 hours. The patient should sit up between the images. Computer acquisition is mandatory, and regions of interest are selected over the stomach and appropriate background areas. Anterior and posterior images can be obtained if one wishes to use the geometric mean value for calculations.

NORMAL AND ABNORMAL STUDIES

In our laboratories, we prefer to label the solid phase study only. The presence of liquids has been reported to accelerate the emptying rates of solids from the stomach. In

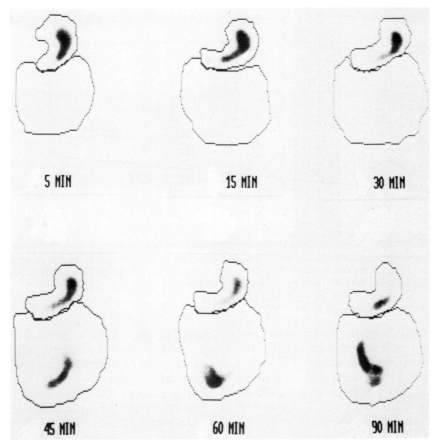

Figure 10–25. Normal gastric emptying. Sequential images are shown with a computer region of interest around the stomach and small bowel. By 45 minutes, the stomach is beginning to empty, and by 90 minutes, well over half of the activity is in the small bowel.

normal persons, the approximate time for half of the activity (using scrambled eggs) to leave the stomach is 90 (45 to 110) minutes (Fig. 10–25). The half-time for emptying of the liquid phase is 40 (12 to 65) minutes. The major use of the study is to monitor the effects of therapy in patients with abnormal gastric motility, such as diabetics. As is the case with esophageal transit studies, the initial workup of a patient with symptoms of gastric outlet obstruction should include a barium examination rather than a scintigraphic study.

SCHILLING TEST

The Schilling test is used to study GI absorption of vitamin B_{12}, which requires the presence of intrinsic factor.

The patient usually fasts the night before the examination, and 0.5 μg of cobalt 57 vitamin B_{12} containing 0.5 μCi (18.5 kBq) is then given orally. This is immediately followed by an intramuscular injection of about 1000 μg of nonlabeled vitamin B_{12}. This intramuscular injection is given to saturate the liver and blood B_{12} binding sites and thus promote urinary excretion of the labeled vitamin B_{12}. A 24-hour urine sample of at least 1 liter is then collected and measured for excreted activity, which would indicate whether there was significant intestinal absorption of radio-labeled B_{12}. Normal 24-hour values for urinary excretion are in the range of 10 to 40 percent of the administered dose. Values lower than 7 percent indicate a significant problem compatible with pernicious anemia (intrinsic factor defect), as well as malabsorption problems. To differentiate between the two, a stage 2 Schilling test is needed.

A stage 2 Schilling test may be performed by repeating the test with labeled vitamin B_{12} and intrinsic factor. If this still reveals low urinary excretion, a malabsorption problem such as sprue, regional enteritis, or blind loop syndrome may exist.

An alternative method is sometimes used in which the Schilling test is performed with a capsule containing both cobalt 57 B_{12} (122 keV) bound to intrinsic factor and a second capsule of cobalt 58 B_{12} (510 and 810 keV). In this instance, each of the radionuclides is measured in the 24-hour urine sample by analysis of the different energies of cobalt 57 and cobalt 58. In the case of pernicious anemia, the 24-hour urinary excretion would be normal for cobalt 57 and low for cobalt 58.

Suggested Readings

Brown CK, Olshaker JS: Meckel's diverticulum. Am Jo Emerg Med 6:157–164, 1988

Freeman LM, Blaufox MD (eds): Gastrointestinal disease update—I: Liver and biliary tracts. Semin Nucl Med 12(1):2–88, 1982

Freeman LM, Blaufox MD (eds): Gastrointestinal disease update—II: Liver and biliary tract. Semin Nucl Med 12(2):104–172, 1982

Freeman LM, Blaufox MD (eds): Nuclear oncology. Part I. Semin Nucl Med 14(4):287–295, 1984

Mettler FA Jr (ed): Contemporary issues in nuclear imaging. Radionuclide imaging of the GI tract, Vol 2. New York, Churchill Livingstone, 1986

Spencer RC (guest editor). In: The spleen. Freeman LM, Blaufox MD (eds): Semin Nucl Med 15(3):229–316, 1985

Zuckier LS, Chervu LR: Schilling evaluation of pernicious anemia: Current status. J Nucl Med 25:1032–1039, 1984

CHAPTER 11

Skeletal System

The availability of stable technetium labeled bone-seeking pharmaceuticals with improved soft tissue clearance has led to sensitive, high-resolution images, which accounts for the widespread use of these agents in bone scanning. It appears likely that bone imaging with these technetium agents will remain clinically useful for a long time, in spite of the rapid advancements in other technologies such as computed tomography and magnetic resonance imaging. The bone scan often provides an earlier diagnosis and demonstrates more lesions than are found by other radiographic procedures. Although the presence of a lesion on a bone scan is nonspecific, its monostotic or polyostotic status and anatomic distribution can usually be determined, and these findings often provide important clues to the differential diagnosis. For optimal performance of bone scans, both the physician and the technologist need to understand the limitations and uses of skeletal imaging procedures.

Anatomy and Physiology

Bone in the diaphyseal region is formed by the periosteum, while longitudinal bone growth emanates from the epiphyseal plate. The basic structure of bone is a crystalline lattice composed of calcium, phosphate, and hydroxyl ions, which form the inorganic mineral hydroxyapatite. The other major constituents of bone include collagen, ground substance, and other minerals. Anatomically, the skeleton is composed of two parts: the axial and the appendicular portions. The axial skeleton includes the skull, spine, and thoracic girdle. The appendicular skeleton includes the upper extremities, pelvis, and lower extremities. This is a relatively important distinction, because some diseases favor either the appendicular or the axial skeleton.

Radiopharmaceuticals

Bone-seeking radiopharmaceuticals are commonly analogues of calcium, hydroxyl groups, or phosphates. Isotopes of strontium have been employed as calcium analogues. These have been primarily strontium 85 and strontium 87m. Strontium 85 is no longer utilized due to the high radiation dose it gives to the bone, and strontium 87m is now rarely used clinically. Fluorine is a hydroxyl analogue. The short half-life (1.87 hours) and positron emission of fluorine 18 limit its clinical application.

By far the most widely utilized radiopharmaceuticals for skeletal imaging are technetium labeled phosphate analogues (Table 11–1). Pyrophosphates and diphosphonate derivatives including ethane-1-hydroxyl-1, 1 diphosphonate (EHDP), methylene diphosphonate (MDP), and methylene hydroxydiphosphonate (MHDP) have proved satisfactory.

Pyrophosphates contain an inorganic P–O–P bond, while diphosphonates contain organic P–C–P bonds, which are more stable in vivo. Of all of these agents, MDP and MHDP have the most rapid blood clearance. Pyrophosphate is the least satisfactory of these radiopharmaceuticals because of slow soft tissue clearance. Because the diphosphonates have greater renal excretion than pyrophosphate, they provide a very high target/nontarget ratio within 2 to 3 hours following injection, with 50 to 60 percent of the activity localizing in bone and the remainder being cleared by the kidneys.

Care should be taken to avoid the injection of air into the mixing vial during preparation of phosphate radiopharmaceuticals because the resultant oxidation of technetium will cause poor tagging of the phosphates. Bone radiopharmaceuticals should be routinely checked with chromatography before injec-

Table 11-1. RADIOPHARMACEUTICALS FOR BONE IMAGING

RADIOPHARMA-CEUTICAL	USUAL DOSE	ROUTE OF ADMINISTRA-TION	PHYSICAL HALF-LIFE	TIME TO IMAGING	ABSORBED DOSE ESTIMATE (rad/mCi)*			REMARKS
					Whole Body	Gonads	Other	
⁹⁹mTc diphosphonates	10–20 mCi (370–740 MBq)	IV	6.0 hr	2–4 hr	0.01	0.01–0.03	Marrow 0.01 Bone 0.02–0.07 Bladder 0.1–0.2†	50–60% in bone at 3–4 hours Frequent voiding and forced fluids reduce bladder dose.

*To obtain absorbed dose in mGy/MBq, divide values by 3.7.
†Indicates critical organ.

tion; a 95 percent tag is acceptable. If the radiopharmaceutical is administered more than 4 to 5 hours after preparation, gastric and thyroid visualization on bone scans may be seen as the result of free pertechnetate.

The initial accumulation of technetium-labeled radiopharmaceuticals in bone is primarily related to blood supply; however, capillary permeability, the local acid-base relationship, fluid pressure within bone, hormones, vitamins, the quantity of mineralized bone, and bone turnover also play a role. Increased radionuclide activity in bone may result from accentuation of any one of these factors. Factors that may be responsible for greater-than-usual activity are listed in Table 11–2. For example, increased blood flow causes increased delivery of the radiopharmaceutical to the bone with resultant increased regional deposition of the agent. The converse is also true: interference with any of these factors may cause decreased skeletal activity. For instance, in cases of decreased cardiac output, bone scans may be of poor quality due to inadequate delivery of radiopharmaceutical to the bone. However, the relationship between blood flow and radionuclide bone activity is not linear; a four-fold increase in blood flow only increases bone uptake by 30 to 40 percent.

Chemisorption may be the initial mechanism of actual binding of technetium labeled phosphates to bone, with some subsequent incorporation into bone crystal and organic matrix. In some patients, this accumulation may be affected by administered drugs.

Technique

The patient is normally injected intravenously with 10 to 20 mCi (370 to 740 MBq) of the technetium phosphate radiopharmaceutical and imaged 2 to 4 hours later. The site of injection should be distant from any suspected osseous pathology and should be recorded. Often even a slight extravasation of isotope at the injection site will cause an area of markedly increased activity. In patients suspected of having either osteomyelitis or cellulitis, a radionuclide angiogram and initial blood pool image are performed after injection, and routine images are obtained at approximately 2 to 3 hours.

Scanning is normally done with a gamma camera and may consist of either multiple spot or whole-body imaging, the latter of which results in a single skeletal image. If multiple spot films are obtained, the entire skeleton should be imaged. The patient is normally scanned in both the anterior and posterior projections. (Detailed spot views of particular regions may be obtained as dictated by history or symptomatology.) Additionally, selective pinhole views allow for enhanced resolution in any areas of interest. Single images obtained with a gamma camera usually require a preset number of counts: approximately 500,000 for a standard camera and 500,000 to 1,000,000 for a large-crystal camera.

The rapid urinary excretion of phosphate radiopharmaceuticals causes large amounts of activity to accumulate within the bladder,

Table 11-2. POSSIBLE MECHANISMS OF INCREASED ACTIVITY ON BONE SCANS

- Increased osteoid formation
- Increased blood flow
- Increased mineralization of osteoid
- Interrupted sympathetic nerve supply

which may obscure pelvic lesions; therefore, voiding prior to imaging should be routine. It should be noted, however, that voiding, particularly in incontinent patients, may result in radioactive contamination of skin or clothing; this may obscure underlying pathology or actually mimic a lesion. Removal of contaminated clothing and cleansing of skin may be necessary to obtain accurate results. Following injection and before scanning, patients should be hydrated. This will decrease the bladder dose of radiation due to more frequent voiding. In patients with renal failure there will be increased soft tissue activity, which may render a suboptimal scan.

Bone single photon emission computed tomography (SPECT) imaging may significantly improve lesion detection in patients with specific regional skeletal complaints and may establish or better localize an abnormality suspected on routine planar images. SPECT is usually of most value in complex bony structures such as large joints, the spine, and the pelvis. A sample protocol for SPECT skeletal imaging is provided in Appendix E.

The Normal Scan

The normal scan (Fig. 11–1) varies significantly in appearance between children and adults. In the child, areas of growth in the region of the epiphyses show intense radionuclide accumulation. In the adult, the quality of the bone scan can be related to age; in general, the older the patient, the higher the proportion of poor-quality scans. There usually is good visualization of the skull, with relatively increased accumulation of activity in the region of the nasopharynx, which may be secondary to the high proportional blood flow in this region. Activity in the skull is often patchy even in normal patients, so care must be taken in assessing skull lesions without an accompanying radiograph. There is activity throughout the spine, and it is quite common to see focal areas of increased activity in the lower cervical spine, usually rep-

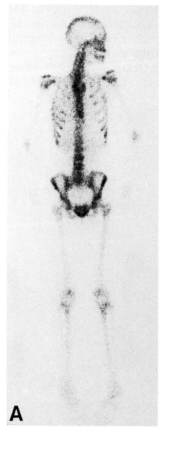
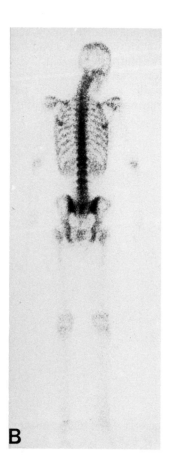

Figure 11–1. Normal adult bone scan. (A) Anterior. (B) Posterior.

A

B

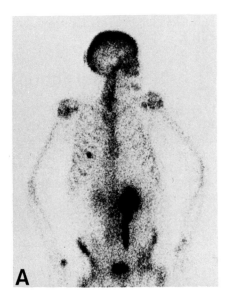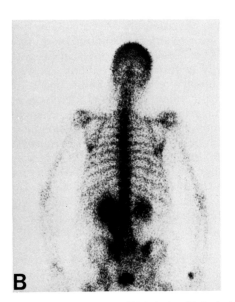

Figure 11-2. Left ureteral obstruction in a female with advanced cervical carcinoma. (A) Anterior. (B) Posterior. A traumatic rib lesion is identified anterolaterally on the right, and the injection site is seen in the right hand.

resenting degenerative changes rather than activity in the thyroid cartilage of the thyroid itself. Areas of tendon insertion, constant stress, and osseous remodeling will also demonstrate increased activity. On the anterior view, there is prominent visualization of the sternum, sternoclavicular joints, shoulders, iliac crests, and hips. Increased activity in the knees in older patients is relatively common because of the propensity for ar-

thritic changes. On the posterior view, the thoracic spine is well seen, as are the tips of the scapulae. The spine often demonstrates increased activity in areas of hypertrophic degenerative change, and the sacroiliac joints are usually pronounced.

Since the human skeleton is symmetric, any asymmetric osseous activity should be viewed with suspicion. In addition, it is important on the posterior view to examine the

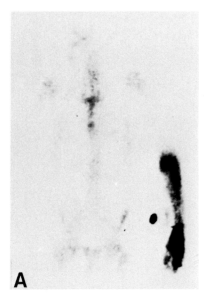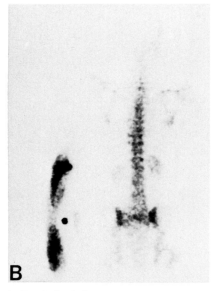

Figure 11-3. The "glove" phenomenon caused by arterial injection in the left antecubital fossa. (A) Anterior. (B) Posterior.

scan for the presence of renal activity, and on the anterior view for bladder activity and possible displacement. Asymmetric renal activity is not uncommon. Since the scans are usually obtained in the supine position, activity may accumulate in extrarenal pelves. If urinary tract obstruction is suspected, views of this area should be repeated after the patient has ambulated. This will ensure that the activity is related to obstruction and not to patient positioning (Fig. 11–2).

Localized areas of increased soft tissue or skeletal activity in an extremity distal to the site of injection (the "glove" phenomenon) may be due to arterial injection of the radionuclide (Fig. 11–3). Regional vascular changes may also be reflected in the scan (either relative ischemia if the activity is decreased or hyperemia if the activity is locally increased). Differential blood flow also may be secondary to neurologically mediated abnormalities (sympathectomy or neuropathy) or even to altered stress. In a patient with a painful extremity that is not being utilized, there may be increased activity throughout the affected limb.

Recognition of the details of normal imaging anatomy becomes even more important when SPECT images of specific skeletal regions are obtained. Reviewing the images in three orthogonal planes generally aids interpreter orientation and thus more accurate localization of pathology. The specific reconstructions of greatest value depend upon the area being evaluated. The complexity of the spine makes it particularly amenable for SPECT imaging in order to localize an abnormality to the vertebral body, disk space, or posterior elements. Transverse images of the spine resemble those of computed tomography sections, whereas coronal and sagittal SPECT images are analogous to anteroposterior and lateral radiographic tomograms, respectively. The curvature of the thoracolumbar spine results in sequential rather than simultaneous visualization of the anatomic parts of adjacent vertebrae. With careful viewing of the sequential images on a computer monitor display, proper orientation generally is not difficult.

Clinical Applications

The following are some common indications for bone scanning:

- Detection and staging of metastatic disease, and follow-up
- Differentiation between osteomyelitis and cellulitis
- Determination of bone viability, infarction, or aseptic necrosis
- Evaluation of roentgenographically difficult fractures (stress fractures and possible fractures in battered children)
- Evaluation of prosthetic joints for infection or loosening
- Determination of biopsy site
- Evaluation of bone pain in patients with normal radiographs

THE ABNORMAL SCAN
Metastatic Disease

The high sensitivity of bone scanning in determining the presence and the extent of metastatic disease makes it an extremely important tool in decision making, particularly since survival rates in patients with multiple distant osseous metastases from many tumors is worse than in those with isolated osseous disease. While the prognostic value of bone scanning for some tumors is disputed, the answer probably depends on the natural history of each tumor type and adequate actuarial analysis. Finding metastases is frequently important to clinical decisions affecting quality of life. Serial bone scanning in patients with known metastases is felt to be valuable in therapeutic decision making (Fig. 11–4), particularly if it is used in combination with other clinical information. This may prove of particular value in the detection of lesions in critical weight-bearing areas such as the femur. Detection of such lesions allows radiation therapy or surgical intervention to prevent pathologic fractures from disabling the patients (Fig. 11–5).

For a lytic lesion to be visualized by radiography, localized demineralization of approximately 30 to 50 percent must occur, and there is little question that bone scans often demonstrate metastatic lesions much earlier than with radiography. The false negative rate of radiographic skeletal surveys may be as high as 50 percent with certain tumors, whereas the overall false negative rate of bone scanning for the most common neoplasms may be as low as 2 percent. Some tumors seem more likely than others to produce a false negative bone scan; these include highly anaplastic tumors, reticulum cell sar-

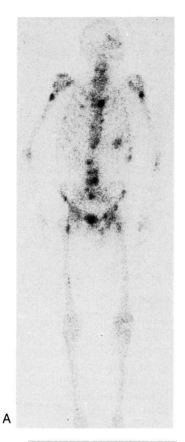 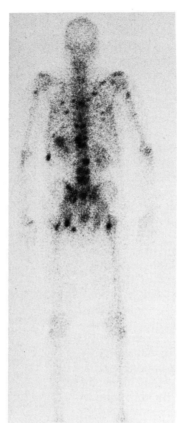

A

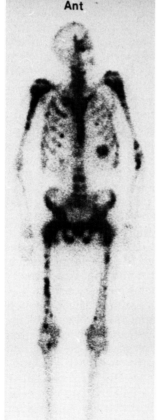 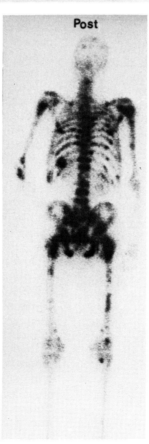

Ant   Post

B

Figure 11–4. Multiple osseous metastases demonstrating progression of lesions from the initial scan (A) to a follow-up scan 9 months later (B). The rapid advancement of these lesions indicates an extremely poor prognosis and may lead to a change in the therapy of this patient.

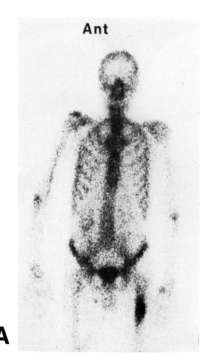
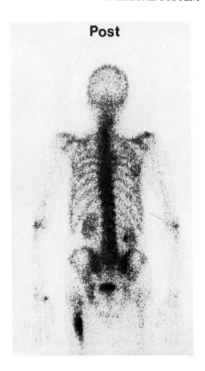

Ant   **Post**

A

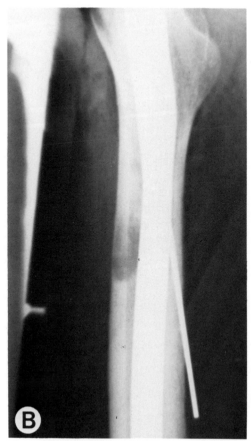

B

Figure 11–5. (A) A single metastasis in the proximal left femur of a patient with breast carcinoma. Early identification of this lesion allowed placement of an intramedullary rod (B) so that a pathologic fracture would not occur in this location.

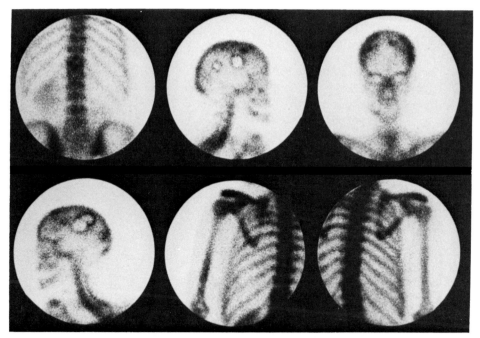

Figure 11–6. Multiple mixed bone metastases from leiomyosarcoma.

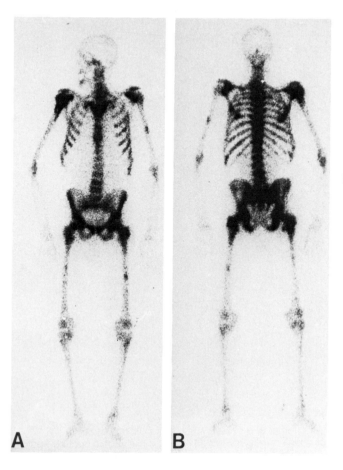

Figure 11–7. Diffuse osteoblastic metastases from carcinoma of the prostate, causing a superscan. There is involvement of the entire axial and proximal appendicular skeleton. Essentially no renal or bladder activity is identified, due to the fact that the metastases have accumulated most of the radionuclide. Several smaller lesions are identified in the long bones as well. (A) Anterior. (B) Posterior.

coma, renal cell carcinoma, thyroid carcinoma, histiocytosis, neuroblastoma, and multiple myeloma. When multiple myeloma causes a positive scan, this often is secondary to a fracture or impending fracture. For patients in whom some lesions cannot be identified easily by bone scanning, the skeletal survey remains the procedure of choice.

Approximately 80 percent of patients with known neoplasms and bone pain will have metastases documented by the bone scan. Although 30 to 50 percent of patients with metastases do not have bone pain, a good case may be made for scanning asymptomatic patients with tumors that have a propensity to metastasize to bone (e.g., breast, lung, and prostate); but for tumors with low rates of osseous metastases (e.g., cervix, head, and neck) the procedure is not cost-effective.

Even though most metastases are multiple (Fig. 11–6) and relatively obvious, there are times when the interpretation may be difficult. If a single lesion is identified, the false positive rate for attributing the finding to metastases is high. In patients with proven metastases, only about 15 percent have a single lesion. A single focus of increased activity is often secondary to benign disease. If two consecutive ribs are involved it is almost always secondary to trauma. However, when multifocal areas of increased activity are seen in noncontiguous bones, the chances of metastatic disease being present become extremely high. In multifocal metastatic disease, the regional distribution of lesions for common bone-seeking primaries is thorax and ribs (37 percent), spine (26 percent), pelvis (16 percent), limbs (15 percent), and skull (6 percent).

Diffuse involvement of the axial skeleton by metastases can be deceptive; it may initially appear as though there has been remarkably good, relatively uniform uptake in all the bones. This has been referred to as a "superscan" (Fig. 11–7). As originally described on rectilinear scans, a hallmark of the superscan was significantly decreased renal activity. However, on current whole-body or spot images, renal activity may appear normal with only diffusely increased bony activity noted, which is frequently more pronounced in the axial skeleton. A superscan is most commonly due to prostatic carcinoma, although diffuse metastases from other tumors such as breast cancer and lymphoma may also cause this appearance. In the absence of neoplasm, a superscan involv-

Table 11–3. CAUSES OF HOT LESIONS ON BONE SCAN

Localized
- Primary malignant bone tumor
- Metastatic disease
- Osteomyelitis
- Trauma
    Stress fractures
    Battering
    Fractures
    Postsurgical osseous changes
    Loose prosthesis
    Degenerative changes
- Osteoid osteoma
- Paget's disease, melorheostosis, fibrous dysplasia
- Arthritis
- Locally increased blood flow
    Hyperemia
    Decreased sympathetic control
- Decreased overlying soft tissue
    (e.g., post-mastectomy)
- Soft tissue activity

Generalized (Superscan)
- Primary hyperparathyroidism
- Secondary hyperparathyroidism
- Renal osteodystrophy
- Metastases
    Prostate
    Lung
    Breast
- Hematologic disorders

ing bones throughout the entire skeleton should raise a suspicion of metabolic conditions such as primary or secondary hyperparathyroidism. Increased activity primarily in the peripheral skeleton may be seen in hematologic disorders.

In searching for metastatic disease, it is important not only to delineate the areas of increased activity (hot spots; Table 11–3) but also to look for cold lesions (Table 11–4), which are usually much more difficult to identify. Focal photon-deficient lesions are

Table 11–4. CAUSES OF COLD LESIONS ON BONE SCAN

- Overlying attenuation artifact caused by pacemaker, barium, etc.
- Radiation therapy
- Local vascular compromise
    Infarction
    Intrinsic vascular lesion
    Early aseptic necrosis
    Marrow involvement by tumor
- Early osteomyelitis
- Tumor
    Neuroblastoma
    Renal cell carcinoma
    Thyroid carcinoma
    Anaplastic tumors (e.g., reticulum cell sarcoma)

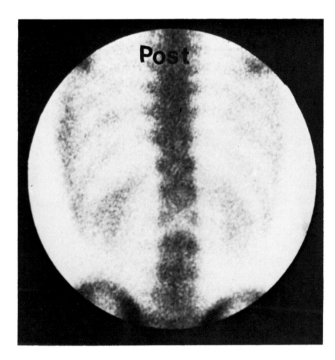

Figure 11–8. Cold lesion seen in the midportion of the lumbar spine, due to marrow involvement by embryonal cell carcinoma.

Figure 11–9. Decreased activity in the upper half of the thoracic spine due to radiation therapy. A liver–spleen scan performed the previous day accounts for hepatic activity. Multiple metastases are noted in the spine and pelvis. (A) Anterior. (B) Posterior.

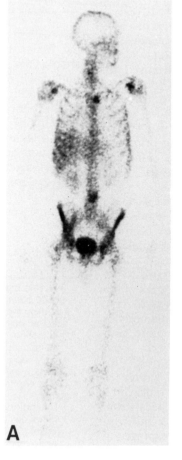

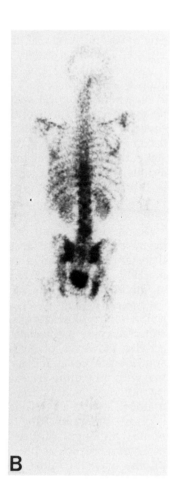

A

B

due to metastatic disease in over 80 percent of cases. They may occur if the tumor is extremely aggressive, if there is disruption of the blood supply to the bone, or if there is significant marrow involvement, particularly in a vertebral body (Fig. 11–8). When multiple adjacent bones have a decreased radionuclide accumulation, other etiologies such as radiation therapy should be considered (Fig. 11–9). Other causes of cold lesions include infarction (particularly in patients with sickle cell anemia) and aseptic necrosis.

Malignant Bone Tumors

The bone scan appearance of *osteogenic sarcoma* varies widely, depending on the tumor's vascularity and aggressiveness and upon the amount of neoplastic and reactive bone production. Only about 2 percent of these patients present with osseous lesions other than the primary. Exact assessment of tumor extent by bone scanning is often complicated by reactive hyperemia in the affected limb, which may produce increased activity in the entire extremity (Fig. 11–10A). In this

setting, computed tomography or magnetic resonance imaging may provide more exact information regarding tumor extent, particularly in soft tissues.

In the past, follow-up bone scans were not felt to be particularly worthwhile in patients with osteosarcoma, since pulmonary metastases almost always developed before osseous metastases. Aggressive chemotherapy, however, seems to be altering the natural history of osteosarcoma, and there are now reports of patients developing osseous metastases without visible pulmonary disease. In interpreting follow-up scans, care must be taken not to mistake postamputation reactive changes at the amputation site for tumor recurrence (Fig. 11–10B).

Ewing's sarcoma is a relatively common primary bone tumor. Up to 11 percent of patients present with osseous metastases (Fig. 11–11). Forty to fifty percent of patients with either Ewing's tumor or osteosarcoma develop osseous metastases within 2 years of presentation, and follow-up bone scans are recommended. Reactive hyperemia is not usually seen with Ewing's tumor.

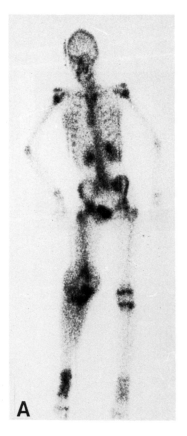 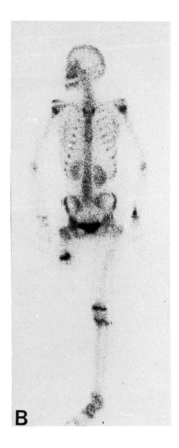

Figure 11–10. (A) Preamputation and (B) postamputation anterior view scans for osteogenic sarcoma of the distal right femur. (A) The scan demonstrates marked epiphyseal activity bilaterally, which is common in children; however, there is also markedly increased activity in the entire right lower extremity, probably due to hyperemia from the tumor. (B) The follow-up scan performed 2 months following amputation demonstrates activity in the bone consistent with healing of the amputation stump. The injection site for the follow-up scan was made over the left wrist.

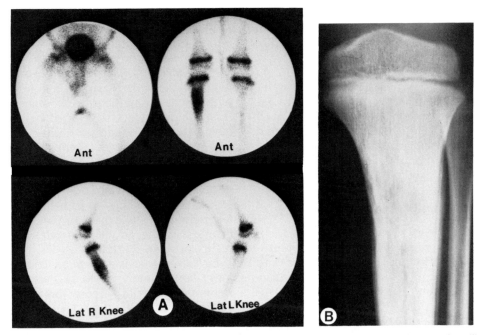

Figure 11–11. Ewing's sarcoma of the proximal right tibia. On the camera spot views of the lower extremities (A), there is marked epiphyseal activity due to the patient's age and soft tissue contamination by urine along the medial and posterior aspects of the left leg. (B) The radiograph demonstrates a mixed lytic and sclerotic lesion with periosteal reaction.

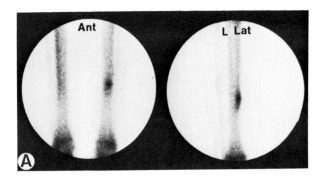

Figure 11–12. (A) Osteoid osteoma of the left mid tibia. The intense uptake is characteristic of these lesions. (B) Lateral tomogram demonstrates the cortical thickening, the lucent lesion, and the nidus.

Benign Osseous Neoplasms

Images obtained shortly after injection of bone scanning agents indicate that most malignant lesions are hyperemic and that most benign lesions have very little initial accumulation of radiopharmaceuticals. An early blood pool image may therefore be helpful in identifying benign lesions, since it may show little or no increased uptake. The major exception to this is in patients with osteoid osteoma (Fig. 11–12), who demonstrate intense activity at the site of the vascular nidus. Bone scans are often of value in detecting such lesions when they occur in difficult to radiograph sites such as the spine.

Soft Tissue Uptake

There may be visualization of activity in soft tissue structures on the bone scan. There are many possibilities to be considered when this is seen (Table 11–5). Soft tissue activity may be secondary to any process that evokes soft tissue calcification or infarction. However, the first and most obvious cause is surface contamination by urine or by the radionuclide during injection.

Soft tissue neoplasms or their metastases may calcify, resulting in soft tissue activity. Such tumors are usually breast cancer (Fig. 11–13), tumors of the gastrointestinal tract (Fig. 11–14) and ovary (particularly mucin-producing tumors), osteogenic sarcoma, and neuroblastoma. Pleural effusions or ascites secondary to such tumors may also be demonstrated on bone scans as diffusely increased activity in the chest or abdomen.

Other causes of soft tissue activity include (1) calcification in dystrophic soft tissues, such as occurs around joints in paraplegics, (2) tumorous as well as pulmonary calcification in patients with renal failure, and (3) dermatomyositis (Fig. 11–15). Calcific tendinitis, postoperative scars, chronic inflammatory change, amyloidosis, and uterine fibroids also may be responsible for soft tissue activity.

In addition, areas of infarction in muscle, brain, heart, and so on (Fig. 11–16) may often be demonstrated on the bone scan. Hyperparathyroidism or renal failure may cause localized activity within the walls of the gastrointestinal tract (particularly in the stomach), lungs, and kidneys, presumably due to excessive parathormone production and sub-

Table 11–5. CAUSES OF EXTRA-OSSEOUS ACTIVITY ON BONE SCANS

- Generalized
  - Poor radiopharmaceutical preparation
  - Renal failure
  - Chronic iron overload
- Localized
  - Injection sites
  - Kidney (normal)
  - Urine contamination
  - Instrument contamination
  - Tissue infarction
  - Myositis ossificans
  - Polymyositis
  - Pulmonary calcification or ossification
  - Hematoma
  - Hyperparathyroidism
  - Steroids (breast uptake)
  - Sites of IM iron injection or calcium injection extravasation
  - Chemotherapy (kidneys)
  - Radiotherapy treatment portals
  - Tumoral calcinosis, dystrophic, and metastatic calcification
  - Calcific tendinitis
  - Free pertechnetate
  - Obstructed kidney or ureter
  - Amyloidosis
  - Abscess/effusion
  - Tumors
    - Breast
    - Ovary (especially mucinous)
    - Gastrointestinal (especially colon)
    - Neuroblastoma
    - Endometrial carcinoma
    - Uterine fibroids
    - Gastrointestinal lymphoma
    - Malignant ascites
    - Hepatic metastases

Adapted from Heck LL: Gamuts: Extra-osseous localization of phosphate bone agents. Semin Nucl Med 10(3):311–312, 1980.

sequent calcium deposition (Fig. 11–17). Infiltration of skeletal and cardiac muscle, liver, and skin by amyloid can likewise cause soft tissue activity. Calcification in regions of trauma, secondary to calcifying hematomas or myositis ossificans, has also been reported as a cause of soft tissue accumulation of bone-imaging radiopharmaceuticals.

An increase in soft tissue or blood pool activity is seen in some patients receiving chemotherapy or with chronic iron overload. Delayed blood clearance and overall increased soft tissue activity are to be expected in patients with renal failure. Poor skeletal uptake and markedly increased renal activity have been reported in patients with thalas-

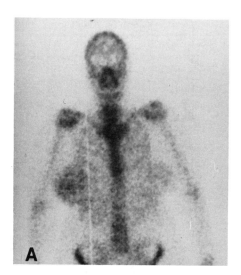
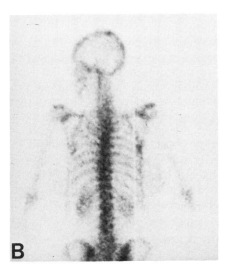

Figure 11–13. Bone scan demonstrating relatively increased soft tissue activity in the right breast due to a large calcified breast carcinoma. (A) Anterior. (B) Posterior.

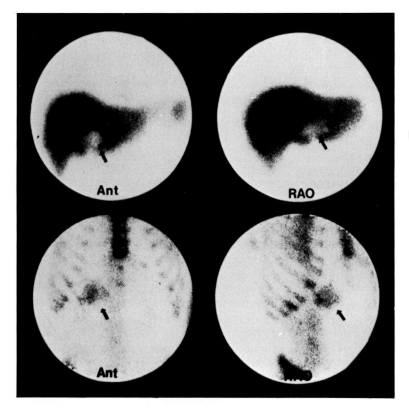

Figure 11–14. Focal liver uptake of bone scan agent. Images from a sulfur colloid liver scan (top row) show a focal lesion in the medial aspect of the left lobe of the liver. This area is clearly seen to concentrate the technetium 99m bone scanning agent on a subsequent bone scan (bottom row) in this patient with adenocarcinoma of the colon.

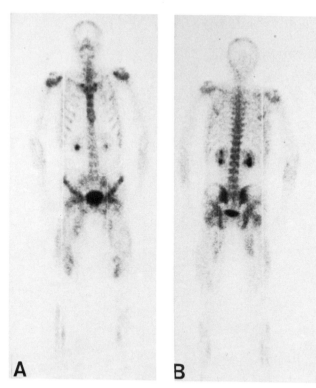

Figure 11–15. Soft tissue activity in both lower extremities in a patient with dermatomyositis. (A) Anterior. (B) Posterior.

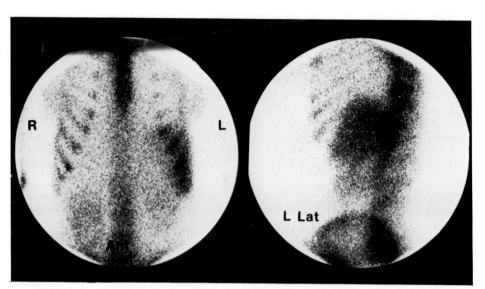

Figure 11–16. Selected images from a diphosphonate bone scan demonstrate increased activity in the spleen in a patient with sickle cell disease. This activity has been attributed to ongoing splenic infarctions.

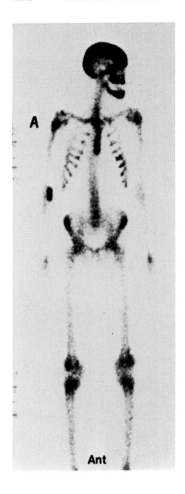

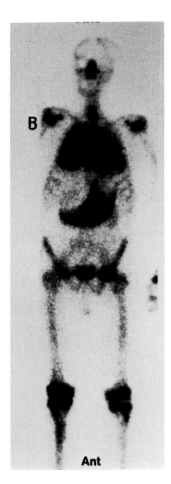

Figure 11–17. Anterior bone scans in two different patients with hyperparathyroidism. (A) The first case demonstrates a typical superscan with lack of significant renal activity and with increased activity diffusely throughout the skeleton. Of note is the particularly increased activity in the calvarium, facial bones, and mandible that has been described in patients with hyperparathyroidism. (B) A second patient with hyperparathyroidism demonstrates not only a superscan appearance but also significantly increased activity in the lungs and stomach compatible with so-called metastatic calcification that may be found in certain soft tissue organs in severe cases of this disease.

semia major and in patients receiving certain kinds of chemotherapy (Fig. 11–18). Some reported causes of increased hepatic and renal activity on bone scans are given in Tables 11–6 and 11–7. Soft tissue changes can be noted on bone scans following mastectomy. The ribs are usually more clearly seen on the mastectomy side, probably since there is less overlying soft tissue.

Trauma

The time of initial appearance of an area of increased activity at the site of a fracture is in part dependent on the patient's age. Occasionally older and debilitated or osteoporotic patients may not show increased activity for several days, although the test is sensitive enough in the first 24 hours to warrant early scanning (Fig. 11–19). Normally, however, 80 percent of bone scans are abnormal by 24 hours after a fracture and 95 percent by 72 hours. The return of the bone

scan appearance to normal following fracture or surgical trauma may also be age-dependent. Fractures and even craniotomy defects in older patients may be visible on bone scans for several years. Very few fractures of weight-bearing bones will have returned to a normal scan appearance within 5 months, whereas approximately 90 percent will be normal within 2 years. More intense and prolonged uptake has been demonstrated in those fractures that have had an open reduction or fixation device applied.

The bone scan appearance after fracture may be divided into acute, subacute, and healing phases. The acute phase usually lasts from 3 to 4 weeks and demonstrates a generalized diffuse increase in radionuclide activity about the fracture site. The subacute phase follows and lasts 2 to 3 months, with the activity more localized and intense. The healing phase may occur over a much longer period and is accompanied by a gradual decline in intensity of radiotracer activity. The

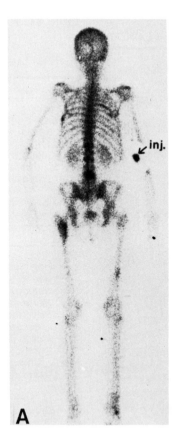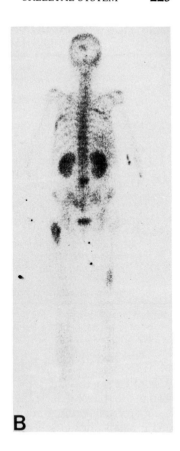

Figure 11-18. Posterior bone scans in a patient on vincristine chemotherapy for osseous metastases. (A) The initial scan demonstrates the osseous metastases. (B) The follow-up scan 2 months later shows markedly decreased bone activity and relatively increased activity in both kidneys.

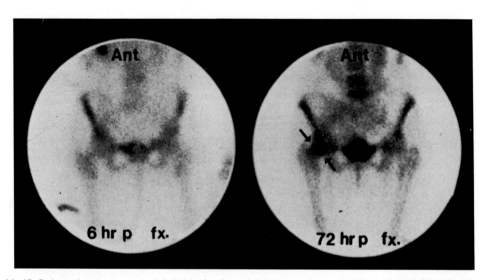

Figure 11-19. Delayed appearance of right hip fracture. A bone scan image of the pelvis obtained at 6 hours post-trauma in an elderly patient with a suspected right hip fracture demonstrates no significant abnormality. However, a repeat study performed 72 hours post-trauma clearly demonstrates a focal band of increased activity in the right femoral neck compatible with a nondisplaced fracture (arrow).

Table 11–6. HEPATIC UPTAKE OF ^{99m}Tc PHOSPHATE COMPOUNDS

- *Common*
    Artifactual—after ^{99m}Tc sulfur colloid study (diffuse activity)
    Apparent—due to abdominal wall or rib uptake (focal activity)
    Metastatic carcinoma (focal)
      Colon
      Breast
      Squamous cell carcinoma of esophagus
      Oat cell carcinoma of lung
      Malignant melanoma
- *Uncommon*
    Diffuse hepatic necrosis (diffuse activity)
    Elevated serum Al^{+3} (diffuse activity)
- *Rare*
    Cholangiocarcinoma (focal activity)
    Improper preparation of radiopharmaceutical causing microcolloid formation (diffuse activity)
    Amyloidosis (diffuse activity)

Adapted from Hansen S, Stadalnick RC: Gamut: Liver uptake of Tc-pyrophosphate. Semin Nucl Med 12(1):89–90, 1982. With permission.

time after fracture at which the bone scan becomes abnormal is shown in Table 11–8. The percentage returning to normal at various times is shown in Table 11–9.

Subtle trauma, such as that from stress fractures, is often difficult to visualize on a plain radiograph. Often such fractures are not visualized for 7 to 10 days, by which time interval decalcification has occurred about the fracture site. On the other hand, radionuclide bone scans are frequently positive at the time of clinical presentation and offer a means of early diagnosis and treatment (Fig. 11–20).

Because fractures may be identified by bone scans as early as 24 hours after occurrence in young patients, bone imaging has been useful in the assessment of suspected battered children. Failure to find areas of increased activity is useful in excluding the diagnosis of child-battering. In elderly patients, the bone scan may not show the fracture for 7 to 10 days. However, a negative bone scan obtained a week after trauma effectively excludes an occult fracture. SPECT scanning may be useful for demonstration of occult fractures, particularly in the spine (Fig. 11–21).

Another use of bone scanning in trauma is in the assessment of hip prostheses. In the initial postsurgical period, activity is noted around the prosthesis, although this usually rapidly decreases and returns to normal

Table 11–7. INCREASED UPTAKE OF TECHNETIUM 99m LABELED BONE IMAGING AGENTS IN THE KIDNEYS

FOCAL

- *Common*
    Urinary tract obstruction
    Normal variant
- *Uncommon*
    Metastatic calcification (breast cancer, poorly differentiated lymphocytic lymphoma)
    Radiation therapy to the kidney
- *Rare*
    Renal carcinoma
    Renal metastasis from carcinoma of the lung

DIFFUSE

- *Common*
    Urinary tract obstruction
    Unknown
- *Uncommon*
    Metastatic calcification
    Malignant (transitional cell carcinoma of bladder, malignant melanoma)
    Benign (hyperparathyroidism)
    Chemotherapy with cyclophosphamide, vincristine, and doxorubicin
    Thalassemia major
- *Rare*
    Multiple myeloma
    Crossed renal ectopia
    Iron overload
    Administration of sodium diatrizoate after the injection of ^{99m}Tc phosphate compound
    Paroxysmal nocturnal hemoglobinuria
    Acute pyelonephritis

Reprinted with minor modifications from Siddiqui AR: Gamut: Increased uptake of technetium-99m labeled bone imaging agents in the kidneys. Semin Nucl Med 12(1):101–102, 1982. With permission.

within 6 months. Persistent activity at the trochanter and the tip of the prosthesis may be taken as an indication of loosening (77 percent specific and 100 percent sensitive) (Fig. 11–22). More generalized activity may be indicative of osteomyelitis. If there is a question of infection, a gallium scan may be

Table 11–8. TIME AFTER FRACTURE AT WHICH BONE SCAN BECOMES ABNORMAL

TIME AFTER FRACTURE	PERCENTAGE ABNORMAL	
	Patients Under 65 Years of Age	*All Patients*
1 Day	95	80
3 Days	100	95
1 Week	100	98

Table 11–9. TIME AFTER FRACTURE AT WHICH BONE SCAN RETURNS TO NORMAL

FRACTURE SITE	PERCENTAGE NORMAL AT			MINIMUM TIME TO RETURN TO NORMAL
	1 Year	2 Years	3 Years	
Vertebrae	59	90	97	7 Months
Long bones	64	91	97	6 Months
Ribs	79	93	100	5 Months

Tables 11–8 and 11–9 are adapted from Matin P: Bone scintigraphy in the diagnosis and management of traumatic injury. Semin Nucl Med 13(2):104–122, 1983.

useful, because a normal scan probably excludes osteomyelitis as the cause of symptoms. Post-surgical heterotopic calcification may be visualized on bone scans, but this usually is lateral to the acetabulum.

Bone scans have also been employed in the assessment of *aseptic necrosis.* Avascular necrosis is often due to trauma, but it may be caused by a variety of etiologies, such as steroid administration, vascular diseases, or others. Generally, a decrease in tracer activity is identified first in the affected area. This is followed by a hyperemic or repair phase, which is characterized by an increase in activity (Fig. 11–23). Correlation with the x-rays is mandatory to accurately diagnose aseptic necrosis. If properly performed, bone scans are almost as accurate as magnetic resonance imaging for this diagnosis.

Some laboratories have used bone scans to demonstrate the vascularity or viability of the femoral head in patients with femoral neck fractures. Either phosphate radiopharmaceuticals or sulfur colloid scanning may be used to evaluate blood supply. The usual procedure is to compare the normal side with the suspected abnormal side. For such studies, high-quality images may be obtained only by using a pinhole collimator, which provides the detail needed for accurate diagnosis.

Radiation therapy constitutes a form of calculated iatrogenic trauma. Following fractionated radiation doses of 4000 to 5000 rad (40 to 50 Gy) to bone, there is a decrease in

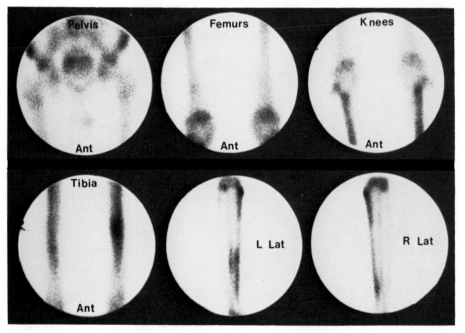

Figure 11–20. Multiple views of the lower extremities in a 32-year-old male jogger. The scans demonstrate increased activity anteriorly in both tibias consistent with shin splints, as well as a stress fracture in the midportion of the left tibia.

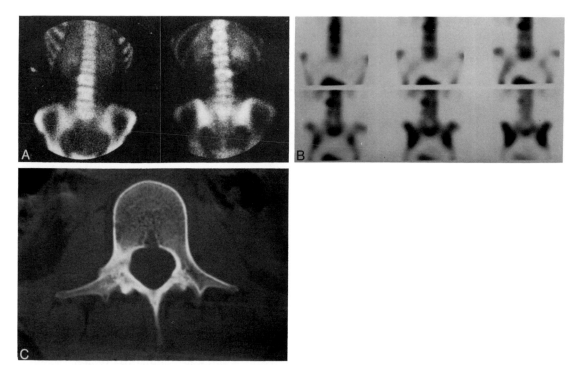

Figure 11–21. (A) A 15-year-old female acrobat with back pain and normal lumbar radiographs had a referral for a bone scan. Planar scintigrams of the lumbar spine in the anterior and posterior projections that show a small area of increased activity along the right lateral aspect of the L4 vertebra. (B,C) Coronal reformatted images from anterior to posterior and triangulation views show the intense activity convincingly centered in a pedicle. (From Hartshorne MF: SPECT orthopedic applications. In Mettler FA Jr (ed): Radionuclide Bone Imaging and Densitometry. New York, Churchill Livingstone, 1988.)

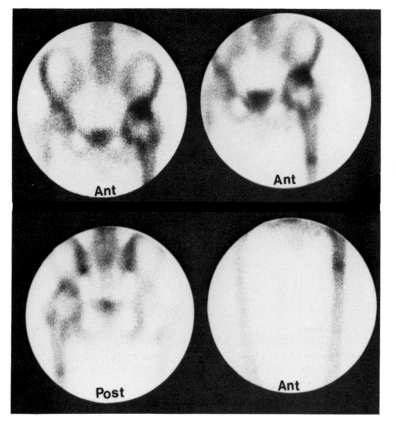

Figure 11–22. Hip prosthesis with loosening. The activity at the distal tip of the prosthesis is increased. The activity about the region of the acetabulum may be secondary to heterotopic calcification.

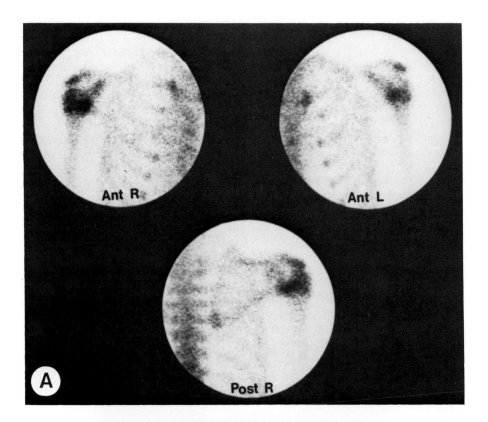

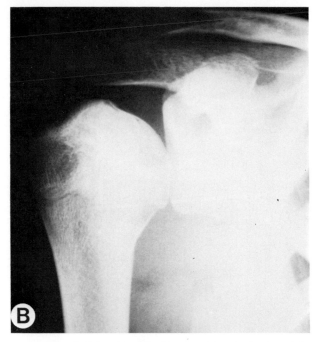

Figure 11–23. Aseptic necrosis of the right shoulder in a 23-year-old male on steroid therapy. (A) The bone scan images show relatively increased activity of the right shoulder, indicating that the aseptic necrosis is in the healing phase. The left shoulder shows some increased activity in the region of the epiphysis, which is normal. (B) The radiograph of the right shoulder demonstrates the deformity and sclerosis seen in aseptic necrosis.

localized vascular patency within the first month. The vascularity may return to near normal in about 6 months and then is reduced again due to endothelial proliferation and arteriolar narrowing. An abrupt geometric area of decreased osseous activity should raise the suspicion of skeletal trauma due to radiation therapy.

Reflex sympathetic dystrophy syndrome (RSDS) consists of pain, tenderness, swelling, and vasomotor instability. The etiology is obscure but it is usually precipitated by trauma, myocardial infarction, or neurologic abnormality. The most common variants are Sudeck's atrophy and shoulder–hand syndrome. Radiographically, there is usually osteoporosis. Classically three-phase bone scanning demonstrates increased blood flow to the affected limb with enhanced asymmetric periarticular radionuclide activity. Diffusely increased juxta-articular activity about all joints of the hand or foot on delayed images may be the most sensitive indicator of RSDS.

Osteomyelitis Versus Cellulitis

Early involvement of the bone by an inflammatory disease process is often difficult to detect on plain radiographs. The earliest radiographic signs of osteomyelitis are nonspecific and include demineralization and loss of the soft tissue fascial margins. At this stage scanning with radionuclides often demonstrates strikingly increased activity (Fig. 11–24), both in the soft tissues and the underlying bony structures. However, if soft tissue inflammation is a prominent feature, it may be difficult to distinguish primary bone involvement from bone activity secondary to the hyperemia that accompanies simple cellulitis.

To differentiate osteomyelitis from cellulitis, a radionuclide angiogram and an immediate blood pool image should be obtained following injection, and routine images should be taken at 2 to 3 hours. Such three-phase scintigraphy has been widely advocated to improve bone scan specificity. Cel-

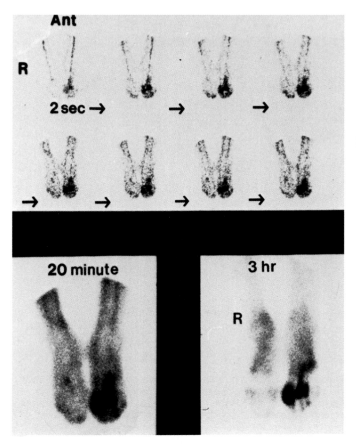

Figure 11–24. Three-phase bone scan and osteomyelitis. The first phase (perfusion) of the scan demonstrates increased perfusion to the digits of the left foot with subsequent increased activity in the first and third metatarsal regions seen during the second phase (blood pool) of the study. An image from the final (delayed) phase of the scan demonstrates intense focally increased activity in the areas of bony involvement. The three phases considered together are compatible with a diagnosis of osteomyelitis.

lulitis presents as diffusely increased soft tissue and bone activity on early images, with decreasing activity on later scans. Osteomyelitis, on the other hand, demonstrates continued accumulation of activity that becomes more focal on delayed scans. In patients with osteomyelitis, focally increased blood flow is seen on the radionuclide angiogram. The absence of such a finding casts serious doubt on a diagnosis of osteomyelitis. Although scintigraphy is extremely sensitive, some false negative scans have been reported early in the disease, perhaps secondary to disruption of the blood supply to the bone. If osteomyelitis is strongly suspected on a clinical basis and if the radionuclide bone scan is negative, a gallium scan may prove useful. When the gallium 67 citrate study is normal, osteomyelitis is very unlikely, but if the uptake of gallium exceeds the uptake of bone agent in the same location, osteomyelitis is probable. The use of labeled white blood cells in the evaluation of osteomyelitis is discussed in Chapter 13.

Benign Non-neoplastic Disease

Paget's disease characteristically displays a marked increase in activity in the involved bones (Fig. 11–25). This is due in part to the greatly increased regional blood flow. While the lytic phase of the disease is often difficult to appreciate on radiographs, it is almost always represented by increased activity on the bone scan. The dense sclerotic lesions seen late in the disease may demonstrate varying degrees of increased activity, and some "burned out" lesions may show normal activity. At some institutions, serial quantitative bone scans employing computer assessment of bone activity are performed to evaluate response of Paget's disease to therapy.

Fibrous dysplasia is another benign disease of bone that may present as single (Fig. 11–26) or multiple areas of increased activity. Both polyostotic fibrous dysplasia and Paget's disease are sometimes confused with multifocal metastatic disease, although the distribution and radiographic presentation of lesions are frequently characteristic.

Bone scanning may be used as a method for documenting the early presence of *arthritis* as well as assessing serial changes in the disease (Fig. 11–27). The bone scan can often delineate the extent of disease activity and symmetry of change better than radiographs. Both ^{99m}Tc pertechnetate and the phosphate bone imaging agents have been used for arthritis imaging. Technetium 99m pertechnetate is probably more specific for regions of synovial inflammation because it is able to diffuse across the synovial surface and into joint effusions, whereas phosphate compounds localize primarily in adjacent bone. Bone scanning for arthritis is limited by lack of specificity, and radiologic correlation of results is mandatory. Quantitative scintigraphic evaluation of clinically inaccessible joints, such as the sacroiliac joints, has been attempted, but has not proven particularly useful to clinicians.

Bone Marrow Scanning

Bone marrow scans can be used to identify marrow replacement by tumor (Fig. 11–28), to define abnormal marrow distribution or locate active sites for marrow biopsy, and occasionally to assess femoral head vascular supply. They may be obtained utilizing either the reticuloendothelial or hematologic functions of the marrow. In the latter instance, iron 59 may be used, but it is difficult to image due to its high photon energy. The most common agent is ^{99m}Tc sulfur colloid, which localizes in marrow because the particles are phagocytized by the resident reticuloendothelial cells. Although the correlation between the hematologic and reticuloendothelial function of the marrow is felt to be generally good, if accurate erythroid studies are needed an iron tracer should be used.

In a sulfur colloid marrow scan, the liver and spleen may need to be shielded during imaging. In the adult, the marrow is usually restricted to the ribs, sternum, vertebral bodies, pelvis, and proximal femurs. In children, the normal marrow extends more peripherally into the extremities.

Bone Mineral Measurements

The accurate measurement of bone mineral density using noninvasive methods can be of value in the detection and evaluation of primary and secondary causes of decreased bone mass. This includes primary osteoporosis and secondary disorders such as hyperparathyroidism, osteomalacia, multiple mye-

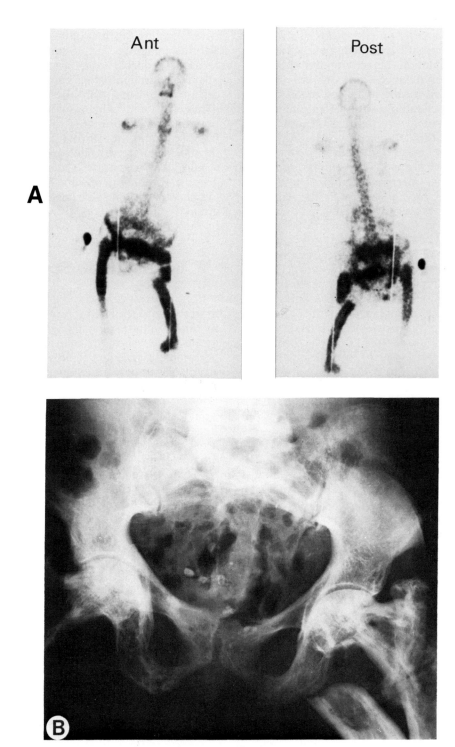

Figure 11–25. Paget's disease with a pathologic fracture. (A) The bone scan demonstrates intense uptake in the affected areas. Such changes are most common in the pelvis, proximal femurs, and skull. (B) The radiograph of the pelvis demonstrates the markedly abnormal trabecular pattern, as well as fracture of the left proximal femur.

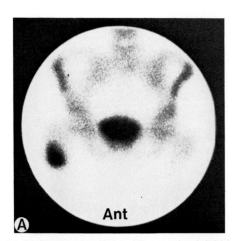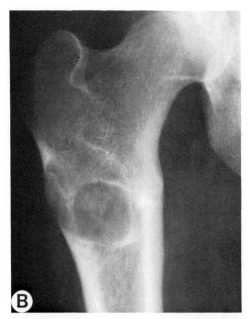

Figure 11–26. Fibrous dysplasia of the proximal right femur. (A) The anterior view of the pelvis shows markedly increased activity in the metaphysis of the proximal right femur. (B) The radiograph shows a well-demarcated expansile and lucent lesion.

loma, diffuse metastases, and glucocorticoid therapy or intrinsic excess.

By far the largest patient population is that encompassed by primary osteoporosis. Osteoporosis is an age-related disorder characterized by decreased bone mass and by increased susceptibility to fractures in the absence of other recognizable causes of bone loss. Primary osteoporosis is generally subdivided into type 1 or postmenopausal osteoporosis, which is related to estrogen deprivation, and type 2 or senile osteoporosis, which occurs secondary to aging.

Primary osteoporosis is a common clinical disorder and a major public health problem because of the significant number of related bone fractures occurring annually. Because the risk of vertebral and femoral neck fractures rises dramatically as bone mineral density falls below 1 gm/cm^2, fracture risk in individual patients may be estimated. Furthermore, in estrogen-deficient women, bone mineral density values may be used to make rational decisions about hormone replacement therapy and as follow-up in assessing the success of such treatment.

Risk factors for osteoporosis in women include being postmenopausal (especially prematurely), being of Caucasian or Asian race, having a positive family history, being of short stature with a small skeleton, having

a lifelong low calcium intake, being inactive, and being nulliparous. In addition, there are a number of other medically related risk factors such as bowel resection and steroid or anticonvulsive therapy. On the contrary, certain characteristics such as obesity are associated with a lower incidence of osteoporosis. In some young males, the disease has been related to alcohol and tobacco abuse.

A number of methods have been devised in order to permit the accurate and reproducible determination of bone mineral content. Plain radiographs generally require a loss of 30 percent or more of bone mineral in order for a change in density to be appreciated and are thus insensitive for the detection of the disease. Other radiographic techniques such as radiogrammetry and radiographic photodensitometry represent improvements but lack sufficient accuracy or reproducibility to be of widespread value.

Quantitative computed tomography (QCT) can be performed with about 10 percent of the absorbed dose that is usually utilized for routine diagnostic imaging, with measurements generally obtained through the centers of the L-1 through L-4 vertebral bodies. Unfortunately, this technique is not readily applicable to the femoral neck and is relatively costly.

Radionuclide photon absorptiometry using

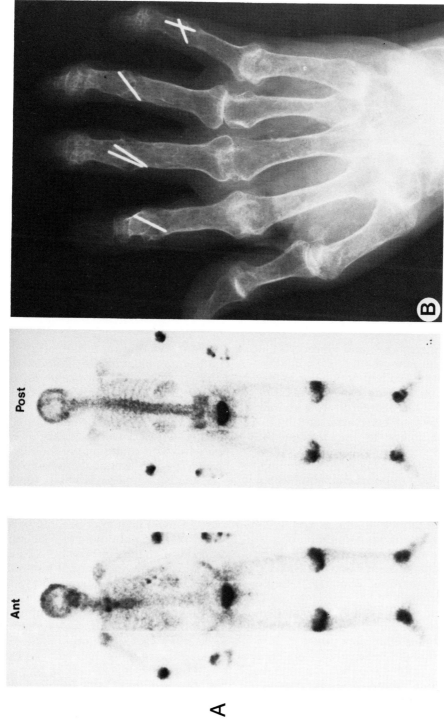

Figure 11–27. Severe rheumatoid arthritis. (A) Bone scans show marked symmetric activity about the joints. (B) A radiograph of the right hand shows postoperative changes as well as loss of joint spaces.

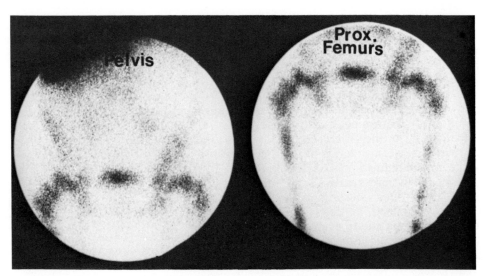

Figure 11–28. Marrow scans in a patient with carcinoma of the prostate. Multiple photon-deficient areas compatible with tumor replacement are identified in the marrow.

either single photon or dual photon technique appears to be a reliable and cost-effective method for the noninvasive determination of bone mineral. Both single photon absorptiometry (SPA) and dual photon absorptiometry (DPA) utilize a highly collimated beam of photons that pass through the soft tissue and bony components of the body to be detected on the opposite side by a scintillation detector. Because absorption by the body part examined (primarily by bone mineral) attenuates the photon beam, the intensity of the beam exiting the body part is indirectly proportional to the density of the bony structure being evaluated. The intensity of the exit beam is then compared with exit beam intensity from standard phantoms of known density so that a bone mineral density can be determined.

Because SPA uses a monoenergetic beam of low-energy photons, it is generally used only for small body parts such as the distal radius or calcaneus. In addition, because only a single energy of photon is employed, the method is incapable of correcting for varying soft tissue attenuation. Thus, the distal limb being examined must be surrounded by or immersed in a tissue equivalent material (such as a water bath) of known geometry so that the soft tissue shape of the limb with its varying thickness does not interfere with the measurements. Results are given in units of gm/cm or, if normalized, in gm/cm^2. SPA generally employs an iodine 125 photon source that emits a 27 keV characteristic x-ray. SPA may have significant repositioning errors, and the iodine 125 sources must be replaced every 6 months.

In contrast, the DPA beam consists of photons of two discrete energies, which obviates the need for assumptions about soft tissue shape and attenuation. It also allows for evaluation of thicker body parts and bones involving complex geometry, such as the femoral neck and the spine.

The most common photon source is gadolinium 153 with emissions from europium 153 and gadolinium in the range of 44 to 100 keV. The source has a useful life of 13 to 15 months. DPA has accuracy rates between 94 and 98 percent and variation of 2 to 4 percent in terms of reproducibility. The absorbed dose from SPA is approximately 5 mrad (50 μGy) and from DPA is 15 mrad (150 μGy).

When the spine is examined using DPA, the hips are flexed to flatten the normal lumbar lordosis. When scans of the femoral neck are performed, the femur should be in slight internal rotation. The results are expressed in gm/cm^2. Falsely elevated bone mineral content when evaluating the spine may result from marked aortic calcification, hypertrophic degenerative disease, compression fractures, calcium within the gastrointestinal tract, renal lithiasis, bone grafts, focal sclerotic bone lesions, or recent intake of aluminum-containing antacids. Falsely low bone mineral results may be obtained in patients who have had a laminectomy or who have scoliosis or lytic bone lesions. Most of the time these problems can be identified from the plain radiograph, which usually is obtained prior to the test.

The use of bone mineral measurement has been controversial. Some of this is due to the wide variation of measurements in the normal population. Also, the criteria for selecting the optimal skeletal site for evaluation have not been well-defined, since bone mineral loss does not progress at the same rate at different body sites. In any case, the method can be utilized to determine the presence of osteopenia and to evaluate effectiveness of a therapeutic maneuver by employing serial scans in which the patient acts as her own control. A normal result, or a bone mineral content in the upper portion of the normal range, represents patients in whom therapy may not be needed.

Suggested Readings

Freeman LM, Blaufox MD (eds): Bone density studies. Semin Nucl Med 17(4):283–333, 1987

Freeman LM, Blaufox MD (eds): Nuclear orthopedics. Semin Nucl Med 18(2):78–168, 1987

Hall FM, Davis MA, Barand DT: Bone mineral screening for osteoporosis. N Engl J Med 316:212–214, 1987

Freeman LM, Blaufox MD (eds): Nuclear oncology. Part I. Semin Nucl Med 14(4):277–286, 1984

Mettler FA Jr (ed): Contemporary Issues in Nuclear Imaging. vol 4. Radionuclide bone imaging and densitometry. New York, Churchill Livingstone, 1988

CHAPTER 12

Genitourinary System

Radionuclide evaluation of the genitourinary system includes the imaging of structural abnormalities as well as making semiquantitative estimates of renal perfusion and function. With the widespread use of ultrasound and computed tomography, the evaluation of renal anatomy by nuclear techniques is rapidly diminishing and the role of nuclear renal imaging is becoming more confined to functional analysis.

Indications for renal scanning include sensitivity to radiographic contrast material, assessment of renal blood flow, and differential or quantitative function of both native and transplanted kidneys. Nuclear techniques have also proved of value in evaluating functional problems such as ureteral or renal pelvic obstruction, assessment of vesicoureteral reflux, and serial evaluation of postoperative patients. Some previous indications for renal scanning, such as assessment of renal size, evaluation of renal masses, and determination of the etiology of nonvisualizing kidneys by excretory urography, have generally been replaced by ultrasound as the initial procedure of choice.

Physiology

In order to understand renal imaging, it is important to briefly review the physiology of the kidneys.

The excretory function of the kidneys consists of two primary mechanisms: passive filtration through the glomerulus and active secretion by the tubules. These processes are tempered by varying reabsorption of certain substances by the tubules. The glomerulus acts as a semi-permeable membrane, allowing only those compounds of a relatively small molecular size to pass through. Larger materials such as proteins do not pass through the glomerulus but may reach the urine by tubular secretion.

The rate at which a particular substance is cleared (C) from the plasma by these mechanisms is determined by utilizing a relationship

$$C = \frac{UV}{P}$$

where U and P represent the urine and plasma concentrations of the substance and V is the rate of urine production in milliliters per minute. The model compound for determining glomerular filtration is inulin, which is freely filtered at the glomerulus and is neither secreted nor reabsorbed by the tubules. Diethylenetriamine-pentacetic acid (DTPA) and other chelates are also cleared by glomerular filtration and may be used as a measure of glomerular function. The normal glomerular filtration rate is 125 ml/min. The compound usually utilized for evaluation of renal tubular secretion is iodohippurate sodium (Hippuran). Approximately 80 percent of Hippuran is eliminated by the tubular secretion pathway, although a very rapid component (approximately 20 percent) reaches the urine through glomerular filtration. In nuclear radiology practice, DTPA tagged with ^{99m}Tc and ^{123}I or ^{131}I labeled Hippuran (orthoiodohippurate) are routinely employed for assessment of glomerular and tubular function, respectively.

Radiopharmaceuticals

The ^{99m}Tc labeled agents commonly used for renal imaging are DTPA, 2,3-dimercaptosuccinic acid (DMSA), and glucoheptonate (Table 12–1). DTPA is normally administered in doses of 10 to 20 mCi (370 to 740 MBq).

Table 12–1. RADIOPHARMACEUTICAL AGENTS FOR RENAL IMAGING

RADIO-PHARMA-CEUTICAL	USUAL DOSE	ROUTE OF ADMINIS-TRATION	PHYSICAL HALF-LIFE	TIME TO IMAGING	ABSORBED DOSE ESTIMATE (rad/mCi)*			REMARKS
					Whole Body	Gonads	Other	
99mTc DTPA	10–20 mCi (370–740 MBq)	IV	6 hr	0–2 hr	0.01–0.02	0.01–0.04	Kidneys (0.03–0.30) Bladder† (0.07–0.60)	Renal dose with obstruction may reach 1.40 rad/mCi. Shelf life 8 hr after preparation
99mTc glucohepto-nate	10–20 mCi (370–740 MBq)	IV	6 hr	0–4 hr	0.01	0.004–0.007	Kidneys (0.15–0.30)	6–8 hr shelf life after preparation
99mTc DMSA	1–5 mCi (37–185 MBq)	IV	6 hr	0–6 hr	0.02	0.01–0.2	Kidneys† (0.55–0.80) Renal cortex (0.56–1.40)	30-min shelf life after preparation
131I O-hippurate	0.1–0.4 mCi (3.7–14.8 MBq)	IV	8 days	0–3 hr	0.03–0.20	0.02–0.10	Kidneys (0.03–0.20) Bladder (2.05–10.00) Thyroid† (10.00–30.00)	Renal dose may reach 13.0 rad/mCi in ob-structed states.
99mTc-mertiatide	5–10 mCi	IV	6 hr	0–1 hr	0.007	0.02–0.03	Kidneys (0.02) Bladder (0.48)	

*To obtain absorbed dose in mGy/MBq, divide values by 3.7.
†Indicates critical organ.

The DTPA complex is useful for both evaluation of renal perfusion as well as renal and urinary tract imaging. A small amount (approximately 5 to 10 percent) is plasma-bound; therefore, it tends to slightly underestimate the glomerular filtration rate. About 90 percent of DTPA is filtered by simple exchange or diffusion into the urine within 4 hours; therefore, excretory function may be measured with serial gamma camera images. 99mTc DTPA is sometimes used for studying renal anatomy, although because of its rapid clearance, it is far from an ideal agent for demonstrating intraparenchymal renal lesions. 99mTc pertechnetate also can be used to examine renal perfusion but is otherwise not useful for imaging the kidneys or urinary tract, since 85 percent of the filtered activity is reabsorbed by the tubules and interfering secretion into the bowel is rapid.

99mTc glucoheptonate is a labeled carbohydrate with renal cortical uptake as well as glomerular filtration. It is quite stable and may be used for up to 5 hours following preparation. Thirteen percent of the injected dose is retained in the kidneys, and 40 percent is cleared through urine at 1 hour. Early camera images demonstrate the renal cortex and the collecting system, although the renal cortex remains well visualized even at 2 to 4 hours. The dose of glucoheptonate is normally 10 to 20 mCi (370 to 740 MBq).

99mTc DMSA is slowly cleared from the blood and concentrates in the renal cortex; 42 percent of the injected dose remains in the renal cortex at 6 hours. DMSA is of particular value when high-resolution images of the renal cortex are needed and when there is no need to identify abnormalities in the ureters or bladder. DMSA localizes by binding to the sulfhydryl groups in the proximal renal tubules. Only 10 percent of the injected dose is excreted in the urine during the first several hours. The dose is normally 1 to 5 mCi (37 to 185 MBq). The radiation dose to the kidneys with DMSA is high, since there is a long effective half-life of the radiopharmaceutical in the kidneys. Another disadvantage of 99mTc DMSA is its 30-minute shelf life after preparation.

Excretion function studies are best performed with orthoiodohippurate tagged with radioiodine. As mentioned previously, this compound is excreted mostly by tubular secretion (80 percent) and to a much lesser extent by glomerular filtration (20 percent). Clearance measurements of this radiopharmaceutical reflect effective renal plasma flow. 131I Hippuran studies follow the dynamic perfusion or glomerular studies because the photopeak of 131I (364 keV) is much higher than that of 99mTc. Although the 131I Hippuran complex is stable, some authors recommend treatment prior to such examinations with potassium iodide, in order to minimize thyroid radiation from unbound [131]I. This is usually less than 1 percent in commercial preparations.

Recently a technetium labeled agent has been synthesized as a substitute for [131]I Hippuran—[99m]Tc-mercaptoacetyltriglycine (mertiatide or MAG3). It is cleared predominantly by the proximal tubules and acts very much like Hippuran, although it produces much better images. MAG3 is not metabolized by the body. It has a lower extraction efficiency than Hippuran, but accurate measurements of effective renal plasma flow (ERPF) can be made.

Renal Imaging Techniques

Functional imaging of the kidneys may be divided into assessment of blood flow, parenchyma, and excretion. Normally, both kidneys can easily be imaged on a 12-inch diameter crystal with a parallel-hole collimator.

Evaluation of renal blood flow and function of native kidneys is performed from the pos-terior projection, while evaluation of transplant blood flow and function is performed from the anterior projection. Normally, a small bolus of high-activity, technetium-labeled radiopharmaceutical (most often ^{99m}Tc DTPA) is intravenously injected by the Oldendorf technique. The initial image is usually obtained as the bolus is visualized in the proximal abdominal aorta, with subsequent serial images being made every 1 to 5 seconds depending on the instrumentation available. A typical renal blood flow study is seen in Figure 12–1. The activity reaches the kidneys approximately 1 second after the bolus in the abdominal aorta passes the renal arteries. At the end of the dynamic images, a single blood pool scintigram is routinely obtained. If a computer is used, time–activity curves may be generated by flagging areas of interest, usually over the aorta and each kidney. Each of the bilateral renal curves may then be compared with the time–activity curve of the abdominal aorta to assess relative renal perfusion. When ^{99m}Tc DTPA is used, sequential static 3-minute images are then obtained over 15 minutes (Fig. 12–2).

Static parenchymal renal imaging is usually

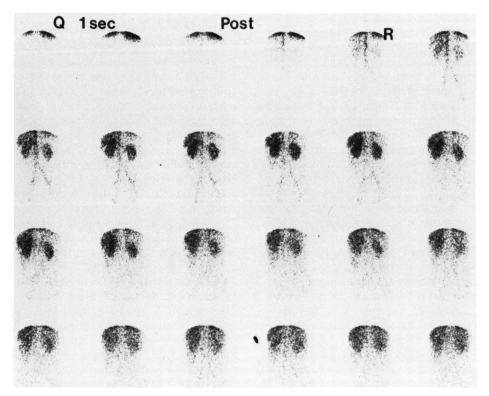

Figure 12–1. Normal renal blood flow study performed with ^{99m}Tc DTPA. There is symmetric and prompt visualization of both kidneys at essentially the same time that the abdominal aorta is visualized.

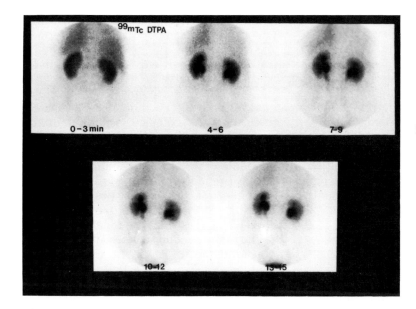

Figure 12–2. Normal ^{99m}Tc DTPA renogram performed over 15 minutes reflects glomerular function and collecting system patency.

performed for evaluation of space-occupying lesions such as tumors, cysts, infarcts, hematomas, and abscesses. These images of the renal cortex are generally taken using DMSA or glucoheptonate and a pinhole collimator.

For evaluation of renal tubular function, 200 to 400 μCi (7.4 to 14.8 MBq) of ^{131}I Hippuran are administered intravenously, and images are normally obtained with a parallel-hole, medium-energy collimator. Images are usually obtained at 2-minute intervals for a total of 30 minutes. A normal renogram is seen in Figure 12–3. Evaluation is similar to that of an intravenous pyelogram. The maximum parenchymal activity is seen at 3 to 5 minutes, with activity usually seen in the collecting system and bladder by 4 minutes. The initial rise in activity, although termed the "vascular phase," reflects not only renal blood flow but also various aspects of tubular function. Following a brief "concentration phase," the renal parenchymal activity should progressively decrease (excretion phase) after 5 minutes. Normally half of the parenchymal activity is gone every 7 to 10 minutes during the excretion phase. With a computer system, a time–activity curve may be generated reflecting the phases described above (Fig. 12–4). A dehydrated patient will demonstrate peak parenchymal activity slightly later and may have delayed clearance. Therefore, renograms should be performed only on normally hydrated patients so that false positive studies may be minimized.

Renal excretion also may be evaluated pharmacologically to maximize or further elucidate abnormalities. Examples of this procedure are the furosemide and captopril renograms, which will be discussed later in this chapter.

Imaging Techniques for the Ureters and Bladder

These procedures are normally done in children with recurrent infections to identify ureterovesicular reflux. One method is to catheterize the child under aseptic conditions and insert 0.5 to 1.0 mCi (18.5 to 37 MBq) of ^{99m}Tc pertechnetate or ^{99m}Tc sulfur colloid (in several milliliters of saline) into the bladder. Use of pertechnetate may be complicated by absorption through the bladder wall, but when this happens stomach activity is easily identified. A single image is obtained to localize the activity in the unfilled bladder. Saline is then introduced in the bladder until bladder capacity is reached. Serial 50,000- to 100,000-count images are obtained during saline instillation until the bladder is filled. The patient is next instructed to void and sequential images are obtained during voiding, at which time the renal areas are examined for activity. An easier method has been proposed in which a normal antegrade intravenous ^{99m}Tc DTPA study is performed. Once all significant activity has passed from the kidneys to bladder, the voiding images are obtained.

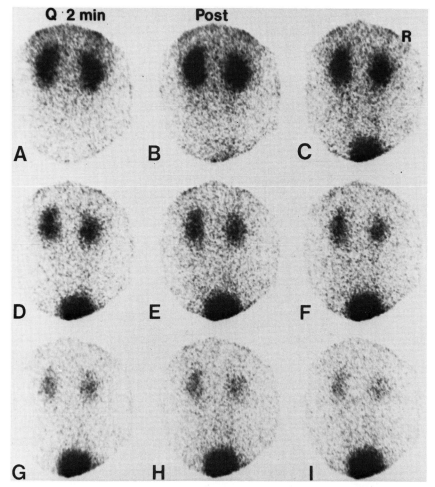

Figure 12–3. Normal renogram performed with ¹³¹I Hippuran. The examination demonstrates symmetric function with the maximum parenchymal phase at approximately 4 minutes (B). Very little activity is left in either the parenchyma or the collecting system by 18 minutes.

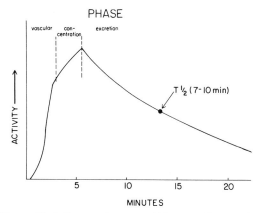

Figure 12–4. Phases of a normal Hippuran time–activity curve.

These methods of evaluation of ureteral reflux generate images that have significantly less resolution than a fluoroscopic voiding cystourethrogram. However, the radiation dose from the nuclear study is usually lower than that from the fluoroscopic or radiographic examinations. Radiographic examinations are also complicated by the proximity of the gonads and the nonphysiologic nature of opaque contrast media. The dose to the bladder wall with most technetium radiopharmaceuticals is usually less than 50 mrad (0.5 mGy). The sensitivity for detection of ureteral reflux by nuclear methods is probably greater than by radiographic methods, and information concerning volume of reflux into the upper tracts also can be calculated. The cases generally missed on radionuclide examinations are those in which the reflux is confined to the distal ureter.

As the bladder volume at which reflux occurs increases in serial studies done on a child, then the patient is more likely to be clinically stable. If reflux occurs at progressively smaller bladder volumes, however, the patient is frequently clinically unstable and may be a candidate for antireflux surgery.

It is possible to calculate the residual urine volume in the bladder following either an antegrade nuclear study or a catheter-type nuclear reflux study. This is done by measuring the voided urine both in volume and counts per milliliter and comparing these with the counts remaining in the bladder. It should be emphasized that examination of residual urine volume is rarely a primary reason for performing a nuclear medicine study, and this information may be more easily obtained by other methods such as ultrasound.

Clinical Applications

ANATOMIC VARIANTS

Renal size, shape, and position may be determined by radionuclide imaging. However, standard contrast radiography, computed tomography, and ultrasound provide more resolution and structural information. Nuclear imaging of the kidney becomes particularly valuable when assessment of function is required or when renal function is seriously impaired. A radionuclide renogram may demonstrate activity in a kidney when the function is only 3 percent of normal.

With congenital anomalies such as horseshoe kidney, clump kidney, or crossed-fused ectopia, it is often difficult, either radiographically or ultrasonographically, to visualize the ectopic kidney, and nuclear scans may be useful. For radionuclide assessment of a clump kidney (which is usually presacral) or pelvic kidney, it is often necessary to have the patient void or to perform the study quickly, before significant bladder activity has accumulated.

INTRARENAL MASS LESIONS

At the present time, nuclear medicine imaging is not often used for evaluation of intrarenal mass lesions alone. Cysts, abscesses, and neoplasms are very difficult to differentiate on the basis of the static image, although a dynamic perfusion study may demonstrate some hypervascularity in a tumor. Lack of vascularity should not be used as a criterion to exclude the possibility of a neoplasm, since many renal cell carcinomas are cystic or centrally necrotic. The limits of resolution are 1-cm lesions in the renal cortex and 2-cm lesions in the central portion of the kidney.

One specific application of nuclear imaging is the differentiation of a renal column (a cortical nodule) from a true space-occupying lesion. Renal columns of Bertin accumulate radionuclide at least as well and sometimes apparently better than the surrounding parenchyma.

VASCULAR ABNORMALITIES

Renal perfusion studies may be performed in an effort to elucidate renal vascular abnormalities without having to resort to intraarterial-catheter angiography. The role of nuclear medicine in perfusion imaging of the kidneys will probably remain useful for patients in whom functional information is also required, such as renal transplant recipients, and in patients with vascular abnormalities or those who have allergies to iodinated contrast material.

Renal artery avulsion, venous thrombosis, and renal infarction can be demonstrated by nuclear techniques, but other radiographic studies remain the procedures of choice. Early in renal vein thrombosis, there is a delay in perfusion and in accumulation and excretion of Hippuran. The image presentations of these disorders and the detection rates are not significantly different from those demonstrated by conventional radiographic techniques.

RENOVASCULAR HYPERTENSION

Renovascular hypertension constitutes approximately 1 to 4 percent of all cases of hypertension, but no discriminating findings allow its diagnosis on clinical grounds. In this setting, radionuclide renography with captopril (angiotensin-converting enzyme inhibitor—ACEI) intervention may be useful.

Significant renal artery stenosis (60 to 75 percent) decreases *afferent* arteriolar blood pressure, which stimulates renin secretion by the juxtaglomerular apparatus. Renin effects the production of angiotensin I, which is acted upon by angiotensin-converting enzyme to yield angiotensin II. Angiotensin II induces vasoconstriction of the *efferent* arterioles, which restores glomerular filtration rate. Angiotensin-converting enzyme inhibitors such as captopril and enalapril prevent the production of angiotensin II, so that in patients with renal artery stenosis and compensated renal function, preglomerular filtration pressures are no longer maintained. This results in a significant sudden decrease in renal function. The severity of renal decompensation induced depends upon a variety of factors including the degree of renal artery stenosis, the level of renin-produced glomerular filtration compensation, and the systemic blood pressure. Such induced decompensation can be documented by performing radioiodinated Hippuran or ^{99m}Tc DTPA studies before and after the administration of captopril. A sample protocol is provided in Appendix E.

Diagnostic criteria reported following captopril administration (single oral dose of 25 to 50 mg) include (1) reduced ^{99m}Tc DTPA accumulation in the affected kidney compared with the base line study, (2) a delay in the time to maximal activity of the Hippuran or DTPA renogram curves, and (3) significant cortical retention of iodinated Hippuran or a delay in Hippuran washout.

In patients with unilateral renal artery stenosis and renal insufficiency, bilateral renal artery stenosis, or stenotic solitary or transplanted kidneys, captopril should be used advisedly for diagnosis, especially if severe stenosis is known to be present. Under these circumstances, acute renal failure may be induced, which is generally self-limited, although persistent anuria may occasionally develop. Furthermore, in any patient undergoing captopril intervention studies, the possibility of severe hypotension induction exists, especially in the presence of intravenous volume depletion. This complication usually responds to intravenous volume expanders (normal saline). Although the technique is promising, further validation will be needed before it can be recommended as a routine screening procedure.

DIFFUSE RENAL DISEASE

In evaluation of diffuse renal diseases such as chronic glomerulonephritis, inflammatory diseases, and radiation nephritis, the radionuclide scan often is sensitive but not disease-specific. Most often there is simply demonstration of poor vascular perfusion and poor tubular secretion on the renogram. In addition, the renogram is of some value in providing quantitative estimates of the function of each individual kidney, information that is not easily obtained by other methods. Radiation therapy may cause a global or localized loss of renal function initially, and over a period of weeks or months there may be a return of some function in the treated areas depending on the dose of radiation given.

Gallium scanning can also be used to localize renal inflammatory lesions. Early physiologic excretion of gallium by the kidneys makes 24- and possibly 48-hour scanning necessary. Such a delay may be unacceptable in acutely ill patients. Activity remaining in kidneys more than 24 hours post-injection should be viewed as abnormal.

In acute renal failure, the isotope perfusion study and renogram are of value. In patients with acute tubular necrosis, there may be relatively good perfusion and accumulation but poor excretion of Hippuran. This frequently presents as bilateral persistent nephrograms with rising curves. Good function on the renogram indicates a favorable prognostic outcome, whereas poor visualization on the renogram is correlated with a low chance of recovery.

OBSTRUCTIVE UROPATHY

The images obtained in patients who have obstructed uropathy are dependent not only on the degree of obstruction but also upon the nature (acute or chronic) of the obstruction. In order for an adequate image to be obtained, there must be relatively good function to allow the radionuclide into the collecting system. With acute unilateral high-grade obstruction, there is generally reduced renal perfusion, although later renogram images may demonstrate more renal symmetry with intact renal extraction of the radiopharmaceutical. It appears that glomerular function is more sensitive to ureteral obstruction than is tubular secretion; however, once tubular changes occur, they take longer to reverse than do glomerular abnormalities (Fig. 12–5).

One of the more popular renal imaging studies performed today is the furosemide

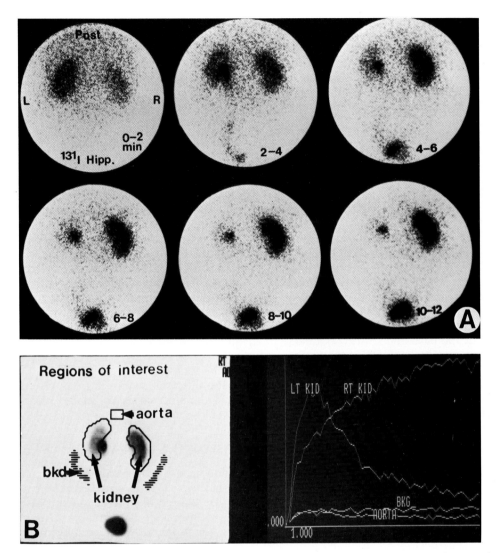

Figure 12–5. Obstructive renogram. (A) Sequential [131]I Hippuran images of the kidneys demonstrate normal concentration, excretion, and clearance of the radiopharmaceutical from the left kidney with delayed but progressively increased concentration of the iodohippuran in an obstructed right kidney. (B) Computer analysis of the study is obtained by flagging the aorta, the renal parenchymal areas (bilaterally), and the background areas to produce bilateral Hippuran curves that show a normal left renogram curve but a progressively rising right renogram curve compatible with acute obstruction. A very similar pattern may be seen in acute tubular necrosis although the changes are usually bilateral.

renogram, which is generally performed on patients in whom collecting system dilatation is questionably due to a true obstruction or secondary to an atonic type of collecting system. The DTPA renal study is initiated in the usual fashion with 10 mCi (370 MBq) of intravenous isotope; however, after approximately 10 to 20 minutes, when the pelvis and calices are visualized, an intravenous injection of furosemide (0.3 mg/kg) is given. Images are obtained for an additional 15 minutes. With this method it is often possible to differentiate between an atonic system and one that has a mechanical obstruction. The

characteristic curves are shown in Figure 12–6.

In the normal patient there is a rapid increase in kidney activity, which peaks at about 6 minutes and is followed by a sharp decline. Injection of furosemide produces another transient increase in activity due to the diuresis (Fig. 12–7). In dilated nonobstructed systems, furosemide causes increased urine flow through the collecting system, which "washes out" the initial increase in activity and causes a decline in the computer-generated time–activity curves. In the case of significant mechanical obstruction there is very

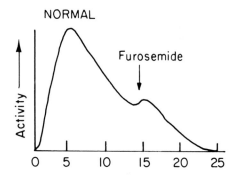

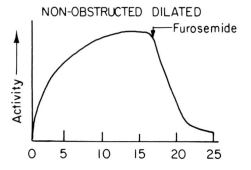

Figure 12–6. Characteristic time–activity curves in a furosemide renogram.

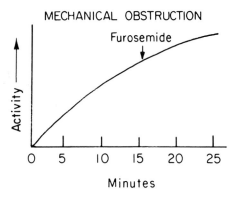

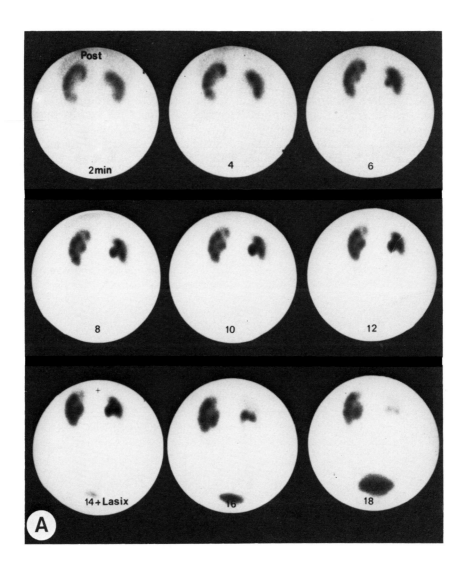

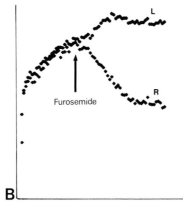

Figure 12–7. (A) Abnormal furosemide renogram. The right kidney demonstrates a dilated central collecting system, which washes out following administration of furosemide. The left kidney remains essentially unchanged, consistent with a ureteropelvic obstruction. (B) The computer-generated time–activity curve confirms this diagnosis.

little decrease in renal collecting system activity following furosemide due to the narrowed fixed lumen of the ureter. Isolated time–activity curves may also be generated for the ureter if necessary. In general, the diuretic renogram is limited when there is poor renal function and thus inadequate response to the furosemide.

EVALUATION OF RENAL TRANSPLANTS

Radionuclide imaging of renal transplants is performed quite frequently in large medical centers. The evaluation normally consists of a renal blood flow dynamic study performed with 10 to 20 mCi (370 to 740 MBq) of ^{99m}Tc DTPA. A series of static images is obtained over a period of 10 to 15 minutes. This is followed by the Hippuran renogram study, with serial 2-minute renogram images taken for a total of 30 minutes.

In the normal transplant perfusion study, the bolus reaches the renal transplant almost exactly at the same time as it is seen in the iliac vessels. As with a renogram of a native kidney, the maximum parenchymal phase is normally seen at 2 to 4 minutes with bladder activity present at 4 to 5 minutes. Immediately following transplant and up to a period of 2 weeks, there may be fairly prominent visualization of the ureter due to edema at the ureterovesicular anastomotic site.

Generally, imaging is performed to help differentiate acute tubular necrosis from renal transplant rejection or to assess other postoperative complications. In those patients with acute tubular necrosis, the vascular perfusion is usually quite well preserved and the tubular clearance demonstrated by the renogram is comparatively poor (Fig. 12–8A, B). Serial studies often demonstrate an improvement in the situation. Acute tubular necrosis is frequently manifested within 4 days following surgery and rarely is this complication seen more than 1 month following transplant surgery. Cyclosporine, which is used to prevent rejection, can cause scintigraphic findings similar to acute tubular necrosis. In a patient who has had a renal transplant for more than 1 month and who presents with relatively good transplant perfusion and poor tubular function, cyclosporine should be suspected as the etiology. Differentiation of acute tubular necrosis from rejection is best done with clinical correlation and serial renal studies.

Renal transplant rejection is classified as hyperacute, acute, or chronic. Hyperacute rejection is due to the presence of an antibody at the time of transplantation and occurs within 24 hours of surgery. Acute (cellular) rejection usually occurs from 1 to 3 weeks following the transplant. Chronic (humoral) rejection is a process that probably occurs in varying degrees in all renal homografts and takes place over a period of months or years. Since renal rejection is physiologically manifested by reduction in perfusion at the small vessel level, the dynamic perfusion study often reveals poor perfusion, which usually gets worse on serial examinations. The renogram is equally poor, demonstrating a diminished nephrogram phase and delayed appearance of bladder activity (Fig. 12–9). A large portion of this may be due to the decreased perfusion and

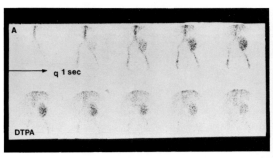
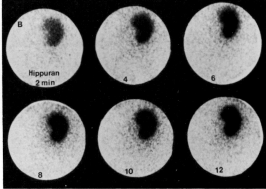

Figure 12–8. Acute tubular necrosis in a left iliac fossa renal transplant. (A) ^{99m}Tc DTPA blood flow study shows excellent perfusion of the transplant. (B) The ^{131}I Hippuran renogram shows accumulation but no tubular clearance of the activity.

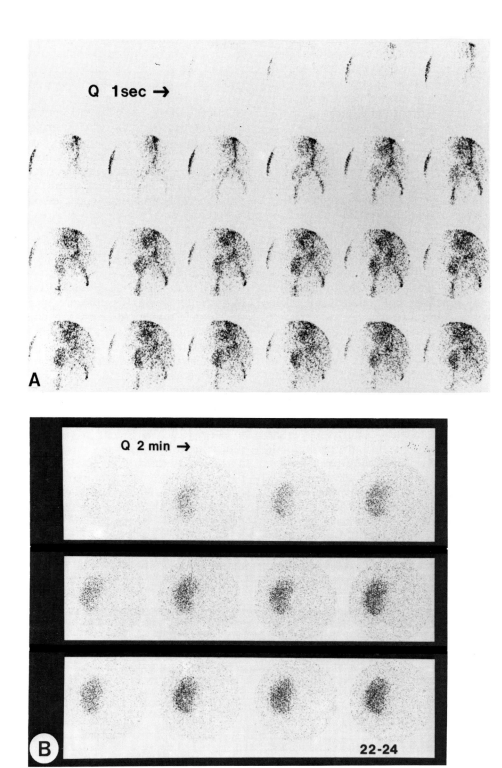

Figure 12–9. Renal transplant rejection. (A) The DTPA flow study demonstrates very poor flow to the transplant, which can be seen several seconds after the iliac vessels. (B) The renogram demonstrates increasing parenchymal activity throughout the course of the study, with no evidence of activity in the collecting system or bladder.

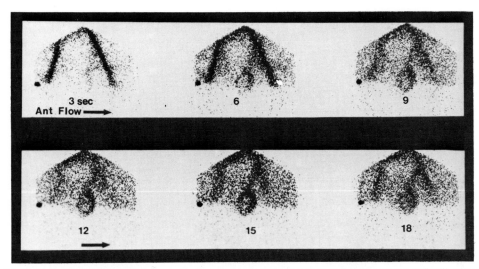

Figure 12–10. Testicular torsion. Serial dynamic images demonstrate hypervascularity on the left with a lucent center consistent with missed testicular torsion.

inability of the radionuclide to reach functional renal structures. A relative increase in perinephric accumulation of ^{99m}Tc DTPA has been felt to signify end-stage rejection as manifested by renal infarction.

It should also be noted that ^{99m}Tc sulfur colloid will accumulate in a renal transplant following an episode of rejection. Although interesting, this has not been particularly useful, since even if the episode of rejection is reversed, the sulfur colloid appears to continue to accumulate in the kidney.

Scrotal Imaging

Scrotal imaging is often requested by clinicians in an effort to differentiate the causes of a swollen or painful testicle. A study is normally performed with 10 to 20 mCi (370 to 740 MBq) of ^{99m}Tc pertechnetate and dynamic scrotal scintiphotos are obtained at 2-second intervals to assess vascular integrity with delayed images obtained every 5 minutes for 20 minutes.

Testicular torsion and hydrocele present as central avascular abnormalities although missed testicular torsion may show a rim of hypervascularity (Fig. 12–10). This "bulls-eye" appearance is not pathognomonic, and it also may be seen with abscess and hematoma. Epididymitis usually is hypervascular. Tumors may be vascular or avascular and are difficult to differentiate with certainty from benign lesions on the basis of the perfusion images (see Table 12–2). Correlation with the clinical findings, particularly the presence of pain, and the acute nature of the symptoms usually provide significant help in the differential diagnosis.

Adrenal Imaging

Adrenal scintigraphy is possible utilizing ^{131}I or ^{123}I 19-iodocholesterol. Mean uptake by

Table 12–2. TESTICULAR TORSION SCINTIGRAPHY

DIAGNOSIS	DYNAMIC STUDY (ACTIVITY)	DELAYED STATIC IMAGE (ACTIVITY)
Acute torsion (<24 hr)	Normal or slightly decreased	Decreased
Late torsion (>24 hr)	Decreased or normal	Cold lesion with surrounding activity
Trauma (hematoma)	Variable	Variable
Epididymitis	Increased	Increased
Abscess	Increased	Cold lesion with surrounding activity
Tumor	Normal or increased	Decreased or increased
Hydrocele	Normal or decreased	Decreased

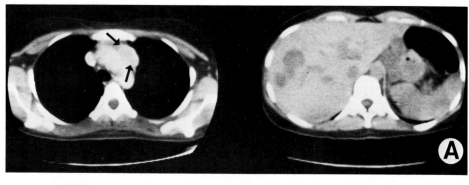

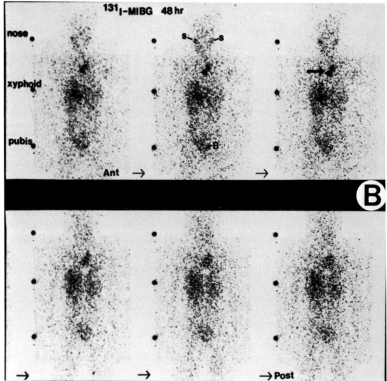

Figure 12–11. Metastatic functioning paraganglioma. (A) A CT scan demonstrates a superior mediastinal mass (arrows) and multiple low-density lesions throughout the liver. (B) A 48-hour tomographic scan of the patient utilizing ^{131}I metaiodobenzylguanidine (MIBG) shows activity in the salivary glands and bladder, which is normal. The mediastinal tumor is clearly identified (arrow). This appearance also can be seen with metastatic pheochromocytoma. (Case courtesy of Manuel Brown, M.D.)

the adrenal glands is very low and is usually less than 1 percent of the injected activity. This method has not achieved wide use, owing to the high radiation dose and a necessary delay of 3 to 15 days after radionuclide injection before scanning can be performed. Distinction between adrenal hyperplasia and adenomas is possible using ^{131}I-iodomethyl 19-norcholesterol (NP-59) and dexamethasone suppression. Nonvisualization of one adrenal gland with increased uptake on the contralateral side is typical of a glucocorti-

coid-producing adenoma. In hyperplasia of the adrenal glands, both glands are usually seen. Currently, however, anatomic visualization of the adrenal gland is best achieved utilizing computed body tomography. If radiopharmaceuticals are utilized, the thyroid should be blocked with potassium iodide prior to administration.

Iodine 123 and 131 meta-iodobenzylguanidine has been used for imaging pheochromocytoma and adrenal medullary hyperplasia. Radioiodinated meta-iodobenzylguanidine (MIBG) is similar to norepi-nephrine and guanethidine in structure but lacks their adrenergic pharmacologic actions. Like norepinephrine, it is taken up from the plasma by chromaffin cells and is therefore useful for the localization of pheochromocy-tomas whether located in the adrenal me-dulla or ectopically. Sensitivity (about 87 per-cent) and specificity (99 percent) are high. Scanning for pheochromocytomas with ^{131}I MIBG is especially helpful in diseases with a high incidence of the following neoplasms: multiple endocrine neoplasms types 2A and 2B, neurofibromatoses, von Hippel-Lindau disease, and Carney's triad. Metastatic le-sions are also imaged.

Drugs such as imipramine, insulin, reser-pine, tricyclic antidepressants, and amphet-amine-like drugs inhibit adrenergic localiza-tion of MIBG and thus interfere with scanning. MIBG is also highly sensitive for localizing neuroblastomas and, to a lesser degree, other neuroendocrine tumors (Fig. 12–11).

Suggested Readings

Beierwaltes WH: Clinical applications of [131]iodine-labeled metaiodobenzylguanidine. In: Hoffer PB (ed): Year-book of Nuclear Medicine. Chicago, Year Book Med-ical Publishers, pp. 17–34, 1987

Fine EJ, Axelrod M, Gorkin J, et al: Measurement of effective renal plasma flow: A comparison of methods. J Nucl Med 28:1393–1400, 1987

Freeman LM, Blaufox MD (eds): Update on radionuclide assessment of the kidney—I. Semin Nucl Med 12(3):224–300, 1982

Freeman LM, Blaufox MD (eds): Update on radionuclide assessment of the kidney—II. Semin Nucl Med 12(4):308–397, 1982

Freeman LM, Blaufox MD (eds): Transplant evaluation. Semin Nucl Med 18(3):181–198, 1988

O'Reilly PH: Diuresis renography eight years later: An update. J Urol 136:993–999, 1986

Russell CD, Dubovsky EV: Measurement of renal func-tion with radionuclides. J Nucl Med 30:2053–2057, 1989

Sfakianakis GN, Sfakianakis ED: Nuclear medicine in pediatric urology and nephrology. J Nucl Med 29:1287–1300, 1988

Tumor and Inflammation Imaging

Gallium

In the past, gallium 67 imaging has been employed as a diagnostic tool in a number of clinical settings. Although many of these applications are no longer considered useful, gallium has survived as a valuable agent in the detection and localization of certain neoplastic and inflammatory lesions. Although other radiopharmaceuticals have been tried in these clinical situations, none has thus far proved as satisfactory as gallium. Until newer agents are fully developed and clinically proven, gallium will remain a front-line agent for tumor and possibly abscess scanning. Therefore, the nuclear imaging physician must possess a thorough understanding of the technical and clinical aspects of gallium scintigraphy.

Gallium 67 is a cyclotron-produced radiopharmaceutical resulting from the bombardment of a zinc target by accelerated protons. The finished product is, for practical purposes, "carrier-free," i.e., free of stable gallium. This is important because significant amounts of carrier gallium will change the biologic distribution of gallium 67 in the body, causing increased concentration in the skeleton.

Gallium 67 has a physical half-life of 78.1 hours and decays by electron capture, emitting gamma radiation over an energy range of 93 to 880 keV. The four principal energy peaks useful in diagnostic imaging are 93, 184, 296, and 388 keV. One or all of these peaks may be used in obtaining a gamma camera image. Chemically, gallium is a group III element with multiple valence states. It is commonly used as a trivalent citrate compound for nuclear medicine imaging and usually arrives in the nuclear medicine laboratory in a carrier-free state ready for intra-venous administration. A dose of 2 to 6 mCi (74 to 222 MBq) is generally employed when imaging adults.

BIOLOGIC BEHAVIOR

When injected intravenously, the majority of gallium 67 is immediately bound to plasma proteins, primarily transferrin. During the first 12 to 24 hours, excretion from the body is primarily through the kidneys, with 20 to 30 percent of the administered dose being excreted by 24 hours. After that time, the intestinal mucosa becomes the major route of elimination, although some is probably excreted via the liver and biliary tract. Overall, these modes of excretion account for the elimination of approximately one-third of the administered dose. The remaining two-thirds are retained in the body for a prolonged period. In addition to activity within the axial skeleton, liver, spleen, and bowel, concentration is also seen in the salivary and lacrimal glands as well as in the breasts and external genitalia (Table 13–1). If imaging is performed in the first 24 hours, kidney and bladder activity may also be noted. As mentioned above, the distribution of gallium in the body is affected by the presence of carrier isotope, which increases activity within the skeleton. In addition, too much stable gallium in the administered dose reduces the likelihood that uptake in the target neoplasms will be sufficient to allow detection.

Although the mechanisms underlying the uptake of gallium are incompletely understood, a few basic principles are known to be associated with the concentration of gallium in inflammatory and neoplastic tissues. In both cases, transport of the gallium 67 to the site of localization appears to be mediated

Table 13–1. RADIOPHARMACEUTICAL AGENTS FOR TUMOR AND ABSCESS IMAGING

RADIO-PHARMA-CEUTICAL	USUAL DOSE	ROUTE OF ADMINIS-TRATION	PHYSICAL HALF-LIFE	TIME TO IMAGING	Whole Body	Gonads	Other	REMARKS
						ABSORBED DOSE ESTIMATES (rad/mCi)*		
^{67}Ga citrate	2–6 mCi (74–222 MBq)	IV	78 hr	6–72 hr	0.2–0.4	0.3	Kidneys 0.4–0.5 Liver 0.4–0.6 Colon† 0.6–0.9	Accumulates in breast milk; renal excretion in first 24 hr; GI excretion after 24 hr.
^{111}In leuko-cytes	0.5–1 mCi (18.5–37 MBq)	IV	67 hr	6–24 hr	0.4	0.4	Spleen† 8.4–18.0 Liver 1.8–5.0	

*To obtain absorbed dose in mGy/MBq, divide values by 3.7.
†Indicates critical organ.

mainly by plasma proteins and gallium-transferrin complexes, which act as carriers for gallium. Once it is taken up by neoplastic cells, gallium 67 is for the most part located in the cytoplasm and is associated predominantly with lysosomes and possibly the endoplasmic reticulum. Although the reason for localization in certain tumors and not in others is not entirely understood, one hypothesis suggests that the mechanism is related to the presence of transferrin receptors on the tumor cells that bind gallium 67-transferrin complexes.

It is clear that the mechanism of gallium citrate localization in inflammatory tissues is complex. In addition to the local deposition of transferrin-bound gallium, migration of labeled white blood cells (which are lactoferrin-rich) to the inflamed areas may also play a role.

IMAGING TECHNIQUE

Gallium imaging may be performed using whole-body techniques or using spot imaging with a wide-field-of-view gamma camera and a medium-energy parallel-hole collimator. A gamma camera with a multichannel analyzer permits the several gallium gamma peaks to be imaged simultaneously. If a single-channel analyzer is used, a wider window (25 to 30 percent) over two adjacent gamma peaks, usually 93 and 184 keV, may be used.

After the intravenous administration of 4 to 6 mCi (148 to 222 MBq) of gallium 67 citrate, initial images are obtained at 4 to 6 hours in the case of suspected inflammatory disease and at 24 hours for tumor imaging. Images are subsequently obtained at 24-hour intervals as needed to allow for improved target/nontarget ratios and for the possible differentiation of normal bowel activity from accumulations in pathologic entities. The progress of excreted gallium through the colon may provide the best evidence of physiologic activity. Persistence of gallium in a given area of the abdomen should be viewed as abnormal.

When spot imaging is performed, anterior and posterior images of the thorax, abdomen, and pelvis are obtained, with anterior or lateral skull views and anterior long bone images taken as needed. The images may be tailored to the particular clinical problem being investigated. For better anatomic localization of an area, lateral or oblique views are frequently helpful. Images are obtained for 300,000 to 500,000 counts.

Use of single-photon emission computed tomography (SPECT) techniques may increase sensitivity relative to planar imaging for both gallium 67 and indium 111 leukocytes. Tomographic techniques should be considered when the results of the planar study are negative and a specific site of inflammation or tumor involvement is suspected or when the planar findings are equivocal or incomplete with respect to defining the extent of disease.

Clinical Applications

NORMAL GALLIUM SCAN

The interpretation of gallium studies is frequently made difficult by the marginal anatomic resolution of the images and by interfering activity in the bowel or in operative sites in postsurgical patients. Thus, careful attention to anatomic orientation and a thorough appreciation of the physiologic distribution of gallium and its excretion patterns are of utmost importance (Fig. 13–1).

Head and Neck Distribution. Normally, gallium activity is noted in the osseous structures of the skull and in the nasopharynx, and variably in the lacrimal and salivary glands. Activity in the salivary glands may be especially prominent in patients who have undergone radiation therapy to that area.

Thorax. Gallium activity is prominent in the skeletal structures of the thorax, including the sternum. If mediastinal pathology is suspected, lateral or oblique chest images may be necessary to differentiate sternal from mediastinal concentrations. In early images (4 to 6 hours), blood pool activity in the heart and great vessels may be noted. Symmetric accumulation of gallium in the breasts occasionally interferes with chest imaging, especially under the stimuli of menarche, pregnancy, or hormonal agents such as birth control pills.

Abdomen. Gallium is normally detected in the liver and to a lesser extent in the spleen. As the primary initial excretory route, the kidneys and bladder may be identified on images obtained up to 24 hours post-injection. After that time, renal activity should be considered abnormal, especially when it is asymmetric.

A common problem seen with image interpretation in the abdomen is the presence of gallium in the bowel, which may mimic lesions or mask disease. Bowel activity is particularly noted in the colon and may be diffuse or focal; frequently activity is seen in the region of the cecum, hepatic and splenic flextures, and rectosigmoid. Such accumulations may appear as early as a few hours after injection. Various bowel preparations have been investigated as possible means of eliminating such interfering activity in the colon, but none has proved consistently successful. Delayed imaging is frequently the best aid in differentiating pathologic localization of gallium from normal bowel activity.

Pelvis. Activity is seen in the osseous pelvis, particularly in the sacrum and sacroiliac joints on posterior views. In early images

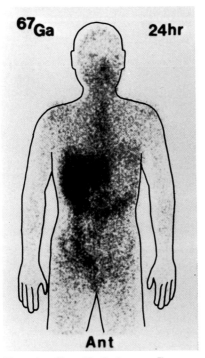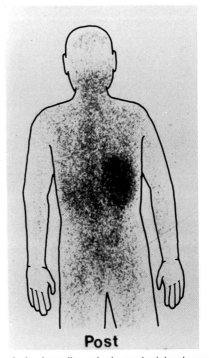

Figure 13–1. Normal gallium 67 citrate scan. The scan demonstrates hepatic, colonic, and minimal osseous and lacrimal gland activity. Scans done earlier may normally show renal and bladder activity.

bladder activity may be noted, and later concentrations may be seen in the region of the vagina or scrotum. As in the abdomen, cecal or rectosigmoid accumulation may present a problem in interpretation.

Extremities. Aside from slightly increased concentration around large joints such as hips and shoulders and in the open epiphyses of children, little activity is normally seen in the long bones.

NEOPLASMS

In the proper clinical setting and with meticulous attention to technique, gallium imaging can be a useful adjunctive tool in the investigation of selected neoplasms. The technique is most successful when clinical findings are correlated with those of other imaging procedures, such as computed tomography (CT) or ultrasound.

Lymphoma. Tumor uptake of gallium 67 has been most extensively studied in lymphoma, the disease in which gallium's usefulness was first recognized. As expected, the sensitivity of gallium in detecting lymphomatous disease is greatly dependent upon the size and location of the lesions.

Lesions of less than 1.0 cm in size are not often detected. Sites of involvement in the abdomen and pelvis may be difficult to identify because of interfering activity within the liver and colon as well as their often deep-seated location. In these areas, computed tomography may provide a more sensitive indicator of disease. More superficial sites such as those in the mediastinum and inguinal and axillary nodal areas are more readily identified (Fig. 13–2). In addition, not all sites of involvement will accumulate gallium, so a normal scan does not reliably exclude the presence of disease.

Various forms of therapy including radiotherapy and chemotherapy have been reported to decrease or eliminate altogether the uptake of gallium in involved sites. Thus, serial gallium scanning may be of value in assessing the effects of therapy as well as in the detection of early disease recurrence.

Hodgkin's Disease. More than 90 percent of patients with untreated Hodgkin's disease show some degree of gallium 67 concentration. This includes all histologic types, although gallium scans are slightly less sensitive for the lymphocyte-predominant category, which may well relate to the generally poor affinity of lymphocytes for gal-

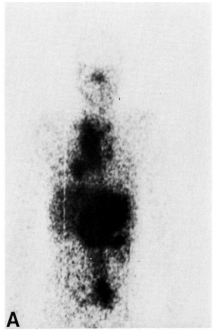 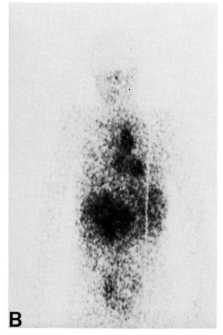

A **B**

Figure 13–2. Hodgkin's disease. This gallium scan was obtained at 72 hours and demonstrates multiple abnormal areas including the mediastinum, right hilum, mid-abdomen, and left pelvis. (A) Anterior. (B) Posterior.

lium. After treatment, the number of patients with positive gallium uptake drops significantly, to approximately 50 percent. The false positive rate in both treated and untreated patients is roughly 5 percent.

Non-Hodgkin's Lymphoma. The sensitivity of gallium 67 imaging for non-Hodgkin's lymphoma demonstrates variability related to histologic type. Sensitivity ranges from approximately 90 percent with the histiocytic cell type to less than 60 percent with the lymphocytic well-differentiated type. The overall detection rate is considerably less than that for Hodgkin's disease, although the false positive rates are comparable.

Bronchogenic Carcinoma. Overall sensitivity of approximately 90 percent has been documented in bronchogenic carcinoma, although there is some evidence that adenocarcinoma is slightly less avid for gallium uptake than squamous cell or undifferentiated types. With current imaging techniques, primary lesions as small as 2 cm may be detected. Identification of regional lymph node metastases is successful at a rate of roughly 50 percent. In general, gallium 67 whole-body scanning is not as sensitive for the evaluation of distant metastases from lung carcinoma as are organ-specific nuclear medicine procedures, including bone and liver radionuclide imaging.

Unfortunately, high false positive rates for gallium detection of lung primaries have been reported. These elevated rates are understandable since gallium has been shown to concentrate in a variety of non-neoplastic pulmonary lesions, including various inflammatory diseases and sarcoidosis (Table 13–2). Therefore, gallium may not be an extremely useful tool in the differential diagnosis of pulmonary disease, but it has been shown to be helpful in determining the activity or extent of selected intrapulmonary lesions and in assessing the effects of therapy.

Some investigators have reported gallium scanning to be of use in determining mediastinal extension of lung tumors. Others have been less enthusiastic, pointing out that the mediastinal uptake cannot be considered specific for neoplastic disease since non-neoplastic lesions including benign lymph nodes have been shown to concentrate the radiopharmaceutical.

Hepatoma. Gallium 67 scanning has proved to be successful in differentiating pri-

Table 13–2. DIFFUSE PULMONARY UPTAKE OF GALLIUM 67

- Idiopathic pulmonary fibrosis
- Diffuse pneumonitis
- Pulmonary sarcoid
- Lymphangitic metastases
- *Pneumocystis carinii* pneumonia
- Miliary tuberculosis
- Bleomycin toxicity
- Lymphangiographic contrast
- Radiation pneumonitis (early exudative phase)

mary hepatocellular carcinoma from regenerating nodules in patients with cirrhosis. Almost always, these studies are preceded by radionuclide or CT scans of the liver. In patients with a defect on the liver–spleen scan that is suspected to be hepatoma, gallium uptake in the defect of greater intensity than elsewhere in the liver is a strong indication of hepatoma. When a sulfur colloid defect with greatly diminished gallium uptake is identified, hepatoma is essentially excluded. Gallium uptake in the area of the defect equal to that of the surrounding liver is equivocal and may be found in both regenerating nodules and hepatoma as well as other etiologies such as metastatic disease. Computer-assisted liver subtraction may significantly aid in the interpretation of gallium images of the liver in this setting.

Other Neoplasms. While the affinity of many other tumors for gallium is variable, a frequent question is the usefulness of gallium scanning in the detection of occult primary malignancies and for locating an unknown primary tumor in a patient with metastases. Gallium imaging is not recommended for the routine screening of such cases. However, in selected patients in whom more conventional methods have revealed no primary tumor, gallium can sometimes be a useful adjunct. It must be emphasized, however, that in patients with proved metastatic disease, a negative scan provides no further information and a positive scan rarely affects therapy or survival.

INFLAMMATORY DISEASE

Gallium 67 imaging has proved important in the investigation of several non-neoplastic lesions, especially inflammatory diseases of pyogenic origin and unknown site of origin (Fig. 13–3). If a particular site is suspected, a

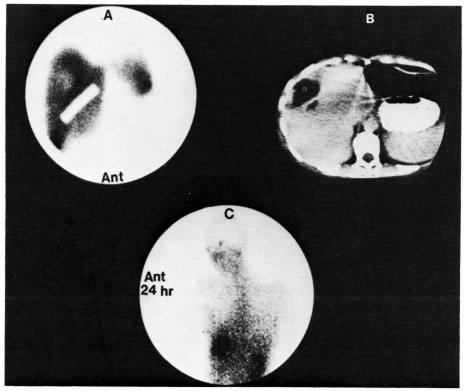

Figure 13–3. Pyogenic liver abscess. (A) A negative defect is seen on the sulfur colloid liver–spleen scan. (B) A lucent defect is seen on the CT scan. (C) The 24-hour gallium scan demonstrates a focus of markedly increased activity in the right upper quadrant.

CT scan or ultrasonography may be more informative. When used in proper perspective and in correlation with CT and ultrasound findings, gallium imaging can lead to early diagnosis and treatment of occult infections.

Because of the avidity of pyogenic abscesses for gallium 67, suitable target/nontarget ratios may be obtained earlier than with neoplastic scanning. Typically, imaging is performed as early as 4 to 6 hours after administration of the radiopharmaceutical.

While a positive gallium scan is certainly not specific for inflammatory disease, in properly selected patients, particularly those with fever of unknown origin and leukocytosis, a focally positive scan may be taken as evidence of abscess. There is a high sensitivity for localized pyogenic disease (80 to 90 percent) and a low false positive rate. To avoid false positive studies, care must be taken to differentiate physiologic activity, such as that in the colon, from truly abnormal accumulations. In addition, in postsurgical patients, possible collections of gallium in

postoperative hematomas or surgically scarred areas must be taken into consideration. The false negative rate in gallium abscess imaging, although higher than the false positive rate, is nevertheless acceptable. The study should be used with caution in patients who have been treated with systemic antibiotics, since false negatives are known to occur under these circumstances.

In general, the proper interpretation of gallium images hinges upon the differentiation of physiologic from abnormal accumulations of the radiopharmaceutical. However, several specific areas that present problems in interpretation should be emphasized. In the abdomen, the presence of liver activity in the right upper quadrant may mask abnormal gallium collection.

While gallium is not specific for any particular type of bacterial infection, amebic abscesses of the liver present a somewhat characteristic appearance—increased gallium accumulation in a ring-like fashion around the periphery of the abscess, with very little or no activity in the central portion of the

Table 13–3. PERSISTENT GALLIUM ACTIVITY IN THE KIDNEYS AFTER 24 HOURS

- Obstruction
- Renal parenchymal pathology
  Neoplasm
  Pyelonephritis
  Vasculitis
  Acute tubular necrosis
- Infiltrative disease
  Leukemia
  Lymphoma
  Amyloid
- Plasma transferrin saturation
  Parenteral iron injections
  Blood transfusions
- Perirenal inflammatory disease
- Faint visualization may be normal

Abnormally increased activity in one or both kidneys can occur in numerous abnormalities and physiologic states and may therefore present a difficult problem of differential diagnosis. Persistence of renal activity after 24 hours, progressively increasing activity, and unilateral discrepancy in gallium activity in the kidneys should all be interpreted as abnormal (Table 13–3). However, persistent renal activity may be seen in patients with compromised renal function and delayed urinary excretion of the radiopharmaceutical and recent transfusions or administration of parenteral iron supplements.

Numerous other disease entities have been reported to produce positive renal gallium scans. The most prominent of these are various nephrides and vasculidites, acute tubular necrosis, and infiltrative disorders such as leukemia and amyloidosis.

In the chest, gallium has been known to accumulate in a variety of inflammatory abnormalities, including pyogenic pneumonias, tuberculosis, sarcoidosis (Fig. 13–4), vasculi-

lesion. This finding may aid in differentiating between amebic and pyogenic disease.

Abscesses in the retroperitoneum are frequently related to associated renal disease.

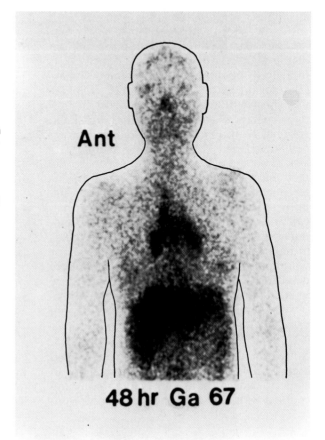

Figure 13–4. Sarcoidosis. A single anterior gallium 67 citrate image obtained at 48 hours demonstrates increased gallium activity in both hilar regions of the lungs extending into the right paratracheal region. In a patient with prominently enlarged nodes on chest radiograph, this finding was compatible with a diagnosis of active sarcoidosis. The absence of significant activity in the lungs excludes significant active parenchymal disease with good reliability.

tis, idiopathic pulmonary fibrosis, and various other pulmonary, pleural, and mediastinal benign diseases. The amount of gallium activity has been used in attempts to determine whether a pulmonary process is in an active or quiescent stage. Acute inflammatory diseases of the heart and pericardium have also been cited as producing positive gallium images.

IMMUNOSUPPRESSED PATIENTS

More recently, gallium 67 scintigraphy has become a valuable tool in the setting of immunologically suppressed patients, especially those with acquired immune deficiency syndrome (AIDS) and AIDS-related complex (ARC). Diffuse pulmonary uptake of gallium has been noted in patients with *Pneumocystis carinii* pneumonia (PCP) before chest radiographs have become positive. Although a positive gallium scan is not diagnostic of PCP, it is approximately 90 percent sensitive for the disease, so that diffuse pulmonary activity in this population should prompt investigation or treatment for the offending organism. The finding that gallium 67 may diagnose PCP even before patients develop symptoms has led some to use the scan as an adjunct for differentiating patients with ARC from those with AIDS.

Other useful patterns of thoracic gallium distribution in patients with AIDS include (1) focal lung uptake in bacterial pneumonias, (2) a negative scan in the presence of abnormal chest radiographs in patients with pulmonary Kaposi's sarcoma, (3) focal uptake in regional lymph nodes in *Mycobacterium avium-intracellulare* (MAI), or pneumonia. The lack of uptake of gallium in Kaposi's sarcoma may make gallium 67 imaging useful in differentiating between infection and sarcoma in these patients. In the abdomen, abnormal gallium accumulation may be seen in bacterial abscess, infection, or enteritis, as well as in regional lymph nodes affected by MAI or lymphoma. In this insidious disease, early detection of infection can make the difference in successful treatment (Fig. 13–5).

OSTEOMYELITIS

^{99m}Tc bone imaging is the most widely used method of detecting early osteomyelitis. In some instances, however, gallium scanning coupled with routine radionuclide bone scanning allows a more definitive diagnosis or a more precise localization of the abnormality. This technique may be particularly useful in differentiating septic arthritis or cellulitis from bony infection and in distinguishing postoperative changes after prosthetic joint replacement from superimposed infection.

Unlike radionuclide bone images, which may remain positive for relatively long periods of time, gallium accumulation in osteomyelitis tends to decrease with successful antibiotic therapy and therefore can be used to determine the results of treatment. Furthermore, active foci of osteomyelitis in chronic lesions may be detected with gallium scanning. Imaging with technetium phosphate analogs may produce positive images in both acute and chronic disease; however, a negative gallium scan in such instances is generally associated with healed infections, whereas a highly positive image usually indicates relapse.

Indium 111 Labeled Leukocytes

In recent years, there have been additional developments in abscess and inflammation scanning. Indium 111 oxine labeled leukocytes have been demonstrated to have relatively high sensitivity and specificity for acute infections, although specificity is somewhat lower for chronic infections or other inflammatory processes. The procedure involves removal of some of the patient's own white cells, labeling them, and reinjecting prior to scanning.

The advantages of indium 111 oxine labeled leukocytes over gallium 67 citrate for the detection of inflammatory disease include less activity in the gastrointestinal tract, kidneys, and normal soft tissues, as well as diminished activity in noninfectious inflammation and tumors and greater concentration in abscessed tissues. However, the indium 111 leukocyte labeling process can be tedious, time-consuming, and especially difficult in patients with depressed white counts.

LABELING AND BIOLOGIC BEHAVIOR

The ability to image leukocyte distribution in the body became possible after the development of successful methods for labeling leukocytes with indium 111 oxine. Oxine (8-

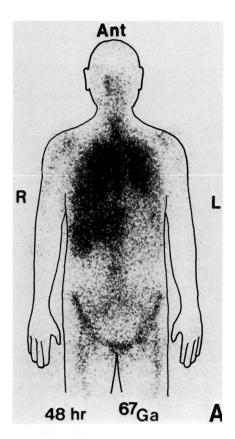

Figure 13–5. (A) Diffuse gallium uptake in the lungs. An anterior gallium image at 48 hours postinjection in an immunosuppressed patient demonstrates increased activity diffusely in both lungs. (B) A pulmonary biopsy diagnosis of *Pneumocystis carinii* was made in this patient with a normal chest radiograph.

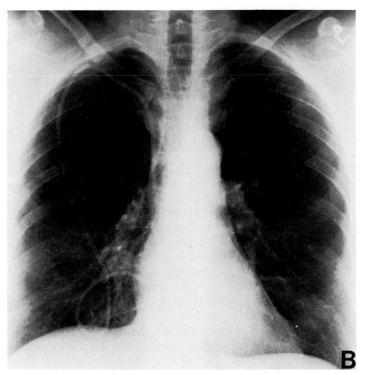

hydroxyquinoline) is a lipophilic ligand capable of chelating metallic ions such as indium. Oxine thus forms a lipid-soluble complex with indium 111, and this complex is capable of diffusing through the leukocyte cell membrane. Once it becomes intracellular, the indium 111 separates from the oxine and binds to the cytoplasmic components. The oxine then elutes from the cell and is removed from the material to be injected by washing the cells. Because the imaging characteristics of indium 111 are inferior to those of ^{99m}Tc, a ^{99m}Tc radiopharmaceutical would certainly be more desirable but has met with only limited success. Thus, at present, indium 111 oxine remains the label of choice.

Several methods of separating leukocytes from the patient's blood have been used, but overall, the method used should permit (1) the separation of as many leukocytes as possible since the efficiency of cell labeling is directly related to the number of cells available; (2) the removal of as many other cellular components as possible, since both red blood cells (RBCs) and platelets will be labeled and have a longer survival in the circulation; and (3) the preservation of leukocyte function to allow the desired results when reinjected into the patient.

The disappearance of reinjected labeled leukocytes from the blood has a half-life of about 5 hours. Blood pool activity is essentially gone in 18 to 24 hours. If one sees blood pool activity after this time, it may be due to excess lymphocyte or RBC labeling because these agents have a longer half-life disappearance from the blood.

IMAGING TECHNIQUE

Because leukocytes can be separated and labeled with indium 111 without significant loss of function, they can be used to image inflammatory processes. Administered activity of 0.5 to 1.0 mCi (18.5 to 37 MBq) may be used. Care should be taken to avoid excessive agitation of the leukocytes because this may cause clumping and focal lung activity. Although some abscesses can be detected as early as 30 minutes after the administration of labeled leukocytes, most imaging is performed 18 to 24 hours after administration. Gamma camera images using a medium energy collimator are obtained of areas of interest, or, if no specific area is indicated, a whole body survey may be performed. Generally, both the 172- and 247-keV gamma emissions are utilized.

NORMAL SCAN

After administration of indium 111 leukocytes, activity is noted in the lungs, liver, spleen, and blood pool. The lung and blood pool activity decreases during the first few hours as spleen and liver activity increases. By 18 hours, no lung or blood pool activity is detected but bone marrow activity is noted (Fig. 13–6).

Twenty-four hours after administration, the indium 111 leukocyte preparation may be found in the liver, spleen, and bone marrow, with the spleen providing the most prominent area of accumulation. It is not known exactly whether the activity in bone marrow represents normal migration of white blood cells or indium chloride eluted from damaged white blood cells. Damaged white blood cells that remain labeled may provide increased activity in the liver if slightly damaged and increased lung activity if severely damaged.

Colonic activity of indium 111 leukocytes has been reported in various entities such as inflammatory bowel disease, vasculitis (including rheumatoid), and cecal abscess draining distally into the colon (Fig. 13–7). Swallowed activity from more proximal inflammation such as in the sinuses, esophagus, and pulmonary lesions has also been reported as a source for colonic activity. Bowel infarction as well as vigorous enemazation prior to imaging may also be a source of colon activity, as may active colonic hemorrhage.

ABNORMAL SCAN

To date, this technique has proved quite useful in the demonstration of pyogenic abscesses with greater success than that reported with gallium 67 citrate. In addition, the evaluation and detection of inflammatory bowel disease, cytomegalovirus and *Pneumocystis* infection (Fig. 13–8), nonspecific inflammation such as acute myocardial infarction, and myocarditis have been reported (see Table 13–4). While indium 111 leukocytes have been proposed for the evaluation of renal transplants, evidence suggests that the radiopharmaceutical may accumulate in both rejecting and normal renal allografts.

Indium 111 leukocytes are useful in detect-

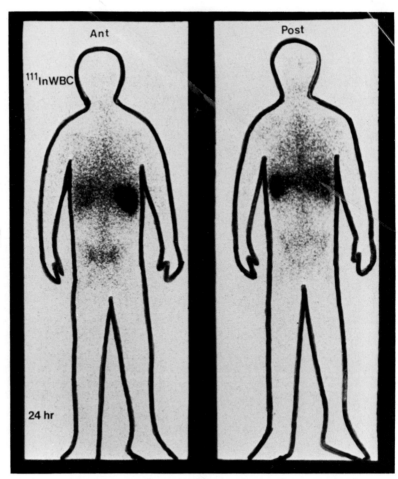

Figure 13–6. Normal indium 111 oxine leukocyte scan. By 24 hours post-injection, there is a minor amount of background activity, moderate hepatic activity, and marked splenic activity.

ing vascular graft infections including dialysis access graft infections. Over 90 percent of patients with positive scans will have subsequently documented culture evidence of infection.

OSTEOMYELITIS

In general, in cases of uncomplicated acute osteomyelitis, if the three-phase bone scan is positive, indium leukocyte scans or gallium scans are usually not needed. In the case of complicated osteomyelitis with fractures or nonunion, the situation becomes much more difficult. Gallium scintigraphy, although sensitive, has limited usefulness, and the criteria for infection in patients usually include local gallium uptake greater than bone agent uptake or in a different spatial pattern. When gallium uptake is equal to bone agent uptake, the results are equivocal.

Indium leukocytes can be positive in early bony trauma without infections, although the uptake is usually mild. Significant focal uptake at a site of suspected osteomyelitis is indicative of bony infection. Reported sensitivity and specificity rates are as high as approximately 90 percent. Overall, indium leukocytes appear to be superior to gallium for detection of bony infection. Leukocytes may also be useful and slightly superior to gallium citrate in detection of infection following insertion of orthopedic prosthetic devices. Note should be made that prior antibiotic therapy or chronic infection may reduce sensitivity of radio-labeled leukocyte imaging. No clear consensus is apparent as to whether gallium or indium leukocyte scanning is the more useful as an adjunct to three-phase bone scanning in cases of complicated osteomyelitis.

IMMUNOSUPPRESSED PATIENTS

In immunosuppressed patients, indium 111 labeled white blood cells may be used to

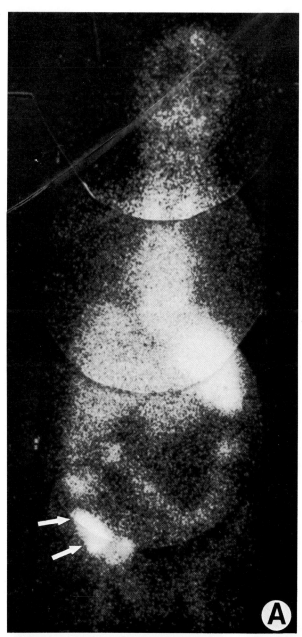

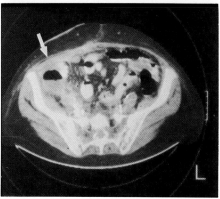

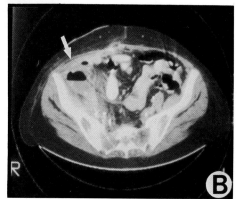

Figure 13–7. Periappendiceal abscess. (A) Indium 111 leukocyte scan done at 24 hours shows intense right lower quadrant activity in a periappendiceal-cecal abscess. The activity more distally in the colon is compatible with drainage into the colon from the abscess (Polaroid images). (B) A correlative CT scan demonstrates the typical finding of an abscess in the right iliac fossa (arrows).

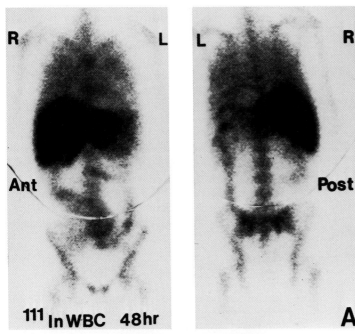

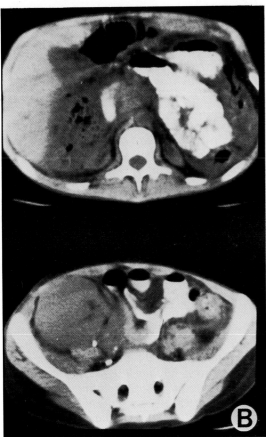

Figure 13–8. Cytomegalic virus pneumonitis and colitis. (A) The indium 111 scan performed at 24 hours demonstrates diffuse pulmonary activity as well as activity throughout the colon. This patient was immunosuppressed due to splenectomy and steroid administration in the course of renal transplantation. The renal transplant is identified on the CT scan (B). (Case courtesy of Manuel Brown, M.D.)

Table 13–4. CAUSES OF INCREASED ACTIVITY ON INDIUM LEUKOCYTE IMAGES

CHEST

Common Causes
- Abscess
- Adult respiratory distress syndrome
- Cellulitis
- Emphysema
- Pleural tubes
- Noninfected intravenous lines
- Pneumonia
- Wound infection

Uncommon Causes
- Aspiration
- Atelectasis
- Cystic fibrosis
- Graft infection
- Hematoma
- Tumor (infected or noninfected)
- Herpes esophagitis

ABDOMEN

Common Causes
- Abscess
- Cellulitis
- Enteric tubes
- Ostomies
- Phlegmon
- Swallowed leukocytes
- Wound infection

Uncommon Causes
- Acute enteritis
- Bowel infarction
- Colitis
- Crohn's disease
- Decubitus ulcer
- Gastrointestinal bleeding
- Graft infection
- Hematoma
- Pancreatitis
- Tumor (infected or noninfected)
- Transplant (with or without rejection)
- Diverticulitis
- Acute cholecystitis

MUSCULOSKELETAL AND SKIN UPTAKE

Common Causes
- Cellulitis
- Intravenous site
- Wound infection
- Osteomyelitis
- Sinusitis

Uncommon Causes
- Lumbar puncture site
- Rheumatoid arthritis
- Septic arthritis

evaluate fevers of unknown origin with a high rate of successful identification of localized infections, including sites of candidiasis and colitis. Indium 111 white cell imaging appears less successful than gallium 67 scans in identifying PCP infections and is insensitive for the detection of secondary lymphomas.

False positive examinations may be caused by nonpyogenic inflammatory diseases such as arthritis, colonic activity as cited above, infarcts, drainage tube sites, and accessory splenic tissue. False negative examinations have been reported in tuberculous and fungal infections, round cell (chronic) reactions, and in patients treated with antibiotics. In addition, false negative studies have been theorized in conditions that alter leukochemotaxis and therefore alter the agent's ability to function properly. Such conditions include hemodialysis, hypoglycemia, and hyperalimentation.

Labeled Antibodies

Over the past several years, much interest has been generated in the development of labeled antibodies for the immunodetection and immunotherapy of a variety of diseases—particularly those of an oncologic nature. However, it was not until the development of methods of producing and labeling monoclonal antibodies that the clinical potential of such agents could be seriously explored. In addition to oncologic agents, radiopharmaceuticals for the evaluation of non-neoplastic diseases such as myocardial infarction (anticardiac myosin monoclonal antibodies) are currently of interest.

Monoclonal antibodies are so named because when developed against a given antigen, they are absolutely identical with one another. The technique for producing monoclonals first involves the immunization of an animal, generally a mouse, with a specific antigen (Fig. 13–9). This antigen can be virtually anything capable of inducing the B lymphocytes to begin producing antibodies against the injected substance. Once this is done, the B lymphocytes are harvested from the mouse and placed in a tube containing mouse myeloma cells. Fusion of these myeloma cells with the B lymphocytes then takes place, forming what is known as a *hybridoma*. This hybridoma has the ability to continue producing antigen-specific antibodies based upon the B lymphocyte parent and at the same time to perpetuate itself based on the characteristic of continual mitosis conferred upon it by the myeloma cells.

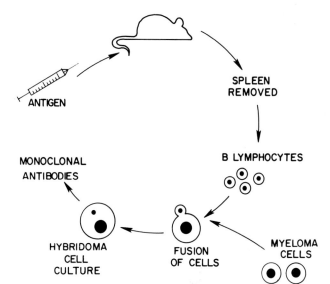

Figure 13–9. Schematic representation of steps involved in production of monoclonal antibodies.

Hybridomas can then be grown in clones and separated out until a clone is developed that produces an antibody of particular interest. When such clones are developed, they are grown in the peritoneal cavities of mice with the antibody produced being secreted into the ascitic fluid. This ascitic fluid is harvested and processed to provide a purified form of the antibody. Large quantities of monoclonal antibodies can be obtained in this way. Bulk production of monoclonal antibodies is also possible employing a synthetic approach in vitro.

Once produced, monoclonal antibodies or fragments thereof may be labeled with radionuclides and used to map the distribution of specific antigens in vivo. Although the concept initially appears quite simple, substantial problems exist that limit the clinical application of monoclonal antibodies for tumor imaging at this time. Not the least of these problems are the selection of an appropriate specific antigen, the successful labeling of the antibody, significant cross-reactivity with other antigens, and poor target-to-nontarget ratios in vivo. Furthermore, immune responses to the foreign antibody protein in humans have provided a further barrier to successful widespread use. It is hoped that eventually a majority of these drawbacks may be circumvented and that monoclonal antibodies will become part of the diagnostic and therapeutic nuclear medicine radiopharmaceutical armamentarium. Radiolabels currently include radioiodines, indium 111, and technetium 99m.

Suggested Readings

Datz FL, Thorne DA: Effect of antibiotic therapy on the sensitivity of indium 111 labeled leukocyte scans. J Nucl Med 27:1849–1853, 1986

Freeman LM, Blaufox MD (eds): Nuclear oncology. Part I. Semin Nucl Med 15(1):2–11, 1985

Freeman LM, Blaufox MD (eds): The role of nuclear medicine in infectious disease. Semin Nucl Med 18(4):273–344, 1988

Ganz WI, Serafini AN: The diagnostic role of nuclear medicine in the acquired immunodeficiency syndrome. J Nucl Med 30:1935–1945, 1989

McAfee JG, Samin A: Indium 111 labeled leukocytes: A review of problems in image interpretation. Radiology 155:221–229, 1985

Tsan M-F: Mechanisms of gallium 67 accumulation in inflammatory lesions. J Nucl Med 26:88–92, 1985

Tsan M-F, Scheffel U: Mechanism of gallium 67 accumulation in tumors. J Nucl Med 27:1215–1219, 1986

Woolfenden JM, Carrasquillo JA, Larson SM, et al: Acquired immunodeficiency syndrome: Gallium 67 citrate imaging. Radiology 162:383–387, 1987

Legal Requirements and Radiation Safety

Regulatory Agencies

The Nuclear Regulatory Commission (NRC) regulates special nuclear material, source material, and by-products. Source material is uranium or thorium, and special nuclear material is plutonium or enriched uranium. By-products are materials made radioactive by exposure to radiation from the use or production of special nuclear material (i.e., reactor-produced radionuclides). The NRC authority does not cover naturally occurring radionuclides (such as radium) or accelerator-produced radioactive material; the individual states are responsible for possession and use of these.

NRC regulations govern most nuclear medicine operations and include the Code of Federal Regulations (CFR) 10, Title I, Parts 20 and 35. Part 20 is concerned with standards for protection against radiation, including permissible doses, levels, concentrations, precautionary procedures, and waste disposal. Part 35 is concerned with the medical use of by-product material, including the ALARA (as low as reasonably achievable) program, types of licenses, required surveys, instrumentation, and training requirements.

Some states have reached an agreement with the NRC and accept the responsibility of regulating by-product, source, and special nuclear materials within their jurisdiction. These are "agreement states," and their regulations are generally compatible with those of the NRC. The agreement states are Alabama, Arizona, Arkansas, California, Colorado, Florida, Georgia, Idaho, Illinois, Iowa, Kansas, Kentucky, Louisiana, Maryland, Mississippi, Nebraska, Nevada, New Hampshire, New Mexico, New York, North Carolina, North Dakota, Oregon, Rhode Island, South Carolina, Tennessee, Texas, Utah, and Washington. In addition to agreement states, there are licensing and registration states. A licensing state is one that licenses only users of naturally occurring and accelerator-produced radioactive material. A registration state registers only those persons or institutions using naturally occurring and accelerator-produced radioactive material.

The philosophy of a radiation protection program, which is now required by the NRC, is that of ALARA. This is designed to keep radiation doses *as low as reasonably achievable*. To satisfy requirements of ALARA, administrative personnel, the radiation safety officer, and all authorized users must participate in an ALARA program as requested by the radiation safety committee or officer. The program must also include notice to the workers of the program's existence and the worker's responsibility to participate in this philosophy.

Radiation Safety Officer

Each licensee must have a radiation safety officer (RSO) who is responsible for implementing the radiation safety program and who ensures that activities are being performed in accordance with approved procedures and regulatory requirements. Duties of the radiation safety officer include investigation of overexposures, accidents, and other mishaps; collecting or establishing written policies and procedures relative to purchasing, receipt and opening, storage, inventory, use, and disposal of by-product material. The RSO is also responsible for training of personnel, performing radiation surveys, keeping copies of reports and policies, briefing management once each year, and establishing investigational levels of personnel exposure, which when exceeded will initiate an investigation by the RSO.

Radiation Safety Committee

Under NRC regulations, each medical institution licensee is required to have a radiation safety committee. Membership must consist of at least three persons, including an authorized user of each type of radiation by-product permitted by the license, the RSO, a representative from nursing services, and a representative of management or administration. The committee must meet at least quarterly, and at least 50 percent of the membership must be present. Minutes must include the date of the meeting, those present and absent, summary of deliberations, discussions, and recommended actions as well as ALARA program review. The committee is required to provide each member with a copy of the minutes and to maintain a copy for the duration of the license.

The committee also reviews for approval or disapproval those who wish to become authorized users, the RSO, and the teletherapy physicist. They may approve or disapprove minor changes in radiation safety procedures. The committee must review quarterly the summary of occupational radiation dose records and all incidents involving by-product material. There must be an annual review of the radiation safety program with the RSO.

Types of Licenses

Possession and use of by-product materials prior to 1987 was allowable with either a general license, a specific license, or a broad license. A *general license* was for physicians and allowed possession and use of limited quantities of prepackaged individual doses or material for in vitro clinical laboratory testing. A *specific license* was for an individual physician utilizing radionuclides in office practice of limited scope. The *broad license* was issued to large qualified research institutions with a full-time RSO.

The 1987 NRC regulations (CFR 35) created three types of broad licenses and six types of Part 35 specific licenses. Broad scope licenses are described in NRC regulations Part 33.11 and are usually reserved for large hospitals and academic institutions. There are type A, B, and C broad scope licenses depending upon the amount of by-product material in possession.

Part 35 specific licenses are usually for small hospitals and office practice. Specific Part 35 licenses are related to the particular use of by-product materials as follows:

CFR 35.100 allows a licensee to use radiopharmaceuticals for uptake, dilution, and excretion studies. The licensee is required to have a portable radiation survey instrument capable of detecting dose rates over the range of 0.1 to 100 mrem (1 μSv to 1 mSv)/hour.

CFR 35.200 is a license for the use of radiopharmaceuticals, generators, and reagent kits for imaging and localization studies. Those licensees using molybdenum 99/technetium 99m generators are required to measure the molybdenum 99 concentration in each eluate and must retain this record for 2 years. The record must contain the time, date, and initials of the person who made the measurement as well as the measured activity of both molybdenum and technetium. In addition, this license requires that radioactive gases be trapped or vented to the atmosphere and used in a room with negative pressure relative to the surrounding area. The licensee must also possess a radiation detection survey instrument capable of detecting dose rates from 0.1 to 100 mrem (1 μSV to 1 mSv)/hour and a portable radiation instrument capable of measuring dose rates from 1 to 1000 mrem (10 μSv to 10 mSv)/hour.

CFR 35.300 is a license for use of radiopharmaceuticals for therapy. The license requires safety inspections for all personnel caring for patients receiving radiopharmaceutical therapy and hospitalization. There must be procedures for patient and visitor contamination and for waste control, as well as for notification of the RSO in case of a medical emergency or a patient's death. There must also be a list of persons receiving such instructions, a description of the instructions, the date, and the name of the person who gave the instruction. A sample protocol for management of such patients is provided in Appendix G. There must be possession of survey instruments similar to those outlined in CFR 35.200.

CFR 35.400 are licenses for use of sealed sources in brachytherapy and for teletherapy.

CFR 35.500 is a license for use of sealed sources for diagnosis. This includes iodine 125, americium 241, and gadolinium 153 as a sealed source for bone mineral analysis, and iodine 125 for use in a portable imaging device. Survey instrument requirements are the same as those for license 35.200.

Training

According to NRC regulations, specific training is required for RSOs and for users of the different types of radiation by-product materials. An RSO is someone who is certified by any of the following: American Board of Health Physics, Comprehensive Health Physics, American Board of Radiology, American Board of Nuclear Medicine, American Board of Science in Nuclear Medicine, or Board of Pharmaceutical Specialists in Nuclear Pharmacy. An alternative to this board certification is 200 hours of classroom and laboratory training in radiation physics, instrumentation, radiation protection, mathematics, radiation biology, and radiopharmaceutical chemistry, as well as one year of full-time experience as a radiation safety technologist under the supervision of an RSO. An alternative is a person who is an authorized user identified on the licensee's license.

Training for imaging and localization studies requires that the authorized user be a physician who meets one or more of the following criteria:

1. Certification by any of the following: American Board of Nuclear Medicine, in diagnostic radiology by the American Board of Radiology, or in diagnostic radiology or radiology by the American Osteopathic Board of Radiology

2. Classroom and laboratory training in handling radioisotopes as follows: 200 hours of classroom and laboratory training in radiation physics, instrumentation, protection, mathematics, radiopharmaceutical chemistry, and radiation biology, as well as 500 hours of experience under an authorized user in ordering, calibration, and preparation of patient doses, administrative control, elution, and kit preparation, as well as an additional 500 hours in supervised clinical experience

3. Successful completion of a 6-month training program in nuclear medicine that has been approved by the Accreditation Council for Graduate Medical Education and has included classroom and clinical experience as stated in item 2.

Training for therapeutic use of radiopharmaceuticals requires a physician who meets one of the following criteria:

1. Certification by the American Board of Nuclear Medicine or the American Board of Radiology in radiology or therapeutic radiology

2. Classroom and laboratory training as well as clinical experience encompassing 80 hours of classroom training in radiation physics, protection, mathematics, and biology. The clinical experience must be under the supervision of an authorized user and include the use of ^{131}I for evaluation of thyroid function and treatment. At least ten hyperthyroid patients must have been treated, and for use in thyroid carcinoma, at least three must have been treated.

Training for use of sealed sources in diagnosis requires that the authorized user be a physician, dentist, or podiatrist who meets one of the following criteria:

1. Certification in radiology, diagnostic radiology, or therapeutic radiology by the American Board of Radiology; certification in nuclear medicine by the American Board of Nuclear Medicine; certification in diagnostic radiology or radiology by the American Osteopathic Board of Radiology

2. Eight hours of classroom and laboratory training including physics, mathematics, radiation biology, radiation protection, and training in the use of the device for the particular uses requested.

All training must have been obtained within 5 years preceding the date of application, or the person must have had related continuing education and experience since the time that required training and experience were completed. It should be noted that physicians or certain podiatrists who were authorized users prior to 1987 need not comply with the above-listed training requirements.

SUPERVISION AND VISITING AUTHORIZED USER

A potential problem must be dealt with when a licensed single authorized user wishes to go on vacation. Receipt, possession, and use of radiopharmaceuticals, as well as interpretation of studies, can be permitted for a person who is periodically reviewed by the authorized user and who has been instructed in radiation safety practices and procedures. This actually allows a user to let one of his or her physician "trainees" be utilized in his or her absence. An alternative is a visiting authorized user who can be employed for 60 days a year and generally comes from another institution. Permission must be granted for this and a copy of the institution's license must be on hand. The clinical procedures must be those for which the visiting authorized user is licensed to perform at his or her institution.

Transportation

Interstate transportation of radioactive materials usually is controlled by regulations of the Department of Transportation (DOT). The NRC requires that DOT regulations be observed when radiopharmaceuticals are returned to a manufacturer or being transported between offices, laboratories, and/or hospitals, with the exception of when materials are being transported by a physician for medical practice.

The DOT has assigned levels of hazardousness to radionuclides based on their toxicity. These levels are different from the NRC license isotope groups mentioned above. Transport group I is reserved for very hazardous radionuclides such as plutonium 239 and americium 241, whereas transport group VI includes radionuclides of very low hazard such as uncompressed krypton 85 gas. Radionuclides used in nuclear medicine are in transport groups III and IV.

The type and amount of isotope determine the hazardousness of the material and therefore the type of packaging required. Packaging of medical radioisotopes is of two common types: type A packaging is designed to prevent loss or disbursement of a limited amount of radioactive material under normal conditions during transport. Type B packaging is for higher activity radioactive material and is more accident-resistant than type A packaging. A type A package may contain up to 3 mCi (111 MBq) of transport group III isotopes, whereas a type B package may contain up to 200 Ci (7400 GBq). In addition, a type A package may contain 20 Ci (740 GBq) of transport group IV radionuclides, and a type B package may contain 200 Ci

(7400 GBq). Less than 1 mCi (37 MBq) of transport group III or IV radionuclide is considered an exempt quantity (does not have to be specially packaged) as long as there is no leakage under normal transport conditions and the radiation dose at the external surface of the package does not exceed 0.5 mrem/hr (5 μSv/hr).

Packages of radioactive materials must be labeled according to one of the three following categories:

- *Radioactive—White I.* No special handling is required. Surface dose rate must not exceed 0.5 mrem/hr (5 μSv/hr).

- *Radioactive—Yellow II.* Special handling is required. Surface dose rate may not exceed 50 mrem/hr (0.5 mSv/hr), and dose rate may not exceed 1 mrem/hr (10 μSv/hr) at 3 feet from any external surface.

- *Radioactive—Yellow III.* Surface dose rate may not exceed 200 mrem/hr (2 mSv/hr) and dose rate may not exceed 10 mrem/hr (100 μSv/hr) at 3 feet from any external surface.

The transportation index (TI) is the number of millirems per hour measured at 3 feet from the package. Thus, any package with a TI from 1 to 10 would be required to have a "Radioactive—Yellow III" label.

Receipt of Radioactive Shipments

When any package of radioactive material is received, it should be checked for contamination and leakage. Its receipt should be noted in a log, and then the package should be stored in an appropriate shielded area. Although most materials being received at a nuclear medicine laboratory are not required to be monitored, it is certainly a good idea to do so. NRC regulations do require monitoring of shipments in liquid form, those with half-lives of more than 30 days, or quantities of more than 100 mCi (3.7 GBq). Molybdenum–technetium generators are normally excluded from this regulation if they do not exceed 3 Ci (111 GBq). It should be noted that although many radioactive materials being received do not need to be monitored, shipments of the following must be surveyed: cobalt 57, cobalt 60, selenium 75, iron 59, strontium 85, iodine 131 (greater than 100 mCi or 3.7 GBq).

To perform a survey, absorbent paper is usually wiped over an area of approximately 100 cm^2 and counted. Removable contamination in excess of 22,000 disintegrations per minute (dpm) over such an area requires notification of the appropriate agency.

RECORD KEEPING

A shipment of arriving radioactive material should be recorded in both a receiving report and in the radionuclide logbook. The receiving report should indicate the shipment identification, including supplier, radionuclide and lot number, measured radiation level, results of surface and internal package wipes for removable contamination, and the amount and type of radionuclide as indicated by manufacturer as well as the nuclear medicine laboratory confirmation of this. Each entry into the logbook should be recorded on a separate page. The inventory record (radiopharmaceutical logbook) should indicate all records of bulk dilutions, use, and disposal so that all the isotope may be accounted for.

Most laboratories also maintain a patient dosage logbook, in which the date, time of calibration, type and amount of radiopharmaceutical, and name of patient and administering technician's name are recorded. Most laboratories also record the quantity of the radiopharmaceutical administered in the patient's hospital or outpatient chart. Record retention times are shown in Table 14–1.

INSTRUMENTATION

NRC regulations also cover instrument calibration.

Dose Calibrator. Even if only unit doses are obtained from an outside radiopharmacy, a dose calibrator is required to measure the amount of activity prior to administration. Dose calibrator calibration requirements include the following:

1. Constancy must be checked at the beginning of each day on a frequently used setting with a sealed source of not less than 10 μCi (0.37 MBq) of radium 226 or 50 μCi (1.85 MBq) of any other photon-emitting radionuclide.

Table 14–1. RECORD RETENTION TIMES INDICATED BY NRC REGULATIONS

Until license termination
  Personnel monitoring records
  Bioassay records
  Radiation accident investigation results
  Radiation safety committee minutes
  Records of receipt of by-product material still in possession

10 years
  Misadministration reports

5 years
  Sealed-source inventory
  Sealed-source checklist

3 years
  Patient dose records
  Records of by-product material transferred to others
  Area surveys
  Disposal survey records of decay-in-storage material
  Molybdenum 99 assay records
  Survey meter calibration
  Dose calibrator constancy, linearity, and accuracy tests (geometry test must be maintained for duration of use of the dose calibrator)

2. Accuracy must be tested upon installation and at least annually with at least two different long-lived sealed sources. One of the sources must have a principal photon energy between 110 and 500 keV.

3. Linearity must be evaluated quarterly over the range of use between 10 μCi (0.37 MBq) and the highest dose that will be administered to a patient.

4. Geometry dependence must be checked upon installation over the range of volumes and volume configurations to be used. All values cannot exceed 10 percent with mathematical corrections for geometry or linearity error.

Repair or replacement of the instrument is required for accuracy or constancy errors greater than 10 percent. A record for each constancy check for the dose calibrator must be maintained for a period of 2 years; this must include the model and serial number of the dose calibrator, the identity of radionuclides, the date of check, the activity measured, and the initials of the person performing the check. Checks of accuracy, linearity, and geometric dependence must in addition be signed by the RSO.

Survey Instruments. Survey instruments must be calibrated before first use, annually, and following repair and must include:

1. Calibration of all scales with readings up to 1000 mrem (10 mSv) per hour
2. Two readings on each scale
3. Conspicuous notation on the instrument of the apparent exposure rate from a dedicated check source as determined at the time of calibration as well as the date of calibration

The instrument can be considered calibrated if it does not differ by more than 20 percent from the calculated exposure rate. Calibration records must be maintained for a period of 3 years. The requirement for determination of an exposure rate from a dedicated check source requires that a check source must be purchased for each survey meter and shipped with it at calibration time. A licensee is required to check each survey instrument for proper operation with the dedicated check source each day of use, although records are not required to be kept of these daily checks.

Preparation of Radiopharmaceuticals

Certain safety requirements need to be observed during the preparation of radiopharmaceuticals. Protection from radiation exposure is achieved primarily by three factors: time, distance, and shielding. Radiation exposure is directly proportional to the amount of time spent in the radiation field. Thus, all preparation procedures should be done as efficiently as possible. Distance is a powerful ally in radiation protection, with the dose to an individual decreasing with the square of the distance. Thus, if one doubles the distance between an individual and a source, the radiation exposure to the individual is reduced to one fourth. If the distance is tripled, the radiation exposure is reduced to one ninth. The converse is also true; therefore, unshielded radioactive materials should never be picked up directly with the fingers since very high doses may result. Instead, such materials should be handled with clamps, forceps, or other holding devices. When time and distance are not adequate or practical for radiation protection, shielding must be utilized. It is important to remember that when dealing with beta radiation, a shield should be made of a low atomic number material. If a high atomic number material such as lead is used, the interaction between the beta particles and the lead may cause the emission of bremsstrahlung radiation, which is highly penetrating.

When utilizing technetium 99m, lead shielding is sufficient. The half-value layer (HVL), which is the amount of lead required to reduce the radiation exposure by half, is 0.2 mm of lead for ^{99m}Tc. A thickness of 2.5 mm of lead will attenuate radiation from ^{99m}Tc by a factor of approximately 1000. Radionuclides with more energetic gamma rays may require much more shielding.

Shielding is of two general types: benchtop, and syringe or vial shields. Benchtop shields are frequently constructed of lead bricks and usually have a viewing portal of lead glass to shield the face and eyes. Direct handling of thin-walled plastic syringes containing short-lived radionuclides can cause skin exposure in the range of 500 to 1000 mrem/hr/mCi (0.14 to 0.27 mGy/hr/MBq). Although brief handling of unshielded radionuclides is usually well within permissible limits, syringe shields will reduce exposure levels by a factor of at least three.

NRC regulations require that the licensee must identify contents of a syringe by a label either on the syringe itself or on the syringe shield bearing at least one of the following: radiopharmaceutical name, clinical procedure, or patient name. Syringe shields are required when preparing a radiopharmaceutical kit or performing a radiopharmaceutical injection unless the use of the shield is contraindicated for that patient. It is not necessary to use a syringe shield for drawing up a dose. If vials are used, the vials must be kept in radiation shields and the shield must be labeled with the radiopharmaceutical name.

Since the basis of imaging procedures is the detection of radiation emanating from the patient, the patient is by definition a source of exposure. Estimates of typical exposure to technologists from standard imaging procedures range from 0.4 mrem to 0.6 mrem (4 to 6 μSv). Between 50 and 90 percent of the dose usually comes from being with the patient while the patient is imaged rather than from the actual injection of dose preparation, assay, or injection. While these are measurable levels, they are not high enough to ever be used as an excuse to keep the technician and physician from providing the patient with the best medical care.

For diagnostic clinical procedures, it is not

necessary to follow the package inserts in the use of a radiopharmaceutical. The only restriction is that the chemical form must not be changed. This allows the user to take an approved radiopharmaceutical and give it in a different form such as gas versus liquid, by a different route of administration, or in a different dose without filing a notice of claimed investigational exemption for a new drug (IND).

The licensee must measure each dose containing more than 10 µCi (0.37 MBq) of a photon-emitting radionuclide before medical use. Doses of 10 µCi (0.37 MBq) or less must be verified to see that in fact the activity is equal to or less than 10 µCi (0.37 MBq). Furthermore, it is necessary to measure low activity items before administration, such as Schilling test capsules.

Records regarding activity of measurement of radiopharmaceutical doses must contain the generic name, trade name or abbreviation of radiopharmaceutical, lot number, expiration date, patient's name and identification number, prescribed dosage, activity at time of measurement, date and time of measurement, and initials of the person who made the record.

Misadministration of Radiopharmaceuticals

The NRC requires that radiopharmaceutical activity be assayed to an accuracy of ± 10 percent of the prescribed dose prior to patient administration. This responsibility resides with the person who will actually be administering the radiopharmaceutical rather than with a centralized radiopharmacy. Thus, an accurate dose calibrator is an essential piece of equipment for a nuclear medicine laboratory. Although diagnostic radioisotopes may be used for calibration of dose calibrators, the more common practice is to use a reference source. Cobalt 57 (122, 136 keV) has a half-life of 250 days and is often used to simulate ^{99m}Tc. Cesium 137 (662 keV) has a half-life of 30 years and is used to simulate molybdenum 99. Barium 133 (356, 302, 80 keV) is used to simulate iodine 131.

Misadministration is defined by the NRC as (1) the administration of a radiopharmaceutical other than the one intended; (2) administration of a radiopharmaceutical to the wrong patient; or (3) administration of a radiopharmaceutical by a route or in a quantity other than that prescribed. An excessive quantity is a diagnostic dosage differing from the prescribed quantity by more than 50 percent or a therapeutic dose differing by more than 10 percent from that prescribed.

A misadministration involving a diagnostic procedure requires that the RSO promptly investigate its cause, make the record for NRC review, and retain the record for 10 years. The licensee must also notify the referring physician and appropriate NRC office within 15 days if the misadministration involved the use of by-product material not intended for medical use, administration of a dose five-fold different from intended dosage, or administration of a by-product material such that the patient is likely to receive an organ dose greater than 2 rem (20 mSv) or a whole-body dose greater than 500 mrem (5 mSv).

With a therapy misadministration, the licensee must notify the NRC regional office by telephone, as well as the referring physician and the patient or a responsible relative or guardian, unless the referring physician agrees to inform the patient or believes that telling the patient or the patient's responsible relative would be harmful to one or the other, respectively. Such notifications must be made within 24 hours after discovery of misadministration. Within 15 days after an initial therapy misadministration report to the NRC, a written report must be sent to the NRC regional office with copies to the referring physician and to the patient or patient's responsible relative if previously notified. The written report must include the licensee's name, the referring physician's name, a brief description of the misadministration, the effect on the patient, the action taken to prevent recurrence, and a statement regarding whether the licensee informed the patient or responsible relative. The report must not include the patient's name or other patient identification.

Laboratory Areas

Nuclear medicine laboratories are generally divided into controlled and noncontrolled areas. Examples of noncontrolled or unrestricted areas are offices, file space, patient waiting areas, and nonradiation laboratory space. These areas must have dose rates of less than 2 mrem/hr (20 μSv/hr) and less than 100 mrem (1 mSv) over 7 consecutive days total. If these limits are exceeded, control of the area is required. A controlled area (also known as restricted area or radiation area) is one in which the occupational exposure of personnel is under the supervision of an individual in charge of radiation protection. Access to the area and working conditions within it are controlled. Controlled areas are not accessible to the general public and must be clearly marked with radiation warning signs. Examples of controlled areas are the radiopharmaceutical preparation area, dispensing area, storage area, administration area, and imaging area. A "Caution—Radioactive materials" sign is required on entrances to areas where radioisotopes are used. A "Radiation Area" sign is required in areas where the dose rate exceeds 5 mrem/hr (50 μSv/hr) or a total of 100 mrem (1 mSv) over 5 consecutive days to a major portion of the body. A "High Radiation Area" sign is required if the dose rate exceeds 100 mrem/hr (1 mSv/hr) to a major portion of the body.

Surveys

Typical radiation detection instruments generally measure either beta or gamma radiation. Only a very sophisticated and expensive piece of equipment can measure alpha particles. The most common piece of equipment found in a nuclear medicine department is either a Geiger-Mueller counter or a low-range survey meter. These survey instruments are usually capable of measuring absorbed dose rates from about 1 to 500 mrad (10 μGy to 5 mGy) per hour. They are useful for detecting small amounts of contamination on persons or on laboratory surfaces. These instruments also can be used to provide an estimate of dose rate at a particular distance from a patient who has received a radionuclide. If dose rates in excess of 500 mrad (5 mGy) per hour are expected, an ionization chamber, such as a "cutie pie," is necessary. Such an instrument is most useful in monitoring patients who have had therapeutic administration of radionuclides.

A licensee possessing sealed sources must leak test the source every 6 months. If more than 0.005 μCi (185 Bq) of removable activity is on a wipe sample, the source is said to be leaking. This procedure is not required if the materials (1) have less than a 30-day half-life, (2) are gases, or (3) consist of less than 100 μCi (3.7 MBq) of beta- or gamma-emitting radionuclide. It is also not required of alpha-emitting radionuclides of less than 10 μCi (0.37 MBq) and of sources stored and not being used. Quarterly inventory of all sealed sources and survey of all stored materials in sealed sources are required.

Surveys for contamination and ambient radiation exposure are covered in NRC Guidelines 35.70. A licensee is required to survey all areas in which radiopharmaceuticals are prepared and administered at the end of each day with a radiation detection instrument. All areas in which radiopharmaceuticals are stored or waste is stored must be surveyed once each week. A licensee can establish trigger levels for the surveys above which there must be notification of the RSO. A survey instrument must be able to detect rates as low as 0.1 mrem (1 μSv) per hour.

Wipe tests for removable contamination must be performed weekly in places where radiopharmaceuticals are prepared, administered, or stored. The licensee must be able to detect contamination on each wipe of 2000 disintegrations per minute and may establish appropriate contamination trigger levels above which the RSO must be notified. Records of each survey must be maintained for a period of 2 years including the date of survey, plan of each area surveyed, trigger level, detected dose rate, and mrem/hr or the contamination expressed in disintegrations/min/100 cm².

Records must also contain the instrument used to make the survey and the initials of persons performing such a survey. In addition, if a licensee utilizes radioactive gases, there is a requirement to check the operation of the traps or collecting systems each month and measure ventilation rates available in areas of use every 6 months.

Personnel Monitoring

In any nuclear medicine laboratory there is potential for exposure from external sources of radiation as well as from possible internal contamination. Although published limits exist for occupational radiation exposure, such dose levels should not be considered completely safe. Although an effort should be made to operate a laboratory with appropriate shielding and periodic surveys, there still needs to be a method of recording the radiation exposure actually received by persons working in the area. Several types of devices are used to measure external exposure, the most common of which is the film badge. After the film is processed and the optical density is determined, the radiation exposure to the individual can be determined. Such film is sensitive down to about 50 to 100 mrem (0.5 to 1.0 mSv).

Another common device for personnel dosimetry is a thermoluminescent dosimeter (TLD). This device is more expensive than a film badge and contains lithium fluoride chips, which, when heated, emit light in proportion to the amount of radiation they have received. TLDs can be made very small and can even be worn as a ring. These devices often are more accurate than film and are sensitive down to levels of 10 mrem (100 μSv). One disadvantage of both the TLD and the film badge is that they require processing and therefore normally are not used for daily exposure measurements.

A device that can be used for daily measurement of doses in the range of 10 to 200 mrem (0.1 to 2 mSv) is the pocket reading or "pen" ionization dosimeter. This device, similar in size to a fountain pen, contains two electrodes. Once the electrodes are charged by a battery pack, the detector indicates no exposure. As ionization from external radiation occurs within the barrel of the pen dosimeter, the electrodes are discharged, thus reflecting the amount of radiation exposure. With the pen dosimeter it is possible to immediately ascertain the amount of radiation received from a given procedure, although the device is not as sensitive or accurate as the other two devices. A pen dosimeter is usually not considered accurate enough to be a legal record of exposure.

Dosimeters are normally worn on the anterior portion of the chest or at the waist, and the exposure registered is usually assigned as "whole-body dose." The Code of Federal Regulations states that all workers who are likely to receive more than approximately 320 mrem (3.2 mSv) whole-body exposure, 4690 mrem (46.9 mSv) to an extremity, or 1880 mrem (18.8 mSv) to the skin in a 3-month period should wear dosimeters. A person under the age of 18 who is likely to receive more than 20 percent of the above values also must wear a dosimeter. Likewise, a person entering an area where the dose rate may be over 100 mrem/hr (1 mSv/hr) must wear a dosimeter.

In general, film badges and TLDs are changed monthly, although this can vary with the particular duties being performed. When not in use, the dosimeter should be stored away from radiation sources. A control dosimeter usually remains in the film badge storage area, so that the background radiation may be subtracted to obtain an accurate occupational dose reading.

The occupational radiation dose limits are shown in Table 14–2.

Waste Disposal

The following methods are available for radioactive waste disposal:

Transfer to an Authorized Commercial Facility for Burial. Waste must be packaged and shipped according to appropriate regulations.

Burial. Burial in the soil may be approved by the NRC or an agreement state. This method is usually not available to nuclear medicine laboratories.

Table 14–2. NRC OCCUPATIONAL RADIATION DOSE LIMITS

BODY PART EXPOSED	DOSE LIMIT
Whole body, head, trunk; active blood-forming organs, lens of eye, gonads	1.25 rem (12.5 mSv) per calendar quarter
Hands, forearms, feet, ankles	18.75 rem (187.5 mSv) per calendar quarter
Skin of whole body	7.5 rem (75 mSv) per calendar quarter
Whole-body exposure	Accumulated dose no more than $5 \times (N - 18)$ rem (50 mSv) where N equals the person's age in years at his/her last birthday

A personnel dosimeter is also required for a person under age 18 years who is likely to receive a dose in excess of .5 percent of the above values; dosimetry also is required for a person who enters a high radiation area.

Release into Sewer System. If the material is readily soluble or disbursable in water, it may be released in the following amounts:

- *Ten times the limit specified* in Appendix C of Title 10 of the Code of Federal Regulations, Part 20 (10 CFR 20), or the quantity of radioactive material that, when diluted by the average daily amount of liquid released by the hospital into the sewer system, results in an average concentration not greater than the amount specified in Appendix B, Table 1, Column 2 of 10 CFR 20. The greater of these two values is permitted.

- *Monthly.* The amount of radioactive material that, when diluted by the average monthly total amount of liquid released into the sewer system, results in an average concentration of not greater than the amount specified in Appendix B, Table 1, Column 2 of 10 CFR 20.

- *Yearly.* A total of not more than 1 Ci (37 GBq) of NRC-licensed or other accelerator-produced materials.

Excreta from persons who have received radioactive materials for medical diagnosis or therapy is not regulated by the NRC.

Other Disposal Methods. Methods such as incineration may be approved by the NRC for disposal of research animals or organic solvents containing radioactive materials. State and local regulations should also be checked.

Decay in Storage. Materials with physical half-lives of less than 65 days can be held in storage and allowed to decay before disposal in ordinary trash. The material must be held for a minimum of 10 half-lives. Before disposal as ordinary trash, the material must be monitored and the radioactivity must be of a level that it cannot be distinguished from background radiation. All radiation labels must be removed or obliterated. A record of each disposal must be retained for 2 years including the date material was disposed of, the date material was placed in storage, the radionuclides disposed of, the survey instrument used, the background dose rate, the dose rate measured at the surface of each waste container, and the name of the person who performed the disposal.

Venting. Many nuclear medicine laboratories use xenon 133 for pulmonary ventilation studies. Although venting into the atmosphere of certain amounts of this material is permissible and gives the least dose to the technologists, it often requires physical plant remodeling for adequate air flow. Another way of disposing of xenon 133 is storage and decay using commercially available activated charcoal traps.

Suggested Reading

Radiation Protection for Medical and Allied Health Personnel. National Council on Radiation Protection and Measurements. Report No. 105. Besthesda, Md, National Council on Radiation Protection and Measurements, 1989

Appendices

Glossary

Accelerator. Device imparting high kinetic energy to a charged particle and directing it toward a target.

Access time. The time required to locate and retrieve information from a specified location in a computer memory.

Accumulator. Register or data buffer used for temporary storage of data.

ADC. *See* Analog digital converters.

A/D converter. *See* Analog digital converter.

Address. Label, name, or number that designates a location where information is stored in a computer memory.

Aggregated albumin. Conglomerates of human serum albumin in a suspension for lung imaging.

ALARA. Nuclear Regulatory Commission operating philosophy for maintaining occupational radiation exposures "as low as is reasonably achievable."

Alpha particle. Fast-moving nucleus of a helium atom ($^4_2$He) emitted by certain radioisotopes upon disintegration.

ALU. *See* Arithmetic unit.

Analog. (1) Representation of a parameter by a signal, the magnitude of which is infinitely variable and which is proportional to the parameter; (2) structure with a similar function.

Analog computer. Computer that parameterizes data in terms of the magnitude of the incoming signals.

Analog digital converter (ADC). Electronic module used to convert an analog signal such as pulse height into digital information recognizable by a computer.

Annihilation. Reaction between a pair of particles resulting in their disintegration and the production of an equivalent amount of energy in the form of photons.

Arithmetic and logical unit (ALU). *See* Arithmetic unit.

Arithmetic unit. Unit within the computer architecture that performs all mathematical and logical operations. Sometimes called "arithmetic and logic unit (ALU)."

Assembler. A program that changes symbolic programs into binary computer form.

Assembly language. Commands for the minicomputer system written in symbolic or mnemonic form. An assembly language program is translated to binary code by an assembler.

Atom. Smallest unit of an element that can exist and still maintain the properties of the element.

Atomic mass. Mass of a neutral atom usually expressed in atomic mass units.

Atomic mass unit. Exactly one-twelfth the mass of carbon 12: 1.661×10^{-24} gm.

Atomic number. Number of protons in an atom, the symbol of which is Z.

Atomic weight. Average weight of the neutral atoms of an element.

Attenuation correction. Procedure for correcting the reconstructed images to counteract the effects of attenuation. This is necessary for quantitative analysis and desirable for visual appearance. Each image point is corrected according to the tissue depth in various view directions.

Auger electron. An orbital electron ejected by a characteristic x-ray, which is usually emitted following electron capture or internal conversion.

Average life. (1) The mean time during which an atom exists in a particular form; (2) 1.44 times the physical half-life.

Avogadro number. Number of atoms in the gram atomic weight of a given element or the number of molecules in the gram molecular weight of a given substance: 6.022×10^{23} per gm mole.

Azimuth position. Stopping position of the camera at any point along the 360° arc of rotation.

Background. Detected disintegration events not emanating from the sample.

Back projection. Process whereby angularly sampled data are distributed, creating a two-dimensional image representing the cross-section of the angularly sampled data.

BASIC. Beginner's All-Purpose Symbolic Instruction Code.

Batch mode. Automatic computer mode that does not require specific programming instruction.

Becquerel (Bq). The International System (SI) unit of radioactivity. One Becquerel is one disintegration per second.

Beta particle. An electron of positive or negative charge.

Binary. Pertaining to the number system with a radix of 2.

Binary digit. One of the symbols 1 or 0; also called a "bit."

Bit. An individual binary digit, either 1 or 0; acronym for binary digit.

Bootstrap loader. Routine whose first instructions are normally sufficient to load the remainder of itself into memory from an input device and start a complex system of programs in a computer.

Bremsstrahlung x-rays. Photonic emissions caused by the slowing down of beta particles in matter.

By-product material. Radioactive material arising from fission in a reactor.

Byte. Group of binary digits usually operated upon as a unit and usually 8 bits long; the maximum number in the decimal system that can be stored in an 8-bit byte is 255.

Carrier. Quantity of stable isotopes of an element mixed with radioactive isotopes of that element. Addition of a carrier often affects biodistribution of a radionuclide.

Carrier-free. Adjective describing a radionuclide that is free of its stable isotopes.

Cathode-ray tube (CRT). Electronic vacuum tube attached to a screen where information is displayed.

Central processor unit (CPU). Unit of a computer system that includes the circuits controlling the interpretation and execution of instructions, that is, the computer proper, excluding I/O and other peripheral devices.

Collimator. A lead device with an arrangement of openings or slits that limits the access of gamma rays to the crystal of a gamma camera. A collimator may be of the parallel or focused type, and is affixed to the crystal face.

Colloid. Molecules in a continuous medium that measure between 1 and 100 nm in diameter. Note that ^{99m}Tc sulfur colloid particles are too large to constitute a true colloid.

Column generator. Column device using a parent radionuclide adsorbed to a medium on the column; the daughter radionuclide is usually obtained by elution of the column with a solution that washes the daughter but not the parent off the column.

Compile. To produce a binary code program from a program written in source (symbolic) language.

Compiler. Device used to change complicated source code to simpler language.

Compton scatter. A process by which a photon loses energy through collisions with electrons.

Computer. Programmable electronic device that can store, retrieve, and process data.

Counting error. (1) The statistical uncertainty associated with counting a radioactive sample based upon the radiation detected in a time interval much shorter than the physical half-life of the radionuclide; (2) the standard deviation for an N count determination equals the square root of N. (For a standard deviation of 1 percent, 10,000 counts must be recorded.)

"Cow." *See* Generator.

CPU. *See* Central processor unit.

Crash. *Hardware crash* is the complete failure of a particular device, sometimes affecting the operation of an entire computer system; *software crash* is the complete failure of an operating system characterized by some failure in the system's protection mechanisms.

Critical organ. Organ (1) receiving the highest dose (2) most affected radiobiologically by an administered radiopharmaceutical.

Crystal, scintillation. Any one of many pure or "doped" crystals that emit visible photons under alpha, beta, or gamma irradiation. Thallium-activated sodium iodide is the material used in most currently available scanning systems.

Curie. Standard measure of rate of radioactive decay; based on the disintegration of 1 gm of radium or 3.7×10^{10} disintegrations/sec.

Cyclotron. Device consisting of two hollow D-shaped chambers for accelerating charged particles to energies up to 15 MeV or more by periodic accelerations through a potential difference.

Daughter radionuclide. Decay product produced by a radionuclide called the "parent."

Debugger. Program to assist in tracking down and eliminating errors that occur in the normal course of computer program development.

Debusser. Device used to erase material from a computer or recording tape.

Decay. Radioactive disintegration of a nucleus of an unstable nuclide.

Decay constant (λ). Probability per unit time that a given radionuclide atom will undergo a radioactive transformation.

Decay schemes. Diagram showing the decay mode or modes of a radionuclide.

Diethylenetriaminepentaacetic acid (DTPA). Chelating agent that can be labeled with ^{99m}Tc and used for scintigraphy.

Digital computer. Device that operates on discrete data, performing sequences of arithmetic and logical operations.

Digital recording system. A system in which counts collected for a predetermined period of time (e.g., time constant) are recorded as actual numbers graphed on a chart or are stored on magnetic medium for recovery and portrayal.

Direct-memory access. Access to data in any location independent of sequential prohibitions.

Discriminator. Circuit that allows only those pulses falling between two specified energies to be recorded.

Distintegration. General process of radioactive decay, usually measured per unit time. (disintegrations per second)

Disk. Form of rotating memory consisting of a platter (either hard or floppy) that can be magnetized or read by a read/write head in proximity to the surface; this is the most common form of bulk memory device.

Dose equivalent. Unit of biologically effective dose, defined as the absorbed dose in rads multiplied by the quality factor. (For all x-rays, gamma rays, beta particles, and positron likely to be used in nuclear medicine, the quality factor is 1.)

DTPA. *See* Diethylenetriaminepentaacetic acid.

ECAT. Emission computed axial tomography.

Editor. Program that permits data or instructions to be manipulated and displayed. Most commonly used in the preparation of new programs or in the revision and correction of old programs.

Efficiency. In detection systems, the ratio of the number of events recorded to the number actually occurring.

Electrode. Positive (anode) or negative (cathode) terminal of an electrical system.

Electron capture. Method of radioactive decay in which the nucleus captures an orbital electron, which then interacts with a proton, effectively negating the proton and transmuting the nucleus to another element.

Electron volt (eV). Unit of energy equal to the kinetic energy acquired by an electron when accelerated through a potential difference of 1 volt (1 eV = 1.60×10^{-19} joules).

Element. Pure substance, consisting of atoms of the same atomic number, which cannot be decomposed by ordinary chemical means.

Exposure. Amount of radiation that is incident upon the surface of the object exposed.

Exposure rate. Rate of exposure to radioactivity, usually expressed in rad/hr.

External contamination. Radioactive material on the body surface; usually refers to unsealed radionuclides.

External exposure. Exposure from any radiation source outside the body or object of interest. An object subjected to external exposure has been "irradiated."

Field of view. Region from which emitted radiation may impinge on the detection system.

Film badge. Photographic film shielded from light; worn by a person to measure radiation exposure.

Filtered back projection. Efficient mathematical algorithm that reconstructs the transverse slice images from the projection images. The projections are first filtered to compensate for the blurring and to control statistical noise. The back projection process estimates each image value by summing the values from the different angular views.

Fission. Splitting of a nucleus accompanied by a release of energy and neutrons.

Fission products. Stable and unstable nuclides resulting from fission.

Focal plane. The plane perpendicular to the axis of symmetry of a collimator contains the focal point.

Focal point. Theoretical spot in front of a focused collimator at which all channels converge. This is the point of maximum sensitivity and resolution.

Gamma emission. Nuclear process in which an excited nuclide de-excites by emission of a nuclear photon.

Gamma ray. Radiation emitted from the nucleus having a wavelength range from 10^{-9} to 10^{-12} cm. (Note: An x-ray is not emitted from the nucleus.)

Gate. Electronic device capable of performing logic operations with a digital circuit. In nuclear medicine it implies a device that can provide a timing signal to the computer. This signal is usually associated with the QRS complex of the electrocardiogram.

Geiger-Müller counter (G-M tube). High-voltage (~1000 V) gas tube used to detect ionizing particles. It is based upon the avalanche effect, which is observed when ions are accelerated by an electric field under appropriate conditions.

Generator. Device that uses a parent radionuclide to obtain its product, the daughter radionuclide, usually by adding a solution that interacts only with the daughter (e.g., ^{99m}Tc from ^{99}Mo).

Geometry factor. That fraction of the total radiation emitted from a point source that impinges on the detector.

G-M tube. *See* Geiger-Müller counter.

Gray (Gy). The International System (SI) of radiation absorbed dose, equal to an energy accumulation of 1 joule/kg (100 rad).

Ground state. The state of lowest energy of a system.

Half-life. (1) *Radioactive:* For a single radioactive decay process, the time required for the activity of a given sample to decrease to half its initial value by that process. (2) *Biologic:* The time required for the amount of a particular substance in a biologic system to be reduced to half of its initial value by biologic processes when the rate of removal is approximately exponential. (3) *Effective:* The time required for the amount of a radionuclide in a system to be reduced to half its initial value as a consequence of both radioactive decay and biologic processes. Note: Radioactive half-life is also called physical half-life.

Half-value layer (HVL). Thickness of absorbing material necessary to reduce the intensity of penetrating radiation by half.

Hamming weighting. Type of co-sinusoidal weight applied to a filter to control or suppress the high-frequency response.

Hexadecimal. Pertaining to the number system with a radix of 16.

HVL. *See* Half-value layer.

ID. *See* Information density.

Image matrix. Corresponds to a collection matrix; a collection of pixels in which an image is stored and displayed.

Information density. The number of counts/cm^2 that is recorded in the field of interest within a particular image. The effect of statistical fluctuations decreases with increasing information density; usually measured per square centimeter of gamma camera crystal face.

Internal contamination. Radioactive material within the body; usually refers to unsealed radionuclides.

Internal conversion. Transition between two energy states of a nucleus in which the energy difference is not emitted as a photon but is given to an orbital electron, which is consequently ejected from the atom.

Internal exposure. Radiation exposure originating from within the object of interest.

Inverse-square law. Rule by which the radiation intensity of any source decreases inversely as the square of the distance between the source and the detector.

I/O (input/output) device. Computer device that accepts input, prints out, records, and displays data.

Ionization. Process whereby a charged portion (usually an electron) of an atom or molecule is given enough kinetic energy to dissociate.

Ionization chamber. Closed vessel used for the detection of radiation energy and containing a gas and two electrodes maintained at a potential difference. Any radiation incidence upon this container forms ions that move to the appropriate electrode, producing a measurable current.

Ionizing radiation. Radiation that produces ion pairs along its path through a substance.

Irradiation. Exposure to radiation.

Isobar. Nuclides that have the same total number of neutrons and protons but that constitute different elements.

Isomeric states. States of a nucleus having different energies and observable half-life.

Isomeric transition (IT). A transition between two isomeric states of a nucleus, involving no elementary change of species.

Isotones. Nuclides having the same number of neutrons but a different number of protons.

Isotopes. Nuclides having the same number of protons but a different number of neutrons. Not all isotopes are radioactive.

keV. One thousand electron volts (10^3 eV).

LET. *See* Linear energy transfer.

Limulus amebocyte lysate (LAL). In vitro test for some pyrogens; it reacts with gram-negative bacterial endotoxins in nanogram or greater concentrations to form an opaque gel.

Linear energy transfer. Amount of energy lost by ionizing radiation by way of interaction with matter per centimeter of path length through the absorbing material.

Load. (1) To store a program or data in memory; (2) to mount a tape on a device such that the read point is at the beginning of the tape; (3) to place a removable disk drive and start the drive.

Lugol's solution. An iodine solution; used in nuclear medicine in some circumstances to block the thyroid from accumulating radioactive iodine.

Maximum permissible dose (MPD). The maximum amount of radiation that may be received by an individual within a specified period of time with expectation of no significantly harmful result. For occupational exposures, MPD = 5 (N − 18) rem, where N is the age, when the worker is older than 18 years. The permissible worker limits for occupational exposure of persons less than 18 years of age are considerably less.

MeV. One million electron volts (10^6 eV).

Memory. (1) Erasable storage in a computer; (2) pertaining to a device in which data can be stored and from which they can be retrieved.

Metastable state. An excited nuclear state of a particular isotope that has a finite half-life and decays by gamma emission (e.g., ^{99m}Tc → ^{99}Tc).

Microcurie (μCi). Quantity of radioactive material having 3.7×10^4 disintegrations per second (one-millionth of a curie).

Micrometer (μm). One-millionth of a meter; formerly "micron."

Millicurie (mCi). Quantity of radioactive material having 3.7×10^7 disintegrations per second (one-thousandth of a curie).

MPD. *See* Maximum permissible dose.

Multiple-gated acquisition. Composite heart-imaging technique performed by synchronizing patient's heartbeat by means of an electrocardiograph connected to a scintillation camera through a physiologic gate.

N. See Neutron number.

Neutron number *(N).* Number of neutrons in a nucleus.

Nuclear Regulatory Commission (NRC). United States government agency regulating radioactive by-product material.

Nucleons. Any particle commonly contained in the nucleus of an atom.

Nuclide. A general term applicable to all atomic forms of the elements. The term is often used erroneously as a synonym for "isotope." Isotopes are the various forms of a single element and therefore are a family of nuclides with the same number of protons. Nuclides are distinguished by their atomic mass and number as well as by energy state.

Nyquist frequency. The highest frequency that can be accurately represented in sampled data; equal to the reciprocal of twice the pixel size.

Operating system. Collection of programs, including a monitor or executive and system programs, that organizes a central processor and peripheral devices into a working unit for the development and execution of application programs.

Operation code. Code used to start the operation of a program.

Parent radionuclide. Radionuclide that decays to a specific daughter nuclide, either directly or as a member of a radioactive series.

Perchlorate. Any chemical compound that contains the ClO_4-group.

Pertechnetate. Any chemical compound containing the TcO_4-group.

PET. Positron-emission tomography.

Phantom. (1) Model of some part of the body in which radioactive material can be placed to simulate in vivo conditions; (2) a device that yields information concerning the performing of an imaging system.

Photocathode. Negative electrode of a photomultiplier tube.

Photomultiplier tube (PMT). Device by which small light flashes are amplified electronically by a cascade process employing secondary emission of electrons. This device detects and amplifies the scintillations produced by the interactions of gamma rays and the crystal in a gamma camera.

Photopeak. The peak (maximum intensity) of a gamma spectrum as measured by scintillation detector.

Pixel. Corresponds to the term "cell"; images are divided into small squares, each of which contains the counts accumulated in that square area of the image.

Point spread function. Image formed of an ideal point object; useful in characterizing the system imaging performance because any object can be represented as a weighted summation of points.

Positron. Particle equal in mass to the electron but with a positive electronic charge.

Program. Complete sequence of instructions and routines necessary to solve a problem.

Proton. Elementary particle with a mass 1873 times that of an electron and a positive charge equal to the basic electronic charge e.

Pulse height analyzer (PHA). Instrument that accepts input from a detector and categorizes the pulses on the basis of signal strength.

Quality factor (QF). Linear energy transfer-dependent factor by which absorbed doses are to be multiplied to account for the varying effectiveness of different radiations.

Rad (radiation absorbed dose; rad). The unit of absorbed dose of ionizating radiation equal to 100 erg/gm of absorbing material. *See also* Gray.

Radioactivity. Radiation emitted by certain nuclides due to the spontaneous transformation of their nuclei.

Radioisotope. Radioactive member of an isotope family (e.g., ^{123}I, ^{131}I).

Radionuclide. Unstable nucleus that de-excites by way of nuclear decay.

Radionuclidic purity. Percent of total radionuclide(s) in a sample that is the desired radionuclide.

Radiopharmaceutical. Radioactive drug used for therapy or diagnosis.

Ramp filter. The name given to the RAM-LAK filter when displayed in frequency space, because the function of the filter resembles a ramp; that is, the value of the filter increases as the spatial frequency increases.

Rate meter. Device, used in conjunction with a detector, that measures the rate of activity of a radioisotope; usually in units of counts/min or counts/sec.

RBE. *See* Relative biologic effectiveness.

Read-only input (ROI). Input only from the memory or from an internal source. (Contrast with Regions of Interest.)

Read-only memory (ROM). Internal acquisition of data from the memory in computers.

Regions of interest (ROI). Portion of the data field that is to be studied. (Contrast with Read-Only Input.)

Register. Division of core memory capable of storing a specified amount of data.

Relative biologic effectiveness (RBE). Ratio of the biologic response derived from a particular type of radiation as compared with another dose of 250 kVp x-rays.

Rem (roentgen equivalent man; rem). Unit of dose equivalent; the absorbed dose in rads multiplied by the relative biologic effectiveness of the type of radiation. *See also* Sievert.

Resolution. Ability of a detection system to separate or discriminate between very similar quantities.

Resolving time. The minimum time interval between two events that will permit them to be counted as distinct events by a given detecting system.

Roentgen (R). Quantity of x or gamma radiation per cubic centimeter of air that produces one electrostatic unit of charge.

ROI. *See* Read-only input and Regions of interest.

Scattered radiation. Radiation that, during its passage through a substance, has deviated in direction, perhaps with an energy loss. *See also* Compton scatter.

Scintillation. Flash of light produced in a phosphor by radiation.

Sensitivity. Count rate observed per unit activity actually present.

Septa. Thickness of lead or other photon-absorbing material in a collimator that defines the field of view of the crystal detector.

Shielding. Any material used to absorb beta, gamma, and x-ray radiation.

Sievert (Sv). The International System (SI) unit of dose equivalent. The absorbed dose in grays multiplied by the RBE of the type of radiation. One sievert equals 100 rem.

Specific activity. Unit pertaining to the disintegrations per gram of a radioisotope.

SPECT. Single photon-emission computed tomography.

Spectrum. Range or distribution of wavelengths of radiation with a lower and upper limit of energy. Particulate radiation may also be included in the designation.

Stannous ion. Ion of tin in the +2 valence state.

Survey meter. Meter that measures rate of radioactive exposure, usually in units of milliroentgens per hour.

Thermoluminescent detector (TLD). Type of crystal used to monitor radiation exposure by emitting light; used in a film badge or ring badge.

Thyroid-binding globulin (TBG). Serum protein that is the primary agent for transport of thyroid hormone.

Thyrotropin (TSH). Hormone stimulating the thyroid. Secreted by the anterior pituitary.

Thyroxine. Hormone of the thyroid gland; 3,5,3',5'-tetraiodothyronine (T_4).

TLD. *See* Thermoluminescent detectors.

Transient equilibrium. Equilibrium reached by a parent-daughter radioisotope pair in which the half-life of the parent is longer than that of the daughter.

United States Pharmacopeia (USP). Official listing of all drugs and medications.

Voxel. Smallest element of a three-dimensional image; cube whose faces are 1 pixel to a side.

Window. (1) Region of interest; (2) limits of radiation energy accepted by a pulse height analyzer.

Window width. The energy range of a gamma ray that when detected will be accepted by the detection system. *See also* Pulse height analyzer.

Word. Unit of data that may be stored in one addressable location (most minicomputers use 16-bit words).

Z number. *See* Atomic number.

Characteristics of Radionuclides for Imaging and Therapy

NUCLIDE	SYMBOL	HALF-LIFE	DECAY MODE*	MAJOR EMISSIONS† (MeV)
Barium 133	$^{133}_{56}$Ba	7.2 yr	E.C.	γ 0.081 (90%) γ 0.356 (63%)
Carbon 11	$^{11}_{6}$C	20.3 min	β +	γ 0.511 (200%)
Cesium 137	$^{137}_{55}$CS	30 yr	β −	γ 0.660 (85%)
Chromium 51	$^{51}_{24}$Cr	27.8 days	E.C.	γ 0.320 (10%)
Cobalt 57	$^{57}_{27}$Co	270.0 days	E.C.	γ 0.122 (86%) γ 0.136 (11%)
Cobalt 58	$^{58}_{27}$Co	71.3 days	E.C. and β +	γ 0.811 (99%) γ 0.511 (31%)
Cobalt 60	$^{60}_{27}$Co	5.26 yr	β −	γ 1.173 (100%) γ 1.332 (100%)
Fluorine 18	$^{18}_{9}$F	109.0 min	E.C. and β +	γ 0.511 (194%)
Gadolinium 153	$^{153}_{64}$Gd	240 days	E.C.	γ 0.100 (55%) γ 0.040 γ 0.048‡
Gallium 67	$^{67}_{31}$Ga	78.1 hr	E.C.	γ 0.093 (38%) γ 0.184 (24%) γ 0.296 (16%) γ 0.388 (4%)
Gallium 68	$^{68}_{31}$Ga	68.3 min	E.C. and β +	γ 0.511 (178%) γ 1.077 (3%)
Indium 111	$^{111}_{49}$In	67 hr	E.C.	γ 0.172 (90%) γ 0.247 (94%)
Indium 113m	$^{113m}_{49}$In	99.0 min	I.T.	γ 0.392 (62%)
Iodine 123	$^{123}_{53}$I	13.0 hr	E.C.	γ 0.159 (83%)
Iodine 125	$^{125}_{53}$I	60 days	E.C.	γ 0.027 (76%)
Iodine 131	$^{131}_{53}$I	8.06 days	β −	γ 0.284 (6%) γ 0.364 (82%) γ 0.637 (7%) β 0.192 (90%)
Iron 52	$^{52}_{26}$Fe	8.3 hr	E.C. and β +	γ 0.511 (116%) γ 0.169 (99%)
Iron 59	$^{59}_{26}$Fe	45.0 days	β −	γ 0.192 (3%) γ 1.099 (55%) γ 1.292 (44%)
Krypton 81m	$^{81m}_{36}$Kr	13.0 sec	I.T.	γ 0.191 (66%)

NUCLIDE	SYMBOL	HALF-LIFE	DECAY MODE*	MAJOR EMISSIONS† (MeV)	
Molybdenum 99	$^{99}_{42}$Mo	66.7 hr	β−	γ 0.181	(8%)
				γ 0.740	(14%)
				γ 0.778	(5%)
Nitrogen 13	$^{13}_{7}$N	10.0 min	β+	γ 0.511	(200%)
Oxygen 15	$^{15}_{8}$O	124.0 sec.	β+	γ 0.511	(200%)
Phosphorus 32	$^{32}_{15}$P	14.3 days	β−	β 0.695	(100%)
Rubidium 82	$^{82}_{37}$Rb	1.3 min	E.C. and β+	γ 0.511	(189%)
				γ 0.777	(13%)
Strontium 87m	$^{87m}_{38}$Sr	2.8 hr	I.T. and E.C.	γ 0.388	(83%)
Technetium 99m	$^{99m}_{43}$Tc	6.03 hr	I.T.	γ 0.140	(88%)
Thallium 201	$^{201}_{81}$Tl	73.0 hr	E.C.	γ 0.135	(2%)
				γ 0.167	(8%)
			(Hg daughter x-rays 0.069–0.081)		
Xenon 127	$^{127}_{54}$Xe	36.4 days	E.C.	γ 0.145	(4%)
				γ 0.172	(25%)
				γ 0.203	(68%)
				γ 0.375	(18%)
Xenon 133	$^{133}_{54}$Xe	5.3 days	β−	γ 0.081	(36%)

Adapted from Dillman LT, Von der Lage FC: Radionuclide Decay Schemes and Nuclear Parameters for use in Radiation Dose Estimation. New York, Society of Nuclear Medicine, 1975.
*Key to symbols: β+ = positron (beta plus) decay. β− = beta decay. E.C. = electron capture. I.T. = isomeric transition.
†Mean energy.
‡From Europium 153.
Information in parentheses refers to the percentage of emissions of that type that occurs from disintegration. For example, carbon 11 gives off a gamma ray of 0.511 MeV 200 percent of the time; i.e., two gamma rays are emitted per disintegration.

Radioactivity Conversion Table for International System (SI) Units (Becquerels to Curies)

0.05 MBq = 1.4 μCi	475. MBq = 12.8 mCi
0.1 MBq = 2.7 μCi	500. MBq = 13.5 mCi
0.2 MBq = 5.4 μCi	525. MBq = 14.2 mCi
0.3 MBq = 8.1 μCi	550. MBq = 14.9 mCi
0.4 MBq = 10.8 μCi	575. MBq = 15.5 mCi
0.5 MBq = 13.5 μCi	600. MBq = 16.2 mCi
0.6 MBq = 16.2 μCi	625. MBq = 16.9 mCi
0.7 MBq = 18.9 μCi	650. MBq = 17.6 mCi
0.8 MBq = 21.6 μCi	675. MBq = 18.2 mCi
0.9 MBq = 24.3 μCi	700. MBq = 18.9 mCi
1.0 MBq = 27.0 μCi	725. MBq = 19.6 mCi
2.0 MBq = 54.1 μCi	750. MBq = 20.3 mCi
3.0 MBq = 81.1 μCi	775. MBq = 20.9 mCi
4.0 MBq = 108 μCi	800. MBq = 21.6 mCi
5.0 MBq = 135 μCi	825. MBq = 22.3 mCi
6.0 MBq = 162 μCi	850. MBq = 23.0 mCi
7.0 MBq = 189 μCi	875. MBq = 23.7 mCi
8.0 MBq = 216 μCi	900. MBq = 24.3 mCi
9.0 MBq = 243 μCi	925. MBq = 25.0 mCi
10. MBq = 270 μCi	950. MBq = 25.7 mCi
15. MBq = 405 μCi	975. MBq = 26.4 mCi
20. MBq = 541 μCi	1.0 GBq = 27.0 mCi
25. MBq = 676 μCi	1.1 GBq = 29.7 mCi
30. MBq = 811 μCi	1.2 GBq = 32.4 mCi
35. MBq = 946 μCi	1.3 GBq = 35.1 mCi
40. MBq = 1.08 mCi	1.4 GBq = 37.8 mCi
45. MBq = 1.22 mCi	1.5 GBq = 40.5 mCi
50. MBq = 1.35 mCi	1.6 GBq = 43.2 mCi
55. MBq = 1.49 mCi	1.7 GBq = 46.0 mCi
60. MBq = 1.62 mCi	1.8 GBq = 48.7 mCi
70. MBq = 1.89 mCi	1.9 GBq = 51.3 mCi
80. MBq = 2.16 mCi	2.0 GBq = 54.1 mCi
90. MBq = 2.43 mCi	2.2 GBq = 59.5 mCi
100. MBq = 2.70 mCi	2.4 GBq = 64.9 mCi
125. MBq = 3.38 mCi	2.6 GBq = 70.3 mCi
150. MBq = 4.05 mCi	2.8 GBq = 75.7 mCi
175. MBq = 4.73 mCi	3.0 GBq = 81.1 mCi
200. MBq = 5.41 mCi	3.2 GBq = 86.5 mCi
225. MBq = 6.08 mCi	3.4 GBq = 91.9 mCi
250. MBq = 6.76 mCi	3.6 GBq = 97.3 mCi
275. MBq = 7.43 mCi	3.8 GBq = 103 mCi
300. MBq = 8.11 mCi	4.0 GBq = 108 mCi
325. MBq = 8.78 mCi	5.0 GBq = 135 mCi
350. MBq = 9.46 mCi	6.0 GBq = 162 mCi
375. MBq = 10.1 mCi	7.0 GBq = 189 mCi
400. MBq = 10.8 mCi	8.0 GBq = 216 mCi
425. MBq = 11.5 mCi	9.0 GBq = 243 mCi
450. MBq = 12.2 mCi	10.0 GBq = 270 mCi

Radioactivity Conversion Table for International System (SI) Units (Curies to Becquerels)

1 µCi = .037 MBq	500 µCi = 18.5 MBq	19 mCi = 703 MBq
2 µCi = .074 MBq	600 µCi = 22.2 MBq	20 mCi = 740 MBq
3 µCi = .111 MBq	700 µCi = 25.9 MBq	21 mCi = 777 MBq
4 µCi = .148 MBq	800 µCi = 29.6 MBq	22 mCi = 814 MBq
5 µCi = .185 MBq	900 µCi = 33.3 MBq	23 mCi = 841 MBq
6 µCi = .222 MBq	1 mCi = 37.0 MBq	24 mCi = 888 MBq
7 µCi = .259 MBq	1.5 mCi = 55.5 MBq	25 mCi = 925 MBq
8 µCi = .296 MBq	2.0 mCi = 74.0 MBq	30 mCi = 1.11 GBq
9 µCi = .333 MBq	2.5 mCi = 92.5 MBq	35 mCi = 1.30 GBq
10 µCi = .370 MBq	3.0 mCi = 111 MBq	40 mCi = 1.48 GBq
15 µCi = .555 MBq	3.5 mCi = 130 MBq	45 mCi = 1.48 GBq
20 µCi = .740 MBq	4.0 mCi = 148 MBq	50 mCi = 1.85 GBq
25 µCi = .925 MBq	4.5 mCi = 167 MBq	60 mCi = 2.22 GBq
30 µCi = 1.11 MBq	5.0 mCi = 185 MBq	65 mCi = 2.41 GBq
35 µCi = 1.30 MBq	5.5 mCi = 204 MBq	70 mCi = 2.59 GBq
40 µCi = 1.48 MBq	6.0 mCi = 222 MBq	80 mCi = 2.96 GBq
45 µCi = 1.67 MBq	6.5 mCi = 241 MBq	90 mCi = 3.33 GBq
50 µCi = 1.85 MBq	7.0 mCi = 259 MBq	95 mCi = 3.52 GBq
60 µCi = 2.22 MBq	7.5 mCi = 278 MBq	100 mCi = 3.70 GBq
70 µCi = 2.59 MBq	8.0 mCi = 296 MBq	110 mCi = 4.07 GBq
80 µCi = 2.96 MBq	8.5 mCi = 315 MBq	120 mCi = 4.44 GBq
90 µCi = 3.33 MBq	9.0 mCi = 333 MBq	130 mCi = 4.81 GBq
100 µCi = 3.70 MBq	9.5 mCi = 366 MBq	140 mCi = 5.18 GBq
125 µCi = 4.63 MBq	10 mCi = 370 MBq	150 mCi = 5.55 GBq
150 µCi = 5.55 MBq	11 mCi = 407 MBq	175 mCi = 6.48 GBq
175 µCi = 6.48 MBq	12 mCi = 444 MBq	200 mCi = 7.40 GBq
200 µCi = 7.40 MBq	13 mCi = 481 MBq	250 mCi = 9.25 GBq
250 µCi = 9.25 MBq	14 mCi = 518 MBq	300 mCi = 11.1 GBq
300 µCi = 11.1 MBq	15 mCi = 555 MBq	400 mCi = 14.8 GBq
350 µCi = 13.0 MBq	16 mCi = 592 MBq	
400 µCi = 14.8 MBq	17 mCi = 629 MBq	
450 µCi = 16.7 MBq	18 mCi = 666 MBq	

Technetium 99m Decay and Generation Tables

^{99m}Tc DECAY CHART*

TIME	DECAY FACTOR	TIME	DECAY FACTOR
0:0	1.000	3:00	.707
0:10	.981	3:10	.694
0:20	.962	3:20	.680
0:30	.944	3:30	.667
0:40	.926	3:40	.655
0:50	.908	3:50	.642
1:00	.891	4:00	.630
1:10	.874	4:10	.618
1:20	.857	4.20	.606
1:30	.841	4:30	.595
1:40	.825	4:40	.583
1:50	.809	4:50	.572
2:00	.794	5:00	.561
2:10	.779	5:10	.551
2:20	.764	5:20	.540
2:30	.749	5:30	.530
2:40	.735	5.40	.520
2:50	.721	5:50	.510

*This table may be used to determine the amount of ^{99m}Tc remaining in a sample after a given period of time using the formula: Original activity (mCi or Bq) at time T × decay factor. Time is given in hours and minutes.

^{99}Mo-^{99m}Tc GENERATOR YIELD

HOURS SINCE PREVIOUS ELUTION	^{99m}Tc YIELD (% OF PREVIOUS ^{99m}Tc ELUTION)
1	9
2	18
3	26
4	33
5	39
6	45
7	50
8	54
10	62
12	69
18	80
24	87

Note: ^{99m}Tc activity reaches maximum activity in 22.9 hours (transient equilibrium).

Iodine 131 Decay Chart

¹³¹I Decay Chart

TIME (DAYS)	DECAY FACTOR
0	1.000
1	.918
2	.841
3	.771
4	.707
5	.648
6	.595
7	.545
8	.500
9	.458
10	.421
11	.386
12	.354
13	.324
14	.297
15	.273
16	.250
17	.229
18	.210
19	.193
20	.177

Appendix D

Injection Techniques and Pediatric Dosage

Injection Techniques

There are two commonly employed rapid bolus injection techniques, either of which, when properly executed, will provide a high quality bolus of radiopharmaceutical, assuming patent venous pathways and adequate cardiac function.

OLDENDORF/TOURNIQUET METHOD

In the Oldendorf method, first the blood pressure is taken to determine diastolic/systolic pressures in the arm to be used for injection. The blood pressure cuff is then inflated to a level above diastolic but less than systolic pressure. The pressure in the cuff is left at this level for 1 to 2 minutes to allow engorgement of the venous system in the lower arm and thereby build up a considerable back pressure that will constitute the forward momentum of the injected bolus. The cuff is then inflated above systolic pressure to prevent further entry of blood into the veins. At this point, a venipuncture of an antecubital vein (preferably a basilic vein) is performed. Next the radiopharmaceutical, in a volume of less than 1 cc, is injected and the cuff is removed from the arm with a single swift motion. It is important to leave the needle in place until the dynamic images are complete so that no pressure on the venipuncture site is instituted.

INTRAVENOUS PUSH METHOD

The intravenous push technique is simpler than the Oldendorf method and has gained in popularity recently. The technique requires a special tubing "set-up" with an additional intravenous (IV) entry site for the introduction of the radiopharmaceutical. Antecubital venipuncture is performed in the usual way, preferably using a large-bore needle. The end of the IV push tubing is connected to a syringe containing 25 to 30 cc of normal saline. Once the needle is in place, the radiopharmaceutical is injected into the distal tubing through the rubber entry portal, immediately followed by rapid injection of the saline, which propels the bolus to the right heart.

296

Pediatric Dosage

Pediatric doses of radiopharmaceuticals ideally should be kept as low as possible. A balance must be achieved between smaller doses due to small patient size and the minimum dose needed to get a statistically valid examination in a reasonable time period. Simple reduction of an adult dose per unit weight will necessitate an extremely long imaging time, and the image may be compromised by patient motion. A modified Young's Rule or Webster's Rule is one method commonly used to estimate pediatric doses. In this case, the adult dose is multiplied by the following fraction:

$$\frac{\text{Age in years} + 1}{\text{Age in years} + 7}$$

An example of this is as follows: If the adult dose of ^{99m}Tc phosphate for a bone scan is 20 mCi (740 MBq), then the dose for a 5-year-old child would be

$$\frac{5 + 1}{5 + 7} = \frac{6}{12} = \frac{1}{2}$$

or 20 mCi (740 MBq) $\times$ ½ = 10 mCi (370 MBq).

The minimum doses needed for various examinations are seen in the table that follows:

EXAMINATION	RADIOPHARMACEUTICAL	DOSE
Gastroesopha-geal reflux	^{99m}Tc sulfur colloid	0.5 mCi (18.5 MBq) p.o.
Brain scan	^{99m}TcO$_4^-$, ^{99m}Tc DTPA	2 mCi (74 MBq)
Meckel scan	^{99m}TcO$_4^-$	2 mCi (74 MBq)
Angiocardi-ogram	^{99m}TcO$_4^-$	2 mCi (74 MBq)
Thyroid uptake	^{123}I	10 μCi (0.37 MBq)
	^{131}I	2 μCi (0.07 MBq)
Thyroid scan	^{99m}TcO$_4^-$	1 mCi (37 MBq)
	^{123}I	30 μCi (1.1 MBq) (newborn)
	^{123}I	60 μCi (2.2 MBq) (to 1 year)
	^{123}I	90 μCi (3.3 MBq) (+1 to 5 years)
	^{123}I	120 μCi (4.6 MBq) (+5 to 10 years)
	^{131}I	170 μCi (6.4 MBq) (+10 to 15 years)
	^{131}I	4 μCi (0.15 MBq) (newborn)
	^{131}I	9 μCi (0.33 MBq) (to 1 year)
	^{131}I	13 μCi (0.48 MBq) (+1 to 5 years)
		18 μCi (0.65 MBq) (+5 to 10 years)
		25 μCi (0.93 MBq) (+10 to 15 years)
Bone scan	^{99m}Tc phosphate	2 mCi (74 MBq)
Lung scan	^{99m}Tc MAA	500 μCi (18.5 MBq) (ventilation
	^{133}Xe	xenon 2.0 mCi/liter or 74 MBq/liter)

Table continued on following page

EXAMINATION	RADIOPHARMACEUTICAL	DOSE
Liver scan	^{99m}Tc sulfur colloid	750 μCi (27.8 MBq)
Renal scan	^{99m}Tc DTPA or DMSA	500 μCi (18.5 MBq)
Cisternogram	^{111}In DTPA	25 μCi (0.93 MBq)
Gallium scan	^{67}Ga citrate	500 μCi (18.5 MBq)
Hepatobiliary scan	^{99m}Tc IDA	1 mCi (37 MBq)

Appendix E

Sample Techniques for Nuclear Imaging

This appendix is provided as a guide to the technical aspects of various imaging procedures. Many of the less common procedures have not been included, and the procedures described herein may need to be adjusted, depending upon the equipment available. Each nuclear medicine laboratory should have a standardized procedures manual, and this appendix may be used as a beginning point for the development of such a manual.

Brain and Cerebral Blood Flow Scan

PROCEDURE IMAGING TIME	20 to 30 minutes
RADIOPHARMACEUTICAL	^{99m}Tc sodium pertechnetate, ^{99m}Tc DTPA, or glucoheptonate
METHOD OF ADMINISTRATION	Bolus intravenous injection in median basilic vein in less than 0.5-ml volume using 19-gauge needle
NORMAL ADULT DOSE	15 to 30 mCi (555 MBq to 1.11 GBq)
INJECTION-TO-IMAGING TIME	Immediate (perfusion); pertechnetate—2 to 4 hours, DTPA—1 to 3 hours, and glucoheptonate—1 to 2 hours for static
CONFLICTING EXAMINATIONS/ MEDICATIONS	1. Potassium perchlorate (KClO$_4$) administration is contraindicated in patients with gastric/duodenal disorders. 2. Brain scans should not be performed with ^{99m}Tc sodium pertechnetate in patients who have had a nuclear procedure using tin-reduced agents in the last 5 days.
PATIENT PREPARATION	200 to 300 mg KClO$_4$ (in 30-ml volume) administered orally 15 minutes prior to intravenous injection of ^{99m}Tc sodium pertechnetate
TECHNIQUE Collimator	Low-energy, all-purpose, parallel-hole
Dynamic Flow Imaging Time	1.5 sec/frame
Preset Count/Time	All static images: 500 to 1000 K counts
Routine Views	Immediate blood pool anterior and delayed views anterior, posterior, and both laterals
Optional Views	1. Vertex 2. Posterior fossa obliques

Patient Positioning	Sitting or supine
Photopeak Selection	140 keV (20% window)
Comments	Use lead shield to mask whole-body activity.

Functional Brain Imaging (SPECT)

PROCEDURE IMAGING TIME	10 minutes (HMPAO*); 30 minutes (IMP†)
INSTRUMENTATION	SPECT camera
RADIOPHARMACEUTICAL	^{99m}Tc HMPAO; ^{123}I IMP
METHOD OF ADMINISTRATION	Intravenous injection
NORMAL ADULT DOSE	HMPAO—5 to 30 mCi (555 MBq to 1.11 GBq); IMP—3 to 5 mCi (111 to 185 MBq)
INJECTION-TO-IMAGING TIME	10 minutes
CONFLICTING EXAMINATIONS/ MEDICATIONS	None
PATIENT PREPARATION	None
TECHNIQUE Collimator	Low-energy, high-resolution (HMPAO); medium-energy (IMP) due to ^{124}I contamination
Counts/Time	60 to 64 stops each for 30 seconds (IMP) and 10 seconds (HMPAO)
Routine Views	360° arc of rotation
Patient Positioning	Supine
Photopeak Selection	159 keV ^{123}I; 140 keV ^{99m}Tc (20% window)
Comments	1. Patient should be in unstimulated state, i.e., in dark, quiet room. 2. Use 64 × 64 matrix.

*Hexamethylpropyleneamine oxime
†N-isopropyl-123-l-p-iodoamphetamine

Cisternogram

PROCEDURE IMAGING TIME	30 minutes for each set
RADIOPHARMACEUTICAL	^{111}In DTPA
METHOD OF ADMINISTRATION	Spinal subarachnoid space injection
NORMAL ADULT DOSE	0.5 mCi (18.5 MBq)
INJECTION-TO-IMAGING TIME	2 hours, 6 hours, 24 hours, 48 hours, and 72 hours (as needed)
CONFLICTING EXAMINATIONS/ MEDICATIONS	None
PATIENT PREPARATION	If the clinical diagnosis is cerebrospinal fluid (CSF) rhinorrhea or otorrhea, the patient's nose and ears should be packed before injection for later counting.

TECHNIQUE

Collimator	Low-energy, all-purpose, parallel-hole
Counts	1. 50 to 100 K counts for ^{111}In 2. ^{57}Co for 50 K counts transmission scan
Routine Views	1. Anterior transmission scan: Position patient between ^{57}Co sheet source and collimator surface. Peak in ^{57}Co by following photopeak determination. Set intensity, but collect only 50 K counts. Do not advance film. Remove sheet source from behind patient. Peak detector for ^{111}In. Collect 100 K counts. 2. Lateral transmission scan 3. Anterior skull 4. Lateral skull (same lateral as transmission scan)
Patient Positioning	Supine. If a large CSF leak is suspected in a specific area, the patient may be positioned with that portion dependent.
Photopeak Selection	^{57}Co (for transmission images); ^{111}In DTPA 173 keV (20% window)
Comments	For CSF rhinorrhea or otorrhea, count all samples in well counter after removal from nose and ears. Note: Remove the pledgets and place each in a separate counting vial at time of removal, labeling each vial.

Thyroid Scan (Technetium 99m)

PROCEDURE IMAGING TIME	15 minutes
RADIOPHARMACEUTICAL	^{99m}Tc sodium pertechnetate
METHOD OF ADMINISTRATION	Intravenous injection
NORMAL ADULT DOSE	6 mCi (222 MBq)
INJECTION-TO-IMAGING TIME	20 minutes
CONFLICTING EXAMINATIONS/ MEDICATIONS	None
PATIENT PREPARATION	None
TECHNIQUE	
Collimator	Low-energy parallel and pinhole
Counts	100 to 250 K counts per image
Patient Positioning	1. Supine 2. Extend neck forward by placing a positioning sponge under back of neck.
Routine Views	1. Anterior view of the thyroid to include salivary glands, using parallel collimator 2. Pinhole views of thyroid only, in anterior and both oblique positions
Photopeak Selection	140 keV (20% window)
Comments	Remind the patient not to swallow while the camera is imaging.

Thyroid Scan (Iodine 123)

PROCEDURE IMAGING TIME	1 hour
RADIOPHARMACEUTICAL	^{123}I sodium iodide
METHOD OF ADMINISTRATION	Oral
NORMAL ADULT DOSE	200 to 400 µCi (7.4 to 14.8 MBq)
ADMINISTRATION-TO-IMAGING TIME	4 to 24 hours
CONFLICTING EXAMINATIONS/ MEDICATIONS	1. Radiographic procedures using intravenous iodine contrast media (e.g., intravenous pyelogram, computed tomogram with contrast)
	2. Other radiographic procedures using iodine contrast media (e.g., myelogram, oral cholecystogram)
	3. Exogenous T_3 or T_4 (liothyronine, levothyroxine)
	4. Thyroid blocking agents such as propylthiouracil, perchlorate, and methimazole
	5. Oral iodides in medications containing iodine (e.g., kelp preparations, vitamins, Lugol's solution)
	6. If necessary, do a $^{99m}TcO_4-$ scan.
PATIENT PREPARATION	Scanning dose to be administered 4 to 24 hours prior to scanning
TECHNIQUE Collimator	Pinhole
Counts	100 to 250 K counts per image
Routine Views	Anterior, right and left oblique
Patient Positioning	Supine, neck extended
Photopeak Selection	159 keV (20% window)
Comments	1. Iodine uptake is normally measured at 24 hours.
	2. Patient's thyroid should be palpated by physician.
	3. Perchlorate washout test: get uptake at 2 hours, then give 800 mg $KClO_4$ orally and measure counts in thyroid every 30 minutes for 2 hours. More than 10% decrease in 2 hours is abnormal.

Thyroid Cancer Scan

PROCEDURE IMAGING TIME	1 to 2 hours
RADIOPHARMACEUTICAL	^{131}I sodium iodide
METHOD OF ADMINISTRATION	Oral
NORMAL ADULT DOSE	1 to 5 mCi (37 to 185 MBq)
INJECTION-TO-IMAGING TIME	72 hours
CONFLICTING EXAMINATIONS/ MEDICATIONS	Iodine-containing medications and contrast agents
PATIENT PREPARATION	2 weeks off T_3 or 4 weeks off T_4 replacement
TECHNIQUE	Whole-body scan
Collimator	Medium- or high-energy
Counts	200 K counts

Routine Views	Anterior and posterior views
Patient Positioning	Supine
Photopeak Selection	364 keV (20% window)
Comments	1. This scan for metastatic disease is done only after ablation of normal thyroid tissue.
	2. Serum thyroid stimulating hormone (TSH) levels should be above 40 mU/ml prior to start.

Ventriculogram at Rest*

PROCEDURE IMAGING TIME	30 minutes
RADIOPHARMACEUTICAL	^{99m}Tc sodium pertechnetate
METHOD OF ADMINISTRATION	Intravenous injection
NORMAL ADULT DOSE	15 to 30 mCi (555 MBq to 111 GBq)
INJECTION-TO-IMAGING TIME	Immediate
CONFLICTING EXAMINATIONS/ MEDICATIONS	None
PATIENT PREPARATION	(See Comments)
TECHNIQUE	
Collimator	Low-energy, all-purpose, parallel-hole
Counts	300 K counts
Patient Positioning	Supine
Photopeak Selection	140 keV (20% window)
Comments	Direct red cell labeling (also see pp. 318–319).

1. Take a vial of cold pyrophosphate and dilute with 1 to 3 cc of *sterile* saline (not bacteriostatic). Shake the mixture and let it stand 5 minutes. Without injecting air into the vial, withdraw the contents into a 3-cc syringe, avoiding inclusion of an air bubble.
2. Inject patient with cold pyrophosphate (0.8 to 1 mg stannous chloride).
3. After 20 minutes, inject the radiopharmaceutical.
4. Connect ECG leads to patient 5 to 10 cm below the axilla bilaterally. Remember to abrade the skin well enough so that the leads have good contact.
5. Place the patient in the supine position on an imaging cart with left side toward the camera.
6. Position the camera over the patient for the first image, an anterior view.

*Stress study and computer operation vary widely and are not presented here.

Myocardial Infarction Scan

PROCEDURE IMAGING TIME	30 minutes
RADIOPHARMACEUTICAL	^{99m}Tc stannous pyrophosphate

METHOD OF ADMINISTRATION	Intravenous injection
NORMAL ADULT DOSE	20 mCi (740 MBq)
INJECTION-TO-IMAGING TIME	2 to 3 hours
CONFLICTING EXAMINATIONS/ MEDICATIONS	None
PATIENT PREPARATION	None
TECHNIQUE	
Collimator	Low-energy, all-purpose, parallel-hole
Counts	All views: 500 K counts (1000 K counts for LFOV).
Routine Views	1. Anterior 2. Left anterior oblique 30° 3. Left anterior oblique 60° 4. Left lateral
Patient Positioning	Supine
Photopeak Selection	140 keV (20% window)
Comments	1. Information density marker must never be placed over heart or kidney. 2. If a large amount of soft tissue activity is present, delayed views may be helpful.

Thallium (^{201}Tl) Scan

PROCEDURE IMAGING TIME	45 minutes per set
RADIOPHARMACEUTICAL	^{201}Tl chloride
METHOD OF ADMINISTRATION	Intravenous injection
NORMAL ADULT DOSE	2 mCi (74 MBq)
INJECTION-TO-IMAGING TIME	Immediate
CONFLICTING EXAMINATIONS/ MEDICATIONS	Discontinue beta-blockers, calcium antagonists, and nitrates, if possible.
PATIENT PREPARATION	Cardiac stress test, if indicated. Intravenous injection at peak of stress and continue exercise for 1 minute.
TECHNIQUE	
Collimator	Low-energy, all-purpose high-resolution or 7 pinhole
Counts	300 K counts on all initial views, and record time. On 3-hour delayed views, use same time as for initial views.
Routine Views	1. Anterior 2. Left anterior oblique (LAO) 45° 3. Left anterior oblique 70°
Patient Positioning	Supine; right lateral decubitus position for 70° left anterior oblique view
Photopeak Selection	85 keV (15% window)
Comments	1. Computer processing is extremely helpful in interpretation of the myocardial perfusion images. 2. Delayed views may occasionally benefit from reinjection. 3. Screen extracardiac structures with lead apron.

EXERCISE-REDISTRIBUTION THALLIUM PROTOCOL EMPLOYING A BRUCE MULTISTAGE OR MODIFIED BRUCE TREADMILL EXERCISE PROTOCOL

Patient Preparation	Fasting; indwelling angiocatheter; discontinue interfering medications
^{201}Tl Injection	1.5 to 2.0 mCi (55 to 74 MBq) thallous chloride injected at peak stress; post-injection exercise, 30 to 60 seconds
Initial Imaging	Within 5 to 10 minutes post-injection 45° LAO; anterior 60° LAO; 8 to 10 min/view (400 K counts)
Post-Exercise Instructions	Only light food intake; minimal physical exertion
Redistribution Imaging	3 to 4 hours post-injection; identical view taken for the same time as initial images

THALLIUM 201 DIPYRIDAMOLE SCINTIGRAPHY PROCEDURE*

Patient Preparation	Nothing by mouth (NPO) 4 to 6 hours, withhold caffeine-containing beverages 24 hours
Drug Administered	Intravenous infusion dipyridamole in antecubital vein with patient supine; rate, 0.5 mg/kg/min over 4 minutes in 20 to 40 cc of normal saline
Thallium Administered	Intravenous administration of ^{201}Tl chloride, 2 mCi; time, 3 minutes post-dipyridamole infusion, patient, supine or upright
Imaging	Begin, 3 to 4 minutes post-thallium injection; views, three standard views; repeat, 3 to 4 hours.
Comments	Side effects may be reversed by intravenous administration of 100 to 200 mg of aminophylline over 1 minute.

*Possibly reinject prior to delayed imaging

SPECT Thallium Imaging

PROCEDURE IMAGING TIME	30 minutes
INSTRUMENTATION	SPECT camera
RADIOPHARMACEUTICAL	^{201}Tl chloride
METHOD OF ADMINISTRATION	Intravenous injection
NORMAL ADULT DOSE	3 to 5 mCi (111 to 185 MBq)
INJECTION-TO-IMAGING TIME	Immediate
CONFLICTING EXAMINATIONS/ MEDICATIONS	Discontinue calcium antagonists, beta-blockers, and nitrates, if possible.
PATIENT PREPARATION	NPO for 2 to 4 hours; exercise, if required
TECHNIQUE Collimator	Low-energy, all-purpose
Counts/Time	30 to 32 stops for 40 seconds each

Routine Views	180° arc of rotation; right anterior oblique to left posterior oblique
Patient Positioning	Supine, left arm overhead
Photopeak Selection	85 keV (15% window) and possibly 135 to 160 keV
Comments	1. Process for short and long axis views.
	2. Parametric images such as "bull's eye" maps can be used to quantitate washout.
	3. Use 64 × 64 matrix.

Pulmonary Ventilation Scan

PROCEDURE IMAGING TIME	5 minutes
INSTRUMENTATION	Large-field-of-view camera, if available
RADIOPHARMACEUTICAL	^{133}Xe
METHOD OF ADMINISTRATION	Gas is inspired via an enclosed ventilation system with appropriate mouthpiece or face mask.
NORMAL ADULT DOSE	10 to 15 mCi (370 to 555 MBq). (If done after perfusion scan, dose may have to be 20 mCi [740 MBq]).
CONFLICTING EXAMINATIONS/ MEDICATIONS	None
PATIENT PREPARATION	None
TECHNIQUE Collimator	Low-energy, all-purpose, parallel-hole
Counts	All images are taken for 10 seconds.
Routine Views	All views are performed in the posterior position unless otherwise specified by the physician.
	1. Begin ^{133}Xe and obtain 10-second inspiration image (1000 K counts).
	2. Record three equilibrium images (300 K counts).
	3. Exhaust ^{133}Xe and record 10-second images until the bulk of the gas has left the lungs.
Patient Positioning	Sitting, preferably. Supine is also acceptable.
Photopeak Selection	81 keV (25% window)
Comments	An exhaust system or xenon trap should be available for expired xenon.

Pulmonary Perfusion Scan

PROCEDURE IMAGING TIME	30 minutes
RADIOPHARMACEUTICAL	^{99m}Tc MAA
METHOD OF ADMINISTRATION	Slow intravenous injection in antecubital vein. Invert syringe immediately before injection to resuspend particles. Inject with patient supine.
NORMAL ADULT DOSE	5 mCi (185 MBq) (Reduce to 3 mCi [111 MBq] if expecting to do xenon study afterwards.)

INJECTION-TO-IMAGING TIME	Immediate
CONFLICTING EXAMINATIONS/ MEDICATIONS	None
PATIENT PREPARATION	None
TECHNIQUE Collimator	Low-energy, all-purpose, parallel-hole
Counts	100 K counts
Routine Views	1. Posterior 2. Left posterior oblique 3. Left lateral 4. Left anterior oblique 5. Anterior 6. Right anterior oblique 7. Right lateral 8. Right posterior oblique
Patient Positioning	Supine or sitting
Photopeak Selection	140 keV (20% window)
Comments	If blood is introduced into the syringe containing the radiopharmaceutical, the injection must be completed immediately or the radiopharmaceutical will cause "hot spots" in the lung.

Liver-Spleen Scan

PROCEDURE IMAGING TIME	30 minutes
RADIOPHARMACEUTICAL	^{99m}Tc sulfur colloid
METHOD OF ADMINISTRATION	Intravenous injection; bolus injection in antecubital vein for dynamic imaging. Invert syringe before injecting to resuspend particles.
NORMAL ADULT DOSE	3 to 5 mCi (111 to 185 MBq)
INJECTION-TO-IMAGING TIME	20 minutes
CONFLICTING EXAMINATIONS/ MEDICATIONS	Recent upper GI series or barium enema with retained barium
PATIENT PREPARATION	None
TECHNIQUE Collimator	Low-energy, all-purpose, parallel-hole
Counts	1. 1000 K counts: anterior supine 2. 500 K counts: all other views
Routine Views	1. Anterior supine 2. Anterior supine with lead marker 3. Anterior erect 4. Right anterior oblique 5. Right lateral 6. Right posterior oblique 7. Posterior with lead marker 8. Posterior 9. Left lateral
Optional Views	On patients who require supine imaging, obtain anterior erect view whenever possible.
Patient Positioning	Supine
Photopeak Selection	140 keV (20% window)
Comments	Breast-shadow artifact is often seen in women. Eliminate artifact by moving right breast away from liver in anterior and right anterior oblique views.

SPECT Liver Imaging

PROCEDURE IMAGING TIME	30 minutes
INSTRUMENTATION	SPECT camera
RADIOPHARMACEUTICAL	^{99m}Tc sulfur colloid
METHOD OF ADMINISTRATION	Intravenous injection
NORMAL ADULT DOSE	5 mCi (185 MBq)
INJECTION-TO-IMAGING TIME	20 minutes
CONFLICTING EXAMINATIONS/ MEDICATIONS	Retained barium
PATIENT PREPARATION	None
TECHNIQUE Collimator	Low-energy, high-resolution
Counts/Time	60 to 64 steps for 30 seconds each
Routine Views	360° arc of rotation
Patient Positioning	Supine; both arms over head
Photopeak Selection	140 keV (20% window)
Comments	128 × 128 matrix, if available

Hepatobiliary Scan

PROCEDURE IMAGING TIME	1 to 4 hours
RADIOPHARMACEUTICAL	^{99m}Tc PIPIDA, HIDA, or DISIDA
METHOD OF ADMINISTRATION	Intravenous injection; bolus injection in antecubital vein for dynamic imaging
NORMAL ADULT DOSE	5 mCi (185 MBq)
INJECTION-TO-IMAGING TIME	5 minutes
CONFLICTING EXAMINATIONS/ MEDICATIONS	1. Retained barium 2. Serum bilirubin level above 20 mg/dl may cause a nondiagnostic examination, due to poor hepatocellular function.
PATIENT PREPARATION	NPO for 6 to 8 hours before procedure
TECHNIQUE Collimator	Low-energy, all-purpose, parallel-hole
Counts	1. Three images (at 5, 10, and 15 minutes) at 500 K counts 2. Record time of third (15-minute) image 3. Remaining images for preset time, taken at 5-minute intervals for 45 minutes
Routine Views	Serial images in anterior position
Optional Views	If visualization of gallbladder is questionable, obtain right lateral view.
Patient Positioning	Supine
Photopeak Selection	140 keV (20% window)

| Comments | 1. If gallbladder is not seen by 45 minutes, delayed images should be taken at 15-minute intervals until 2 hours post-injection, and then hourly for 2 hours. |
| | 2. If gallbladder is visualized but activity is not seen in the small bowel by 1 hour post-injection, 2 oz of a fat solution or cholecystokinin may be considered. Images are taken 15 and 30 minutes after administration. |

Meckel's Diverticulum Scan

PROCEDURE IMAGING TIME	½ to 1 hour
RADIOPHARMACEUTICAL	^{99m}Tc sodium pertechnetate
METHOD OF ADMINISTRATION	Intravenous injection
NORMAL ADULT DOSE	10 mCi (370 MBq) or 200 μCi/kg (7.40 MBq) in children
PEDIATRIC DOSE	At least 2.0 mCi (74 MBq)
INJECTION-TO-IMAGING TIME	Immediate
CONFLICTING EXAMINATIONS/ MEDICATIONS	1. Recent upper GI series
	2. Recent barium enema
PATIENT PREPARATION	None
TECHNIQUE	
Collimator	Low-energy, all-purpose, parallel-hole
Counts	All static images: 500 K counts in the lower midabdomen above the bladder (*not* in stomach or small bowel)
Routine Views	1. Sequential anterior abdominal images at 5-minute intervals for 30 minutes
	2. Right lateral midabdomen at 30 minutes
Patient Positioning	Supine
Photopeak Selection	140 keV (20% window)

Gastrointestinal Scan to Investigate Blood Loss

PROCEDURE IMAGING TIME	30 to 45 minutes
RADIOPHARMACEUTICAL	^{99m}Tc sulfur colloid or red cells
METHOD OF ADMINISTRATION	Intravenous injection (see also pp. 318–319)
NORMAL ADULT DOSE	10 mCi (370 MBq) SC; 20 mCi (740 MBq) RBC.
INJECTION-TO-IMAGING TIME	Immediate
CONFLICTING EXAMINATIONS/ MEDICATIONS	1. Recent upper GI series
	2. Recent barium enema
PATIENT PREPARATION	None
TECHNIQUE	
Collimator	Low-level, all-purpose, parallel-hole

Counts	Collect 500 K counts per image with camera
Routine Views	Sequential anterior abdominal images taken at 5-minute intervals for 30 minutes
Optional Views	Oblique images or images taken in a cephalad angulation may be helpful in locating an abnormality if using sulfur colloid.
Patient Positioning	Supine
Photopeak Selection	140 keV (20%) window)
Comments	24-hour delayed images possible with RBCs

Esophageal Transit

PROCEDURE IMAGING TIME	20 minutes
RADIOPHARMACEUTICAL	^{99m}Tc sulfur colloid in 15 ml of water
METHOD OF ADMINISTRATION	Oral
NORMAL ADULT DOSE	150 to 300 μCi (5.6 to 11.1 MBq)
INGESTION-TO-IMAGING TIME	Immediate
CONFLICTING EXAMINATIONS/ MEDICATIONS	None
PATIENT PREPARATION	NPO for 4 hours
TECHNIQUE	
Collimator	Low-energy
Counts	Computer acquisition
Routine Views	Anterior
Patient Positioning	Sitting
Photopeak Selection	140 keV (20% window)
Comments	1. Computer required 2. In the normal person, 90% of activity should have traversed esophagus in 15 seconds.

Gastroesophageal Reflux

PROCEDURE IMAGING TIME	2 hours
RADIOPHARMACEUTICAL	^{99m}Tc sulfur colloid in 150 ml of orange juice and 150 ml of 0.1 N HCl
METHOD OF ADMINISTRATION	Oral
NORMAL ADULT DOSE	300 μCi (11.1 MBq)
ADMINISTRATION-TO-IMAGING TIME	Immediate
CONFLICTING EXAMINATIONS/ MEDICATIONS	None
PATIENT PREPARATION	NPO for 6 hours
TECHNIQUE Collimator	Low-energy
Counts	30-second images; computer acquisition mandatory
Routine Views	Anterior; image with abdominal binder at 0, 20, 40, 60, 80, and 100 mm Hg in both positions

Patient Positioning	Upright then supine
Photopeak Selection	140 keV (20% window)
Comments	1. Over 4% reflux is abnormal.
	2. A nasogastric (N-G) tube may be used in young children for insertion of sulfur colloid.
	3. To look for pulmonary aspiration in infants use 5 μCi/ml (0.19 MBq) in milk or formula (for a total of 500 μCi or 18.5 MBq). Image at 24 hours.

Gastric Emptying

PROCEDURE IMAGING TIME	2 hours
RADIOPHARMACEUTICAL	Liquid phase, ^{111}In DTPA in 300 ml water; solid phase, ^{99m}Tc sulfur colloid in scrambled eggs or oatmeal
METHOD OF ADMINISTRATION	Oral
NORMAL ADULT DOSE	0.5 to 3 mCi (18.5 to 111 MBq) of ^{99m}Tc sulfur colloid; 125 μCi (4.6 MBq) of ^{111}In DTPA
ADMINISTRATION-TO-IMAGING TIME	Immediate
CONFLICTING EXAMINATIONS/ MEDICATIONS	Drugs affecting gastric motility
PATIENT PREPARATION	NPO for 6 hours
TECHNIQUE Collimator	Low-energy for ^{99m}Tc; medium-energy for ^{111}In
Counts	500 K counts in images at 5, 10, 15, 30, 60, 120, and 180 minutes
Routine Views	Anterior
Patient Positioning	Sitting between images, supine for imaging
Photopeak Selection	140 keV (20% window) for ^{99m}Tc
Comments	1. Normally, for eggs or oatmeal half of the activity will leave the stomach in 90 minutes.
	2. Computer acquisition is essential.

Leveen Shunt Patency

PROCEDURE IMAGING TIME	1 hour
RADIOPHARMACEUTICAL	^{99m}Tc sulfur colloid
METHOD OF ADMINISTRATION	Intraperitoneal
NORMAL ADULT DOSE	1 to 2 mCi (37 to 74 MBq)
INJECTION-TO-IMAGING TIME	Immediate
CONFLICTING EXAMINATIONS/ MEDICATIONS	None
PATIENT PREPARATION	Void before examination; local anesthesia
TECHNIQUE Collimator	Low-energy
Counts	2-second dynamic images. If flow is slow, use 2-minute static images. Image as soon as lower portion of tube is seen. At 1 hour, image liver and spleen

Routine Views	Anterior abdomen and chest
Patient Positioning	Supine
Photopeak Selection	140 keV (20% window)
Comments	1. Flush needle with 3 to 5 ml saline.
	2. Abdominal ballotment may facilitate mixing with ascitic fluid.
	3. If tube does not appear, delayed views up to 5 hours may be necessary.

Bone Scan

PROCEDURE IMAGING TIME	20 to 45 minutes
RADIOPHARMACEUTICAL	^{99m}Tc labeled phosphates
METHOD OF ADMINISTRATION	Intravenous injection
NORMAL ADULT DOSE	20 mCi (740 MBq)
INJECTION-TO-IMAGING TIME	Immediate to 3 hours (see Comments)
CONFLICTING EXAMINATIONS/ MEDICATIONS	None
PATIENT PREPARATION	1. Patient should be hydrated, intravenously or orally, after administration to reduce radiation dose to bladder.
	2. Patient should void prior to imaging.
TECHNIQUE Collimator	Low-energy, all-purpose, parallel-hole
Counts	1. 500 K counts in axial skeleton
	2. 250 K counts in extremities
Routine Views	Anterior and posterior skeleton, lateral skull
Patient Positioning	Supine, prone, or sitting
Photopeak Selection	140 keV (20% window)
Comments	1. Differential diagnosis of cellulitis from osteomyelitis requires flow study (images every 3 seconds for 1 minute) and a blood pool image of area of interest; additional static images at 20 minutes and 3 hours.
	2. Diagnosis of pseudoarthrosis or stress fracture requires area of interest to be imaged at 3 hours.
	3. Prevent "cold spot" artifacts by having patient remove metal objects (e.g., money, lighter, jewelry).
	4. Identify area of interest to be imaged prior to selecting injection site to prevent injection in area of interest.
	5. Urine contamination is the most common "hot spot" artifact. Decontaminate patient and image again.

SPECT Bone Imaging

PROCEDURE IMAGING TIME	30 minutes
INSTRUMENTATION	SPECT camera

RADIOPHARMACEUTICAL	^{99m}Tc diphosphonate
METHOD OF ADMINISTRATION	Intravenous injection
NORMAL ADULT DOSE	20 mCi (740 MBq)
INJECTION-TO-IMAGING TIME	20 minutes
CONFLICTING EXAMINATIONS/ MEDICATIONS	Retained barium
PATIENT PREPARATION	None
TECHNIQUE Collimator	Low-energy, high-resolution
Counts/Time	60 to 64 steps for 30 seconds each
Routine Views	360° arc of rotation
Patient Positioning	Supine
Photopeak Selection	140 keV (20% window)
Comments	Use 128 × 128 matrix, if available.

Bone Marrow Scan

PROCEDURE IMAGING TIME	1 hour
RADIOPHARMACEUTICAL	^{99m}Tc sulfur colloid
METHOD OF ADMINISTRATION	Intravenous injection
NORMAL ADULT DOSE	8 to 10 mCi (296 to 370 MBq)
INJECTION-TO-IMAGING TIME	20 min
CONFLICTING EXAMINATIONS/ MEDICATIONS	None
PATIENT PREPARATION	None
TECHNIQUE Collimator	Low-energy, all-purpose, parallel-hole
Counts	All images: 250 K count in bone marrow
Routine Views	1. Anterior: shoulders, sternum, ribs, pelvis, thighs 2. Posterior: thorax, lumbar spine, pelvis
Patient Positioning	Supine or prone or sitting
Photopeak Selection	140 keV (20% window)
Comments	1. Overlap images of areas of interest to prevent loss of information due to edge-packing. 2. Liver and spleen require lead shielding if within area of interest.

Hip Bone Marrow Scan

PROCEDURE IMAGING TIME	1 hour
RADIOPHARMACEUTICAL	^{99m}Tc sulfur colloid
METHOD OF ADMINISTRATION	Intravenous injection
NORMAL ADULT DOSE	8 to 10 mCi (296 to 370 MBq)
INJECTION-TO-IMAGING TIME	20 minutes
CONFLICTING EXAMINATIONS/ MEDICATIONS	None
PATIENT PREPARATION	None

TECHNIQUE

Collimator	Low-energy, all-purpose, parallel-hole
Counts	250 K counts in images of femoral head
Routine Views	1. Anterior pelvis and hips 2. Posterior pelvis
Optional Views	1. "Frogleg view" of both hips 2. Pinhole collimator views of each hip
Patient Positioning	Supine
Photopeak Selection	140 keV (20% window)
Comments	1. If both hips cannot be imaged at the same time, record time for first image and do second image for the same length of time. 2. Check films to determine whether to perform anterior or "frogleg" pinhole imaging.

Renal Blood Flow Scan

PROCEDURE IMAGING TIME	5 minutes
RADIOPHARMACEUTICAL	^{99m}Tc DTPA
METHOD OF ADMINISTRATION	Intravenous injection; bolus injection in antecubital vein
NORMAL ADULT DOSE	10 mCi (370 MBq)
INJECTION-TO-IMAGING TIME	Immediate
CONFLICTING EXAMINATIONS/ MEDICATIONS	None
PATIENT PREPARATION	None

TECHNIQUE

Collimator	Low-energy, all-purpose, parallel-hole
Counts	500 K count for static image
Routine Views	1. Dynamic (anterior: transplant; posterior: retroperitoneal): 2 to 3 sec/frame for 30 sec 2. Static
Patient Positioning	Sitting or supine
Photopeak Selection	140 keV (20% window)

Renal Scan (A)

PROCEDURE IMAGING TIME	20 minutes
RADIOPHARMACEUTICAL	^{99m}Tc DMSA (cortical agent)
METHOD OF ADMINISTRATION	Intravenous administration: bolus injection in antecubital vein in less than 0.5 ml volume using a 22-gauge needle
NORMAL ADULT DOSE	5 mCi (185 MBq)
INJECTION-TO-IMAGING TIME	Immediate and at 2 hours
CONFLICTING EXAMINATIONS/ MEDICATIONS	None
PATIENT PREPARATION	None

TECHNIQUE

Collimator	Low-energy, all-purpose, parallel-hole
Counts	500 K counts for static image

Routine Views	1. Dynamic (anterior: transplant; posterior: retroperitoneal) 2 to 3 sec/frame for 30 sec 2. Static imaging immediately after flow study 3. Static imaging 2 hours after flow study
Patient Positioning	Supine
Photopeak Selection	140 keV (20% window)

Renal Scan (B)

PROCEDURE IMAGING TIME	45 minutes
RADIOPHARMACEUTICAL	^{99m}Tc glucoheptonate
METHOD OF ADMINISTRATION	Intravenous injection: bolus injection in ante-cubital vein
NORMAL ADULT DOSE	10 mCi (370 MBq)
INJECTION-TO-IMAGING TIME	Immediate
CONFLICTING EXAMINATION/ MEDICATIONS	None
PATIENT PREPARATION	None
TECHNIQUE Collimator	Low-energy, all-purpose, parallel-hole
Counts	1. First dynamic study: 2 sec/frame 2. Second dynamic study: 120 sec/frame 3. Static image for 500 K counts
Routine Views	1. A flow study at 2 sec/image in the anterior position for a transplant kidney and the posterior position for a retroperitoneal kidney (perfusion study) 2. Upon completion of the initial flow study, a second phase of dynamic study is performed at 3 min/frame with the patient in the same position. The second phase is carried out for 20 minutes post-injection (excretion study). 3. A delayed image taken in the same position as the previous studies is performed at 2 hours post-injection (cortical study).
Patient Positioning	Supine or sitting
Photopeak Selection	140 keV (20% window)

Renogram

PROCEDURE IMAGING TIME	30 minutes
RADIOPHARMACEUTICAL	^{131}I or ^{123}I Hippuran
METHOD OF ADMINISTRATION	Intravenous injection
NORMAL ADULT DOSE	250 μCi (9.25 MBq) for ^{131}I; 0.75 to 1 mCi (27.8 to 37 MBq) for ^{123}I
INJECTION-TO-IMAGING TIME	Immediate
CONFLICTING EXAMINATIONS/ MEDICATIONS	None
PATIENT PREPARATION	None
TECHNIQUE Collimator	Medium-energy
Counts	15 dynamic images of 2 minutes each are obtained.

Views	Anterior for transplant evaluation; posterior for native kidneys
Patient Positioning	Supine
Photopeak Selection	364 keV (20% window) for ^{131}I 159 keV (20% window) for ^{123}I
Comments	Erect posterior images may be obtained after the patient has ambulated if ureteral obstruction is suspected

Lasix Renogram

PROCEDURE IMAGING TIME	30 to 60 minutes
RADIOPHARMACEUTICAL	^{99m}Tc DTPA
METHOD OF ADMINISTRATION	Bolus intravenous injection in antecubital vein
NORMAL ADULT DOSE	10 mCi (370 MBq)
INJECTION-TO-IMAGING TIME	Immediate
CONFLICTING EXAMINATIONS/ MEDICATIONS	Intravenous iodine contrast media should not be used on the same day that this examination is performed.
PATIENT PREPARATION	1. See requisition, because many patients must have an indwelling catheter placed prior to this procedure. 2. Patient must void prior to imaging.
TECHNIQUE Collimator	Low-energy, all-purpose, parallel-hole
Counts/Time	120 sec/frame
Routine Views	Posterior
Patient Positioning	Sitting, if possible
Photopeak Selection	140 keV (20% window)
Comments	1. A small quantity of DTPA is infused to be certain that the kidney is within the field of view. 2. Dynamic images are begun on the camera and computer simultaneously. 3. Furosemide (0.3 mg/kg body weight) is given intravenously approximately 10 minutes into the study. Note frame number of administration. 4. Continue with dynamic images for 10 more frames.

Captopril Renogram

PROCEDURE IMAGING TIME	1 hour
RADIOPHARMACEUTICAL	^{99m}Tc DTPA and/or ^{131}I sodium iodohippurate
METHOD OF ADMINISTRATION	Radionuclide administered intravenously 1 hour after 50 mg captopril single oral dose.
NORMAL ADULT DOSE	10 mCi (370 MBq) ^{99m}Tc DTPA, 250 μCi (9.25 MBq) ^{131}I Hippuran
INJECTION-TO-IMAGING TIME	Immediate
CONFLICTING EXAMINATIONS/ MEDICATIONS	Medication withdrawal overnight is advisable and study should not be initiated if blood pressure is below 140 mm Hg.
PATIENT PREPARATION	Patient should be hydrated orally, 10 ml/kg.

TECHNIQUE
Collimator | Low-energy or general all-purpose for DTPA; medium-energy for Hippuran portion

Counts/Time | DTPA flow study at 1 or 2 seconds obtained for 1 minute followed by sequential imaging every 2 to 3 minutes on film or every 30 seconds on computer for 20 minutes. A post-void image is obtained.

Routine Views | Posterior blood flow and sequential imaging as described
For Hippuran study, imaging obtained at 2-minute intervals for 20 minutes in posterior projection. In some protocols, patients may receive furosemide (40 mg) 3 minutes after administration of the Hippuran.

Patient Positioning | Supine

Photopeak Selection | 140 keV (20% window) for ^{99m}Tc DTPA; 364 keV (20% window) for ^{131}I Hippuran

Comments | Patients may become seriously hypotensive with this procedure. It is advisable to establish intravenous infusion of normal saline prior to administration of captopril; blood pressure should be recorded every 15 minutes. Many patients who become hypotensive respond to intravenous fluids without the need for vasopressive drugs.

Testicular Scan

PROCEDURE IMAGING TIME | 30 minutes
RADIOPHARMACEUTICAL | ^{99m}Tc sodium pertechnetate
METHOD OF ADMINISTRATION | Bolus intravenous injection in median basilic vein
NORMAL ADULT DOSE | 30 mCi (1.11 GBq)
INJECTION-TO-IMAGING TIME | Immediate, followed by 15-minute delayed image
CONFLICTING EXAMINATIONS/ MEDICATIONS | None
PATIENT PREPARATION | None
TECHNIQUE
Collimator | Converging low-energy
Counts | 1. Anterior blood flow: 2 sec/frame
2. Static image: 500 K counts
Routine Views | 1. Anterior blood flow study
2. Static anterior immediately after blood flow study
3. Delayed anterior 15 to 20 min post-injection
Patient Positioning | Supine
Photopeak Selection | 140 keV (20% window)

Gallium Scan

PROCEDURE IMAGING TIME | 30 minutes
RADIOPHARMACEUTICAL | ^{67}Ga citrate
METHOD OF ADMINISTRATION | Intravenous injection

NORMAL ADULT DOSE	5 mCi (185 MBq)
INJECTION-TO-IMAGING TIME	6 and 24 hours for abscess; 48 and 72 hours for tumor imaging
CONFLICTING EXAMINATION/ MEDICATIONS	Retained barium
PATIENT PREPARATION	Bowel preparation after initial images
TECHNIQUE	
Collimator	Medium-energy, parallel-hole
Counts	500 K counts
Patient Positioning	Supine
Photopeak Selection	93, 184 keV (20% windows). Other photopeaks can be utilized.
Routine Views	1. Anterior and posterior whole-body images with scanning gamma camera
	2. Spot views (optional)
Comments	1. Occasionally lateral views may be helpful.
	2. Subtraction views with ^{99m}Tc sulfur colloid may be considered.

Indium (^{111}In) Leukocyte Scan

PROCEDURE IMAGING TIME	1 hour
RADIOPHARMACEUTICAL	^{111}In autologous oxine-labeled leukocytes
METHOD OF ADMINISTRATION	Intravenous
NORMAL ADULT DOSE	500 μCi (18.5 MBq)
INJECTION-TO-IMAGING TIME	16 to 24 hours
CONFLICTING EXAMINATIONS/ MEDICATIONS	Patients on antibiotics or with altered chemotaxis may have false negative exams.
PATIENT PREPARATION	None
TECHNIQUE	
Collimator	Medium- or high-energy
Counts	300 K counts per view
Routine Views	Anterior and posterior views of head, chest, abdomen, pelvis
Patient Positioning	Supine
Photopeak Selection	Dual: 173 and 247 keV (20% window)
Comments	Difficult to obtain enough cells to label in leukopenic patients

RBC Labeling Techniques*

1. *In Vivo:* Add 3 ml saline to Mallinkrodt pyrophosphate kit. Wait 5 minutes and inject intravenously. Wait 10 to 20 minutes and inject 20 mCi (740 MBq) ^{99m}TcO$_4$. Results in 60 to 70 percent labeling, with remaining activity in kidneys, bladder, stomach, thyroid, and salivary glands.
2. *Modified In Vivo:* Results in approximately 88 percent labeling. Add 3 ml of normal sterile saline to Mallinkrodt pyrophosphate kit. Wait

---

*Smith TD, Richards PA: A simple kit for the preparation of ^{99m}Tc-labeled red blood cells. J Nucl Med 17(1):126–132, 1976.

5 minutes, then inject 1 ml IV. Wait 20 minutes. Using a 20-gauge needle, draw 10 ml of patient's blood into a syringe containing 20 mCi (740 MBq) of $^{99m}TcO_4^-$ and 0.5 ml of heparin. Allow this mixture to incubate for 10 minutes at room temperature before reinjecting into patient. Patients with low hematocrit counts may need more than 10 minutes of incubation.

3. *Brookhaven In Vitro:* Results in approximately 97 percent labeling. Procedure for using the RBC kit to prepare ^{99m}Tc labeled RBCs (use aseptic techniques throughout):

   A. Add 1 to 5 ml of saline ^{99m}Tc pertechnetate to a sterile and pyrogen-free 15 ml pharmaceutical vial and assay. IMPORTANT: Determine the maximum ^{99m}Tc activity for satisfactory performance of the kit. The technetium atoms added to the kit must not exceed the number of atoms of technetium (^{99}Tc + ^{99m}Tc) generated by the decay of 10 mCi (370 MBq) of ^{99}Mo. Store in a lead shield.

   B. A Vacutainer tube is used to draw about 6 ml of whole venous blood. Use 20-gauge 1½-inch sterile multiple-sample Vacutainer needle and Vacutainer adapter.

   C. Mix immediately to dissolve the freeze-dried solids in the blood and gently mix the tube contents for 5 minutes at room temperature.

   D. Add 4 ml of sterile saline to the blood. CAUTION: To avoid pressure buildup in the Vacutainer tube, draw 4 ml of sterile saline into a 10-ml syringe, push the hypodermic needle through the Vacutainer stopper, and with the tube upright so that the blood will not be drawn back into the syringe, pull the syringe plunger back to the 8-ml mark. Allow the created vacuum to draw the saline into the tube.

   E. Mix briefly and centrifuge the tube stopper end down for 5 minutes at 1300 RPM.

   F. Maintain the tube in inverted position to avoid disturbing the packed RBCs. Withdraw 2 ml of RBCs using a 20-gauge ⁹⁄₃₂-inch needle. This needle length will just penetrate the stopper.

   G. Transfer the RBCs to the premeasured ^{99m}Tc solution prepared in Step A.

   H. Incubate the ^{99m}Tc-RBC mixture for 5 minutes at room temperature, with gentle mixing.

   I. Assay and dilute appropriately for injection. Cell separation and yield determination at this point consistently give 97 percent yield.

Radionuclide Imaging During Pregnancy

Many clinicians are concerned about ordering radionuclide scans for a pregnant patient. The question most frequently arises in connection with lung and hepatobiliary scans. In general, if the scan is medically indicated and would be performed on a nonpregnant female, it is indicated during pregnancy. There are some facts to be kept in mind when considering this issue.

1. Radiation-induced fetal abnormalities have not been reported below absorbed dose levels of 10 rad (0.1 Gy). The risk of "spontaneous" abnormalities is 3 to 6 percent.
2. The risk of radiation carcinogenesis may be higher in children than in adults but is not likely to exceed a risk of 1 in 1000/rad (10 mGy) (spontaneous cancer risk in the United States population is about 1 in 3).
3. The fetal thyroid does not concentrate iodine before 12 weeks of gestation. After this, if iodine radiopharmaceuticals are to be used, the thyroid can be effectively blocked by administering stable iodide to the mother.
4. It is very unlikely that the fetal absorbed dose from ^{133}Xe or a ^{99m}Tc radiopharmaceutical would exceed 0.5 rad (5 mGy).
5. A large portion of the fetal absorbed dose for many radiopharmaceuticals comes from the maternal bladder, so hydration and frequent voiding should be encouraged.
6. In many instances, the administered activity can be reduced by 50 percent, and the imaging time can be increased without significant degradation of the information obtained. Table F-1 can be used to estimate fetal absorbed dose for various scans.

See Table F–2 for recommendations regarding breast feeding following administration of radiopharmaceuticals to mothers.

Table F–1. ESTIMATED ABSORBED DOSE TO EMBRYO FOR SELECTED RADIOPHARMACEUTICALS

RADIOPHARMACEUTICAL	rad PER MILLICURIE ADMINISTERED*
^{67}Ga citrate	0.250
^{99m}Tc human serum albumin	0.020
^{99m}Tc MAA	0.035
^{99m}Tc phosphonate	0.040
^{99m}Tc Na pertechnetate	0.040
^{99m}Tc glucoheptonate	0.040
^{99m}Tc DTPA (IV or aerosol)	0.035
^{99m}Tc sulfur colloid	0.035
^{99m}Tc DISIDA†	0.030
^{99m}Tc RBC†	0.060
^{111}In leukocytes†	0.400
^{123}Na iodide (15% uptake)	0.035
^{131}Na iodide (15% uptake)	0.100‡
^{123}Rose bengal	0.130
^{131}Rose bengal	0.680
^{201}Tl chloride†	0.300
^{127}Xenon†	0.001
^{133}Xenon†	0.001

*To obtain absorbed dose in mGy/MBq, divide values by 3.7.
†In instances in which no data on embryonic or fetal absorbed dose were available, either the maternal whole-body dose or the gonadal dose was utilized. To be conservative, the largest of these two quantities was chosen.
‡0.010 prior to 10 weeks gestational age.
Data adapted from Protection in Nuclear Medicine and Ultrasound Diagnostic Procedures in Children. Washington, DC, National Council on Radiation Protection and Measurements, Report No. 73, 1983 and from Smith EM, Warner GG: Estimates of radiation dose to the embryo from nuclear medicine procedures. J Nucl 17:836, 1976.

Table F–2. RECOMMENDATIONS FOR CESSATION OF BREAST FEEDING AFTER ADMINISTRATION OF RADIOPHARMACEUTICALS TO MOTHERS

RADIOPHARMACEUTICAL	ADMINISTERED ACTIVITY	CESSATION TIME*
^{99m}Tc MAA	2.2 mCi (81.4 MBq)	12 hr
^{99m}Tc sodium pertechnetate	3.1 mCi (115 MBq)	12 hr
^{99m}Tc sodium pertechnetate	20 mCi (740 MBq)	24 hr
^{99m}Tc DTPA	3.8 mCi (141 MBq)	4 hr
^{99m}Tc phosphonate	11 mCi (407 MBq)	4 hr
^{99m}Tc labeled red blood cells	15 mCi (555 MBq)	4 hr
^{131}I orthoiodohippurate	8 μCi	12 hr
^{131}I orthoiodohippurate	200 μCi	4.5 days
^{67}Ga citrate	3 mCi	4 weeks
^{131}Na iodide	5 μCi	8 weeks
^{131}Na iodide	8.6 μCi	46 days
^{131}Na iodide	0.34 μCi	8 days
^{123}Na iodide (carrier-free)	10 to 30 μCi	2 to 3 days
^{123}Na iodide (with ^{124}I or ^{125}I carrier)	30 mCi	Discontinue
^{201}Tl chloride	3 mCi	24 to 48 hr

*All milk expressed prior to this time should be discarded.

APPENDIX G–1

General Considerations for Patients Receiving Radionuclide Therapy

1. It is important for the patient to understand the nature of the radionuclide treatment. Patient cooperation is important in minimizing unnecessary incidents and exposure.
2. Prior to the administration of the radionuclide, the procedures and special precautions should be reviewed with the nursing staff. The nursing staff must have specific written instructions for each procedure and should review them before the patient arrives in the room.
3. Immediately following the return of the patient to the hospital room, or after the administration of the compound or insertion of the sources, a person from the Radiation Safety Office should survey the patient and surrounding areas to determine distance and time restrictions for hospital personnel and visitors in the patient's room. These distances and times are recorded on a form in the patient's chart and listed on the caution sign on the patient's door. These signs and labels should remain posted until removal is ordered by the Radiation Safety Officer (RSO).
4. Hospital personnel and allowed visitors should position themselves as far from the patient as is reasonable except for necessary bedside care. A distance of 2 meters is normally acceptable. In some cases, the RSO may determine that mobile lead shields are needed to reduce exposure to others in adjacent areas. Specific restrictions will be noted by the RSO on the room door and in the hospital chart.
5. It is not advisable for pregnant women or children under age 18 to enter the hospital room.
6. Personnel dosimeters are required for all hospital personnel who are likely to receive in excess of 25 percent of the dose-equivalent limit for radiation workers. The RSO will identify hospital personnel within this category and issue the appropriate dosimeters to them.
7. Pregnant personnel should not routinely be assigned to the care of patients under treatment with radioactive materials.
8. Patients receiving radionuclide therapy should be assigned a private room and restricted to the room unless an exception is authorized by the RSO.

Special Considerations and Requirements for Iodine 131 Therapy

A patient receiving 30 or more mCi (1.11 GBq) of ^{131}I must be hospitalized. NRC regulations require confinement until the dose rate from the patient is less than 5 mrem (50 μSv) per hour at a distance of 1 meter or the activity in the patient is less than 30 mCi (1.11 GBq).

1. All patients in the above category shall be in a private room with a toilet.
2. The door must be posted with a radioactive materials sign, and note must be made on the door or in the patient's chart where and how long visitors may stay in the patient's room.
3. Visits by persons under the age of 18 should be authorized only on a patient-by-patient basis with approval of the authorized user and after consultation with the Radiation Safety Officer (RSO).
4. A survey of the patient's room and surrounding areas should be conducted as soon as practicable after administration of treatment dose. The results of daily surveys can be used to recalculate permitted staying times of different visitors. Film or thermoluminescent dosimeter (TLD) badges should be worn by the nurses attending the patient.
5. Patients containing ^{131}I shall be confined to their rooms except for special medical or nursing purposes approved by the Nuclear Medicine or Radiation Therapy Department and the RSO. The patient should remain in bed during visits.
6. If possible, there should be no pregnant visitors or nurses attending the patient.
7. Staff should wear disposable gloves, discard them in a designated waste container located just inside the room, and wash their hands after leaving the room.
8. Disposable plates, cups, and other disposables should be used and after use discarded in a specifically designated container.
9. All items such as clothing, bed linens, and surgical dressings may either be surveyed prior to removal from the room or placed in a designated container and held for decay.
10. Urine, feces, and vomitus from ^{131}I therapy patients may be disposed of by way of the sewer or stored for decay in the radioactive waste storage area. The method of disposal should be determined by the RSO.
11. If the urine from ^{131}I patients is to be collected (not an NRC requirement), special containers should be provided by the RSO.

The patient should be encouraged to collect his or her urine in the container. If the patient is bedridden, a separate urinal or bedpan should be flushed several times with hot soapy water after each use.

12. The same toilet should be used by the patient at all times and should be flushed several times after each use.

13. Precautions should be taken to ensure that no urine or vomitus is spilled on the floor or bed. If any part of the patient's room is suspected of being contaminated, the RSO should be notified.

14. If a therapy patient should need emergency surgery or should die, the RSO and the Nuclear Medicine or Radiation Therapy Department should be notified immediately.

15. After the patient is released from the room, the room should be surveyed and may not be reassigned until removable contamination is less than 2000 disintegrations/min/100 cm². Final survey of the room should include areas likely to have been contaminated, such as the toilet area, and items likely to have been touched by the patient, such as the telephone and doorknobs.

16. The thyroid burden of each person who helped prepare or administer a liquid dosage of ^{131}I should be measured within 3 days after administration of the doses. The records should include each thyroid burden measurement, the date of measurement, the name of the person measured, and the initials of the person who made the measurements. These records must be maintained indefinitely.

Nursing Instructions

1. Only that amount of time required for ordinary nursing care should be spent near the patient.

2. Visitors should be limited to those 18 years of age or older unless specified.

3. Patient should remain in bed. All visitors should remain at least 2 meters from patient.

4. Patient should be confined to the room, except by special approval of the RSO.

5. No pregnant nurse, visitor, or attendant should be permitted in the room, if possible. Attending personnel should wear disposable gloves.

6. If a spill of urine or radioactive material is encountered, the RSO should be notified.

Appendix H

Emergency Procedures for Radioactive Spills

Accidental spillage of radioactive material is rare; however, spills may occur in the laboratory, in public areas such as the hall, in the freight elevator, or in any hospital room or ward through contamination by a patient's body fluids.

Major radiation accidents or serious spills of radioactive contamination have rarely involved medical or allied health personnel. Usually spills in hospitals involve only small amounts of radioactivity, in which the main concern is the spread of the contamination, e.g., from shoes or contaminated clothing into public areas. The following is a general outline of the procedure to be followed in the event of a radioactive spill:

1. Confine the spill immediately by placing paper towels or other absorbent material onto it.
2. Put on impermeable gloves.
3. Check shoes for visible signs of contamination. If it appears that shoes may be contaminated, remove shoes when leaving the contaminated area.
4. Mark off or isolate in some way the entire suspect area so that no one walks through it.
5. Detain all evacuees from the immediate area in a place where they can be surveyed by the Radiation Safety Officer (RSO).
6. CALL THE RADIATION SAFETY OFFICE. If the RSO's telephone number is not posted in a convenient place, or if you do not know the number, call the telephone operator, report an emergency, and request the RSO or the first accessible person on the radiation emergency call list.
7. In general, inexperienced personnel should not attempt to clean up a spill. It is better to wait for the RSO than to risk spreading the contamination by erroneous procedures. If the spilled material is covered and bystanders are kept at least a few feet away, there is little or no danger from the radiation.
8. If any of the spilled material has splashed onto a person or his or her clothing, immediate steps should be taken to remove it. Laboratory coats or outer garments should be removed and left in the contaminated area. Hands and other exposed skin areas should be washed thoroughly with soap and water in the nearest wash basin, if by doing so the area of contamination is not enlarged. Care should be taken not to abrade or inflame skin

surfaces. If it is uncertain as to whether or not shoes are contaminated, the walkway to a washing facility should be treated as a contaminated area until the RSO has certified that it is uncontaminated.

9. The RSO will provide decontamination materials and a survey meter so that the cleanup operation can proceed.

10. If the RSO is not immediately available and cleanup must be initiated, as few persons as possible should be involved in the actual decontamination efforts. Impermeable gloves, shoe covers, and a surgical face mask should be worn if available. The spilled material should be taken up with absorbent paper, handled with forceps or tongs, and deposited immediately in a waterproof container. After as much contamination as possible has been removed in this way, the surface should be washed with damp—not wet—paper towels held in forceps, always working toward the center of the contaminated area rather than away from it.

11. Careful monitoring with a survey meter of both the area and the personnel should be carried out during this emergency procedure. The survey meter should be operated by someone who is not involved in the cleanup, so that the instrument does not become contaminated. Cover the probe with thin, clear plastic wrap, if possible.

12. Reduction of the count rate to several times background is usually satisfactory. Higher count rate areas can be covered with plastic-backed absorbent paper and held in place with tape to await further evaluation by the RSO. The RSO should survey the area and certify adequate decontamination prior to its return to routine use.

13. When the operation is finished, gloves and other protective garments should be checked carefully for residual contamination. If any contamination is found, the garments should be left with the other contaminated material in plastic bags for ultimate disposal by the RSO.

14. Life-saving efforts and vital first aid have priority over contamination concerns.

15. If necessary, activate the medical radiation emergency plan.

This information is adapted from Radiation Protection for Medical and Allied Health Personnel: Recommendations of the National Council on Radiation Protection and Measurements. NCRP Report No. 105. Issued October 30, 1989. Bethesda, MD: National Council on Radiation Protection and Measurements, 1989.

INDEX

Note: Page numbers in *italics* refer to illustrations;
page numbers followed by (t) refer to tables.

Abdomen, gallium 67 distribution in, 255

Abscess, imaging of, radiopharmaceuticals for, 254(t)
  periappendiceal, indium leukocyte imaging of, *264*
  pyogenic liver, gallium imaging of, *258*

Absorptiometry, dual photon, 235
  single photon, 235

Acquired immune deficiency disease, gallium imaging in, 260

Activity, definition of, 4
  specific, 4

Adenoma, hepatic cell, radionuclide imaging of, 188
  of liver, radionuclide diagnosis of, 203(t)
  of parathyroid gland, 94, 94(t)

Adrenal imaging, 249–251

Adverse reaction, definition of, 10
  of radiopharmaceuticals, 10

Aerosol, in ventilation imaging, 144, *145*
  dosing of, 143(t)

Akinesis, 134

ALARA program, 269

Albumin, macroaggregated, 143, 143(t)
  serum, technetium 99m labeled, 131–132

Alcoholic liver disease, 183–187, *185, 186*

Alpha, 3

Alpha emission, 1

Aminophylline, in dipyridamole thallium imaging, 112

Amplitude, in cardiac function studies, 126, *127, 128*

Analog-to-digital converter, 47

Aneurysm, left ventricular, *125*

Angiocardiography, first–pass radionuclide, interpretation in, 130–131, *131*
  principle of, 129
  radiopharmaceuticals for, 129–130
  technique in, 130–131

Angiogram, radionuclide, abnormal, 59–66, 59(t)
  cerebral death and, 62–63
  imaging technique for, 57
  in cerebrovascular occlusive disease, 60–62
  in intracranial inflammatory disease, 63

Angiogram *(Continued)*
  in trauma, 63–66
  normal, 58–59, *58, 59*
  normal static, 58–59, *59*
  of neoplasms, 59–60

Angiography, pulmonary, *vs.* ventilation–perfusion imaging, 165(t), 166, 166(t)

Antibodies, radiolabeled monoclonal, 266–267, *267*

Aortic valvular regurgitation, gated blood pool imaging in, 138(t)
  thallium exercise imaging in, 116–117

Aortic valvular stenosis, gated blood pool imaging in, 138(t)

Arithmetic and logic unit, of computer, 46

Array processor, 46

Arrhythmia, filtering of, in gated blood pool ventriculography, 133

Arthritis, bone imaging in, 231, *234*

Artifacts, ring, in SPECT, 42

As low as reasonably achievable program, 269

Ascites, in hepatic cirrhosis, radionuclide imaging of, *185*

Asthma, ventilation–perfusion imaging in, 170–173

Asymmetric septal hypertrophy, thallium exercise imaging in, 117

Atom, notation of, 1

Atrial septal defect, gated blood pool imaging of, 138(t)

Average filling rate, assessment of, 135

Axis of rotation, detector head alignment with, 43
  SPECT, 37

Azimuth stops, in SPECT, 38

Back projection, filtered, 39–40
  in SPECT, 39

Backscatter peak, 19

BATO. See *Boronic adducts of technetium oxine.*

Bequerel, 4

Beta particle emission, 1–2, *2*

Biliary tree, atresia of, 202, *203*
  imaging of. See *Hepatobiliary imaging.*
  obstruction of, 201

Binary system, 45

Bit, 45, 48
Bladder, imaging techniques for, 240–242
Bleeding, of gastrointestinal tract, radionuclide imaging in, 193–195
scan for, 309–310
Blood pool imaging, abnormal radiopharmaceutical distribution in, 13(t)
Blood pool radionuclide ventriculography. See also *Ventriculography*.
gating in, 132–133
in acute myocardial infarction, 137–138
in cardiomyopathy, 139
in dyspnea, 138–139
in intracardiac shunts, 140
in left ventricular function monitoring, 139
in noncoronary heart disease, 138–140
findings of, 138(t)
in valvular heart disease, 139–140
interpretation in, 133–134
principle of, 131
qualitative data in, 134, 134(t)
quantitative data in, 134–135
radiopharmaceuticals for, 131–132
technique in, 132–133
Bone, aseptic necrosis of, 227, 229
fibrous dysplasia of, imaging in, 231, 233
fracture of, imaging in, 225
imaging of. See *Bone imaging*.
physiology of, 209
Bone imaging, abnormal radiopharmaceutical distribution in, 11(t)
clinical applications of, 213
cold lesions in, 217(t), 218
for malignant bone tumors, 219–220
hot lesions in, 217(t)
in arthritis, 231, 234
in aseptic necrosis, 227, 229
in cellulitis, 230–231
in chemotherapy, 225
in fibrous dysplasia, 231, 233
in metastatic disease, 213–219, 214–216
in osteomyelitis, 230–231, 230
in Paget's disease, 231, 232
in reflex sympathetic dystrophy syndrome, 230
in trauma, 224–230, 225, 227–229
normal scan in, 211–213, 211
of benign osseous neoplasms, 221
of Ewing's sarcoma, 219, 220
of fractures, 225
of osteogenic sarcoma, 219, 219
of osteoid osteoma, 220
radiation therapy and, 218, 219
radiopharmaceuticals for, 209–210, 210(t)
scan of, 312
soft tissue uptake in, 221–224, 221(t), 222, 223
SPECT, 312–313
technique in, 210–211
Bone marrow scanning, 231, 235, 313
of hip, 313–314
Bone mineral, measurement of, 231–236

Bone mineral (*Continued*)
quantitative computed tomography for, 233
radionuclide photon absorptiometry for, 233, 235
Boronic adducts of technetium oxine, technetium 99m labeled, 122–123
Brain, trauma to, radionuclide imaging and, 63
Brain death, 62–63, 64
Brain imaging. See also *Angiogram, radionuclide*.
clinical applications of, 58–66
conventional, 55
delayed static images in, 57
functional, 66–68, 300
HIPDM in, 66–68
IMP in, 66, 70
in cerebrovascular occlusive disease, 60, 62, 62–64
in pathologic states, 67, 70
iodinated radiopharmaceuticals for, 66
normal brain physiology and, 55
patient preparation for, 57
positron-emitting agents for, 67–68
radiopharmaceuticals for, 55–57
static images in, 57
technique of, 57, 299
Breakthrough, 31
definition of, 5
Breast, carcinoma of, pulmonary lymphangitic spread of, 172
Breast feeding, radiopharmaceutical dosing and, 321
Bronchiectasis, ventilation–perfusion imaging in, 170–173
Bronchitis, acute, 170–173
chronic, 166, 167–170
Budd-Chiari syndrome, 189–190
Buffer, of computer, 46
Bull's eye plot, in thallium SPECT imaging, 121–122, 121
Byte, 45, 48

Calibrator, dose, 26, 26
for quality control, 27–28
NRC regulations for, 273
Camera system, collimator for, 15–17
computer interface of, 52–53
console controls of, 20
crystal for, 17–19
for imaging, 15
gamma, in SPECT, 37–38, 38
quality control of, 28–30, 29–33
specialized, 24
photomultiplier tubes for, 19
pulse height analyzer for, 19–20
resolution of, 20–24
specialized, 24
Captopril renogram, 242–243, 316–317
Carcinoma, bronchogenic, gallium imaging in, 257
of breast, pulmonary lymphangitic spread of, 172
of thyroid, 87–90
iodine-131 therapy of, 93
metastatic disease from, 89

Carcinoma *(Continued)*
    metastatic disease therapy for, 90–91
Cardiac cycle, phases of, 96, *96*
Cardiac function, nuclear medicine tests of, 123
    computers and, 123–124
    functional images for, 124–127
    qualitative data display for, 123–124
    quantitative data display for, 127–129
Cardiac output, 95
Cardiomyopathy, gated blood pool imaging in, 139
    findings of, 138(t)
    thallium exercise imaging in, 117
Cardiovascular system, anatomy of, 95–96
    physiology of, 95–96
Caroli's disease, hepatobiliary imaging in, *203*
Cellulitis, bone imaging in, 230–231
Center of rotation, correction of, 42
    determination of, 42
    in SPECT imaging, 42, *43*
Central processing unit, of computer, 46
Cerebral blood flow scan, technique for, 299–300
Cerebral cisternography, abnormal radiopharmaceutical distribution in, 13(t)
Cerebral death, radionuclide scanning and, 62–63, *64*
Cerebral infarction, radionuclide scanning in, 60, 62, *62–64*
Cerebrospinal fluid imaging, 68–70
    in cerebrospinal fluid leaks, 73–74, *73*
    in communicating hydrocephalus, 71, *72*, *73*
    in noncommunicating hydrocephalus, 73
    in normal examination, 71, *71*
    in pathologic states, 71–74
    radiopharmaceuticals for, 70
    technique for, 70
Cerebrovascular occlusive disease, radionuclide scanning in, 60, 62, *62–64*
Chemotherapy, bone imaging and, 225
Cholecystitis, hepatobiliary imaging in, acute, 198–200, *199*
    chronic, 200–201
Cholecystokinin, in hepatobiliary imaging, 200
Chronic obstructive pulmonary disease, ventilation–perfusion imaging in, 166–170
Cirrhosis, of liver, radionuclide imaging in, 183–187, *185*, *186*
Cisternogram, normal, 71
    radionuclide, 300–301
        in cerebrospinal fluid leak, 73–74, *73*
Colitis, cytomegalic virus, indium leukocyte imaging in, *265*
Collimator, converging, 17, *17*
    diverging, 17, *17*
    for imaging, 15–17
    in SPECT imaging, 43

Collimator *(Continued)*
    integrity of, quality control protocol for, 33(t)
    line spread of, 22–23
    multihole, 15–16, *17*
    parallel-hole, 16–17, *17*
    pinhole, 15, *17*
        seven-, *17*
    quality control of, 43
    resolution and, *18*
    rotating slant hole, 17
    septa, 15–16
Compton scatter, 20–21, *20*, *21*
Computed tomography, quantitative, in bone mineral measurement, 233–235
Computer, analog, 45
    bulk information storage in, 51, *52*
        purchase considerations for, 53
    camera interface with, 47, 52–53
    central processing unit of, 46
        purchase considerations for, 53
    digital, 45
    display of, 46–47
        purchase considerations for, 53
    hardware for, 46–47, *46*
    hard-wired, 45
    image acquisition in, 48–49
    in cardiac function testing, 123–124
        functional images of, 124–127
        qualitative data display of, 123–124
        quantitative data display of, 127–129
    in gated blood pool radionuclide ventriculography, 132–133, *132*
    in image display, 49–50, *50*
    in image processing, 49–50, *50*
    matrix size of, 48–49, 48(t)
    memory size of, 48–49, 48(t)
    operator interaction with, 50–51
    program for, 45
    purchase of, considerations in, 51–53
    service of, 52
    software for, 47–48
        purchase considerations for, 52
    terminal of, 47
    turn-key system for, 45
Congestive heart failure, pulmonary perfusion imaging in, 175, 175(t)
Console controls, 20
Contour mapping, 173
Conversion, internal, 2–3
Coronary artery disease, exercise radionuclide ventriculography in, 135–138
    prognosis in, 116
    risk stratification in, 116
    thallium exercise imaging in, 113–116
Count rate response, quality control protocol for, 33(t)
Counter, Geiger–Müller, 276
Counting system, single probe, 26
Crystal, of imaging camera, 17–19
Curie, 4
Cyst, of liver, 188–189

Data display, qualitative, 123–124
    quantitative, 127–129
        classical approach to, 127

Data display (Continued)
    count-volume approach to, 127–128
    geometric approach to, 127
    time-activity approach to, 127–128
Dead time, 24
Decay, nuclear, 1–3, 2
Deep venous imaging, thrombus detection and, 175–176, 176
Diastasis, 96
Diastolic function, assessment of, 135
Diethylenetriamine-pentacetic acid, indium 111, in brain imaging, 56(t)
    in cerebrospinal imaging, 70
    technetium 99m, dosing of, 143(t)
    in first-pass radionuclide angiocardiography, 129–130
    in renal imaging, 237–239, 238(t)
    in ventilation imaging, 144–145
    characteristics of, 148(t)
    for pulmonary emboli, 155
    normal scan of, 152
2,3–Dimercaptosuccinic acid, technetium 99m labeled, 237–239, 238(t)
Diphosphonates, technetium 99m labeled, derivatives of, 209–210, 210(t)
Dipyridamole thallium imaging, need for, 111
    scan interpretation in, 112
    technique in, 112
Disk, floppy computer, 51
    hard computer, 51
DMSA. See 2,3–Dimercaptosuccinic acid.
Dose calibrator, 26, 26
    for quality control, 27–28
    NRC regulation for, 273
Dosimeter, pen ionization, 276
    thermoluminescent, 276
Doughnut sign, 63, 101
Drug(s), abnormal radiopharmaceutical distribution due to, 11(t)–13(t)
    effects of, on thallium exercise imaging, 107(t)
DTPA. See Diethylenetriamine-pentacetic acid.
Dyskinesis, 134
Dyspnea, gated blood pool imaging in, 138–139

Edge-packing, 28–29
Ejection fraction, 95
    calculation of, 128–129
    images of, 125, 125
    left ventricular, exercise and, 136, 136
Electron, capture of, 2, 2
    internal conversion of, 3
Elution, quality control of, 32
Embolism, pulmonary, ventilation–perfusion imaging of, 151–152, 167, 171
Embryos, radionuclide imaging and, 321
Emission-computed tomography, 24
Emphysema, ventilation–perfusion imaging in, 166, 167–170
End-diastolic volume, typical values for, 95(t)
Equilibrium, transient, 5
Esophageal transit, radionuclide imaging of, 202–204

Esophageal transit (Continued)
    scan of, 310
Ethylenediaminetetra-acetate, in radionuclide quality control, 32
Ewing's sarcoma, imaging of, 219, 220
Exercise scintigraphy. See Thallium exercise imaging.
    ventriculogram in. See Ventriculography, exercise.

Fibrinogen, radiolabeled, 176
Filling rate, 135
Film badge, 276–277
Filtering, of SPECT image, 39–40, 41
    spatial, 50
    temporal, 50
First-pass radionuclide angiocardiography, interpretation in, 130–131, 131
    principle of, 129
    radiopharmaceuticals for, 129–130
    technique in, 130–131
Fissure sign, 149, 150
Floppy disk, 51
Fluorodeoxyglucose, in brain imaging, 67–68
Formatter, performance of, quality control protocol for, 33(t)
Fourier technique, in cardiac function studies, 126
Fracture, time frame following, abnormal scan and, 226, 226(t)
    normal scan and, 227(t)
Frame mode, 123
Frame subtraction, 50
Frequency filtering, of SPECT image, 40
Functional images, 124–127
Furosemide renogram, 245
    abnormal, 246
    time-activity curve in, 245

Gallbladder imaging. See Hepatobiliary imaging.
Gallium 67, biologic behavior of, 253–254
    citrate, in abscess imaging, 254(t)
    in tumor imaging, 254(t)
    diffuse pulmonary uptake of, 261
    imaging characteristics of, 253
    imaging with. See Gallium imaging.
    normal distribution of, 255–256
    renal activity of, after 24 hours, 259(t)
Gallium 68, imaging characteristics of, 8–9
Gallium imaging, diffuse pulmonary uptake of, 257(t)
    in AIDS, 260
    in bronchogenic carcinoma, 257
    in hepatoma, 257
    in Hodgkin's disease, 256–257, 257
    in immunosuppressed patients, 260
    in inflammatory disease, 257–260
    in lymphoma, 256
    in neoplasms, 256–257, 257
    in non-Hodgkin's lymphoma, 257
    in osteomyelitis, 260

Gallium imaging *(Continued)*
  in pyogenic liver abscess, 258
  normal, 254–256, *255*
  scan of, 317–318
  technique in, 254
Gamma ray, photon, 3
Gamma scintillation camera, for imaging, 15, *16*
Gamma variate function method, in shunt size calculation, 140
Gastric emptying, scintigraphic studies of, 205–206, *206*
  abnormal radiopharmaceutical distribution in, 13(t)
Gastroesophageal function, radionuclide imaging of, 202–204
Gastroesophageal reflux studies, 204–205, *205*
  scan in, 310–311
Gastrointestinal tract. See also specific organs.
  bleeding from, radionuclide imaging in, 193–195
  scan for, 309–310
Geiger-Müller counter, 276
Generator system, alumina, 6
  for radionuclide production, 5, *6*
  solvent extraction, 6
Glioma, radionuclide angiogram of, *61*
Glossary, 281–289
Glove phenomenon, 212
Graves' disease, iodine 131 therapy in, 91–93
  thyroid imaging in, 78–79, 85, 87, *87, 88*

Half-life, biologic, 4
  effective, 4–5
  physical, 4
Hard disk, 51, *52*
Hashimoto's thyroiditis, thyroid imaging in, 87
Head, gallium 67 distribution in, 255
Heart, anatomy of, 95–96
  chambers of, typical end–diastolic volume for, 95(t)
  circulation of, 96, *97*
  phased cycles of, 96, *96*
  physiology of, 95–96
Hemangioma, of liver, 188–189, *190*
  radionuclide diagnosis of, 203(t)
Hematoma, subdural, radionuclide imaging of, 65, *65*
Hemocytometer, 36
Hemorrhage, of gastrointestinal tract, 193–195
  scan for, 309–310
Hepatic cell adenoma, radionuclide imaging of, 188
Hepatic vein, thrombosis of, 189–190
Hepatitis, radionuclide imaging in, *186*
Hepatobiliary imaging, abnormal radiopharmaceutical distribution in, 12(t)–13(t)
  cholecystokinin in, 200
  in acute cholecystitis, 198–200, *199*
  interpretative difficulties of, 199(t)

Hepatobiliary imaging *(Continued)*
  in Caroli's disease, 203
  in chronic cholecystitis, 200–201
  normal scan in, 198, *198*
  post-surgical, 201–202
  post-traumatic, 201–202
  radiopharmaceuticals for, 196–197
  scan for, 308–309
  sincalide in, 200
  technique in, 197–198
Hepatocellular dysfunction, radionuclide imaging in, 182, *182*
Hepatoma, gallium imaging in, 257
  radionuclide imaging of, 188, *189*
Hepatomegaly, causes of, 187(t)
  radionuclide imaging of, 183, 187
Hexadecimal system, 45
Hexamethylpropyleneamine oxine, 56(t), 66–68
Hip bone marrow scan, 313–314
HIPDM, 66–68
Hippuran, iodine 131 labeled, 237–239, 238(t)
  time-activity curve of, *241*
HMPAO. See *Hexamethylpropyleneamine oxine.*
Hodgkin's disease, gallium imaging in, 256–257, *257*
Hot nose sign, 62, *64*
Hot spot imaging, 96–97
Hybridoma, 266–267, *267*
Hydrocephalus, cerebrospinal fluid imaging in, 71–73
  communicating, 71, *72, 73*
  noncommunicating, 73
  normal pressure, *72*
Hyperparathyroidism, bone imaging in, *224*
Hypertension, myocardial hypertrophy due to, thallium exercise imaging in, 117
  renovascular, renal imaging in, 242–243
Hyperthyroidism, iodine 131 therapy of, 91–93
  thyroid imaging in, 78–79
Hypokinesis, 134

IDA. See *Iminodiacetate complexes.*
Idiopathic hypertrophic subaortic stenosis, thallium exercise imaging in, 117
Image memory, 47
Iminodiacetate complexes, technetium 99m labeled, derivatives of, 196(t)
  dimethyl derivatives of, 196(t), 197
  in biliary atresia, 202
  in gastrointestinal imaging, 177
  in hepatobiliary imaging, 196–197
IMP, 66, *70*
Indium 111, DTPA, for brain imaging, 56(t)
  in cerebrospinal imaging, 70
  imaging characteristics of, 9
  leukocytes. See also *Indium leukocyte imaging.*
  biologic behavior of, 260–262

Indium 111 (Continued)
in abscess imaging, 254(t)
in osteomyelitis, 263–266
in tumor imaging, 254(t)
Indium 113m, imaging characteristics of, 9
Indium leukocyte imaging, abnormal scan in, 262–263
in abscess imaging, 254(t)
in cytomegalic virus pneumonitis, 265
in immunosuppressed patients, 263–266
in osteomyelitis, 263–266
in periappendiceal abscess, 264
in tumor imaging, 254(t)
increased activity in, causes of, 266(t)
normal scan in, 262, 263
scan in, 318
technique in, 262
Infarct-avid imaging, 96–97
monoclonal antibodies in, 99
pyrophosphate studies in, diffuse uptake in, 100–101
focal uptake in, 101–102, 101(t)
Holman interpretation of, 100(t)
Parkey interpretation of, 100(t)
persistent uptake in, 102
prognosis and, 103
risk stratification and, 103
scan interpretation for, 99, 100(t), 100
sensitivity and specificity of, 102
technetium 99m pyrophosphate in, 99
Inflammatory disease, ventilation–perfusion imaging and, 173–175, 174
Information density, 20, 22
Instruments, radiopharmaceutical, NRC regulations concerning, 273–274
survey, 273–274
Internal conversion, 2–3
Intracardiac shunt(s), calculation of, gamma variate function method for, 140
gated blood pool imaging of, 140
Intracranial inflammatory disease, static radionuclide brain imaging in, 63
Iodide, trapping of, 75
Iodine 123, imaging characteristics of, 7–8
in thyroid imaging, 75–76, 302
dosing of, 77(t)
Iodine 125, in thyroid imaging, 76
dosing of, 77(t)
Iodine 131, decay chart for, 295
imaging characteristics of, 7–8
in thyroid imaging, 75
dosing of, 77(t)
MIBG, in adrenal imaging, 249–251
orthoiodohippurate labeled with, in renal imaging, 237–239, 238(t)
therapy with, considerations in, 323–324
in hyperthyroidism, 91–92
in thyroid carcinoma, 93
in thyroid disease, 90–91
patient preparation for, 92–93
Iodine escape peak, 19
Iodine rebound phenomenon, 79

Iodine uptake test, clinical considerations in, 78
elevated iodine 131 uptake in, 78–79
iodine uptake in, 78–79, 79(t)
principles of, 77
procedure of, 77–78
reduced iodine 131 uptake in, 79
Isomeric transition, 2
Isonitrile, technetium 99m, 122–123
N-Isopropyl-123-I-p-iodoamphetamine, in brain imaging, 66, 70
Isotope(s), carrier–free, 3–4
fission, 4
metastable, 3, 3
notation of, 1
Isovolumic relaxation, 96

Kidney, imaging of. See Renal imaging.
physiology of, 237
renogram of, 240, 240
Captopril, 242–243, 316–317
furosemide, 245, 245, 246
lasix, 316
scan of, 314–315
technetium 99m uptake by, 226(t)
transplant of, radionuclide monitoring of, 182, 183
renal imaging in, 247–249, 247, 248
Krypton 81m, in ventilation imaging, 144–145
characteristics of, 148(t)
dosing of, 143(t)

Lasix renogram, 316
Lead x-ray peak, 19
Left bundle branch block, thallium exercise imaging in, 117
Left ventricular function, monitoring of, gated blood pool imaging for, 139
Legal requirements, for radiation safety, 269–278
Leukocyte, indium 111 labeled, abnormal radiopharmaceutical distribution in, 11(t)
biologic behavior of, 260–262
in abscess imaging, 254(t)
in osteomyelitis, 263–266
in tumor imaging, 254(t)
scan of, 318
LeVeen shunt patency, 311–312
Licenses, for radiopharmaceutical usage, 270–271
Linearity, quality control protocol for, 33(t)
Lingual thyroid, 82, 83
List mode, 123
Liver, abnormal radiopharmaceutical distribution in, 11(t)–12(t)
abnormal sulfur colloid scan of, 180–183, 181, 182
cysts of, 188–189
fatty infiltrations of, 186
focal lesions of, 188
focal nodular hyperplasia of, 188, 189
hemangiomas of, 188–189, 190

Liver *(Continued)*
  metastases to, 187–188, *187*
  normal sulfur colloid scan of, 179–180,
    179, 180
  primary neoplasms of, 188, *189*
  radionuclide imaging of, 177–178
    radiopharmaceutical dosing in,
      178(t)
    radiopharmaceuticals for, 177
    technique in, 177–178
  scan of, 307
  solitary cold lesions of, causes of,
    181(t)
  SPECT imaging of, 178–179
  trauma to, 189
Lung, anatomy of, 141–143, *142*
  decreased perfusion to, causes of,
    155(t)
  imaging of, radiopharmaceutical
    agents for, 143(t)
  inflammatory disease of, 173–175, *174*
  neoplasms of, 173, *174*
  perfusion imaging of, radiopharma-
    ceutical distribution in, 11(t)–12(t)
  physiology of, 141–143
  thallium 201 accumulation in, 111
  ventilation-perfusion imaging of, 173–
    175
Lymphoma, gallium imaging of, 256

MAA. See *Macroaggregated albumin*.
Macroaggregated albumin, technetium
    99m, dosing of, 143(t)
  in pulmonary imaging, 143
Magnetic tape, 51
Marrow scanning, 231, *235*, 313–314
Matrix size, 48–49, 48(t)
Meckel's diverticulum, radionuclide im-
    aging of, 195–196, *196*
  radiopharmaceutical distribution in,
    13(t)
  scan of, 309
Medication, abnormal radiopharmaceuti-
    cal distribution due to, 11(t)–13(t)
  effects of, on thallium exercise imag-
    ing, 107(t)
Memory, main, of computer, 46
Metaiodobenzylguanidine, iodine 131 la-
    beled, in adrenal imaging, 249–251
Mitral valve prolapse syndrome, thal-
    lium exercise imaging in, 116–117
Mitral valvular regurgitation, gated
    blood pool imaging in, 138(t)
Mitral valvular stenosis, gated blood
    pool imaging in, 138(t)
Molybdenum 99, in technetium 99m
    production, 6–7
Monoclonal antibody, in infarct avid im-
    aging, 99
  radiolabeled, 266–267, *267*
Multichannel analyzer display, 20
Myocardial activity, rating of, 99, 100(t)
Myocardial hypertrophy, hypertensive,
    thallium exercise imaging in, 117
Myocardial infarction, acute, gated
    blood pool imaging in, 137–138

Myocardial infarction *(Continued)*
  dipyridamole thallium imaging follow-
    ing, 111–112
  exercise imaging following, 104–111
  pathophysiology in, 97
  perfusion following. See *Myocardial
    perfusion imaging*.
  pyrophosphate imaging in, 96–97
    diffuse uptake in, 100–101
    focal uptake in, 101–102, 101(t)
    Holman interpretation of, 100(t)
    Parkey interpretation of, 100(t)
    persistent uptake in, 102
    prognosis and, 103
    risk stratification and, 103
    scan interpretation for, 99, 100(t),
      100
    sensitivity and specificity of, 102
  radiopharmaceutical distribution in,
    13(t)
  resting thallium scintigraphy follow-
    ing, 122
Myocardial perfusion imaging, abnormal
    radiopharmaceutical distribution in,
    13(t)
  dipyridamole in, 111–112
  in exercise, 104–106
    abnormal scans in, 107–111
    clinical applications of, 113
    drug effect on, 107(t)
    error sources in, 108(t)
    lung-to-heart thallium index in, 111
    nonreversible abnormality patterns
      in, 109–110, *110*
    normal planar scan in, *107*
    planar image interpretation in, 106–
      107, *107*
    planar technique in, 104–106
    redistribution image interpretation
      in, 109(t)
    reversible redistribution patterns in,
      110–111
    reversible abnormality patterns in,
      107–109, *108*
    right ventricular activity in, 111
    technical error sources in, 106(t)
    thallium 201 quantitative analysis
      in, 112–113, *113*
    thallium 201 washout profile in,
      113, *113*
  thallium 201 for, 103–104
Myosin, 99

N-isopropyl-123-I-p-iodoamphetamine,
    in brain imaging, 66, *70*
N-trimethyl-N-(2-hydroxyl-3-methyl-5-io-
    dobenzyl)-1,3-propa–nediamine, in
    brain imaging, 66–68
Neck, gallium 67 distribution in, 255
Neoplasm(s), benign osseous, 221
  gallium imaging in, 256–257, *257*
  of brain, 59–60
    radionuclide scanning for, *61*
  of liver, radionuclide imaging of, 188,
    189
  of lung, ventilation–perfusion imaging
    of, 173, *174*

Neutrino, 2
Neutron, notation of, 1
Non-Hodgkin's disease, gallium imaging in, 257
Nuclear decay, 1–3, 2
Nuclear medicine laboratory, 275–276
  instrument calibration in, 273
  occupational radiation dose limits in, 277(t)
  personnel radiation monitoring in, 276–277
  radiation surveys in, 276
  radioactive waste disposal in, 277–278
  radiopharamaceutical preparation in, 274–275
  venting of, 278
Nuclear Regulatory Commission, 269
  licensure requirements of, 270
Nuclear stability, 1–3

Obstructive renogram, 243–247, 244
Obstructive uropathy, renal imaging in, 243–247
Octal system, 45
Osteogenic sarcoma, imaging of, 219, 219
Osteoma, osteoid, imaging of, 220
Osteomyelitis, bone imaging in, 230–231, 230
  gallium imaging in, 260
Osteoporosis, bone mineral measurement for, 233

Paget's disease, bone imaging in, 231, 232
Paradox image, 125–126
Parametric images, 124–127
Parathyroid gland, adenoma of, 94, 94(t)
  imaging of, 93–94
Peak filling rate, assessment of, 135
Pelvis, gallium 67 distribution in, 255–256
Pen ionization dosimeter, 277
Perchlorate washout test, 81
Perfusion agent, in pulmonary imaging, 143
  dosing of, 143(t)
  myocardial, 122–123
Perfusion imaging, of lungs. See Pulmonary perfusion imaging.
  of myocardium. See Myocardial perfusion imaging.
Pericholecystic hepatic activity sign, 200, 200
Pertechnetate, technetium 99m labeled, in gastrointestinal imaging, 177, 178(t)
Phase analysis, in cardiac function studies, 126–127, 127, 128
Phosphate compound, technetium 99m labeled, hepatic uptake of, 226(t)
Photoelectric absorption, 18
Photomultiplier tube, 18–19
Photon, gamma ray, 3

Photopeak, full width at half–maximum of, 22–23, 23
  z-mode display of, 32
Pixel size, in SPECT imaging, 42–43
Plummer's disease, iodine-131 therapy in, 91–93
  thyroid imaging in, 78–79
Pneumonia, ventilation–perfusion imaging in, 174
Pneumonitis, cytomegalic virus, indium leukocyte imaging in, 265
Pointed head sign, 65
Positron emission, 2
Positron-emission tomography, 24
  of brain, 67–68
Positron-emitting agent, in brain imaging, 67–68
Prefiltering, of SPECT image, 40
Pregnancy, radionuclide imaging during, 320–321
Probe counting system, single, 26
Proton, notation of, 1
Pulmonary embolism(i), multiple, 151–152, 153
  perfusion scan for, 154
  ventilation-perfusion imaging of, 167, 171
Pulmonary perfusion imaging. See also Ventilation-perfusion imaging.
  agents for, 143
  clinical applications of, 151–164
  defects identified by, causes of, 155(t)
  hot spots in, 146
  in congestive heart failure, 175, 175(t)
  normal lung scan in, 148–151, 149, 150
  of embolism, 171, 172
  perfusion agent in, right–to–left shunting of, 147
  scan, 306–307
  technique in, 146–147
Pulse height analyzer, 19, 20
Pyrophosphate imaging, clinical applications of, 102–103
  imaging technique in, 98–99
  in myocardial infarction, 96–97
    diffuse uptake in, 100–101
    focal uptake in, 101–102, 101(t)
    Holman interpretation of, 100(t)
    Parkey interpretation of, 100(t)
    persistent uptake in, 102
    prognosis and, 103
    risk stratification and, 103
    scan, 303–304
    scan interpretation for, 99, 100(t), 100
    sensitivity and specificity of, 102
  radiopharmaceutical dosing in, 98(t)

Quality control, dose calibrator for, 27–28
  for instrumentation, 27
  in radiopharmaceutical preparation, 30–31
  in SPECT, 40–43
  of gamma cameras, 28–30, 29–33
  of radionuclide purity, 31–32
  parameters of, 33(t)

Quality control *(Continued)*
  radiochemical tagging and, 32–36
  sterility and, 36
Quantitative computed tomography, in
    bone mineral measurement, 233–235

Radiation, occupational dose limits of,
    277(t)
Radiation safety committee, 270
Radiation safety officer, 269–270
Radiation therapy, bone imaging and,
    218, 219
  radionuclide monitoring of, *181*
Radioactive spill, 325–326
Radioactive waste, disposal of, 277–278
Radioactivity, accidental spillage and,
    325–326
  conversion of, from Becquerels to
    Curies, 292–293
  decay of, 4–5
  definition of, 4
Radiochemical tagging, 32–36
Radionuclide(s), decay of, 1–2, *2*
  definition of, 1
  imaging characteristics of, 5, 290–291
  positron-emitting, 9
  production of, 3–4
    generator systems for, 5, *6*
  purity of, quality control for, 31–32
  therapy with, considerations in, 322
Radionuclide imaging. See also specific
    test and site.
  in alcoholic liver disease, 183–187,
    185, 186
  in gastrointestinal bleeding, 193–195
  in hepatitis, *186*
  in Meckel's diverticulum, 195–196, *196*
  in pregnancy, 320–321
  of esophageal transit, 202–204
  of fatty liver infiltrations, *186*
  of gastroesophageal function, 202–204
  of hepatic cirrhosis ascites, *185*
  of liver, 177–190
  of superior vena caval obstruction, *184*
Radiopharmaceutical(s), abnormal distri-
    bution of, 11(t)–13(t)
  adverse reactions of, 10
  brain distribution of, 67, *68*
  breast feeding and, 321
  dosing of, for cardiac imaging, 98(t)
  fetal absorption of, 321
  for bone imaging, 209–210, 210(t)
  for brain imaging, 55–57, 56(t)
  for cerebrospinal fluid imaging, 70
  for hepatobiliary imaging, 196–197
  for renal imaging, 237–239, 238(t)
  in liver-spleen imaging, 177
    dosing of, 178(t)
  in myocardial infarction imaging, 98,
    98(t)
  in thyroid imaging, 75–76, *76*
  infarct-avid, 96–99
    monoclonal antibody as, 99
  injection techniques for, 296
  instrumentation for, 273–274
  investigational, 10
  iodinated, in brain imaging, 66–68

Radiopharmaceutical(s) *(Continued)*
  labeling of, 272
  laboratory areas for, 275–276
  localization mechanisms of, 9–10, 10(t)
  misadministration of, 275
  personnel radiation monitoring and,
    276–277
  preparation of, 274–275
    quality control in, 30–31
  radiation surveys and, 276
  receipt of, 272–273
    record keeping for, 273
    record retention for, 273(t)
  transportation of, 272
  usage of, licenses for, 270–271
    supervised, 271–272
    training for, 271–272
  waste disposal and, 277–278
Radius of rotation, SPECT, 37, 39
Random-access-memory, 46
Read-only-memory, 45
Record keeping, for radioactive materi-
    als, 273
Red blood cell, technetium 99m labeled,
    in blood pool ventriculography,
    131–132
  in gastrointestinal bleeding, 194, *195*
  in gastrointestinal imaging, 177
  technique in, 318–319
Reflex sympathetic dystrophy syn-
    drome, bone imaging in, 230
Reflux studies, gastroesophageal, 204–
    205, *205*
  scan in, 310–311
  ureterovesicular, 240–242
Register, of computer, 46
Regulatory agencies, 269
Renal imaging, clinical applications of,
    242–249
  in diffuse renal disease, 243
  in obstructive uropathy, 243–247
  in renal transplant evaluation, 247–
    249, *247, 248*
  normal scan in, *239, 240*
  of anatomic variants, 242
  of blood flow, 314
  of intrarenal mass lesions, 242
  of renovascular hypertension, 242–243
  of vascular abnormalities, 242
  radiopharmaceuticals for, 237–239,
    238(t)
  static parenchymal, 239–240
  techniques in, 239–240
Renal scan, 314–315
Renogram, 240, *240,* 315–316
  Captopril, 242–243, 316–317
  furosemide, 245, *245, 246*
  Lasix, 316
Resolution, energy, 20, 23–24
  quality control protocol for, 33(t)
  spatial, 20–24
Resting thallium scintigraphy, 122
Rhinorrhea, cerebrospinal fluid, 73–74,
    73
Rim sign, 66
  in acute cholecystitis, 199–200, *200*
Ring artifact, in SPECT, 42
Rotating man image, of SPECT, 40
R-wave trigger, 132

Safety regulations, for radioactive materials, 269–278
Sarcoidosis, gallium imaging in, *259*
Sarcoma, Ewing's, 219, *220*
    osteogenic, 219, *219*
Schilling test, 206–207
Scintillation event, 18
Scrotal imaging, 249, *249*, 249(t)
Sensitivity, quality control protocol for, 33(t)
Septa, of collimator, 15–16
Shielding, in radiopharmaceutical preparation, 274
Shine through, 148
Sincalide, in hepatobiliary imaging, 200
Single photon emission computed tomography, 24
    bone imaging, 312–313
    functional brain imaging with, 300
    of liver, 178–179
    of spleen, 178–179
    pyrophosphate imaging with, 99
    rotational, acquisition time in, 39
        center of rotation in, 42, *43*
        collimator evaluation in, 43
        collimator in, 43
        correction of, 41–42
        data acquisition in, 38–39
        detector head alignment in, 43
        field uniformity assessment of, 41–42
        image display in, 40
        image filtering for, 39–40
        image matrix size in, 39
        instrumentation for, 37–38
        number of views in, 39
        pixel size calibration in, 42–43
        pixel size in, 42–43
        principles of, 37–39
        quality control in, 40–43
        ring artifact in, 42
        rotational center correction in, 42
        rotational center determination in, 42
        system performance in, 43
        x and y gain calibration in, 42–43
    thallium imaging with, 117–118, *118, 119*
        artifacts of, 120(t)
        bull's eye plot in, 121–122, *121*
        technique in, 118–122
Skeletal system, anatomy of, 209
    imaging of. See *Bone imaging.*
Sodium pertechnetate, in technetium 99m production, 6–7, *7, 8*
SPECT. See *Single photon emission computed tomography.*
SPECT thallium imaging, 117–118, *118, 119*
    artifacts of, 120(t)
    bull's eye plot in, 121–122, *121*
    technique in, 118–122
Spleen, focal lesion of, 190–192
    imaging of, abnormal radiopharmaceutical distribution in, 11(t)–12(t)
        normal scan in, 190
    lymphoma of, *191*
    nonvisualization of, 193, 193(t)
    radionuclide imaging of, 177–178

Spleen *(Continued)*
    radiopharmaceutical dosing in, 178(t)
    radiopharmaceuticals for, 177
    technique in, 177–178
    scan of, 307
    size of, disease affecting, 193(t)
    SPECT imaging of, 178–179
    trauma to, 192–193
    upside-down image of, 190, *191*
Splenomegaly, radionuclide imaging in, 192, *192*
Stability, nuclear, 1–3
Step and shoot technique, of SPECT, 38
Sterility, 36
Stomach, emptying of, scintigraphic studies of, 205–206, *206*
Stress imaging. See *Thallium exercise imaging.*
Stress test. See *Thallium exercise imaging.*
Stripe sign, 155
Stroke volume, 95
Stroke volume image, 124
Struma ovarii, 82
Sulfur colloid, technetium 99m labeled, diffuse pulmonary uptake of, 183(t)
    in bone marrow scanning, 231
    in esophageal transit evaluation, 203
    in first-pass radionuclide angiocardiography, 129–130
    in gastrointestinal bleeding, 194
    in gastrointestinal imaging, 177
    in hepatobiliary imaging, 202
    in solid hepatic lesion diagnosis, 203(t)
    splenic defects on, 193(t)
Supervisor, of computer, 46
Survey instruments, NRC regulation for, 273–274
Systolic function, assessment of, 134

Technetium 99m, albumin, 131–132
    BATO, 122–123
    bone imaging agents, renal uptake of, 226(t)
    decay scheme of, 3, *3*
    decay table for, 294
    diphosphonates, derivatives of, 209–210, 210(t)
    DMSA, for renal imaging, 237–239, 238(t)
    DTPA, dosing of, 143(t)
        for brain imaging, 56(t)
        for renal imaging, 237–239, 238(t)
        in first-pass radionuclide angiocardiography, 129–130
        in ventilation imaging, 144–145
        characteristics of, 148(t)
        for pulmonary emboli, *155*
        normal scan of, *152*
    generation table for, 294
    glucoheptonate, for brain imaging, 56(t)
        for renal imaging, 237–239, 238(t)
    HMPAO, for brain imaging, 56(t), 66–68

Technetium 99m *(Continued)*
  IDA, derivatives of, 196(t)
    in biliary atresia, 202
    in gastrointestinal imaging, 177
    in hepatobiliary imaging, 196–197
  imaging characteristics of, 5–7
  isonitriles, 122–123
  MAA, dosing of, 143(t)
    in pulmonary imaging, 143
  mertiatide, for renal imaging, 237–239,
      238(t)
  pertechnetate, biodistribution of, 6–7,
      7, 8
    dosing of, 77(t)
    for brain imaging, 56(t)
    in gastrointestinal imaging, 177
    in thyroid imaging, 76
  phosphate compounds of, hepatic up-
      take of, 226(t)
  production of, 6
  pyrophosphate, dosing of, 98(t)
    in myocardial infarctions, 96–97
  red blood cells labeled with, in blood
      pool ventriculography, 131–132
    in gastrointestinal bleeding, 194, 195
    in gastrointestinal imaging, 177
    radiopharmaceutical dosing for,
        98(t)
  serum albumin labeled with, in blood
      pool ventriculography, 131–132
  sulfur colloid, diffuse pulmonary up-
      take of, 183(t)
    in bone marrow scanning, 231
    in esophageal transit evaluation, 203
    in first-pass radionuclide angiocar-
        diography, 129–130
    in gastrointestinal bleeding, 194
    in gastrointestinal imaging, 177
    in hepatobiliary imaging, 202
    in solid hepatic lesion diagnosis,
        203(t)
    splenic defects on, 193(t)
  valence states of, 6
Temporal analysis, 135
Testicular scan, 317
Testicular torsion scintigraphy, 249, 249,
    249(t)
Thallium 201, biokinetics of, 103–104
  for cardiac imaging, dosing of, 98(t)
  imaging characteristics of, 9
  in dipyridamole testing, 111–112
  in exercise imaging, 104–111
  lung accumulation of, 111
  physical characteristics of, 103
  resting scintigraphy with, 122
  scan, 304
Thallium exercise imaging, 305
  abnormal scans in, 107–111
  clinical applications of, 113
  drug effect on, 107(t)
  error sources in, 108(t)
  in aortic valvular regurgitation, 116–
      117
  in aortic valvular stenosis, 116–117
  in cardiomyopathy, 117
  in coronary artery disease, 113–116
  in hypertensive myocardial hypertro-
      phy, 117

Thallium exercise imaging *(Continued)*
  in idiopathic hypertrophic subaortic
      stenosis, 117
  in left bundle branch block, 117
  in mitral valve prolapse syndrome,
      116–117
  lung-to-heart thallium index in, 111
  nonreversible abnormality patterns in,
      109–110, 110
  normal planar scan in, 107
  planar image interpretation in, 106–
      107, 107
  planar technique in, 104–106
  redistribution image interpretation in,
      109(t)
  reverse redistribution patterns in,
      110–111
  reversible abnormality patterns in,
      107–109, 108
  right ventricular activity in, 111
  technical error sources in, 106(t)
  thallium 201 quantitative analysis in,
      112–113, 113
  thallium 201 washout profile in, 113,
      113
Thallium SPECT imaging, 117–118, 118,
    119, 305–306
  artifacts of, 120(t)
  bull's eye plot in, 121–122, 121
  technique in, 118–122
Thallium stress imaging. See *Thallium
    exercise imaging.*
Thermoluminescent dosimeter, 277
Thorax, gallium 67 distribution in, 255
Thrombus, detection of, deep venous
    imaging for, 175–176, 176
  of hepatic vein, 189–190
Thyroid, lingual, 82, 83
Thyroid function testing, clinical consid-
    erations in, 78
  elevated iodine 131 uptake in, 78–79
  iodine uptake in, 78–79, 79(t)
  perchlorate washout in, 81
  principles of, 77
  procedure of, 77–78
  reduced iodine 131 uptake in, 79
  thyroid stimulating hormone in, 80–81
  thyroid suppression in, 79–80, 80
Thyroid gland, carcinoma of, 87–90
  functioning metastases of, 93
  iodine 131 therapy of, 93
  metastatic disease from, 89
  metastatic disease therapy in, 90–91
  scan for, 302–303
  iodine 131 ablation of, 90–91
  post-surgical ablation of, 93
Thyroid imaging, abnormal radiophar-
    maceutical distribution in, 13(t)
  clinical, 81
  for thyroid function. See *Thyroid func-
    tion testing.*
  in chronic thyroiditis, 87
  in diffuse toxic goiter, 85, 87, 87, 88
  of cold nodule, 83, 84(t), 85
  of discordant thyroid nodule, 84, 86
  in Graves' disease, 85, 87, 87, 88
  in Hashimoto's thyroiditis, 87
  of histologically normal ectopic thy-
      roid tissue, 82

Thyroid imaging (Continued)
  of hot nodule, 83–84
  of multinodular gland, 84–85, 86
  of normal thyroid, 82
  of thyroid carcinoma, 87–90, 89, 90
  of thyroid nodules, 83–85
  of warm nodule, 84
  radiopharmaceutical dosing in, 76–77, 77(t)
  radiopharmaceuticals in, 75–76, 76
  scan, for cancer, 302–303
    iodine, 123, 302
    technetium 99m, 301
  technical considerations in, 81–82
Thyroid stimulating hormone, in TSH stimulation test, 80–81
Thyroid suppression test, 79–80, 80
Thyroid uptake study, abnormal radiopharmaceutical distribution in, 13(t)
Thyroiditis, chronic, thyroid imaging in, 87
Training, for radiopharmaceutical imaging, 271–272
Transmutation, definition of, 1
Tricuspid regurgitation, gated blood pool imaging in, 138(t)
N-Trimethyl-N-(2-hydroxyl-3-methyl-5-iodobenzyl)-1,3–propa–nediamine, in brain imaging, 66–68
TSH (thyroid stimulating hormone), 80–81
TSH stimulation test, 80–81
Tumor, imaging of, radiopharmaceuticals for, 254(t)

Uniformity, quality control protocol for, 33(t)
Ureter, imaging techniques for, 240–242
Ureterovesicular reflux, imaging in, 240–242
Urinary bladder, imaging techniques for, 240–242

Valvular heart disease, gated blood pool imaging in, 139–140
  thallium exercise imaging in, 116–117
Vena cava, superior, obstruction of, radionuclide imaging of, 184
Ventilation agent, in pulmonary imaging, 143–145
  dosing of, 143(t)
Ventilation-perfusion imaging, 306
  aerosols in, 144, 145
  agents for, 143–145, 143(t)
    characteristics of, 148(t)
  clinical applications of, 151–164
  for pulmonary embolism, 151
    mismatch in, 152, 153, 154
    scan findings in, 152
  for segmental perfusion defects, 156
  in asthma, 170–173
  in bronchiectasis, 170–173
  in bronchitis, 170–173
  in chronic obstructive pulmonary disease, 166, 167–170
  in emphysema, 170–173

Ventilation-perfusion imaging (Continued)
  in hypoplastic left pulmonary artery, 162
  in inflammatory disease, 173–175
  in perfusion defects, 162, 163
  in pulmonary embolism follow-up, 167
  interpretation scheme for, 164(t)
  normal lung scan in, 150, 151
  of anterior basal segment, 159
  of anterior segment, 158, 160
  of cardiovascular abnormalities, 175
  of inferior lingular segment, 158
  of lateral basal segment, 159
  of lateral segment, 160
  of lung neoplasms, 173
  of medial segment, 160
  of posterior basal segment, 158
  of posterior segment, 160
  of pulmonary embolism, 171, 172
  of superior lingular segment, 157
  of superior segment, 159
  scan interpretation in, 164–166
  technique in, 147–148
  vs. pulmonary angiography, 165(t), 166, 166(t)
Ventricular filling rate, assessment of, 135
Ventricular septal defect, gated blood pool imaging of, 138(t)
Ventriculography, exercise, in coronary artery disease, 135–138
    sensitivity of, 137
    specificity of, 137, 137(t)
  gated blood pool, gating in, 124, 132–133
    in acute myocardial infarction, 137–138
    in cardiomyopathy, 139
    in dyspnea, 138–139
    in intracardiac shunts, 140
    in left ventricular function monitoring, 139
    in noncoronary heart disease, 138–140
    findings in, 138(t)
    in valvular heart disease, 139–140
    interpretation in, 133–134
    normal, 129
    principle of, 131
    qualitative data in, 134, 134(t)
    quantitative data in, 134–135
    radiopharmaceuticals for, 131–132
    technique in, 132–133
  resting, 303
Vitamin B$_{12}$, gastrointestinal absorption of, Schilling test for, 206–207

Waste disposal, radionuclear, 277–278
Well counter, sodium iodide, 24–26, 25
Whole-body accessory, quality control protocol for, 33(t)
Whole-body imaging, following thyroid carcinoma therapy, 88–89, 90
Window, energy, asymmetric, 20, 21
  improper setting of, 33
  symmetric, 21

Window *(Continued)*
 width of, 19
Wipe test, 276
Word, 45, 48

X, 1
Xenon, imaging characteristics of, 8
Xenon 127, in ventilation imaging, 144
 characteristics of, 148(t)
 dosing of, 143(t)

Xenon 133, in ventilation imaging, 143
 characteristics of, 148(t)
 dosing of, 143(t)
 normal lung scan in, *150,* 151

Z, 1
Z pulse, 47
Z pulse display, 20
Zoom capability, 47